DATE DUE

GAYLORD			PRINTED IN U.S.A.

INTERNATIONAL TRADE AND FINANCE

FRONTIERS FOR RESEARCH

INTERNATIONAL TRADE AND FINANCE

FRONTIERS FOR RESEARCH

EDITED BY

PETER B. KENEN

*Walker Professor of Economics and International Finance
Princeton University*

CAMBRIDGE UNIVERSITY PRESS

CAMBRIDGE

LONDON · NEW YORK · MELBOURNE

Published by the Syndics of the Cambridge University Press

The Pitt Building, Trumpington Street, Cambridge CB2 1RP

32 East 57th Street, New York, NY 10022, USA

Bentley House, 200 Euston Road, London NW1 2DB

296 Beaconsfield Parade, Middle Park, Melbourne 3206, Australia

© Cambridge University Press 1975

Library of Congress Catalogue Card Number: 75-2717

ISBN: 0 521 20719 3

First published 1975

Printed in the United States of America

The economist, as such, is under no obligation to assume the role of the statesman, and he is doing his full duty if he supplies the statesman with sound advice with respect to economic means and economic ends. But he owes it to the statesman to take into account as full a range of the economic means and ends as he can recognize and has the skills to analyze and deal with, and to be aware of and to make evident to others the limitations of his analysis and the possible significance of what he has not taken into account. We should be suspicious ourselves, and we should encourage suspicion on the part of non-economists, of a trend toward greater simplicity and rigour of models in economics at a time when it is apparent to even the man in the street that the real economic world has been getting more complicated and its problems less susceptible of exact and clean-cut solutions.

Jacob Viner
International Trade and
Economic Development, 1953

CONTENTS

LIST OF CONTRIBUTORS

Bela Balassa	Johns Hopkins University
	International Bank for Reconstruction and Development
Robert E. Baldwin	University of Wisconsin – Madison
Jagdish Bhagwati	Massachusetts Institute of Technology
Ralph C. Bryant	Board of Governors of the Federal Reserve System
Richard E. Caves	Harvard University
Hollis B. Chenery	International Bank for Reconstruction and Development
Benjamin J. Cohen	Fletcher School of Law and Diplomacy, Tufts University
Richard N. Cooper	Yale University
W. M. Corden	Nuffield College, Oxford University
Carlos F. Diaz-Alejandro	Yale University
Ronald Findlay	Columbia University
Milton Gilbert	Bank for International Settlements
John Helliwell	University of British Columbia
Thomas Horst	Harvard University
G. C. Hufbauer	Office of Tax Analysis, Department of the Treasury
Harry G. Johnson	University of Chicago
Ronald W. Jones	University of Rochester
Charles P. Kindleberger	Massachusetts Institute of Technology
L. R. Klein	Wharton School of Finance and Commerce, University of Pennsylvania
Lawrence B. Krause	The Brookings Institution
Ronald I. McKinnon	Stanford University
Stephen P. Magee	Graduate School of Business, University of Chicago
Norman C. Miller	University of Pittsburgh
C. Moriguchi	Kyoto University
Rudolf R. Rhomberg	International Monetary Fund
Wilson Schmidt	Virginia Polytechnic Institute and State University
Robert M. Stern	University of Michigan at Ann Arbor
Grant B. Taplin	International Monetary Fund
A. Van Peeterssen	Ecole des Hautes Etudes Commerciales, l'Université de Montréal
Thomas D. Willett	Department of the Treasury

PREFACE

International trade and finance are among the oldest subjects studied by economists. Along with public finance, money, and what we would now call economic development, they were the chief concerns of the "consultant administrators" whose doctrines and advice for emerging nation-states too many of us know only through their critics' eyes. And because so much of classical economics was written on and for an island, the international aspects of economic life played an extraordinary role in the development of economic thought and the theory of economic policy.

The concentration on problems and policies relating to foreign trade inspired many major contributions to analytical economics. Mill's treatment of price determination, the first full formulation of the law of supply and demand, appeared in his essay, *Of the Laws of Interchange between Nations,* to round out Ricardo's account of international specialization. Edgeworth's taxonomic work on tariffs and the terms of trade contained and contributed importantly to the theory of tax incidence in general equilibrium. Positive and normative concerns with the gains from trade gave birth to classical welfare economics, a contribution which Schumpeter described as the "most important exploit" of the trade theorists. And, on the monetary side, debates about bullion and the balance of trade, going back to Hume and earlier writers, furnished the first formal statement of the quantity theory of money.

In our own century, of course, international economics, like most other specialties, has been a net importer of techniques. The most important innovations in trade theory, the opportunity-cost approach set forth by Haberler and the factor-endowments approach developed by Heckscher and Ohlin, are adaptations of more general ideas – the Austrian theory of value and the Walrasian theory of markets (especially in its Casselian variant). International monetary theory has been a borrower too. It has used Keynesian propensities and multipliers to analyze balance-of-payments adjustment, the transfer problem, and the international propagation of business fluctuations. Most recently, portfolio and monetary theories constructed to do other work have been applied to the analysis of capital movements and the implications of changes in exchange rates.

In one vital respect, however, there was too little borrowing for too long. A full decade after other specialties had been transformed by the application of econometric methods, international trade and finance displayed a stubborn immunity to quantification. They became the last refuge of the speculative theorist. One can cite several significant exceptions, including early efforts to measure the price elasticities and income propensities pertaining to import demand. But little was done to verify the fundamental propositions of trade theory or to measure the effects of trade restrictions. The theory was deemed to be immutably true. The task of the trade theorist, then, was merely to spell out its implications for welfare and policy. Recall, for example, the manner in which Leontief interpreted his own results on the factor content of U.S. trade. Because the Heckscher–Ohlin theorem *had* to be true, one would have to set aside common-sense judgments about the American factor endowment. Or read again the closing lines of Richard Caves's *Trade and Economic Structure,* published in 1960:

Even if a massive breakthrough comes in the statistical testing of economic models, surely statistical verifiability will never be the only test for keeping a theory on the books. Indeed, should such a standard come to rule, one can predict that the audience for professional airings of economic ideas may be reduced to statistical clerks and baseball fans between seasons.

Quantification cannot get ahead of speculation. When indeed it tends to do so, its practitioners are reduced to rerunning equations with one more year's data. Theorists must keep on throwing off ideas, not only as grist for the computers, but also to keep up with human ingenuity. But speculation without quantification, even the most rigorous derivation of theoretical propositions, cannot tell us how an economy functions or what we should do in case of a malfunction.

It is fun to speculate about the reasons for the long delay in the coming of econometrics to international economic research. I can think of three. First, trade theory is a species of general-equilibrium theory, and, in the multi-country, multi-commodity form that has to be used as the framework for estimation, it is wonderfully complex. Trade theorists enamored of their complicated constructs have been loathe to simplify those constructs sufficiently, to make do with partial-equilibrium approximations. Trade theory is very hard to test in ways that do justice to its sophistication. Second, trade data are notoriously poor. They may be no worse than the other statistics economists use all the time, often incautiously, but their flaws are more conspicuous because the statistics exist in ubiquitous pairs. One country's exports of goods, services, or assets are another country's imports, yet the two numbers never agree. Third, economists attracted to the subject have often come with normative, not positive, inclinations. My own meticulous investigation, conducted late one evening at a famous conference site, disclosed that four of seven well-known colleagues were fugitives from political science. They had been told that they must master international economics in order to understand international politics. This background may not be a handicap. Anyone who studies international economics without noticing that governments are decisive actors has missed the distinguishing characteristic of his subject. It is the clash of sovereignties, not the role of distance, that causes us to study international transactions separately from other economic phenomena. But someone who approaches the subject from this vantage point is apt to disdain the study of numbers and to shun the acquisition of quantitative tools.

Reasons like these, however, no longer matter much. Quantification has come, late but massively. Ten years ago, few papers on international trade or finance contained a single regression equation. Papers published today look naked without them. I have just compared the reading list I use in a graduate course with the one I used a decade ago. Half of the articles on the current list were written in the last ten years, and half of those contain regression equations or other quantitative work. Half of the articles on the old list are not on the new one, and most of those that I deleted had no numbers.

Right now, in fact, we face the danger I mentioned before. Quantification is getting ahead of speculation. Too many papers are written to show that some colleague's test of someone else's theory can be refined, but that the test is inconclusive even when refined. One longs to know where we are – what we have learned during the last decade, what else we might learn from the numbers, and what the theorist should be doing next to pave the way for subsequent rounds of testing and measurement. These are the questions I asked of the authors whose papers appear in this book.

Emerging from two years of university administration, I spent a year of intellectual rest and recuperation trying to catch up with my subject. Like most of us, I had already fallen behind being a full-time economist. But my plight had grown worse while I was away from the subject, and I did not have the usual excuse – that I was too busy writing to read. Eventually, I thought it best to ask for help. I organized a conference.

The meeting took place at Princeton University in March 1973, under the joint auspices of the International Finance Section and the Woodrow Wilson School of Public and International Affairs. My colleague, William Branson, served as co-chairman. The program was much like the table of contents of this volume.

The first session was devoted to the three papers published in Part I, Robert Stern's paper on the testing of hypotheses concerning the sources of comparative advantage and the structure of merchandise trade, Max Corden's paper on the costs and consequences of protection, and Carlos Diaz-Alejandro's survey of the implications of trade policies for efficiency and growth in the less developed countries. Drafts were circulated in advance, and one discussant was assigned to each of the three papers. The fourth discussant was allowed to roam more freely, to look at the broad issues raised by the three papers taken together.

The second session was devoted to econometric work on international payments, the papers published in Part II. Stephen Magee was asked to look at econometric models of merchandise trade, with special attention to the problems of specification and the testing of hypotheses concerning the role of exchange rates. Gary Hufbauer was asked to look at recent research on the determinants and implications of direct investment, including the broad economic issues raised by the growth of multinational production. Ralph Bryant was asked to review and appraise studies of capital flows, linkages between capital markets, and the external effects of monetary policies. Again, one discussant was assigned to each paper, and one was urged to wander at will.

The third session of the conference, Part III of this book, was devoted to a heterogeneous collection of questions. John Helliwell was asked what we have learned about balance-of-payments adjustment under fixed and flexible exchange rates, especially to tell us whether and to what extent inferences drawn from Canadian experience are susceptible of generalization. Jerry Cohen was assigned to survey positive and normative work on international liquidity, to ask if economists have useful things to say about the management of world reserves. And Lawrence Klein was invited to furnish a progress report on Project LINK, including an estimate of the costs and benefits of this ambitious multinational enterprise. Discussants were assigned to each of these three papers, but, as you will see, they took some useful liberties.

The fourth session was devoted to a stock-taking. A panel of academic and government economists, under the chairmanship of Charles Kindleberger, was asked to survey what we know and what we need most urgently to know from the standpoint of policy formation. The summary of the discussion, in Part IV, will give you some idea of what transpired, even though it contains only the comments of the appointed oracles, not of the self-appointed who spoke from the floor.

I dislike editors who comment invidiously on the efforts of their authors, and I will not do so here. It is, in fact, my duty to shoulder the blame for some of the flaws you may detect.

When I commissioned the papers that appear in this book, I asked the authors a number of questions. Some of these were very broad: What has recent research told us about the causes and effects of international transactions and international economic policies? What more do we need to know, and how do we go about learning it? Where, in other words, is the frontier of ignorance right now, and how can we push it back most efficiently? Some of my questions were more technical: What does the most recent theoretical work tell us we should test or measure? And what has recent empirical work taught about designing theories? Do we pay sufficient attention to the institutional and political environment? Do we specify carefully enough the structures of national and world markets? Or are we apt to neglect certain important realities, political and economic, merely because they are difficult to model or measure? Finally, I asked a series of questions that were meant to elicit cost–benefit analyses of research strategies: Have we been responding effectively to the requirements of those who make policy? Or have we perhaps been responding too well to their short-run needs and neglecting the long-run problems of the international economy? Most important, have we allowed our skills to define our priorities, choosing to study only the problems we can solve with techniques we have at hand instead of trying to fashion the techniques required to study the problems we ought to be solving?

None of the nine authors whose papers appear here has tried to answer all my questions. Some of the questions were not germane to their special topics. Each of us, moreover, has his own comparative advantage. Some of us are better at surveying what others have done, some at doing and describing their own work, and some at telling others what they should be doing. And no one, regardless of versatility, could answer every one of my questions in a single paper of the size I allowed. You will find, then, that some of the papers are long on descriptions of recent research but short on suggestions for further work, while others are long on suggestions for new tests and estimates but short on descriptions of work done to date. (None of the papers, I trust, is just plain long.)

I have also to take responsibility for the form of the book. The choice of topics to be surveyed is to some extent a reflection of my personal curiosity. The choice, moreover, has a backward bias. It is much easier to map and subdivide the world we already know than one we have not yet explored.

Finally, I must take responsibility for a decision that some readers will deplore. Although I asked the authors to appraise the implications of our knowledge and ignorance for the conduct of public policy, my instructions emphasized positive economics – the relationships between pure theory and quantification. This is not a book about political economy or about international economic relations. It can perhaps be viewed as a complement to Bergsten's recent study for the Ford Foundation, *The Future of the International Economic Order,* not as a competitor.

Although I promised to refrain from comment on the papers, I am moved to end this Preface with two observations inspired by my reading of the manuscript. First, I detect a dangerous ambiguity in our quantitative work. We do not distinguish carefully enough between the *testing* of hypotheses and the *estimation* of structural relationships. The ambiguity is rampant in economics, partly because the development of econometric method has been so heavily influenced by the requirements of economic forecasting. But this is no reason to perpetuate it. We should be spending more time and thought on the construction of tests that will help us to discriminate between hypotheses having very different economic implications. It is not enough to show that our favorite theory does as well as – or better than – some other theory when it comes to accounting retrospectively for the available evidence. Second, I would echo Kindleberger's plea for the resurrection of historical studies – and not just cliometric studies. Regression equations are not the only forms of scientific evidence, the contents of this book notwithstanding. The phenomena with which we deal and those with which we should be dealing are far too complicated to be investigated by a single method. To answer affirmatively the question I posed earlier, we *do* tend often to neglect those aspects of our subject that defy analysis by techniques we have at hand. This is a sure road to triviality.

I accumulated many debts planning for the conference and editing this volume. I am especially grateful to John P. Lewis,

Dean of the Woodrow Wilson School, for joining the resources of the School to those of the International Finance Section as co-sponsor of the conference. I am grateful to Jane Armistead and Elizabeth Search of the International Finance Section for managing flows of paper and people before, during, and after the conference, and to Ellen Seiler, our expert and patient editor, who prepared this volume for publication. Above all, I am grateful to the authors of the papers and to the discussants. They were remarkably responsive to my questions, delivered their manuscripts on time, and, after the conference, dealt graciously and energetically with my extravagant suggestions for revision.

PETER B. KENEN

PART I

TRADE, PROTECTION, AND DOMESTIC PRODUCTION

TESTING TRADE THEORIES*

Robert M. Stern

International trade theory is mainly concerned with determining what goods and services countries will buy and sell in foreign trade, the gains from trade, and how the gains are divided within and among the trading countries. These concerns are of course positive and normative. In theorizing about such matters, we construct abstract models with the presumption that these models will be coherent, logical, interesting, and relevant. While empirical considerations have some bearing on model construction, they obviously become more crucial when a model is to be confronted by observation. At this juncture, what counts most are empirical specification and interpretation of results. These considerations will constitute the primary focus of this paper.

Section 1 begins with a brief discussion of the various theoretical models that purport to explain the commodity composition and direction of trade. Sections 2 to 5 contain a review of the major recent developments in the empirical testing of these models.[1] Some suggestions for future research are then given in section 6. Section 7 deals with empirical investigation of the relations between international trade and returns to factors, and section 8 with economic expansion and trade.[2] Some concluding remarks are made in section 9.

1. THEORIES OF THE COMMODITY COMPOSITION AND DIRECTION OF TRADE

The classical determination of what goods and services countries will buy and sell in foreign trade is based on the theory of

* I am indebted to B. Balassa, J. N. Bhagwati, A. V. Deardorff, P. S. Heller, E. E. Leamer, J. D. Richardson, G. Saxonhouse, H. T. Shapiro, C. P. Staelin, and members of the Research Seminar in International Economics at the University of Michigan for helpful comments on earlier versions of this paper.

1 My focus will be primarily on developments from about 1968 onward. Accounts of prior research efforts are to be found especially in Bhagwati (1964, 1969) and the references cited therein.

2 In order to reduce the scope of the paper, I shall not discuss several important areas for research, for example, the theory and measurement of trade creation and diversion in the context of customs-union and other preferential arrangements, computational models for assessing the effects of multilateral trade liberalization, and the microfoundations of macroeconometric models of trade and the balance of payments. Nor shall I deal systematically with the effects of international labor migration and direct foreign investment upon trade.

comparative advantage. As formulated by Ricardo and subsequently further elaborated and refined by the neoclassicists, the theory identified and arrayed goods in each country according to their unit costs. The precise pattern of specialization in production and trade depended on comparative costs, with the dividing line between imports and exports determined by reciprocal demand, subject to monetary equilibrium in the balance of trade. As simple as it is, the comparative-cost principle has profound implications for maximizing economic efficiency and welfare.[3]

From the empirical standpoint, the hypothesis suggested by the Ricardian model is that the observed composition of trade can be explained by intercountry variations in comparative costs. The information on trade patterns needed to test this hypothesis can generally be obtained from official published sources. However, the cost data required have to be searched out or specially constructed for the occasion. Since labor is the key productive factor in the Ricardian model, measures of comparative labor productivity have been designed to serve as a proxy for comparative costs. Given the existence of other productive factors and the fact that, in actuality, trade is determined by differences in absolute money prices among countries, the question becomes: How good is comparative labor productivity as an approximation of comparative total factor productivity and of comparative selling prices? As we shall note below, empirical testing of the Ricardian model has foundered on this particular issue, and interest has increasingly focused on more comprehensive measures of intercountry differences in efficiency, especially in the context of estimating production functions.

But even supposing that an empirical relationship is established between specialization in trade and variations in comparative costs, this does not answer the more fundamental question of what determines these variations in costs. The Ricardian model is not of much help here, since it presumes that comparative-cost differences are a fact of life and thus do not require separate investigation.

It is concern for a more complete understanding of the sources of comparative advantage that distinguishes the Heckscher–Ohlin model from its forebears. In the form of the model that was popularized especially by Samuelson and others, intercountry variations in comparative costs were determined by differential endowments of productive factors, with the quality of factors and

---

3 While we shall not be concerned directly with the gains from trade, welfare considerations will of course be implicit throughout the discussion.

production functions for given goods taken to be the same everywhere. Two well-known theorems have emerged from the Heckscher–Ohlin model: (1) countries will tend to export goods embodying their relatively most abundant factors and import goods embodying their relatively most scarce factors; and (2) under certain specified conditions, international trade will result in the equalization of returns to factors among countries.

As noted below, empirical work on the Heckscher–Ohlin model has been confined mainly to testing the factor-endowments hypothesis. Because information on factor endowments is not gathered systematically in most countries, researchers have had to rely especially upon data compiled from national input–output tables and on their own special constructs for the investigation at hand. Lacking internationally comparable data, tests of the factor-endowments hypothesis have typically been concentrated on individual nations. The early tests by Leontief and others, conducted within the framework of a two-factor version of the model, estimated the capital and labor requirements of exports and imports, but often yielded results that suggested incorrect or incomplete specification and measurement. Some of these difficulties were subsequently dealt with by redefining and expanding the number of factors in order to distinguish physical capital, human capital, raw (uneducated) labor, and natural resources.

While the foregoing line of research has enhanced significantly our understanding of the sources of comparative advantage, the subject has by no means been exhausted; there are apparently other important influences on comparative advantage that lie outside the Heckscher–Ohlin model. These other influences relate mainly to technological differences, which the model assumes away, economies of scale, and market imperfections of various kinds. Moreover, the model has come under increasingly critical scrutiny because it does not offer an explanation of what determines a country's initial factor endowment and how this endowment may change through time.

Since phenomena like technological influences, scale economies, and market imperfections cannot be readily observed, they have to be approximated. Technological influences have been represented by such measures as R & D expenditures, the employment of scientists and engineers, and total and per capita GNP. Scale economies have been approximated on the basis of value added per man in different-sized establishments and on the basis of GNP measures. Market imperfections, such as tariffs, have been represented by averages of nominal and effective rates.

As we shall see, a wide latitude has been used in the selection of these proxy measures, depending upon the data available and the framework in which the hypotheses are posed for investigation. This makes it difficult at times to evaluate and compare the results of particular studies. In addition, most of the studies relate to specific points in time, thus affording only limited insight into the initial determination of comparative advantage and the process of change through time.

It should be clear from this discussion that inquiry into the determinants of comparative advantage has progressed considerably beyond the frameworks of the simplified Ricardian and Heckscher–Ohlin models. In particular, technological and other phenomena not embraced by the traditional models have been found to be important. At the same time, much of the work emphasizing these "newer" forces appears ad hoc in character. This is due, in part, to data problems, but it also reflects deficiencies especially in the theoretical analysis of the process and the impact of technical change and factor accumulation upon production and trade.

2. TESTING THE RICARDIAN–NEOCLASSICAL MODEL OF COMPARATIVE COSTS

The early empirical tests of the Ricardian model of comparative costs were markedly simplistic.[4] Assuming a Ricardian world in which labor was the only factor of production, it was hypothesized that the relative export performance of the United States and United Kingdom in third markets depended upon differences in output per man by industry, which in turn would be reflected successively in differences in unit wage costs, unit value added, and unit prices.

In his 1964 survey of trade theory, Bhagwati (pp. 4–17) examined the logic and underlying assumptions of the Ricardian model and the empirical procedure whereby the hypothesis was tested in successive steps. He argued that the procedure was defective insofar as relative export prices could not necessarily be approximated by labor productivities and the other measures. He went on to demonstrate this point using correlation methods and concluded (p. 16) that "there is yet no evidence in favor of the Ricardian hypothesis."

In subsequent reflection on this issue, Daly (1972) attributed

---

4 These tests were conducted by MacDougall, Stern, and Balassa. The precise references are given in Bhagwati (1964, 1969).

the lack of relationship between labor-productivity and export-price ratios in part to the fact that the labor-productivity calculations were based on measures of net value added, thus excluding intermediate inputs, while the export-price ratios were derived from measures conceptually closer to gross output. In his reaction to Daly's interpretation, Bhagwati (1972, p. 136) reiterated his skepticism about the labor-productivity approach to comparative advantage and expressed reservations as to whether the productivity data were in fact calculated on a net-value-added basis. On this same occasion, Balassa (1972, pp. 128–129) took issue with Bhagwati's contention about labor productivities and export prices, arguing that the unit values used as proxies for export prices reflected quality differences and were thus not good measures of price, and that, in any case, the hypothesis presupposed the existence of intercountry productivity differences.

A separate empirical investigation would be required to evaluate Balassa's assertion concerning the appropriateness of unit values. But even if they are appropriate, prediction based on the Ricardian model may be of limited interest, since, as Bhagwati (1964, pp. 16–17) and Johnson (1968, p. 28) have noted, it does not shed much light on the nature and sources of comparative advantage.

The foregoing discussion brings out the limitations of treating labor productivity as exogenous and as the most important determinant of comparative-cost differences.[5] It would be no less arbitrary, as Bhagwati (1972, p. 134) noted, to focus on the productivity of capital as the crucial factor, especially in view of the importance of human capital and capital inputs into natural resources. What this suggests, therefore, is that we should adopt a multifactor view of the world and premise the Ricardian–neoclassical model on the existence of intercountry differences in total factor productivity, that is, on intercountry differences in production functions for given goods.

Thus, the model could be tested by fitting production functions for industries in different countries, with the expectation that a country's exports would be concentrated in its relatively most efficient industries and its imports in its least efficient ones. The

---

5 For a study in which essentially negative conclusions were reached concerning the hypothesis that changes in labor productivity governed changes in export performance, see Kreinin (1969). Glejser (1972) has examined relative prices and market shares prior and subsequent to the formation of the European Common Market and concluded that relatively high elasticities of substitution between competitors served to confirm the theory of comparative costs. His interpretation of the theory, however, is quite different from what we are discussing.

problem is, however, that the model offers no guide in choosing the most appropriate production function for estimating purposes. Since different production functions exhibit different properties, the choice of any particular type may well color the results. In order to illustrate these points and to provide some indication of possible directions for future research, it may be fruitful to review some recent work that has been done on inter-country efficiency differences.[6]

Intercountry Efficiency Differences

Stryker (1968), using a Cobb–Douglas framework, constructed a model to explain differences over time in the growth of exports for the United States and Canada in twenty-four manufacturing industries in terms of differing rates of technological progress, scale effects, and factor-price changes. While his results were suggestive, they were not particularly strong for a variety of reasons, such as the framework chosen, the assumption that technological change was disembodied and could be approximated by a linear time trend, and the application of U.S. industry coefficients to industries in Canada. There may have been some problem, moreover, in making Canadian–U.S. comparisons for manufactured exports, since the United States is dominant in Canadian markets, and the countries do not compete extensively in exports to third markets. Despite these qualifications, Stryker's work was certainly a marked improvement on the earlier simplistic tests of the one-factor Ricardian model.

Several other studies have dealt with intercountry differences in efficiency per se, although they have not related these differences to observed differences in the commodity composition of trade. In this sense, these efforts amount to testing one of the major differences between assumptions of the Ricardo–neoclassical and Heckscher–Ohlin models: Are production functions for given goods and industries different or the same among countries? Some investigators, however, have been asking how important different factor endowments are in comparison with technological differences, scale economies, and other influences upon the commodity composition of trade. We shall review these latter efforts after we have discussed the various empirical tests of the Heckscher–Ohlin model.

6 Perhaps of greatest influence is the pioneering research on the CES production function by Arrow *et al.* (1962), in which Hicks–neutral efficiency scalars were estimated for certain comparable U.S. and Japanese industries.

Among the investigations of efficiency differences among countries, the efforts of Clague (1967), Nelson (1968), Daniels (1969), Gehrels (1970), and Hayami and Ruttan (1970) are worthy of note. Clague's work involved fitting a CES production function to a cross-section of eleven manufacturing industries in the United States and Peru. The question he asked was: What would the productivity of Peruvian labor be relative to U.S. labor if Peru had the same capital–labor ratio as the United States, with allowance being made for economies of scale? The various observations on labor and capital inputs were centered around 1960. Subject to caveats concerning the fact that the Peruvian observations were drawn from the urban–industrial sector only, the possibility of substitution between labor and other inputs, differences in economic environment, and differences in the average age of equipment in the two countries, Clague observed that Peruvian efficiency was substantially less than that of the United States.[7] The smallest differences were found in the more capital-intensive industries such as raw sugar, cement, and chemicals, and the largest differences in the less capital-intensive industries such as leather tanning, cotton textiles, and glass containers.

Nelson's point of departure was similar to Clague's in that only about one-third of the observed differences in labor productivity in manufacturing industry between Colombia and the United States could be explained by differences in the capital–labor ratio alone. In order to comprehend these vast differences in productivity, Nelson invoked the role that technology and new-product development play, especially in developed countries. He suggested that one should view technological change dynamically as a diffusion process, with the economic system adapting over time toward (but not reaching) equilibrium. Firms would therefore exhibit different efficiency characteristics within as well as between countries in terms of the technology they were using. By comparing cross sections of Colombian and U.S. value added by firm size in 1958 and examining the composition of employment and output by firm size within Colombia in 1958 and 1964, Nelson concluded that the largest firms in Colombia were closest in terms of productivity to their U.S. counterparts and more favorably situated than smaller firms within Colombia.

Gehrels investigated efficiency differences in a cross section of manufacturing for the United States and Germany in 1962 and

---

[7] Clague's (1969) estimates of the elasticities of substitution for Peruvian manufacturing were challenged by Witte (1971) on the grounds that they excluded the traditional sector. See Clague (1971) for a defense of his results.

for the United States and the United Kingdom in 1958, again trying to determine the extent to which differences in relative labor-input coefficients were due to differences in capital per man or in resource effectiveness. He estimated that somewhat less than half the German–U.S. labor-productivity differences were due to differences in resource effectiveness, whereas most of the U.S.–U.K. productivity differences were attributable to such differences. Daniels's objective was to estimate efficiency differences in seventeen 2-digit SIC manufacturing industries for eight less developed countries, using aggregated and disaggregated national cross-section data from the 1950s and early 1960s. He employed a CES production function and assumed constant returns to scale. For want of better data, he chose as a proxy for capital input the rated horsepower capacity of installed prime movers and electric motors in operation. Testing the significance of the calculated efficiency scalars across industries by country, he concluded that Spain was the most efficient of the group and Paraguay the least efficient, but that it was not possible to make efficiency distinctions among El Salvador, Argentina, Korea, Chile, and Peru.

Finally, Hayami and Ruttan sought to explain agricultural productivity differences among countries. They fitted a Cobb–Douglas production function to three separate cross sections of thirty-eight developed and less developed countries for averages of years centered on 1955, 1960, and 1965. In contrast to the studies noted immediately above, Hayami and Ruttan did not seek to measure directly intercountry differences in agricultural efficiency. They nevertheless conceived of their model in the same sense as Nelson's model of the diffusion process, arguing that the full range of technological alternatives was only partially available to individual producers and countries. While such an observation may be correct, their production-function estimates did not test this contention directly. It might be interesting, accordingly, to conduct explicit cross-country studies of differences in agricultural efficiency.

While these various studies offer numerous insights, they are difficult to compare because of intercountry differences in the stage of development, the time periods covered, and the empirical proxies used. Furthermore, these studies offer little guidance in selecting for estimation one production function over another, and, from the standpoint of the international-trade models that concern us here, they have not yet been connected systematically with the observed composition and direction of trade. Granted all these limitations, there nevertheless appears to be substantial evidence of intercountry efficiency differences, as posited by the Ricardian–neoclassical model. As will be noted below, this conclusion is further borne out by the "newer" explanations of comparative advantage in which technological factors play a substantial role.

3. TESTING THE HECKSCHER–OHLIN FACTOR-ENDOWMENTS MODEL

Following the unveiling of Leontief's paradox in his test of the Heckscher–Ohlin factor-endowments model for U.S. trade, the literature was filled with both theoretical and empirical efforts to resolve the paradox and to determine whether it applied to other countries. The thrust of these efforts was directed in large measure at the simplicity of Leontief's test and to the nature of the production conditions subsumed in the model. In particular, the empirical specification of the explanatory variables was expanded beyond just capital and labor to include the natural-resource content of trade and to distinguish human capital from physical capital and raw (uneducated) labor. Also, as noted above, a great deal of work on production functions has been generated out of concern with the empirical foundations of the Heckscher–Ohlin model. The foregoing and certain other issues connected with the factor-endowments model will occupy our attention in this section.

Natural Resources

The composition of trade includes, of course, both primary commodities and manufactures at different stages of processing. Most observers have asserted that, since trade in primary commodities is so obviously dependent upon differences in natural endowments, there is no need to test the Heckscher–Ohlin theory for this component of trade. In a formal sense, this is not correct, because both capital and labor are required to improve natural resources to give them economic value, and countries may certainly combine these factors in somewhat different proportions when producing natural-resource products. Moreover, since primary commodities move in raw and processed form, there may be a need to explain the basis for such specialization.

Because of the importance of natural-resource products, it is difficult to know where to draw the line in defining industries for analytical purposes. Tests of the Heckscher–Ohlin model may therefore be confounded on both the export and import sides unless the investigator takes pains to recognize this issue. Leontief himself made allowance for this factor in his subsequent work on the subject, as have later investigators.[8] In other studies, an attempt is made to minimize the impact of natural-resource products by concentrating strictly on trade in manufactures as classified in SITC classes 5–8.[9] The influence of natural-resource considerations nevertheless remains a matter of central concern in evaluating empirical studies of comparative advantage.[10]

Human Capital

The inclusion of human capital as a major determinant of the commodity structure of trade was recognized by Leontief and later became a prime focus in empirical implementation of the Heckscher–Ohlin model.[11] There seems to be little question now that U.S. exports are relatively more human-capital intensive than imports. Similarly, in studying the factor content of trade of other countries, the analysis is enriched when human capital is considered apart from physical capital and raw (uneducated) labor. Given the recognized importance of human capital, the main issues at present involve how best to approximate it, how to relate it to other factor inputs, and how to distinguish it especially from the technological characteristics of trade.

More precisely, if human capital is reflected in earned income,

8 Thus, for example, Baldwin (1971) found in his comprehensive study of the determinants of the commodity structure of U.S. trade, using 1958 input–output data and 1962 trade data, that the ratio of capital per man-year in import-competing production to that in export production was 1.27, reconfirming the Leontief paradox. However, when natural-resource products were excluded, the ratio fell to 1.04. See Baldwin (p. 135, note a) for his "arbitrary" definition of natural-resource products. In examining the factor content of the U.S. bilateral trade pattern by selected regions, the importance of natural-resource products in trade with Canada and the less developed countries was evident (p. 140).

9 See, for example, Hufbauer (1970) and Leamer (forthcoming a).

10 Using 1947 and 1958 input–output data as applied to the 1947 and 1962 composition of U.S. trade, Weiser (1968) concluded that U.S. imports were still relatively more natural-resource intensive than exports, but that the natural-resource scarcity had been reduced in the intervening years. Williams (1970) used a conceptual framework designed explicitly to measure the notion of the "plentifulness" of labor, capital, and natural resources in terms of the ratio of domestic endowments to those in the rest of the world and to explain the volume and direction of the factor content of trade. He concluded that capital was the abundant factor in the United States and that the Leontief paradox was therefore invalid.

11 See Kenen (1970) for a review of the major empirical considerations in and results of introducing human capital into the analysis, and for suggestions on possible avenues for further theoretical exploration.

wage differentials should reflect differences in human capital per person. The procedure here is to calculate wage differentials relative to unskilled or uneducated labor and to capitalize these differentials at some appropriate discount rate. Another measure, based on the returns to all factors, involves the use of data on factor incomes to calculate the returns to human capital, physical capital, and raw labor. A third measure is to calculate the cost of human capital based on the sum of the direct costs of education and training plus foregone earnings. Finally, some index of skills can be constructed on the basis of the importance of different occupational groups in producing exports and imports. As Bhagwati has noted (1969, p. 107), the first three measures should, in principle, yield identical results. A skill index may be less satisfactory than these other measures to the extent that it may not reflect fully the capital accumulation involved.[12]

The main problem in using wage differentials is the difficulty of isolating the influences of market imperfections from the returns to investment in human capital. Working directly with returns to factors involves serious valuation problems, especially in terms of differential profit rates and interest returns by industry. Finally, if formal education is used as the basis for calculating the cost of human-capital investment, insufficient allowance may be made for other types of investment, such as on-the-job training. Since we are dealing with basically empirical issues, more than one type of calculation would appear to be in order to reduce the possibility of measurement error.

In this respect, Baldwin's (1971) work already mentioned is interesting, for he tested a number of alternative measures of human-capital investment and indexes for skill groups by occupation and educational attainment. He found in general that the skill-group measures had greater explanatory value than the human-capital measures.[13] These results are not definitive, however, since Baldwin did not test directly in his regressions the wage-differential concept of human capital. On this point, Branson (1971) concluded on the basis of a much more highly aggregated sample of U.S. industries and trade that both wage differentials and skill mix were important determinants of the commodity structure of U.S. trade. Skill mix may thus reflect human-capital

12 Krueger (1970, p. 232) has additional comment on this point.
13 On the basis of calculations of the cost of formal schooling plus foregone earnings, Fareed (1972) found that U.S. exports in 1947 were relatively human-capital intensive. Baldwin reached essentially the same conclusion when natural-resource industries were excluded. Neither author made allowance for on-the-job training costs, so that their measures of human capital are understated.

differences that are not captured by wage differentials.[14] But it is also likely that a higher skill mix is characteristic of high-technology U.S. industries that specialize in the introduction of improved and new products and processes.

Baldwin (1971, p. 128) also asked whether physical and human capital should be added together or treated separately, the point being whether to regard different forms of capital as substitutes or complements. Since there was no a priori reason to accept one assumption or the other, he included the variables both ways in his regressions and the results were generally statistically significant. Branson (1973) has argued, however, that physical and human capital should not be aggregated, since they are neither perfect substitutes nor perfect complements in production. The fact that the variables reflected quite different coefficients of opposite sign in Branson's regression explaining U.S. trade would seem to support his contention. Nevertheless, the relationship of the different forms of capital to each other and to other factors of production is still an open question.

It may also be of interest here to cite some recent studies of other countries in which human capital has been treated separately. Thus, Bhagwati and Bharadwaj (1970) calculated measures of human capital for India for 1953–54 based on wage differentials and on the returns to physical capital, human capital, and unskilled labor. Combining human- with physical-capital estimates, they concluded that Indian exports were relatively labor intensive.[15] They obtained conflicting results, however, for their alternative measures, with the wage differentials showing exports to be relatively human-capital intensive and the returns calculations indicating the opposite. The authors attributed these differences in part to data problems encountered in measuring physical capital and to interindustry variations in unskilled wages and profit rates. While they stated a preference for the results based on the returns calculations because of the lesser reliability of the capital-stock estimates, they also pointed out that insofar as

14 In a more recent paper, Branson (1973) tested the finding noted by Waehrer (1968) that skill mix was a better predictor than wages of the variation in U.S. trade balances by industry. Using Hufbauer's (1970) data on wage differentials and the industry proportions of scientific, professional, or technical workers, Branson concluded that Waehrer's results did not hold. Branson's conclusion is clouded, however, because Waehrer's measure of skill mix was much more comprehensive than Hufbauer's, and her calculations of wages were based on skill classes rather than a simple wage differential.

15 They also made calculations of value added per employee, which may be a proxy for capital–labor intensity, and reached a similar conclusion. But see Bhagwati (1969, p. 106–107) for some critical remarks on the interpretation of this composite measure in view of problems arising from monopoly profits and factor-price distortions.

human capital and physical capital are not directly related, exports could be both labor and human-capital intensive. This would appear consistent with our earlier observation that skill measures impart information additional to that conveyed by wage differentials, insofar as the authors used a skill ratio by industry in their human-capital estimates.

In a study designed to yield insights into possible changes in the industry mix to stimulate LDC industrialization and exports, Fels (1972) had occasion to correlate trade balances per employee with total physical and human capital per employee for 1962 and 1969, for nineteen West German industries. By separating West German trade with less developed countries from its trade with other industrialized countries, he obtained R^2's of 0.59 and 0.71 for the former countries as compared with 0.18 and 0.30 for the latter. Because Fels did not use input–output data and calculated human capital by wage differentials, it is difficult to compare his work directly with the earlier work by Roskamp and McMeekin (1968), in which West German exports were found to be relatively human-capital intensive. It might be interesting, therefore, to replicate Fels's study using input–output data, to determine whether the factor intensity of West German exports differed by region. Since Fels presented additional data on industry-skill proportions, their influence could be tested as well.

Two studies have been made for Brazil. Lowinger (1971) used the percentage of skilled employees in an industry earning more than an assumed wage for unskilled workers as an approximation of human capital in twenty manufacturing industries in 1959. He found a rank correlation of 0.70 between this measure and the 1966 industry ratios of net imports (from the United States, Canada, and Western Europe) to domestic sales in Brazil. Rank correlations with respect to physical capital as measured by horsepower per employee and by value added per employee were not statistically significant. Lowinger concluded, therefore, that Brazil's net imports of manufactures were human-capital intensive based on his skill index.[16]

Tyler (1972) made two calculations of the skill requirements of Brazil's exports and imports based upon U.S. and Brazilian census data for 1960. He obtained a rank correlation of 0.79

16 Lowinger also obtained significant rank correlations when he correlated the ratio of industry imports to total imports with his skill index and his proxy measure of physical capital. Strictly speaking, this does not constitute a test of the Heckscher–Ohlin theory, which is concerned rather with net exports (imports). This same comment applies to Tyler's work (1972) noted below.

between Brazil's skill mix (using U.S. coefficients for forty-six industries) and net imports as a proportion of total imports and exports by industry, thereby reaching the same conclusion as Lowinger concerning the human-capital intensity of Brazil's net imports of manufactures. He also found a weak indication that Brazil's industrial exports to members of the Latin American Free Trade Association (LAFTA) were relatively more skill-intensive than to developed countries.[17]

The foregoing studies by Bhagwati and Bharadwaj, Fels, Lowinger, and Tyler focused narrowly on the role of human capital in determining comparative advantage. We have made reference already to the importance of technological factors that may be responsible for intercountry differences in product improvement and development. Several studies have addressed themselves to these explanations as well as to the role of factor endowments. We shall leave such studies for separate discussion below. At this point, let us consider some of the issues arising in the empirical measurement of factor intensities and capital–labor substitution.

Factor Intensities and Capital–Labor Substitution

For the factor-endowments explanation of trade to be valid, there must be no factor-intensity reversals in the capital–labor combinations for industries in different countries. The first systematic investigation of this assumption was by Minhas (1962), who concluded that there was a significant empirical likelihood that such reversals might in fact occur. Minhas's conclusions have been criticized by several authors on a number of scores, as noted by Bhagwati (1969, pp. 100–107), and the consensus is that the strong-factor-intensity assumption seems to hold empirically.[18] On the other hand, a more recent investigation by Yeung and Tsang (1972), who employed a form of variable-elasticity-of-substitution (VES) production function for U.S. manufacturing data, found strong indications that factor-intensity reversals were likely. If this type of production function were fitted to the inter-

17 Tyler observed that the skill mix of Brazil's manufactured exports was in about the same range as those for France, Austria, Belgium, and Italy. He cited as possible explanations, although his statistical results were poor, the fact that manufacturing is concentrated in the relatively high per capita income states of Brazil, the importance of natural-resource products in Brazilian exports, the superior relative efficiency of these industries, and factor-market distortions that have worked against the relatively more labor-intensive industries in Brazil.

18 For additional criticisms of Minhas's results, see Hutcheson (1969), Gehrels (1970), and Philpot (1970).

national cross-section data used by Minhas and others, the presumption is that reversals would similarly be observed. In such an event, we would still be in an ambiguous situation concerning the empirical likelihood of factor reversals.

This research brings out the point already mentioned that the Heckscher–Ohlin and other trade models in themselves do not offer any guidance in selecting the form of production function to be estimated. So long as this is the case, we may continue to get conflicting results like those just noted. Nonetheless, there may be some interesting questions bearing on trade models that are worth pursuing in the context of estimating production functions. For example, the attempts by Yahr (1968), Mitchell (1968), and Philpot (1970) to introduce labor quality as a separate factor in production-function estimation could be explored further, following Bhagwati's suggestion (1969, p. 104) that distinctions be made between different classes of skills as different factor inputs. It might also be of interest to test whether the elasticity of substitution in particular industries is the same across countries. A directly related question is whether intercountry differences in efficiency are neutral or biased toward labor or capital augmentation.[19] Finally, experimentation in an intercountry context with such recent innovations as the translog production frontier developed by Christensen *et al.* (1973) might yield insights concerning production relationships that go beyond the CES and related representations.

Further research on the intercountry aspects of production functions can be viewed within the strict confines of the factor-endowments model as a means of determining if the assumption of identical production functions is valid. Alternatively, given the evidence of intercountry differences in efficiency, there may be no compelling reason to accept this assumption. In such an event, production-function research might best be conceived in a broader framework as a potentially useful approach in isolating the phenomena that shape comparative advantage.

Tariffs and Other Distortions

Any model that purports to explain the composition and direction of trade must obviously take into account the existing level and

19 Yahr (1968) concluded on the basis of her CES cross-section production-function estimates, which included a variable for labor quality, that the availability of high-quality labor induced entrepreneurs to substitute labor for physical capital, at given factor prices.

structure of protection afforded by tariff and nontariff barriers to trade. In this connection, Travis (1972) especially has argued that tariffs may have an important effect on Heckscher–Ohlin-type trade for the United States inasmuch as U.S. imports of labor-intensive goods are restricted. In reaching this conclusion, Travis relied on a model with capital and labor inputs, with no distinction being drawn between physical and human capital. Labor was thus considered the scarce factor and the beneficiary of protection.

In order to test Travis's contention more generally, Baldwin (1971, p. 138) sought to estimate the change in the capital–labor ratio of the new commodity composition of U.S. imports that would result if all tariff and nontariff barriers were removed, subject to guesstimates about the import-price elasticities of demand. Baldwin concluded that the new capital–labor ratio would be about 5 per cent lower than the ratio that he computed with the barriers intact. Travis's contention was thus borne out to some extent, although certainly not as powerfully as he had claimed.

Trade barriers outside the United States also affect trade, and, as Baldwin noted (p. 138), it would be interesting as well to determine what impact their removal would have on the commodity composition and factor content of trade. He also made the same point (pp. 130–131) with respect to the various market imperfections and distortions existing in the United States and elsewhere that affect trade.

International Factor Movements

The assumptions of static trade models that factors are in fixed supply and do not move internationally have been questioned on numerous occasions, especially in theoretical inquiries. Thus, the structure and factor content of trade will change over time, especially in response to differential rates in the accumulation of physical and human capital. International labor migration and direct foreign investment will also affect factor endowments and trade. In this latter regard, the geographic and sectoral composition of U.S. direct investment has received some attention, especially inasmuch as investment in extractive industries abroad is reflected in the composition of U.S. imports. Direct investment in maufacturing will also, of course, have an impact on the composition of trade. A more complete understanding of the evolution of the structure and factor content of trade thus requires explicit recognition of differential factor accumulation and international factor movements.[20]

Methodology

In the tests of the Heckscher–Ohlin model referred to above, two procedures were followed. The first was to calculate the direct and indirect factor requirements of a bundle of exports and imports using input–output data and to compare the capital–labor ratios. The second was to use cross-section regression or rank-correlation methods in order to explain interindustry variations in net exports (imports) by means of capital–labor ratios, skill mix, etc.

With regard to the "Leontief type" tests, Finger (1969) has asked whether, in a multicommodity world, there is sufficient variation in capital–labor ratios so that export industries can be distinguished from import industries. He classified export industries according to whether an industry's exports per million dollars of total exports exceeded imports comparably measured, and conversely for import industries. Industries were designated as capital- or labor-intensive relative to the median ratio for all industries. He then tested by chi square the null hypothesis that the trade classifications and factor-intensity classifications were independent. The null hypothesis could not be rejected for most of Leontief's calculations based on 1947 and 1951 data. Finger also computed the mean capital–labor ratio of the export and import industries and tested the hypothesis that the means were equal in the cases of Leontief-type studies for the United States, Japan, West Germany, and India. Using Fisher exact probabilities, he concluded that in general the null hypothesis of equal means could not be rejected. It appeared to him, therefore, that the results of many of the Leontief-type tests were attributable to chance.

In order to pose this issue more clearly, we may note that the calculations of factor requirements per million dollars of exports and competitive imports, as in Baldwin (1971, p. 134), reveal that

20 See Kenen (1970, pp. 206–212) for some pertinent comments and references on these issues. Of particular interest is the work that he cites by Yudin (1968) on borrowing skills and the literature on the brain drain relating to importing skills. Horst (1972) has called attention to the factors influencing decisions by U.S. manufacturers to expand their Canadian subsidiaries as an alternative to exporting from U.S. facilities. See also Schmitz and Helmberger (1970) for some pertinent comments on the effects of direct investment on trade.

the import–export ratios hover on either side of unity. Given these results, Finger would propose to determine whether the capital–labor ratios in *exports* and *competitive imports* can be distinguished from one another. This differs, however, from the hypothesis that Finger in fact tested, which, as noted above, was framed in terms of the dichotomy between export and import industries according to their trade balances. It would appear therefore that his rejection of the Leontief-type tests is not warranted, since he did not test a Leontief-type classification. It is still conceivable, of course, that Leontief-type results could be due to chance: One way to try to resolve this issue would be to calculate the capital–labor requirements for exports and competitive imports for different points in time using different input–output data. If the regularities persisted, we could then have more confidence in the observed differences.

Both the Leontief and correlation tests raise the usual sorts of econometric questions concerning aggregation and measurement error. There is some evidence in Branson's work (1971, p. 756) that differences in levels of aggregation affect regression results attempting to explain interindustry variations in trade balances. We have already mentioned the crudity especially of the capital-stock and returns measures. One final point worth mentioning here is the matter of scaling the trade-balance measurements in order to neutralize the effects of differences in industry size. Again, Branson's work (1971) indicates that scaling affects regression results.[21]

Conclusion

It should be evident from our discussion that the simple Heckscher–Ohlin model does not rest on strong empirical foundations. When natural resources and human capital are taken explicitly into account, the model affords greater insights. It should be stressed, however, that the data used in most investigations refer to individual countries, and that these data consequently offer no basis for inferring the factor-endowment characteristics of other trading countries. Moreover, it is not altogether clear how the various productive factors identified are interrelated in the process of production and trade.

---

21 In this regard, Branson (1971, p. 758) has noted that Baldwin's (1971) results may be biased because Baldwin's measure of industry exports and imports was not scaled in cases where trade was roughly balanced. However, Branson's scaling has problems of its own, as Leamer (forthcoming a, Appendix) has pointed out, because it assumes constancy in the general level of trade across commodities.

Some investigators have sought to evaluate the Heckscher–Ohlin model by subjecting the strong-factor-intensity assumption to
empirical test. There is an intrinsic difficulty here, however, since
the production functions used for estimating purposes may yield
conflicting results. In any event, intercountry differences in
efficiency seem sufficiently well established to make it most unlikely that the factor-endowments hypothesis is empirically valid
universally. We have then to go beyond factor endowments per se
to determine what other influences determine the composition
and direction of trade. This is what the "newer" theories of trade
have attempted to do. Let us see how they have fared.

4. TECHNOLOGICAL-GAP, PRODUCT-CYCLE, AND
SCALE-ECONOMY EXPLANATIONS OF THE
COMMODITY COMPOSITION OF TRADE

We have already indicated that attention has focused increasingly
on the influences that the traditional trade models take for granted or ignore. As mentioned, these influences involve chiefly intercountry differences in technological change with respect to the
introduction of improved and new products and processes and
the realization of scale economies in the domestic market. Because
these phenomena are essentially dynamic in character, it has been
relatively difficult to date to incorporate them endogenously into
theoretical models. Serious obstacles are then bound to be
encountered in hypothesis formulation and empirical testing.
Typically, the empirical problem is posed in terms of explaining
trade composition at a point in time in terms of factor endowments, technological variables, scale economies, demand influences, and other special factors such as tariffs and distance to
markets. With so many forces at work, there are bound to be difficulties in the interpretation and comparison of empirical results,
as we shall see.

In the subsections immediately following, I have grouped the
most important recent studies according to their focus on the
composition of exports, imports, and net exports (imports).
Thereafter I discuss some industry studies. Research dealing
explicitly with demand influences and intraindustry specialization
will be treated in section 5.

The Determinants of Export Composition

An especially ambitious and noteworthy effort to incorporate the
newer explanations of trade along with the older ones into an

empirical analysis has been made by Hufbauer (1970). He sought to explain the characteristics embodied in 1965 exports for twenty-four developed and less developed countries. Using 3-digit SITC trade data for manufactures and assuming that U.S. coefficients could be applied to all other countries, he calculated export characteristics for each country that were designed to reflect (1) capital per man, skill ratios, and wage differentials in accordance with the factor-endowments theory; (2) the "first trade date," to represent the introduction of new products according to the theory of the technological gap; (3) product differentiation, to represent a stage of specialization in the product cycle; (4) scale economies arising from specialization for the home market; and (5) the ratio of consumer-goods to total-industry sales, to capture the stage of economic development. These national export characteristics were then related by rank-correlation methods to various national attributes: fixed capital per man in manufacturing and skilled employees as a percentage of the labor force, to approximate factor endowments; gross domestic product per capita, to reflect technological sophistication; and total manufacturing output, to represent the possible realization of scale economies and the stage of development in production.

Despite the crudity of his measures, Hufbauer found that the various explanations did relatively well. This was due in part to certain strong intercorrelations involving wages and human skills, human and physical capital, the consumer-producer goods and the light–heavy industry classification, standardized and skilled goods, and scale economies and skilled goods. There was, nevertheless, a remarkable ordering of the country rankings in terms of the various characteristics, indicating that the commodity composition of exports of different countries did reflect different national attributes. Hufbauer thus concluded that both factor endowments and technological influences were important in explaining the composition of exports.

A study by Gruber and Vernon (1970) was designed to focus more explicitly on technolgical factors. They constructed a matrix for the 1964 exports of manufactures in twenty-four industrial categories, with respect to ten major exporting areas and twelve major importing areas. Eight industries were characterized as technology-intensive on the basis of having more than 6 per cent of their employment comprised of scientists and engineers: aircraft, office machines, drugs, chemicals, electrical machinery, instruments, agricultural machinery, and petroleum and coal. Each area's exports were normalized in relation to the exports for all areas. The variables chosen to explain these normalized exports were derived from U.S. experience and included (1) employees per dollar of value added, (2) scientists and engineers as a percentage of total employment, (3) fixed assets as a percentage of sales, (4) output delivered to other business as a percentage of total output, (5) industry concentration, and (6) import of crude materials as a percentage of total output.

Despite the data mining in which the authors apparently indulged, multiple regressions yielded significant results for only three countries: the United States, Japan, and Mexico. For the United States, the factor-intensity (1 and 3) and technological-intensity (2) variables were significant. The factor-intensity variables (1 and 3) were significant for Japan. The Mexican results made little sense intuitively. Given such meager pickings, one suspects that most of the variation in the dependent variable was probably averaged out by the normalization procedure that they followed. It would also appear that several of their industries were intensive in the use of natural resources or concentrated in the production of nontraded goods.

Partial tests of the product-cycle model have been carried out by Wells (1969) and Adler (1970).[22] Wells identified the stages of the product cycle in terms of the changes in U.S. exports of high-income products, with the timing of the expansion of foreign production depending upon the significance of scale economies and transport costs. He attempted to verify that the change in U.S. exports of consumer durables from 1952–53 to 1962–63 could be explained by the income elasticity of ownership of these goods, that the industries involved were subject to scale economies, and that unit transportation costs were low. Wells's formulations were unfortunately rather vague and his empiricism so casual that his results do not seem well grounded.

Adler sought to distinguish among U.S. exports of manufactures (SITC 5–8) to thirteen countries at different stages of development during 1953–63 according to differences in their income and price elasticities. His contention was that U.S. exports are more income-elastic as well as less price-elastic than those of competing suppliers in countries with different per capita incomes. His assumption about the relations involving price elas-

22 References to earlier studies of the technological-gap and product-cycle models for the cases of motion pictures, synthetic materials, and electronic capital goods are given in Wells (1969) and Morrall (1972). Studies of learning-by-doing as an important source of dynamic scale economies are also pertinent here, as, for example, Dudley (1972) and Klein (1973), which is discussed below.

ticities was shown to be invalid, however, by Deppler (1971), and, despite some further ruminations on the matter by Adler (1971), the differential income- and price-elasticity assumptions of the product-cycle model remain unresolved empirically. In a similar vein, Hufbauer and O'Neill (1972) tried without much success to determine the extent to which per-capita-income differences among countries and other factors explained the observed variation in the unit values of U.S. machinery exports.

The Determinants of Import Composition

Leamer's (forthcoming a) work is especially noteworthy, since it goes significantly beyond the works just described in terms of its approach and methodological innovations. Using a comparative cross-section regression analysis, Leamer sought to explain the commodity imports of twenty-eight 2-digit SITC manufactures across twelve industrialized Atlantic-area countries for 1958 in terms of three major types of variables: development variables, resistance variables, and various measures of national attributes. The development variables included the levels of GNP and population in the exporting and importing countries. These variables were considered to reflect both technological sophistication and possible scale economies arising from size differences. The resistance variables were tariff levels and distance to markets. National attributes of the Heckscher–Ohlin type included fixed capital per employee, installed electric capacity, and public expenditure on education as a percentage of national income. National technological attributes were represented by national R & D expenditures as a percentage of GNP.

There are several novelties in Leamer's work. First, he did not have to impose U.S. coefficients on other countries.[23] Second, his framework permitted the multiple testing of competing theories and he offered an explicit procedure for selecting the "best" theory. This is in contrast to Hufbauer's procedure of testing theories one by one.[24] Finally, Leamer allowed the "best" theory to vary

---

23 There has always been some question as to whether U.S. coefficients are applicable to other countries. In this regard, Keesing (1971) concluded that very similar results are obtained for the skill intensity of manufactured exports using the labor-skill coefficients of the nine leading industrial countries, based on 1965 data.

24 Thus, as Hufbauer (1970, pp. 160–172) noted: "It must be acknowledged that the chosen statistical tools [rank correlations] afford little more than a crude screen for eliminating unsatisfactory theories. No real attempt can be made, using such measures, to say which of several closely competing theories is 'best'."

with commodity class while assuming it constant across countries, and he then profiled each country's characteristics on the basis of the commodity-cross-section results. This is also in contrast to Hufbauer, who searched for a single theory for all commodities that could vary from country to country.

Because each of Leamer's twenty-eight equations involved more than twelve parameters, he relied on prior information from the literature to introduce constraints on these parameters and then employed Bayesian methods of estimation.[25] His best estimates based on posterior-mean elasticities were in reasonable agreement with other studies, indicating, for example, that the importing country's elasticity of GNP with respect to imports was below the GNP elasticity of the exporting region, that commodities could be characterized by differences in their capital–labor ratios in a way similar to Hufbauer's findings, and that the education coefficients were similar to Hufbauer's.

In mapping out his search for a best theory, Leamer's objective was to identify a subset of explanatory variables that provided an accurate and causally correct prediction.[26] He chose to formulate his predictions in terms of the import–GNP ratio, which will be closely related to the import share of the domestic market, on the assumption that the best theory would vary by commodity class. His conclusion was that the GNP and population variables offered the best predictions of the import–GNP ratio, and the distance and tariff variables the next best predictions. The measures of national attributes were, as a group, not significant. Leamer then made separate calculations by country in order to compare the country characteristics implied by the commodity cross sections. For the United States, for example, GNP and R & D expenditures were especially important. Benelux was distinguished only by its closeness to markets; the United Kingdom and France were

25 One important advantage of Bayesian methods is in dealing with multicollinearity, something that Hufbauer could not cope with and that consequently (pp. 165–166) led him to the methodological position that "a confluence of theory makes for good results."

26 The issue here has to do with classical hypothesis testing, which is designed to test the "truthfulness" of a theory. In carrying out such tests, it is common to add and drop variables in the estimating process. It is Leamer's (forthcoming b) contention that dropped variables should not be compensated for by reestimating, since this procedure inadvertently assumes that the included variables cause the excluded ones. If this assumption is incorrect, recomputation may thus distort causality. It follows that the restricted equation is adequate only if the correlation structure of the explanatory variables remains unchanged. His procedure attempts, therefore, to deal explicitly with these objections.

distinguished by large GNPs, R & D, and population; and Germany was distinguished by a large GNP, R & D, and its closeness to markets.[27]

Given his emphasis on the choice of a best theory in terms of a particular decision problem, Leamer redefined the problem as one of explaining the ratio of imports to exports as the dependent variable. This is, in fact, much closer to the Heckscher–Ohlin variant of net imports that other investigators have chosen for studying the determinants of comparative advantage. It turned out that the group of factor-endowment and technological measures of national attributes was uniformly superior to the resistance and development groups, with the R & D measure most often performing the best. As Leamer noted, this change in performance of the various groups can be traced to the netting out of the development and resistance variables in terms of the ratio formulation and to the doubling of the impact of the national-attribute measures. While this result may not occasion surprise, it nevertheless brings out clearly how a change in the prediction problem will make for differences in the performance of particular types of explanatory variables.

The Determinants of Net Exports

Studies by Baldwin (1971), Branson and Junz (1971), and Morrall (1972) have focused on the determinants of U.S. net exports.[28] As mentioned, this formulation should provide a better approximation of comparative advantage than the study of exports or imports alone.

Baldwin found that the percentage or the absolute numbers of engineers and scientists employed in different industries were positively correlated with net exports and that U.S. exports were relatively R & D intensive. He interpreted this finding to reflect the importance of both skill factors and the activities of export industries that result in new and improved products. Baldwin also constructed separate measures of scale economies, the degree of unionization, and the degree of concentration. These were found

27 It bears repeating that Leamer's procedure for identifying commodities exported by countries relatively rich in the attributes being measured is to be distinguished from Hufbauer, Gruber and Vernon, and others. Their procedures amount to assuming that there are certain attributes of countries that are common across commodities. For additional comment, see Leamer (forthcoming a, Appendix).

28 See Katrak (1969) for an examination of the extent to which efficiency differences offset differences in factor endowments, based upon Japan/U.S., Peru/U.S., and U.K./U.S. comparisons in a simplified Ricardo–Heckscher–Ohlin framework.

to be more important in exports than in competitive imports, but they were not statistically significant in the regression analyses.[29] The final noteworthy feature of Baldwin's work was his examination of the determinants of U.S. net exports by region. The importance of natural-resource and capital complementarities was revealed for the United States vis-à-vis Canada and the less developed countries, with the skill and other human-capital influences being clearly discernible vis-à-vis Western Europe and Japan. Branson and Junz's results were broadly similar to Baldwin's, with physical capital, human capital, and the skill ratio explaining most of the variation in net exports.[30]

Morrall's objective was to assess the relative explanatory power of the human-capital and product-cycle (technology) explanations of U.S. trade. Using 1965 data for twenty 2-digit SIC industries, he found that a skill index, extrapolated from the 1960 ratio of professional, technical, and kindred workers to total employment, together with a dummy variable for four natural-resource-intensive industries, accounted for about one-half the variation in the ratio of net exports to total industry shipments. Measuring human capital by average wage and salary per employee gave similar results. Separate tests of the product-cycle model were then made, with the percentage increase in value added between 1947 and 1965, the labor-saving bias by industry, and the ratio of materials plus payroll to industry shipments explaining about one-half the variation in net exports by industry. These latter measures were designed to capture the product-cycle characteristics of industry growth, capital–labor substitution, and external economies by industry.

29 In a comment on Baldwin's work, Weiser and Jay (1972) took issue with Baldwin's measure of scale economies, which was based on the percentage of employees in establishments with 250 or more employees in each industry. Instead, they proposed using Hufbauer's (1970) measures, in which establishment size was more explicitly related to productivity differences. They then tested the importance of scale economies in a regression model in which the dependent variable was the U.S. export share of the total exports of the eleven leading exporting countries, and found scale economies to be important. These results are not comparable with Baldwin's, however, since, as he pointed out in his reply (1972), his dependent variable was net exports, which would appear to be a preferable measure for the model that he was testing. Thus, the importance of scale economies per se remains an open question for investigation, and it would be useful to determine if more comprehensive measures could be constructed for firms and industries rather than strictly for establishments.

30 Weiser and Jay (1972) also attempted to isolate more precisely the effects of productivity change and scale economies on differences in the export performance of the United States and other industrial countries. While their results were highly suggestive, Baldwin (1972) noted that they were unable to distinguish the relative importance of technical factors per se from improvements in the quality of labor in terms of increased skills. The issue of the relative importance of innovational activities, skills, and scale economies thus remains unresolved at the aggregate level.

He then tested the models jointly, concluding that the product-cycle model added significantly to the explanation provided by the human-capital model. There is a problem in interpreting his results, however, because his skill index was very highly correlated with the percentage increase in value added (0.74) and with the measure of the ratio of scientists and engineers (0.87) that was supposed to capture the innovating characteristics of different industries. Since Morrall may not really have discriminated between the two theories, his results may simply reflect the differential performance of alternative measures of skill mix.[31]

Industry Studies

In addition to the aggregative studies just described, some works focusing on particular industries and products are worth mentioning because they may bring out more clearly the micro-oriented forces at work, particularly with regard to the diffusion of technology. Thus, Tilton (1971) has studied the remarkable speed with which semiconductor technology has been diffused within the United States and then internationally to the United Kingdom, France, Germany, and Japan in the period, 1951–68. He found that, while most of the creation of semiconductor technology was due to relatively large firms with substantial R & D capacity, the rapid diffusion within the United States was accomplished by newer firms that were strongly motivated by profit and related considerations and were adept in exploiting new technology for commercial purposes within the U.S. market. The success of the newer firms was encouraged by relatively easy entry conditions, including liberal licensing arrangements, and substantial interfirm mobility of scientific personnel. The U.S. Government was also instrumental in encouraging these firms through its defense contracts. In contrast, in Europe and Japan the rapid diffusion was undertaken by larger and more established firms, including U.S. subsidiaries that served to prod local European firms that lagged behind. The larger firms in Japan were strongly export-oriented and, with the help of liberal arrangements for

31 Morrall also attempted to prove that human capital was not the truly abundant factor in the United States. His argument is unconvincing, however, since his national measures of wage dispersion were not derived from internationally uniform data, and especially since he offered no estimates of physical capital and labor or of the relative returns to the different factors. While cognizant of the relation between human and physical capital, he persisted in keeping them separate in his discussion. If instead he had treated them jointly, the United States would appear to be capital abundant, especially when natural-resource industries are removed.

licensing, were able to achieve rapid diffusion. The semiconductor industry is thus an interesting example in which scale economies have not been important, whereas new firms have overcome entry barriers arising from learning economies associated with R & D mainly by concentrating on commercial applications.

Two somewhat different industries, chemicals and heavy electrical-engineering equipment, have been studied in depth by Burn and Epstein (1972). Comparative advantage in chemicals is apparently related to significant differences between U.S. and European firms with respect to the use of skilled personnel, expenditures on R & D, and scale economies. In contrast, comparative advantage in producing and exporting heavy power plant on a competitive basis has been severely modified because of international differences in public procurement policies and national technical standards.

Ault's (1972) work focused on differential rates of diffusion of process innovations in the steel industry and the effects upon the relative export performance of twenty-five countries for the period, 1957–66. He found that wage costs per unit of output (taken as a proxy for total unit costs), the kind of process used, and domestic market size explained a substantial amount of the year-by-year variations in export performance across countries. In particular, the newly developed oxygen process was observed to play an increasingly important role during the period, but some of the older processes continued to be used because they were apparently still relatively efficient in coping with certain technical problems.

Klein (1973) developed a model of a firm with a two-part production function. One part was a learning or knowledge function that depended upon past cumulative output to reflect learning by doing and upon cumulative real R & D expenditures. He termed the second part the "static production function," which depended on traditional inputs of capital and labor. It was assumed that U.S. domestic firms initially enjoyed a learning advantage over foreign firms that was great enough to overcome any foreign static cost advantage. As the learning advantage was more fully exploited domestically, U.S. comparative advantage would diminish and there would be an increasing tendency for U.S. firms to invest abroad for cost reasons. Klein applied his model to a pooled cross section of four U.S. nonproprietary drug firms during the 1960s. While his results gave modest support to the learning hypothesis advanced, he was not able to capture effectively the micro aspects of the relationship between existing drug products marketed and the introduction of new products and product ingredients. More intensive analysis on the firm and product level would accordingly be required to determine whether his model was applicable to the behavior of the U.S. drug industry.

While industry studies are interesting and informative, they are, of course, difficult to undertake because of the detailed knowledge required. In addition, such studies may not lend themselves easily to generalization. It does not follow, however, that we need to confine our efforts to more highly aggregative studies, since such studies may founder on the search for empirical proxies that are designed to capture the essence of microeconomic phenomena. If we accept the notion that given industries differ across countries in terms of their technological characteristics and the rate at which technological adaptations occur, this would suggest studying these matters directly. A country's net exports might then be more effectively profiled according to the determinants of its industry-specific characteristics.

Conclusion

Because the studies just reviewed differ somewhat in focus and specification, they are difficult to compare. Thus, while it is abundantly clear that technological influences are important, they need to be distinguished more carefully, especially in relation to the human-capital endowments that determine comparative advantage. This is in part a question of theory and also one of empirical methodology. As far as theory is concerned, the issue is that the factor-endowments model has yet to be integrated systematically with an endogenous mechanism of technological change and diffusion. Until more progress is made along these lines, it will be difficult to sort out the various determinants of trade. The methodological issue is to devise ways of discriminating among the various theories and choosing the "best" explanations in the face of highly collinear data sets. Leamer's work is an important beginning here.

5. PREFERENCE SIMILARITY AND INTRAINDUSTRY SPECIALIZATION

The influence of demand has thus far been treated only indirectly in terms of the returns to factors that provide some clue to relative factor abundance, differences in the factor content of trade according to regions of destination, the influence of market size on scale economies, and differential income and price elasticities that characterize a country's trade. If one observes actual trade flows, it is evident that a very substantial and increasing proportion of these flows is accounted for by the advanced industrial countries. Moreover, much of this trade involves the exchange of products within the same industrial categories. Since these are phenomena that may not be fully accounted for by the explanations already discussed, they deserve additional comment.

Preference Similarity

The main issue here is whether countries that are close to or distant from one another in terms of per capita income levels and economic structure exchange manufactured goods that are similar or dissimilar in terms of factor content. This question, which purportedly stems from Linder (1961), was tested by Hufbauer (1970) by comparing the relative commodity composition of the export and import vectors of individual countries with different economic structures as distinguished by GDP per capita. Whether this is in fact Linder's hypothesis is not clear, however, since Linder dealt more explicitly with the idea that trade in manufactures between countries with similar per capita incomes and consumption patterns would be larger than between countries with dissimilar per capita incomes. Export and import vectors would thus tend to become more alike as per capita incomes converged. The proper test, therefore, would be to compare each country's export and import vectors across countries with differing per capita incomes.

In any event, Hufbauer's formulation led him to expect a sharp distinction in the compositional patterns. He found, however (p. 201), that the relative composition of the typical export vector grew *continuously* more similar to the import vector of an opposing nation as the importing nation was more developed. As he pointed out, this is not surprising, for what it says is that both exports and imports·become more diversified as countries get richer, whereas poorer countries have more sharply defined export specializations. As the poorer countries get richer, their trade vectors can thus be expected to become more similar, which is more or less in line with our interpretation of Linder.

The findings just noted are descriptively interesting but in themselves do not explain the underlying basis of trade. In this connection, Hufbauer (1970, pp. 206–207) compared by means of rank correlations the various factor-endowment and technological characteristics embodied in exports and imports across nations. While the results were not statistically significant, they all had negative signs, indicating (p. 210) that "trade does involve some exchange of characteristics." As Hufbauer noted (p. 210), it would be interesting to investigate this question further on a bilateral basis for countries and regions with different per capita income levels, and to extend the analysis through time to see how the sources of comparative advantage have evolved.[32]

Intraindustry Specialization

As already noted, the fact that a substantial amount of trade, particularly among the advanced countries, falls into the same product and industry categories has led some investigators to ask why this is so. Drawing especially upon work by Balassa (1966), Grubel (1970) has suggested that this kind of trade may occur because of locational, time, or other special factors that characterize particular goods; differences in income-distribution profiles and consumer tastes; and differences in the rate of technological adaptations for improved and new products and processes. Grubel also mentioned that there are underlying supply forces at work involving the usual types of factor endowments and impediments, but coupled with possible differences in scale economies and productive efficiency.

In a study of Australian trade data for 1968–69, Grubel and Lloyd (1971) have calculated the intraindustry flows for the 7-, 5-, 3-, 2-, and 1-digit SITC commodity groupings with respect to Australia's main trading partners. While Australia's economic structure does not typify that of other advanced countries, there is nevertheless a clearly discernible pattern of intraindustry trade across SITC groupings and with respect to particular countries. The question is how to account for this. Since it is extraordinarily difficult and time-consuming to collect highly disaggregated information by industry, Grubel and Lloyd were not able to test any of the possible explanations noted above. However, in the case of iron and steel products, they attributed the two-way trade to specialization along narrow product lines, and, for petroleum products, technical and legal factors were important. They also

32 The recent studies of the United States by Baldwin (1971) and of Japan by Kojima (1970) and Heller (forthcoming), and the bilateral analyses by Gruber and Vernon (1970) and Hodd (1967, 1970) are instructive here.

demonstrated, using data on trade flows involving stone, sand, and gravel among OECD countries, that these flows were essentially "border" trade arising especially from transport-cost considerations.

The focus on intraindustry trade is worthwhile, if for no other reason than to remind us that the different levels of aggregation of trade and industry data are worrisome matters that deserve careful attention in the design and interpretation of research. Having said this, the issue is whether intraindustry trade should be considered a phenomenon in its own right or one that arises because we are unable to define product categories to capture all the underlying nuances that are reflected in the differences in production costs, technical design, and consumer preferences that lead to trade.[33]

6. FUTURE DIRECTIONS FOR RESEARCH ON THE COMMODITY COMPOSITION AND DIRECTION OF TRADE

It should occasion little surprise that neither the simple Ricardian nor the Heckscher–Ohlin model provides a satisfactory explanation of the commodity composition and direction of trade, since these models are characterizations of the world that seek to emphasize particular forces to the exclusion of others. These characterizations have proven to be extremely useful for theoretical purposes and have suggested important normative conclusions with respect to the maximization of economic welfare. But while the scientific mind yearns understandably for simplicity in model construction, empirical verification, and applications to policy, there may be great risk in overlooking many forces that are important and yet lie outside normal inquiry. The significance of the empirical developments described above is that the discourse has been lifted to a much higher plane, for we are now investigating directly why comparative-cost differences exist among nations, rather than taking them for granted, and are inquiring more

---

33 For some pertinent remarks on the suitability of trade and industry data and on factors leading to intraindustry trade, see Kravis (1970). Kenen (1970, p. 212) has also suggested that it would be interesting to determine if the tendency toward larger flows of two-way trade could be accounted for by the very special technologies and thus the specific skill requirements of the newer types of manufactures involved. A directly related question of interest is the extent of product standardization or differentiation that characterizes a country's trade. This question was first investigated by Drèze (1960, 1961). Balassa (1969) later showed that smaller countries tend to specialize relatively in standardized semimanufactures and larger countries in finished manufactures.

deeply into the forces that are responsible for such differences.

Our review of recent research suggests that the determinants of comparative advantage can be classified into the following major groups: factor endowments, technological differences, scale economies, market impediments and imperfections, and demand influences. To obtain a better understanding of how these forces operate, the following questions deserve further study:

1. Do alternative measures of human capital lead to differences in calculations of the factor content of trade at a single point and different points in time? Is human capital a substitute or complement with respect to physical capital and unskilled labor?[34]

2. Are efficiency differences across countries due to variations in the quality of human and physical capital?[35] What is the relationship between human capital and R & D intensity? What determines the rate of technological diffusion within industries and among countries? Has this rate changed significantly across industries since World War II?

3. How important are economies of scale? Can measures of scale economies be constructed that incorporate company and industry-wide production and nonproduction characteristics, and would these be better than the more narrow measures based on production data for establishments?[36]

4. How do tariffs and other distortions affect the commodity composition and factor content of trade? How do international labor migration and direct foreign investment affect factor endowments and technology?

5. How do differences in per capita incomes and other demand characteristics interact with the foregoing determinants of the commodity and geographic distribution of trade?

There have been numerous references in our discussion to the estimation of production functions in the context of trade models. Even though the trade models themselves do not suggest the most appropriate type of production function to be estimated, some interesting investigations can nevertheless be carried out in this framework that may shed light on some of the questions posed above:

1. Can the Ricardian–neoclassical model be best depicted in

---

34 This and other issues relating to the measurement of human capital are treated in Griliches (1970).

35 Some attention has been given to this question, especially by Kenen (1966), Mitchell (1968), Yahr (1968), and Philpot (1970).

36 See Silberston (1972) for a useful review of the problems of measuring scale economies and some calculations for British industries.

terms of differences in Hicks–neutral efficiency parameters, or are there biases present with respect to differential factor savings?[37]

2. The issue here can be posed in another way: Do production functions for an industry differ across countries with respect both to the scale and the curvature of the industry isoquants?[38]

The final area for concern is methodological:

1. In attempting to assess the importance of the various determinants of comparative advantage, are there acceptable procedures for handling problems of multicollinearity and for choosing the "best" theory?

2. How important are aggregation and measurement error in the estimation and interpretation of results?

Of the various questions listed above, the ones relating to technological influences, scale economies, market impediments, and international factor movements represent our areas of greatest substantive ignorance. It may be too much to expect that these phenomena can be incorporated all at once into theoretical models and their relative importance assessed empirically. But unless we strive consciously to deal with these phenomena, there is a real danger of molding our conception of reality on the basis of oversimplified and incomplete characterizations.

7. INTERNATIONAL TRADE AND RETURNS TO FACTORS

In addition to its emphasis upon relative factor endowments as a major determinant of trade, the Heckscher–Ohlin model called attention to the impact of trade on the returns to factors. This culminated, of course, in the factor-price-equalization theorem that was developed in rigorous fashion by Samuelson. While the factor-price-equalization theorem has subsequently generated great theoretical interest, it has never been subjected to direct empirical investigation, presumably because it appears so obviously violated by the sizable differences in factor prices that exist among countries. If factor prices are, in fact, not equalized, this signifies that one or more of the assumptions underlying the

37 Besides the references cited in Section 2 with regard to the study of intercountry differences in efficiency, see the interesting exchange on this issue between Gupta (1968) and Minsol (1968). As noted above, Morrall (1972) used a measure of labor-saving bias in his test of the product-cycle model.

38 There is the further question examined by Atkinson and Stiglitz (1969) as to whether technological change in relatively high-wage countries may shift part of the isoquant inward while leaving the remainder unchanged. For a useful recent review of the empirical aspects of technical progress, see Kennedy and Thirlwall (1972).

Heckscher–Ohlin model are not applicable. It might therefore be interesting to investigate the reasons for observed differences in factor prices in terms of the influences suggested by the Heckscher –Ohlin model. A directly related question is whether these influences can explain the wide differences in per capita incomes among countries.

The impact of trade on factor prices and incomes has been analyzed extensively in theoretical inquiries, especially in connection with the literature on offer curves and the Stolper–Samuelson argument. It is surprising, then, that there has been so little empirical investigation of this impact generally or in the context of changes in protection.

Factor-Price and Per Capita Income Differences among Countries

The simple Heckscher–Ohlin model deals with two factors, capital and labor. Working within this simple model, Minhas (1963, pp. 38 and 86) observed that, for 1953–58, average wages ranged from $250 in poor countries to $3,600 in rich countries, whereas the average returns on capital were about 15 per cent in the former as compared with 19 per cent in the latter. We should not put too much stock in such comparisons, however, because they do not take into account the fact that average wage differences reflect to a large extent returns to human capital.[39]

Human-capital considerations are important as well in per capita income comparisons. In an especially interesting study, Krueger (1968) concluded that human capital explained more than half the difference in per capita income levels in 1959 between the United States and a selection of other countries. She reached this conclusion by applying U.S. median-income measures as approximations of marginal productivities to populations stratified according to age, sex, educational attainment, and sector, in order to compute the incomes for each country. Differences in the age and educational characteristics were especially important in explaining the wide disparities observed between the United

---

[39] It may therefore be misleading to draw inferences from uncorrected estimates of comparative returns to factors. For example, Haitani (1970) has suggested that wage-rental disparities can be explained by much greater variation across countries in output–labor as compared with output–capital ratios. His explanation was that production isoquants may become much flatter toward the higher labor–capital ratio end and that there may also be (neutral) differences in efficiency. Whether or not isoquants have this shape is, of course, an empirical question that would be interesting to investigate when both physical and human capital are taken into account.

States and the poor countries. Assuming next that unexplained differences in income could be attributed in great part to nonhuman resource differences that were not measured, Krueger (p. 658) suggested that perhaps we were not as far from factor-price equalization as might have been thought. This is an intriguing suggestion that would be interesting to investigate further, especially if it were possible to develop reliable measures of tangible capital. It might also be of interest to extend Krueger's human-capital measures over time and to examine the international-trade characteristics of the countries involved.[40]

International Trade and the Distribution of Income

While it is difficult to isolate empirically the effects of trade from other influences on the distribution of income, it is surprising that so little work has been done on this question. We had occasion above to note Travis's (1972) contention that the U.S. tariff tends to shut off Heckscher–Ohlin type trade and thus to make U.S. imports relatively more capital intensive. Some evidence supporting this contention was cited in Baldwin's (1971) work. A similar conclusion emerges from an earlier study by Ball (1967), in which he found that U.S. effective tariff rates for thirty-one manufacturing industries in 1962 suggested that somewhat heavier protection was being given to lower-wage than higher-wage industries.[41] Given the similarity of the tariff and wage structures across developed countries, Ball also surmised that this situation would exist elsewhere, although he did not investigate the matter directly.

In order to assess the full distributional impact, one would also want to consider the consumption effects of tariffs. In this regard, Fieleke (1971) has estimated that the U.S. tariff weighs somewhat more heavily on the lower-income groups of consumers, based on 1967 and 1972 tariffs, although it seems likely that the impact may be understated because nontariff barriers were not included in his measures.

Another interesting study is by Evans (1971). Using a multisectoral growth model based upon 1958–59 input–output relation-

---

40 Interregional analysis constitutes another possible focus for trying to explain income differences, as, for example, in Olsen (1971). But since relatively little information is available on regional trade flows, such analysis seems of limited interest in the context of testing trade theories.

41 Balassa (1965) and Basevi (1966) had concluded previously that there was no relation between effective tariff rates and labor intensity. However, they did not make any allowance for skill and wage differences among industries.

ships and data, he estimated the optimal pattern of Australian production, investment, and trade over the ensuing decade. He then generated alternative solutions of the model under the assumed condition of free trade, with the exchange rate permitted to vary, and under the condition of a uniform ad valorem tariff designed to keep the exchange rate constant. He estimated that the free-trade and uniform-tariff alternatives would increase total consumption by an additional 0.8 and 1.8 per cent after ten years of growth and that average wage rates would rise between 2.3 and 4.6 per cent, that domestically owned firms would lose more than foreign-owned firms and that unskilled labor would undergo income losses. While these results are suggestive, Evans noted that they had to be interpreted subject to the quality of the data and the fixed coefficients of the model. Moreover, he noted that no account was taken of other policies besides tariff changes that could affect the outcomes. Granted all of these qualifications, Evans's work should nevertheless be lauded for being one of the first attempts of its kind to grapple directly with the impact of changes in trade and commercial policies on the return to factors.

Given the importance of these issues, there is a clear need for more research on distributional effects with respect to functional shares and consumption by different income groups.[42] The further development of computational models of general equilibrium and the adaptation of the several existing descriptive studies of income distribution and consumer budgets for various countries would provide useful points of departure for incorporating international trade effects.

8. ECONOMIC EXPANSION AND INTERNATIONAL TRADE

A substantial amount of research has been done on models and estimation of international trade dependence. The object has been to isolate those influences that operate cross-sectionally and over time for countries at different stages of development. There have also been much theoretical discussion and empirical measurement of the terms of trade, although interest in these issues seems to have waned in recent years. Finally, some efforts have been made to give greater empirical content to the relations involving trade and growth. Some brief comments will be made on each of these subjects.

---

42 Some work is presently underway by Richardson and Baade (forthcoming) on the effects of commercial policy on the functional distribution of income in the United States. Another fruitful area for investigation might be the effects of customs unions on factor returns and per capita incomes in member countries.

Patterns of Growth and Trade
Interdependence–Dependence

Leamer's (forthcoming a) work on the commodity composition of trade is an example of the kind of model used to explain trade flows. As mentioned earlier, his variables included the income and population levels of the trading countries, certain resistance factors such as distance and tariff levels, and various national attributes that reflected endowments of physical and human capital and technological capabilities.[43] It will be recalled that he found that the income and population variables provided the best explanation for variations in the import ratio for the manufactured commodities studied. Gruber and Vernon (1970) relied on a similar model, but their conceptualization and choice of variables made their results somewhat difficult to interpret.

An additional recent example of this type of research is by Keesing and Sherk (1971), who introduced a measure of population density into a model with per capita income and population size in order to determine how natural-resource influences affected the percentage composition of trade of different countries. Their hypothesis was that densely populated countries would have a comparative advantage in manufactures along lines suggested by a land-labor version of the Heckscher–Ohlin model. Country and domestic-market size and development effects operating through scale economies and the accumulation of human capital would be reflected in the population-size and per capita income measures. For twenty-six less developed countries, they found that the percentage composition of manufactured exports, based on 1965 data, was well explained by their three variables, but the composition of imports was not well explained. A similar pattern was observed in regressions for twenty-two industrial countries. While Keesing and Sherk's results are suggestive for exports, their results for imports indicate that there are apparently other forces at work that their model does not clearly portray.[44]

---

43 A detailed treatment of models of trade dependence and trade interdependence, with bibliographic citations of work published through 1968, is given in Leamer and Stern (1970, pp. 145–170).

44 The authors also presented sets of results for per capita exports and imports using the same explanatory variables. These results are difficult to interpret, however, since population is contained in the dependent variable and in two of the independent variables. Results similar to Keesing and Sherk are to be found in Banerji (1972) for a larger number of countries. Banerji introduced an additional variable to measure the degree of industrialization in terms of the deviation of the actual share of manufactures in GDP from an estimated share, obtained by regressing the actual shares on per capita incomes for all countries. This seemed to improve the results. He also investigated Indian exports in detail and obtained results that were similar to his seventy-country cross section.

Since one country's exports are another country's imports, surely we need a model of comparative advantage that encompasses them both.

Because models of trade dependence and interdependence are conceived in general-equilibrium terms and their empirical measurement is in reduced form, it is difficult to distinguish how the demand and supply influences operate, particularly with reference to the population and per capita income variables. These variables are presumably intended to capture the effects of market size and resultant scale economies, as well as the technological sophistication that promotes the development of improved and new products and processes. The measures are so gross, however, that they cannot discriminate among the various explanations. It would be desirable therefore to search for more refined empirical proxies in future work and to clarify more precisely how this line of research is related to the determinants of comparative advantage.[45]

Economic Expansion and the Terms of Trade

There is an abundance of theoretical literature on the terms-of-trade effects of output changes due to factor accumulation, technical change, changes in demand, and other phenomena. Many of these considerations relate directly to the issue of whether there is any secular tendency for the terms of trade to move favorably or unfavorably between primary products and manufactures and between the less developed and the advanced countries.[46] While these issues are still capable of arousing great emotion, they seem to have dropped from the limelight as the economic and policy environments have changed, particularly in many less developed countries that are now more outward-looking than in the past. The exposure of the logical weaknesses in the Singer–Prebisch theory of the terms of trade and the weight of empirical evidence against the secular-deterioration hypothesis have no doubt played a part in diminishing the attention given to this area of study.

The terms of trade are nonetheless of continuing interest because they may provide some indication of the gains that countries derive from participating in trade. In this regard, two issues

45 For some additional remarks along these lines, see Leamer and Stern (1970, pp. 147–157).
46 The product and country distinction is made because there are several advanced countries that are important exporters of primary products.

may merit further study. The first is productivity change and how it is reflected in changes in the net-barter and single-factoral terms of trade. The second is how quality change and the introduction of new goods are reflected in the price indexes used to calculate changes in the terms of trade. The close connection between these issues has been stressed in the technology explanations of trade referred to earlier. What is being proposed now is to tie in these explanations more closely with measurements of the forces that manifest themselves in the gains from trade.

In particular, developments in the theory and measurement of the determinants of economic growth suggest ways of analyzing changes in total factor productivity that might in turn be related to changes in the foreign sector.[47] The treatment of quality change in the construction of hedonic price indexes and in the attributes framework of the "new" theory of demand might also be more explicitly related to price-index comparisons among countries.[48]

Export-Led Growth

While it may be difficult to distinguish among the various components of aggregate demand in terms of their contribution to growth, there have been numerous historical experiences in which exports seem to have been unusually important in stimulating growth. In this light, Caves (1965) analyzed two types of "vent for surplus" models of trade and growth in which hitherto unutilized or underutilized supplies of natural resources or labor are brought into production and furnish the basis for rapid growth. As he pointed out (pp. 110–114), the creation of externalities and linkage effects is important in determining how strong the transmission effects will be from the export sector to other producing sectors.

In a subsequent article, Caves (1971) elaborated on these matters at greater length, using the "staple" or "export-led" model of growth that was originally formulated by Canadian economic historians to explain the successive stages in Canadian development. In this connection, he made some illustrative calcula-

---

47 The works mentioned earlier by Stryker (1968) and Weiser and Jay (1972) represent a modest beginning on these lines. Some of the research on export-led growth in advanced countries may also warant greater attention here, as, for example, Stern (1967) and Caves (1970), where certain post-World War II interindustry and country variations are examined theoretically and empirically.

48 On problems of treating quality change in internationally traded goods, see Alexander (1971, pp. 49–51), Chan-Lee (1971, pp. 346–350), and the references cited therein.

tions of the impact of the Canadian wheat boom during 1901–11 on per capita income, taking into account the differential effects of induced immigration, scale economies, gains in efficiency, capital formation, and induced savings. These effects, which were manifested both within and outside the wheat sector, accounted for more than one-fifth of the increase in per capita income during that decade, an estimate substantially above that obtained in earlier research in which the export stimulus was more narrowly conceived.

Caves then went on to point out how this model could be applied fruitfully to a variety of historical experiences. In doing so, he set forth the key relationships of the model in an empirically operational sequence and offered many practical suggestions for applying the model and interpreting the results. His suggestions for investigating the various linkages stemming from exports are especially insightful. They call attention to such influences as changes in skill mix, scale economies, intrastructure, factor intensities and efficient use of factors, entrepreneurial skills, and the characteristics of saving behavior that may be affected in the process of export expansion.

While many of the forces just mentioned are operative over time in general circumstances, the thrust of the export-led model is to call attention to the unusual circumstances that may generate rapid growth and thereby set into motion a pattern and rate of development that might otherwise not have occurred. It is for this reason that export-led models are deserving of separate attention.

9. CONCLUSION

It is abundantly clear from our discussion that comparative advantage cannot be viewed in the simple Ricardian sense of intercountry differences in labor productivity. Rather, we must set this model in a multifactor framework that is premised on the existence of intercountry differences in total factor productivity. As we have noted, there is considerable empirical evidence, especially from the estimation of production functions, to support this broader formulation. There is still room for additional research on the estimation of productivity differences, particularly with respect to the effects of technological change and the relationships among the various productive factors. However, what is needed more is to improve our understanding of the processes whereby technology and other forces determine comparative advantage at a point in time and alter its structure over time. To accomplish this, these various forces must be treated endogenously in our theoretical models.

The importance of natural-resource and human-capital endowments, together with the accumulated evidence on intercountry efficiency differences, makes continued reliance on the simple Heckscher–Ohlin model a somewhat dubious proposition. While the theoretical and empirical work on technological and related explanations of trade has filled some of the void of the factor-endowments model, it is evident from our discussion of recent empirical research that results were often difficult to interpret and compare. This was due especially to conceptual inadequacies in specifying the interrelationships among the various determinants of comparative advantage.

In studying international trade, we must deal with a variety of highly complex phenomena, and we are continually faced with severe limitations on the availability of relevant data. Even if we could remedy the data situation, however, the conceptual inadequacies would remain. What is needed in particular is to broaden the theoretical conception of the factor-endowments model to incorporate human-capital and natural-resource endowments and especially to relax the assumptions of the model with respect to the international transfer of technology and the international mobility of investment.[49]

As indicated in the two sections just preceding, the impact of trade on factor returns and income distribution and the relationships involving trade and growth offer unusual scope for further empirical study. Most of our past concern has been with obtaining a better understanding of the determinants of the composition and direction of trade. Since distributional questions are particularly important in assessing the impact of changes in policy, we should seek to make greater efforts along these lines as well.

REFERENCES

Adler, F. M., "The Relationship between the Income and Price Elasticities of Demand for United States Exports," *Review of Economics and Statistics,* 52 (August 1970), pp. 313–319.

"Elasticities of Demand for U.S. Exports: A Reply," *Review of Economics and Statistics,* 53 (May 1971), pp. 203–204.

Alexander, W. E., "The Theory and Measurement of Quality-Corrected Price Indexes, with Possible Applications to the U.S. Foreign Sector," Seminar Discussion Paper No. 29, University of Michigan, Research Seminar in International Economics, Ann Arbor, 1971.

49 I am grateful to Baldwin for pointing this out (see his comment below).

Arrow, K. J., H. Chenery, B. Minhas, and R. Solow, "Capital-Labor Substitution and Economic Efficiency," *Review of Economics and Statistics,* 43 (August 1962), pp. 225–250.

Atkinson, A. B., and J. E. Stiglitz, "A New View of Technological Change," *Economic Journal,* 79 (September 1969), pp. 573–578.

Ault, D., "The Determinants of World Steel Exports: An Empirical Study," *Review of Economics and Statistics,* 54 (February 1972), pp. 38–46.

Balassa, B., "Tariff Protection in Industrial Countries: An Evaluation," *Journal of Political Economy,* 73 (December 1965), pp. 573–594.

"Tariff Reductions and Trade in Manufactures among the Industrial Countries," *American Economic Review,* 56 (June 1966), pp. 466–473.

"Country Size and Trade Patterns: Comment," *American Economic Review,* 59 (March 1969), pp. 201–204.

Comment on D. J. Daly, in Daly (1972).

Baldwin, R. E., "Determinants of the Commodity Structure of U.S. Trade," *American Economic Review,* 61 (March 1971), pp. 126–146.

"Determinants of the Commodity Structure of U.S. Trade: Reply," *American Economic Review,* 62 (June 1972), p. 465.

Ball, D. S., "United States Effective Tariffs and Labor's Share," *Journal of Political Economy,* 75 (April 1967), pp. 183–187.

Banerji, R., "Major Determinants of the Share of Manufactures in Exports: A Cross-Section Analysis and Case Study of India," *Weltwirtschaftliches Archiv,* Band 108 (Heft 3, 1972), pp. 345–381.

Basevi, G., "The United States Tariff Structure: Estimates of Effective Rates of Protection of United States Industries and Industrial Labor," *Review of Economics and Statistics,* 48 (May 1966), pp. 147–160.

Bhagwati, J., "The Pure Theory of International Trade: A Survey," *Economic Journal,* 74 (March 1964), pp. 1–84. Reprinted with an Addendum in J. Bhagwati, *Trade, Tariffs and Growth,* Cambridge, Mass., M.I.T. Press, 1969.

Comment on D. J. Daly, in Daly (1972).

Bhagwati, J., and R. Bharadwaj, "Human Capital and the Indian Pattern of Foreign Trade," M.I.T. Working Paper Number 57 (1970), forthcoming in the *Indian Economic Review.*

Branson, W. H., "U.S. Comparative Advantage: Some Further Results," *Brookings Papers on Economic Activity,* No. 3, pp. 754–759.

"Factor Inputs, U.S. Trade, and the Heckscher–Ohlin Model," Seminar Paper No. 27, University of Stockholm, Institute for International Economic Studies, Stockholm, 1973.

Branson, W. H., and H. B. Junz, "Trends in U.S. Trade and Comparative Advantage," *Brookings Papers on Economic Activity,* No. 2, 1971, pp. 285–338.

Burn, D., and B. Epstein, *Realities of Free Trade: Two Industry Studies,* Toronto, University of Toronto Press, 1972.

Caves, R. E., " 'Vent for Surplus' Models of Trade and Growth," in R. E. Baldwin *et al.,* eds., *Trade, Growth, and the Balance of Payments: Essays in Honor of Gottfried Haberler,* Amsterdam, North-Holland, 1965.

"Export-Led Growth: The Post-War Industrial Setting," in W. A. Eltis *et al.,* eds., *Induction, Growth and Trade: Essays in Honour of Sir Roy Harrod,* Oxford, Clarendon Press, 1970.

"Export-Led Growth and the New Economic History," in J. N. Bhagwati *et al.,* eds., *Trade, Balance of Payments, and Growth: Essays in Honor of Charles P. Kindleberger*, Amsterdam, North-Holland, 1971.

Chan-Lee, J. H., "Intercountry Cost and Price Comparisons," *IMF Staff Papers*, 18 (July 1971), pp. 332–388.

Christensen, L. R., D. W. Jorgenson, and L. J. Lau, "Transcendental Logarithmic Production Frontiers," *Review of Economics and Statistics*, 55 (February 1973), pp. 28–45.

Clague, C. K., "An International Comparison of Industrial Efficiency: Peru and the United States," *Review of Economics and Statistics*, 49 (November 1967), pp. 487–493.

"Capital-Labor Substitution in Manufacturing in Underdeveloped Countries," *Econometrica*, 37 (July 1969), pp. 528–537.

"Alternative Estimates of Capital-Labor Substitution in Manufacturing in Developing Economies – Reply," *Econometrica*, 39 (November 1971), pp. 1055–1056.

Daly, D. J., "Uses of International Price and Output Data," in D. J. Daly, ed., *International Comparisons of Prices and Output*, Studies in Income and Wealth, Vol. 27, New York, Columbia University Press for National Bureau of Economic Research, 1972.

Daniels, M. R., "Differences in Efficiency among Industries in Developing Countries," *American Economic Review*, 59 (March 1969), pp. 159–171.

Deppler, M. C., "Elasticities of Demand for U.S. Exports: A Comment," *Review of Economics and Statistics*, 53 (May 1971), pp. 201–203.

Drèze, J., "Quelques réflexions sereines sur l'adaptation de l'industrie belge au Marché Commun," *Comptes Rendus des Travaux de la Societé Royale d'Economie Politique de Belgique*, 275 (December 1960), pp. 4–26.

"Les exportations intra-CEE au 1958 et la position belge," and J. Drèze, J. van Der Rest, and J. van Overbeke, "Analyse de la balance commerciale de l'U.E.B.L. en 1958-59," *Recherches Economiques de Louvain*, 8 (1961), pp. 715–766.

Dudley, L., "Learning and Productivity Change in Metal Products," *American Economic Review*, 62 (September 1972), pp. 662–669.

Evans, H. D., "Income Distribution, Welfare and the Australian Tariff," *Australian Economic Papers*, 10 (December 1971), pp. 89–113.

Fareed, A. E., "Formal Schooling and the Human-Capital Intensity of American Foreign Trade: A Cost Approach," *Economic Journal*, 82 (June 1972), pp. 629–640.

Fels, G., "The Choice of Industry Mix in the Division of Labour between Developed and Developing Countries," *Weltwirtschaftliches Archiv*, Band 108 (Heft 1, 1972), pp. 71–121.

Fieleke, N. S., "The Cost of Tariffs to Consumers," *New England Economic Review*, Federal Reserve Bank of Boston (Sept./Oct. 1971), pp. 13–19.

Finger, J. M., "Factor Intensity and 'Leontief Type' Tests of the Factor Proportions Theory," *Economia Internazionale*, 22 (August 1969), pp. 405–422.

Gehrels, F., "Factor Efficiency, Substitution, and the Basis for Trade: Some Empirical Evidence," *Kyklos*, 23 (Fasc. 2, 1970), pp. 279–302.

Glejser, H., "Empirical Evidence on Comparative Cost Theory from the European Common Market Experience," *European Economic Review,* 3 (November 1972), pp. 247–258.

Griliches, Z., "Notes on the Role of Education in Production Functions and Growth Accounting," in Hansen (1970).

Grubel, H. G., "The Theory of Intra-Industry Trade," in I. A. McDougall and R. H. Snape, eds., *Studies in International Economics,* Amsterdam, North-Holland, 1970.

Grubel, H. G., and P. J. Lloyd, "The Empirical Measurement of Intra-Industry Trade," *Economic Record,* 47 (December 1971), pp. 494–517.

Gruber, W. H., and R. Vernon, "The Technology Factor in a World Trade Matrix," in Vernon (1970).

Gupta, S. B., "Some Tests of the International Comparisons of Factor Efficiency with the CES Production Function," *Review of Economics and Statistics,* 50 (November 1968), pp. 470–476.

Haitani, K., "International Differences in Capital Returns and Wage Rates," *Kyklos,* 23 (Fasc. 2, 1970), pp. 272–278.

Hansen, W. L., ed., *Education, Income, and Human Capital,* Conference on Research in Income and Wealth, Studies in Income and Wealth, Vol. 35, New York, Columbia University Press for National Bureau of Economic Research, 1970.

Hayami, Y., and V. W. Ruttan, "Agricultural Productivity Differences among Countries," *American Economic Review,* 60 (December 1970), pp. 895–911.

Heller, P. S., "The Neofactor Proportions Theory and Rapid Structural Change: The Case of Japan, 1956–1969" (forthcoming).

Hodd, M., "An Empirical Investigation of the Heckscher–Ohlin Theory," *Economica,* 34 (February 1967), pp. 20–29.

"An Empirical Investigation of the Heckscher–Ohlin Theory: Reply," *Economica,* 37 (November 1970), pp. 420–421.

Horst, T., "The Industrial Composition of U.S. Exports and Subsidiary Sales to the Canadian Market," *American Economic Review,* 62 (March 1972), pp. 37–45.

Hufbauer, G. C., "The Impact of National Characteristics and Technology on the Commodity Composition of Trade in Manufactured Goods," in Vernon (1970).

Hufbauer, G. C., and J. P. O'Neill, "Unit Values of U.S. Machinery Exports," *Journal of International Economics,* 2 (August 1972), pp. 265–276.

Hutcheson, T. L., "Factor Intensity Reversals and the CES Production Function," *Review of Economics and Statistics,* 51 (November 1969), pp. 468–470.

Johnson, H. G., *Comparative Cost and Commercial Policy Theory for a Developing World Economy,* Wicksell Lectures 1968, Almqvist & Wiksell, Stockholm, 1968.

Katrak, H., "An Empirical Test of Comparative Cost Theories: Japan, Peru, the United Kingdom, and the United States," *Economica,* 36 (November 1969), pp. 389–399.

Keesing, D. B., "Different Countries' Labor Skill Coefficients and the Skill Intensity of International Trade Flows," *Journal of International Economics,* 1 (November 1971), pp. 453–460.

Keesing, D. B., and D. R. Sherk, "Population Density in Patterns of Trade and Development," *American Economic Review,* 61 (December 1971), pp. 956–961.

Kenen, P. B., "Efficiency Differences and Factor Intensities in the CES Production Function: An Interpretation," *Journal of Political Economy,* 74 (December 1966), pp. 635–636.

"Skills, Human Capital, and Comparative Advantage," in W. L. Hansen, ed. (1970).

Kenen, P. B., and R. Lawrence, eds., *The Open Economy: Essays on International Trade and Finance,* New York, Columbia University Press, 1968.

Kennedy, C., and A. P. Thirlwall, "Surveys in Applied Economics: Technical Progress," *Economic Journal,* 82 (March 1972), pp. 11–72.

Klein, R. W., "A Dynamic Theory of Comparative Advantage," *American Economic Review,* 63 (March 1973), pp. 173–184.

Kojima, K., "Structure of Comparative Advantage in Industrial Countries: A Verification of the Factor-Proportions Theorem," *Hitotsubashi Journal of Economics,* 10 (June 1970), pp. 1–29.

Kravis, I. B., Comment on Hufbauer and Gruber and Vernon, in Vernon (1970).

Kreinin, M. E., "The Theory of Comparative Cost–Further Empirical Evidence," *Economia Internazionale,* 22 (November 1969), pp. 3–15.

Krueger, A. O., "Factor Endowments and *Per Capita* Income Differences among Countries," *Economic Journal,* 78 (September 1968), pp. 641–659.

Comment on P. B. Kenen, in Hansen (1970).

Leamer, E. E., "The Commodity Composition of International Trade in Manufactures: An Empirical Analysis," *Oxford Economic Papers* (forthcoming a).

"Tests for Simplifying Linear Models" (forthcoming b).

Leamer, E. E., and R. M. Stern, *Quantitative International Economics,* Boston, Allyn and Bacon, 1970.

Linder, S. B., *An Essay on Trade and Transformation,* Stockholm, Almqvist & Wiksell, 1961.

Lowinger, T. C., "The Neo-Factor Proportions Theory of International Trade: An Empirical Investigation," *American Economic Review,* 61 (September 1971), pp. 675–681.

Minhas, B. S., "The Homohypallagic Production Function, Factor Intensity Reversals, and the Heckscher–Ohlin Theorem," *Journal of Political Economy,* 70 (April 1962), pp. 138–156. Reprinted as Chap. 4 in B. S. Minhas, *An International Comparison of Factor Costs and Factor Use,* Amsterdam, North-Holland, 1963.

Minsol, Archen, "Some Tests of the International Comparisons of Factor Efficiency with the CES Production Function: A Reply," *Review of Economics and Statistics,* 50 (November 1968), pp. 477–479.

Mitchell, E. J., "Explaining the International Pattern of Labor Productivity and Wages: A Production Model with Two Labor Inputs," *Review of Economics and Statistics,* 50 (November 1968), pp. 461–469.

Morrall, J. F., III, *Human Capital, Technology, and the Role of the United States in International Trade,* Gainesville, University of Florida Press, 1972.

Nelson, R. R., "A 'Diffusion' Model of International Productivity Differences in Manufacturing Industry," *American Economic Review*, 58 (December 1968), pp. 1219–1248.

Olsen, E., *International Trade Theory and Regional Income Differences: United States 1880–1950*, Amsterdam, North-Holland, 1971.

Philpot, G., "Labor Quality, Returns to Scale and the Elasticity of Factor Substitution," *Review of Economics and Statistics*, 52 (May 1970), pp. 194–199.

Richardson, J. D., and R. Baade, "The Effects of Commercial Policy on Functional Income Distribution" (forthcoming).
Roskamp, K. W., and G. C. McMeekin, "Factor Proportions, Human Capital and Foreign Trade: The Case of West Germany Reconsidered," *Quarterly Journal of Economics*, 82 (February 1968), pp. 152–160.

Schmitz, A., and P. Helmberger, "Factor Mobility and International Trade: The Case of Complementarity," *American Economic Review*, 60 (September 1970), pp. 761–767.
Silberston, A., "Economies of Scale in Theory and Practice," *Economic Journal*, 82 (March 1972, Supplement), pp. 369–391.
Stern, R. M., *Foreign Trade and Economic Growth in Italy*, New York, Praeger, 1967.
Stryker, J. D., "The Sources of Change in Export Performance: The United States and Canada," in Kenen and Lawrence (1968).

Tilton, J. E., *International Diffusion of Technology: The Case of Semiconductors*, Washington, The Brookings Institution, 1971.
Travis, W. P., "Production, Trade, and Protection When There Are Many Commodities and Two Factors," *American Economic Review*, 62 (March 1972), pp. 87–106.
Tyler, W. G., "Trade in Manufactures and Labor Skill Content: The Brazilian Case," *Economia Internazionale*, 25 (May 1972), pp. 314–334.

Vernon, R., ed., *The Technology Factor in International Trade*, New York, Columbia University Press for National Bureau of Economic Research, 1970.

Waehrer, H., "Wage Rates, Labor Skills, and United States Foreign Trade," in Kenen and Lawrence (1968).
Weiser, L. A., "Changing Factor Requirements of United States Foreign Trade," *Review of Economics and Statistics*, 50 (August 1968), pp. 356–360.
Weiser, L., and K. Jay, "Determinants of the Commodity Structure of U.S. Trade: Comment," *American Economic Review*, 62 (June 1972), pp. 459–464.
Wells, L. T., Jr., "Test of a Product Cycle Model of International Trade: U.S. Exports of Consumer Durables," *Quarterly Journal of Economics*, 82 (February 1969), pp. 152–162.
Williams, J. R., "The Resource Content in International Trade," *Canadian Journal of Economics*, 3 (February 1970), pp. 111–122.
Witte, A. D., "Alternative Estimates of Capital-Labor Substitution in Manufac-

turing in Developing Countries: Comments on Professor Clague," *Economet-rica,* 39 (November 1971), pp. 1053–1054.

Yahr, M., "Human Capital and Factor Substitution in the CES Production Func-tion," in Kenen and Lawrence (1968).
Yeung, P., and H. Tsang, "Generalized Production Function and Factor-Intensity Crossovers: An Empirical Analysis," *Economic Record,* 48 (September 1972), pp. 387–399.
Yudin, E. B., "Americans Abroad: A Transfer of Capital," in Kenen and Lawrence (1968).

THE COSTS AND CONSEQUENCES OF PROTECTION: A SURVEY OF EMPIRICAL WORK*

W. M. Corden

This paper surveys empirical research concerned with protection, including the consequences of regional and nondiscriminatory trade liberalization. The relationship between theory and empirical work is discussed, but no attempt is made to provide a comprehensive survey of protection theory.

Let us start with an overview, distinguishing between research on developing and developed countries, and beginning with the former. In the postwar period, protection, especially through import quotas and exchange control, has been much more important for the economies of less developed countries than for those of developed countries. It would probably not be disputed that in India and Pakistan import quotas have really made a difference – at least in the nonagricultural sector of the economy – to an extent that cannot be found with respect to tariffs or quotas in any developed country (except possibly New Zealand). It is thus surprising that, until Bhagwati and Desai (1970), a description and analysis of the Indian import-control system was not publicly available. Indeed, until the last few years very little was available on protection in the less developed countries.[1]

What were the reasons for this? Perhaps there is an inevitable lag before new situations – such as industrialization by import substitution as a result of the aftermath of the Korean boom – are recognized as requiring study, and before research is organized. Perhaps there was a tendency for economists working on less developed countries to be preoccupied with doubtfully relevant problems and techniques popular in the United States and the United Kingdom. Finally, perhaps standard theory had not provided convenient techniques for describing and analyzing the complicated systems of protection, multiple rates, and exchange control prevalent in many countries.

---

* This is a substantially revised and extended version of the paper presented at the Conference (the section on trade integration was not included in the original paper). I am indebted to John Martin for valuable comments.

[1] One of the few comprehensive pieces of description was by Macario (1964) on Latin-American protectionism.

51

In any case, since about 1967 there has been a remarkable burst of policy-oriented empirical work on protection and industrialization in less developed countries. We know a lot more about protection in these countries than we did ten years ago. Two important projects have stimulated a great deal of work – the OECD project organized by Little on industrialization and trade in six developing countries[2] and the IBRD project involving comprehensive calculations of effective protection in another (overlapping) group of developing countries (Balassa, 1971). The OECD studies all make use of effective-protection calculations, and Bergsman (1970) also has a rough cost-of-protection calculation. But these studies go well beyond this and have provided, often for the first time, much-needed descriptions of protective systems and of changes in industrial structure and associated trade flows.

Quite apart from these projects, effective-protection calculations have been made for numerous less developed countries. These will be discussed further below. In addition, two other major projects are under way at the moment. Bhagwati and Krueger have organized a project for the National Bureau of Economic Research on exchange control, liberalization, and economic development, involving ten country studies,[3] while Balassa has organized another project for the IBRD that will involve a comprehensive description and analysis of the systems of resource-allocation incentives in six countries,[4] going well beyond tariffs and import quotas.

In the case of developed countries, there have been attempts to quantify the costs of protection, notably for Canada and the United States, and also the effects of actual or hypothetical trade liberalization. But the most important development by far has derived from the establishment of the EEC and EFTA. The formation of these trading blocs has given rise to an extensive literature analyzing the effects, particularly of the EEC, on trade flows. It will be reviewed more fully below.[5]

2 See the comprehensive overall study by Little, Scitovsky, and Scott (1970), and the country studies on India by Bhagwati and Desai (1970), Brazil by Bergsman (1970), Pakistan by Lewis (1970), Mexico by King (1970), and Taiwan and the Philippines by Hsing, Power, and Sicat (1970).
3 Brazil, Chile, Colombia, Egypt, Ghana, India, Israel, the Philippines, South Korea, and Turkey.
4 Argentina, Colombia, Israel, Singapore, South Korea, and Taiwan.
5 As liberalization has reduced the importance of tariffs in the main industrial countries, attention has correctly shifted to "nontariff" barriers, a rather omnibus term that includes, above all, quantitative import restrictions and voluntary export restraints. The significant literature growing up here has so far been mainly descriptive. See Bald-

Let us now turn to theory. In terms of impact on empirical work as well as on theoretical writings, the most important development here has been the theory of effective protection. Possibly of equal importance is the theory of customs unions, which is, of course, of considerably earlier origin. Predating effective-protection theory, but closely related to it, is the theory of the cost of protection. We shall look at all of these below. Another important theoretical development, with significant policy implications, is the theory of domestic distortions, which makes a general argument in favor of subsidies rather than tariffs as policy interventions. But this has not had a great deal of policy impact and has not led to empirical work, a matter that will have to be discussed.

1. THE COST OF PROTECTION

The cost of protection can be conceived of either in Marshallian partial-equilibrium terms or in general-equilibrium terms. In Corden (1957), an analysis was presented in both partial-equilibrium and two-sector general-equilibrium terms. The aim was to clarify the concept of "excess cost" of protection used in Brigden (1929). With given terms of trade, and assuming no reciprocal tariff reductions, the cost of protection consists of a *production-cost* and a *consumption-cost* component, both of which are triangles if one assumes linear curves. This is illustrated in Figure 1, which can be interpreted to refer either to a single importable good (partial equilibrium) or to the sole importable in a two-sector model (general equilibrium). In the latter case, the export price is the numeraire, and the demand curve must be explicitly defined as a constant-utility one. The tariff is *ST*. Area I is the production cost and area II the consumption cost. The Brigden excess cost is different from the cost of protection, being areas I plus III. It is easier to calculate because it does not require knowledge of elasticities. It is what we now call the "cash cost" or "subsidy equivalent" – the cash cost to the Treasury of the production subsidy to protected industry that would have the same protective effect as the tariff.

The major theoretical paper is by Johnson (1960), who generalized the cost-of-protection concept to the general-equilibrium many-good case and brought out a variety of crucial assumptions.

win (1970) and Walter (1972), especially, as well as Bergsten (forthcoming) on voluntary export restraints, which are particularly significant for the United States. The cost-of-protection work of Magee (1972), to be discussed below, takes quotas and export restraints into account.

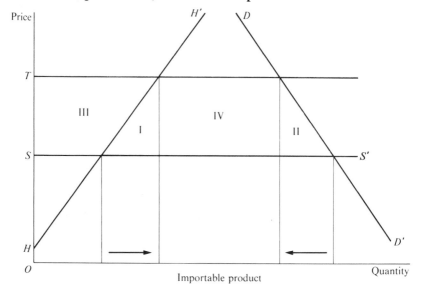

Figure 1. *SS'* is the foreign supply curve of the import, assumed to be a perfect substitute for the competing domestically produced product. *HH'* is the import-competing supply curve. *DD'* is the domestic demand curve for imports and domestic production combined. *ST/OS* is the ad valorem tariff rate.

An extensive discussion, taking into account increasing returns, is in Wonnacott and Wonnacott (1967, Chap. 15).

We shall come back to various theoretical problems shortly. Let us first note the main empirical work, distinguishing comprehensive calculations designed to estimate the cost of the whole tariff or protection system of a country from calculations concerned with particular industries or limited sectors.

Empirical work began with calculations of cash cost (or subsidy equivalent) in Australia (Brigden, 1929) and Canada (Young, 1957).[6] Today, by "cost of protection" calculations we usually understand the familiar Marshallian triangles calculations. In international trade, these were initiated by Johnson (1958), who worked out on the basis of some *ex ante* figures estimated by the Economist Intelligence Unit the gains to the United Kingdom from freer trade with Europe – though these cannot strictly be described as comprehensive cost-of-protection computations.

6 The Australian study, the product of a semiofficial committee, is really the pioneering work in this area. There was also a postwar exercise by a similar committee in Australia (Vernon, 1965).

The only comprehensive calculations of this type for a developed country, as far as I am aware, have been done for the United States, first by Stern (1964), who pioneered this work in the United States but assumed constant import and export prices (the small-country assumption), and then by Basevi (1968) and Magee (1972).

Basevi used U.S. foreign-trade elasticities from Floyd (1965), allowed for finite export-demand and import-supply elasticities, and assumed an average U.S. tariff of 15 per cent. He found that there was a gain to the United States from her tariff, the average tariff rate indeed being below the optimum. Walker (1969) reviewed Basevi's work. Using later elasticity estimates, he found that, assuming no reciprocal tariff reductions, the optimum tariff (and/or export tax) would be even higher than that which came out of Basevi's figures, but, allowing for reciprocal tariff elimination, he concluded there would be a net gain from free trade. The use of a single average tariff figure for the U.S. tariff and quota structure represents a degree of aggregation that makes these sorts of calculations of rather modest value: all one can say is that, *if* there were a single tariff of 15 per cent and the elasticities were of such an order of magnitude, then this *might be* the welfare effect.

The recent work of Magee (1972) on the welfare effects of the U.S. tariff is thus a big step forward, since he has disaggregated somewhat, especially the items restricted by import quotas or voluntary export restraints abroad. He distinguishes short-run from long-run effects, allows for adjustment costs, and, importantly, includes as an element of cost to the United States that part of the tariff equivalent of U.S. import quotas and of voluntary export restrictions by suppliers to the United States that is likely to go to foreign suppliers. (The tariff equivalent is the customs revenue that an equivalent tariff would have yielded and is represented by area IV in Figure 1.) This is in addition to the two triangles.

Magee finds that the cost to the United States of quotas and voluntary restraints, including the cost of the tariff equivalent, on six major import-quota items dominates the total cost of U.S. protection. His quota-cost estimates are based on more detailed work by others, notably Bergsten and Mintz; his tariff-cost estimates, which come out quite small, are rather tenuous: they are based on guesses about elasticities, notably on the supply side, and on tariff averages derived from customs revenue. In addition, he takes into account the costs of foreign-trade restrictions on the U.S. terms of trade; for agriculture the cost is estimated as substantial, higher than the cost to the United States of her quotas. The total cost to the United States of U.S. and foreign restrictions combined consists mainly of these two categories.

There have been many cost-of-protection calculations for particular industries, notably in the agricultural field.[7] The "triangles" method has become as conventional as drawing demand and supply curves. This modern revival of Alfred Marshall has been particularly fostered by Arnold Harberger. He pioneered the bold approach to welfare-cost calculations for less developed countries with a celebrated rough estimate for Chile (Harberger, 1959), though this applied to the whole protected sector, not just to one industry, and also involved calculations of the effects of other distortions. An important contribution, to which I shall refer again later, has come from Krueger (1966), who calculated the "domestic resource cost" – essentially the cost-of-protection concept – for some Turkish industries and made some methodological innovations.

Let us now look at a number of aspects of the cost-of-protection topic, all of which are relevant for empirical work.

a. There is the familiar problem that, for consumers'-surplus calculations, one must make use of a constant-utility demand curve and so must choose between the existing (protection) utility level and that of free trade, or perhaps of an alternative optimum or lower protection situation. In practice, when elasticity figures have such high margins of errors and are often just guesses, and since income effects do not generally appear to be very large anyway, this is probably not worth worrying about.

b. What is the meaning of "cost"? There are three possible interpretations: (i) It is the cost of official foolishness or ignorance, of a failure to adjust policies to changes, and so on. A positive cost figure means, then, that removal or reduction of protection would raise welfare in the Pareto-efficiency sense, and possibly in a wider sense, even allowing for income-distribution effects. (ii) It is the current cost of achieving economic objectives, such as income redistribution or raising future incomes, and this cost must be set both against the costs of alternative ways of attaining the same objectives and against the benefits from the objectives; it is thus an

---

7 Interesting examples of the use of the method are Snape's (1969) calculation of the cost of protection and taxation of sugar in some developing countries; Munk (1969), who worked out the welfare costs of content-protection systems in the Latin-American automotive industry; and Dardis (1967) on the cost of livestock protection in West Germany. All these take intermediate goods into account. Dardis applies elasticities derived from U.S. data to her German problem.

element in a cost–benefit calculation. (iii) It is the cost of attaining specified noneconomic objectives.

c. The simplest expositions assume given terms of trade. Except in the small-country case, or possibly when tariff reductions are reciprocal, this is not legitimate. But terms-of-trade effects can be allowed for. This consideration distinguishes the U.S. calculations of Basevi (1968) from those of Stern (1964). Magee (1972) disregards terms-of-trade effects of U.S. tariffs, but does allow for terms-of-trade effects of quotas and foreign tariffs.

d. A potential source of confusion is the role of the exchange rate in the analysis (see Basevi, 1968, for clarification). The analysis is *real* and assumes balance-of-payments equilibrium at all times, or at least a constant deficit or surplus. The exchange rate is no more than the instrument of adjustment, which ensures that exports do rise when the tariff is removed and imports rise. The elasticities that are used for calculations in a general-equilibrium exercise should take into account the consequences of exchange-rate adjustment. If reciprocal tariff adjustment is assumed – that is, if the cost of domestic and foreign protection combined is being calculated – it may be reasonable to disregard the exchange-rate adjustment on the grounds that, broadly, the balance-of-payments effects of domestic and foreign tariff and quota adjustments would offset each other. This may justify Young (1957) and Magee (1972) ignoring this adjustment.

e. The practical implications of the multi-commodity case where tariffs are not uniform are not often appreciated. In fact, I suspect that Johnson's (1960) analysis is not always understood. The cost of protection can be thought of as having two parts: the first is the cost of the uniform-tariff equivalent of the existing tariff system – that is, the uniform tariff that would have the same effect on total imports as the existing tariff structure; the second is the additional cost owing to nonuniformity. If the elasticity of supply of exports were zero, the whole cost would consist of the second part. It is thus not sufficient to look at the possible effects on exports if free trade were established. One must also allow for cases in which the move to free trade would cause some imports to fall.

This problem does not arise, of course, in the usual partial-equilibrium calculations. Magee (1972) handles it explicitly by allowing for aggregation bias with the use of tariff-dispersion data. The greater the dispersion, the more a simple average understates the welfare effect. One of the features of most protective systems is their nonuniformity. This has been highlighted by effective-protection calculations, which suggest that effective tariff dispersion may be an important generator of costs of protection. This dispersion problem is distinct from another problem, to which I shall refer again later, that tariff averages based on import weights will be less than the uniform-tariff equivalent, and so also a source of understatement of welfare effects.

f. If one is studying the effects of some tariffs or quotas while others are held constant, and if the others are nonoptimal and affect the demand or supply curves entering into the calculations, then market demand and supply curves cannot be used in the calculations. There is a divergence between private and social costs or benefits, or both, and *social* benefit or cost curves must be used. Hence, one has a typical second-best situation; a particular tariff would inflict a cost, as calculated in the usual way, if all other (nonoptimal) tariffs were removed; but if other tariffs are given, the cost may be less or more, or there may actually be a gain from this particular tariff. This is an important consideration for all partial-equilibrium calculations.

g. Amendments must be made in the presence of any divergence (distortion) between private and social cost or benefit, for example, a divergence between the actual wage payable and the shadow wage, indicating a social opportunity cost of labor. These complications may not be important for calculations in developed countries (and it must be remembered that Australia and Canada originated this subject), but are very relevant for less developed countries.

In fact, the subject becomes part of modern cost–benefit analysis. Krueger (1966), in her work on Turkey, has taken such divergences into account. She has also stressed that domestic costs (her "domestic resource cost") should not include monopoly profits. One must compare domestic average costs, not prices, with import prices. Modern cost–benefit analysts might go further and, following Meade (1955a), attach distributional weights to different incomes. If wage income is used as the numeraire, monopoly profits might then create "costs."[8]

h. The calculations are often criticized for being static. If econ-

---

[8] Here one should note the recent development of cost–benefit analysis for open less developed economies (Little and Mirrlees, 1969), which in its *ex ante* form may turn into an influential technique for guiding policy decisions, and in its *ex post* form might be regarded as a more sophisticated version of standard cost-of-protection analysis. Empirical work applying the Little–Mirrlees method to various projects in less developed countries is currently under way at Nuffield College, Oxford, and modified forms of the method are coming to be widely used.

omies of scale are meant (and these are not essentially dynamic in nature), the effects of changes in trade policy on trade itself – and the welfare consequences of these effects – should in principle be captured by the calculations. What is not captured is the "cost-reduction effect" of trade: when the size of the market expands owing to opening up an economy to trade or reducing protection, the costs of domestically produced products sold domestically may fall.

A genuinely dynamic consideration is to take into account the general growth of the economy. A nonoptimal tariff or quota imposes a cost of protection every year. The cost is likely to grow absolutely with the size of the economy, and it may rise or fall in relation to GNP. The cost of a tariff (or of a tariff reduction) that is expected to be sustained into future periods is then the discounted sum of the costs in every year. One can thus calculate present values, as Magee (1972) has done, using various discount rates. A tariff may have very little effect for some years but might impose large costs in later years, when domestic producers become capable of taking advantage of it; this can be taken into account when calculating the present value of a tariff or quota *decision*. Of course, this assumes, perhaps realistically, that a tariff or quota once imposed cannot easily be removed.

If there is a cost of protection, so that protection reduces real GNP, it is likely that savings will be reduced (compared with savings in the cost-free situation) and this may bring about a lower rate of capital accumulation and hence lower rate of growth. While this adverse growth effect is distinct from the one mentioned above, it cannot be regarded as giving rise to a separate cost; rather, it is one way in which the static cost in any given year is borne.

An important dynamic element is the adjustment cost of making changes in trade policy. Here one must distinguish the adverse effects of tariff reduction (or quota expansion) on national output – through causing temporary unemployment and underutilization of capacity – from the effects in creating unwelcome temporary or permanent *income redistribution*. If factor prices were completely flexible, there would be only the second problem (the country would stay on its production-possibility frontier). If adjustment assistance were very generous, there would only be the first. In practice the two go together. Baldwin and Mutti (1973) and Magee (1972), following the method of Baldwin and Mutti, have pioneered here in putting some figures to these costs. Their estimates are rough (to put it mildly): Magee uses as a proxy for the cost the estimated income expected to be lost by labor during a five-year transitional period. The result is, of course, to reduce the costs of existing protection relative to the free-trade alternative; in the short run, indeed, the costs may be turned into a gain.

i. Finally, there is the big issue raised by all the cost-of-protection calculations. The static costs always seem to come out "small." In some less developed countries, they are unlikely to come out "small" in relation to value added at world prices in the industrial sector, or to incomes in the urban sector, but in some of the largest countries, notably India and Pakistan, the industrial sector is, of course, a small part of the national economy. Bergsman (1970), in a very rough calculation, came up with a small figure for Brazil, as did Harberger (1959) for Chile, and I have already referred to Krueger's (1966) work on Turkey, but it may be worth making even rough estimates for other less developed countries.

In any case, let us consider why the cost of protection may appear to be small for developed countries. First, some relevant effects, sometimes described as "dynamic," may have been left out of the calculations. I shall come back to this later. Second, there is the question of what is "small." In relation to GNP, most policies other than macroeconomic ones have small effects. Johnson (1958) produced figures of possible gains to the United Kingdom from joining the EEC industrial customs union; these are somewhat equivalent, allowing for price changes, to the possible cost to the United Kingdom of joining the agricultural common market, with its income transfers from the United Kingdom to some fellow members. The latter cost, which can be calculated somewhat more reliably, is small in relation to GNP but a justified source of indignation. There are many good things that can be done with £250 million per annum. What *is* true is that the effects of trade-policy changes are often overrated, notably in the case of Britain and the Common Market.

At the same time, effects on sectional incomes may not be small. Even when a tariff increase has no effect in increasing output of a protected industry or reducing consumption of protected products, it will still redistribute incomes between consumers and producers of the protected products and have further income-distribution effects through its general-equilibrium repercussions. The domestic income-distribution effects may be the main effects of protection, and these effects are not captured by cost-of-protection calculations. We shall come back to income-distribution effects of protection later.

2. EFFECTIVE PROTECTION

Since the pioneering empirical work of Balassa (1965) and Basevi (1966), there has been a boom in the calculation of effective protective rates and, more generally, in descriptive and analytical studies of the protective systems of many countries.

Effective-protection theory has developed rapidly since the first theoretical papers by Johnson (1965b) and Corden (1966a). Newcomers to this field can be offered a large journal literature, a conference book (Grubel and Johnson, 1971), and a book by the present author attempting to consolidate and clarify the theory (Corden, 1971). The latter also contains a comprehensive bibliography of theoretical and empirical work and a history of the concept. We have here a genuine interaction between theory and empirical work: empirical work has been stimulated by theory, theoretical problems have been raised by empirical work, and theoretical contributions have been made as a by-product of empirical work.

The great attraction of the effective-rate concept – which no doubt helps to explain its worldwide and very rapid impact – is that it allows a single figure to sum up the net result of various trade and other taxes and subsidies affecting any particular activity. It makes it possible to describe neatly very complicated systems of trade and other interventions in many countries. But it would be wrong to interpret this new development as being concerned only with the effective protective rate; it goes beyond this in being a theory of tariff or protective structure aimed to bring out the interaction between different rates of protection for different commodities that may not be vertically related at all. It is an attempt to break out of the orthodox two-sector, general-equilibrium mold, and so make trade theory more relevant – even though various theorists have gone back to the methods of the two-sector model to clarify some problems in this new branch of theory.

This is a sympathetic way of putting the new developments. There has been a good deal of controversy and also some misunderstandings. Here let us focus on the empirical side and list some of the difficulties and criticisms. First, what problems have arisen in the calculations? Second, what are the uses, if any, of the figures when they have been calculated? The latter question raises, of course, some of the questions discussed by the theorists.

I list now a number of difficulties that have been found important by researchers and that have sometimes meant considerable

differences in the figures produced by different researchers for
the protective structures of the same country in similar time periods. A good reference on all this is Balassa *et al.* (1971), but much
is to be learned from many other country studies. In general,
these difficulties entitle one to be highly skeptical of greatly aggregated figures or figures obtained quickly. More value can be
placed on detailed calculations for particular cases, perhaps as
parts of industry studies, or on thorough, comprehensive calculations drawing on considerable resources. Furthermore, one
should not place much emphasis on small variations or differences
between calculated rates; there is always bound to be a rather
large margin of error due to measurement error alone. But this
does not mean that some carefully calculated figures are worse
than no figures! Sometimes it is useful to have rough orders of
magnitude.

a. When quotas are the principal method of protection,
comparisons between domestic and world market prices must be
made in order to obtain implicit nominal rates of protection,
which must be the starting point for any calculations. A country
may have a tariff system, but calculations on the basis of tariffs
alone have little meaning when imports are effectively restricted
by quotas. This is relevant for many developing countries. [9] The
margin for error is vast here. With a given quota structure or policy, and with demand and supply curves shifting over time, implicit effective rates may vary greatly year by year.

b. Even when tariffs alone are used, there may be much tariff
redundancy, also necessitating price comparisons. A difficulty in
these comparisons is that the quality of the local product and the
substitute import may differ. If the price of the local product is
below the tariff-inclusive price of the import, one cannot auto-
matically assume that there is tariff redundancy. This raises the
wider issue of product differentiation. Effective rates are calculated for *traded* goods, that is, goods where the domestic product and
the import are, in theory, perfect substitutes. In the case of manufactures, substitution is rarely perfect, though it may be high. This
presents no real difficulty if there is simply a constant quality difference between the products. But a problem does arise if they
are differentiated products in the true sense, the consumers'
choice between them depending on relative prices. The elasticity

---

[9] For India, Pakistan, and Mexico, calculations have had to be made starting with such
price comparisons. See Panchmukhi in Bhagwati and Desai (1970), and the Mexico and
Pakistan chapters in Balassa *et al.* (1971).

of substitution on the demand side will then bear on the impact of the tariff on the domestic producer.

c. Available input–output coefficients in most countries are rarely sufficiently disaggregated for the purpose. Indeed, coefficients are likely to differ between firms in the same industry. The method of using the coefficients of one country (Balassa *et al.*, 1971) for calculating effective rates of another hinges mainly on the doubtful assumption that production functions are the same between countries.

d. All effective-rate calculations involve tariff averaging of some kind. The whole question of tariff averages is a large subject of its own. The choice of averaging method can be a major source of error or at least divergence between different figures, and the more aggregated they are, the greater the difficulty (see Tumlir and Till, 1971). I have attempted to clarify the theory of tariff averaging by developing the concept of the "uniform tariff equivalent" (Corden, 1966b; see also Balassa, 1965, and Basevi, 1971). The uniform ad valorem tariff that would have the same effect on the total value of imports as the existing tariff structure is, ideally, the figure one is seeking (though, in principle, there are many other possible uniform tariff equivalents, for example, the one that leads to the same amount of protected production). This concept does not resolve the practical problems. In most calculations, it is customary to obtain the basic nominal tariffs required to calculate effective rates in a given category from import and customs revenue data, and so obtain import-weighted averages. For well-known reasons, these data lead to understatements. The effective rates themselves, once calculated, may then be averaged on some other basis, perhaps with domestic production weights, but an averaging error is built in at the source.[10]

e. The treatment of nontraded inputs has been shown to make a considerable difference to the figures. Various methods have been suggested and used: the simple Corden (1966a) method, which lumps nontraded inputs with value added; the more complex (and, in my view, correct) Corden (1971) method, which lumps the nontraded and primary-factor content of nontraded

[10] In effective-rate calculations for the United Kingdom by Barker and Han (1971) and Oulton (1973), account is taken of the fact that one cannot use the same average tariff for a commodity group when it is employed as an input as when it is a final good; though both industries and final consumers pay the same tariff rates on individual products, the weighted average tariffs paid on commodity groups differ because the product mixes differ. Oulton (1973) also notes that there will be an error if the mix of products imported is not the same as the mix of products produced domestically.

inputs with value added, but groups the traded-input content of nontraded inputs with direct traded inputs; the simple Balassa (1965) method, which groups nontraded inputs with traded inputs, and treats the former as if they were traded inputs with zero tariffs; the later Balassa *et al.* (1971) method, which allows for tariffs on traded inputs contained in nontraded inputs; and, finally, the Scott method (Little *et al.,* 1970, and Corden, 1971), which treats the nontraded and primary-factor content of nontraded inputs as if they were traded inputs with a uniform tariff equal to the equilibrium exchange-rate adjustment.

The simple Corden method is often used, but Balassa *et al.* (1971) produce figures on the basis of both the complex Corden and the later Balassa methods. The choice of method seems to make a substantial difference to levels, though not necessarily to ordering. Perhaps more important, even if one method comes generally to be accepted, and unless it is the simple Balassa method (which Balassa has abandoned), there is the crucial empirical problem of deciding which are traded and which nontraded goods. In theory the line cannot be clearly drawn.[11]

So much for what seem to be the main empirical problems. There are, of course, others also. The treatment of indirect taxes has given rise to some discussion.[12] Sometimes, particular industries are both import-competing and exporters. More disaggregation would eliminate or at least reduce this problem, but if one wants to calculate the effective rate for an activity or industry, rather than just the protection it obtains on the home market, one needs to have a weighted average of the import-protective rate and the rate applying to exports (often zero or negative). On this basis, one can obtain "adjusted" effective rates.[13] If firms and products within the industry were homogeneous, then the existence of exports would suggest that tariffs were redundant; nonhomogeneity and monopoly give rise to the complication.

I turn now to the meaning and uses of the figures once they have been calculated. Indeed, before embarking on the statistical exercise, one needs to consider whether they are likely to be of any use at all! Broadly, one can see a positive and a normative role for them. The theory for the positive role has been more rigorously developed (Corden, 1966a and 1971), but the real interest is

11 I have discussed these questions at a theoretical level and compared the methods in Corden (1971, Chap. 7).
12 The original article here is Grubel and Johnson (1967). See also Gamir (1971), who correctly criticizes the methods in the original article. A discussion of the issues, with calculations, is in Oulton (1973).
13 As McAleese (1971) has for Ireland, and as Balassa is doing in his new IBRD project.

in the normative implications, and large resources would not have been sunk into this empirical work if normative implications had not been seen. The positive theory must be a foundation for the normative theory, but the latter must go beyond the former; possibly it can avoid some of the positive theory's problems.

The essence of the positive role is that the scale of effective rates should give some indication of the direction of resource pulls of the protective structure (and if factor intensities differ between activities – as surely they do – also of functional or sectional income-distribution effects). But it cannot actually tell us what the resource changes are, so perhaps we should attempt instead complete general-equilibrium programming exercises to give us total rather than partial answers – which is the approach of Evans (1972).

The emphasis on the scale of effective rates suggests that *rankings* of industries on the basis of effective rates are crucial for assessing resource-allocation effects of protection. A number of authors, notably Cohen (1971) and Guisinger and Schydlowsky (1971), have compared rankings of nominal rates with rankings of effective rates for many countries, and found them to be similar, at least when the degree of aggregation is high. This has suggested to Cohen that it may be sufficient to know nominal rates. This would appear to be true broadly, if one just wants to know rankings and is not concerned with detailed disaggregated tariff making. But the *extent* of protection – notably the size of the bias against exports indicated by average effective rates for import-competing manufacturing – is also important. Because the relationship between nominal and effective rates is not consistent as *between* countries, one cannot just calculate nominal rates, then feed the result into some common intercountry equation, and so deduce levels of effective rates.

It has generally been found that effective rates for protected industry far exceed nominal rates.[14] This suggests that the resource pulls are much greater than nominal rates on their own would indicate. And the larger the resource-allocation effects of the protective structure, the higher the cost of protection is likely to be. All this implies the need to calculate effective rates, as Guisinger and Schydlowsky stress (1971).

The critics have questioned whether anything at all can be said about resource pulls and have produced theoretical counter-

14 For example (and, of course, there could be no end of examples), McAleese (1971) found the average nominal rate for Irish manufacturing to be 25 per cent and the average effective rate 79 per cent.

examples.[15] I have reviewed all this in Corden (1971). In theory, all things are indeed possible. In practice, it must be remembered that, even if effective rates give a reasonable indication of the direction of resource pulls, they cannot on their own tell one what the responses to the pulls will be; one also needs supply elasticities. This point is obvious, but often neglected. If the elasticity of supply is zero there will be no resource movement, however high the effective rate.

More fundamentally, Travis (1968) has queried the whole concept of value added. Value added has no natural units, so how can it have a price? And if it really has no price, then relative price changes of so-called value added cannot indicate resource pulls. This argument hinges in large measure on the substitution problem, to which I shall turn in a moment.

I am afraid that much of this debate reminds one of a certain British school of thought's preoccupation with whether one can or should measure capital. If one is purist, one will not do so, and it is not difficult to produce paradoxes and counterexamples. Clearly, one must not place too much value on the calculations or estimated figures. Theory certainly has a useful role in bringing out various possible paradoxes, implicit assumptions, and so on, but finally some judgment is required as to what is important or probable, and there will never be enough empirical information to give one certain answers.

Furthermore, one has to consider the alternatives. Travis produced the first substantial study that drew attention to the importance of intermediate goods and the input–output relationships in the analysis of tariffs (Travis, 1964). But he avoided the effective rate because he felt that only nominal tariffs are real, since value added as such cannot have a price (Travis, 1968). He seems to suggest that one should base one's empirical research and policy judgments on nominal rates only; it is this alternative that, in spite of the difficulties of the effective-rate concept, many people would reject.

Let us now look at the substitution problem for a moment.[16] First, suppose that the relevant production functions are "separable," or, in other words, that produced inputs are equally substitutable for the various factors which together make up the "value-added product" (substitution is "unbiased"). This means that a three-input production function is of the form $j = J[V(K,L), i]$,

15 Tan (1970); Ramaswami and Srinivasan (1971). Bhagwati is also very skeptical, his views and models being in Bhagwati and Srinivasan (1973).
16 This discussion is based on Corden (1971, Chap. 6).

where K and L are capital and labor and i is the produced traded input. There is then no conceptual problem about the meaning of value added and hence of effective rates. The degree of error will depend on substitution elasticities and spreads between nominal protective rates on final products and inputs. Empirical work on the importance of substitution is required here, or at least an exploration of plausible figures. A start has been made by Leith (1968) and by Grubel and Lloyd (1971). Travis (1964) stressed substitution effects, and Balassa *et al.* (1970) reexamined Travis's data and concluded that substitution was not important. Humphrey (1973), on the basis of U.S. data, has found very little substitution.

Second, a problem arises if production functions cannot be regarded as "separable," so that the production function takes the general form $j = J\,(K, L, i)$. Substitution may then be "biased." For example, the produced input may be a closer substitute for capital than for labor. There are then, in turn, two issues. One is conceptual: Does "value added" continue to have a meaning, a question originally posed by Travis. The problem has also been discussed in the national-income literature. Jones (1971) argues that it can still be given a meaning.[17] The other issue is whether effective rates are, in such a case, of any use for resource-pull analysis. Ramaswami and Srinivasan (1971) produced a counterexample with biased substitution where resources moved in a paradoxical way. But Jones (1971) analyzed this in detail and showed the result to depend on extreme and improbable figures.

Empirical work on this subject is being done by Humphrey and Wolkowitz (1971). They have studied substitution between capital, labor, and all intermediate inputs for the aggregate U.S. manufacturing sector from 1947 to 1958 and have found some substitution but unbiased, supporting the separability hypothesis. More recently, Humphrey (1973) has disaggregated, making the same calculations for six U.S. manufacturing sectors, and found not only absence of bias but also, for five sectors, no statistically significant primary-factor intermediate-product substitution at all. His work is continuing, and these results must be regarded as preliminary.

Effective-protection figures can be of some use for normative purposes, and such a purpose was certainly in the minds of its

---

17 His argument cannot be briefly summarized. Essentially, he treats "bias" as a particular form of technical change in the activity producing value added, and the effective rate is "the distributive-share weighted average of the relative changes in the wage rate and rental" (p. 75).

pioneers. The case where the normative implications are clearest is that of *negative value added*. It is a contribution of the effective-protection approach that it has uncovered this phenomenon, which has been found in many countries (see Corden, 1971, p. 51, and the references given there). This is a case where the value of inputs at world prices exceeds the value of the final product, also at world prices. Protection systems may create economic inefficiency even when value added at world prices is always positive, but negative value added is a particularly clear case of economic inefficiency: no general-equilibrium analysis is needed to suggest that negative-value-added activities are likely to be socially inefficient, though privately profitable owing to high protection of final goods.

More generally, for normative uses of effective protection one has to envisage second-best situations, for example, where the exchange rate is constrained (an assumption that is less realistic now than some years ago); where a target size of import-competing manufacturing is exogenously given; where there is some uniform externality believed to attach to certain economic activities, say manufacturing, relative to others; or where free trade is first-best, but only partial tariff reductions or tariff elimination is possible (Corden, 1971, chap. 8, and 1974).

An important case is one in which the purpose of protection is to increase employment in manufacturing because the shadow wage is below the market wage, so that labor-intensive industries should be protected relatively more. This clearly applies to some less developed countries. The normative reference point cannot then be a uniform effective rate but must rather be a closely related concept, the uniform *effective protective rate for labor*. In general, it must be appreciated that if there are many uncorrected and uncorrectable domestic distortions, effective-rate calculations cannot provide adequate guidance for allocation of resources. Ideally, complete cost–benefit calculations are required, but to make these for more than a few projects or activities involves even greater human-resource cost than to make effective-rate calculations. Thus the latter may be a feasible second-best when a complete overview of the protective structure is required, provided one realizes that they give only *some* guidance for policy decisions rather than final guidelines.

3. TRADE INTEGRATION

The theory of customs unions, pioneered by Viner (1950) and Meade (1955b), has been so often and well surveyed (see Lipsey,

1960; Robson, 1971; and Krauss, 1972) that it is hardly necessary to do so again. It is concerned primarily with the effects of trade discrimination and stresses the distinction between *trade creation* and *trade diversion*. Recent contributions have also emphasized the terms-of-trade implications of customs unions.

But a customs union also involves the establishment of a common external tariff, and the effects of this have tended to be neglected in the theory. The earlier writers analyzed only the effects of freeing trade within the union, not of aligning external tariffs, implicitly assuming that union members' tariffs for particular products were initially identical. This external tariff alignment could expand trade with the outside world (as a result of member countries with initially high tariffs having to reduce their external tariffs); hence there may, on balance, be "external trade creation" in spite of trade diversion brought about by freeing trade within the union. Empirical studies suggest that this has been a significant effect of the EEC.

The welfare analysis of customs unions involves more than just looking at effects on trade flows. Even if one grants the assumptions of the simplest analysis – which assumes away domestic distortions and is concerned only with a potential Pareto improvement for the world as a whole (and hence ignores internal and international income-distribution effects) – one cannot say for certain that an increase in trade will always raise welfare and a decrease lower it. Furthermore, even when it is a reasonable approximation to suppose this, welfare analysis still requires weights to be attached to various changes in trade, the weights depending essentially on discrepancies between costs of original and of new suppliers and on changes in tariff rates. It is not sufficient to look at the effects on total trade, hence implying equal weights for all trade changes.

A great deal of empirical work has been done on estimating the effects of the EEC and EFTA on trade flows. Recently, this has been surveyed by Williamson and Bottrill (1971), Kreinin (1972), and Sellekaerts (1973). Let us just summarize the main methods and problems.

First, one must distinguish between *ex ante* and *ex post* studies. The former sought to study the effects of the EEC in advance of its formation and required estimates of relevant average tariff reductions or rates of discrimination, as well as estimates of elasticities. These estimates tended to be somewhat broad and rough.[18]

18 The best-known *ex ante* studies are those of Verdoorn (1954), who pioneered this type of work, and of Krause (1963), who predicted the effects of the EEC on U.S. trade.

As is to be expected, there have by now been a large number of *ex post* studies. These seek to isolate the Common Market effect in changes that have actually taken place and ideally require allowances for "other things" that, regrettably, do not stay equal, such as technical progress, changing commodity composition of final demands, and – above all – increases in incomes. The problem is to construct an *anti-monde* with which actual flows of trade can be compared, the difference being the integration effect.

One approach is simply to look at changes in trade shares for various commodity groups. If the share of intra-EEC trade for any given member country has increased relative to its trade with the world as a whole, then there is an "integration effect." The convenience of this approach is that it requires only trade data. But the increased share of intra-area trade does not tell us whether there has been trade creation or trade diversion, since both will raise the share of intra trade. Furthermore, the implicit assumption is that, in the absence of integration, the shares would have stayed constant.

The latter difficulty is possibly overcome by a slight variant of this method. One looks at the changing shares that various suppliers have in markets where there have been no preferential tariff changes, and assumes that these shares apply in the *anti-monde*. For example, if the share of German exports in the imports of countries outside the EEC has gone up, one assumes that even in the absence of integration the German share would have gone up in imports to France. This approach, pioneered by Lamfalussy (1963), has recently been used by Williamson and Bottrill (1971) to study the effects of both the EEC and EFTA. But it still suffers from the disability that it fails to separate trade-creation and trade-diversion effects, yielding only a total "integration effect."

A preferable approach, fully developed by Truman (1969 and 1972), analyzes changes in shares of apparent consumption rather than shares of imports. If the share of total imports in apparent consumption of members of the union increases, there is trade creation; if the share of imports from nonpartner countries falls, there is trade diversion. In his analysis of the effects of the EEC, Truman found that the share of imports from outside the EEC actually increased, so that there was presumably "external trade creation" owing to tariff reduction vis-à-vis outsiders. The fundamental assumption is that in the absence of integration the shares would have stayed constant. This presents three difficulties: (a) income elasticities of demand for imports may not be unity –

there is some reason to believe that they are often greater than unity; (b) other policy changes, notably general tariff reductions associated with the Dillon and Kennedy rounds, may have affected shares; and (c) relative prices may have changed.

In an earlier paper, Balassa (1967b) sought to deal with the first problem. He assumed that in the *anti-monde* the income elasticities of demand of the pre-integration period would have ruled. With income elasticities of demand for imports in this earlier period (1953–59) greater than unity, the shares of imports in apparent consumption would have increased even in the absence of integration. Nevertheless, he found evidence of substantial trade creation and very little trade diversion (and some external trade creation). His calculations have been analyzed by Clavaux (1969) and Sellekaerts (1973); there is some doubt whether the income elasticities of 1953–59 would have stayed constant, and, in fact, during that period there was a change in income elasticities. Above all, the method fails to allow for the second difficulty, the effects of general trade liberalization proceeding at varying rates in both the pre- and the post-integration period. One might regard the Kennedy-round liberalization in the post-integration period as simply part of the adjustment of the common external tariff, and hence part of the integration process, but there remains the problem of trade liberalization (including removal of quantitative restrictions) in the 1953–59 period.

Kreinin (1969) tried to allow for relative price effects. He calculated import functions for the EEC and EFTA countries for the period 1953–61, allowing for income and price effects and for lags in the impact of price changes. But many of the price coefficients turned out to have the wrong sign. (His methods are criticized in Williamson and Bottrill, 1971, p. 332.) Taking into account also his own work, Sellekaerts (1973) concludes that the exclusion of relative prices is not a major loss, because the estimates of relative price elasticities are often statistically nonsignificant and carry the wrong sign, and because variations in real income can explain a great deal.

In two very thorough studies, the EFTA Secretariat (1969, 1972) used a method rather similar to that of Balassa to analyze the effects of both the EEC and EFTA. The *anti-monde* was again constructed on the basis of data from the pre-integration period. Import shares in apparent consumption for the period 1954–59 were extrapolated by fitting straight lines. This was done for each commodity group, and adjustments were made where the result produced an integration effect clearly of the wrong sign. The extrapolation captured not just income effects but also any other trends, but may imply, without good reason, varying income elasticities of demand. The advantage of the EFTA approach compared with Balassa's is that it allows for a trend in the pre-integration period rather than just using a single income-elasticity figure for each commodity group to represent the whole period.[19]

Kreinin (1972) has constructed an *anti-monde* in which shares of apparent consumption are determined not by data of the pre-integration period but rather by actual changes in these shares in the same period in a "normalizing" country, namely, the United States. He also took some account of differences in income and price movements between the United States and the EEC during this period and excluded certain sectors, notably agriculture and petroleum products, which were clearly special cases. Like the authors of all the other studies, he found trade creation to be far in excess of trade diversion.

The most recent contribution in this field, by Aitken (1973), has gone back to utilizing only trade data, but the method is quite different from earlier studies. (He uses the "gravity"-type model of international flows developed by Linnemann, 1966.) Bilateral trade flows between the twelve countries making up the original EEC and EFTA for each of the years from 1951 to 1967 form the basic raw material; they are explained by yearly cross-section regressions with GNP, population of each country, distance, and a dummy variable representing the trade-preference effect. Relative prices are *not* taken into account. The question is whether the preference effect causes trade across groups to be proportionately less than trade within groups, allowing for income, population, etc. (There is also a dummy variable for adjacent countries.) This approach, like the earlier methods that relied on trade data alone, will reveal an integration effect but will not distinguish trade creation from trade diversion.

Since trade across groups is likely to be reduced by trade diversion, it cannot be regarded as "normal" trade against which trade within groups can be measured. To isolate the trade-diversion effect, an intertemporal comparison is made, and the last year when there was no trade-preference effect (1958) is used as a base year. The results turn out as expected for total trade of the two blocs and for each country separately (except the United Kingdom): there has been substantial trade creation and some trade diversion. While this study is limited to aggregative trade flows

---

19 A similar method is used in McAleese and Martin (1973) to analyze the effects on Irish-manufactured imports of the Anglo-Irish Free Trade Area Agreement.

(with no commodity breakdowns) and is so new that it has not yet been subject to detailed criticism in the literature, it is worth noting as one of the few detailed econometric studies of the effects of European integration on trade flows.

In general, it is easy to point to all the limitations of these studies. They tell us about trade effects, not welfare effects, and obviously need to be supplemented by theoretical and qualitative analysis. Some of them are based on rather far-fetched assumptions. Nevertheless, seen as a whole, the work is impressive. Many possible considerations have been allowed for and explored with great care, and without exception the authors have stressed the limitations of their own work. The conclusion emerges pretty clearly that trade creation has far outweighed trade diversion, and some approaches suggest that there has indeed been a great deal of external trade creation.

4. TRADE LIBERALIZATION

Effective-protection calculations are supposed to give some indication of the consequences of a movement from an existing protection situation to free trade. But it has been a central theme of the effective-protection literature that effective rates can only be ingredients in explaining how the protective structure has shifted resources and how a movement to free trade would move resources the other way. The fact that effective rates themselves are quite complicated to calculate accurately is an indication of the complexity of the *ex ante* analysis of one country's trade liberalization. Let us now look at more ambitious approaches.[20]

There have been three important *ex ante* studies of trade liberalization. It is interesting to compare their methods. The most ambitious – because it covers many countries and considers several trade-liberalization or bloc options – is the work done by Balassa and associates under the auspices of the Council of Foreign Relations (Balassa, 1967a; Balassa *et al.*, 1967). He analyzed both "static" and so-called "dynamic" (mainly economies of scale) effects. He made extensive use of U.S. import-demand elasticities calculated by Ball and Marwah (1962) and, with various modifica-

20 Apart from the three studies discussed here, other work in the general area should be noted. An important *ex ante* study by Salant and Vaccara (1961) was concerned with the potential effects of U.S. trade liberalization on U.S. employment. On the *ex post* front, Kreinin (1961) studied the effects on U.S. import prices and volumes of the tariff reductions negotiated in 1956. Wemelsfelder (1960) analyzed the effects of German tariff reductions in the same period. Krause (1962) made a similar study for an earlier set of tariff changes.

tions, also applied these to countries other than the United States. While there is a substantial qualitative element in this work, the main object is to predict effects of trade liberalization on trade flows. There are also calculations of welfare effects. The ingredients are estimates – very bold estimates – of tariff averages and of elasticities. The general philosophy, it would appear, is to obtain a broad picture, that some figures are better than no figures, and that, in the absence of better data, one must be prepared to use elasticities that were calculated from data for one country in making trade estimates for another.

An outstanding trade-liberalization study – probably one of the most impressive contributions to applied international economics in recent years – is the Wonnacotts' *ex ante* study of the consequences of free trade between the United States and Canada (Wonnacott and Wonnacott, 1967). The approach is very detailed, resting on intensive industry studies. There is much less emphasis on obtaining a neat set of figures at the end, and the book conveys some of the untidiness and complexity of the real world, traits some readers may find unsatisfactory but which I find rather appealing. The general idea is to combine location theory and international economics.

The authors ask first how various industries would be affected by North American free trade, with given money wages and a given exchange rate. This involves a detailed analysis of many elements of comparative advantage. The Wonnacotts place stress (as does Balassa) on economies of scale, arguing that if the U.S. market were opened to Canadian industries, the latter could expand output or specialize more, and so their costs would fall significantly. Such benefits would not be obtained by U.S.-located firms, which are already likely to be operating on a large scale. Thus the competitive position of Canadian industry would improve; on balance, the Wonnacotts expect that Canadian exports would expand more than imports (with a given money-wage level and exchange rate). They stress that the main repercussion would be on the *pattern* of manufacturing in Canada, not on the total size of the manufacturing sector.

The Wonnacotts then analyze the process of adjustment: money-wage levels in Canada would rise or the exchange rate would appreciate, or there would be some combination of the two, and they pursue the consequences. They allow time for adjustment and, indeed, in a qualitative, piecemeal way allow for almost every possible consideration. They end up with very rough estimates (on which they do not place much emphasis) of the cost to Canada of both Canadian and U.S. tariffs.

Finally, Evans has been engaged in the construction of a programming model for Australia to analyze the consequences to Australia of a unilateral movement to free trade over a period of years. He has already published a pilot study (Evans, 1972), but with a group of colleagues he is engaged in a much more thorough and detailed project that should soon be finished. The intended methodology is described concisely, and the difficulties stressed, in Evans (1971). The approach is to use an explicit general-equilibrium linear programming model (with some nonlinear constraints), employing a 110-sector input–output table. Fixed coefficients are assumed. The main aim is to predict output changes resulting from free trade, but estimates of welfare changes, exchange-rate devaluation, and factor-price changes are also supposed to fall out. Perhaps the most interesting feature is that Evans and associates assume a ten-year planning period that will eliminate the problem of short-run resource constraints and allow time for new investment to flow into industries that would expand under free trade.

The whole conception seems very ambitious and is governed by the same philosophy as Balassa's – that some figures are better than no figures and, notably, that "bad data are no excuse for an incomplete model." It is more ambitious, because less piecemeal, than the usual effective-protection approach. The group is trying to do the same sort of thing as the Wonnacotts, and yet their approach is remarkably different, at least in the manner of presentation, in the emphasis on tidiness and formal model building.

5. THEORY OF DOMESTIC DISTORTIONS

The main argument of the theory of "optimal trade intervention in the presence of domestic distortions" is that, when there are divergences between private and social costs or benefits that are *domestic* in nature, first-best policy is never to use trade interventions but rather to tax or subsidize directly at the point of the divergence. The only first-best argument for tariffs is the optimum tariff (terms of trade) argument. Hence, practically all arguments for tariffs or export taxes, at least as first-best arguments, are disposed of.[21]

---

21 This approach was most fully developed and highlighted by Johnson (1965a), but the main elements of the general approach can be found earlier – notably in Meade (1955a) and Bhagwati and Ramaswami (1963). There has been a large literature since, drawing out the theoretical implications of this approach; it is consolidated in Bhagwati (1971), where there is also a fuller bibliography.

This approach is of great significance. Leaving aside the terms-of-trade argument – about which one can have some doubts in many practical cases – it really suggests that, if there is any valid basis for intervention at all, subsidies of various kinds should generally replace tariffs. It breaks the traditional link between advocacy of free trade and advocacy of laissez-faire. One can be an interventionist and yet a free trader, at least when advocating first-best policies. It would suggest that there is little point in calculating effective rates or costs of protection except to describe nonoptimal policies; to get to the optimum, one should just work toward getting rid of all trade interventions.[22]

Theorists have labored to produce rigorous proofs and explore numerous possible cases, and the implications are radical. Yet this new approach seems to have had little or no impact on practical policy and none on empirical work. Does it not rest on any empirical assumptions that could be tested? Can one not study empirically why it has made no impact, why governments and practical economists remain unconvinced? I shall come to these questions in a moment, but first let me note a possible exception to the argument that there has been no impact.

Little, Scitovsky, and Scott (1971), in a book that is likely to be influential, do argue that wage subsidies are preferable to protection if there is a divergence between the actual and the shadow wage, and in general that one should intervene as close as possible to the point of a distortion, rather than use trade restrictions. Their main thrust is that protection of manufacturing industry by tariffs or import quotas fails to encourage exports of manufactures; hence, given the desire to foster manufacturing, subsidies either on production or (preferably) on labor use should replace tariffs and quotas, or, alternatively, tariffs should be supplemented by export subsidies. Thus, industry should be *promoted* rather than protected.

The theoretical literature does not concern itself with this problem. It is concerned rather with the consumption cost created by a tariff compared with a production subsidy, the assumption being that the protected industries are not potential export industries. Little *et al.* do not regard consumption distortion as important but are concerned with the distortion cost owing to (what I would call) *home-market bias* within the manufacturing sector. Both kinds of distortion will be avoided by a first-best subsidy policy.

The formal theoretical literature rests on three assumptions:

22 Indeed, this was one element in the Ramaswami and Srinivasan (1971) criticism of effective rates.

absence of collection (administrative) costs of taxes; concern with Pareto efficiency, implying that income distribution is taken care of through costless transfers; and absence of subsidy-disbursement costs. Let us consider each of these in turn.[23]

a. Once collection costs are allowed for, and especially the likelihood that in many countries, notably less developed countries, these are much less for trade taxes than for other taxes, one can obtain a first-best fiscal argument for trade taxes. Thus the Johnson (1965a) view that the terms-of-trade argument is the only valid argument for tariffs (and export taxes) has to be qualified. But the interesting point is that a domestic distortion that requires encouragement of production of an import-competing industry should still be dealt with by a subsidy, not a tariff. The subsidy may well be financed by tariffs, and this may include some tariff on imports of products also produced by the protected industry (so that the rate of subsidy may not need to be as high as otherwise). Furthermore, the act of financing will impose inevitable distortion and collection costs, so that (as Meade, 1955a, pointed out) it will not be optimal to correct the original distortion completely. But it remains true that first-best policy still requires correction of a domestic divergence by subsidies or taxes directed close to the point of the divergence, even though tariffs and export taxes may figure in a first-best financing package.

b. Removing the income-distribution assumption does not really upset the main conclusion either. It would not be appropriate here to develop this argument rigorously, but a little thought will suggest that any given income-distribution target can be attained with less distortion cost by use of a subsidy financed by first-best income taxes than by use of a tariff. But this argument falls apart once we assume that the financing of subsidies would not be first-best, in terms of income distribution. We then enter again a typical second-best situation.

c. Finally, subsidy-disbursement costs may restore the case for a tariff in preference to a subsidy as a first-best method of protection. A tariff is a device that, in effect, taxes consumers of a particular product and refunds part or all of the revenue to subsidize producers. In the absence of collection and disbursement costs, it is entirely equivalent to a consumption tax and production subsidy at the same rate. It brings about the collection and disbursement in the same act, so that, in effect, no disbursement is required. The point is obvious and is clearly in the minds of prac-

---

23 I have developed the subsequent lines of thought further in Corden (1974).

tical people who reject the "subsidy biased" approach where protection of import-competing industries is desired, but it has been ignored by theorists.

What are the implications of all this for empirical work? Some research might be done into collection costs of various taxes, to compare collection and distortion costs for alternative tax packages. The role of trade taxes in an optimum revenue package of taxes might then be clarified. Subsidy-disbursement costs could also be investigated. In addition, the income-distribution implications of protective systems could be analyzed and compared with the income-distribution implications of alternative ways of achieving the same protection, promotion, or manufacturing employment targets. In all this I have in mind less developed countries, where these things really matter. One might also investigate official and political attitudes. One would no doubt find that tariffs and quotas are preferred to subsidies because the implicit subsidization through trade restrictions is not obvious and the extent of it is not clear, and because it does not pass through the budget, does not require annual review, and hence is more assured.

6. ARGUMENTS FOR PROTECTION

The theory of protection might be regarded as including all arguments for public assistance, direct or indirect, to traded-goods industries, even if the first-best arguments are for nontrade interventions, such as subsidies. In that case, the familiar "arguments for protection" continue to be relevant for the present discussion. But once one appreciates that most arguments for protection rest on *domestic* distortions of some kind, one can see that most relevant research will have to do with *domestic* conditions and will not be specifically *trade* in nature. Trade theory can build on the outcome of research on the domestic economy. Since the relevant research deals essentially with the domestic economy and mainly falls within the sphere of development economics, it will not be discussed at length here.

The two arguments perhaps most widely accepted by economists as providing some basis for assistance to manufacturing industries in less developed countries are the infant-industry and the wage-differentials (employment) arguments (see, e.g., Little *et al.*, 1970). Theoretical work has helped to clarify these arguments in recent years.

The infant-industry argument can be based on either internal or external dynamic economies. In the former case, an argument could rest on imperfection of private information or on imperfection of the capital market. In the latter case, it could rest on the inability of firms to retain the labor they train, on diffusion of knowledge by firms for which they do not receive rewards, or on "social atmosphere" creation (creating a suitable environment for factory work, or, more generally, for entrepreneurial activity). Insofar as labor training really does give rise to market failure, it can be attributed to a form of capital-market imperfection (Becker, 1964), namely, in the market for human capital.

Johnson (1970) has tried to redefine the infant argument rather narrowly so as to separate it from the argument based on imperfection of the labor or capital markets, and to confine it to one resting on externalities generated through diffusion of knowledge. Baldwin (1969) has stressed that protection provides no further incentive for firms to acquire more knowledge or to diffuse it than they would have otherwise, even though the social gains exceed the private gains. All protection can do is to favor those firms that create and diffuse knowledge more than others. A subsidy related directly to creation or diffusion of knowledge would be preferable. Leaving aside Johnson's attempt to narrow the argument, one can conclude that there is certainly scope for more empirical research about capital and information imperfections in less developed countries in order to shed light on the popular versions of the infant-industry argument. This is a large area for potential (and some actual) research.[24]

The wage-differentials argument rests on a divergence between the shadow wage and the actual wage facing the manufacturing sector in less developed countries. This is one of the central issues of development economics, and especially of the new literature on cost–benefit analysis for less developed countries (Little and Mirrlees, 1969). Even if one grants such a divergence, a tariff, or even a production subsidy to manufacturing industry, will clearly not be first-best. Even an employment subsidy may not be first-best if one bears in mind income-distribution effects. Recent theoretical and empirical work on migration and urban unemployment (Todaro, 1969, and Harris and Todaro, 1970) may turn out to have serious implications for, and possibly even destroy, the wage-differentials argument for protection of manufacturing, at least for some countries. The point is that an expansion of manufacturing would actually increase urban unemployment, or would increase employment in a low-productivity urban sector, while

---

24 A discussion of the many problems caused by policy-induced capital-market imperfections in less developed countries is in McKinnon (1973).

subsidization of the agricultural sector may, by contrast, reduce unemployment by reducing the wage differential that in this type of model gives rise to the unemployment.

Finally, one might just note the two main arguments for protection used currently in developed countries. One, a special version of the infant-industry argument, is concerned to demonstrate the case for public assistance to "high technology" industries. There does not seem to be a serious literature in this field, other than that concerned with "science policy." The other is the "senescent industry" argument and rests on adjustment costs and income-distribution effects. It has been attracting a good deal of attention lately. Adjustment assistance is a currently fashionable subject, and in a few years' time it will be possible to survey an extensive analytical and empirical literature.[25] Let us look at the issues involved a little more closely.

There is clearly no point in preserving or protecting a declining industry – such as the textile industry in developed countries – for its own sake. Two distinct arguments for protection of such an industry can be made: First, a fall in demand owing to increased import competition may create unemployment, and this represents a resource loss in Pareto-efficiency terms. If labor were mobile or wages were flexible downward, this problem would not arise. In the short run, protection will raise output above what it would otherwise be. On the other hand, in the long run it eliminates the incentive for labor outflow, and so reduces the efficiency of resource allocation. Second, a fall in demand owing to increased import competition reduces incomes of factors intensive in the industry concerned. It is this adverse sectional income effect which undoubtedly explains the prevalence of this type of protection. The logic is the "conservative social-welfare function" (discussed further at the end of this paper). Protection is designed to modify or even avoid completely the adverse income-distribution effect.

The case for adjustment assistance is that it may attain the desired effect on sectional incomes without the adverse effect on resource allocation. Protection embalms the existing pattern of production, while adjustment assistance encourages changes. But if income distribution were the only consideration – private deci-

25 On the U.S. situation, a useful reference is Murray and Egmond (1970); see also Hughes (1973) for discussion of adjustment issues affecting many countries, and various papers in Vol. I of the Compendium of Papers in the Williams Commission Report (1971).

sion makers having correct expectations and private and social adjustment costs coinciding – optimal policy would be to compensate with lump-sum transfers. Labor and capital in the declining industries would then make whatever adjustments they wished, and this would be socially optimal. While protection of existing production would distort resource allocation by *dis*couraging adjustment, adjustment assistance that takes the form of subsidizing outward factor movement and labor training would distort allocation by inducing *over*adjustment. The logic of adjustment assistance hinges both on income-distribution considerations and on a natural private tendency to underadjust owing to various distortions and, perhaps, lack of information.

It is arguable that a case for adjustment assistance cannot be concerned only with adjustment to import competition. In principle, assistance for adjustment to any changes, especially sudden or unexpected ones, would seem to be justified once the basic arguments are granted. The only possible argument for limiting assistance to industries suffering from import competition is this: Import competition is likely to provoke protection with tariffs or quotas, leading to prolonged resource-allocation losses, unless adjustment assistance is provided. On the other hand, changes that do not originate abroad do not normally provoke such costly policy responses. The case for adjustment assistance is then essentially that it avoids protection, or makes it politically possible to reduce protection. Thus, one reason the topic of adjustment assistance is currently fashionable is that it is hoped that the availability of assistance will make it easier to achieve reduction in trade restrictions in forthcoming international negotiations.

7. "DYNAMIC" AND SIMILAR EFFECTS OF TRADE AND PROTECTION

As one reads the empirical literature on trade liberalization and the effects of the EEC, and even more the semipopular economic discussions about Britain joining the EEC, as well as some writing on the Canadian tariff, one comes across an interesting set of theories, some of them implicit. Practical-minded economists have improvised models because orthodox theory has proved inadequate. Because they are writing for wider audiences or their main interest is empirical, they rarely spell out these models fully. Nevertheless, there are clear signposts here for theorists to follow.

The models they would produce might then lead to specification of further necessary empirical work.[26]

The main theme is the importance of economies of scale. The various Canadian writers, notably Eastman and Stykolt (1967) and English (1964), stress that freeing trade would increase the scale of output and so lower costs of Canadian industries, and this would be the main source of gains from trade. Their argument that tariffs lead to undue fragmentation of production and to production at high cost – much empirical evidence is given – can logically have two bases, and both strands of the argument seem to be used: too many firms are producing a basically similar product behind a tariff wall to satisfy the domestic Canadian market (presumably an oligopolistic phenomenon); and too many varieties of product are produced in Canada because the combination of Canadian and U.S. tariffs discourages specialization. The second strand of the argument can, of course, be explained readily in terms of standard trade theory (and originated with Adam Smith), though in recent times theorists have tended to neglect it.

Economies of scale also play an important role in Balassa's work. When he refers to "static" effects of trade liberalization, he appears to refer only to consumption or exchange effects, with production in each firm or industry given. Is this what other writers mean? "Dynamic" effects apparently refer to effects that increase specialization of production and so lower costs.[27]

Another theme in this literature is the effect of trade liberalization on competitiveness and, by implication at least, on profits and on X-efficiency. This also offers scope for further theoretical and empirical work. At the theoretical level, I have attempted to make a start on the relationship between X-efficiency and trade in Corden (1970), using the concept of "managerial leisure." Empirical work on corporate behavior may shed light on these matters.

Do so-called dynamic effects – namely, effects on the degree of competition and on X-efficiency – bulk large in the true cost of protection? These effects would then resolve the puzzle that the static figures always come out small in relation to GNP, even

---

26 The main professional references are English (1964), Eastman and Stykolt (1967), and Wonnacott and Wonnacott (1967), all in Canada. The Wonnacotts, in Chaps. 13 and 15, are actually much more explicit in their models than others. Outside Canada, there are Scitovsky (1958) and Balassa (various writings, but particularly 1967a). Chapter 5 of the latter book, concerned especially with economies of scale, raises a whole range of interesting issues.

27 In a letter commenting on my remarks here, Balassa appears to disagree with this interpretation. He states that he defines static effects to include both production and consumption effects, while dynamic effects involve shifts in the supply curve.

though many people instinctively believe that trade and protection must be much more important than the triangles suggest. The central point is that tariffs and trade may set the price structure for the whole economy, and tariff reduction may thus be a form of price control for import-competing industries. A tariff reduction can have very large effects on the distribution of domestic income even when the effects on output and demand are small; as competitiveness is increased, there may be redistribution both from factors intensive in importables to factors intensive in exportables and from profits to wages. In turn, a monetary change in income of a factor may become transmuted into an X-efficiency change: instead of losing money profits, a firm may raise X-efficiency, presumably losing something, perhaps "managerial leisure" or achievement of other corporate objectives. It is also possible that the X-efficiency of gainers may fall. Furthermore, this approach suggests that a trade-induced (or otherwise-induced) rise in X-efficiency may not be a pure welfare gain, if indeed it is a welfare gain at all.

Finally, is the term "dynamic," which is so widely used for this mass of effects – competitiveness, X-efficiency, economies of scale – really suitable? Many of these effects can be analyzed in terms of static models, and, in any case, it is useful to distinguish the various effects. They will certainly have genuinely dynamic implications, since there will be time lags in adjustment and capital accumulation may be affected in various ways, but this also applies to what are usually called "static" effects, namely, effects that are highlighted by orthodox static trade theory.

8. EXPLAINING ACTUAL POLICIES

Why do countries *actually* protect their industries? Why are some countries protectionist at some times and not others? Which sorts of arguments have carried most weight, and why does an argument carry weight in one country and not another? If – as is suggested by the theory of domestic distortions – tariffs are hardly ever first-best, why do countries nevertheless use them? Furthermore, if the effects of tariffs, as represented by the cost of protection, are often so small, why is it so difficult to get rid of tariffs? Economists' sentiments since the time of Adam Smith have been overwhelmingly against tariffs, and yet our arguments have "fallen on stony ground" (Graham, 1934). Of course, in the postwar period there have been substantial tariff reductions by developed countries, especially as a result of the Kennedy round, and trade liberalization in Europe since the early 1950s has been remarkable. Nevertheless, an important question remains: What is the logic of actual policies at different times? This is an interesting potential area of research. It may guide us to new, valid arguments or perhaps to better ways of putting old arguments. It may simply help us to understand history. Yet, as far as I know, not much work has been done along these lines.

One notable exception is Kindleberger (1951), who compared the responses of different European countries to the fall in grain prices in the late nineteenth century. Motives, attitudes, and pressures affecting recent U.S. trade policies have been analyzed with a political-science approach by Bauer, Pool, and Dexter (1972). Both Macario (1964) and Hirschman (1968) bring out some pattern and motives in the postwar protectionism of Latin America. Detailed country studies, for example on Canada, Australia, and India, are available (Young, 1957; Corden, 1963; Desai, 1970). But one would hope to discover some consistencies over time and many countries, and hence some valid generalizations.

Clearly, hypotheses are needed. One hypothesis is that some less developed countries want industrialization for its own sake: Industrial production within the frontiers of the country is a public good for that country (Johnson, 1965c). This attributes a considerable degree of irrationality to the decision makers of the countries concerned. It may be a convenient approach to describe industrial output as a proximate target and analyze the consequences and least-cost ways of seeking to attain it. But the economic decision makers probably believe – perhaps erroneously – that there will be economic gains from industrialization under protection, perhaps on the basis of some kind of infant-industry argument. It is at least a hypothesis worth investigating.

Another popular argument is that protection reflects the triumph of producer over consumer interests, the triumph of the tightly organized small group over the diffused large group. This means that one must analyze protection policy in terms of its income-distribution effects and compare the various interests involved. A weakness of this approach is that, if one takes general-equilibrium effects of tariffs into account, protection benefits some producers at the expense of others, especially exporters, and damages some consumers but favors others, especially consumers of exportables. Thus the producer-consumer dichotomy is essentially a partial-equilibrium one. Of course, affected interests may not always readily see general-equilibrium implications.

Nevertheless, one does need to go deeper. It is not sufficient to make the obvious point that a tariff, quota, or subsidy benefits a particular producer interest group and is possibly the reward for successful political activity by that group. One needs to know why tariffs are imposed on some goods and not others or are higher on some than others, and thus why some producers are more successful than others in obtaining an income-distribution shift in their favor. Why are the textile interests so energetic and successful in this respect compared with, say, the automobile interests?

In the United States, it appears that effective protection tends to be higher for activities that pay wages at rates below the average and are thus probably unskilled-labor intensive (Ball, 1967), and in particular that the tariff system discriminates against natural-resource-intensive products (Travis, 1964). It seems that U.S. tariffs protect the "scarce" factor. But this does not tell us much about motives. Indeed, in a two-good, two-factor model a tariff could do nothing else (defining the "scarce" factor as the factor intensive in the importable). In a multi-factor, multi-commodity world this is not so: there is scope for a tariff system to discriminate between different goods and hence different factors of production.

It has been argued that protection in the United States is generally either prohibitive or zero, and thus that protected industries get all the protection they need to obtain the whole domestic market (Vaccara, 1960, and Travis, 1964). One might think in terms of differentiated products subject to economies of scale; if domestic production exists, the tariff will normally be high enough to give the domestic producers the whole domestic market. But presumably there is some upper limit to the amount of protection that is provided, and this will help to determine whether an industry survives. If there is no domestic production, there will normally be no tariff. With such a policy, activities intensive in the scarcest factor are likely to obtain (because they "need") the highest protection.

I would put forth another hypothesis: The aim of many protective policies throughout history has been maintenance of sectional incomes or, literally, *income protection* (see Corden, 1974). Thus the purpose is redistribution of incomes toward those sections of the population that would otherwise suffer absolute falls in real income as a result of market forces such as falls in import prices. A particular type of social-welfare function – one that places much more weight on decreases in incomes than on increases – can rationalize such policies. I would call this a "conservative social-welfare function." It tells us that society – whether public opinion or particular individuals or groups exercising power – has some sense of justice that makes it much more ready to help a producer group that would otherwise suffer a loss in income than one that would obtain a net rise. Pressure-group politics may still be needed to obtain a tariff or subsidy, but this concept helps to explain why some pressures are more successful than others, and indeed why some industries but not others apply pressure for assistance.

There is clearly scope for analyzing in these terms the recent revival of American protectionism (see Bergsten, 1971). More generally, the effects of protection on the distribution of domestic income may be crucial to understanding motivations for actual policies, especially in developed countries. Casual empiricism suggests much historical evidence to support this possibility. More work might be done in analyzing income-distribution effects, in relating these to tariff policies, and perhaps in considering least-cost ways of achieving given income-distribution objectives, for example through the use of adjustment assistance and escape-clause arrangements in preference to permanent tariff or nontariff barriers.

REFERENCES

Aitken, Norman D., "The Effect of the EEC and EFTA on European Trade: A Temporal Cross-Section Analysis," *American Economic Review,* 63 (December 1973), pp. 881–892.

Balassa, Bela, "Tariff Protection in Industrial Countries: An Evaluation," *Journal of Political Economy,* 73 (December 1965), pp. 573–594.
　Trade Liberalization among Industrial Countries, New York, McGraw-Hill, 1967a.
　"Trade Creation and Trade Diversion in the European Common Market," *Economic Journal,* 77 (March 1967b), pp. 1–21.
Balassa, Bela, *et al., Studies in Trade Liberalization,* Baltimore, The Johns Hopkins Press, 1967.
　"The Effective Rates of Protection and the Question of Labor Protection in the United States: A Comment," *Journal of Political Economy,* 78 (September/October 1970), pp. 1150-1162.
　The Structure of Protection in Developing Countries, Baltimore, The Johns Hopkins Press, 1971.
Baldwin, R. E., "The Case against Infant-Industry Tariff Protection," *Journal of Political Economy,* 77 (May/June 1969), pp. 295–305.
　Nontariff Distortions of International Trade, Washington, The Brookings Institution, 1970.

Baldwin, R. E., and J. H. Mutti, "Policy Problems in the Adjustment Process," in Hughes (1973).

Ball, D. S., "United States Effective Tariffs and Labor's Share," *Journal of Political Economy*, 75 (April 1967), pp. 183–187.

Ball, R. J., and K. Marwah, "The U.S. Demand for Imports 1948-1958," *Review of Economics and Statistics*, 44 (November 1962), pp. 395–401.

Barker, T. S., and S. S. Han, "Effective Rates of Protection for United Kingdom Production," *Economic Journal*, 81 (June 1971), pp. 282–293.

Basevi, Giorgio, "The United States Tariff Structure: Estimates of Effective Rates ·of Protection of United States Industries and Industrial Labor," *Review of Economics and Statistics*, 48 (May 1966), pp. 147–160.

"The Restrictive Effect of the U.S. Tariff and Its Welfare Value," *American Economic Review*, 58 (September 1968), pp. 840–852.

"Aggregation Problems in the Measurement of Effective Protection," in Grubel and Johnson (1971).

Bauer, R. A., I. S. Pool, and L. A. Dexter, *American Business and Public Policy: The Politics of Foreign Trade*, Chicago, Aldine-Atherton, 1972.

Becker, Gary, *Human Capital*, New York, Columbia University Press, 1964.

Bergsman, Joel, *Brazil: Industrialization and Trade Policies*, London, Oxford University Press, 1970.

Bergsten, C. Fred, "Crisis in U.S. Trade Policy," *Foreign Affairs*, 49 (July 1971), pp. 619–635.

"On the Equivalence of Import Quotas and Voluntary Export Restraints," in C. Fred Bergsten, ed., *Toward a New World Trade Policy: The Maidenhead Papers*, Washington, The Brookings Institution, forthcoming.

Bhagwati, Jagdish, "The Generalized Theory of Distortions and Welfare," in Bhagwati *et al.*, eds., *Trade, Balance of Payments and Growth*, Amsterdam, North-Holland, 1971.

Bhagwati, Jagdish, and Padma Desai, *India: Planning for Industrialization*, London, Oxford University Press, 1970.

Bhagwati, Jagdish, and V. K. Ramaswami, "Domestic Distortions, Tariffs and the Theory of Optimum Subsidy," *Journal of Political Economy*, 71 (February 1963), pp. 44–50.

Bhagwati, Jagdish, and T. N. Srinivasan, "The General Equilibrium Theory of Effective Protection and Resource Allocation," *Journal of International Economics*, 3 (August 1973), pp. 259–281.

Brigden, J. B., *et al.*, *The Australian Tariff: An Economic Enquiry*, Melbourne, Melbourne University Press, 1929.

Clavaux, F. J., "The Import Elasticity as a Yardstick for Measuring Trade Creation," *Economia Internazionale*, 22 (November 1969), pp. 606–612.

Cohen, B. I., "The Use of Effective Tariffs," *Journal of Political Economy*, 79 (January/February 1971), pp. 128–141.

Corden, W. M., "The Calculation of the Cost of Protection," *Economic Record*, 33 (April 1957), pp. 29–51.

"The Tariff," in A. Hunter, ed., *The Economics of Australian Industry*, Melbourne, Melbourne University Press, 1963.

"The Structure of a Tariff System and the Effective Protective Rate," *Journal of Political Economy*, 74 (June 1966a), pp. 221–237.

"The Effective Protective Rate, the Uniform Tariff Equivalent and the Average Tariff," *Economic Record*, 42 (June 1966b), pp. 200–216.

"The Efficiency Effects of Trade and Protection," in I. A. McDougall and R. H. Snape, *Studies in International Economics,* Amsterdam, North-Holland, 1970.
The Theory of Protection, Oxford, Clarendon Press, 1971.
Trade Policy and Economic Welfare, Oxford, Clarendon Press, 1974.

Dardis, Rachel, "Intermediate Goods and the Gains from Trade," *Review of Economics and Statistics,* 19 (November 1967), pp. 502–509.
Desai, Padma, *Tariff Protection and Industrialization,* Delhi, Hindustan Publishing Corporation, 1970.

Eastman, H. C., and S. Stykolt, *The Tariff and Competition in Canada,* Toronto, University of Toronto Press, 1967.
English, H. E., *Industrial Structure in Canada's International Competitive Position,* Montreal, Private Planning Association of Canada, 1964.
European Free Trade Association Secretariat, *The Effects of EFTA on the Economies of Member States,* Geneva, 1969.
The Trade Effects of EFTA and the EEC 1959-1967, Geneva, 1972.
Evans, H. D., "The Empirical Specification of a General Equilibrium Model of Protection in Australia," in Grubel and Johnson (1971).
A General Equilibrium Analysis of Protection, Amsterdam, North-Holland, 1972.

Floyd, J. E., "The Overvaluation of the Dollar: A Note on the International Price Mechanism," *American Economic Review,* 55 (March 1965), pp. 95–107.

Gamir, Luis, "The Calculation of Effective Rates of Protection in Spain," in Grubel and Johnson (1971).
Graham, Frank D., *Protective Tariffs,* New York, Harper, 1934.
Grubel, H. G., and H. G. Johnson, "Nominal Tariffs, Indirect Taxes and Effective Rates of Protection: The Common Market Countries 1959," *Economic Journal,* 77 (December 1967), pp. 761–776.
Grubel, H. G., and H. G. Johnson, eds., *Effective Tariff Protection,* Geneva, GATT, 1971.
Grubel, H. G., and P. J. Lloyd, "Factor Substitution and Effective Tariff Rates," *Review of Economic Studies,* 38 (January 1971), pp. 95–103.
Guisinger, S., and D. Schydlowsky, "The Empirical Relationship between Nominal and Effective Rates of Protection," in Grubel and Johnson (1971).

Harberger, A. C., "Using the Resources at Hand More Effectively," *American Economic Review, Proceedings,* 49 (May 1959), pp. 134–146.
Harris, J. R., and M. P. Todaro, "Migration, Unemployment and Development: A Two-Sector Analysis," *American Economic Review,* 60 (March 1970), pp. 126–142.
Hirschman, Albert O., "The Political Economy of Import-Substituting Industrialization in Latin America," *Quarterly Journal of Economics,* 82 (February 1968), pp. 2–32.
Hsing, M-H., J. Power, and G. P. Sicat, *Taiwan and the Philippines: Industrialization and Trade Policies,* London, Oxford University Press, 1970.
Hughes, Helen, *Prospects for Partnership: Industrialization and Trade Policies in the 1970s,* Washington, International Bank for Reconstruction and Development, 1973.
Humphrey, D. B., "Factor and Intermediate Input Substitution in Groups of

American Manufacturing Sectors: 1947–58" (January 1973), mimeographed.

Humphrey, D. B., and B. Wolkowitz, "Substitution of Capital, Labor and Intermediates in U.S. Manufacturing: An Aggregate Study" (December 1972), mimeographed.

Johnson, Harry G., "The Gains from Freer Trade with Europe: An Estimate," *Manchester School of Economics and Social Studies*, 26 (September 1958), pp. 247–255.

"The Cost of Protection and the Scientific Tariff," *Journal of Political Economy*, 68 (August 1960), pp. 327–345.

"Optimal Trade Intervention in the Presence of Domestic Distortions," in R. Baldwin *et al.*, *Trade, Growth and the Balance of Payments*, Chicago, Rand McNally, 1965a.

"The Theory of Tariff Structure, with Special Reference to World Trade and Development," in H. G. Johnson and P. Kenen, *Trade and Development*, Geneva, Librairie Droz, 1965b.

"An Economic Theory of Protectionism, Tariff Bargaining, and the Formation of Customs Unions," *Journal of Political Economy*, 72 (June 1965c), pp. 256–283.

"A New View of the Infant-Industry Argument," in I. A. McDougall and R. H. Snape, eds., *Studies in International Economics*, Amsterdam, North-Holland, 1970.

Jones, R. W., "Effective Protection and Substitution," *Journal of International Economics*, 1 (January 1971), pp. 59–81.

Kindleberger, C. P., "Group Behavior and International Trade," *Journal of Political Economy*, 59 (February 1951), pp. 30–47.

King, Timothy, *Mexico: Industrialization and Trade Policies since 1940*, London, Oxford University Press, 1970.

Krause, L. B., "United States Imports, 1947–1958," *Econometrica*, 30 (April 1962), pp. 221–238.

"European Economic Integration and the United States," *American Economic Review, Proceedings*, 53 (May 1963), pp. 185–196.

Krauss, Melvyn B., "Recent Developments in Customs Union Theory: An Interpretive Survey," *Journal of Economic Literature*, 10 (June 1972), pp. 413–436.

Kreinin, M. E., "Effect of Tariff Changes on the Prices and Volume of Imports," *American Economic Review*, 51 (June 1961), pp. 310–324.

"Trade Creation and Diversion by the EEC and EFTA," *Economia Internazionale*, 22 (May 1969), pp. 273–280.

"Effects of the EEC on Imports of Manufactures," *Economic Journal*, 82 (September 1972), pp. 897–920.

Krueger, Anne O., "Some Economic Costs of Exchange Control: The Turkish Case," *Journal of Political Economy*, 74 (October 1966), pp. 466–480.

Lamfalussy, A., "Intra-European Trade and the Competitive Position of the E.E.C.," *Manchester Statistical Society Transactions* (March 1963).

Leith, J. C., "Substitution and Supply Elasticities in Calculating the Effective Protective Rate," *Quarterly Journal of Economics*, 82 (November 1968), pp. 588–601.

Lewis, S. R., *Pakistan: Industrialization and Trade Policies*, London, Oxford University Press, 1970.

Linnemann, H. J., *An Econometric Study of International Trade Flows*, Amsterdam, North-Holland, 1966.

Lipsey, R. G., "The Theory of Customs Unions: A General Survey," *Economic Journal*, 70 (September 1960), pp. 498–513.

Little, I. M. D., and J. A. Mirrlees, *Manual of Industrial Project Analysis in Developing Countries*, Paris, OECD, 1969.

Little, Ian, Tibor Scitovsky, and Maurice Scott, *Industry and Trade in Some Developing Countries*, London, Oxford University Press, 1970.

McAleese, Dermot, *Effective Tariffs and the Structure of Industrial Protection in Ireland*, Dublin, Economic and Social Research Institute, June 1971.

McAleese, Dermot, and John Martin, *Irish Manufactured Imports from the UK in the Sixties: The Effects of AIFTA*, Dublin, Economic and Social Research Institute, May 1973.

Macario, S., "Protectionism and Industrialization in Latin America," *Economic Bulletin for Latin America*, 9 (March 1964), pp. 61–101.

McKinnon, R. I., *Money and Capital in Economic Development*, Washington, The Brookings Institution, 1973.

Magee, S. P., "The Welfare Effects of Restrictions on U.S. Trade," *Brookings Papers on Economic Activity*, 3 (1972), pp. 645–707.

Meade, J. E., *Trade and Welfare*, London, Oxford University Press, 1955a.

The Theory of Customs Unions, Amsterdam, North-Holland, 1955b.

Munk, B., "The Welfare Costs of Content Protection: The Automotive Industry in Latin America," *Journal of Political Economy*, 77 (November 1969), pp. 85–98.

Murray, T. W., and M. R. Egmond, "Full Employment, Trade Expansion, and Adjustment Assistance," *Southern Economic Journal*, 36 (April 1970), pp. 404–424.

Oulton, Nicholas, *Tariffs, Taxes and Trade in the U.K.: The Effective Protection Approach*, London, Her Majesty's Stationery Office, 1973.

Ramaswami, V. K., and T. N. Srinivasan, "Tariff Structure and Resource Allocation in the Presence of Factor Substitution," in J. Bhagwati *et al.*, eds., *Trade, Balance of Payments and Growth*, Amsterdam, North-Holland, 1971.

Robson, P., *International Economic Integration*, Harmondsworth, Penguin Books, 1971.

Salant, Walter S., and Beatrice Vaccara, *Import Liberalization and Employment*, Washington, The Brookings Institution, 1961.

Scitovsky, Tibor, *Economic Theory and Western European Integration*, Stanford, Stanford University Press, 1958.

Sellekaerts, W., "How Meaningful Are Empirical Studies on Trade Creation and Diversion?" *Weltwirtschaftliches Archiv*, 109 (Heft 4, 1973), pp. 519–553.

Snape, R. H., "Sugar: Costs of Protection and Taxation," *Economica*, 36 (February 1969), pp. 29–41.

Stern, R. M., "The U.S. Tariff and the Efficiency of the U.S. Economy," *American Economic Review, Proceedings*, 54 (May 1964), pp. 459–470.

Tan, A. H. H., "Differential Tariffs, Negative Value-Added and the Theory of Effective Protection," *American Economic Review*, 60 (March 1970), pp. 107–116.

Todaro, M. P., "A Model of Labor Migration and Urban Unemployment in Less Developed Countries," *American Economic Review*, 59 (March 1969), pp. 138–148.

Travis, W. P., *The Theory of Trade and Protection*, Cambridge, Mass., Harvard University Press, 1964.

"The Effective Rate of Protection and the Question of Labor Protection in the United States," *Journal of Political Economy*, 76 (May/June 1968), pp. 433–461.

Truman, E. M., "The European Economic Community: Trade Creation and Trade Diversion," *Yale Economic Essays*, 9 (Spring 1969), pp. 201–257.

"The Production and Trade of Manufactured Products in the EEC and EFTA: A Comparison," *European Economic Review*, 3 (November 1972), pp. 271–290.

Tumlir, Jan, and L. Till, "Tariff Averaging in International Comparisons," in Grubel and Johnson (1971).

Vaccara, Beatrice N., *Employment and Output in Protected Manufacturing Industries*, Washington, The Brookings Institution, 1960.

Verdoorn, P. J., "A Customs Union for Western Europe: Advantages and Feasibility," *World Politics*, 6 (July 1954), pp. 482–500.

Vernon, J., et al., *Report of the Committee of Economic Enquiry*, Canberra, Commonwealth of Australia, 1965.

Viner, Jacob, *The Customs Union Issue*, New York, Carnegie Endowment for International Peace, 1950.

Walker, F. V., "The Restrictive Effect of the U.S. Tariff: Comment," *American Economic Review*, 59 (December 1969), pp. 963–966.

Walter, Ingo, "Non-Tariff Protection among Industrial Countries: Some Preliminary Evidence," *Economia Internazionale*, 25 (May 1972), pp. 333–353.

Wemelsfelder, J., "The Short-Term Effect of the Lowering of Import Duties in Germany," *Economic Journal*, 70 (March 1960), pp. 94–104.

Williams Commission, *United States International Economic Policy in an Interdependent World*, Report to the President submitted by the Commission on International Trade and Investment Policy, Washington, 1971.

Williamson, John, and A. Bottrill, "The Impact of Customs Unions on Trade in Manufactures," *Oxford Economic Papers*, 23 (November 1971), pp. 323–351.

Wonnacott, R. J., and P. Wonnacott, *Free Trade between the United States and Canada: The Potential Economic Effects*, Cambridge, Mass., Harvard University Press, 1967.

Young, John H., *Canadian Commercial Policy*, Ottawa, Royal Commission on Canada's Economic Prospects, 1957.

TRADE POLICIES AND ECONOMIC DEVELOPMENT*

Carlos F. Diaz-Alejandro

The stagnation of international trade between the world wars gave rise, with a lag, to a reconsideration of pre-1914 classical orthodoxy regarding the role of trade policies on economic development. Even as Nurkse, Prebisch, and Myrdal wrote, however, the post–World War II trade boom was gathering momentum. By the 1960s, it was clear that such a boom was not a passing cyclical phenomenon, and, not surprisingly, a substantial neoclassical revival followed in the applied trade and development literature, although pure trade theory was becoming increasingly agnostic regarding free trade. This paper will survey primarily what has been written since 1960 on the impact of trade policies of less developed countries on their growth and development. It will, on the whole, leave aside the literature on trade policies of developed countries.

What is to be included among "trade policies"? Pride of place will be given to those influencing significantly the level and composition of exports of goods and services, although those associated with inducing import substitution beyond the levels dictated by market forces will also be discussed. Most less developed countries can influence their long-run import level by encouraging or discouraging exports, while they are unlikely to expand exports just by increasing their imports, a simple point ignored by some import-liberalization attempts of the 1960s. In other words, although one can imagine increases in imports triggering mechanisms that will lead to higher exports, the lags and frictions of that process are likely to be substantially greater than those involved between an export rise and the ensuing import expansion. Exchange-rate policy, taxes and subsidies on merchandise trade, and special credit programs are obvious examples of trade policies influencing exports. There are, however, other policies that will influence exports, and not just in the trivial sense that everything depends on everything else in general equilibrium. It is an old point, recently re-emphasized and quantified by Birn-

* Friends and colleagues at the Yale Economic Growth Center have been a great help in the preparation of this paper. Richard Brecher, Benjamin I. Cohen, Richard Cooper, Ernestine Jones, Christina Lanfer, Vahid Nowshirvani, and Gustav Ranis deserve special thanks, but no blame if their efforts are not well reflected by this survey. Helpful and extensive comments from Jagdish Bhagwati and I.M.D. Little are also gratefully acknowledged.

93

berg and Resnick (1971), that infrastructure financed by government can be more or less trade-biased. Moreover, policies toward multinational corporations have become for many countries a key element of their export-promotion plans.

Indeed, the classroom distinction between the current and capital accounts (and the corresponding separation between policies toward trade and toward capital flows) is becoming increasingly irrelevant in world markets dominated by multinational corporations, even more so than it was in 1929, when John H. Williams chided the classical theory of international trade for neglecting, in spite of Adam Smith's insights, the relation between international trade and capital migration. However, space allows us only superficial incursions into these broader interactions between the current and capital accounts, and between traditional trade and other development policies. Subjects like LDC management of external debt and international reserves will be totally ignored.

Even if the foreign exchange available for imports of goods and services is regarded as given, the mechanisms used to allocate such an amount among competing uses still have important repercussions on the development of a country. Some of the most interesting recent research in the field of trade and development has dealt precisely with the details and consequences of different policies for repressing and controlling imports of goods *and* services.

Discussions of import-repressing policies, like tariffs and quotas, tend to assign them an autonomous or trigger role, from which certain resource-allocation decisions are supposed to follow. Yet, in most contemporary developing countries, those policies are only one weapon in the planning arsenal of the state, and frequently only an accommodating instrument that follows decisions taken elsewhere. For example, a public investment bank may decide, as part of an industrialization program, to set up a petrochemical plant with or without private-sector help; once that decision is approved, tariffs or quotas will be adjusted and changed as frequently as necessary to enable the new plant to sell all its output domestically. Tax rebates, low-interest loans, etc., will also help the new plant. Thus, research on LDC trade policies should ideally be carried out in the context of their domestic development policies (Bhagwati and Krueger, 1973).

Trade-policy instruments are far easier to describe than targets of economic development. By now everyone knows that for most less developed countries growth of per capita GNP is only one of several development targets. A more equal income distribution

among families and regions and a greater degree of national autonomy are others; the several targets, moreover, sometimes
conflict with one another, even when they do not include lofty
desires to create a "New Man." Glib references to different targets
are frequently used to justify all kinds of trade policies that are
most unlikely to serve the efficient pursuit of any goal. Nevertheless, real trade-offs do remain.

Less developed countries differ not only in the weight they, or
their ruling groups, give to various development targets, but also,
of course, in size, resource endowment, per capita income, etc.
This reminder of the limitations of purely qualitative arguments
is sometimes lost in the fury of the ancient debate between protectionists and free traders. And these typological considerations can
be more important for trade policies than differences in development targets. Many aspects of the trade experience of Taiwan, for
example, may be more relevant to Cuba than those of the
U.S.S.R., while India is unlikely to find much inspiration in the
Hong Kong model.

The traditional central question in the field of trade and development, as put by Meier (1968), is: Are the gains from trade in
conflict with the gains from growth? Or, more simply, is international trade good or bad for growth and development? Kindleberger's (1962, p. 211) answer indicates that the question
should be rephrased. The relevant queries seem to be the following:

a. Under what conditions will free trade (or more trade)
   increase per capita growth?
b. Under what conditions will free trade (or more trade) bring
   less developed countries closer to their other development
   targets?
c. Can the less developed countries, by their own actions, influence how much they trade?
d. Can these qualitative effects be quantified even roughly, and
   what does such quantification tell us about the importance of
   trade policies (for good and evil) in achieving the different
   development targets?

The rest of the paper will be organized as follows: In section 1,
recent theoretical work will be reviewed, to see what answers it
suggests to the above questions and what guidance it gives to
empirical studies. In sections 2 and 3, research on economic history and on long-term and cross-section patterns will be surveyed. It

will be seen that theoretical studies cast an uncertain light primarily on the first question, while providing some tools that can be used, although they seldom are, to analyze the second. Research on pre–World War II economic history and cross-section studies yield scattered and contradictory hints of answers to the first three questions. In section 4, the paper will examine empirical work bearing on whether and by how much the less developed countries can affect the level and composition of their exports, focusing on the rout of export pessimism during the 1960s. Recent work on some perennial issues surrounding the export sector will be discussed in section 5. Attention will turn in section 6 to work discussing mechanisms for suppressing import demand. In section 7, the paper discusses attempts at quantification that have been or need to be made on the several links between trade and development, in the world as it exists circa 1973. Some cranky conclusions, in the spirit of self-criticism, close the paper.

1. GUIDANCE FROM THEORETICAL DEVELOPMENTS

In the trade and development literature there has existed for a long time, going back at least to John Stuart Mill, a striking difference between the rigor of formal proofs on the static advantages of free trade, typically involving careful assumptions and caveats, and the impetuous enthusiasm with which most of the professional mainstream advocates free or freer trade policies, on both static and dynamic grounds, for all times and places. Positive theories of trade and of balance-of-payments adjustment mechanisms have come and gone, but whether one subscribes to "vent for surplus," Ricardian, Heckscher–Ohlin, or product-cycle theories of trade or to monetarist, absorption, or elasticities approaches to balance-of-payments adjustment, the typical normative advice on trade policy comes out pretty much the same. The literature leaps with remarkable ease from the sensible proposition that some trade can potentially make everyone better off, as compared with no trade, to the conviction that more trade is always likely to do just that.

The mainstream has tended to minimize what Mill called "the temporary inconvenience of the change" toward freer trade. It is ironic that one of the few recent efforts to conceptualize and quantify the burden of adjusting to freer trade policies has been done for one of the richest countries in the world, the United States of America (Baldwin and Mutti, 1972).

Even if adjustment costs are left aside, the tension between guarded theoretical results and the ultra-pro-trade-biased obiter dicta of the professional mainstream has sharply increased during the 1950s and 1960s, as a result of general theoretical developments and what may be called the Indian planner's revenge. The Pandora's box of distortions and the second-best was opened by professionally respectable hands (Haberler, 1950; Little, 1950; Lipsey and Lancaster, 1956-57). Furthermore, modern analytical tools were falling into the hands of economists whose backgrounds made them skeptical of traditional free-trade verities and who rightfully resented the glib conventional wisdom of bureaucrats in aid-granting organizations. These new tools and biases, combined with intellectual curiosity, generated consistent theoretical models embodying more or less realistic distortions, in which free trade need not always be the best policy available.

It is true that in these static models (for example, Johnson, 1965a; Bhagwati, 1971) taxes or subsidies on international trade are not the optimal policies, except in the old-fashioned case of monopoly power in international markets, if there are other policy instruments at hand that can tackle distortions directly. But it is easy to see that different assumptions regarding the availability, effectiveness, and real costs of different policy instruments can yield a disconcerting variety of heterodox conclusions. By now any bright graduate student, by choosing his assumptions regarding distortions and policy instruments carefully, can produce a consistent model yielding just about any policy recommendation he favored at the start. To reach his conclusion, moreover, he need not introduce development targets additional to static efficiency. The conclusion, of course, applies a fortiori when other targets are brought in.

Algebra and consistent models can prove nothing about the real world, but perhaps the major contribution of these models, and of those sure to follow them, is to force a discussion of the realism of assumptions that are crucial to theoretical demonstrations. Given our professional discipline and prejudices, this result could not have been accomplished only by outside critics, who did not frame their doubts and skepticism in accepted mainstream theoretical language.

Postwar theoretical developments (Meade, 1955; Johnson, 1960) have also provided neoclassical frameworks for quantifying costs and benefits of trade policies for small or large countries. Typically, the strict application of this methodology to actual situations yields the result that contemplated changes in trade policy will raise or lower the nation's GNP by a few percentage points at most (see, for example, Harberger, 1959). Introducing effective rates of protection into these calculations, making alternative assumptions as to whether protected industries will disappear under free trade (Balassa, 1966), computing the present discounted value of all future benefits of liberalization (Magee, 1972), etc., can raise the percentages somewhat, but not by much. The standard model can be made to generate hypothetical situations in which the costs of protection and self-sufficiency loom large, partly by assuming low elasticities of substitution in consumption and production (Johnson, 1965b).[1] But in countries where those elasticities are indeed very low, might it not be better to work with structuralist or two-gap models, which after all are designed to emphasize inflexible economic structures?

At this point, many authors quickly add that static effects are not the only positive effects of free trade and are probably the least important. They are likely to be right, but this defense implies that the standard neoclassical theoretical framework has some serious flaws and fails to capture key aspects of the real world (Leibenstein, 1966). Faced with the alternatives of strict adherence to the pure model yielding small quantitative effects or adding to it epicycles that make free trade look quantitatively better, most authors have chosen to do the latter. This situation has a number of similarities to that in growth accounting and in the explanation of cross-country productivity differences, where Nelson (1973) has shown the weaknesses of the pure neoclassical methodology. In all cases, the pure neoclassical model is a poor guide to entrepreneurial behavior, especially regarding productivity control and the search for and diffusion of innovations; the latter are likely to explain both growth and productivity differences better than are variations in such things as capital–labor ratios and static allocation. With few exceptions (Brainard and Cooper, 1968), uncertainty and costs of information have also been left out of neoclassical trade models.

While competition from world markets can, under the right conditions, ensure that no major departures from static efficiency will survive in an industry, it will not necessarily promote innovation and adaptation. On the other hand, protected entrepreneurs can turn lazy and complacent, or they can use market safety to devote their energies to innovation and exports, depending on their "animal spirits." Compare, for example, the textile indus-

---

1 This result is somewhat peculiar, as Ronald Findlay argues in this volume. Less ambiguously, low elasticities of substitution in consumption and production will make the short-run adjustment problem more complicated.

tries in Brazil and Colombia, both of which have been over-protected for a long time. The former turned X-inefficient (Bergsman, 1970, Chap. 8), while the latter was known for its progressiveness even before it began exporting in substantial amounts. Or compare quota-protected Japanese corporations and entrepreneurs with British firms, who are exposed to greater import competition and who are at best protected with tariffs.

International trade in knowledge and technological services – a topic of particular interest for developing countries whether those services are embodied in direct investment or are hired directly – cannot be handled adequately within neoclassical models that assume identical production functions and yield free-trade conclusions, even if one is willing to neglect Schumpeterian considerations. As put by Johnson (1970a), ". . . the essential problem is that reliance on the market principle of rewarding investment in the discovery of knowledge, which has the nature of a public good, by granting a temporary monopoly of the use of the knowledge. . . . is inherently inefficient" (p. 20). (See also Katz, 1972, Chap. 2.)

Structural models of trade and development (Chenery and Bruno, 1962; McKinnon, 1964; Chenery and Strout, 1966), formalizing insights developed also within the United Nations Economic Commission for Latin America during the 1950s (see, for example, United Nations, 1959), tended since their birth to sacrifice theoretical rigor for the sake of empirical applicability. This fact, their tendency to *ex ante, ex post* confusion, plus their assumptions of low elasticities of substitution in consumption and production and of exogenously given growth rates for exports, generated considerable criticism during the increasingly elasticity-optimistic 1960s, when the structural models came to be regarded as the intellectual underpinning for import-substitution strategies (Fei and Ranis, 1968; Bruton, 1969). Nevertheless, the simplifications involved in structural models still exert considerable intellectual and practical appeal. Their intellectual appeal is illustrated by Findlay's (1971) theoretical tidying up of the two-gap model; their practical appeal is illustrated by fresh empirical applications of revised and extended two-gap models (Weisskopf, 1972a; Chenery and Carter, 1972).

A promising development is the introduction of some nonzero substitution possibilities into planning models that generate two-gap situations, and the quantification of the impact of the change in assumptions. This route seems to lead to a convergence of neoclassical and structuralist models; compare, for example, the

Johnson (1965b and 1966) simulations with the Chenery and Raduchel (1971) arguments and calculations. Neither, of course, can quantify X-efficiency effects, induced technical change, and costs of obtaining information. Furthermore, Chenery and Raduchel, while admitting that policy variables such as the exchange rate can help to utilize fully domestic resources, remain doubtful that indirect factor substitution via demand and trade can be extensive enough to accommodate very wide variations in factor proportions. But their last sentence is worthy of full quotation: "This formulation offers the hope for shifting policy discussions from the ideological level to empirical questions of estimating structural relations and determining policy choices from them. In that context, there need be no inconsistency between the structuralist diagnoses of the causes of underdevelopment and the use of neoclassical guidelines for planners" (p. 47). Two-gappers and neoclassicists agree that the shadow price of foreign exchange in less developed countries is generally greater than its official value and that the two-gap problem is typically a symptom of inefficient allocation policies (Chenery, ed., 1971, p. 92).

The suggested convergence is likely to be aided by fresh work on models in the neoclassical spirit, which directly embody possible effects of trade on growth, and which subdivide output not only into importables and exportables but also into consumption and investment. While the effects of growth on trade have been exhaustively analyzed using the Heckscher–Ohlin–Samuelson framework, much less has been done on the trade-on-growth link. Corden (1971) has explored the growth effects of trade, which ". . . are not necessarily the most important ones in practice but are those that emerge most clearly from the simple neoclassical model" (p. 117). His emphasis on the impact of trade policies on the relative price and/or availability of investment goods is, however, likely to be of very great practical relevance and offers an important link to the structural models.

Bardhan's (1970) and Findlay's (1972) dynamization of several aspects of trade theory, and their rigorous analysis of trade and development problems, are also important steps toward incorporating development insights into more or less formal trade and development models, although it is not always clear how those models could be quantified and used for policy purposes. The extension of the distortion literature into more dynamic contexts should also yield interesting results, as already indicated by the work of Johnson (1967 and 1970b) and Bhagwati (1968b). More could also be done to bring the link between income distribution, consumption patterns, and savings into such models.[2]

Theoretical work is likely, alas, to continue generating interesting parameters and relationships at a much faster rate than such things are quantified. But a bringing together of theoretical work on distortions and policy instruments, on the one hand, and on dualistic models (where the "modern" sector is split into import-competing and exporting parts), on the other, may yield scenarios useful in guiding empirical research on historical and contemporary cases where more trade yielded poor or ambiguous development results. Those models promise to be more in accordance with the known facts about less developed countries[3] than are most of the present pure trade or pure development models. It would be a matter of pinpointing and selecting the key circumstances under which the unavoidable (and the avoidable) rigidities, imperfections, and distortions in LDC markets set the stage for a failure to capture the potential gains from trade for development purposes.

Many of the possible building blocks are at hand; besides the standard staple or vent-for-surplus models (Caves, 1965; Findlay, 1970, Chap. 4) and dualistic models (Ranis and Fei, 1961), one can mention Brecher's (1972) work on the role of minimum wages in trade theory, showing the possibility that larger exports lead to greater unemployment. Also worth noting are the Hymer and Resnick (1969) model of agrarian economies with nonagricultural activities, and the Birnberg and Cohen (1971) second-best analysis in the context of distorted development conditions. The beautiful W. A. Lewis (1969) model explains trends in terms of trade for tropical exports, as well as relative standards of living, on the basis of average labor productivity in food production in tropical and temperate countries. It lends itself to a number of extensions, and also to different interpretations, some of which are of a neo-Marxist radical character (Emmanuel, 1972, pp. 87–90). Except for Emmanuel, neo-Marxist contributions to pure trade theory, in contrast with those to economic history and the theory of capital movements, are scanty.

Further exploration of differences in production functions

---

2 Ricardo's dictum to the effect that income distribution is the major concern of political economy was largely unheeded, until very recently, in postwar mainstream research, theoretical or empirical, on trade policies and development.

3 Such as less than full employment, profit rates not very different from those in rich countries, but much lower real wages.

between developed and underdeveloped countries, which may vary from sector to sector, could also yield relevant insights, combined with research along the product-cycle line (Vernon, 1971). The works of Linder (1961) and Nelson (1968) also contain a number of ideas and hypotheses waiting to be further expanded. The old complaint that comparative-advantage models were insufficiently "dynamic" is on the way to being met, probably with a vengeance. As in the case of recent explorations of the infant-industry argument for protection, more empirical studies could greatly enrich theoretical analysis.

This kind of work can be extended to the analysis of the impact of direct foreign investment on LDC economies.[4] See, for example, the paper by Cohen (1972b), which generates cases in the context of development-dualistic models, where the impact of incoming foreign investment on the host economy can be negative. The concept of an optimal tax or subsidy on international capital movements, developed by·Kemp (1966) and Jones (1967), should also be of interest to empirical researchers and economic historians, and particularly to those with a radical bent.

Another line of theoretical endeavor in which fruitful interactions with empirical research will continue to occur is the analysis of illegal foreign-trade transactions, such as smuggling and fake invoicing (Bhagwati and Hansen, 1973a). An interesting political-economy sidelight in this field would explore asymmetries in what countries regard as legal transactions, or at least differences in the vigor with which various illegal transactions are prosecuted. The importation of some commodities (for example, marijuana) is actively repressed in most rich countries, which complain that many less developed countries tolerate such exports from their territories. On the other hand, most less developed countries ban the export of archeological items deemed part of their heritage, while the same items have entered into rich countries either legally, according to their own laws, or using illegal routes not zealously guarded by authorities preferring not to upset wealthy collectors.

The application to international trade and development of theories involving externalities and the misuse of valuable but

---

4 The growing role of multinational corporations, and to a lesser extent of state-owned enterprises, in international trade will make the borderlines between trade, location, and industrial-organization theories increasingly blurred (Caves, 1971b). The internal rules of large bureaucratic units will necessarily influence trade theories as such units spread their activities across several countries. The analytical problems raised by the study of such administrative rules are remarkably similar to those arising from research on nonmarket socialist economies.

unclaimed assets is likely to grow, as a result of the desire of some less developed countries to gain comparative advantage in pollution-intensive activities and to share mankind's "commons," such as oceans and space. This desire explains some preemptive enclosure movements (the 200-miles issue). The optimal rate of exploitation of nonrenewable resources, internationally traded by nations with different expectations and discount rates, should also receive increased attention.

This review of theoretical developments has, following custom, dealt with real, or long-run, trade theory. As will be seen below, much recent empirical work on less developed country trade problems calls attention to the need for work on short-run adjustment mechanisms. Development theorists have tended to ignore the cyclical macroeconomic problems of less developed countries, which are typically closely tied to balance-of-payments management, while theorists of adjustment mechanisms for rich countries have paid little attention to the less developed countries. As a result, theoretical analysis of less developed countries' short-term policies for simultaneously achieving internal and external balance, as well as income-distribution and growth targets, has been neglected. A notable exception is the recent paper of Taylor (1973), which correctly emphasizes the particularly difficult dilemmas faced by policy makers in many semi-industrialized economies.

2. RE-EXAMINATION OF THE PRE-WORLD WAR II ECONOMIC HISTORY OF TRADE POLICIES AND DEVELOPMENT

In the nineteenth century, freer trade played a role in weakening the position of unprogressive British landlords, the real targets of Ricardo, and accompanied the settlement and/or prosperity of some predominantly Anglo-Saxon or Scandinavian developing countries. These facts have had a disproportionate influence in tilting the mainstream literature, dominated by Anglo-Saxon and Scandinavian authors, toward a benign and optimistic view of the trade and growth nexus. The combined population of Australia, Canada, New Zealand, Denmark, and Sweden around 1900 was 18 million, a figure roughly equal to the combined population of Taiwan and Hong Kong today. If to those five successful countries one adds Argentina, South Africa, and Uruguay, their total 1900 population reaches 31 million, or less than 2 per cent of the world population at that time, and about the demographic size of today's South Korea.

The Nurksian notion of trade as the historical engine of growth has recently been challenged even for some "countries of recent settlement." Kravis (1972) rejects the view that external demand factors predominate in accounting for nineteenth-century U.S. economic growth; he also argues (Kravis, 1970) that international-trade policies and performance cannot explain varying growth records of countries in the nineteenth century. Trade, at best, was a handmaiden of a growth whose mainsprings were internal and, it may be added, difficult to locate exactly. In a Kindlebergerian spirit, Kravis also suggests that both trade and investment can be fickle and opportunistic handmaidens; they *may* serve growth, but they could also serve structures perpetuating underdevelopment.

For the Canadian case, Chambers and Gordon (1966) applied a strict neoclassical model to quantify the share of the increase in per capita income from 1901 to 1911 that could be attributed to the wheat-export boom. Not surprisingly, given the methodology, that share came out small, about 6 per cent. Although Caves (1971a) accepts their conclusion that advances in international technological knowledge and its application are likely to comprise the main source of income gains for small nations, a conclusion whose policy implications are unclear, he adjusts the Chambers and Gordon calculation in mildly heterodox ways, raising that share to 21 per cent. In the same article, Caves has also provided a thorough survey (with extensive bibliography) and stimulating discussion of possible uses of the export-led growth model as a research tool, concluding that it is best applied to national or regional time series but difficult to handle in cross-country studies. The important difference between extensive and per capita growth also receives attention from Caves and from Chambers and Gordon.

Skepticism regarding the historical predominance of beneficial links between trade and development has always increased when attention has shifted to countries that even today remain under-developed. In many of those countries, freer trade policies were adopted during the nineteenth century and up to 1930, not always simply as a result of the persuasive powers of Mill and Ricardo but mainly as a consequence of unequal treaties imposed forcibly by colonial and neocolonial powers (see, for example, Hansen and Nashashibi, 1972, Chap. 1). Little wonder, then, that free-trade policies which had to be buttressed by foreign gunboats failed to be viewed universally by less developed countries as obvious handmaidens of *their* development.

Caves (1971a) discusses some of the reasons usually given for the failure of rising exports to induce significant and self-sustained growth in developing countries, listing (pp. 433–437) ten possible and more or less positive linkages between staple export expansion and intensive growth. He tentatively adds an interesting eleventh effect, which, contrary to the typical assumption in the literature on LDC export instability, suggests in a Schumpeter–Hirschman spirit that irregular (supply-induced) bursts of staple exports will ". . . spur a larger quantity of capital formation and more diverse type of projects, than a growth process not attended by windfalls . . ." (p. 437). Leff (1972a and 1972b) blames economic retardation in nineteenth-century Brazil on too few, rather than too many, exports; lack of internal capacity to transform and reallocate resources led to Brazilian failures to adapt and profit fully from shifts in comparative advantage. He also introduces into the historical discussion the notion of optimum currency areas, suggesting that populations in large less developed countries would have been better off had they been distributed among several smaller nation-states rather than one large country with poor internal factor mobility.

W. A. Lewis (1969, Lecture 1) indicates that pessimism regarding the historical trade and development link is largely an optical illusion. Trade, he argues, was indeed an engine of growth for most of the tropics having "a stable and modern type of government," at least from 1880 to 1913. The illusion arises from failing to realize that, given large subsistence sectors, trade was a smaller proportion of tropical economies than manufacturing was of temperate economies; from disregarding the fact that the starting point for less developed countries was very low, owing mainly to poor agricultural productivity; from placing too much emphasis on the "special" cases of land-poor India and the sugar islands; and from failing to put the dismal interwar period in proper historical perspective. It should be noted that Lewis is not so much trying to give new life to the thesis of trade as an engine of growth as to combat the argument that tropical growth is not possible until deep spiritual and social transformations occur in those countries.

Other authors, unlike Lewis, have emphasized the disruptive effects of expanding trade on underdeveloped economies, as well as the weaknesses or negative nature of backward linkages, the uneven distribution of gains from trade, etc. Several have noted that, contrary to the British experience, freer trade strengthened the economic and political position of landlords and regressive elements in LDC societies.

The upsurge of radical economics during the 1960s gave fresh impetus to such historical views and research. See, for example, the work of Resnick (1970) on the decline of rural industry under export expansion in Southeast Asia, the Hymer and Resnick (1971) paper on international trade and uneven development, and that of A. G. Frank (1970) on Latin America. These and other authors, not all "radical," stress that asymmetries in political and military power will be reflected not only in asymmetries in the distribution of the burden of adjusting to equilibrium disturbances but also in the determination of equilibrium itself. The more extreme thesis is that markets grow out of the barrel of a gun, so the powerful can play the market following the rule of "heads I win, tails you lose." Although this extreme version appears to be an exaggeration, it is clearly incorrect to assume that markets exist independent of sociopolitical and power realities, as shown by the experience of markets under colonialism. The colonial experience with markets, in turn, varied according to the policies of hegemonic powers (Birnberg, 1972). See also the discussion by Triffin (1968) of the actual workings of the gold standard during the nineteenth century, showing how Britain thrust the major burden of adjusting to her cyclical balance-of-payments difficulties onto the countries of the periphery.

Drawing heavily on pre-World War II historical experience, Sunkel (1969) and Furtado (1971) have elaborated building blocks of the Latin American "dependence" school, which examines not only the purely economic links between trade and growth, including the inducement to technological change, but also re-emphasizes negative long-run effects of export-led growth on the autonomous development of LDC social and political institutions. Contrary to Mill, who celebrated the impact on LDC tastes of the introduction of new products, these authors point to negative economic and social repercussions of international demonstration effects in consumption. Other authors have also lamented the spread of "consumerism" implicit in outward-looking trade policies, suspecting undesirable shifts in indigenous tastes. Girvan (1972) has noted the independent but related development of similar ideas in the sugar ex-colonies or plantation economies of the Caribbean. The dependence school, although providing numerous interdisciplinary insights, still contains several ambiguities (Pinto, 1972). It remains unclear, for example, whether dependence has more to do with economic size than with social system, and whether only less developed countries are dependent. Indeed, a fully satisfactory definition of "dependence" is hard to find, and the policy prescriptions flowing from this school are vague.

A. G. Frank (1970) has emphasized the healthy response of several Latin-American economies to the Great Depression of the 1930s, as well as to the two world wars, suggesting that, contrary to orthodoxy, less developed countries do best when the rich are weakest. But he seems to have interpreted a situation in which the more advanced of poor countries were making the best of a bad thing in the trade field as one absolutely preferable, from the LDC viewpoint, to worldwide prosperity. Frank's thesis is stronger in the area of direct foreign investment; for example, several less developed countries took advantage of conditions during World War II to buy back rather cheaply European assets within their territories. Further comparative work on various LDC reactions to the depression and the world wars should provide insights comparable to those of Kindleberger (1951) regarding group behavior and international trade. Frank also has given historical examples of regions geographically remote and isolated from metropolitan centers, claiming that they initiated and experienced the most promising self-generating economic development in Latin America before they were stopped by lower transport costs and freer trade.

It should be clear by now that historical research yields no less ambiguous results than the theoretical work surveyed in section 1. The problem is not only the different ideologies and nationalities of the authors but also the different weights placed by them on the various dimensions of development, and their nontestable views on "what could have been" had the countries remained isolated from international trade currents. In history, as in the cross-section research to be reviewed below, our small and young planet does not seem to provide enough variance or degrees of freedom to test our theories unambiguously.

It has been the practice of many economists, when faced with historical or contemporary situations in which it appears at first glance that growing trade led to weak or negative development results, to blame lack of LDC "preconditions," or market imperfections and distortions, or weak "societal responses" to development opportunities, etc., usually without bothering to define and analyze further these factors and explanations. These approaches verge on the tautological. Two avenues seem worth exploring to cast further light on the absolute or relative failures in the historical literature on trade and development.

One, already mentioned, would be to set up realistic models useful in isolating market frictions and distortions that account for unsatisfactory LDC reactions to trade stimuli, and to contrast those imperfections with the policy tools that LDC governments had at hand before 1930. It is often forgotten that, whether independent or not, most of those governments had little control over their exchange rates, owing to their commitment to the gold standard, that most did not even have a central bank, and that their fiscal machinery was rudimentary. Little wonder, then, that in less developed countries characterized by large subsistence sectors and imperfect markets, governments were often loathe to abandon autonomy in tariff policy – one of the few tools available to them.

A second and more difficult step would be to look at the social and political institutions which lie behind market distortions and imperfections and which could also explain the degree and speed of the spread of educative effects arising from a more open economy (Myint, 1969). Why did LDC governments, for example, show greater interest in breaking .some domestic bottlenecks than others? Who, if anyone, gained, and who lost from market imperfections and institutional arrangements? Were those imperfections a result of policies? If not, could they have been removed by policy?

3. THE POST-WORLD WAR II EXPERIENCE WITH TRADE POLICIES AND DEVELOPMENTS; EMPIRICAL RESEARCH ON THE OVERALL PERFORMANCE

Three major styles can be noted in scholarly empirical work looking at overall LDC postwar trade and development performance: the econometric analysis of cross-section and time-series data for many countries, more specific country or sector studies, and grand summaries. On the whole, these three styles look at the aggregate picture and skip exhaustive discussion of the details in the trade and development nexus.

Inspired by the monumental work of Kuznets (see, for example, 1966 and 1967), the econometric analysis of LDC cross-section and time-series data starts with the hypothesis that there are uniform patterns of change in the structure of production as income levels rise, subject to secular shifts due to innovational changes. The paper by Chenery and Taylor (1968) may be taken as the best published example of this school. Three LDC development patterns are isolated – for large countries (more than fifteen to twenty-five million inhabitants), for small industry-oriented countries, and for small primary-oriented countries. From the viewpoint of this survey, the most striking result of Chenery and Taylor is that so much can be explained without reference to variations in trade policies, once differences in size and resource endowments are taken into account.[5] While many less developed countries have followed roughly similar trade policies, there has been a fair degree of variance among them (Mexico vs. Brazil, Philippines vs. Egypt, etc.), so the Chenery and Taylor results cannot be explained by saying that no policy effect is detected because all LDC policies were the same. Size and resources seem to be destiny, and all that policy appears to do is speed or delay a given less developed country along its preordained development path. It cannot much change the structural pattern of production. This will not bother those most interested in the link between trade policies and per capita growth, but it will disturb those hoping to use trade policies to alter significantly the output profile associated with a given per capita income. Trying to give a small primary-oriented country the industrial structure of a diversified large country will simply stop or slow down growth. But it is also implied that India and Brazil, liberalize as they may, will maintain a diversified and "heavy" industrial structure.[6]

The quantification of the more short-term structural models generated by the Chenery planning school has focused on the identification of major development bottlenecks for a given country, usually either savings or foreign exchange, and on the measurement of the impact of foreign-resource inflows on growth and, more recently, on domestic savings. For many countries, these efforts have yielded the measurement of important functions, such as those for imports and savings, as well as for the link between investment and output. An interesting summary of the latest refinements for these functions can be found in Chenery

5 In a cross-country study of industrial concentration ratios, Pryor (1972) found that average four-firm, four-digit concentration ratios among large industrial nations are roughly the same, in spite of alleged policy differences in antitrust policies. Concentration in those large nations, however, was less than among smaller industrialized nations. Rank orders of concentration ratios by specific industries were found to be roughly the same in all nations. A difficulty in all cross-country studies, but of particular importance to those involving less developed countries, is the difference in relative price structures from country to country. For example, in comparing investment rates in GNP, cross-country studies seldom take into account differences in the relative prices of capital goods, which can be large.

6 In more recent, unpublished work, Chenery (1970a and 1970b) explicitly introduces trade-policy orientation, as well as capital inflow, as explanatory variables of the trade and development patterns he isolates. For example, he blames a policy of import substitution at the expense of export promotion for the abnormally low levels of exports, not offset by substantial capital inflows, observed for Argentina, Uruguay, Chile, and Turkey. Nevertheless, size of country still emerges as the most important difference explaining various patterns. In this kind of analysis, the level of aggregation and the time span one has in mind very much influence the judgment regarding how much "policy matters" for both the speed of growth and its structure.

and Carter (1972). Unfortunately, export functions continue to be a weak spot in these constructions, which typically make exports depend simply on time.

Weisskopf (1972a) has proposed and applied an econometric test to determine whether the growth of a given less developed country is constrained by lack of savings or of foreign exchange. He concludes that a binding trade constraint, contrary to the usual belief, has been a relatively infrequent phenomenon in LDC postwar experience. Some of his results are puzzling; for example, Peru comes out dominated by a trade constraint, while Colombia appears bound by a savings constraint. His *ex ante* savings function, however, makes exports one of the independent variables, on the ground that, for many countries, a strong *ex post* link has been observed between exports and savings. There are also a priori reasons to expect some connection between exports and savings; for example, public savings often rely heavily on trade taxes. This formulation is now common in Chenery-style models; see Landau (1971), and, for an earlier formulation, Vanek (1967). Such specification appears to blur further the distinction between the savings and foreign-exchange constraints. It could be argued that a close link between fluctuating savings and exports is observed simply because the latter allow the importation of machinery, otherwise unavailable, which national accounts register as investment, and therefore, given accounting procedures, as residual domestic savings.

The Chenery-style savings function has also generated controversy in the related area of the impact of capital inflows, or just aid, on domestic savings. Weisskopf (1972b) and others have argued that the evidence indicates a strong negative correlation between savings and foreign aid. Papanek (1972 and 1973) has provided a convincing critique of the methodology used in reaching those results. He notes that, given the misleading definition of domestic savings as equal to investment minus all foreign resource inflows, any increase in investment that is smaller than the increase in foreign inflows will by definition imply an absolute drop in recorded domestic savings. A pure grant from abroad, for example, used fully for relief (i.e., consumption), which leaves domestic investment unchanged, will lead by the illogic of this accounting to a recorded drop in domestic savings. Papanek urges separate treatment of different capital inflows and also observes that many other realistic considerations indicate that factors which produce below-average savings rates will produce above-average foreign inflows. On the whole, these and other econometric exercises are on more solid ground when working directly with investment data than with those ill-defined residuals now labeled "domestic savings." Clearer definitions of domestic savings and disposable income are needed, with the latter incorporating not only domestic output but also the "grant element" of capital inflows.

During the 1960s, there was a voluminous outpouring of country and sector studies for less developed countries; these typically devote substantial sections to discussing trade policies and development. In many cases, pre-World War II trends are discussed at least as background to postwar developments. While these studies emphasize the experience and institutions of particular countries, they generally rely, implicitly or explicitly, tightly or loosely, on one or several of the standard trade and development models. The Yale Economic Growth Center, for example, has sponsored a series of ambitious country studies having both a historical and trade orientation. No grand summing up of these country studies has yet appeared, and, if any such ever comes along, it will have to emphasize the variety of trade and development experiences found in those volumes.

Criticism of LDC trade policies hampering export expansion, of delayed and sporadic devaluations under inflationary conditions, and of erratic and excessive protectionism appears in some of the Yale country studies, particularly in the study of Argentina. This theme is also developed in the Nelson, Schultz, and Slighton (1971) volume on Colombia, and in that of S. R. Lewis (1969) for labor-rich Pakistan. Other country studies have been written around open dualistic *land*-surplus models. Examples include the work of Helleiner (1966) on Nigeria, and that of Hicks and McNicoll (1971) on the Philippines. The latter authors not only warn against excessive import substitution but also against continued reliance on resource-intensive export growth.

Interesting examples of sectoral studies emphasizing the trade and development nexus include Roemer (1970), C. Reynolds (in Mamalakis and Reynolds, 1965) and Leff (1968). The major contribution of the first book lies in its analytical description of the Peruvian fishmeal industry, blending applied theory, straightforward econometrics, and interesting narrative. The book's weakness is typical of many recent works on trade and development; together with scientific analysis of a specific case, the author gives us an evangelical description of the benefits of the export-led development in general. The capricious anchovies, alas, have decided to jolt this particular success story by mysteriously disappearing from Peruvian coasts throughout 1972. Reynolds's study of the interactions between the foreign-owned copper sector and the Chilean economy developed the concept of "returned value" (i.e., that part of copper sales abroad paid locally in the form of wages, taxes, purchase of materials, etc.) and showed it to be a more significant magnitude than the gross exports of those enterprises. This concept, incidentally, could be fruitfully applied to some new LDC manufacturing export activities which are dominated by multinational corporations and rely heavily on foreign inputs.

While Roemer and Reynolds expanded the established export-economy research line, Leff's study of the Brazilian capital-goods industry analyzes in depth the historical evolution of import-substituting activities, a relatively new and much-needed research endeavor. The growth of the capital-goods industry, he found, was achieved without import restrictions, thanks partly to an elastic domestic supply of the required inputs, including technical and skilled personnel. He is also skeptical of the thesis that the development of a domestic capital-goods industry by itself will lead to accelerated rates of capital formation, at least for big Brazil. A related study (Baer, 1969) analyzes the expansion of the Brazilian steel industry, giving it high marks for efficiency and growth effects.

As a result of the outpouring of country and sectoral studies, as well as more specialized articles, on which more below, survey articles and books began to appear in the middle 1960s attempting to evaluate overall LDC development and trade strategies. Import-substituting industrialization received early and mostly critical attention, as in the paper by Macario (1964). Criticism came from both neoclassicists and some Latin-American structuralists, who argued that import substitution would inevitably lead to economic stagnation unless incomes were drastically redistributed. The Williams College group also provided, besides original research, valuable surveys, such as those of Bruton (1970) and Sheahan (1972). The weaknesses of the "import-substitution syndrome" are by now being repeated ad nauseum, and fairly sympathetic reviews of that strategy, such as those by Hirschman (1968) and Baer (1972), are grossly outnumbered by orthodox and structuralist critiques.

The attack on LDC policies designed to induce import-substituting industrialization reached a climax with the publication of the Little, Scitovsky, and Scott comparative volume (1970), to be referred to hereafter as LSS, together with accompanying country studies on Brazil (Bergsman, 1970), India (Bhagwati and Desai, 1970), Mexico (King, 1970), Pakistan (S. R. Lewis, 1970), and Taiwan and the Philippines (Hsing, Power, and Sicat, 1970). (It should be noted, however, that, as could be expected, not all the country volumes fully share the precise critical stance or all the views of the comparative work; this is particularly true for the Bergsman book.)

LSS argue that near-first-best efficient policies are more practical than people in developing countries realize, and that these policies would also improve income distribution. LDC industry has been overencouraged relative to agriculture, they charge, and the selection of activities to be favored *within* industry has been careless. They recognize some arguments for special encouragement of industry, such as the infant-industry thesis, unskilled industrial wages higher than opportunity costs, and the external economies arising from knowledge or training spillovers for which industry cannot charge fully and from complementarities in industrial investments. But these and other arguments do not necessarily justify taxes on foreign trade. Instead, on grounds of wage distortion, they recommend the equivalent of a general labor subsidy of up to 50 per cent, which – depending on the labor intensity of each industry – would imply "promotion" of up to roughly 20 per cent of value added. Other arguments could increase the subsidy in rare and ad hoc cases up to 50 per cent of value added, but they expect the average justifiable subsidy to be no more than about 20 per cent. They add that in the more advanced developing countries there may be no justification for promotion at all. In all cases, quantitative controls would be abolished eventually, or kept for use only under emergency conditions, and import and export taxes, unless justified on optimum tariff or fiscal grounds, would be gradually phased out. Any remaining import duties would be matched by (equivalent) internal indirect taxes. The exchange rate would be allowed to seek its optimum-trade equilibrium, with small but frequent changes if necessary. The optimum amount of import substitution would then come out as a by-product of this system.

LSS find that the major distortion in the seven countries they and their collaborators studied results from the very high level of protection afforded by various forms of restrictions on imports and from the uneven nature of such protection. They blame a number of undesirable LDC trends on the use of protection against imports to encourage industrialization. Industrialization policies are said to have aggravated inequalities in income distribution, benefiting mainly a small group of industrialists, plus a working-class aristocracy. Adding insult to injury, it turns out that many "infant" industries are run by large multinational corporations. Untaxed excess profits, which when captured by local entrepreneurs represent domestic income redistribution, can further tilt the balance toward an unfavorable national result when foreign-owned activities are heavily subsidized by protection. Local industrialists have not always been induced to accumulate more domestic capital out of their high profits, choosing instead good living more appropriate to affluent societies, or foreign bank accounts. Tariff levels and structures, with low duties on capital goods, and arbitrary import-control rules are said to have encouraged capital-intensive industries and techniques, as well as widespread excess industrial capacity, aggravating the problem of unemployment. Employment in agriculture and labor-intensive exports has been discouraged. Import controls are said to have induced corruption.

Agricultural output naturally has also suffered, and at least in some countries social-overhead capital is said to have been neglected because of excessive preoccupation with protection of industry. The bias against exports created by protection, the overvaluation of exchange rates, and the excessive import demand that paradoxically was generated by import-substituting industrialization led to persistent balance-of-payments difficulties and to exchange bottlenecks that LSS would not call structural. They also note that possibilities for easy import substitution will sooner or later be exhausted; at that point, however, the necessary export growth will be hampered by expensive and shoddy domestic inputs to potential exporters and by overvalued exchange rates inherited from the earlier stages of import substitution. In short, many less developed countries have neglected comparative advantage and have failed to reap the full benefits of a decentralized price system.

LSS and the companion volumes contain advice for a gradual transition between present and recommended policies. LSS also question the validity of recorded postwar LDC growth rates, which at first view appear impressive, and take pains to show that the industrialized countries never had the astronomical protective rates in effect now in many developing countries.

The LSS volume brilliantly captures professional exasperation with the errors and missed opportunities in LDC planning and policy making, particularly in trade policy, which accumulated during the late 1950s and the 1960s, as LDC exports lagged behind booming world trade. Had world trade stagnated during the 1960s, however, we would now be reviewing books praising LDC import-substituting policies, as indeed such policies are praised for the 1930s. LSS policy recommendations do not rely on booming world trade, and they would argue that under less buoyant circumstances their proposals would have resulted in more healthy import substitution. But the consequences of different choices among trade policies become relatively less important when world trade is stagnating than when it is expanding vigorously.

The LSS volume is not intended as a rigorous presentation of either theory or empirical evidence, and it is written with a clear desire to influence policy as soon as possible. This makes it highly readable, given its subject matter, and influential among policy makers. Sympathy for its fundamental cause, however, should not keep us from listing some criticisms. Before going into those, it should be noted that LSS attempted, even if roughly, to translate arguments about externalities and distortions into concrete quantitative justifications for different policies. This attempt deserves praise; it is seldom made by those who casually invoke this or that imperfection to justify just about any level of protection or any other policy that happens to come into the head of a policy maker to whom they wish to be sympathetic. The leap from vague qualitative arguments to impetuous policy advocacy is no monopoly of the orthodox, and it raises important questions regarding the role of theory and its influence on policy advice and empirical research.

It is perhaps the LSS interest in influencing policy that leads them to couch their presentation too much in terms of old debates, such as industry versus agriculture or free trade versus protection, rather than exploring more subtly the various links between trade policy and development. Like many other authors (including Diaz-Alejandro, 1970), they lump together all features of the import-substitution syndrome, such as import and other controls, tariffs, overvalued and pegged exchange rates, spectacular balance-of-payments crises, inflationary pressures, and stop–go cycles. Following a "guilt by association" procedure, they then tend to blame much of what is going wrong in less developed countries on that ill-defined syndrome. Unsophisticated readers may indeed conclude that nearly everything gone wrong in those countries is due to that wicked syndrome.

Consider a mental experiment: What would have happened if, say, Argentina and Colombia had adopted flexible exchange rates back in 1945, *while adopting also an across-the-board import tariff of 150 per cent ad valorem?* I suspect their record, at least on growth and exports, would have been much better. Their harmful stop–go policies may be blamed to a large extent on exchange-rate mismanagement, as in the case of the United Kingdom, and on other short-run policies that could be analytically separated from the long-run effects of protection (although, of course, a more flexible exchange-rate policy would also tend to decrease the political muscle of protectionists). Similarly, LSS could have separated in a rough quantitative way the effects of the level of protection from the impact of dispersion in protective rates, as well as from effects arising from year-to-year changes in rates.

LSS *do* note the various aspects of the syndrome, as well as country-to-country variations, and are careful to say that problems such as unemployment or skewed income distribution are aggravated (not created) by protective policies. But the reader is left with the impression that the whole "infamous thing" must be eliminated before developing countries can achieve sound progress, and that income distribution, the employment picture, administrative honesty, etc., will be *much* better if the LSS policy advice is followed. The authors further expect X-efficiency and technological change to improve and accelerate if their policies are followed. It is perhaps revealing of the state of our science that LSS decline to quantify the gains countries may expect from following their policies, much less to separate quantitatively the costs of the various features of the syndrome. The impact on world trade if all less developed countries followed the LSS advice is of course another nice matter left unquantified, although the authors devote a good chapter to a discussion of actions by which developed countries could pave the way for such contingency.

Other attempts to sum up at least parts of the postwar LDC trade and development experience typically share the LSS stance. See, for example, Keesing (1967), Cohen and Ranis (1971), and Schydlowsky (1972). Discussion at that level of generality faces sharply diminishing returns, so it is wiser to turn to the various empirical building blocks of the consensus to see how solid are its foundations.

4. CAN LESS DEVELOPED COUNTRIES AFFECT THE LEVEL AND COMPOSITION OF THEIR EXPORTS? THE 1960s ROUT OF EXPORT PESSIMISM

No complicated models are needed to show that if one expects LDC exports to grow much below their desired GNP growth rates, import substitution, however induced, will be a very important part of the development program. And if the supply of foreign exchange is, say, perfectly inelastic with respect to changes in the exchange rate, then import duties and even quotas can be made to have the same impact as equilibrium exchange rates on resource allocation, although not on income distribution. The period between 1914 and 1945 generated an export pessimism that lasted well into the 1950s, based on two mutually reinforcing strands of thought. First, the supply-price elasticity of exportables in less developed countries, a domestic parameter, was deemed by many to be low, because of institutional rigidities in the case of rural exportables or because of difficulties of entry and quality in the case of nontraditional manufactured goods. Second, both income and price elasticities of the foreign demand for LDC exports were considered to be very low. Engel's law, synthetics, etc., were the key code words. So export pessimists saw little point in trying to use domestic policy tools, such as the exchange rate, to coax a few more exportables out of inelastic domestic activities (which were frequently owned either by foreigners or by nationals regarded as socially unprogressive and already above average in income); one would have had to push the additional staples on reluctant foreign buyers, inducing what could be immiserizing terms-of-trade declines.

Empirical research has been blasting away those two major props of export pessimism, at least in their most extreme form. In the first place, numerous studies have shown that where markets exist (i.e., for commercial agriculture) LDC farmers will respond to relative prices. Nowshirvani (1971) surveys this literature, noting also that high prices will induce the spread of markets, so that their total economic effect includes a movement along a given supply schedule, plus a rightward schedule shift due to induced organizational changes. He notes, however, that such total price responsiveness is far from an unmixed blessing, as the social consequences of the uncontrolled spread of markets can be quite undesirable. Econometric research on supply response has become ever more refined, as in Nowshirvani's (1971) study of some food crops in northern India, in which *subsistence* crops showed no price response, while *cash* crops generally showed positive and significant price elasticities of supply. Also noteworthy is Behrman's (1968) book on four crops in Thailand, using as independent variables not only mean prices but also their variances. In the short run supply responses may be weak or even apparently perverse, as with Argentine beef, but most studies show a significant and substantial long-run positive supply response for individual crops and rural activities. For large groups of such activities, or for the rural sector as a whole, however, the evidence on price responsiveness is much less clear.

The trade boom of the 1960s, during which the purchasing power of nonpetroleum LDC exports rose about three times as rapidly as in the 1950s, has provided abundant raw materials for empirical workers trying to show that external demand for LDC exports is much more price- and income-elastic than the pessimists thought (De Vries, 1967). With the possible exception of old staples, such as coffee and sugar, whose international marketing can be handled with ad hoc policies, it has been shown that, even within the area of primary products, all kinds of new developed-country demands have opened up (Cohen, 1970; but see Hicks and McNicoll, 1971, who remain skeptical and warn of resource exhaustion). The small share of total world trade accounted for by most LDC exports of manufactured goods, and the rapid growth of these exports in "success stories" such as South Korea, have been powerful arguments in routing both demand and supply pessimism (LSS, Chap. 7).

Cohen and Sisler (1971) have provided a detailed analysis of LDC shares in the world market for their major exports during the 1960s. They show that for commodities being imported by industrial countries at the most rapidly growing rates, developing countries experienced the largest losses in potential exports; they failed to maintain their market shares. Cohen and Sisler take this fact as *prima facie* evidence that low growth rates for LDC exports were due primarily to domestic supply problems, often induced or aggravated by incorrect domestic policies, rather than to lack of external demand. An extreme example of a domestically induced decline in market shares would be the meat and grain exports of the Argentine Republic; with hindsight, it is hard to believe that, quite late into the 1960s, many in that country justified just about any import-substituting project on the grounds that there was no future in world markets for primary products such as beef, corn, and wheat. And as one watches the United States, the U.S.S.R., China, Japan, and Western Europe plan growing trade among themselves in cotton, wheat, natural gas, and oil, it is hard to remember that such trade was and is regarded by many as an infallible symptom of colonial dependency. Indeed, growing preoccupation in rich countries with resource exhaustion and undesirable side effects of synthetics puts us back, at least for a while, in a neo-Ricardian–Malthusian world.

The pessimists also missed the rapid 1960s expansion in the

demand of rich countries for LDC tourist services, which transformed previously untradeable LDC "home goods" into earners of foreign exchange. The demand for LDC tourist services appears to have a high income elasticity, and for some areas also a high price elasticity. For several less and semi-developed countries in the Mediterranean basin, migrant remittances have also become a substantial source of foreign exchange.

There is an invincible pessimism even in countries that are now dramatically expanding their exports, such as Brazil and Colombia. It argues that the expansion cannot continue or that it is bound to collapse. Others simply ignore the facts and continue to repeat the a priori arguments for pessimism, eagerly greeting each new international monetary storm.[7] Nobody, of course, can say for sure that trade wars among Europe, Japan, and the United States could not radically alter the outlook for world trade. Another view, reflected in W. A. Lewis's (1969) second lecture, is that the expected export expansion to developed-country markets, although substantial, will still not be enough to achieve LDC growth targets, so further import substitution, at the regional or all-LDC level, is still required. But Lewis does not discuss the optimum way of inducing such import substitution. Helleiner (1972, Chap. 2) argues that LDC supply policies and random difficulties account in large part for country-to-country differences in export performance, but only within constraints imposed by traditional world commodity-demand factors.

The direct testing of the link between exchange-rate policies and the supply responses of nontraditional LDC exports has generally yielded significantly positive elasticities, showing that exchange-rate policy typically does matter. See, for example, the survey and fresh work of Eaton (1972). There are, however, some unresolved problems. While the time-series econometric work shows that the exchange rate matters, it frequently suggests that it does not matter very much, explaining only a relatively small part of export growth rates. Indeed, as the monetarists would expect, examples of countries that have substantially changed their *real* exchange rate for a sustained number of years are few. More sophisticated lag structures, exchange-rate variances, etc., could in some cases boost the quantitative weight of exchange-rate variables.

---

7 Some recalcitrant export pessimists make the aesthetically understandable point that it is difficult to wax enthusiastic about a boom in exchange earnings that is partly based on items such as wigs, false teeth, dog toys, plastic flowers, and, in some countries, blood and cadavers, not to mention earnings from the sale of tourist services, not all of which originate in ticket sales at the local anthropological and historical museums.

For many countries, the *stability* of the real exchange rate may turn out to be more important for expanding nontraditional exports than the *level* of such a variable. But the separate effects, as well as the interaction of exchange-rate policy with the many other LDC export-promotion policies, remains very difficult to quantify, at least using time series. Halevi (1972) notes the crucial problem of establishing the functional links between relative prices and the structure of capital formation, as well as possible scale effects. There is also the fact, emphasized by Krueger's (1972a, Chap. 7) work on Turkish exports, that many LDC exports are determined mainly by government domestic policies (e.g., agricultural policies), as well as by direct public interventions in the export market, rather than by the trade regime itself.

Cross-section studies on export performance rarely go beyond casual empiricism; a promising avenue could be to quantify degrees of under- or overvaluation across less developed countries, using either a modified purchasing-power-parity approach[8] or shadow exchange-rate benchmarks, and formally relating those measures to export performance.

Many promotion policies have a net impact per dollar of exports that varies substantially from industry to industry, or even firm to firm, while others promote exports mainly by providing market and technical information inside and outside the country. The former include tax and credit subsidies, exemption from import duties, and the creation of free-trade zones. The latter refer to such things as fairs and can also include direct government pressures to export "or else." Either type of policy presents its own difficulties for quantifying supply responses. As already noted, some export-promotion plans are closely coordinated with policies toward foreign investors. As my colleague Benjamin Cohen has pointed out to me, and as noted long ago by Williams

---

[8] Assuming that LDC nontradeables are on balance more intensive in unskilled labor than tradeable goods, and that the importance of the subsistence sector that makes up a good share of nontradeables declines with development, it is to be expected that the ratio of unskilled wage rates to the exchange rate will be positively correlated with per capita incomes. Departures from such "normal" relationships could provide clues regarding degrees of over- or undevaluation of currencies (see also Balassa, 1964). Much remains to be done in making the distinction between tradeables and nontradeables both more empirically useful and more theoretically integrated with the traditional models used to derive the showpiece theorems of international trade. It is not clear, for example, whether the share of nontradeables in the absorption basket depends only on per capita income, or also on country size. Size, in turn, can be defined in terms of geographical extension, population, or total output. The precise degree of "tradeability" of different commodities is a difficult matter to establish precisely, but it is probably a mistake to regard all agricultural and manufactured goods as 100 per cent "tradeable."

(1929), this complementarity between trade and capital movements contrasts with the standard textbook thesis that trade and factor movements are substitutes, as indeed they have been in import-substituting activities.

The multiplicity of export-promoting policies has raised the issue of the effectiveness of the different instruments in expanding exports. The example of South Korea (C. Frank, 1972) suggests that export success is not simply a matter of following neoclassical textbook recipes. Export promotion may involve as much haphazard government interventionism as import substitution (Bhagwati, 1968a). Cuba offers an extreme example of an export-promotion strategy with highly centralized socialist planning techniques. Thus the issue of the *efficiency* of the different tools and techniques must also be raised.

Examples of excesses in export promotion, symmetrical to excesses in import substitution, can be given at the theoretical as well as the empirical level. Bhagwati and Krueger (1973) argue, however, that the situation is unlikely to be wholly symmetrical, and that export promotion may be the superior strategy. Generally, the costs of excessive export promotion are more visible to policy makers than those of import substitution. Exporting firms must face price and quality competition in international markets; insofar as the persistence of inadequate competitiveness is less likely under the export-oriented strategy, export promotion is superior simply because it reduces the incidence of the problem. Finally, if there are significant indivisibilities or economies of scale, an export-oriented strategy will enable firms of adequate size to realize them. The various symmetries and asymmetries between export-promotion and import-substituting strategies are likely to remain an important focus of research.

The spread of preferential trading agreements among less developed countries, and between some developed and less developed countries, presents measurement problems not yet adequately tackled by the empirical literature on LDC export expansion. LDC common markets or free-trade areas provide the conditions under which apparent export expansion could be hiding the repetition at regional levels of national import-substitution excesses. In other words, a dollar earned exporting from Colombia to Peru, or to Bulgaria, may not be worth as much as a dollar earned by exporting to Germany if the former carries with it the obligation to buy in return goods that are overpriced relative to alternative least-cost sources. Differential effects in other fields, such as employment, could also be expected between exports to common-market partners, or to centrally planned economies under bilateral arrangements, and those to the rest of the world. A related point arises when growing exports are closely linked to heavy use of imported inputs, as in free-trade zones on the Mexican border with the United States. In either circumstance, using gross export data may yield misleading impressions.

Although customs unions and free-trade areas among developing countries have received a fair amount of theoretical, speculative, and descriptive attention, as in Cooper and Massel (1965), Grunwald *et al.* (1972), and Morawetz (1972), analyses of the economic consequences of their actual trade flows have been relatively rare, owing perhaps to their recent creation and/or precarious existence. Exceptions include the Hansen (1967) and Willmore (1972) studies on the Central American Common Market.

5. RECENT WORK ON OTHER PERENNIAL ISSUES OF LDC EXPORT SECTORS

Two aged theses emphasized by some species of export pessimists also came in for rude attack during the 1960s from empirical research and contemporary reality. One identified LDC export instability, independent of trend, as another obstacle to growth, while the other preferred to express its export pessimism by arguing that the long-term trend in the terms of trade for primary products (or for developing countries) was inevitably downward.

Looking systematically at relevant 1946-58 numbers in an area where few had done so, MacBean (1966) created a minor scandal when he showed that export instability was not that much greater in less developed than in rich countries. Leaving aside such cases as Brazilian coffee and Ghanaian cocoa, he also argued that primary-product exports are no more unstable than manufactured exports. When data showed acute export fluctuations, he found that the responsibility lay with domestic factors – including weather, pests, political turmoil, and economic errors – rather than with shifts in world demand. Finally, there was little econometric evidence showing a significant link between export instability and the stability and growth of GDP and capital formation.

Examining the period 1950–66, Massel (1970) tested a number of possible explanations for export instability in rich and poor countries. The only explanatory variables showing significant coefficients were concentration in few export products, associated with increasing instability, and absolutely large export sectors and unusual reliance on food exports, associated with less instability.

A result related to the absolute size of the export sector is that of Erb and Schiavo-Campo (1969), who found for 1954–66 a negative correlation among less developed countries between export instability and the absolute size of their GDPs. These authors also found that between 1946 and 1958, the MacBean period, and 1954 and 1966, there was an important decline in export instability both in less developed and in rich countries, but in the latter more than in the former.

Kenen and Voivodas (1972) conclude that the choice among various methods of measuring export instability and among plausible country samples does not affect their major results, which on the whole agree with those of MacBean, but the results are somewhat more sensitive to the choice of time period. For example, contrary to MacBean, they find a strong and plausible negative connection between export instability and the level of investment during the 1960s, which reopens the question of how much and how export instability reduces investment levels.

Mathieson and McKinnon (1972) focus on the instability not only of exports and aggregate GDP but also of several GDP components, arguing that measurement techniques tend to hide important LDC instability in large aggregates. They find that instability in less developed countries is indeed substantially larger than in rich countries, but that there is no persuasive evidence that the international economy generally exerted a net destabilizing influence on the former from 1950 to 1968, partly because rich countries did not experience their business cycles in unison during these years. Mathieson and McKinnon find that instability decreases with per capita income but, contrary to Erb and Schiavo-Campo, that the country size per se, as measured by absolute GDP levels, bears no significant link with instability. They also obtain some weak evidence indicating that the more open an economy, as measured by the ratio of exports to GDP, the lower will be the instability. Although that link is not strong statistically, they certainly can say that there is no basis in their results for supporting the traditional view linking instability with openness and outward-looking trade policies.

The main thrust of the above is to undercut *general* contemporary arguments for international commodity schemes and for restrictionist and interventionist domestic trade policies, which are justified by the alleged harmful effects of presumed export instability on LDC economies. Of course, ad hoc cases of instability that require particular policies, just like ad hoc grounds for optimum export taxes, are not weakened by the results surveyed.

Studies of pre-World War II LDC export instability should yield interesting results; they are likely to indicate that declines in that instability, and in its negative impact on development, are due to improved macro and sectoral economic management, both in developed and developing countries.

As noted by Helleiner (1972, Chap. 5), the focus on exports as a source of instability in LDC economies has usually been based on the belief that other elements in aggregate demand within those countries were not as important, in the short run, in determining the level of aggregate economic activity. LDC exports are supposed to influence economic activity not only through their effects on demand but also through their effects on feasible import supplies. At least for the study of business cycles in the larger developing countries, such traditional focus is clearly out of date. The fact that in many developing countries imports show greater instability than exports cannot be explained without a closer examination of the interplay between domestic policy instruments (including monetary and fiscal policy) on the one hand, and external demand conditions and foreign-trade policy instruments (particularly the exchange rate) on the other. The stop–go macro policies observed in several semi-industrialized countries and the induced domestic instability have more to do with the sporadic and reluctant way in which devaluations have been handled than with disturbances arising in world markets. In other words, postwar instability in, say, Argentine or Turkish investment, particularly in construction, has a lot in common with that found in the United Kingdom, a hypothesis hardly illuminated by the traditional focus on export instability.

Theoretical and empirical work on the determinants of secular trends for LDC terms of trade, so popular during the 1950s, was on the whole neglected during the 1960s, perhaps because of general agreement that the terms of trade, whatever their trend, were not the key variables to focus on when discussing trade policy and development. On the theoretical front, the works of Arthur Lewis (1969) and Emmanuel (1972) have already been mentioned. Lewis adds a historical-empirical test to his theoretical model. He concludes that the reason tropical countries were experiencing net barter terms of trade in 1965 that were unfavorable compared with the situation before World War I was fundamentally that the world price of wheat had risen less than the price of manufactures, owing to sharp increases in U.S. agricultural productivity in the context of relatively immobile farm populations (pp. 24–25).

Emmanuel presents a Marxian model of the terms of trade, based on the labor theory of value. It has a number of similarities with the Lewis view anchored in "unlimited" supplies of labor generated by low-productivity LDC subsistence food sectors, and with the Kindleberger (1956) emphasis on the terms of trade between developing and rich countries, rather than on those between primary and manufactured products. Emmanuel also emphasizes the relatively greater contemporary international mobility of capital (which could include human capital) than of unskilled labor. Empirical work on terms of trade based on the "unequal exchange" thesis has been mostly polemical; of particular interest is the use made by Romanians of this thesis in their arguments with COMECON, as described by Montias (1967, Chap. 4). In this debate, the less developed Romanians argued that they had to spend more labor time to produce a unit of value at world prices than, say, the Czechs, who produce their exports with higher labor productivity. Not surprisingly, the Czechs argued that, so long as world prices were free of monopolistic elements, there was nothing exploitative about such a situation. One may remark, in passing, on the curious fact that some of the Western observers who are the most admiring of the protectionist Romanians are the same who sneer with the most zeal at LDC inward-oriented policies.

On the empirical front, nothing as monumental as Kindleberger's (1956) terms-of-trade study has been forthcoming during the 1960s. The empirical aspects of the Lewis lectures and the Porter (1970) study of postwar price movements of primary products are the main contributions. For the period between the late 1940s through the early 1960s, Porter documents a generally falling trend for the prices of forty-six primary products. He also finds that demand for primary products typically may be very price-inelastic *or* very income-inelastic, but not both. In an interpretation in line with that of Lewis, he suggests that the greater ability of the advanced countries to raise productivity in primary products, presumably nontropicals, is part of the explanation of their increasing domination of the more income-elastic products, a domination which has tended to increase since the late 1930s. Evenson (1973), in turn, suggests that differential productivity advances are partly explained by variations in expenditures on agricultural research and development, a field in which many less developed countries have seriously lagged, particularly outside traditional staples.

The recovery of LDC terms of trade since the early 1960s,

perhaps a partly offsetting consequence of past import-substitution excesses, may also account for the recent scarcity of terms-of-trade studies and the quiet filing of policy proposals linking terms-of-trade movements to domestic or international (e.g., aid) policies. On the other hand, the spectacular success of the Organization of Petroleum Exporting Countries has encouraged those wishing to use commodity agreements to raise selected LDC export prices, while alarming some who only a few years ago emphasized LDC inability to do any such thing.

6. MANAGING LDC FOREIGN-EXCHANGE AVAILABILITIES DURING THE POSTWAR PERIOD: MECHANISMS FOR SUPPRESSING IMPORT DEMAND AND THEIR CONSEQUENCES

Even if the supply of foreign exchange had a zero elasticity with respect to the export exchange rate, the precise nature of the trade regime and of the mechanisms used to repress import demand could have important repercussions for efficiency, income distribution, and growth. For many less developed countries, their postwar trade regimes, featuring differential import exchange rates, high and uneven import duties, import and exchange controls, and prior import deposits, in fact evolved from their policy reaction to the Great Depression of the 1930s, when their supply of foreign exchange was highly inelastic to their export exchange rate, if indeed it did not have a negative elasticity. But once such complex restrictionist regimes were in place, first legitimized by the balance-of-payments crisis, they gradually took on a more openly protectionist nature.

The measurement of the costs and consequences of tariff protection is to be discussed in detail elsewhere in this volume, so two long paragraphs on the subject will suffice here. The use during the 1960s of the concept of effective rates of protection provided additional quantitative tools that documented and dramatized, first, the high and uneven nature of the LDC tariff structure and, later, the same characteristics in the overall net impact of all the import-repressing mechanisms. The recent work of Balassa *et al.* (1971) summarizes and extends this type of research. Balassa finds a considerable degree of discrimination in favor of manufacturing and against primary activities in four of the six developing countries studied in depth, which also have the largest interindustry variation in effective rates of protection. Such variation, it is argued, is *not* the result of conscious and systematic planning decisions, a conclusion also reached by the Desai (1970) study of the Indian Tariff Commission. There may be some political method in such economic madness, however. For the cases of Mexico and Pakistan, Balassa finds large differences between rates of tariff and implicit protection, showing that tariff data will not by themselves appropriately describe the structure of protection in countries that employ quantitative restrictions to limit imports.

Another approach for measuring the extent and consequences of trade restrictionist regimes was pioneered by Bruno (1967) and Krueger (1966), using the concept of domestic resource costs. The relationship of this concept to measures of effective protection have recently been explored (Bruno, 1972, and Krueger, 1972b). In her in-depth study of ten Turkish industries, Krueger has found a significant gap in real domestic resource costs per dollar earned or saved between the lowest-cost import-substitution activity and the most costly potential export industry. She has also found a spread of about 10 to 1 between the highest (an import-substitution firm) and lowest (a potential export firm) domestic resource costs estimated. Yet she notes that Turkish trade policies removed virtually all incentive for the potential export firms studied. Rejecting export pessimism, she tentatively suggests that twice as much output, in value terms, could be obtained from the same resources with a liberalized trade regime and an equilibrium exchange rate. Her results, of course, depend heavily on the across-the-board application of the small-country assumption to all Turkish activities, as well as on the assumption of constant costs. Other related detailed studies of the impact of restrictionist trade regimes in developing countries include those of S. R. Lewis (1969) for Pakistan, L. L. Johnson (1967) for the Chilean automobile industry, and Baranson (1969) for a larger sample of automobile firms in developing countries.

A good part of the typical LDC restrictive trade regime relies neither on general signals transmitted via tariffs and subsidies nor on clear and universal administrative rules but on a maze of ad hoc bureaucratic decisions and obscure rules of thumb. Not without reason, most researchers have tended to stay away from a careful study of this disconcerting reality, preferring to limit themselves to a few well-chosen critical generalizations sure to be received with approval by the rest of the profession. Writers associated with Anglo-Saxon traditions have usually found the labyrinths of quantitative controls somewhat more Kafkaesque and damaging than authors used to Latin bureaucracies but, as

Italy shows, such controls may be compatible with and may survive economic development. Nevertheless, serious studies of these matters have begun to appear, as may be seen in Chapters 15 and 16 of the Bhagwati and Desai (1970) volume for India, and Chapter 8 in the new Krueger (1972a) study of Turkey. Studies on exchange control, liberalization, and economic development, sponsored by the National Bureau of Economic Research (Bhagwati and Krueger, 1973), are on the way. It is generally agreed that quota protection, even more than tariff protection, has been granted and used indiscriminately.

Administrative import and exchange controls are typically blamed for a large number of inefficiencies, many difficult to quantify. Delays and red tape are said to waste private and public entrepreneurial time and energy; require additional clerical staff to handle paperwork in both government and industry; give rise to other extra expenses (e.g., flying back and forth to capital cities to deal with bureaucrats); lead to excessive domestic inventories; have peculiar rules of thumb stimulating overbuilding, capital intensity, and excess capacity; favor large firms and discriminate against new and small entrepreneurs; encourage administrative corruption and smuggling; help to extinguish competition and technological change in domestic markets; slow down the inflow of foreign technology; arbitrarily alter the composition of imports; encourage industrial concentration in the capital city; and, of course, lose potential tax revenue for the state.

Solid empirical documentation of these charges is still scanty. Some of the generalizations may reflect too much the complex psychology of Indian civil servants. Brazilian and Colombian postwar import controls, for example, did not display the Indian tendency to use installed capacity as rigid criteria for allocating import permits, and to encourage machinery rather than intermediate imports in spite of excess capacity due to input shortages. Perhaps the costs of administrative controls become very high only for very large countries or when they are not complemented by substantial reliance on other, more orthodox, import-repressing mechanisms.

At any rate, the key question continues to be how much difference it would make if controls were replaced by more orthodox mechanisms. Noting that under import controls, for example, 100 large firms receive 50 per cent of a country's import permits hardly proves that controls lead to economic concentration, although it may show that controls do not prevent concentration. Observing that import controls coexist with excess capacity or corruption is also not very enlightening. One would have to show, or give persuasive reasons to indicate, that matters would be different in an LSS world, or that they are different in countries without such controls (adjusting for other differences). More on this in the next section.

The study of import-control mechanisms has typically focused on merchandise trade, often leaving aside imports of services. Yet the handling of service payments usually offers *prima facie* evidence of gross inefficiencies and inequities. Without paying the equivalent of import duties, the following persons frequently have access, even if limited, to foreign exchange at overvalued exchange rates: foreign investors in import-substituting activities, tourists, parents of students abroad, users of foreign ships, and users of foreign patents. Particularly in the field of optimal control of imports of technological services, where world markets can hardly be said to be competitive, much empirical and theoretical work remains to be done, in spite of the pioneering work of Vaitsos (1970) and Katz (1972).

One subject receiving increasing empirical attention is illicit transactions, primarily under restrictionist trade regimes. Such illicit transactions include old-fashioned smuggling, inward and outward, and under- or overinvoicing of imports and exports as a way to avoid exchange controls and other departures from unified and equilibrium exchange rates. When alternative trade policies are being weighed, their vulnerability to evasions and corruption is an important consideration (Bhagwati, 1968a). Going beyond unreliable anecdotes, systematic empirical work in this area includes Bhagwati's (1969) study on alleged Turkish fake invoicing, which uses partner-country trade data to obtain presumptive evidence on the degree of faking. For the Pakistani case, Winston (1970) has found that the effective price to the firm of imported capital goods was reduced by more than 45 per cent below its recorded value, as a result of fake overinvoicing of those goods and subsequent illegal exchange transactions. More is expected from the National Bureau of Economic Research project already mentioned, and from a collection of papers on the subject edited by Bhagwati. It may be noted that not only questionable trade policies are vulnerable to corruption and evasion: Colombian and Ghanaian export taxes on coffee and cocoa, respectively, which could be defended on optimum tariff grounds, are also bedeviled by outward smuggling.

Much of the 1960s debate on LDC trade policies suffered from the use of terms such as "import-substitution," "protection," and "promotion," whose exact definitions were often ambiguous. The typical definition of import substitution, that used by Chenery (1960), was devoid of welfare implications. The proportion of total supply of a particular good obtained from imports rather than from domestic production can decrease (i.e., import substitution occurs) either because a tariff is placed on that good, or because devaluation makes imports more expensive, or for a number of other reasons.

Desai (1969) has clarified and called attention to possible alternative definitions of import substitution, some based on optimality notions, and explored various ways of calculating the purely descriptive measure. Alternative descriptive statistical procedures arise from different ways of handling departures from base-year import-availability ratios, degrees of aggregation, and ways of handling intermediate demands generated by import substitution. Both Desai and Diaz-Alejandro (1970, Chap. 4) note the importance of aggregation. The commonly heard remark that import substitution has stopped in many less developed countries because they have been unable to lower their aggregate ratio of imports to supplies can hide two conflicting tendencies: an across-the-board decline in each industry's imports-to-supplies ratio, *and* an increase in the weights of the more import-intensive industries, which may benefit from high income elasticities of demand.

Morley and Smith (1970) note that a given imported good substitutes for the output of many domestic value-adding activities, and that the standard measures for import substitution in a given sector do not quantify the two components of total supply, imports and domestic production, on the same gross-production basis. They show for the Brazilian case that the usual measures underestimate import substitution by domestic intermediate-goods industries, which now supply intermediate value added previously embodied in imports.

7. AFTER THE ROUT: THE NEW TRADE POLICIES AND DEVELOPMENT

On the whole and in spite of theoretical and empirical *lacunae*, evidence does appear robust for the proposition that trade policies in many developing countries during the 1950s and the 1960s left much to be desired. But even under the assumptions that world trade will continue to expand, i.e., that no new 1929s are to be feared, and that most less developed countries have now a variety of policy tools and choices allowing them to tackle distortions directly, important research and policy questions remain: How easy or difficult is the transition between old and new trade policies, both economically and politically? How far must old policies be dismantled and new ones installed to achieve significantly positive developmental results? Even if the old are totally abandoned, how much can be expected from the new trade policies?

Starting already in the late 1950s, many of the semi-industrialized developing countries attempted to liberalize their restrictive trade regimes, while in some cases attempting to check inflation. "Liberalization" is here defined in the Bhagwati and Krueger (1973) sense; it is said to be attempted when there exists the intention to let the official price of foreign exchange assume an increased role in the domestic allocation of resources. Diaz-Alejandro (1965) examined the painful Argentine stabilization and liberalization attempts up to that date, focusing on the large redistributions of income triggered by massive devaluations, and the unsurprising failure of domestic supplies to respond quickly to highly unstable relative prices. The stop–go macro policies arising from the commitment to a pegged rate, sporadically and dramatically devalued every two or three years, were also analyzed in that book. The Turkish case, like that of Argentina, also illustrates the difficulty of distinguishing transitional problems arising from the fight against inflation from those arising from liberalization (Krueger, 1972a, Chap. 4). This, of course, is related to the difficulty of parceling blame for excess costs between uneven inflation and restrictive trade regimes while that not unusual combination is in full bloom.

Somewhat different issues have been raised by the analysis of the 1966 Indian devaluation (Bhagwati and Srinivasan, 1973). In that case, as in the Turkish 1958 devaluation, the impact of the parity change was more than offset by the reduction and removal of surcharges, taxes, and export premia leading to a major difference between nominal and effective devaluations. Assessing the nominal devaluation as if it were also an effective devaluation leads to confusion in public opinion. The 1966 Indian case also illustrates the dangers of liberalizing under pressure from donors of aid, and the importance of timing liberalization attempts with relatively favorable exogenous factors, e.g., good harvests and terms of trade. These two points are also highly relevant for studying the short-run failure of the Colombian 1965–66 liberalization attempt and the friction between many Latin-American governments and institutions such as the IMF. The links between aid, liberalization, and stabilization in Latin America have been examined with particular verve by Hayter (1971).

R. N. Cooper's (1971a and 1971c) impressive review of about three dozen recent devaluations in developing countries also concludes by emphasizing that managing a devaluation through the transition phase to final success requires both judgment and delicacy of handling. He confirms that, although the price level often rises, real aggregate demand frequently falls following a devaluation, and so does the public official linked to the devaluation decision.

By now there is general agreement that stabilization and liberalization attempts should be managed gradually (LSS, Chap. 10); few share the orthodox enthusiasm of the 1950s and early 1960s for shock therapy, which left more than one patient wondering whether the net present discounted benefits of the cure were higher than the present discounted costs of the disease. The recessionary tendencies which frequently accompany stabilization and liberalization plans, contrary to what is expected from devaluation and resource-allocation theory, and which occur even as the rise in the price level accelerates,[9] have been blamed on a variety of factors that seem to operate with different force from country to country. A large redistribution of income may transfer purchasing power from those with high to those with low propensities to spend on locally produced goods. The rise in domestic prices of tradeable goods triggered by devaluation will exert downward pressure on real cash balances, a tendency that may be aggravated by overly restrictive fiscal and monetary policies. In developing countries with rigid and segmented capital markets, this can put severe strains on various compartments of the credit market, such as those providing working capital for industrial firms and for housing and construction, leading to supply-induced output declines in addition to the standard cash-balance effects.

---

9 During the late 1950s and early 1960s many economists from industrialized countries looked upon explanations of the alleged coexistence of output recession with price inflation in semi-industrialized countries with a mixture of amusement and doubts about both the economists proposing explanations and the peculiar economies where such queer happenings were said to occur. As the Argentinization of first the United Kingdom and then the United States advanced during the 1960s and 1970s, one began to hear even from rigorous macroeconomists in the rich countries rather mystical explanations for "stagflation" that were not so different from those offered in semi-industrialized economies in the 1950s.

Cooper (1971b) also notes how devaluation can lower aggregate demand in aid-receiving countries, acting essentially as an excise tax, at least in the short run, and explores wealth effects arising from devaluations in countries with foreign debts. There may also simply be an asymmetrical response to the new incentive structure: sectors subject to new negative signals may pick those up more quickly and effectively than do sectors that should be expanding in response to positive signals.

Not all stabilization and liberalization attempts have led to catastrophe, even if all had to undergo difficulties, and research on happier experiences can tell us something regarding the other two questions raised at the beginning of this section. As noted before, a major point emerges from the successful cases: To reach rapid growth in exports it was *not* necessary to dismantle totally the paraphernalia of controls inherited from the stage of import substitution, nor to enter fully into an orthodox neoclassical, decentralized world. Indeed, as shown in the cases of South Korea (C. Frank, 1972) and, more recently, Colombia, many administrative rules can be quickly turned around and used to encourage new exports, just as they were used before to promote new import-replacing activities. The authorities, in fact, can use existing market distortions (e.g., in the credit market) to give their export-promoting policies greater leverage. As shown by the post-1967 Brazilian example, it is not necessary to eliminate inflation, or even to lower it below 15 per cent per annum, to generate an export boom. Many successful liberalization attempts did not really try to eliminate or massively reduce protection to truly import-competing industries, limiting import-liberalization efforts mainly to goods and services that do not compete with established domestic industry (Michaely, 1973). At any rate, the least-risk strategy is clearly *first* to get exports up and *then* to liberalize imports. This does not appear to be as difficult as many thought a few years ago.

The above gives substance to the earlier suggestion that the conceptualization of trade and development problems of many less developed countries is on firmer ground in "vent for surplus" or in three-sector models (with some factor-market imperfections) in which the competition for resources between the export and the import-competing sectors is mitigated by the existence of a home-good or subsistence sector that can gradually yield resources to both (if the price is right).

This view of liberalization, which is gradualist regarding its timing and marginalist (!) with respect to the degree of change needed in policy instruments to achieve higher export growth rates, gets some support from the argument (Schydlowsky, 1972; Dudley, 1972) that many LDC import-substituting industries developed during the last thirty years are not as inefficient, uncompetitive, and technologically stagnant as the most extreme critics of import substitution suggest. One need not argue, as some do, that the stage of import substitution was a necessary precondition to the development of new exports, to notice that much of the productive capacity created during that stage can be turned around fairly readily toward export expansion. This argument, of course, while tending to decrease the urgency of drastic changes, also indicates that full adoption of neoclassical policies, including devaluations that will partly compensate for lower protection will hurt only the real white elephants, which may not be so numerous.

This view also implies that LDC postwar growth rates have been mostly real after all, even measured at world prices.[10] There is another reason why even developing countries convinced of the excesses of past policies and the need for greater exports may be reluctant to abandon suddenly all exchange and other controls: As one looks around the world in early 1973, one observes many developed countries returning to such practices as exchange controls and dual exchange rates, not to mention wage-price controls. In an uncertain world, it may be wise to hang on to a variety of policy tools.

A lesson emerging from both successful and unsuccessful liberalization attempts, particularly in medium and large countries subject to inflationary pressures, is the great importance of handling devaluations by using crawling pegs rather than the Bretton Woods system of infrequent and large parity changes. Brazilian and Colombian growth rates for exports and GNP, for example, have recently become not only higher but also less unstable, and their crawling pegs seem to have more to do with those results than any profound revision of their protectionist system (Donges, 1971). In other words, improved short-term macroeconomic and balance-of-payments management in inflation-prone, semi-industrialized developing countries may explain

10 As shown by Bhagwati and Hansen (1973b), the usual measure of growth rates based on data at domestic market prices is the correct one if one is looking for an indicator of the development of actual welfare, assuming a well-behaved community-preference map. For other purposes, valuation at international prices is more desirable. But, in general, these authors argue, we cannot tell whether a particular measure "exaggerates" the growth rate.

a larger share of their higher growth rates than does the presumed reallocation of resources from inefficient import-substitution activities toward efficient export lines.

The new policies are clearly yielding higher per capita growth rates in capitalistic developing countries as diverse as South Korea, Brazil, Taiwan, and Colombia. Higher exports have permitted sharply expanded imports of machinery and equipment, and therefore of capital formation. It is noteworthy that Cuban economic authorities, not widely regarded as orthodox neoclassicists, put great emphasis on the link between expanding exports and growing capital formation. The results have been a domestic resource allocation and a Cuban plan that can be characterized as an export-oriented staple-growth strategy.[11] But the impact of new trade policies on LDC domestic savings, other than the impact of easier access to imported capital goods, is unclear and appears secondary to results flowing from policies regarding local capital markets.

Evidence on whether the new policies are reducing the marginal capital-output ratio and, if so, through which mechanisms, is not yet robust. Higher growth rates, by themselves, are known to reduce that ratio. But the new policies could further reduce it by improving resource allocation (Krueger 1972a, Chap. 9) and by using up excess capacity. Reduction of average excess capacity, in turn, can result from the dampening of stop-go cycles, and/or from the elimination of mechanisms through which protectionist trade regimes allegedly stimulated idle installed capital.

The study of excess capacity in less developed countries has picked up considerable steam recently (Winston, 1971; Thoumi, 1972; and Calvo, 1972). But the precise extent to which incorrect LDC trade policies can be blamed for such idle capacity remains obscure. There are several complementary explanations for excess capacity, and many have little or nothing to do with trade policies. It does seem plausible that excess profits induced or renewed by protection could lead to excess entry and Chamberlinian coexistence, or that small domestic markets and indivisibilities could cause many import-replacing projects to have a capacity

---

11 The development consequences of the bizarre blockade imposed on that island by some members of the world trading community, incidentally, have not been yet carefully analyzed. The issues are similar, but hardly identical, to those involved in the study of the impact of wars and the 1930s depression on less developed countries. To study the even more complex issues surrounding massive reorientation in LDC trade links as a result of domestic and foreign political decisions, it is necessary to go way beyond the pure theory of foreign trade, as Hansen and Nashashibi (1972) emphasize in their study of Egypt.

unlikely to be fully used for many years. But the quantitative impact of these and other hypotheses is far from established.

Similar considerations apply to the impact of the new trade policies on LDC employment. Krueger (1972a, Chap. 9) shows that if Turkish investment in manufacturing had been allocated according to sectoral shares in value added or in investment in 1963, not according to the development plan, the same investment volume would have generated greatly increased employment opportunities in manufacturing, besides reducing marginal capital-output ratios and import requirements (see also Power and Sicat, 1971). The evidence on employment growth in Taiwan and South Korea is also impressive (Ranis, 1972), but once again it is difficult to sort out exactly which part can be credited to higher growth rates of aggregate output and which part to other effects, such as the changing composition of output, changing capital-labor ratios, etc.

Sweeping the Leontief paradox under the carpet, even though Baldwin (1971) has pinpointed its source mainly on U.S. trade with Canada, Oceania, and less developed countries, we tend to assume that new LDC exports will be labor intensive, although there are skeptics, such as Sheahan (1971). As many such exports, even those going to world markets and not to free-trade-area partners, come from large (often foreign) firms, which have also been active in import substitution, skepticism regarding the quantitative impact on employment of the change in output mix is further justified.[12] Differences in capital–labor ratios between large and small firms within the same industry can be larger than such differences between sectors. Furthermore, a good share of the new exports are made up, directly or indirectly, by land-intensive primary products, whose labor use may or may not be greater than in import-substituting activities.

There is, after all, one small-country "success story" that has for a long time followed free-trade policies, at least vis-à-vis a major industrial center, and where unemployment continues to be a serious problem. The case of Puerto Rico could be fruitfully used as a near-free-trade comparative benchmark for excess-capacity, capital-intensity, and income-distribution studies, even though (or perhaps because) that island has other notorious market imper-

---

12 Many new LDC exports come from firms which, thanks to protection, still rely on captive domestic markets for most of their sales, and which "dump," say, 10 per cent of their output at marginal cost in world markets. This fact raises the paradoxical possibility that a lowering of protection for the output of such firms may *decrease* their exports, for a given installed capacity.

fections (Reynolds and Gregory, 1965). It should also be noted that there are sound theoretical reasons, besides sticky wages, to expect some LDC unemployment even in small countries that follow optimal trade policies (Fields, 1972). Furthermore, in some developing countries fast export expansion could lead to a relaxation of controls over imports of labor-replacing machinery.

As in the case of LDC rural-supply responses, evidence has been accumulating that substitution possibilities between capital and labor in LDC productive activities are generally *not* zero (Clague, 1969; Fei and Ranis, 1971). But beyond this weak statement, interpretations differ and generalizations become shakier; Behrman (1972), for example, interprets his estimates to imply that Chilean flexibility in response to changes in international markets is limited and that adjustment takes a long time, giving some support to the structuralist view. Behrman also concludes that Eckaus's (1955) technological explanation for LDC unemployment is supported by his results, and finds that sectors generally thought to serve as the predominant absorbers of surplus labor are among those with the most limited estimated substitution possibilities.

Firmer answers to these doubts should also help settle the quantification of how LDC income distributions are likely to react to the new trade policies. As with industrial structure and concentration ratios, differences in income distribution turned up by cross-section studies are not plausibly explained by differences in trade policies (Weisskoff, 1970). Even the allegedly favorable Taiwanese income distribution could have more to do with previous land and educational reforms than with trade policies. Note that, even if the new trade policies trigger massive labor-intensive exports, they are also likely to accelerate GNP growth, and periods of accelerating growth are generally regarded as conducive to growing inequality (Despres, 1973). It is not clear that Stolper–Samuelson will dominate Schumpeter. Furthermore, new land-intensive primary-product exports often come from less developed countries where land ownership is far from evenly distributed. It should be recalled that, even at the theoretical level, generalizations of the Stolper–Samuelson theorem to more than two goods and factors are difficult to interpret, and that the distributional implications of "vent for surplus" and product-cycle trade theories are ambiguous. These skeptical remarks can be extended to the impact of the new trade policies on regional distributions of income and economic activities.

Whether the new trade policies and higher exports significantly stimulate X-efficiency and technological change remains also an empirically open and researchable question. Much seems to depend on the institutional environment in which the new exports are being generated, and on what is regarded as the likely alternative scenario. For example, if those exports are mainly forthcoming from foreign firms training large numbers of local workers and managers, who rapidly leave to work for local firms, the diffusion of new techniques will be greater than if such turnover is low (Cohen, 1972a). But foreign firms, whose great asset is typically "know-how," are unlikely to go out of their way to promote the spread and diffusion of the knowledge on which their power is based. The mechanism through which the bargain on patents and licenses for new exports is struck and the differences between it and the equivalent mechanism for import substitution are also obviously important. Will foreign firms spend more on adapting to local conditions in export or in import-substitution activities, and what does the difference, if any, imply for domestic welfare? Will the new price structure arising from the reformed trade policies induce local and foreign entrepreneurs to search for the "right" innovations in significant amounts, even if credit and labor markets remain imperfect?

The most fundamental doubts about the new trade policies arise not on purely economic grounds, however, but on those related to fuzzier, but no less important, development targets and aspirations. The large role of foreign investors in new export activities, larger perhaps in Latin America than in the Far East, has been already documented (Vernon, 1971) and is likely to become greater than it was under the import-substitution strategy (Helleiner, 1973; de la Torre, 1972). Many LDC exports will consist not of finished products but of semi-finished commodities, which are also imported in a somewhat less finished state, both being part of vertically integrated international industries. Like workers in an assembly line, less developed countries will, in those cases, have little knowledge of what comes before or after them in the production process; that knowledge will be reserved for those running the whole operation from abroad. Thus, even as LDC control over traditional natural-resource exports tends to grow, their control over new exports could start from a very low base, renewing a sense of dependency and frustration. Even intra-LDC trade stimulated by customs unions could easily become dominated by non-LDC firms.

If large exports of labor-intensive goods materialize, the need for wage and labor "discipline" will grow, a discipline likely to be exerted either by the reserve army of the unemployed or, particularly when surplus labor dries up, by the *other* army. Indeed, it is disconcerting that neoclassical liberal policies are more often than not pursued by LDC regimes with notoriously illiberal politics, while democratic LDC governments typically provide a good share of horror-show inefficiency stories. It is also a bit unseemly that some of those who are eager to promote the new exports, and who become outraged at income inequalities arising from the higher wages of the "aristocracy of the proletariat," appear to get much less excited about other income inequalities.

8. CONCLUDING REMARKS

The scholarly community should be kept busy documenting and analyzing the various possible development consequences of the new LDC trade policies. The task must include improving and extending the available data base. In particular, fresh insights are most likely to come from disaggregated and sample data than from further manipulation of rather dog-eared national accounts and other macroeconomic aggregates. Meanwhile, as always, LDC trade policies will react, and should react, to trends in the world economy. In spite of recurrent monetary crises and threats of commercial wars among the rich, the less developed countries face a world market on the whole prosperous and diversified. It is in their interest to stimulate such diversification and, in particular, to fight trends toward domination of the world market for trade, finance, and technology by either a few countries or a few multinational corporations. In trade-policy discussions, it is frequently too glibly assumed that domestic monopoly problems can be resolved simply by pulling down import barriers and letting "world competition" do the job. Alas, in some sectors even the whole world market may not be big enough and diversified enough to allow sufficient competition. LDC investments in expanding their own networks of information and intelligence gathering about imperfect and uncertain world markets for commodities, technology, and finance (i.e., a kind of LDC "Consumer Reports") should become a key element of their trade policies. These countries could profitably rethink their acceptance of world arrangements such as the Paris patents convention, which appear to benefit mainly the rich. They also have an interest in new international monetary rules which minimize the possibility that rich countries will thrust the burden of adjusting their balance of payments onto less developed ones. Sudden unilateral import surcharges, defaults on the convertibility of debts, etc., are no monopoly of developing countries, as recent actions by rich countries faced with payments problems show.[13]

How willing the rich will be to accommodate their economies to new LDC exports remains a difficult matter to forecast exactly. Yet a good share of the heated debate on how far less developed countries should go in adopting this or that trade policy typically depends on often implicit assumptions regarding world demand. The key "staple" for many resource-poor contemporary developing countries is simply unskilled labor; particularly for the large ones, it is unlikely that exports of this "staple" can reach the relative development significance that wheat, timber, meat, etc., had in the last century for the development of the success stories of that time, when their populations represented tiny fractions of world totals. It is also unclear to what extent the rich will permit those developing countries choosing to be outward-oriented in trade, but reluctant to permit foreigners to handle their new exports, to take advantage of wealthy markets. Yet this combination is perhaps the most appealing to developing countries worried about both exchange earnings and national autonomy (Myint, 1969). In view of these uncertainties, developing countries would do well to continue working toward the creation and expansion of common markets among themselves, in ways that minimize the repetition of past errors in import substitution.

Much empirical research remains to be done on the exact impact of the new export expansion on growth, employment, income distribution, and national autonomy in different types of developing countries. But it should be added that the rout of export pessimism has not been a pyrrhic victory,[14] nor are the

---

13 World financial disorder and inflation during the late 1960s and early 1970s probably had a positive net effect on less developed countries, however. When the 1930s Depression hit, and the world price level fell unexpectedly, LDC long-term foreign debts typically exceeded their short-term foreign-exchange assets. During World War II and its aftermath, when the world price level rose, LDC exchange reserves exceeded their foreign debts. For a change, during the recent world inflation the long-term foreign debt exceeded exchange reserves in most developing countries, excepting mainly oil countries, thus partly providing the real debt relief sought by many (see, e.g., Pearson, et al., 1969, Chap. 8).

14 Although written while discussing rich-country policies, the following warning by Samuelson (1972, p. 450) is relevant here: "There are correctly formulated systems in which elasticity pessimism is a correct doctrine rooted in irremovable real elements. Our world may not be like such models. And no doubt many writers of the late 1940s were paranoid on this subject. That does not mean we can take as established, either by valid deductive reasoning or plausible inference from the experiences of the last two decades, that 'elasticity optimism' is assuredly correct. The jury is still out on this empirical question...."

achievements described in the recent trade and development literature to be dismissed lightly. The air has been cleared of nightmarish myths dreamed up mainly in the 1930s, and important analytical tools have been developed to help LDC authorities avoid, if the political will exists, at least the worst errors in evaluating projects related to the foreign sector (Bacha and Taylor, 1971; Little and Mirrlees, 1969). Suitably employed, economists who know the shadow price of everything and the social worth of nothing are more useful than bureaucrats who know neither. Studies on crawling pegs led to gradual acceptance of that technique. Indeed, it can be argued that the major contribution of research on trade policies during the 1960s has been to provide concepts and tools that should make exchange crises, trade problems, etc., less of a pressing preoccupation to LDC policy makers during the 1970s. The ridiculous extent to which LDC public opinion followed every new local balance-of-payments crisis can be made largely a thing of the past, allowing policy makers to turn, if they have the will, to really basic development problems such as mass poverty and low rural productivity. We have little to say on those problems, but perhaps our conscience is saved by showing policy makers how to avoid letting the basically small problems of trade and payments policy absorb too much of their attention. Many of us who look at development through international-trade glasses may have trouble accepting the fact that trade policies are a small part of the development problem for most large and medium-sized less developed countries. Furthermore, as good firemen, our efforts during the 1960s have already helped to make such part even smaller, freeing development planning from the tyranny of avoidable payments crises. But only those aspiring to use their knowledge of trade theory to play the role of world savior should object to being labeled simply honest craftsmen, with few magic formulas and much empirical homework to do.[15]

REFERENCES

Bacha, E., and L. Taylor, "Foreign Exchange Shadow Prices: A Critical Review of Current Theories," *Quarterly Journal of Economics*, 85 (May 1971), pp. 197–224.

[15] A reviewer of books on the lives of G. D. H. Cole and Lord Robbins recently suggested that "....economics is more a matter of temperament than the research of scientific conclusions from an objective survey of the evidence" (Paul Johnson, *The New York Times*, book review section, Jan. 7, 1973). I hope this will be less true in the future than it has been in the past for the field of trade policy and development.

Baer, W., *The Development of the Brazilian Steel Industry*, Nashville, Vanderbilt University Press, 1969.

"Import Substitution Industrialization in Latin America: Experiences and Interpretations," *Latin American Research Review*, 7 (Spring 1972), pp. 95–122.

Balassa, B., "The Purchasing-Power Parity Doctrine: A Reappraisal," *Journal of Political Economy*, 72 (December 1964), pp. 584–596.

"Resource Allocation and Economic Integration in Latin America," mimeographed, 1966.

Balassa, B., *et al.*, *The Structure of Protection in Developing Countries*, Baltimore, The Johns Hopkins Press, 1971.

Baldwin, R. E., "Determinants of the Commodity Structure of U.S. Trade," *American Economic Review*, 61 (March 1971), pp. 126–47.

Baldwin, R. E., *et al.*, eds., *Trade, Growth and the Balance of Payments*, Chicago, Rand McNally, 1965.

Baldwin, R. E., and J. H. Mutti, "Policy Problems in the Adjustment Process (U.S.)," mimeographed, University of Wisconsin, 1972.

Baranson, J., *Automotive Industries in Developing Countries*, World Bank Occasional and Staff Papers, No. 8, Washington, 1969.

Bardhan, P. K., *Economic Growth, Development and Foreign Trade*, New York, Wiley, 1970.

Behrman, J. R., *Supply Response in Underdeveloped Agriculture*, Amsterdam, North-Holland, 1968.

"Sectoral Elasticities of Substitution between Capital and Labor in a Developing Economy: Time Series Analysis in the Case of Postwar Chile," *Econometrica*, 40 (March 1972), pp. 311–327.

Bergsman, J., *Brazil: Industrialization and Trade Policies*, London, Oxford University Press, 1970.

Bhagwati, J., *The Theory and Practice of Commercial Policy: Departures from Unified Exchange Rates*, Special Papers in International Economics No. 8, Princeton, N.J., 1968a.

"Distortions and Immiserising Growth: A Generalization," *Review of Economic Studies*, 35 (October 1968b), pp. 481–485.

Trade, Tariffs and Growth, Cambridge, Mass., M.I.T. Press, 1969.

"The Generalized Theory of Distortions and Welfare," in Bhagwati *et al.*, eds., (1971, pp. 69–90).

Bhagwati, J., *et al.*, eds., *Trade, Balance of Payments and Growth*, Amsterdam, North-Holland, 1971.

Bhagwati, J., and P. Desai, *India, Planning for Industrialization: Industrialization and Trade Policies since 1951*, London, Oxford University Press, 1970.

Bhagwati, J., and B. Hansen, "A Theoretical Analysis of Smuggling," *Quarterly Journal of Economics*, 87 (May 1973a), pp. 172–188.

"Should Growth Rates Be Evaluated at International Prices?" in J. Bhagwati and R. S. Eckaus, eds., *Development and Planning*, London, Allen & Unwin, 1973b.

Bhagwati, J., and A. O. Krueger, "Exchange Control, Liberalization, and Economic Development," *American Economic Review*, 63 (May 1973), pp. 419–427.

Bhagwati, J., and T. N. Srinivasan, "Exchange Control, Liberalization and Development: India," mimeographed, 1973.

Birnberg, T., "Dynamic Properties of Colonial Development," Yale Growth Center Discussion Paper No. 156, New Haven, 1972.

Birnberg, T., and B. Cohen, "A Theoretical Analysis of Partial Economic Reform," Yale Growth Center Discussion Paper No. 135, New Haven, 1971.

Birnberg, T., and S. Resnick, "A Model of the Trade and Government Sectors in Colonial Economies," Yale Growth Center Discussion Paper No. 130, New Haven, 1971.

Brainard, W., and R. N. Cooper, "Uncertainty and Diversification in International Trade," *Food Research Institute Studies in Agricultural Economics, Trade, and Development,* 8 (1968), pp. 257–285.

Brecher, R., "Minimum Wage Rates and the Pure Theory of International Trade," Yale Growth Center Discussion Paper No. 140, New Haven, 1972.

Bruno, M., "The Optimal Selection of Export-Promoting and Import-Substituting Projects," in *Planning the External Sector: Techniques, Problems, Policies,* New York, United Nations, 1967, pp. 88–135.

"Domestic Resource Costs and Effective Protection: Clarification and Synthesis," *Journal of Political Economy,* 80 (January/February 1972), pp. 16–33.

Bruton, H., "The Two-Gap Approach to Aid and Development," *American Economic Review,* 59)june 1969), pp. 439–446.

"The Import Substitution Strategy of Economic Development," *Pakistan Development Review,* 10 (Summer 1970), pp. 123–146.

Calvo, G., "A Theory of Capacity Utilization with an Application to Electricity Generation in Colombia," mimeographed, Columbia University, 1972.

Caves, R. E., "'Vent for Surplus' Models of Trade and Growth," in Baldwin *et al.,* eds. (1965, pp. 95–115).

"Export-Led Growth and the New Economic History," in Bhagwati *et al.,* eds. (1971a, pp. 403–443).

"International Corporations: The Industrial Economics of Foreign Investment," *Economica,* 38 (February 1971b), pp. 1–27.

Chambers, E., and D. F. Gordon, "Primary Products and Economic Growth: An Empirical Measurement," *Journal of Political Economy,* 74 (August 1966), pp. 315–322.

Chenery, H., "Patterns of Industrial Growth," *American Economic Review,* 50 (September 1960), pp. 624–654.

"The Normally Developing Country," mimeographed, Harvard University, 1970a.

"Alternative Patterns of Development," mimeographed, Harvard University, 1970b.

Chenery, H. B., ed., *Studies in Development Planning,* Cambridge, Mass., Harvard University Press, 1971.

Chenery, H., and M. Bruno, "Development Alternatives in an Open Economy: The Case of Israel," *Economic Journal,* 72 (March 1962), pp. 79–103.

Chenery, H., and Nicholas Carter, "International External Aspects of Development Plans and Performance," mimeographed, Washington, 1972.

Chenery, H., and W. J. Raduchel, "Substitution in Planning Models," in Chenery, ed. (1971, pp. 29–47).

Chenery, H., and A. M. Strout, "Foreign Assistance and Economic Development," *American Economic Review,* 56 (September 1966), pp. 679–733.

Chenery, H., and L. Taylor, "Development Patterns: Among Countries and Over Time," *Review of Economics and Statistics,* 50 (November 1968), pp. 391–417.

Clague, C. K., "Capital-Labor Substitution in Manufacturing in Underdeveloped Countries," *Econometrica* 37 (July 1969), pp. 528–537.

144 Trade, protection, and domestic production

Cohen, B. I., "The Less-Developed Countries' Exports of Primary Products," *Economic Journal*, 78 (June 1970), pp. 334–343.

"The Economic Impact of Foreign Investments for the Export of Manufactures: A Tentative Study of South Korea," Yale Growth Center Discussion Paper No. 136, New Haven, 1972a.

"An Alternative Theoretical Approach to the Impact of Foreign Investment on The Host Country," Yale Growth Center Discussion Paper No. 164, New Haven, 1972b.

Cohen, B. I., and G. Ranis, "The Second Postwar Restructuring," in Ranis, ed., (1971).

Cohen, B. I., and D. Sisler, "Exports of Developing Countries in the 1960s," *Review of Economics and Statistics*, 53 (November 1971), pp. 354–362.

Cooper, C., and B. Massel, "Towards a General Theory of Customs Unions for Developing Countries," *Journal of Political Economy*, 78 (October 1965), pp. 461–476.

Cooper, R. N., "An Assessment of Currency Devaluation in Developing Countries," in Ranis, ed., (1971a, pp. 472–512).

"Devaluation and Aggregate Demand in Aid-Receiving Countries," in Bhagwati *et al.*, eds. (1971b, pp. 355–377).

Currency Devaluation in Developing Countries, Princeton Essays in International Finance No. 86, Princeton, N.J., 1971c.

Corden, W. M., "The Effects of Trade on the Rate of Growth," in Bhagwati *et al.*, eds. (1971, pp. 117–144).

de la Torre, J. R., "Foreign Investment and Export Dependency," mimeographed, Harvard University, 1972.

Despres, E., "Dimensions and Dilemmas of Economic Development," in G. M. Meier, ed., *International Monetary Reform: Collected Papers of Emile Despres*, New York, Oxford University Press, 1973, pp. 89–99 (written in 1963).

Desai, P., "Alternative Measures of Import Substitution," *Oxford Economic Papers*, 21 (November 1969), pp. 312–325.

Tariff Protection and Industrialization, Delhi, Hindustan Publishing, 1970.

De Vries, B. A., *Export Experiences of Developing Countries*, World Bank Staff Occasional Paper, No. 3, Baltimore, Johns Hopkins Press, 1967.

Diaz-Alejandro, C. F., *Exchange Rate Devaluation in a Semi-Industrialized Country*, Cambridge, Mass., M.I.T. Press, 1965.

Essays on the Economic History of the Argentine Republic, New Haven, Yale University Press, 1970.

Donges, J. B., *Brazil's Trotting Peg: A New Approach to Greater Exchange Rate Flexibility in Less Developed Countries*, Washington, American Enterprise Institute, 1971.

Dudley, L., "Learning and Productivity Change in Metal Products," *American Economic Review*, 62 (September 1972), pp. 662–669.

Eaton, J. W. "Effective Devaluation as an Export Incentive in Less Developed Countries," senior thesis, Harvard University, March 1972.

Eckaus, R. S., "The Factor Proportions Problem in Underdeveloped Areas," *American Economic Review*, 45 (September 1955), pp. 539–565.

Emmanuel, A., *Unequal Exchange: A Study of the Imperialism of Trade*, New York, MR Press, 1972.

Erb, G. F., and S. Schiavo-Campo, "Export Instability, Level of Development, and Economic Size of Less Developed Countries," *Bulletin of the Oxford*

University Institute of Economics and Statistics, 31 (November 1969), pp. 263–283.

Evenson, R., "Agricultural Trade and Shifting Comparative Advantage," mimeographed, Yale University, 1973.

Fei, J. C. H., and G. Ranis, "Foreign Assistance and Economic Development," *American Economic Review,* 58 (September 1968), pp. 897–912.
"Development and Employment in the Open Dualistic Economy," Yale Growth Center Discussion Paper No. 110, New Haven, 1971.

Fields, G. S., "Rural-Urban Migration, Urban Unemployment and Underemployment, and Job Search Activity in LDCs," Yale Growth Center Discussion Paper No. 168, New Haven, 1972.

Findlay, R., *Trade and Specialization,* Baltimore, Penguin Books, 1970.
"The 'Foreign Exchange Gap' and Growth in Developing Countries," in Bhagwati *et al.,* eds. (1971, pp. 168–183).
"Primary Exports and Manufacturing Production in the Development of a Dual Economy," mimeographed, Columbia University, 1972.

Frank, A. G., "The Development of Underdevelopment," In R. I. Rhoades, ed., *Imperialism and Underdevelopment,* New York, MR Press, 1970.

Frank, Jr., C., *Exchange Control, Liberalization and Economic Development: South Korea,* mimeographed, Princeton University, 1972.

Furtado, C., "Dependencia Externa y Teoria Economica," *El Trimestre Económico,* 38 (April–June 1971), pp. 335–351.

Girvan, N., "The Development of Dependency Economics in the Caribbean and Latin America: Review and Comparison," mimeographed, University of the West Indies, Mona, Jamaica, 1972.

Grunwald, J., M. S. Wionczek, and M. Carnoy, *Latin American Economic Integration and U. S. Policy,* Washington, The Brookings Institution, 1972.

Haberler, G., "Some Problems in the Pure Theory of International Trade," *Economic Journal,* 60 (June 1950), pp. 223–240.

Halevi, N., "Effective Devaluation and Exports: Some Issues in Empirical Analysis, with illustrations from Israel," *Economica,* 39 (August 1972), pp. 292–300.

Hansen, B., and K. Nashashibi, "Exchange Control, Liberalization and Economic Development: Egypt, from Free Trade to Arab Socialism," mimeographed, University of California, Berkeley, 1972.

Hansen, R., *Central America: Regional Integration and Economic Development,* National Planning Association Studies in Development Progress, No. 1, Washington, 1967.

Harberger, A. C. "Using the Resources at Hand More Effectively," *American Economic Review,* 49 (May 1959), pp. 134–146.

Hayter, T., *Aid as Imperialism,* Baltimore, Penguin Books, 1971.

Helleiner, G. K., *Peasant Agriculture, Government and Economic Growth in Nigeria,* Homewood, Ill., Irwin, 1966.
International Trade and Economic Development, Baltimore, Penguin Books, 1972.
"Manufactured Exports from Less Developed Countries and Multinational Firms," *Economic Journal,* 83 (March 1973), pp. 21–48.

Hicks, G. L., and G. McNicoll, *Trade and Growth in the Philippines,* Ithaca, Cornell University Press, 1971.

Hirschman, A. O., "The Political Economy of Import Substituting Industrialization in Latin America," *Quarterly Journal of Economics*, 87 (February 1968), pp. 1–32.

Hsing, M., J. Power, and G. P. Sicat, *Taiwan and the Philippines; Industrialization and Trade Policies*, London, Oxford University Press, 1970.

Hymer, S., and S. Resnick, "A Model of an Agrarian Economy with Non-Agricultural Activities," *American Economic Review*, 59 (September 1969), pp. 493–506.

"International Trade and Uneven Development," in Bhagwati *et al.*, eds. (1971, pp. 473–494).

Johnson, H. G., "The Cost of Protection and the Scientific Tariff," *Journal of Political Economy*, 68 (August 1960), pp. 327–345.

"Optimal Trade Intervention in the Presence of Domestic Distortions," in Baldwin *et al.*, eds., (1965a, pp. 3–34).

"The Costs of Protection and Self-Sufficiency," *Quarterly Journal of Economics*, 79 (August 1965b), pp. 356–372.

"Factor Market Distortions and the Shape of the Transformation Curve," *Econometrica*, 34 (July 1966), pp. 686–698.

"The Possibility of Income Losses from Increased Efficiency or Factor Accumulation in the Presence of Tariffs," *Economic Journal*, 77 (March 1967), pp. 151–154.

"The State of Theory in Relation to the Empirical Analysis," in R. Vernon, ed., *The Technology Factor in International Trade*, New York, Columbia University Press, 1970a, pp. 9–21.

"A Note on Distortions and the Rate of Growth of an Open Economy," *Economic Journal*, 80 (December 1970b), pp. 990–992.

Johnson, L. L., "Problems of Import Substitution: The Chilean Automobile Industry," *Economic Development and Cultural Change*, 15 (January 1967), pp. 202–216.

Jones, R. W., "International Capital Movements and the Theory of Tariffs and Trade," *Quarterly Journal of Economics*, 81 (February 1967), pp. 1–38.

Katz, J., *Importacion de Tecnologia, Aprendizaje Local e Industrializacion Dependiente*, Buenos Aires, Instituto Torcuato Di Tella, 1972.

Keesing, D. B., "Outward-Looking Policies and Economic Development," *Economic Journal*, 77 (June 1967), pp. 303–320.

Kemp, M., "The Gain from International Trade and Investment: A Neo-Heckscher-Ohlin Approach," *American Economic Review*, 56 (September 1966), pp. 788–809.

Kenen, P. B., and C. S. Voivodas, "Export Instability and Economic Growth," *Kyklos*, 25 (Fasc. 4, 1972), pp. 791–805.

Kindleberger, C. P., "Group Behavior and International Trade," *Journal of Political Economy*, 59 (February 1951), pp. 30–47.

The Terms of Trade: A European Case Study, Cambridge, Mass., M.I.T. Press, 1956.

Foreign Trade and the National Economy, New Haven, Yale University Press, 1962.

King, T., *Mexico: Industrialization and Trade Policies since 1940*, London, Oxford University Press, 1970.

Kravis, I. B., "Trade as a Handmaiden of Growth: Similarities between the Nineteenth and Twentieth Centuries," *Economic Journal*, 80 (December 1970), pp. 850–873.

"The Role of Exports in Nineteenth Century United States Growth," *Economic Development and Cultural Change*, 20 (April 1972), pp. 387–406.

Krueger, A. O., "Some Economic Costs of Exchange Control: The Turkish Case," *Journal of Political Economy*, 74 (October 1966), pp. 466–480.

Exchange Control, Liberalization and Development: Turkey, mimeographed, University of Minnesota, Minneapolis, 1972a.

"Evaluating Restrictionist Trade Regimes: Theory and Measurement," *Journal of Political Economy*, 80 (January/February 1972b), pp. 48–62.

Kuznets, S., *Modern Economic Growth*, New Haven, Yale University Press, 1966.

"Quantitative Aspects of the Economic Growth of Nations: X. Level and Structure of Foreign Trade: Long-Term Trends," *Economic Development and Cultural Change*, 15 (January 1967, part 2), pp. 1–140.

Landau, L., "Saving Functions for Latin America," in Chenery, ed., (1971, pp. 299–321).

Leff, N. H., *The Brazilian Capital Goods Industry, 1929–1964*, Cambridge, Mass., Harvard University Press, 1968.

"Economic Development and Regional Inequality: Origins of the Brazilian Case," *Quarterly Journal of Economics*, 86 (May 1972a), pp. 243–263.

"Economic Retardation in Nineteenth Century Brazil," *Economic History Review*, 25 (August 1972b), pp. 489–507.

Leibenstein, H., "Allocative Efficiency vs. 'X-efficiency'," *American Economic Review*, 56 (June 1966), pp. 392–415.

Lewis, S. R., *Economic Policy and Industrial Growth in Pakistan*, Cambridge, Mass., M.I.T. Press, 1969.

Pakistan: Industrialization and Trade Policy, London, Oxford University Press, 1970.

Lewis, W. A., *Aspects of Tropical Trade, 1883–1965*, Stockholm, Almquist and Wiksell, 1969.

Linder, S. B., *An Essay on Trade and Transformation*, Stockholm, Almquist and Wiksell, 1961.

Lipsey, R. G., and K. Lancaster, "The General Theory of the Second Best," *Review of Economic Studies*, 24 (1956–57), pp. 11–32.

Little, I. M. D., *A Critique of Welfare Economics*, Oxford, Oxford University Press, 1950.

Little, I. M. D., and J. A. Mirrlees, *Social Cost-Benefit Analysis, Manual of Industrial Project Analysis in Developing Countries*, Vol. II, Paris, OECD Development Centre, 1969.

Little, I. M. D., T. Scitovsky, and M. Scott, *Industry and Trade in Some Developing Countries*, London, Oxford University Press, 1970.

Macario, S., "Protectionism and Industrialization in Latin America," *Economic Bulletin for Latin America*, 9 (March 1964), pp. 61–102.

MacBean, A. I., *Export Instability and Economic Development*, Cambridge, Mass., Harvard University Press, 1966.

McKinnon, R., "Foreign Exchange Constraints in Economic Development and Efficient Aid Allocation," *Economic Journal*, 74 (June 1964), pp. 388–409.

Magee, S. P., "The Welfare Effects of Restrictions on U.S. Trade," *Brookings Papers on Economic Activity* 3 (1972), pp. 645–702.

Mamalakis, M. J., and C. W. Reynolds, *Essays on the Chilean Economy,* Homewood, Ill., Irwin, 1965.

Massel, B. F., "Export Instability and Economic Structure," *American Economic Review,* 60 (September 1970), pp. 618–630.

Mathieson, D., and R. McKinnon, "Instability in Underdeveloped Countries: The Impact of the International Economy," mimeographed, Stanford University, 1972.

Meade, J. E., *Trade and Welfare,* London, Oxford University Press, 1955.

Meier, G. M., *The International Economics of Development,* New York, Harper and Row, 1968.

Michaely, M., *Exchange Control, Liberalization and Development: Israel,* mimeographed, The Hebrew University, Jerusalem, 1973.

Montias, J. M., *Economic Development in Communist Rumania,* Cambridge, Mass., M.I.T. Press, 1967.

Morawetz, D., "Economic Integration among Less Developed Countries with Special Reference to the Andean Group," Ph.D. thesis, Cambridge, Mass., M.I.T., 1972.

Morley, S. A., and G. W. Smith, "On the Measurement of Import Substitution," *American Economic Review,* 60 (September 1970), pp. 728–735.

Myint, H., "International Trade and the Developing Countries," in P. A. Samuelson, ed., *International Economic Relations,* New York, St. Martin's Press, 1969, pp. 15–35.

Myrdal, G., *An International Economy,* New York, Harper, 1956.

Nelson, R. R., "A 'Diffusion' Model of International Productivity Differences in Manufacturing Industry," *American Economic Review,* 58 (December 1968), pp. 1219–1248.

"Recent Exercises in Growth Accounting: New Understanding or Dead End?" *American Economic Review,* 63 (June 1973), pp. 462–468.

Nelson, R. R., T. Paul Schultz, and R. Slighton, *Structural Change in a Developing Economy,* Princeton, Princeton University Press, 1971.

Nelson, R. R., and S. Winter, "Evolutionary vs. Neoclassical Theories of Economic Growth," mimeographed, Yale University, 1972.

Nowshirvani, V., "The Efficacy of the Market Mechanism in Traditional Agriculture: A Reexamination of an Old Controversy," Yale Growth Center Discussion Paper No. 106, (New Haven, 1971).

Papanek, G. F., "The Effect of Aid and Other Resource Transfers on Savings and Growth in Less Developed Countries," *Economic Journal,* 82 (September 1972), pp. 934–951.

"Aid, Foreign Private Investment, Savings, and Growth in Less Developed Countries," *Journal of Political Economy,* 81 (January/February 1973), pp. 120–131.

Pearson, L. B., *et al., Partners in Development,* New York, Praeger, 1969.

Pinto, A., "Notas Sobre Desarrollo, Subdesarrollo y Dependencias," *El Trimestre Económico,* 39 (April-June 1972), pp. 243–265.

Porter, R. C., "Some Implications of Post-War Primary-Product Trends," *Journal of Political Economy,* 78 (May/June 1970), pp. 586–597.

Power, J. H., and G. P. Sicat, *The Philippines: Industrialization and Trade Policies,* London, Oxford University Press, 1971.

Prebisch, R., "Commercial Policy in the Underdeveloped Countries," *American Economic Review*, 49 (May 1959), pp. 251–273.

Pryor, F. L., "An International Comparison of Concentration Ratios," *Review of Economics and Statistics*, 54 (May 1972), pp. 130–141.

Ranis, G., "Technology Choice, Adaptation and Its Impact on Industrial Sector Labor Absorption in Developing Countries: A Review of Evidence," mimeographed, Yale University, 1972.

Ranis, G., ed., *Government and Economic Development*, New Haven, Yale University Press, 1971.

Ranis, G., and J. C. H. Fei, "A Theory of Economic Development," *American Economic Review*, 51 (September 1961), pp. 533–565.

Resnick, S., "The Decline of Rural Industry under Export Expansion: A Comparison among Burma, Philippines and Thailand," *Journal of Economic History*, 30 (March 1970), pp. 51–73.

Reynolds, L. G., and P. Gregory, *Wages, Productivity and Industrialization in Puerto Rico*, Homewood, Ill., Irwin, 1965.

Roemer, M., *Fishing for Growth: Export-Led Development in Peru, 1950–1967*, Cambridge, Mass., Harvard University Press, 1970.

Samuelson, P. A., "Heretical Doubts about the International Mechanism," *Journal of International Economics*, 2 (September 1972), pp. 443–455.

Schydlowsky, D. M., "Latin American Trade Policies in the 1970s," *Quarterly Journal of Economics*, 86 (May 1972), pp. 263–290.

Sheahan, J., "Trade and Employment: Industrial Exports Compared to Import Substitution in Mexico," mimeographed, Williams College, 1971.

"Import Substitution and Economic Policy: A Second Review," mimeographed, Williams College, 1972.

Sunkel, O., "National Development Policy and External Dependence in Latin America," *Journal of Development Studies*, 6 (October 1969), pp. 23–48.

Taylor, L., "Short-Term Policy in Open Developing Economies: The Narrow Limits of the Possible," mimeographed, Harvard University, 1973.

Thoumi, F. E., "Industrial Capacity Utilization in Colombia: Some Empirical Findings," mimeographed, Washington, April 1972.

Triffin, R., "The Myth and Realities of the So-Called Gold Standard," Chap. 1 in *Our International Monetary System: Yesterday, Today and Tomorrow*, New York, Random House, 1968, pp. 3–28.

United Nations, Economic Commission for Latin America, *El Desarrollo Económico de la Argentina*, Mexico, Naciones Unidas, 1959.

Vaitsos, C., "Transfer of Resources and Preservation of Monopoly Rent," Center for International Affairs, Economic Development Report No. 168, Cambridge, Mass., Harvard University, 1970.

Vanek, J., *Estimating Foreign Resource Needs for Economic Development*, New York, McGraw-Hill, 1967.

Vernon, R., *Sovereignty at Bay: The Multinational Spread of U.S. Enterprises*, New York, Basic Books, 1971.

Weisskoff, R., "Income Distribution and Economic Growth in Puerto Rico, Argentina, and Mexico," *Review of Income and Wealth,* 16 (December 1970), pp. 303–333.

Weisskopf, T. E., "An Econometric Test of Alternative Constraints on the Growth of Underdeveloped Countries," *Review of Economics and Statistics,* 54 (February 1972a), pp. 67–78.

"The Impact of Foreign Capital Inflow on Domestic Savings in Under- developed Countries," *Journal of International Economics,* 2 (February 1972b), pp. 25–38.

Williams, J. H., "The Theory of International Trade Reconsidered," *Economic Journal,* 39 (June 1929), 195–209.

Willmore, L. N., "Free Trade in Manufactures among Developing Countries: The Central American Experience," *Economic Development and Cultural Change,* 20 (July 1972), pp. 659–670.

Winston, G. C., "Overinvoicing, Underutilization and Distorted Industrial Growth," *Pakistan Development Review,* 10 (Winter 1970), pp. 405–421.

"Capital Utilization in Economic Development," *Economic Journal,* 81 (March 1971), pp. 36–60.

DISCUSSION

TESTING TRADE THEORIES: A COMMENT

Robert E. Baldwin

I have been asked to focus particular attention on Stern's paper. Stern has, I think, provided us with an excellent, comprehensive survey of trade theories, together with the results and the difficulties of testing these theories. I shall therefore limit my comments to some of the issues he raises concerning the directions in which we should now try to move on both the theoretical and empirical levels.

The present state of trade theory is far from satisfactory. Tests of the Heckscher–Ohlin factor-proportions theory have shown that, at least in its simple form, it does not perform very well in predicting the commodity composition and direction of trade. As yet, however, we do not have a well worked out theory to replace it. We have lots of bits and pieces with which to amend the Heckscher–Ohlin approach, but we do not know how significant each part is or how the parts are tied together. Consequently, most of us, in presenting the pure-theory side of trade to our students, still spend considerable time carefully building up the simple Heckscher–Ohlin–Samuelson trade model and then examining such theorems as the Stopler–Samuelson proposition, the Rybczynski effect, and the factor-price equalization theorem. The appeal of the model, of course, is that it enables us to relate price changes all the way back to the distribution of income. However, when we finally talk about empirical tests of trade theories, students are not the only ones who wonder if all the time spent on the model was worthwhile.

Yet the so-called "new" theories of trade involve not too much more than a listing of various factors that affect comparative costs. This is not a great deal better than starting with labor-productivity differences to explain trade patterns. A helpful development on the empirical level would be the acquisition of better measures of these various factors affecting comparative costs. This would enable us to make better estimates of their relative importance in shaping trade patterns. The human-capital and technology variables illustrate this need. As Stern points out, trying to measure the human-capital variable by differences in wages has the drawback that part of these differences may simply be due to market imper-

151

fections. Similarly, years or costs of education do not take account of on-the-job training. Using ratios of, say, professional and technical workers to total workers also has drawbacks. One might find this ratio to be low in a particular industry, yet the ratio of craftsmen to total workers in the industry to be high. What then do we conclude from such arbitrary classifications about the overall skill or human-capital requirements in the industry? The technology factor is even more difficult to measure. Often the relative importance of scientists and engineers in an industry is used as a proxy for this variable. One difficulty with this measure is that, except on a quite aggregative level, it is not possible to separate the scientists and engineers undertaking research from those using their skills to facilitate production under known techniques. Even if we could obtain these figures or obtain estimates of R & D expenditures by industry on a detailed basis, we would still have to assume a proportional relationship between these figures and the technological developments that are currently affecting market behavior.

In order to obtain better measures of the various factors that influence trade patterns and thereby make scientific progress, economists must play a larger role in determining the nature of the information collected by the government in such surveys as the Population Census and the Survey of Manufactures. Perhaps through an organization such as the American Economic Association, economists in all fields should decide what kinds of data are needed to help improve their particular branch of social science and then lobby actively in an effort to get the government to obtain the data. Some efforts along these lines have already been made, but a more systematic approach seems needed.

Although a better empirical base with which to test alternative trade theories will lead to improvement in the state of trade theory, developments on an analytical level are most needed at the present time. In particular, we must broaden the framework within which we have traditionally theorized and undertaken empirical testing exercises. The problems encountered with regard to so-called "natural resource" industries illustrate the difficulties of working within the traditional framework. The imports of the United States and most other industrial countries include a considerable volume of nonagricultural natural-resource products (e.g., minerals) that tend to be produced in a fairly capital-intensive manner. In some cases, these imports are sufficient to make a representative bundle of imports more capital-intensive than a representative bundle of export commodities. The fact that the industrial countries importing these goods are undoubtedly capital-abundant compared with the many less developed countries exporting them makes the result appear to be inconsistent with the factor-proportion theory. However, in most cases much of the capital, technology, and management needed for mineral production in the less developed countries was furnished by the industrial countries. In other words, the assumption of international factor immobility is not warranted and is what clouds the usefulness of the test. The relative abundance of capital in the industrial countries may be playing a role in shaping trade patterns that is perfectly consistent with standard theory when we expand our model to include international capital flows but appears inconsistent when we implicitly assume that the developing countries furnished all the capital for their export industries.

The need to develop a not-too-complex model in which there are international movements of commodities, capital, labor, and technology is also apparent when we try to explain trade in manufactures among industrial countries. As the contributions of economists with specialized knowledge in the industrial-organization field indicate, analysis must include notions of imperfect markets, differentiated products, and economies of scale. The standard factor-proportions approach, even when we include differences in human-capital supplies, does not come up with particularly interesting results when it is used to try to explain this industrial trade. In part, this is due to the fact that the volume of intra-industry trade is made to seem high by the basis of our usual classification schemes. However, even if we eliminate most intra-industry trade by using a finer industry classification, it is not clear that we possess either the theoretical or the empirical distinctions among productive factors to be able to explain industrial trade.

Clearly, the development and international movement of new technology is an important factor influencing this industrial trade as well as the trade between developed and developing countries. And it is in this area that trade theory, as well as most other branches of economics, is particularly unsatisfactory. I have already mentioned the problem of obtaining even a crude measure of the flow of new technology. More fundamentally, we are unable to answer very well such questions as what are the underlying factors that determine its rate of change, why it is more rapid in some industries than in others, what determines its bias toward particular productive factors, and what determines the rate at which it spreads among nations. It is not a very high level of theorizing to introduce these various ways that technology can affect trade patterns as exogenous variables.

A closely related point is that we must seek to understand better the forces that influence the accumulation of human capital, particularly those that lead to economic innovations. A simple mechanistic theory of human-capital accumulation along traditional neoclassical lines is clearly inadequate. Yet this variable together with technology are turning out to be the most significant factors affecting the nature of international trade, especially on the part of the industrialized nations. In other words, the most important causal factors are the ones for which our understanding of the process of change is the weakest. In a simple physical-capital–labor model, our analysis of the growth process was none too good, but at least a reasonably acceptable model of physical-capital accumulation and population growth can be added to standard trade theory.

All this leads to the conclusion that trade theory should be integrated much more closely with general development theory. I was pleased to see that Stern emphasizes this point by devoting his last section to economic expansion and international trade. This approach is already well-accepted in the analysis of trade patterns of the less developed countries. Trade in these countries is almost always discussed within the framework of their general development efforts. While the need for this approach is less obvious for developed countries, I think we will gain considerably by trying to integrate more development analysis into trade theory for these countries also. Such factors as international flows of capital, technology, and skilled labor, as well as the development of new technology and the growth of human capital – all of which are excluded from most standard trade theory – should be integrated more closely with the traditional determinants of trade. Significant changes in these dynamic factors do take place in time periods of interest to us for both predictive and public-policy purposes; we must broaden our framework if we are going to satisfy this interest.

TRADE, PROTECTION, AND DOMESTIC PRODUCTION:
A COMMENT*

Bela Balassa

It is tempting to comment on all three papers presented at this session, as each of them provides an interesting discussion of a

* The results reported here have been obtained in the course of research carried out by the author as a consultant to the International Bank for Reconstruction and Development.

wide variety of issues. I will try to resist the temptation, however, and concentrate on two issues raised by Corden, although these will necessarily take me into Diaz-Alejandro's territory. The issues concern the costs of, and the arguments for, protection, with the latter leading to the more general question of the choice of optimal policies.

The Cost of Protection in Developing Countries

Corden, as well as Diaz-Alejandro, suggest that estimates of the cost of protection always seem to come out "small." Such results are not surprising for developed countries, where tariffs and their dispersion are low. But this is hardly the case in developing countries, where tariffs – and the tariff equivalent of quantitative restrictions – are generally high and show considerable dispersion. Thus while, in United States and Common Market manufacturing, post-Kennedy Round unweighted tariff averages are 7 per cent, and their standard deviation 2 per cent, the corresponding figures for Argentina are 161 and 73 per cent; for Chile 172 and 68 per cent (Balassa, 1973).

Corden claims that the cost of protection in countries such as India and Pakistan will nevertheless be small, as the manufacturing sector is a small part of their economies. The share of manufacturing is considerably higher, however, in all other developing countries that have established an industrial base. In fact, in some of these countries the share of manufacturing in GDP, expressed in domestic factor prices, is comparable to that in the industrial nations. In 1969, this share was 28 per cent in Argentina and Chile, equaling that for the United States (United Nations, 1972).

At any rate, protection is not necessarily confined to manufacturing industries. Chile, for example, protects its agriculture, with mining and basic metals being the unprotected sectors; particular sectors in agriculture are also protected in other developing countries. At the same time, effective-protection calculations show the share of manufacturing – and of other protected sectors – to be much smaller at world prices than at domestic prices, with the difference between the two providing an indication of the cost of protection.

This last remark brings me to the measurement of the cost of protection. It seems appropriate to start out with the Marshallian triangles referred to repeatedly by Corden. The use of these triangles is predicated on the assumptions, among others, that protected industries will not disappear following the elimination of tariffs and that their efficiency will not improve under free trade.

In view of the high effective protection observed in many developing countries, the two assumptions appear to be conflicting. With effective rates of protection in manufacturing (adjusted for overvaluation) averaging 60 to 70 per cent in Brazil and in Chile, and exceeding 100 per cent in Pakistan (Balassa and Associates, 1971, p. 56), one wonders if these industries could survive without protection. This is indeed the corollary of Krueger's (1966) conclusions for the Turkish import-substituting industries she has studied. Given her assumptions of constant costs and no terms-of-trade effects, the industries in question would disappear if import restrictions were removed.

We face a dilemma, however, since we can hardly expect the manufacturing sector – or a substantial part of this sector – in major developing countries to disappear if they adopt a policy of free trade. A possible solution to the dilemma has been suggested by Bergsman (1970), according to whom the elimination of protection would bring improvements in X-efficiency by inducing a more efficient organization of production that would permit the survival of industries in which a country has an intrinsic comparative advantage. Another factor contributing to the survival of firms would be the adoption of large-scale production methods under free trade, a question to which I will return at a later point.

I have amended Bergsman's method of estimating the cost of protection to include consumption costs, the terms-of-trade loss due to reductions in export prices, and the cost of increased exports under free trade. The results show the cost of protection in the mid-1960s in countries following policies of import substitution to range from 3.7 per cent of GNP in the Philippines, to 6.2 per cent in Chile and Pakistan, to 9.5 per cent in Brazil (Balassa and Associates, 1971, p. 82).

It is noteworthy that the estimated cost of protection in Pakistan is the same as in Chile, although the manufacturing sector accounts for only one-tenth of Pakistani GNP, as against 28 per cent in Chile. At the same time, the figure for Chile is considerably higher than the Harberger (1959) estimate that Corden cites; I had earlier (1966) shown that Harberger understates the cost of protection in Chile by using erroneous figures for tariff averages and the share of imports in national income and by neglecting the possibility that some industries may disappear under free trade. Finally, Corden apparently refers to Bergsman's estimate of the cost of protection for 1967, the year of temporary import liberalization, while I use his estimate for 1966, which is representative of the postwar period as a whole. In this I have followed Bergsman (1970, p. 179) who relies on the 1966 figure when he concludes that, for the period 1954–64, "the cost due only to misallocation amounted to at least 4 per cent of GNP, with the total cost rising to perhaps 10–20 per cent of GNP." ("Total cost" is defined to include the cost of X-inefficiencies associated with protection, as well as monopoly profits.)

These figures are understandably higher than those obtained for developed countries, although the Wonnacotts (1967, p. 300) estimated the cost of protection to be about 4 per cent of GNP in Canada. They are comparable to Krueger's (1966, p. 475) estimate for Turkey. Extrapolating the results obtained for a sample of manufactured industries, she suggested that the world market value of Turkish manufacturing output may double under free trade, following the reallocation of resources from import-substituting to export industries. With manufacturing accounting for one-seventh of GNP (United Nations, 1972), this is equivalent to a cost of protection of 7 per cent of Turkey's GNP.

The above results have been derived in the traditional two-commodity model, with Marshallian partial-equilibrium demand and supply curves. In order to analyze the relationship of tariffs and the cost of protection in the case of high tariffs and to indicate the implications of the dispersion of tariffs, a general-equilibrium framework would have to be employed.

Using indifference and production-possibility surfaces in a two-commodity general-equilibrium model, Johnson (1965) has shown that the cost of protection rises more than proportionately with the rate of the tariff. Thus, assuming that the two goods are consumed in equal quantities under free trade, that the elasticity of substitution in consumption is 1, and that the supply elasticity of the importable is 1.5, the cost of protection, as a proportion of GNP, will increase from 1.6 to 9.8 per cent, and again to 19.1 per cent, as the tariffs on the import goods rise from 20, to 60, to 100 per cent.

Johnson's results have been confirmed by Nugent in the framework of a three-commodity model. Moreover, following an earlier contribution by Johnson (1960), Nugent (1971, Appendix B) has shown that tariff dispersion and the cost of protection are positively correlated. With three commodities consumed in equal quantities under free trade and the stated values of the elasticities, he has found that the cost of protection will increase from 12.0 to 15.7 per cent of GNP if the two protected goods have tariffs of 20 and 100 per cent, averaging 60 per cent, rather than a 60 per cent tariff on each.

The Cost of Protection and Economic Growth

These conclusions are of special interest to developing countries, where tariffs and their dispersion are high. Discrimination in favor of import substitution and against exports in individual industries also entails a cost in these countries. Still, we have to try to provide an answer to Corden's question of what is "small."

It has been claimed that the cost of protection in developing countries is small in the sense that it can be recouped with a few years of rapid growth. But excessive protection will also have adverse effects on economic growth. Johnson (1967) has shown that capital accumulation may lead to a decline in real incomes in a country that faces constant world market prices and protects capital-intensive commodities. And while the assumptions on the shape of the production isoquants necessary for "immiserization through growth" to occur may not be fulfilled (Bertrand and Flatters, 1971), high protection will tend to affect economic growth adversely through its effects on productivity and savings.

In the event that capital is the only scarce factor of production, the cost of protection will entail a lowering of output-capital ratios. The resulting decline in incomes will, in turn, lead to lower domestic savings and investment, thus compounding the adverse effects of protection on economic growth. If, for example, the incremental output–capital ratio is 0.33, the average saving ratio 15 per cent, and the marginal saving ratio 30 per cent, a cost of protection amounting to 6 per cent of GNP will lower the rate of economic growth from 5 to 4 per cent. And, if population is growing at a rate of 3 per cent, the increase in per capita incomes will be halved as a result of protection.

Abstracting from the effects of the cost of protection on savings and introducing additional factors of production, the analysis can be conducted in terms of total factor productivity. For the 1955–1964 period, this has been estimated to rise at an annual rate of -0.6 per cent a year in Argentina; 1.4 per cent in Brazil; and 0.5 per cent in Chile (Bruton, 1967, p. 1103). Even aside from the case of Argentina, it would thus take quite a number of years to recoup the cost of protection through increases in total factor productivity. At any rate, the relevant comparison is with *gains* in factor productivity under protection. The question is then if such gains are forthcoming as a result of protection.

For highly protected economies, this does not appear to be the case. To begin with, the growth rate of average factor productivity tends to be smaller in developing countries with high protection than in the developed nations (Bruton, 1967, p. 1104). The economic distance between the two groups of countries has thus widened, rather than narrowed – which, however, was the purpose of the application of protective measures. Developing countries relying on import substitution behind high protective barriers have also had a poorer growth performance than countries following more outward-looking policies (Balassa, 1971). Moreover, in countries such as Brazil and Colombia, increased incentives to exports have improved growth performance in recent years. In this connection, it should be recalled that, under continuing balance-of-payments equilibrium, greater incentives to exports reduce the protection of import substitution.

I differ on this point with Diaz-Alejandro, who takes an agnostic view as to what policy can do. In fact, comparisons of individual countries (Little, Scitovsky, and Scott, 1970; Balassa, 1971; Balassa and Associates, 1971), as well as a recent large-scale, cross-country investigation by Chenery and Carter (1973), provide results that are inconsistent with Diaz-Alejandro's contention that "size and resources seem to be destiny, and all that policy appears to do is speed or delay a given less developed country along its preordained development path. It cannot much change the structural pattern of production" (p. 109). Chenery and Carter (1973, p. 20) conclude that in Korea 40 per cent, and in Taiwan 50 per cent, of the acceleration of economic growth during the 1960s is explained by increases in exports, which, in turn, resulted from the application of export-incentive schemes. And this estimate does not include the effects of export-induced growth on the productivity of capital and on domestic savings. Yet savings effects are likely to be substantial in both Korea and Taiwan, where the marginal propensity to save is high.

These results are hardly surprising, since, apart from increasingly involving the production of commodities in which a country has a comparative disadvantage, continuing import substitution does not permit exploiting large-scale economies and provides little incentive for technical and organizational improvements. Conversely, not only does export orientation entail specialization according to comparative advantage, but it gives rise to large-scale production and is conducive to technological change. Now, while Corden raises the question whether these factors should be considered static or dynamic, a more important question is how significant they are in practice.

Technical studies have shown that, in a variety of industries, economies of scale can be substantial. This is especially the case in process industries, where a doubling of output tends to be accompanied by a 20 to 30 per cent decline in unit costs (Moore, 1959; Pratten, 1971). Cost reductions, obtainable through the freeing of tariff barriers in developing countries, are also indicated by the results of a study of Latin America; taking into account transportation costs, the elimination of tariffs within the area was estimated to entail cost savings of 10 to 20 per cent for the six commodities studied (Carnoy, 1972).

While these results relate to cost reductions due to increases in the output of particular products, further gains can be obtained through reducing product variety (horizontal specialization) and establishing ancillary industries to produce parts, components, accessories, and various services (vertical specialization). Horizontal specialization has been the subject of empirical studies in the aircraft, machine-tool, and shipbuilding industries, and its theoretical underpinnings have been provided by Arrow (1962) in his famous paper on learning by doing. The gains from vertical specialization are more difficult to quantify, although an interesting effort has recently been made by Rocca (1970). He has found that about 50 per cent of interstate differences in labor productivity in Brazil are explained by differences in the size of the manufacturing sector, with the remainder being due to differences in capital per worker and in plant scale. The size of the manufacturing sector, in turn, has been taken to reflect the external economies obtainable through the existence of ancillary industries.

The Choice of Optimal Policies for Developing Countries

If high protection adversely affects economic growth, one may easily slip into the conclusion that free trade, or free trade with some rather unimportant modifications, will be the appropriate policy for developing countries. This is the thrust of the Little, Scitovsky, and Scott (1970) recommendations, which Diaz-Alejandro justly criticizes for oversimplification. But he does not provide reasons for departures from the free-trade norm, whereas Corden confines himself to brief references to wage differentials and the infant-industry argument.

I find that our knowledge in this area is woefully inadequate. Apart from the case when foreign demand is less than infinitely elastic, we have little to say as regards the optimal degree of protection, its time dimension, and the measures through which it should be provided. And while we can list the reasons for the protection of manufacturing industry – including the "production" of knowledge and skills, industry linkages, and imperfections in factor markets – we are ignorant as to the quantitative importance of these factors.

Nor can the analysis be limited to protection, i.e., discrimination between domestic and foreign goods. Rather, it should be extended to cover other forms of discrimination, including discrimination between industry and agriculture, among individual industries, between import substitution and exports in particular industries, and between foreign and domestic investment. In all these cases, we would need to examine the extent of optimal interventions and the cost of nonoptimal policies.

Also, optimal policies, as well as the move from nonoptimal to optimal policies, have to be considered in a time frame. First, the extent of optimal intervention varies over time because of changes in both external conditions (foreign demand) and domestic supply conditions, especially in resource-using industries. Second, infant-industry arguments call for temporary incentives; a time schedule must be established for their elimination, lest the industry never grow up. Third, in the event that nonoptimal policies are applied, one would have to inquire as to the optimal path for policy improvements.

At the same time, optimal policies and the cost of nonoptimal interventions will vary, depending on the characteristics of particular countries, including size, natural-resource endowment, preferential access to foreign markets, the stage of development, and political and social conditions. The size of national markets will affect the optimal extent of import substitution (e.g., India can better afford to proceed in import substitution and to neglect exports than can Chile or Korea). Optimal policies will differ depending on the availability of natural resources, which, if abundant, "loosen" the foreign-exchange constraint and penalize manufacturing industries through higher wages. Preferential access to developed-country markets reduces discrimination against a country's exports, whereas mutual preferences among developing countries are a double-edged weapon: they provide export markets and also raise the cost of imports.

Special attention must be given to the relationship of optimal policies and the stage of development. Studies of developing countries have so far concentrated on countries that have already established an industrial base. Yet the extent of optimal intervention, and the instruments to be employed, are likely to be quite different in countries at lower stages of development. Given their neglect in the past, these countries should receive priority in future research.

The last point leads me to the question of the multiplicity of instruments. Apart from protection in the form of tariffs, quotas, and import licenses, use may be made of export, production, and wage subsidies, tax and credit preferences, and government expenditures benefiting particular activities. One would need to study the effectiveness of these instruments and the relationships between policy instruments and policy objectives. Among the latter, income distribution and employment, as well as the trade-off between objectives and economic growth, would need to be analyzed.

The pursuit of these research objectives calls for theoretical research, comparative investigations, and case studies of individual countries. Both comparative investigations and case studies will require the application of econometric techniques. However, in intercountry comparisons as well as in country studies, one will often have to work with relatively few observations. This limits the use of formal methods and necessitates relying, in part, on what may be called, for lack of a better expression, "informal judgment."

REFERENCES

Arrow, Kenneth, "The Economic Implications of Learning by Doing," *Review of Economic Studies*, 29 (June 1962), pp. 155–173.

Balassa, Bela, "Integracion regional y asignacion de recursos en America Latina," *Comercio Exterior*, 16 (September 1966), pp. 672–685.

"Trade Policies in Developing Countries," *American Economic Review*, 61 (May 1971), pp. 178–187.

"Tariffs and Trade Policy for the Andean Common Market," *Journal of Common Market Studies*, 11 (December 1973), pp. 176–195.

Balassa, Bela, and Associates, *The Structure of Protection in Developing Countries*, Baltimore, The Johns Hopkins Press, 1971.

Bergsman, Joel, *Brazil: Industrialization and Trade Policies*, London, Oxford University Press, 1970.

Bertrand, T. J., and Frank Flatters, "Tariffs, Capital Accumulation and Immiserizing Growth," *Journal of International Economics*, 1 (November 1971), pp. 453–460.

Bruton, H. J., "Productivity Growth in Latin America," *American Economic Review*, 57 (December 1967), pp. 1099–1116.

Carnoy, Martin, *Industrialization in a Latin American Common Market*, Washington, The Brookings Institution, 1972.

Chenery, H. B., and N. G. Carter, "Foreign Assistance and Development Performance, 1960–1970," *American Economic Review*, 63 (May 1973), pp. 459–468.

Harberger, A. C., "Using the Resources at Hand More Effectively," *American Economic Review*, 49 (May 1959), pp. 134–146.

Johnson, H. G., "The Cost of Protection and the Scientific Tariffs," *Journal of Political Economy*, 68 (August 1960), pp. 327–345.

"The Costs of Protection and Self-Sufficiency," *Quarterly Journal of Economics*, 79 (August 1965), pp. 356–362.

"The Possibility of Income Losses from Increased Efficiency or Factor Accumulation in the Presence of Tariffs," *Economic Journal*, 77 (March 1967), pp. 151–154.

Krueger, Anne, "Some Economic Costs of Exchange Control: The Turkish Case," *Journal of Political Economy*, 74 (October 1966), pp. 466–480.

Little, I. M. D., T. Scitovsky, and M. Scott, *Industry and Trade in Some Developing Countries*, London, Oxford University Press, 1970.

Moore, F. T., "Economies of Scale: Some Statistical Evidence," *Quarterly Journal of Economics*, 73 (March 1959), pp. 232–245.

Nugent, Jeffrey, *Empirical Investigtions in Economic Integration: The Central American Case*, mimeographed, 1971. (To be published by The Johns Hopkins Press.)

Pratten, D. F., *Economies of Scale in Manufacturing Industry*, London, Cambridge University Press, 1971.

Rocca, C. H., "Productivity in Brazilian Manufacturing Industries." An abbreviated English translation published as Appendix 2 in Bergsman (1970, pp. 222–241).

United Nations, *Yearbook of National Accounts Statistics, 1970*, Vol. II, New York, 1972.

Wonnacott, R. J., and G. P. Wonnacott, *Free Trade between the United States and Canada: The Potential Economic Effects*, Cambridge, Mass., Harvard University Press, 1967.

TRADE POLICIES AND ECONOMIC DEVELOPMENT:
A COMMENT

Ronald Findlay

Our field has had more than its fair share of survey papers. However, most of these have been on the pure theory of trade and commercial policy. The vast grey area which, with apologies to Henry Miller, can be described as the trade-development nexus has never to my knowledge had an adequate survey article devoted to it. Diaz-Alejandro has therefore performed a most useful service in his broad and perceptive contribution, which ranges in scope from high theory to grubby fact. His placing of the contemporary literature in its historical context by contrasting it with the interwar experience is particularly to be welcomed. A survey paper is especially difficult to write when there is wide disparity in the assumptions and methods of the literature, which in the present case vary all the way from Marxism to neoclassical orthodoxy and from historical narrative to the most sophisticated mathematical and econometric model building. Diaz-Alejandro not only succeeds in integrating all this material into a coherent story but in addition offers several insights of his own into the trade-development nexus.

Since I agree with the general thrust of his appraisal of the major trend in the literature, which is the vindication, mostly by contradiction, of the virtues of the principle of comparative advantage and an equilibrium exchange rate and with his guarded endorsement of it, I shall confine my remarks to a few particular points.

1. In connection with import-liberalization programs, Diaz-Alejandro says that there would be a considerable lag between the increase of imports and the rise of exports. He therefore advocates a strategy of export promotion to precede the liberalization of imports. He does not appear to give sufficient attention to the question of where the resources for the export expansion are to come from. The mechanism usually envisaged is one in which the additional imports displace production of importables, which releases resources for expansion of exportables. Diaz-Alejandro is quite right in contending that this might be a long and painful process. I wonder whether the alternative of trying to expand exports first, however, would not simply generate excess demand and inflation.

2. It appears that in most countries tariffs are not levied in an economic vacuum, waiting for some entrepreneurs to come along eventually and take advantage of them. Instead, they tend to be levied *ex post*, at whatever level is necessary, to support a project that has already won acceptance from the relevant authorities. It might therefore appear that the theory of trade and commercial policy has nothing to contribute in such a case. Such a conclusion, however, would be quite unjustified. All that happens is that the analysis has to be shifted from the *post hoc* assessment of the welfare effects of the tariff to the prior cost–benefit analysis of the project. The logic of both these analyses should in principle be identical. There is now a rapidly growing literature on project evaluation in less developed countries, in which the OECD volume by Little and Mirrlees is perhaps best known. The Little and Mirrlees recommendation that the shadow prices for project evaluation should be actual world prices (or, where monopoly power exists, marginal cost and revenue in terms of foreign

exchange) is really nothing but the principle of comparative advantage. The case for a shadow wage to industry below the market wage, also made by these authors, is the Manoilesco–Hagen argument in another guise. Recognition of the direct correspondence between the welfare economics of trade, tariffs, and domestic distortions, on the one hand, and of project evaluation, on the other, should reduce some unnecessary duplication of effort by workers in the two areas.

3. On the basis of a 1965 paper by Johnson, Diaz-Alejandro mentions that the gains from trade (and hence the costs of protection) will be smaller the greater is the flexibility of production in the economy. This proposition was derived by Johnson on the basis of a model with some very special assumptions. He uses a two-good model with CES indifference curves to represent tastes and a quadratic transformation curve which, depending upon the value of a parameter, can range from a quarter-circle at one extreme to linearity at the other. The quarter-circle is the maximum rigidity of production structure that the form of the function used allows, while the linear case, of course, corresponds to perfect flexibility. Moreover, units are chosen such that the transformation curve coincides with the given world terms-of-trade line in the linear case. With this model, gains from trade and costs of protection are zero in the linear case and at a maximum in the quarter-circle case. This is the sense in which it can be said that the gains from trade are an increasing function of the inflexibility of production in the economy. That this proposition is not generally valid, however, can be seen once it is realized that in the case of total inflexibility (i.e. a rectangular production block) the production gain from trade is zero. If the Johnson model is expanded to permit the transformation curve to range all the way from linearity to rectangularity, I conjecture that the production cost of protection will rise as we go from linearity to the quarter-circle and then fall as we go from the quarter-circle to complete inflexibility. Perfect flexibility is by no means inconsistent in general with substantial production costs of protection, if the given world terms-of-trade line does not coincide with the linear transformation curve, as it does in the Johnson model.

4. Of all the items in Diaz-Alejandro's extensive bibliography, the most influential and widely read will undoubtedly be the Little, Scitovsky, and Scott volume. His own attitude toward this work is somewhat ambivalent. He apparently agrees with its main thesis, but also seems to feel that it overstates the case against the

"import-substitution syndrome" and the virtues of its own case for "promotion." Together with Diaz-Alejandro, I find the volume an extraordinarily skillful blend of theory, history, and analysis of data. For a work devoted to a survey of industrialization in less developed countries over more than a decade, however, I find the framework used by the authors overly static in character. The essence of their story is the evils of twisting internal relative prices too much against agriculture, pushing the economy to a lower value of production at world prices. This has undoubtedly happened to an excessive degree in many developing countries. However, Little *et al.* say too little about capital accumulation, technical change, education and training, and other factors that augment productive capacity. Their recomputation of growth rates at world prices is a valuable counterweight to measuring them at the internal price ratio, which artificially raises the relative price of industrial output. This should not, however, be the end of the story. As Diaz-Alejandro points out, the capacity built up during the import-substitution phase can and has been put to good use later when a more rational strategy is adopted. In principle, the *potential* increase of GNP at world prices is a better measure of the extent to which development has taken place than the *actual* increase, since the former captures the effects of capital accumulation, technical change, and improved quality of the labor force, which are offset by misallocation of resources resulting from explicit and implicit protection of industry. It is possible for the actual growth of GNP at world prices to be substantially negative while its potential growth is substantially positive. Needless to say, the concept of potential GNP at world prices would present a host of difficulties to empirical research, but it would not be beyond the ingenuity of the most skilled at the arts of our profession.

5. My last point concerns the Corden paper as well, since it relates to the use of the effective rate of protection to rank industries in terms of efficiency. In principle, it is perfectly possible for an industry that would be viable under free trade to require *more* protection than an industry that would not. This is because protection itself can alter relative factor prices in a manner that discriminates relatively more against some industries viable under free trade. This can happen even if there are fixed coefficients for the intermediate inputs. The same criticism applies to the concept of domestic resource cost of foreign exchange. Such rankings as are computed should therefore be interpreted with some care.

TRADE THEORY, TRADE POLICY, AND PROTECTION:
A COMMENT*

Ronald W. Jones

The three papers presented at this session, by Stern, Corden, and Diaz-Alejandro, each present a detailed and admirable review of the mass of recent contributions to testing trade theories, to the application of theories of protection generally, and to problems of economic development in particular. One could, in discussing these papers, literally "review the reviews." The doctrine of comparative advantage, however, suggests to me an alternative approach: Given the huge amount of theoretical and empirical work attested to by these authors, where would a trade theorist like myself like to see advances made in the basic models?

Specifically, I wish to focus upon two of the basic reasons why a country – developed or underdeveloped – may wish to pursue an active commercial policy. The first is a concern with the distribution of income and the second involves the balance of payments. In what follows, I propose to make a few subjective remarks on each of these, ignoring the variety of other possible motivations for a protectionist stance, e.g., the infant-industry argument, a desire for diversification, or the use of commercial policy as an admitted second-best device to raise revenues or correct domestic distortions. Furthermore, these remarks betray my own current preoccupation with emphasizing more than has been done the role of specific factors and nontraded commodities in the standard theoretical literature on protection.

The familiar Heckscher–Ohlin arguments concerning protection seem to pit one basic factor of production, such as labor, against another, say capital. The Stolper–Samuelson argument encourages us to identify the factor used intensively in a country's import-competing industry. This factor would gain from protection (barring a Metzler-paradoxical lowering of relative domestic import prices by a tariff), and the other factor would lose. Does this argument correspond to our view of the pro- and antiprotectionist sentiments in this (or any other) country, even assuming that advocates of protection have not been confused by the literature concerning the Leontief paradox so that they know with confidence which factor is indeed used intensively in the import-

---

* I wish to thank Rudiger Dornbusch for conversations on these remarks.

competing sector? A more likely stereotype, in my view, is the notion that factors of production most *specific* to productive activity in an industry are most likely to push for protection if that industry faces active import competition, or for freer trade if it is an export industry. A model that highlights the distinction between factors specific to an industry and factors that are more mobile as between industries is consistent with this stereotype.[1]

Such a model may also help make sense of a problem that has long bothered me in the literature on effective protection. There the focus is upon the distinction between domestic value added and the value of imported intermediate goods. But why should an entrepreneur in industry j be concerned with whether his costs are rising because the price he has to pay for an imported intermediate good rises or because the wages he must pay have increased? It may be that in focusing upon the bundle of factors comprising domestic value added in an industry, the theory of effective protection has failed to capture the motivation for protection possessed by the domestic factors most specific to an industry. And the theory is simple: An increase in the effective rate of protection to industry j (assuming unchanged effective rates to all other industries) unambiguously improves the real return to the factor used specifically in the jth industry.[2]

A standard message about commercial policy in most courses on the pure theory of trade concerns the Lerner symmetry theorem, or the equivalence between an import tariff and an export tax. Each, it is argued, would lead to the same improvement in a country's terms of trade, the same tax collections (to be reimbursed to the private sector), and the same wider spread between domestic prices of imports and exports. Yet what of the balance-of-payments argument for commercial policy? Should a small underdeveloped country wishing to cure a trade deficit look with indifference upon advice to tax its imports and to tax its exports? Most would not, and this points to the importance in basic theory of carefully specifying the underlying assumptions of the model and distinguishing between alternative causes of a trade deficit or surplus.

Properly pursued, this is a topic too lengthy to be discussed here, and I shall therefore follow the advice often given by my col-

---

1 Such a model was suggested by Kenen (1965). The structure of this model was explored by Jones (1971) and Samuelson (1971).

2 In an N–commodity setting, let each industry employ one factor specific to that industry (e.g., vested capital or entrepreneurship) and one mobile domestic factor (say, labor), together with any number of imported intermediate products.

league, Rudiger Dornbusch: "Draw a pciture."[3] To keep matters simple, suppose we are analyzing commercial policy in a small country facing fixed world prices for its imports and exports.[4] The country produces importables (x_M), exportables (x_X), and nontraded goods (x_N).[5] Expenditure is restricted to income, the classical budget constraint that allows me to ignore monetary factors as well. In both consumption and production, all goods are assumed to be substitutes and to depend upon relative domestic prices. The tariff or export tax is initially zero, so that a small tax, rebated to the private sector, does not alter real incomes, since the small country's terms of trade are constant.

The "$N = 0$" downward-sloping curve in Figure 1 shows the locus of domestic relative prices of exports (compared with home goods) and imports (also compared with home goods) that will clear the home-goods market. It is downward-sloping because all commodities are substitutes in production and consumption: To clear the nontraded home-goods market when imports have risen in relative price, attracting resources away from home goods and demand toward home goods, the price of exports must fall in order to attract resources back toward, and demand away from, home goods.

The OT and OT' rays from the origin indicate, by their respective slopes, the initial and post-tariff or post-export-tax domestic-price ratios between imports and exports. Initially, the small-country economy is at A. A duty on imports at unchanged prices of exports and nontradeables raises the p_M/p_N ratio to point D. This creates a surplus in the trade account for the small country, as resources are pulled into the import-competing sector and demand for imports falls. This is why countries look upon import duties as a device to improve the trade account. But if desired expenditures at home are kept equal to full-employment income, as assumed, the trade surplus is matched by an excess demand for nontradeables. This tends to force the price of nontradeables upward, reducing *both* p_M/p_N and p_X/p_N along OT' toward point B. At B, the trade surplus disappears and the nontraded-goods sector is in equilibrium.

---

3 Indeed it is *his* picture, from an unpublished article, "Tariffs, Non-traded Commodities, and Resource Allocation."

4 Assume fixed exchange rates.

5 The underlying productive structure could exhibit a distinct factor specific to each industry and a mobile factor common to all, as suggested earlier in this note. Unlike the Heckscher–Ohlin structure with two mobile factors, the small country need not be forced to specialize in only two commodities, and all commodities are substitutes for each other in production.

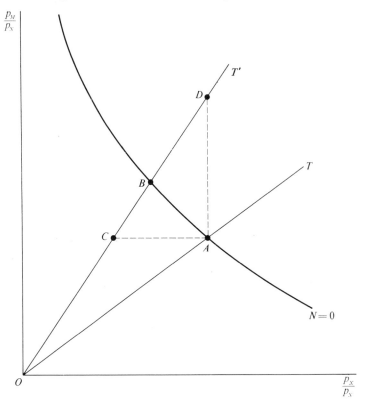

Figure 1. Growth with a negative income elasticity of demand for imports.

An export tax also moves the economy from *A* to *B*. But the transition process is different. At given world prices for the small country, the export tax initially lowers the p_X/p_N ratio from *A* to *C*. At *C* the country suffers a trade deficit, as the prices of traded goods domestically serve to push resources toward the nontraded-goods sector and cause demanders to switch toward consuming more of the country's exportables. A country anxious to use commercial policy to create a trade surplus would understandably prefer the import-duty route (leading to point *D*) to the export-tax path (eventuating at point *C*). The pure theorist of trade, insistent that all markets be cleared, would point out that *C* involves disequilibrium in the nontraded-goods market. The excess supply of nontradeables would soften their price relative to tradeables and lead to point *B*. An import duty is indeed equivalent to an export tax, if you can convince policy makers that it takes little time to move from A to B.

I wish to conclude by putting all this on a more general level. Let a country's demand vector for exportables, importables, and nontraded goods be represented by D_X, D_M, and D_N, and let E represent the excess of aggregate demand over aggregate value of production in units of nontradeables:

$$E \equiv \frac{P_X}{P_N}(D_X - x_X) + \frac{P_M}{P_N}(D_M - x_M) + (D_N - x_N).$$

Some assumptions must be made about disequilibrium behavior, and the ones I choose are asymmetric: Local firms hold inventories of the country's exportables and of its nontradeable goods (but not of importables) and are willing to satisfy demanders (at least in the short run) in the event that demand and supply are not equal. Therefore, a country's actual exports, X, equal its intended export supply, $x_X - D_X$, minus any unintended inventory accumulation, I_X. Its imports, M, equal its excess demand, $D_M - x_M$, while I_N represents any unintended accumulation of inventories of nontraded goods, $x_N - D_N$. Let Q denote the country's actual balance-of-trade deficit in units of the nontraded good:

$$Q \equiv \frac{P_M}{P_N}M - \frac{P_X}{P_N}X.$$

By substitution,

$$Q = \left(\frac{P_X}{P_N}I_X + I_N\right) + E.$$

This shows the trade deficit as some combination of overspending, E, or unintended inventory accumulation, either of its exportables, $(p_X/p_N)I_X$, or of its nontradeable good, I_N.

The assumptions for the small country levying a tariff or export tax were that aggregate expenditures equaled the value of production ($E = 0$) and that all its desired exports could be sold on world markets at given world prices ($I_X = 0$). Thus trade deficits and surpluses must reflect disequilibrium in the market for home goods.

There are many alternative stories that could be told in this framework. Monetary assumptions could be introduced to explain overspending or underspending. There is room for changing levels of production in response to inventory changes. Exchange-rate changes can be analyzed in several different ways. My concluding point bears upon possible empirical tests. Stern has described in detail the efforts made to test trade theories by distinguishing among alternative sources of comparative advantage. By analogy, it should be possible to test whether countries' actual trade imbalances are of the "overspending" type ($E > 0$) or "overvaluation" type (unintended inventory accumulation reflecting too high prices for a country's goods).[6]

REFERENCES

Caves, R. E., and R. W. Jones, *World Trade and Payments,* Boston, Little, Brown, 1973.

Jones, Ronald, "A Three Factor Model in Theory, Trade, and History," Chap. 1 in Jagdish Bhagwati *et al.,* eds., *Trade, Balance of Payments, and Growth,* Amsterdam, North-Holland, 1971.

Kenen, Peter, "Nature, Capital, and Trade," *Journal of Political Economy,* 73 (October 1965), pp. 437–460.

Samuelson, Paul, "Ohlin Was Right," *Swedish Journal of Economics* (1971), pp. 365–384.

---

[6] This distinction between the two interpretations of a trade imbalance is stressed in Chap. 4 of Caves and Jones (1973).

PART II

ECONOMETRIC MODELS OF TRADE AND PAYMENTS

PRICES, INCOMES, AND FOREIGN TRADE*

Stephen P. Magee

This paper examines econometric models that relate prices and incomes to aggregate international trade flows. A number of trade surveys should be mentioned. Harley (1966) surveyed empirical work done in the 1960s on U.S. trade, and Taplin (1967) has surveyed world trade models. Prais (1962) did an earlier paper on econometric work in international trade, and Cheng (1959) did an exhaustive survey of empirical estimates of international trade elasticities and propensities. Hultman (1967) has examined the relationship between exports and growth. Both Bloomfield (1969) and Krueger (1969) have surveyed international economics generally, and the Krueger study has a good, though somewhat dated, discussion of the effects of devaluations on the trade balance.

The most extensive survey of econometric work in international trade is contained in Leamer and Stern (1970). I will try to avoid duplicating their rather thorough treatment of specification and estimation problems, the relationship between demand and substitution elasticities, and other topics.

There are both positive and normative reasons for interest in econometric trade models. From a purely scholarly point of view, we are interested in the relationship between the international and domestic sectors of national econometric models (see Buckler and Almon, 1972; Helliwell *et al.*, 1969; Hooper, 1972; Klein's report on project LINK in this volume; and Rhomberg and Boissonneault, (1965). There is also a positive interest in the international transmission of economic activity (in addition to Klein, see Brems, 1956, and T.R. Robinson, 1968).

Normative interest in international trade models is based on their usefulness in measuring the welfare costs of fluctuations in international trade (Berry and Hymer, 1969); the welfare effects of macroeconomic restrictions on trade (Johnson, 1972a, Chap. 6,

* I am indebted to Jacques R. Artus, Rudiger Dornbusch, J. David Richardson, Grant Taplin and William H. White for helpful suggestions; to Christine Hekman, Carl Hubbard, Nan Magee, and Jeffrey Schott for research assistance; to the Department of Economics at Texas Tech University for research facilities in the summer of 1973; to Virginia Crum, Ida Mae Hope, and Carol Nackenoff for typing; and to the National Science Foundation (Grant GS-35620), the Graduate School of Business at the University of Chicago, The Brookings Institution and the Rockefeller Foundation for research support in the preparation of this paper.

175

and Magee, 1972a); the effects of international trade on domestic growth (Ball and Drake, 1962; Emery, 1967; Hultman, 1967; and Severn, 1968); the policies available for obtaining internal or external balance (Helliwell, *et al.*, 1969; Kwack and Schink, 1972; and Magee, 1971b); and the policy effects of exchange-rate changes and trade restrictions on external balance (Artus, 1970; Barker, 1968; Branson, 1972; Johnston and Henderson, 1967; Laffer, 1973b; Magee, 1971a, 1972a, 1973b; and Perkins, 1968).

What is interesting about most of the empirical studies reviewed in this paper is the preoccupation with testing either an individual hypothesis or a policy effect; few tests seek to evaluate alternative theories. This may explain why part of trade theory has run for so long in a vacuum. Little competition among alternative macroeconomic theories of trade surfaces at the empirical level: for example, there is nothing to rival the Keynesian versus monetarist controversy over domestic stabilization policy, the stock versus flow approach to international capital movements, or the Ricardian versus Heckscher–Ohlin versus modern theories explaining the commodity composition of international trade. There have been extended theoretical controversies over rival theories of devaluation – elasticity, absorption, and monetary approaches – but these controversies have not been subjected to extensive empirical scrutiny.

Another area of continuing empirical interest is investigation of the international transmission of economic activity (this research is continuing in Project LINK). However, there has not been comparable interest in the international transmission of nominal price changes. Recent developments in the United States and abroad should stimulate work in this area.

Another neglected area is the investigation of the degree of imperfection in international goods markets. There has been no research comparable to the empirical studies of domestic securities markets, testing the efficient-market hypothesis, although work by Junz and Rhomberg (1965) and by Kravis and Lipsey (1971) are suggestive in this regard. While this might seem to be the domain for microeconomic research, the results may have important implications for the international transmission of price changes and the path of adjustment following exchange-rate changes.

I turn now from these areas for future research to the strengths and weaknesses of existing studies. Section 1 is a semi-chronological review of past studies, trade-model specification, and the conventional wisdom surrounding these models. Section 2 discusses the theoretical limitations of the studies in section 1 and ways to narrow the gap between the pure theory of international trade and monetary approaches to international trade theory, on the one hand, and empirical studies, on the other. Several propositions in both theoretical areas challenge relationships assumed in the conventional studies, but these have not been tested. Propositions from the pure theory of international trade pose aggregation problems for empirical studies, while results from the monetary theory suggest that the real models are misspecified. Section 3 deals with practical and methodological considerations that have plagued empirical studies. These include modifications of Orcutt's (1950) famous list, the implications of empirical evidence on lags, the response of trade to the business cycle, and a counter-list to Orcutt's points. Section 4 deals with policy considerations: specifically, using trade models for tariff policy, evaluating changes in "competitiveness," and simulating exchange-rate changes. Section 5 provides a summary and some concluding remarks.

1. A CHRONOLOGY OF EMPIRICAL TRADE STUDIES

Single-Equation Models

In this subsection I shall deal primarily with the single-equation import–demand model. (In some cases, supply factors will be introduced.)[1] In the next subsection, I shall discuss world trade models.

The advent of the Keynesian approach to the open economy was an important historical factor in the development of empirical work in international trade (see Kennedy, 1966, for a theoretical discussion and T. R. Robinson, 1968, for an application of the Keynesian model to Canada). Disaggregated versions of this approach are embodied in open-economy input–output models (see Buckler and Almon, 1972). At some point, the interwar and postwar interest in the effect of prices on trade was merged with

---

1 I will not consider in this paper the demand specification for imports by the less developed countries. There is a large literature on this question, extending back at least as far as Polak's (1953) discussion of "reflection ratios," and continuing in studies by Rhomberg and Boissenneault (1964), Rhomberg (1968), and Hemphill (1973). The reason for an alternative specification for LDC import equations is that their reserves are typically low and foreign-exchange authorities limit imports to prevent them from falling further. The logic and problems in using "foreign exchange availability" rather than income as the activity variable in determining imports is well discussed in Hemphill's paper.

the income determinant.[2] But the specification of import demand functions raises problems, especially on the theoretical level.

In perfectly competitive models, imports equal domestic demand less domestic supply. However, if constant costs prevail for each good in domestic and foreign markets, we should observe for any given product either complete domination of the market by imports (in which case, estimation of import demand functions is reduced to estimation of a domestic demand function) or complete domination by domestic production. Yet these phenomena do not appear in the aggregate data; changes in relative prices do not appear to cause large movements toward either complete import domination or complete domestic domination of markets, even in the long run. (This is true both for total trade and for disaggregated trade.) This observation has been deemed to justify an imperfect-substitution view of international trade patterns, in which imports and domestic production are taken to be sufficiently nonsubstitutable to generate finite price elasticities. In this case, the demand by region j for imports from region i can be written as follows:

$$ QM_{ij} = f(Y_j, PM_{ij}, PM_{kj}, P_j) $$

$$ f_1 > o \quad f_2 < o \quad f_3, \; f_4 \gtrless o, \tag{1} $$

where QM_{ij} is the quantity of goods moving from region i to region j; Y_j is real income, expenditure, or another activity variable in region j; PM_{ij} is the price of goods moving from region i to region j; PM_{kj} is the price of goods moving from all other regions to region j; and P_j is the price of goods in region j. The partial derivative with respect to PM_{ij} reflects the direct price effect, and those pertaining to PM_{kj} and P_j are cross-price effects. If we consider total imports into region j, the demand function reduces to

$$ QM_j = g(Y_j, PM_j, P_j), $$

$$ g_1 > o \quad g_2 < o \quad g_3 > o, \tag{2} $$

---

2 While the Keynesian apparatus stresses a macroeconomic income effect on imports, the use of per capital data in estimation emphasizes a microeconomic foundation.

where the variables are the same as before except that the subscript i has been removed, so that the competition among world suppliers is eliminated. The signs indicated for the partial derivatives are those assumed most frequently in the literature; they will be discussed at length in section 2. The usual expectation is for imports to increase with income. In comparing the two equations, note that in equation (2), with only two goods, gross substitutability is required (if the equation is homogeneous of degree zero in nominal prices), whereas, with three goods, complementarity is possible [it leaves indeterminate the signs of f_3 and f_4 in equation (1)].

While the imperfect-substitutability approach eliminated the theoretical problems raised by the perfectly competitive model, a new empirical problem arose. A number of studies in the late 1940s found that the price elasticities of demand for imports were not only finite but were so low that the Marshall-Lerner condition was not fulfilled. For example, Neisser's (1953) study indicated that only U.S. imports of manufactured merchandise showed any important degree of price responsiveness. These empirical studies had sinister implications for the stability of foreign-exchange markets and led to pessimism regarding the usefulness of exchange-rate policy to correct trade imbalances.

The elasticity pessimism of the postwar period was dissipated after 1960 by Ball and Marwah (1962), Junz and Rhomberg (1965), Kreinin (1967), Houthakker and Magee (1969), Prachowny (1969), Magee (1970), Gregory (1971), Buckler and Almon (1972), Hooper (1972), Kwack (1972), Richardson (1972), and by work in project LINK reported by Basevi (1973), Taplin (1973), and Hickman and Lau (1973). Not all the evidence was uniform, however. Mixed evidence was presented by Rhomberg and Boissonneault (1965), and continued elasticity pessimism was generated by Johnston and Henderson (1967) and Klein (1972).

Some generally "elasticity optimist" results are reported in Table 1. They are price and activity elasticities of demand for the exports and imports of ten countries taken from four studies covering the postwar period. The sum of the absolute values of the export and import elasticities exceeds unity for 7 out of 9 LINK cases (excepting the United Kingdom and Belgium), 5 out of 10 Houthakker–Magee cases (excepting West Germany, United Kingdom, Italy, the Netherlands, and Sweden) and 9 out of 10 Taplin–Hickman and Lau cases combined (excepting the Netherlands). [After adjustment for serial correlation, 9 out of 10 Houthakker–Magee (1969, Table 8, p. 125) cases conform; the

TABLE 1 *Price and Activity Elasticities for Total Trade, by Country[a]*

| | Price Elasticities | | | | | | Activity Elasticities | | | | |
| | Imports | | | Exports | | | Imports | | | Exports | |
Country	LINK	Houthak-ker-Magee	Taplin	LINK	Houthak-ker-Magee	Hick-man-Lau	LINK	Houthak-ker-Magee	Taplin	LINK	Houthak-ker-Magee
Belgium	−0.20	−1.02	−0.65	0.00	0.00	−1.02	1.64	1.94	1.27	1.29[b]	1.83
Canada	−1.98	−1.46	−1.59	−0.59	−0.59	−0.84	0.99	1.20	1.18	1.16	1.41
France	n.a.	+0.17	−0.39	n.a.	−2.27	−1.09	n.a.	1.66	1.30	n.a.	1.53
Italy	−0.95	−0.13	−1.03	−0.72	−0.03	−0.93	2.05	2.19	1.26	1.18	2.95
Japan	−0.17	−0.72	−0.81	−2.38	−0.80	−0.49	1.15	1.23	1.12	1.62	3.55
Netherlands	−0.41	+0.23	−0.02	−2.39	−0.82	−0.95	1.06	1.89	1.27	0.85	1.88
Sweden	0.00	−0.79	−0.76[c]	−1.92	0.00	−1.99	1.21	1.42	1.02	1.22	1.76
United Kingdom	0.00	+0.22	−0.22	−0.71	−0.44	−1.27	1.20	1.66	1.24	0.61	0.86
United States	−0.52	−0.54	−1.05	−1.44	−1.51	−1.38	1.26	1.51	1.81	0.92	0.99
West Germany	−1.21	−0.24	−0.61[c]	−1.68	0.00	−1.04	1.30	1.80	1.35	1.33	2.08

n.a. = Not available.

[a] All elasticities are long-run elasticities in cases where a short-run, long-run distinction is drawn.

[b] The elasticity for exports of commodities and services.

[c] The sum of the $P_t + P_{t-1}$ elasticities.

SOURCES:

LINK: See Basevi (1973); the import elasticities are weighted averages (using 1963 weights) of the four commodity elasticities reported in Table 7 on p. 250. The export elasticities are reported in Table 8, p. 251. The models for Canada, Italy, Japan, United Kingdom, and United States are quarterly, while those for Belgium, Germany, Netherlands, and Sweden are annual (see Ball, ed., 1973, p. 69).

The Houthakker and Magee (1969, Table 1, p. 113) elasticities are from annual data with no lags estimated from 1951 to 1966. None of the results for Houthakker–Magee included their price elasticities change to the following values after Cochrane–Orcutt estimation was applied: for imports, the United States moved to −1.03 and the United Kingdom to −0.21; for exports, the United Kingdom moved to −1.24; Germany, −1.25; Italy, −1.12; Sweden, −0.47, and Belgium–Luxembourg, 0.42.

Taplin's (1973, Tables 1 and 2, pp. 188–189) model was estimated from annual data, 1953 or 1954 to 1969 or 1970.

Hickman and Lau's (1973, Table 5, col. 3, p. 41) estimates are based on Taplin's (1973) annual export trade matrices for 1961–69.

Netherlands does not.] Another interesting feature of Table 1 is that the LINK, Houthakker–Magee, and combined Taplin–Hickman–Lau results all indicate that U.S. exports are more price elastic than imports.[3] Vernon's (1966) product cycle implies that the reverse is true for U.S. trade in manufactued equipment. The results together imply that world demand for U.S. nonmanufactured goods must be more price elastic than U.S. demand for world nonmanufactured goods.

Income and price elasticities for U.S. trade taken from five studies are shown in Table 2.[4] These elasticities are based on specifications similar to those in equation (2). Notice that the price elasticities for finished manufactures and (to some extent) manufactured foods are uniformly higher than those for crude materials, crude foods, and semimanufactures. The income elasticities of demand for U.S. imports tend also to be higher for finished manufactures and semimanufactures than for crude materials and crude foods. Vernon's (1966) implication that the U.S. import price elasticity for manufactures should exceed the export price elasticity is confirmed (-5.02 vs. -1.76).

Estimation of Koyck distributed lags permitted Houthakker and Magee (1969) to estimate the short-run and long-run demand elasticities. In all cases the long-run elasticities were larger, indicating that "habit formation" dominated "inventory behavior" over the period (see Houthakker and Taylor, 1970, who found that short-run elasticities can exceed long-run elasticities if buyers purchase for inventory purposes). In the case of semimanufactures, finished manufactures, and total trade, the long-run elasticities are much higher than the short-run elasticities. Except for the study by Rhomberg and Boissonneault (1965), Table 2 also indicates that the long-run price elasticities of demand are sufficient to guarantee stability via the Marshall–Lerner condition. One defect in the Koyck approach, however, is its imposition of uniform lag patterns on all variables in an equation.

Simultaneous-equation techniques have been used by Magee (1970), Hooper (1972), Richardson (1972), and others to correct for simultaneous-equation bias in the estimation of the import price elasticities of demand. Consider a division of the world into two regions, import region j and export region i. Equations (3)

---

3 On the other hand, Buckler and Almon (1972) report a weighted average U.S. import price elasticity of -1.97 and an export price elasticity of $-.86$ (using 1970 trade weights).

4 See Leamer and Stern (1970, p. 35, Fig. 2.12) for confidence intervals on some of the income and price elasticities reported in Table 2.

TABLE 2 *Elasticities of Real U.S. Imports with Respect to Real Income and Relative Prices*[a]

Study and Period of Estimation	Crude Materials		Crude Foodstuffs		Manufactured Food		Semi-Manufactures		Finished Manufactures		Total Trade	
	Y	P	Y	P	Y	P	Y	P	Y	P	Y	P
1. Ball and Marwah (1962) (quarterly, 1948–58)	0.87	−0.26	0.49	−0.34	0.96	−1.87	1.22	−1.38	2.47	−3.50		
2. Rhomberg and Boissonneault (1965) (quarterly, 1948–61)	0.62	−0.21	0.60	−1.10	3.00	−2.30	0.93	−0.73	0.58	−0.48		
3. Kreinin (1967) (annual, 1954–1964)			0.27	−0.40	0.60	−1.67	1.05	−0.61	2.25	−5.03		
4. Houthakker and Magee (1969) (quarterly, 1947–66)												
a. Short-run	0.18	−0.05	0.12	−0.09	0.47	−0.51	0.14	−0.18	0.29	−0.45	0.33	−0.20
b. Long-run	0.61	−0.18	0.30	−0.21	1.28	−1.40	1.11	−1.83	2.63	−4.05	1.42	−0.88
5. Magee (1970) (annual, 1951–69)												
a. U.S. imports	0.72		0.05	−0.40	1.39	−1.14	1.38	−0.78	2.45	−5.02	1.45	−1.35
b. U.S. exports	1.06	−1.21	0.36	−2.09	0.87	−2.62	1.62		1.44	−1.76	1.45	−2.00

[a] All are for imports except Magee (1970), which gives both exports and imports.

through (6) furnish a simple model of the demand for imports into region j, the supply of exports from region i, the market-clearing equilibrium condition, and the relative-price equation, which links the export and import price:

$$QM_j^d = f_3\,(Y_j, PM_j^d, P_j) \tag{3}$$

$$QX_i^s = f_4\,(PX_i^s, P_i) \tag{4}$$

$$QM_j^d = QX_i^s \tag{5}$$

$$PM_j^d = FX_{ij}\,(1 + T_j)\,PX_i^s. \tag{6}$$

The *endogenous variables* are QM_j^d, the quantity of imports demanded in region j; QX_i^s, the quantity of exports supplied by region i; PM_j^d, the price of imports facing demanders in region j, in j's currency; and PX_i^s, the export price received by suppliers in region i, in i's currency. *The exogenous variables are* Y_j, income in region j; P_j, the price of goods produced in region j; P_i, the price of goods sold in region i; FX_{ij}, the foreign-exchange rate linking currency i to j (j's currency/i's currency); and T_j, the proportional tariff rate in region j.

This approach was used by Magee (1970) to estimate the demand and supply for the five categories of products shown in Table 2 and total exports to the world. The simultaneous-equation approach appeared superior to ordinary least squares only for finished manufactures and total exports. (For finished manufactures, the structural price elasticity of demand equaled -1.8 and the elasticity of supply, 5.2. For total exports, the demand elasticity in the structural equation equaled -2.0 and the supply elasticity equaled 11.5.) The use of instrumental variables to reduce simultaneous-equation bias in the estimation of export and import price elasticities of demand for U.S. trade disaggregated by country significantly increased a number of the demand elasticities.

Conceptually, the variable T_j should represent tariffs, transport costs, insurance, and all other differences between the price received by the supplier and the price paid by the demander in the importing region. One defect of Magee's (1970) work was that only the foreign-exchange rate was used in equation (6). Hooper (1972) improved upon this by also including tariff rates.[5] His work indicates that the income elasticity of demand for U.S. imports is high relative to the income elasticity of U.S. exports, a result similar to that of Houthakker and Magee (1969).

An even more elaborate model for U.S. imports has been constructed by Richardson (1972). Domestic prices as well as import prices are endogenous, and the determination of supply and demand includes all of the variables in equations (3) through (6) plus unit costs, productivity, inventory levels, and inventory backlogs.

World Trade Models

I turn now to a review of some recent world trade models. Taplin (1967) has surveyed pre–1967 world trade models, such as those by Neisser and Modigliani (1954) and Rhomberg and Bois-sonneault (1964).

The world trade models discussed here can be illustrated by the trade matrix in Table 3 (see Taplin, 1967). Variable x_{ij} represents exports flowing from region i to j. The sum of each row gives the total exports of region i, X_i; the sum of each column gives total imports into region j, M_j. We have assumed that all trade flows are measured either f.o.b or c.i.f., so that the sum of world imports, T, is equal to the sum of world exports.

I shall not discuss in this section cross-section world-trade models. These models attempt to explain each of the bilateral trade flows, x_{ij}, at a fixed point in time in terms of the relative distances between regions, region sizes, and other variables. Models of this type have been estimated by Savage and Deutsch (1960), Poyhonen (1963), Pulliaian (1963), and Linnemann (1966). I am concerned here not with explaining the pattern of trade flows at any point in time, but their changes through time.

I shall discuss three models that have been constructed in a time-series framework (the fourth, the LINK model, is described in Klein's paper). The first is the OECD world trade model developed by Adams *et al.* (1969) and extended in subsequent work. (A good summary of this model and the Armington model, discussed

5 Hooper disaggregates U.S. imports into eight commodity categories and U.S. exports into four commodity categories; he uses five geographic regions (Canada, Japan, the United Kingdom, Western Europe, and the rest of the world). His model is estimated quarterly from 1961–I to 1972–II (in some cases, the starting point is 1964–I) and is a part of the Michigan Quarterly Forecasting Model of the U.S. economy, DHL-III.

TABLE 3   *A Matrix of World Trade Flows*

Exporting Region	Importing Region							Total Exports
	1	2	3	...	j	...	n	
1	x_{11}	x_{12}	x_{13}	...	x_{1j}	...	x_{1n}	X_1
2	x_{21}	x_{22}	x_{23}	...	x_{2j}	...	x_{2n}	X_2
3	x_{31}	x_{32}	x_{33}	...	x_{3j}	...	x_{3n}	X_3
...	...							...
i	x_{i1}	x_{i2}	x_{i3}	...	x_{ij}	...	x_{in}	X_i
...	...							...
n	x_{n1}	x_{n2}	x_{n3}	...	x_{nj}	...	x_{nn}	X_n
Total imports	M_1	M_2	M_3	...	M_j	...	M_n	T

next, is given in Branson, 1972.) The Adams model was originally estimated using quarterly data for the period 1955–IV to 1965–IV. An updated version reported in Branson (1972) used semiannual data covering the period 1955 through 1968. The model operates as follows. First, it estimates total imports into each of nine regions (United States, Canada, Japan, France, Germany, Italy, the United Kingdom, other OECD, and non-OECD). In Table 3, this is equivalent to estimating each of the column sums, M_1 through M_9. Second, it sums total imports into each of the nine regions to give total world trade, T. Third, it estimates the individual exports of each of the nine regions to the world, X_1 through X_9, using equations that predict export shares in world trade. The total trade balance for any given region simply equals X_i minus M_i. Notice that none of the bilateral trade flows, x_{ij}, is determined in this model; it deals entirely with the marginal totals in Table 3.

The second model is the Armington model (1969a, 1969b, and 1970), developed at the IMF. It is more elaborate theoretically than the OECD trade model, since it explains each bilateral flow in Table 3. Unfortunately, the Armington model has not been estimated empirically and uses assumed elasticities of demand and substitution. The logic of the Armington model proceeds as follows. Individuals in region j are given money income and two prices, the price of traded goods and the price of nontraded goods, to determine the total value of traded goods they will consume; this is a column sum in Table 3. Next, the individuals distribute their demands for the components of M_j across each of the i suppliers (exporters) according to a CES function. Thus, Armington is able to write the distribution function as

$$x_{ij}/M_j = b_{ij}^{e_j} (P_{ij}/P_j)^{-e_j}, \tag{7}$$

where e_j is the elasticity of substitution. This framework allows computation of both the direct elasticity of demand and cross price elasticities of demand.

The third model, the Taplin (1973) model, was built for short-term forecasting purposes at the IMF. There are 27 regions in the model – 25 developed countries, a group consisting of the Communist countries, and the rest of the world. Here, total imports into each region j, M_j, depend on the autonomous determinants of income (government expenditure, gross investment, and exports) and prices.[6] Then the total exports of region i, X_i, are obtained as the sum across j of the share of exporter i in market j *times* imports in region j *times* an f.o.b.–c.i.f. adjustment factor. (In some cases base-year share and adjustment factors are used; in others the $27 \times 27 = 729$ export shares are estimated from time-series equations, with relative prices as the prime movers.) Finally, the trade balance of region i equals $X_i - M_i$. The first two steps involve the simultaneous determination of trade flows.[7] An important virtue of this approach is that it captures the world wide feedback effect of a change in autonomous expenditure in any region (see Kindleberger, 1973, Chap. 20, for a discussion of the foreign-trade multiplier and Piekarz and Stekler, 1967, for an earlier application of the Taplin approach). Another virtue is that there is explicit, albeit rather crude, consideration of the f.o.b.–c.i.f. problem.

The Taplin model was used to predict trade in the last six years

---

6 The import equations were estimated using ordinary least squares from annual data, 1953 or 1954 to 1969 or 1970.

7 Linearized, the model can be written in matrix form as follows (see Taplin, 1973, p. 179n). First, $M = CX + Z$, where M is a column vector of imports, and Z is a matrix of the coefficients of autonomous exports in determining imports, and Z is a column vector of the other determinants of imports (including their coefficients). Second, $X = ADM$, where A is the 27×27 share matrix with components a_{ij} (a_{ij} is the share of exporter i in imports into j) and D is a vector of f.o.b.–c.i.f. adjustment factors. Third, $B = X - M$. The system can be solved for each of the three endogenous trade vectors, M, X, and B. For example, trade balances can be expressed in terms of Z as $B = (AD - I)(I - CAD)^{-1} Z$, where the superscript -1 indicates matrix inversion.

of the estimating period (1964–69) under alternative assumptions regarding actual versus 1963 export shares and actual versus 1963 f.o.b.–c.i.f. adjustment factors (in all cases, predicted values of country imports were used). Taplin (1973, Table 6, p. 207) found that when actual export shares and actual adjustment factors were used, the model yielded an average error on imports of 3.5 per cent.[8] When actual adjustment factors were used with 1963 export shares, the import error increased to 8.85 per cent. When both 1963 export shares and 1963 adjustment factors were used, the import error increased to 9.04 per cent. Taplin concluded that the use of constant 1963 export shares contributed substantially to the total forecast error. He was able to reduce this error by attempting to approximate actual export shares in the forecasting period, using seven different approaches. An important finding was that the use of export shares in period t to predict total exports in period $t+1$ did as well or better than any of the more sophisticated approaches.

2. SOME THEORETICAL PITFALLS IN THE EMPIRICAL STUDIES

I shall review the studies cited in the previous section for problems in two areas: (a) aggregation problems related to propositions in the pure theory of international trade and (b) specification problems caused by the interaction of trade with securities and money markets. Both areas are extremely important, but the second is of special importance for policy purposes, since most trade-stabilization policy is directed not toward trade per se but toward the entire balance of payments. *I shall emphasize here ways in which to link the pure theory of international trade with macroeconomic studies. Pure theory may be especially helpful in explaining structural shifts and instability through time in both income and price coefficients.*

I shall examine the sign of the income coefficient in the import demand function; the stability of the import-income relationship; some structural effects of taxes and various market distortions on the aggregate levels of trade; comparative advantage, price changes, and aggregate trade flows; and the implications of monetary and general-equilibrium models for international trade flows.

8 The average error was calculated as the square root of the weighted-squared-proportional errors of the individual regions, using 1963 trade weights (see Taplin, 1973, p. 205). Taplin used both a total trade model and a four-commodity trade model (SITC $0+1$, $2+4$, 3, and $5-9$). The errors reported in the text are for the total trade model.

The Sign of the Income Coefficient

In the Keynesian nonprice model of international trade flows, the income coefficient in the structural import demand equation must be positive. In the empirical import demand function, equation (2), the sign of the income coefficient is usually specified as being "positive unless imports are inferior in consumption." This statement is true only if imports can be treated like any other good in the consumer demand function (i.e., it is a substitute for some products and a complement to others) or if there is no domestic production of the good so that the import demand function is the demand function for the good itself.

However, the assertions regarding the sign of the income coefficient from both the Keynesian and the "usual" approach can be false if the imported good has a relatively close domestic substitute. Theoretically, the relationship between the growth of real income and the growth of real imports is not necessarily positive; in fact, the importable could even be *superior* in consumption (as income grew, the consumption of this good would increase while the consumption of the other product would decrease), yet the true income elasticity of demand for imports could be *negative*. This assertion rests on Johnson's (1967b) study of trade and growth. The demand for imports is the excess of domestic consumption over domestic production, and variations in the latter can dominate variations in the former. This admittedly extreme case is illustrated for a small country in Figure 1, where good Y, the importable good, is shown on the vertical axis and good X, the exportable, on the horizontal axis. Before income grows from OI to OI' (expressed in terms of good X), the quantity of good Y imported is equal to AB. After the country grows, consumption moves from point C_0 to C_1 and production moves from P_0 to P_1. The ultra pro-trade-biased growth in consumption from C_0 to C_1 is more than offset by ultra anti-trade-biased growth in production from P_0 to P_1, so that the quantity of real imports actually declines from AB to $A'B'$. Mathematically (see Ikema, 1969, for a discussion of the mathematics behind Johnson's argument), the excess demand for imports can be expressed as

$$M(Y) = D(Y) - S(Y). \tag{8}$$

Taking the derivative of (8) with respect to income (Y) and substituting, we can derive the income elasticity of demand for imports (e_{my}) in terms of the domestic demand for the importable

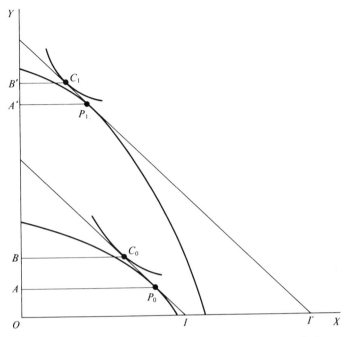

Figure 1. Growth with a negative income elasticity of demand for imports.

in terms of income (e_{dy}) and the elasticity of domestic supply with respect to income (e_{sy}),

$$e_{my} = (D/M)\,(e_{dy}) - (S/M)\,(e_{sy})$$

$$= (D/M)\,(e_{dy} - e_{sy}) + e_{sy}\,, \tag{9}$$

where D, S, and M are demand, supply, and imports, respectively. In general, e_{my} will be negative when

$$\frac{D}{S} < \frac{e_{sy}}{e_{dy}}. \tag{10}$$

Thus, when the domestic demand and supply elasticities are of the same sign, in order to have a negative income elasticity of demand for imports, the value of the domestic supply elasticity must be sufficiently higher than the domestic demand elasticity so that their ratio exceeds the ratio of domestic demand to domestic supply (the latter exceeds one, since $D/S = 1 + M/S$).

In short, the Keynesian model led us to expect positive income elasticities of demand for imports. The pure theory indicates that the import–income relationship can go either way. Is there any empirical evidence of negative income elasticities of demand for imports?

I have been unable to find any import-income elasticities that are significantly negative at the *aggregate* level. For example, Houthakker and Magee (1969) found that the income elasticities of demand for imports into 15 countries were highly significant and positive; 7 out of 15 had income elasticities with t values in excess of 10. However, there is a methodological problem with the use of this type of study to test the pure-theory hypothesis. It lumps together the cyclical and secular income elasticities. Since structural changes occur slowly through time and imports respond quickly to short-run variations in income, the cyclical component of the income elasticity should be removed in testing for the sign of the long-run elasticity (e_{my}). Johnson's (1967a) approach applies only to the secular income elasticity; for a discussion of the cyclical-secular behavior of trade, see section 3. *A useful taxonomy for future modeling would be to relate the cyclical income effect to Keynesian factors and the secular effect to pure-theory and structural factors.*

We might expect that tendencies toward import substitution, which are more common in the less developed countries, would increase the relative elasticity of supply of importables (e_{sy}), and this might push the income elasticity of demand for imports toward zero or negative values. Khan (1973, Table A2) has used the specification in equation (2) and two-stage least squares adjusted for serial correlation to estimate imports into less developed countries. For 7 out of 15 less developed countries, the income elasticities of demand for imports were significantly positive (Brazil, Ceylon, Colombia, Costa Rica, Equador, Pakistan, and the Phillipines); for 5 of 15, the income elasticities were nonsignificant though positive (Argentina, Chile, Ghana, Morroco, and Turkey); and for 3 of the 15, the income elasticities were negative and nonsignificant (India, Peru, and Uruguay). (These estimates were derived from annual data, 1951–69, and were not purged of the cyclical component in the income elasticity.) However, these somewhat lower and less significant income elasticities do not necessarily point to anti-trade-biased growth attributable to the behavior of the domestic supply of importables; there may be other reasons for these results related to the specification of import demand functions into less developed countries, such as the treatment or omission of import controls and foreign-exchange availability (see Hemphill, 1973).

The only evidence I could muster for negative income elasticities of demand for imports in developed countries came from commodity studies, and this evidence is scant. A necessary but not sufficient condition for $e_{my} < 0$ is that, when m/y is the dependent variable, the coefficient on trend income must be negative. Both Marston (1971) and Branson (1968a) used m/y as their dependent variable and had trend income as an independent variable. Marston's study of five commodity categories of British imports found no negative coefficients. Branson's study of ten commodity categories of U.S. imports found one significantly negative coefficient on trend income (coffee, cocoa, and sugar) and one insignificantly negative coefficient (industrial supplies and materials); seven of the other categories had significantly positive coefficients. For U.S. exports to Japan, Branson found a significantly negative trend-income coefficient. Neither of these studies is entirely satisfactory for present purposes, however, since the coefficient on trend income could be negative and yet e_{my} could still be positive. Buckler and Almon (1972) present more direct evidence. They found that for one category, meat animals, U.S. imports respond negatively to domestic demand. While it is a relatively large import item, it was the only one of fifty import categories to do so. When they substituted a time trend in place of domestic demand, it had a significant and negative coefficient, confirming that the negative elasticity was a secular and not a cyclical phenomenon.[9]

The difficulty of finding negative income elasticities of demand for imports may be due to (a) reluctance on the part of empiricists to report such findings; (b) systematic tendencies in the growth patterns of demand and supply of import-competing products, which guarantee positive import-income elasticities; (c) misspecification of import demand functions, so that the omission of variables which reflect trade liberalization causes upward biases in estimates of e_{my}; or (d) failure to distinguish cyclical and secular elasticities in trade studies. There is some merit to the first explanation. Buckler and Almon showed commendable candor in revealing their negative result, especially since they did not

---

9 Buckler and Almon (1972) present stronger evidence for $e_{my} < 0$ for U.S. exports, but their specification of the export equations made these results less amenable to the type of analysis pursued here.

believe it and changed the specification when running their forecasts. More of this candor is needed. Points (b) and (c) deserve systematic empirical examination. If (b) is the explanation, then the "systematic tendencies" should be explored and explained. I suspect, however, that (c) and (d) are the major reasons for the consistently positive income elasticities.

Stability of the Import-Income Relationship

Another implication of equation (9) is that, in addition to the possibility of negative signs, there is increased likelihood of *instability* in import demand functions relative to domestic demand functions, because (9) represents excess demand. Shifts in the domestic demand elasticity or the domestic supply elasticity or secular changes in D/M and S/M can cause changes through time in the income elasticity of import demand. This point is important for two reasons: it provides another potential link between the pure theory and empirical macroeconomic trade studies, and the pure theory can provide testable hypotheses to explain the frustrating empirical problem of shifts in import-income relationships.[10]

Consider, first, characteristics of the supply side that lead to instability in e_{sy} and therefore to instability in e_{my} in equation (9). The causes of growth in income are important for the observed trade-income relationship. Assume that income grew at a constant rate over some period, that import-competing production was labor intensive, and that demand was homothetic and identical for every consumer (that e_{dy} was constant). If growth in income were caused by capital accumulation alone in the first half of the period and by labor accumulation alone in the second half [this is Rybczynski (1955) type growth], we would observe a positive income elasticity of demand for imports in the first half and a negative income elasticity of demand for imports in the second.

Next, let us hold the supply side constant and examine instability in e_{my} caused by demand factors. Growth because of factor augmentation or technical change can lead to new distributions of income within a country and thus change the income elasticity of demand for the importable good. This could be due to (a) all consumers being identical but having nonhomothetic preference patterns or (b) all consumers having homothetic demand (i.e.,

---

10 Remember that this analysis applies to product areas in which imports have close
   domestic substitutes.

income elasticities of demand equal to 1) but not being identical or (c) some combination of nonhomothetic preferences and non-identical individuals. Thus, the pure theory does not lead us to expect stable empirical estimates of the income elasticity of demand for aggregate imports.

There is a third factor which can cause secular changes in the income elasticity of demand for imports. Even if domestic demand and supply elasticities are constant through time with respect to income, there may still be systematic changes in the income elasticity of imports, since the ratio of domestic demand to imports [D/M in equation (9)] changes through time if the domestic demand and supply elasticities are unequal. The larger the disparity between the two elasticities, the greater the long-term change in the income elasticity of demand for imports.

If we include the possibility of international factor movements, Vernon's (1966) product cycle provides a fourth reason to expect long-term instability in import-demand relationships. In Vernon's product cycle, goods move in some periods, but factors become the dominant force in others, so that the trade–income relationship is altered. Vernon's model also implies long-term reversals of the pattern of trade. New and technology-intensive goods are exported early in their life cycle by developed countries like the United States. As the goods complete the cycle, becoming standardized, they are imported by the United States. Vernon's model applies only to manufactured goods, however, and the length of his cycle for most goods will be longer than the ten- to twenty-year periods over which existing international trade models are estimated.

As might be expected, the empirical evidence on the stability of the income coefficient is mixed. Kemp (1962b) broke Canadian imports into two periods, 1926–39 and 1947–55, and found that the income elasticity of demand rose from .65 in the first period to 1.30 in the second. Some agnostic evidence for the United States has also been presented by Rhomberg and Boissoneault (1965). They separated U.S. import demand for the five commodity categories in Table 2 into two periods: 1948–53 and 1954–61. They found the "income" variable not significant in both periods for crude materials and finished manufactures and significant in only one period for crude foodstuffs. The income elasticities declined between periods for manufactured foodstuffs and rather significantly for semimanufactures. Magee (1972a), using analysis of variance, tested a fifteen-region bilateral trade model for U.S.

exports and imports reported in Magee (1970); he found that the income elasticities declined significantly from the first period (1952–60) to the second period (1961–69) for U.S. imports from four countries (United Kingdom, Germany, Netherlands and Japan) and for U.S. exports to four countries (Belgium–Luxembourg, Denmark, Netherlands, and Japan). In no case did the income elasticities increase significantly.

Unfortunately, I know of no studies that have attempted to explain such aggregate shifts in import-income elasticities in terms of the pure-theory hypotheses advanced earlier. Though the effect of Vernon's product cycle on income elasticities has not been tested directly, there is the aforementioned indirect confirmation of Vernon's hypothesis that U.S. import price elasticities of demand for manufactured goods are higher than U.S. export price elasticities (see Branson, 1968a; Houthakker and Magee, 1969; Adler, 1970; and Magee, 1970). Thus, we cannot rule out the possibility that the product cycle may imply long-term instability in the import-income coefficients.

Other Structural Effects on the Levels of Trade

Thus far, we have emphasized structural reasons for pure theory to suggest that the income elasticity of demand for imports can be either negative or unstable. This analysis can be generalized to the following statement: Any secular change in the economy that moves the system toward trade reversal (the export good becomes the importable, and vice versa) will give a negative income elasticity of demand for imports, while factors moving the economy away from trade reversals will give a positive elasticity.[11] This statement applies not only to international trade studies based on time-series analysis, but also to cross-section studies that attempt to explain the importance of trade in a national economy. Models of this sort were mentioned earlier (see Savage and Deutsch, 1960; Poyhonen, 1963; Pulliainen, 1963; and Linnemann, 1966). In these studies, the share, rather than the level of trade in a national economy, would be increased by events that moved the economy away from trade reversals and decreased by events that

---

11 For the small-country case, if the Engel's curve intersects the Rybczynski expansion path in output space, a trade reversal occurs at the intersection. If both curves are linear, we are guaranteed a negative income elasticity of demand for imports before reversal and a positive income elasticity after reversal. The reason, of course, is the changed composition of trade.

moved it toward trade reversals. These events would include changes in consumption taxes, production taxes, factor taxes, unionization, etc. The literature on explanations of the Leontief paradox abounds with explanations of trade reversals. For a description of the effects of distortions in factor markets on the level and importance of trade in a national economy, see Magee (1973a).

Comparative Advantage, Price Changes, and Aggregate Trade Flows

A number of the problems discussed in the import-income category apply to import price elasticities as well. For imports that have close domestic substitutes (the "perfect substitution" group), we can derive a relationship between the import price elasticity of demand and the domestic elasticities that is similar to equation (9):

$$e_{mp} = (D/M)\,e_{dp} - (S/M)\,e_{sp}$$

$$= (D/M)\,(e_{dp} - e_{sp}) + e_{sp}\,, \tag{11}$$

where e_{mp} is the price elasticity of demand for imports, e_{dp} is the domestic demand elasticity with respect to the price of importables, e_{sp} is the domestic supply elasticity with respect to the price of importables, and D, S, and M, are demand, supply, and imports in real terms, respectively. We do not face the problem of ambiguity in the sign of the import price elasticity (in the usual case in which the domestic demand and supply elasticities are negative and positive, respectively). However, the problem of stability through time may be more critical for the import-price relationship than for the import-income relationship. First, the lags in response of supply and demand are believed to be longer with respect to price than they are with respect to income. Second, the lags accompanying the response to domestic supply are probably much longer than those related to domestic demand, so that e_{mp} will appear to be more structurally unstable in time-series analysis than either the domestic demand or supply elasticity (since it is a combination of both). Third, there is forced interaction among the own and cross-price elasticities and their lag patterns in the estimation of equation (1) when the sum of the elasticities of real imports with respect to all nominal prices is constrained to equal zero (the no-money-illusion case). The homogeneity constraint is imposed empirically by estimating import equations in which prices enter only as price ratios. Unfortunately, the imposition of zero degree homogeneity is a very strong condition, since it generally requires that there be no money illusion on the part of *both* demanders and suppliers in the domestic market. This is a more stringent assumption than lack of money illusion on the part of either group separately.

If we move from the perfect substitution model into the imperfectly substitutable situation, we can specify in equation (1) that consumers in region j consider three categories of goods for consumption: those from country i, those from all other countries (from k), and domestic goods (from j). Consider a uniform price increase in all domestic goods (the P_j's). From the macro approach given in equation (1), we would predict that the percentage increase in the domestic price times the cross-price elasticity of demand for imports with respect to that price will give the effect on the quantity of goods imported. Whether imports will rise or fall depends on whether imports are substitutable or complementary with domestic goods. We know, however, that this scenario is a macroeconomic fiction, since the world is a complicated assortment of thousands of goods.

What can the pure theory of international trade tell us about the behavior of these many goods when prices change? Will this knowledge give us insights into the limitations of the macro approach? Will these facts throw suspicion on the stability of the estimated macroeconomic trade-price relationships?

Let us consider comparative advantage in this situation. Using the simple multiproduct model of Ricardian comparative advantage, we can rank all n products, from those with the lowest ratio of U.S. to foreign price to those with the highest ratio. The United States will have a comparative advantage in low cost-ratio goods; a middle category of goods in the ranking will be nontradeables; and products with the highest cost ratios, at the bottom of the list, will be U.S. importables. The effect of a uniform inflation of all prices in the United States or of revaluation of the dollar is to move up the dividing lines between exportables, nontradeables, and importables, so that fewer U.S. goods are exported, goods that were previously on the margin of being exported become nontraded, and goods that formerly did not face import competition are now imported. If the U.S. comparative advantage is defined as simply the *ranking* of goods according to ratio of U.S.

to foreign costs, uniform rates of inflation in the United States or abroad and exchange-rate changes would have no effect on comparative advantage in the Ricardian model.[12]

The implications of this discussion for the stability of the price effects is clear: The export supply elasticity will be modified by the parameters pertaining to the products that became nontradeables, while the import demand elasticity will be modified by the parameters for previously nontraded goods that are now imported. The important point is that uniform rates of inflation, changes in exchange rates, and other monetary phenomena shift the composition of exportables, nontradeables, and importables in the short run. In most models, there would be no real long-term effects of monetary or exchange-rate changes. Houthakker (1973) is now using the Ricardian approach to link the pure theory with aggregate trade behavior.

What empirical evidence do we have on the size and stability of the price effects? On size, we know from equation (11) that if the domestic supply elasticity exceeds zero, then the estimated elasticity of imports with respect to price will exceed the domestic demand elasticity with respect to price. This observation is confirmed by the data. [Compare the domestic U.S. price elasticities of demand in Houthakker and Taylor (1970, pp. 166–167) with the international price elasticities in Houthakker and Magee (1969, Tables 1, 4, 6, and 8).]

I turn next to several studies of the stability question. Rhomberg and Boissonneault (1965) have evidence from quarterly data on the five commodity categories of U.S. imports listed in Table 2. Their data were divided into two subperiods – 1948–53 and 1954–

---

12 This is a more useful definition of comparative advantage for empirical analysis, particularly with monetary disturbances, etc. In the long run, real forces (demand) determine the cut-off points between the three commodity groups. However, in the short and medium run, overvalued exchange rates, differential rates of inflation, imperfect knowledge, lags in the adjustment of prices to market forces through nonprice rationing and queuing, all lead to cut-off points that do not coincide with the long-run equilibrium.

One way of organizing the analysis of the effects of price and exchange-rate changes in this model is to establish the following definitions: A country has a competitive advantage in the list of products it exports and a competitive disadvantage in the list of goods it imports. Adverse home price movements and exchange-rates changes hurt a country's competitive advantage (the list of exportables shrinks and of importables expands) in the short run; however, these factors do not affect long-run competitive advantage, since real demand determines the long-run cut-off points, and comparative advantage (the ranking of the entire list) is independent of both.

Perhaps this nomenclature would help sharpen policy discussions in the trade area. For example, a U.S. government official once remarked that "the United States was losing its comparative advantage in everything."

61.[13] For both crude materials and crude foods, there were no significant changes in the relative import-price relationships [the specification was similar to that noted in equation (2) above, in which import prices relative to domestic prices form the price variable]. For manufactured foods and semimanufactures, there appeared to be shifts in the price relationships between the two subperiods, although the shifts may be marginal in their statistical significance. Finished manufactures is the one category in which a very definite change appears to have occurred; imports were much more price elastic in the second period than in the first.

Kemp (1962b) has studied Canadian imports using annual data. He found that the price elasticity of demand "fell" from −3.18 to +0.75 from the period 1926–39 to 1947–55, indicating substantial instability.

The study by Heien (1968) dealt with imports by eleven countries from the late 1940s until 1964. Again, the specification was similar to that in equation (2); the price variable in the equation is the ratio of import prices to domestic prices in each country. Heien found that, for seven of the eleven countries, the price elasticities in the first subperiod (roughly 1950–54) differed from those in the 1955–64 period. For Germany, the import-price relationship was extremely unstable; it differed in three subperiods: 1949–53, 1954–57, and 1958–64. Only for Canada, France, and the Netherlands was the price relationship stable throughout the entire period. The instability of the price relationship for 1950–54 compared with the later period for the remaining seven countries is not surprising and is probably due more to exogenous factors such as postwar rebuilding, the Korean War, and other disruptions than to the purely economic and structural factors discussed above.

As another check of the trade-price relationship, I have tested U.S. exports to 15 countries for the period 1951–69. The specification is similar to that given in equation (1): i is the United States, j is the foreign market involved, and k is non-U.S. suppliers. The subperiods tested were 1951–60 and 1961–69.[14] The

---

13 While they did not test the stability of the coefficients explicitly, we can infer stability from the standard errors of the equation for the total period and the information given in the equations for the two subperiods.

14 In most of the equations, the zero-degree homogeneity constraint was imposed on the price coefficients. The testing proceeded as follows. First, tests were made to see if there were changes in the relationships between the subperiods in equations subject to the homogeneity constraint. Second, if the analysis of variance revealed that significant price changes had occurred, the homogeneity constraint was relaxed and the analysis of variance was repeated in order to pinpoint which price variable was responsible for the change in the relative price relationship in the first step.

results indicate that for seven of the fifteen countries there were significant changes in the effects of prices. In two of these seven cases (the United Kingdom and Denmark), when the individual price coefficients were tested separately I found that neither the own- nor the cross-price effect had changed *individually* in a statistically significant way, even though the relative price coefficient changed significantly. Thus, while the change in neither of the individual price coefficients was large enough to indicate a significant change, the sum of the two effects combined with the homogeneity constraint did reveal a significant change in the relative price approach. In the Japanese case, there was no change in the own-price relationship [coefficient f_2 in equation (1)], but there were significant changes in both cross-price effects (f_3 and f_4 changed). In the remaining four of seven cases the own-price elasticity changed significantly, and in all cases the elasticity declined from relatively large and negative values to insignificance, or in one case to a significantly positive price elasticity.

In summary, the evidence does not refute the hypothesis that there is substantial instability in trade-price relationships in the postwar period. This may warrant, inter alia, direct estimation of e_{dp} and e_{sp} in equation (11) and better integration of the pure theory into future empirical work.

Money, Factor Flows, and General-Equilibrium Models

I turn to models that incorporate bond markets and money markets. Studies by Mundell (1968), Komiya (1969), Dornbusch (1971b), and Frenkel (1971) have produced some interesting propositions regarding the relationships between the growth of income, trade, and the balance of payments, while Johnson (1972b) has related the balance of payments to strictly monetary variables.

Consider a small country producing a single good. If absorption exceeds output, the economy has an excess demand for goods and a trade-balance deficit:

$$Y = A + (X - M), \tag{12}$$

where Y is income, A is absorption (expenditure), and $(X - M)$ is the value of net exports, or the trade balance. Since there are two other markets, a bond market and a money market, if $(X - M) < 0$, there must be excess flow supply in the other two markets combined, implying a gap between desired and actual stocks in those markets (see Johnson, 1967a) for flow and stock concepts of disequilibrium. Let us consider two polar cases, given the trade-balance deficit. First, if the bond market is in equilibrium, there must be an excess flow supply of money. Cash balances will be run down by exporting money (i.e., running a balance-of-payments deficit). Since the sum of the excess flow demands in the three markets must equal zero, the net import of goods must equal the net export of money (or the loss in foreign-exchange reserves). Second, if the money market is in equilibrium but the bond market is not, then the balance of payments will be in equilibrium; the trade-balance deficit (the excess demand for goods) will be offset by a capital-account surplus (an excess supply of bonds). The power of the small-country assumption should be apparent here. Since all prices are fixed in world markets, net excess demands in the three markets are immediately reflected in the corresponding balance-of-payments category.

These considerations imply that an increase in population growth, for example, leads to an increase in the flow demand for cash balances, and, if there is no increase in the flow supply by the domestic monetary authorities, an improvement in the balance of payments. The trade balance improves if at the same time absorption declines relative to income (savings increase more than investment) and deteriorates in the opposite case. The capital account can also go either way (see Dornbusch, 1971b). *This result, based on a macro model, reinforces the case made earlier in the discussion of the pure theory that the relationship between income growth and the trade balance can be positive or negative.*

There have been few attempts to identify empirically exogenous factors that could be used to predict secular trends in the pattern of excess flow demands in the three markets (goods, securities, and money). Houthakker and Magee (1969) attempted to isolate factors in real markets that might predict secularly either an excess supply or demand for tradeable goods. They tested whether the income elasticity of demand for a country's exports was significantly different from the income elasticity of demand for its imports. If the import income elasticity was significantly greater than the export income elasticity, as was found in the case of the United States and the United Kingdom, this was hypothesized to indicate a possible net excess *demand* for tradeable goods in the long run, and a forecast of secular trade-balance deterioration. An asymmetry in which the export income elasticity exceeded the import income elasticity would indicate possible excess *supply* in the tradeable-goods sector in the long run; statistical tests found that only Japan was in this category (Germany had a similar pattern, but the differences in the elasticities were not statistically significant). The equations on which these results were based were estimated from 1951 to 1966. Subsequent developments in the trade balances of the United Kingdom, United States, and Japan are not inconsistent with the hypothesis.

Two criticisms can be leveled at the Houthakker and Magee results. First, Morgan (1971) questioned the adequacy of the price data used and noted how aggregation bias could influence the results. Second, there is no consideration of the interaction of the goods markets with either the money or securities markets. Even if the prediction holds that the trade balance will decline, the model is not capable of determining the composition of the implied excess flow supply of securities and money; it is powerless to make categorical statements about the balance of payments. The trade-balance deficit leads to a balance-of-payments deficit only to the extent that it is converted into an excess supply of money. For this same reason, as Johnson (1972b) and others have shown, the balance of payments is controllable through control of domestic credit creation. Starting from stock equilibrium in money markets, growth leads to a deterioration in a country's balance of payments only if domestic credit creation exceeds the growth in the domestic demand for money.

A trade model incorporating this monetary approach to the balance of payments was constructed by Schotta (1966); it built on earlier work at the International Monetary Fund by Polak and White (1954–55), Polak (1957), Polak and Boissonneault (1960), Fleming and Boissonneault (1961), and Prais (1961). Schotta's model is not directed at trade per se, but rather at testing monetary versus Keynesian approaches to the determination of domestic income in Mexico. He found that the Keynesian multiplier approach explained between 44 and 50 per cent of the variance in money national income in Mexico, while the monetary model explained 70 per cent of the variance. There are a number of studies under way which find the monetary approach to the balance of payments promising empirically. The key to success is the ability to estimate the demand for money in the economy in question. The change in the country's international reserves follows immediately from this demand equation, together with an identity and the behavior of the monetary authorities.

A Patinkin (1965) type of general-equilibrium model of trade, bond, and money flows was constructed by Courchene (1970). It incorporates explicitly the theoretical links between commodity markets, bond markets, and money markets in a multicountry world. Unfortunately, the model was not estimated empirically.

At least two empirical studies link trade and capital flows explicitly. Sedjo (1971) used annual data from 1926–39 and 1950–63 to explain changes in the Canadian trade balance. He found that autonomous capital inflows into Canada are highly significant in explaining these changes (they have a negative coefficient). In most of the second part of the estimation period, Canada's excess demand for currency is constrained to zero by the floating Canadian dollar. Thus, the excess supply of items on current account must equal the excess demand for securities. As Sedjo was aware, there is therefore a problem in relating trade and capital flows in a floating system. Care must be taken to estimate meaningful behavioral relations rather than an identity.

A study by Niehans (1965) derived the impact of trade-balance changes on the capital account. He found a strong positive relationship between the Swiss trade-balance deficit for merchandise and the Swiss interest rate. He reasoned that an increase in imports relative to exports owing to an increase in national income results in a contraction of the money supply as reserves flow out. At the same time, the increase in national income brings about an increase in the demand for transactions balances. The reduced flow supply of money to domestic residents and the increased flow demand for money cause the interest rate to rise. He found that the interest-rate changes lagged four to five months behind the trade-balance changes and noted that both of these variables are endogenous and only a part of a larger macro-economic model.

Financial capital flows that involve some control over foreign operations (direct investment as opposed to portfolio investment) have implications for trade (apart from the general-equilibrium properties just enumerated); the technology used by foreign affiliates of U.S. multinational corporations, for example, frequently involves use of goods from the home country. This factor partially offsets the reduction in exports caused by increases in direct investment and may explain results reported by Lipsey and Weiss (1972). They found that the activity of foreign affiliates of U.S. firms in foreign markets is negatively related to exports to that market by non-U.S. countries, but the relationship between U.S. affiliates and U.S. exports was ambiguous. In general, direct investment may either substitute for or complement trade.

Finally, I shall discuss the relationship between trade flows and factor movements. Much of the early pure-theory literature (e.g., Samuelson on factor-price equalization), as well as the empirical specification of trade flows in equations (1) through (6), assumes international factor immobility. However, the only motivation for trade is to accommodate the lack of correlation between the locations of production and consumption. As Ohlin (1970, p. 18) stated, "The flows of commodites are chiefly the result of the . . . economic location of production and the distribution of population." Through time, increases in income lead to increases in imported goods, imported factors, or both. There is no theoretical reason why excess product demand should be supplied by trade instead of by increased factor movements. Empirical studies have largely ignored these interactions of the goods market and factor markets in accommodating differential demand growth among regions. The relationship between factor augmentation and production was examined theoretically by Rybczynski (1955). His work was extended by Mundell (1968, Chap. 6), who showed that a small country could reach the same level of welfare with a prohibitive tariff that was possible·with free trade if one of the factors of production was perfectly mobile. Olivera (1967) showed that even though either free trade or free factor mobility will lead to a complete equalization of factor prices, this does not by itself imply that the two approaches will lead to equalization of factor prices at the same levels. This is important for econometric work, since it means that the composition of world output and employment may differ in the two situations.

Since increases in aggregate income may be supplied by either increased trade, increased factor movements, or both, then, technically, empirical trade studies should incorporate changes in relative transport costs as an explanatory variable. There are also data problems. Movements of physical capital are reported as trade flows, and labor movements are subject to the vagaries of national immigration policies; the effects of both on trade occur with long lags. Trade in existing capital goods, à la Rybczynski, is a reshuffling of endowments which will eventually reduce trade in the standard well-behaved static model.

3. SOME PRACTICAL AND METHODOLOGICAL CONSIDERATIONS

This section is a miscellany of comments on problems arising in estimation and specification of international trade equations, evidence on lags, trade behavior over the business cycle, and factors that would cause estimated price elasticities to *exceed* true values.

The Orcuttization of Empirical Studies

Orcutt (1950), Machlup (1950), and Harberger (1953) have shown why empirically estimated price elasticities of demand for internationally traded goods are downward biased.[15] Orcutt's famous list consisted of five factors. Estimated price elasticities could be biased downward because of *simultaneity,* random *observation errors* in the price indices, *aggregation, timing* (short-run elasticities are smaller than long-run elasticities), and *quantum effects* (elasticities are larger for large price changes than for small price changes). While these were important observations, unfortunately they have led to what might be called "Orcuttization" of empirical work in international trade (due not so much to Orcutt as to those of us who followed). The emphasis in empirical work on international trade inadvertently shifted from theoretical and logical improvements to the mechanics of refining estimation techniques. What started as a preoccupation rapidly turned into an obsession over the coefficient of one variable in the entire system – the price coefficient. A normative discussion of some of the reasons for the profession's extended interest in the price coefficient, and the implications of this fascination, will be pursued at the conclusion of this paper. I shall focus here on the positive aspects of Orcutt's five points.

The findings on *simultaneous-equation bias* are somewhat mixed. Both Magee (1970) and Richardson (1972) found evidence that the standard techniques for eliminating simultaneous-equation bias succeeded in increasing the price elasticities of demand. However, in this process Magee (1970) found that the estimated elasticity of supply for U.S. imports was 8.5 (with a t value of 3.7) and for U.S. exports was 11.5 (with a t value of 3.6).[16] While I have some reservations about these estimates (both the specification and the statistical results had problems, such as a Durbin–Watson statistic for the import supply equation of 0.44), they are sufficiently high, if valid, to reduce concern about the simultaneous-equation problem in estimating international demand functions. One of the greatest dangers of continued emphasis on the simultaneous-equation problem is that researchers (including this one) sometimes incorrectly conclude that any reasonable specification that increases estimated international price elasticities of demand must be a step in the right direction. Incorrect functional

---

15 At one time, the procedure in vogue for obtaining the "true" import price elasticity of demand was to add 1 or 2 standard errors to the estimated price coefficient.
16 The corresponding price elasticity of demand was -0.3 for U.S. imports (with a t-value of -0.8) and -2.0 for exports (with a t-value of -2.3).

forms, data mining, and excessive experimentation with lags can lead to upward rather than downward bias in the price coefficients (see the end of this section).

There are problems with three of Orcutt's points, on observation errors, timing, and the quantum effect. Orcutt was right that *observation errors* in the own price variable will cause the own price elasticity to be biased toward zero, but only on his assumption that "errors in the [dependent] quantity variable . . . are uncorrelated with the observed price and income variables" (Orcutt, 1950, p. 548). In many empirical studies, however, errors in the quantity variable are negatively correlated with the price variable. This is because the quantity indices used as the dependent variables in import demand equations are derived by deflating an error-free value series by an import price variable subject to random errors. Kemp (1962a) has shown that, in this case, the estimated import price elasticity will be biased toward -1 rather than toward zero. Hence, empirically estimated price elasticities that fall between 0 and -1 are too large in absolute value and elasticities greater absolutely than -1 are too small in absolute value. (Kemp's proof assumes "exact" demand and large samples.) Orcutt was not strictly correct on the *timing* issue, since short-run elasticities will be larger than long-run elasticities if the purchases are made for inventories. Houthakker and Taylor (1970, p. 164) found that in 28 per cent of the categories for which they estimated domestic U.S. demand equations, this inventory behavior dominates. While Orcutt's a priori arguments were persuasive with regard to the *quantum effect* (that elasticities are larger for large price changes than for small price changes), I do not find much empirical support for this effect in events following the 1971 currency realignments. In the period from the end of the Korean War until 1971, annual changes in the international prices of goods traded by developed countries were modest compared to the price changes implied by the 1971 currency realignments. Yet a number of models (including my own) estimated over this period predicted, *ex ante,* that the realignment would have much larger effects on 1972 trade than actually occurred (see Branson, 1972). One explanation is that we underestimated the length of the lags relating trade and prices and that this error offset the quantum effect. Another explanation relates to the "passthrough" problem and the speed with which the relative prices of traded goods between countries respond to exchange-rate changes (see section 4 on "Devaluation"). However, some skepticism of the empirical relevance of Orcutt's quantum effect is warranted, particularly in light of the study of Laffer (1973b) (again, see section 4 on

"Devaluation"). There are also technical reasons why researchers might incorrectly infer larger effects of exchange-rate changes than actually occur (see the end of this section). These errors also weaken the quantum effect.

Of Orcutt's five points, the *aggregation* problem still remains the most troubling problem in empirical work on international trade.[17] For that reason, it merits extended discussion (see Appendix A for an elaboration of the discussion here).

Consider the effects of policy-induced import price increases. Assume that there are n imported products and we know the "true" product price elasticities, price changes, and trade weights for individual imports. If we use the trade weights to construct an average aggregate price elasticity and an average aggregate price change, will the product of these two yield the "true" aggregate quantity change? Because of the aggregation problem, the answer is usually "No."

A simple explanation can be given if we assume that all the component products have equal weights (see the numerical example in Appendix A). If there is strong negative correlation between the component-product price changes and their elasticities, the actual total quantity change will be less than the product of the total elasticity and the aggregate price change. The reason is that products with large price changes should receive smaller effective weights because their effect on total trade operates through a small elasticity. This correlation between the disaggregated price changes and elasticities is lost when the two are aggregated separately and then multiplied together (see Barker, 1969, for a good discussion of this problem).

A "true" aggregate price elasticity which incorporates all the information that disaggregation can provide (and which, when multiplied by the aggregate price change, gives an estimate of the total quantity change free of aggregation error) is shown in equation (13):

$$e_p = \sum_i e_{pi} \, (m_i/m) \frac{dp_i/p_i}{dp/p} \tag{13}$$

$$\text{(a)} \qquad \text{(b)} \qquad \text{(c)}$$

---

17 The problem exists for both aggregation over time (see Zellner and Montmarquette, 1971) and aggregation over commodities (see Grunfeld and Griliches, 1960). The latter felt that aggregation error over commodities may be partially offset by the reduction in the specification bias that occurs with relationships estimated at a disaggregated level. Edwards and Orcutt (1969) feel that, for forecasting, disaggregated estimation is always better.

where e_p is the "correct" aggregate price elasticity, i indicates the component number in the total (the product number, country number, etc.), m_i/m is the share of component i in total imports, and the final term (c) is the "distribution elasticity," that is, the percentage change in price component i relative to the percentage change in the aggregate price index (see Appendix A for the derivation of this formula). I have calculated three aggregate price elasticities using the five commodity categories for U.S. imports listed in Table 2. The price and distribution elasticities were estimated from annual data, 1951–69, and the trade weights are for 1963. The results of estimating the U.S. import price elasticity from a single total equation yielded a value of −1.35; a weighted average of the five component elasticities was −2.23; calculation of an aggregate price elasticity using equation (13) yielded a value of −1.15. Comparison of the last two elasticities illustrates Orcutt's point: historically, items with high demand elasticity tend to have small variations in their price indices, so that the distribution elasticities for high-elasticity items are low.

If a policy change is being considered, such as a tariff cut, the "policy relevant" aggregate price elasticity is a function of the disaggregated elasticities, recent weights, and the distribution elasticities that are implied by the tariff cuts themselves. The "historical" price elasticity estimated either from a single total equation or from equation (13) [if historical distribution elasticities were used in (13)] would be inappropriate, since the distribution elasticities implied by the policy change may differ considerably from the historical elasticities. In short, there is no such thing as "the" elasticity of demand; calculation of an accurate aggregate price elasticity requires knowledge of disaggregated behavior. An example of nonuniform disaggregated price changes caused by a policy decision was the U.S. import surcharge of 10 per cent imposed on 15 August, 1971. The application of the surcharge to U.S. imports varied considerably by country, from about a third for U.S. imports from Canada to over 90 per cent for U.S. imports from Japan.

In general, the rule is to work at a disaggregated level, if possible, and sum the effects of prices on trade as the last step. If estimates must be done at an aggregate level, then the aggregate elasticity should approximate the disaggregated information contained in equation (13), rather than a simple weighted average of the component elasticities.

Lags

In this subsection I will consider the empirical evidence on the time lags between changes in independent variables and their effects on international trade flows. Junz and Rhomberg (1965, p. 259) pooled cross-section and time-series data to estimate the effects of relative price changes on international market shares. They found that, on average, a 1 per cent increase in a country's relative price would lead to a 3 per cent decrease in the quantity of its exports within two years, and to a decrease of approximately 5 per cent after four years.[18] In a more recent paper, Junz and Rhomberg (1973) updated their earlier work and discussed the reasons why price changes will have relatively slow effects on internationally traded goods: there may be recognition lags, decision lags, delivery lags,[19] replacement lags, and production lags. Again, using a combination of cross-section and time-series data, they found that the price elasticities of market shares in international trade increased for the three years following the year of the price change, then declined. They showed that there are statistically significant effects of price changes on trade for five years after a price change. In effect, the lags are six years long (including the year in which the price change occurred), and within the last five years, the peak occurs in the third year.

There is evidence on lags derived from Koyck estimation in the Houthakker and Magee (1969) results in Table 2. It is interesting to compare the long-run elasticities derived from the quarterly data, line 4b of Table 2, with the unlagged annual elasticities derived in line 5a (reported in Magee, 1970). For the *income* variable, the long-run elasticities in line 4b and the annual elasticities in line 5a are remarkably similar, with the single exception of crude foodstuffs. It would appear that most of the long-run effects occur within the first four quarters. On the other hand, the long-run price elasticities in line 4b and the annual price elasticities in line 5a show much less correspondence. One problem is that the period of estimation differs for the two studies. Another is that the Koyck lags in line 4b may be dominated by the income variable and these lags are inappropriate for the price variable.

18 The corresponding changes in the value of exports would be 2 per cent and 4 per cent, respectively.

19 Artus (1973) calculated the average export *delivery* delays in days from three countries in the fourth quarter of 1971 to be: for machinery – 400 for Germany, 297 for the United Kingdom and 107 for the United States; for machine tools – 308 for the United Kingdom and 217 for the United States. He stresses that these figures are not strictly comparable across countries because of differences in statistical coverage.

Grimm (1968) has estimated lag patterns for the effects of prices on U.S. trade using the polynomial-distributed-lag (Almon) technique (see Branson, 1972, Table 15, p. 56, for a summary of Grimm's price lags). Using quarterly data from 1954 to 1962, Grimm found that for U.S. imports of food, beef, feed and beverages, consumer goods, and "other imports," the price effect had a total lag length of one to two quarters (excluding the quarter of the price change), while for industrial supplies and materials, capital goods, and autos and parts, the lag length was three to five quarters. For U.S. exports, the lag length was one quarter for crude materials and manufactures, while it was five to seven quarters for food stuffs and manufactures, electrical machinery, and autos and parts.

Buckler and Almon (1972) have estimated price elasticities for a large number of commodity categories for their U.S. input–output model. Several lag structures were attempted for U.S. imports; the most satisfactory results gave a weight of 0.25 to the current price, 0.65 to the price lagged one year, and 0.10 to the price lagged two years (the price variable being the ratio of the foreign to the domestic price).

A study by Heien (1968) estimated import functions for seven countries. The specification of the equation was similar to equation (2), except that consumption rather than income was the activity variable. Heien's procedure was to choose seven arbitrary lag structures, set the lag length at three years (including the current year), construct a single consumption variable and price variable using the alternative lag structures for both, and run the equations using the alternative lag structures to find the best fit. Since there were two variables and seven alternative lag patterns for each, he estimated 7^2, or 49, equations for each country. The best equation from the 49 for each country presumably gives the "correct" lag pattern for the effects of consumption and relative prices on its imports. The lag structures for the best equations are reported in Table 4.

Several comments are in order. First, there is an unfortunate amount of data mining involved in this exercise, as in the Almon procedure. Second, Heien's results appear to refute the notion that price lags are longer than income or expenditure lags (see the means for the lags at the bottom of Table 4). The results also indicate that three-fourths of the effect of a price or consumption change occurs within one year, while the bulk of the remainder occurs within the second year. Since 48 other equations were estimated for each country, it would be of some interest to know

TABLE 4   *Lag Structures Estimated by Heien (1968) for the Effects on Real Imports of Real Consumption and the Relative Price of Imports*[a] (annual data)

Country	Period of Estimation	Weight Attached to the Variable by Year[b]					
		Real Consumption			Relative Prices		
		t	$t-1$	$t-2$	t	$t-1$	$t-2$
Austria	1950–64	0.42	0.46	0.12	0.90	0.10	0.00
Belgium–Lux.	1953–64	0.90	0.10	0.00	0.72	0.26	0.02
Canada	1951–65	0.90	0.10	0.00	0.56	0.38	0.06
Denmark	1949–64	1.00	0.00	0.00	0.72	0.38	0.02
France	1950–64	1.00	0.00	0.00	1.00	0.00	0.00
Germany	1949–64	1.00	0.00	0.00	0.72	0.26	0.02
Italy	1950–64	0.56	0.38	0.06	0.42	0.46	0.12
Netherlands	1950–64	0.72	0.26	0.02	1.00	0.00	0.00
Norway	1950–65	0.25	0.50	0.25	0.56	0.38	0.06
Sweden	1950–64	0.90	0.10	0.00	1.00	0.00	0.00
United States	1947–65	0.56	0.38	0.06	1.00	0.00	0.00
Unweighted average		0.75	0.20	0.05	0.77	0.20	0.03

[a]The relative price is the ratio of the country's import price index to its cost-of-living index.

[b]Notice that there are six different lag patterns reported in this table. A seventh lag pattern, 0.09, 0.42, and 0.49, did not give a "best" fit for any of the countries.

how many of these equations explained almost as much variance in imports as the best equations reported in Table 4. It would also have been interesting to test the patterns in Table 4 against a Koyck or truncated Koyck-type lag to see if there was a statistically significant difference between the two lag patterns. This could be done ad hoc by (a) estimating each of the country equations with the lagged dependent variable on the right-hand side; (b) taking its coefficient, say a, and estimating an alternative equation for each country which used the weights 1, a, and a^2 on both the consumption and relative price variables; and then (c) comparing these fits with the equations in Table 4, using an analysis of variance.

One problem with estimating lags is that the time series are generally too short, at least on an annual basis, to permit a precise estimate of the effect of price and income changes on trade patterns. Most of the success reported in finding lag lengths longer than three years has been through the pooling of cross-section and time-series data by Junz and Rhomberg (1965, 1973).

Another problem in estimating lags relates to the price data.

Unit values are sometimes the only price series available for traded goods. The unit value for goods crossing the border in any given month is constructed by dividing the value of the goods by the quantity. But this price may not equal the current price at which the goods could be obtained; the unit value is the price that was negotiated when the goods were contracted. For example, if there is a five-year time lag in ship construction and delivery, then the unit value of a ship imported in January of 1970 reflects the price of ships when they were contracted for in January of 1965. Each component in trade has its own separate lag distribution, and the lag between contract and delivery dates cannot be determined by regressing the quantity of imports on present and past unit values.

This is an important problem and plagues all trade studies that have used unit values. [See the report of The Review Committee for Balance of Payments Statistics (1965, pp. 27–31) for general problems in trade valuation which affect unit values.] Since an import price index based on unit values and a domestic price index may refer to very different points in time, it is improper to impose homogeneity through the use of relative price variables.

The Cyclical Behavior of Trade

The merchandise trade balance fluctuates a great deal over the business cycle. This is usually due more to variation in the demand for imports in the country experiencing the business fluctuations than in the supply of its exports, although there is evidence that the latter contributes some variation to the trade balance. Import functions such as equation (2), which are either linear or log-linear in income and prices, usually do not capture the extent to which imports vary over the cycle. I shall discuss three studies that attempt to explain the cyclical component in the demand for imports[20] and three that focus on export behavior.

Branson (1968a) investigated U.S. imports quarterly from 1955 to 1966. His dependent variable is the ratio of money imports to money GNP; his activity variables are trend GNP (which captures the secular income effect) and a nonlinear transformation of the Federal Reserve Board index of U.S. utilization of manufacturing capacity (which captures the cyclical component). The nonlinear transformation causes the proxy utilization variable to increase dramatically as actual utilization of capacity approaches 95 per

[20] For an earlier study on this subject, see Harberger (1953) and revisions to the original arguments in Harberger (1957, p. 510n).

cent, to represent the fact that, as the economy reaches full capacity, prices are sticky and do not rise enough to reflect accurately the tightness of commodity markets.

Gregory (1971) studied the same problem in a quarterly model of U.S. merchandise imports from 1948 to 1968. He, too, used as his dependent variable the ratio of imports to domestic goods production, but both were defined in real terms. He was expressly interested in the fact that, in the short run, producers do not adjust their prices to meet fluctuations in demand but use waiting times, credit terms, and other nonprice methods to make fluctuations in demand correspond with their supplies. Gregory found considerable evidence that the response of demanders was to increase the ratio of imports to domestic production in upswings. He found that delivery lags and other nonprice variables were significant in capturing the increased waiting time faced by domestic consumers and in explaining the cyclical variation in imports. He also found that these measures were superior to the rate of capacity utilization used by Branson (1968a). When proxy variables for waiting time were used to calculate "effective prices," higher estimates of the elasticity of substitution between foreign and domestic goods were obtained than those derived from more traditional specifications of import demand that used actual prices as market-clearing variables.

Marston's (1971) study of quarterly U.K. imports (1955-I through 1967-III) cited other reasons why we might expect import demand to vary over the cycle. Through the accelerator, the demand for investment goods rises faster than income in the upswing, and if imports of investment goods have a higher than average import coefficient, we might expect them to contribute some variability to the import/income ratio. Imports for inventories also show great volatility over the business cycle. (Johnston and Henderson, 1967, and Burns, 1969, have also included inventory behavior as an important cyclical component.) Marston found that both the trend and cyclical income variables were significant in explaining imports. He estimated polynomial distributed lags on the cyclical income variable and found that they were shorter than lags estimated in previous studies of both British and American imports. An important implication of all of these studies is that failure to separate cyclical and secular components can lead to overestimation of the secular income elasticity of demand for imports.

I turn now from the effects of the cycle on the *demand for imports* to variables affecting the *supply of exports*. Steuer *et al.* (1966) found that the flow of foreign orders received by the U.K. machine-tool industry was influenced more by large delivery delays (caused by rising home demand) than by relative prices. They found that a one-month increase in waiting time for U.K. exports of machine tools resulted in a reduction in foreign orders of about 10 per cent. However, they did not extend their analysis to calculate the effect of increased waiting time on the delivery of exports.

This extension was provided by Artus (1973), who investigated the export production behavior of machinery industries in Germany, the United Kingdom, and the United States, using quarterly data from 1956 to 1971 (or appropriate subperiods for which data were available). He calculated that a 10 per cent increase in domestic demand resulted ultimately in an increase in export delivery delays of 18 days for German machinery (4.5 per cent), 20 days for U.K. machinery (6.7 per cent), 5 days for U.S. machinery (4.7 per cent), 8 days for U.K. machine tools (2.6 per cent) and 10 days for U.S. machine tools (4.6 per cent).[21] Artus then linked his results with Steuer *et al.* (1966) to conclude that a 10 per cent increase in U.K. domestic demand will ultimately reduce the level of British exports of machine tools by 3 per cent.

Mintz (1967) provides some interesting noneconometric evidence on the effects of cyclical fluctuations on the supply of U.S. exports. She observed that, assuming constant world demand from 1921 to 1961, expansions in domestic business activity in the United States were associated with decreases in the quantity of exports and increases in export prices.[22] Furthermore, the price effect was sufficiently strong to raise the total value of U.S. exports during U.S. expansions. This rather interesting behavior was examined at a more disaggregated level by dividing U.S. exports into four broad commodity classes: crude materials, food, semimanufactures, and finished manufactures. Mintz found that domestic U.S. expansions would retard the quantities exported in the first three groups, while the quantities of finished manufactures would increase slightly. The strength of the positive correlation between business activity and export prices varied across product groups. Expansions would coincide very closely with increases in the prices of semimanufactured exports, to a lesser degree with prices of finished manufactured exports, and less regularly with the other two categories. The paradoxical positive relationship between the value of total exports and

21 See footnote 19 for the average export delays for these cases.
22 The summary of Mintz's work reported here deals with the supply side only: "world demand" is held constant in her study.

domestic expansions was due to the fact that the increases in the quantity of finished manufactures and the prices of semimanufactures more than offset the declines in the quantities of crude materials and foods.

The Mintz study is important for three reasons. First, it is rich with hypotheses to be tested and extended by econometric work on the supply of traded goods. Second, it indicates that policies designed to cut absorption by reducing U.S. domestic activity have, as a rule, not been translated into increases in the value of U.S. exports. Third, it is a useful starting point for future empirical studies of the monetary-absorption analysis of the balance of payments.

Orcutt: A Counterlist

Orcutt's famous list dealt with reasons why empirically estimated import price elasticities might be lower than the actual elasticities. His paper responded to the extremely low estimates of price elasticities obtained from data on the interwar period, which, when inserted in the elasticities formulas of Joan Robinson and others, led to pessimism about the ability of exchange-rate changes to exert a stabilizing influence on trade. The postwar price elasticities reported in this paper are much higher than those obtained from data on the 1920s and 1930s, and, as we shall see, generally satisfy the Marshall–Lerner condition.

There is increasing evidence that perhaps we should balance Orcutt's list with considerations to the contrary, namely, *under what conditions will empirically estimated price elasticities be too high or their effects overstated?* At least eight cases can be cited, some of them coming from points made earlier in this section and some coming from work by MacDougall (1952) and White (1970).

1. *Nonprice rationing.* Since prices are relatively sticky in the short run, nonprice rationing, changes in delivery dates, length of queues, etc., are variables that assist prices in clearing markets. If the length of queues and prices move together, and if we misspecify import demand functions by failing to include the queueing factor, then the quantity movements caused by both prices and queues will be attributed to the price variable alone. This leads to an overstatement of the price effect and upward bias in the estimated price elasticity of import demand.

Orcutt's (1950) quantum effect was based on the psychological and economic costs of switching sources. These would cause price elasticities to be lower for small price changes than for large ones, such as those occasioned by changes in foreign-exchange rates. It is not necessarily true, however, that predictions of effects on trade of changes in prices (such as exchange-rate changes) will be too low if based on elasticities estimated over a period of small price changes. We turn now to two errors which economists can make in estimating the trade effects of large price changes which may more than offset Orcutt's quantum effect. While these two points are stated in terms of the elasticities of substitution, they carry over directly to the elasticities of demand [see Leamer and Stern (1970, p. 60), who show that the elasticity of substitution is implicitly equal to the direct less the cross-price elasticities of demand].

2. *Cross-price effects.* White (1970) has shown that the price effect on exports of exchange-rate changes can be overstated when calculations are performed at a disaggregated level, if elasticities of substitution differ by market. If an elasticity of substitution for the United States versus all other suppliers were estimated by pooling cross-section and/or time-series data for U.S. exports by country, as in MacDougall (1951, 1952), Junz and Rhomberg (1965), and others, then the overall elasticity of substitution obtained from the regression, say −4, would be an average of the elasticities across markets. Assume that there is a 10 per cent devaluation of the dollar, that the U.S. export supply elasticity is high, and that we predict a 5 per cent decrease in the average export price of all non-U.S. suppliers to each market, so that, in total, the U.S. relative price falls by 5 per cent in terms of foreign currencies. Does this imply a 20 per cent increase in the relative quantity of total U.S. exports (-4×-5)? The answer is "No": The increase will be less than 20 per cent, since non-U.S. supplier prices will fall by *more* than 5 per cent in highly competitive markets with high substitution elasticities and by *less* than 5 per cent in markets with low substitution elasticities. This negative correlation between the substitution elasticities and price changes explains the reduced overall effect in the same way that the negative correlation between the demand elasticities and distribution elasticities in equation (13) at the beginning of this section reduces the true aggregate price elasticity below a weighted average of the component elasticities.

3. *Structural effects.* MacDougall (1952) and White (1970) give another reason why pooled time-series and cross-section data will yield an overestimate of the total elasticity of substitution between the trade of two competitors into several markets. This bias holds

even when the elasticity of substitution is identical across all markets, the values of total exports by the two competitors are identical, the markets are of equal size, and the relative price change induced by a devaluation causes relative prices to change by the same amount in each market. The bias arises because exporters specialize in different markets and is best explained by a slight modification of MacDougall's (1952, p. 493) example. Assume that U.S. and U.K. prices are initially unity and that the total value of U.S. and U.K. trade equals $100 in each case. Assume further that $99 of U.S. trade goes to Canada and $1 to Europe, while the reverse is true for the United Kingdom. If the elasticity of substitution equals −4 between U.S. and U.K. exports to both markets (and the total market size remains unchanged with relative price changes), a 1 per cent decrease in U.S. prices relative to U.K. prices results in a rise in the ratio of U.S. to U.K. exports to Canada from 99/1 to roughly 99.04/.96, or 4 per cent. Similarly, there is a rise in the ratio of U.S. to U.K. exports to Europe from 1/99 to roughly 1.04/98.96, or 4 per cent. However, the rise in the ratio of total U.S. to total U.K. exports to both markets is from 100/100 to roughly 100.08/99.92, which is only a fraction of 1 per cent.

Thus it is improper to derive an elasticity of substitution across several markets (and/or products) and use this elasticity to calculate the effect of a price change on the two countries' total trade. MacDougall (1952, Appendix C) derives a formula to correct for such structural differences in the patterns of trade. He finds that *the elasticity derived from individual submarkets* (−4 in the example) *forms the upper limit on the "total" elasticity*: the *total* elasticity equals −4 only if the two countries have the *same* pattern of exports across markets. Otherwise, the total elasticity must be less than −4 in absolute value. This mathematical phenomenon also makes economic sense: Even though the total trade of the United States and the United Kingdom is of the same size, they do not really compete in total, since they specialize in different markets.

4. *Understated lags.* The use of unit values in estimating import demand functions leads us to understate the true length of the lags in effects of price changes on quantity, because unit values reflect prices prevailing when the goods were contracted. (See the subsection above on "Lags.") This causes us to be overly optimistic about the speed with which exchange-rate changes will affect trade (although not necessarily about the ultimate effects).

5. *Inversely correlated measurement errors.* For estimated price elasticities that are less than unity in absolute value, I restate

Kemp's (1962a) point, noted at the beginning of this section: If the quantity variable is obtained by dividing a value series by a price index that is subject to random measurement errors, the estimated demand elasticity will exceed the actual elasticity in absolute value. (The reverse is true for elasticities above unity.)

6. *Aggregate prices in submarkets.* Assume, following White (1970), that one attempts to explain exports from the United States to a number of foreign countries and that price indices of exports to each market are not available. Assume that we attempt to explain the quantity of exports to each market using the total price index of all U.S. exports as the own price variable in each of the country equations. We shall distinguish two cases.

a. Assume that we have somehow obtained the true quantity of exports to each market and use an error-free aggregate export price index as the price variable. Assume also that the component prices move in the same direction as the aggregate price index. The true component price changes for countries with low elasticities of demand are apt to be high relative to component price changes for countries with high elasticities of demand. This implies that the *overall* price index will show less variation than the *component* prices for countries with low demand elasticities, and greater variation than the component prices for countries with high demand elasticities. For low-elasticity countries, the quantity of trade is regressed on a price index with smaller variations than actually occurred, biasing upward the estimated price elasticity. (For high-elasticity countries, the quantity is regressed on a price index with larger variations than actually occurred, leading to downward bias.)

b. Assume next that the values of exports to each market are deflated by the total export price index. This situation is similar to Kemp's (1962a). In cases in which the properties here are identical to those with random errors in variables, the results in point 5 hold here as well.

7. *Positive component elasticities.* This point follows a suggestion made by Jacques Artus. Assume that price elasticities are estimated for many components of total trade (either by product or by country). If all *true* direct price elasticities are negative, then any *estimated* price elasticity that is positive is due to error (misspecification, etc.). But if the estimation errors are random, an average of the estimated price elasticities, appropriately weighted to take care of aggregation problems, will yield a correct aggregate price elasticity. However, there is a tendency for researchers to throw out or set equal to zero all estimated compo-

nent price elasticities that are positive before performing the aggregation. This throws out part of the positive tail *only* of the random-error distribution. Thus, the average aggregate elasticity computed from such component price elasticities yields an upward bias in the aggregate elasticity.

8. *Orcuttization.* This point is more psychological than technical. Orcutt's (1950) list produced the assumption that estimated price elasticites could only be biased downward. As noted earlier, this has led to data mining and use of alternative specifications and lag patterns in an effort to increase the size of the price coefficient. When maximizing the size of the price coefficient becomes an important criterion for statistical acceptability (along with goodness of fit), we are in danger of overcompensating for Orcutt's causes of downward bias.

The statistical importance of these factors, compared with Orcutt's causes of downward bias, can be determined only by future research. The important point is that the bias may go either way and the direction depends on the problem at hand and the techniques involved. There is an overstatement of the price effects in points 1, 2, 3, 7, and 8, an overstatement of the speed of price effects in 4, and the possibility of an overstatement or an understatement of price effects in points 5 and 6.

4. POLICY CONSIDERATIONS

This section investigates the use of empirical trade studies for policy questions: the trade balance and welfare effects of tariff cuts, the use of constant-market-share analysis to evaluate trends in the excess demand for tradeable goods, and alternative approaches to devaluation.

One concept frequently discussed by policy-makers is the "full-employment trade balance." However, this term has no unique value for a country with at least two policy tools, since one can be used for internal equilibrium and one for extenal equilibrium (see, inter alia, Mundell, 1968, and Swan, 1963). When internal and external equilibrium schedules are plotted geometrically with the two policy tools on the axes, full employment occurs at every point on the internal-equilibrium schedule (if that schedule is defined in terms of full employment). Yet the value of the trade balance varies continuously along the "full employment" schedule; it equals zero only at the intersection of this schedule with the external-equilibrium schedule (defined here as a zero trade balance). Thus, the term "full-employment trade balance" should either be dropped as meaningless or defined as a precise point on an internal-equilibrium schedule that cannot be altered because of a constraint on one of the policy tools (see Magee, 1971b).

Tariff Policies

Countries change their overall tariff levels for a variety of reasons: to improve world welfare through mutually negotiated tariff reductions, to improve national welfare through optimal tariffs, to achieve external balance, and to achieve internal redistribution effects. I shall discuss briefly two papers that have used empirical trade models to investigate tariff questions (see Corden's paper in this volume for comprehensive coverage).

Officer and Hurtubise (1969) investigated the effect of the Kennedy Round tariff cuts on Canadian imports and exports. They estimated disaggregated equations by commodity group, using quarterly data from 1953 to 1965. Their study was useful in an elasticities context in that they calculated both price and activity elasticities by commodity groups. They found that, because of the relatively small changes in tariff rates involved, there would be a small impact on Canadian imports. The cuts would imply a reduction in Canadian exports to the United Kingdom because of reductions in Commonwealth Preference margins, while exports to the United States would expand.

Johnston and Henderson (1967) evaluated the effect on United Kingdom imports of a 15 per cent surcharge (with certain exclusions) imposed in October 1964 and reduced to 10 per cent in February 1965, with the reduction to become effective in late April 1965. Using quarterly equations for imports (which did not include price terms), estimated from 1955-I through 1964-III, they examined the residuals from 1964-IV through 1966-II. They found an immediate effect in the quarters when the surcharge was first imposed, 1964-IV and 1965-I, but for the remaining quarters of the analysis there were some perverse residuals. This led them to experiment with alternative explanatory variables, investigating deseasonalized data, checking the patterns of imports subject to and exempt from the surcharge, and checking biases due to failure to use simultaneous-equation techniques. After some interesting work on these problems, the unexpected residuals in the four quarters after 1965-I were reduced, and the authors concluded that there would be an import reduction equal to approximately 1 or 2 per cent of total imports for the five quarters ending in 1965-IV. These estimates were lower than those previously announced by the British Government.

There is a danger in using empirically estimated import-price relationships to calculate permanent structural or welfare effects of tariff changes if the tariffs are to be maintained for a long period (see Magee, 1973b). In the long run, the effects of a tariff can be completely undone by international factor movements (as noted by Mundell, 1968). Thus the time pattern of the adjustments of the economy to factor movements becomes important in the calculations.

Constant-Market-Share Analysis

A justification frequently heard for international market-share analysis is the interest of policy makers in keeping abreast of the "competitiveness" of their country's internationally traded goods. This concern is reflected in the following statement:

The true performance of the UK on current account merely reflects the general uncompetitiveness of the country in world trade in manufactures. It will be recalled that the UK share of "world" exports of manufactures declined from 20% in 1954 to 13.7% in 1964. This implies an average annual growth rate over the period of 5.3% for the UK as compared with 9.3% for the "world" (Coppock, 1965).

The interest of policy makers in following the growth rates of trade is partially based on the realization that, in the medium run, changes in the trade balance may not correctly reflect trends in the external demand for tradeables if the initial trade balance is large absolutely. For example, the trade balance of the United States in 1958 was $3.46 billion; by 1967 it had increased to $3.82 billion. Policy makers were generally aware, however, that this did not mean there was no deterioration in the position of U.S. tradeables, because imports grew by 107 per cent over the 1958–67 period, while exports grew by only 87 per cent. Thus, in the medium run, growth rates of exports and imports may be better indications of trends in net excess demands for goods than changes in the trade balance. These net excess demands, in turn, are best reflected *relative* to other countries in the market shares of the countries through time.

If aggregate market shares convey any useful information, can their disaggregation provide further insight? A vast literature has arisen in the past twenty years which disaggregates market-share changes ex post into three components: a market component, a product component, and an "other factors" effect that has been loosely called a "competitive" component (see, inter alia, Baldwin, 1962; Cooper, 1962; Junz and Rhomberg, 1965; and Romanis, 1961). The technique reveals that, even if a country maintains its share of every product in every market, it can still have a decrease in its aggregate market share if it exports to markets that grow more slowly than the world average and/or if it exports products for which demand is growing more slowly than average (see Appendix B).

Richardson (1971b, 1971c) has done important work questioning the usefulness of constant-market-share analysis because of variance he found in the three-way allocation of market-share changes caused by (a) different levels of commodity disaggregation, (b) the base year from which the calculations were made, (c) the order in which the product and market components were calculated, and (d) the world area used for comparison.[23] The first factor is not surprising, being simply a manifestation of the classical aggregation problem. It does not condemn constant-market-share analysis relative to any other aggregation technique; in fact, we should be surprised if the results were invariant to the level of aggregation. The purpose of disaggregation is to get different and, it is hoped, better information than was obtained at a more macro level. The interesting question is not *that* the results vary with the level of aggregation but *why* they vary. (This calls for research analogous to that reported in Appendix A, in which low aggregate price elasticities can be explained by negative correlation between the component demand elasticities and distribution elasticities.) On the other hand, Richardson's results are important in finding large changes with alternative levels of aggregation, so that there is much to be explained. Richardson recognizes that the second factor, the question of the appropriate base year, is simply an index-number problem. As such, it, too, is not a problem unique to constant-market-share analysis. The third factor is more troublesome in that it is specific to constant-market-share analysis. Richardson (1971b) found that reversing the order in which the product and market components were calculated changed the results noticeably for Switzerland, Canada, the United States, and Japan; for only three of seven remaining countries were the results relatively stable.

What conclusions are we to draw from these results? First, for this one body of data, the results are sensitive to the order of the

---

23 Richardson had eleven countries, four different levels of commodity aggregation, and both initial- and final-year weights.

calculation. But if data are being used to evaluate a technique, many data sets should be tested to obtain a crude distribution of the "order sensitivity" of the results. We do not know whether Richardson's data set is typical, so that order sensitivity is a pervasive problem, or whether his results are several standard deviations from a norm that would be obtained if the experiment were performed on a large number of data sets (equal in size to Richardson's). Second, if the order-sensitivity problem persists in such an experiment, the next step should be a mathematical investigation of the reasons for the sensitivity rather than abandonment of the technique.

If we can dispose of the methodological problems,[24] constant-market-share analysis still stands or falls on whether, as an identity, it yields a useful organization of the data. If this identity, like the GNP identity, contains behavioral components that can be explained by other independent variables, and if this process gives expanded insight into the behavior of international trade flows, then more research is warranted, on both method and application.

I think it is premature to kill the technique with methodological criticism. On the other hand, it would be healthy to bury normative misuse by policy makers. Beyond indicating medium-term trends in the net excess demand for tradeables, which, using the technique, might be decomposed and related causally to explanatory variables, I have never been able to fathom what policy questions would be answered by an analysis of market shares. The technique is too often used as an indicator of whether we are "winning the war in international markets," and, if not, why not? The greatest potential misuse is for policy makers to convert this macro index into a guide for distorting micro policies (aimed at restoring "our competitive position" in certain products in order to "improve our balance of payments").

Devaluation

There are a number of theoretical approaches to exchange-rate changes (see the surveys by Negishi, 1968; Krueger, 1969; and Cooper, 1971). Cooper's study stresses three approaches: the elasticity, the absorption, and the monetary. While there has been a long theoretical debate over reconciliation of the various ap-

---

24 There is another limitation not mentioned: from a theoretical standpoint, constant-market-share analysis imposes an excessive number of constraints on the underlying behavioral parameters (see Leamer and Stern, 1970).

proaches, that literature will not be discussed here. Since Dornbusch and others have combined the absorption and monetary approaches, they will be considered here as one approach. (The absorption approach emphasizes the flow aspect of short-run stock disequilibrium, while the monetary approach stresses long-run stock equilibrium itself.) There is also a rigid-price approach to devaluation that has received insufficient attention in the literature. For the present purposes, I shall consider three divisions: the elasticities approach; the absorption-monetary approach; and the imperfect-competition–rigid-price approach, concluding this section by comparing and contrasting the three.

While many papers have been written on the *elasticities* approach to devaluation, I will follow the early paper by Joan Robinson (1950). The assumptions here are a two-region model with two goods, in which all cross-price effects are ignored, and in which the relative-price equation holds:

$$\%\Delta P^{\$} = \%\Delta FX + \%\Delta P^{fc}, \tag{14}$$

where FX is the foreign-exchange rate, expressed in terms of dollars per unit of foreign currency, $P^{\$}$ is the price of goods in dollars, and P^{fc} is the price of goods in foreign currency. A devaluation of the dollar raises the dollar price and lowers the foreign-currency price by a differential equal to the percentage change in the foreign-exchange rate.

Assume that there is a proportional devaluation of the dollar equal to k ($k = .10$, for example, implies a 10 per cent devaluation). The effect of this change on the trade balance in terms of dollars is shown in the following equation:

$$dTB = k \left[(P_x X) \frac{d_x (1 + s_x)}{d_x + s_x} - (P_m M) \frac{s_m (1 - d_m)}{s_m + d_m} \right], \tag{15}$$

where P_x and P_m are export and import prices, X and M are the quantities of exports and imports, d_x and d_m are the demand elasticities of exports and imports, and s_x and s_m are the supply elasticities for exports and imports. Both demand elasticities, d_x and d_m, are defined as positive.

We shall consider two cases. The first is the traditional one in which supply for both exports and imports is perfectly elastic. This requires either the assumption of underemployment in both the home and foreign country or a nontraded good in the background that can provide perfectly elastic supplies of factors (Dornbusch, 1973c). In this case, equation (15) reduces to

$$dTB = kP_x X \left[d_x + d_m (P_m M/P_x X) - (P_m M/P_x X) \right]. \quad (16)$$

If trade is initially balanced, equation (16) can be written in the familiar form:

$$dTB = kP_x X (d_x + d_m - 1), \quad (17)$$

which is the simple Marshall–Lerner condition that if the sum of the absolute values of the demand elasticities exceeds unity, a devaluation will lead to an improvement in a country's trade balance.

While this first case has a long tradition, it is plagued by certain logical inconsistencies. The assumptions that the foreign supply of the home country's imports is perfectly elastic and that the home country's supply of exports is perfectly elastic are based on justifications which also imply that the supply of factors to the other two industries is perfectly elastic in both countries. This, in turn, implies that the elasticity of demand for imports in both regions is infinite [both d_x and d_m equal infinity in equation (17)]. Thus, these assumptions lead to the logical collapse of the simplest Marshall–Lerner criterion in equation (17). More plausible assumptions must be made regarding the high supply elasticities required to derive equation (17).

The second case deals with the classic situation of the theoretically small country that is a price taker in world markets for both its exports and imports. In this case, the elasticity of demand for the country's exports, d_x, and the elasticity of supply of its imports, s_m, equal infinity. If trade is initially balanced, from equation (15) we have the following effect on a country's trade balance when it devalues:

$$dTB = kP_x X (s_x + d_m). \quad (18)$$

Clearly, for the small country, if either the elasticity of supply of exports or the elasticity of demand for imports exceeds zero in absolute value, the trade balance unambiguously improves (the trade balance cannot deteriorate).

There are several problems with the elasticities approach generally. The biggest theoretical problem is its partial-equilibrium approach. It ignores the behavioral effects of the currency change on money markets and, hence, on absorption. Since a foreign-exchange rate change is a change in a nominal variable (the relative price of two currencies), the omission of monetary considerations is serious. The elasticities approach in its simplest form also ignores the market for nontradeable goods.

These problems notwithstanding, I turn now to empirical elasticity studies that might be used to analyze the effects of changes in exchange rates. Nearly a dozen studies have provided evidence that the simple Marshall–Lerner condition in equation (17) is satisfied for the United States [see Ball and Marwah, 1962; Branson, 1968a; Buckler and Almon, 1972; Gregory, 1971; Houthakker and Magee, 1969; Kreinen, 1967; Kwack, 1972; Magee, 1970, as well as Branson's (1972) simulation of the 1971 exchange-rate changes; Prachowney, 1969; and Rhomberg and Boissonneault, 1964, 1965]. The studies by Sedjo (1971), and Officer and Hurtubise (1969) indicate elasticity optimism with respect to Canada. Rather ambiguous results were obtained for the United Kingdom by Marston (1971), and some interesting points were made by Turnovsky (1968); he found that an exchange-rate change would increase New Zealand's trade balance in the short run but cause it to deteriorate in the long run. Khan (1973) estimated import and export price elasticities of demand for 15 less developed countries. He found that only 2 countries (Chile and Uruguay) had absolute values of the elasticities summing to less than unity (although Colombia was a borderline case). There are a number of multicountry studies of elasticities. Heien's (1968) study of import price elasticities for 11 developed countries yielded the following results for the long-run price elasticities (the maximum lag length was three years): 2 countries had elasticities between 0 and -0.5, 6 countries had elasticities between -0.5 and -1.0, while 3 had elasticities that exceeded -1.0 (in absolute value).

Table 5 provides distributions for the sums of the price elasticities for the studies reported in Table 1: LINK, Houthakker and Magee, and a combination of Taplin (for imports) and Hickman and Lau (for exports). Two of the studies rate Belgium and the Netherlands as elasticity pessimistic from a Marshall–Lerner viewpoint. The problem for the Netherlands appears to be on the import side in both Houthakker and Magee and Taplin. This may be due to a combination of data and cross-price effects. Imports into Rotterdam and Amsterdam that are re-exported to other European countries but are not so reported cannot be expected to respond to domestic price developments in the Netherlands itself.

TABLE 5 *Distributions of the Sums of Price Elasticities for Exports and Imports*

Absolute Value of the Sum of the Elasticities	LINK	Houthakker–Magee	Taplin (Imports) Hickman–Lau (Exports)
0–0.5	Belgium		
0.5–1.0	United Kingdom	Belgium–Lux. Netherlands	Netherlands
1.0–1.5		Germany Italy Sweden United Kingdom	France Japan United Kingdom
1.5–2.0	Italy Sweden United States	Japan	Belgium Germany Italy
2.0–2.5		Canada France	Canada United States
2.5–3.0	Canada Germany Japan Netherlands	United States	Sweden

Source: See Table 1. For Houthakker and Magee, the Cochrane–Orcutt estimates in the notes to Table 1 are used.

Since the import price elasticity is derived from a ratio of import prices to Dutch domestic prices, the low import price elasticity may merely mean that unreported re-exports and Dutch domestic prices are uncorrelated. The Belgian case is less clear; while LINK and Houthakker and Magee agree that the export price elasticity is low, there is a larger spread between the two studies on the import elasticity. The United Kingdom is the only major country with consistent evidence of possible elasticity pessimism.

The large cross-section–time-series studies by Junz and Rhomberg (1965, 1973) are genuinely elasticity-optimist, although the lags involved are substantial.[25] Substitution elasticities close to the Junz and Rhomberg estimates were used in the world trade model developed by Armington (1969a, 1969b, and 1970) to simulate

25 Of course, the substitution elasticities they estimate are larger than the demand elasticities implicit in them (see Leamer and Stern, 1970). Nevertheless, the implicit demand elasticities are high.

the 1971 currency realignment (see Branson, 1972). The Waelbroeck (1972) model also shows elasticity optimism. A world trade
model that is less "price optimistic" has been constructed by
Adams *et al.* (1969) [see Branson's (1972) simulation of the 1971
currency realignments using this model].

In summary, the empirical evidence indicates, with few exceptions, that international price elasticities of demand satisfy the
simple Marshall–Lerner condition for stability expressed in equation (17), suggesting that currency realignments will move trade
balances in the desired directions. Some counterevidence will be
presented below in the comparison of the three devaluation
models.

The *absorption-monetary* approach to devaluation has a somewhat shorter history than the elasticities approach (see Meade,
1951; Alexander, 1952; Johnson, 1967a and the efforts to reconcile the elasticity and absorption approaches by Alexander, 1959,
and Tsiang, 1961). The best recent theoretical work on devaluation is the extensive analysis by Dornbusch (1971a, 1971c, 1972,
1973a, 1973b, 1973c, 1974), which grows out of earlier work by
Mundell (1971) and others.[26]

A good exposition of devaluation applied to the small country is
presented by Dornbusch (1974). Because of its elegance and
simplicity, this paper will be described briefly here; it contains
elements of the elasticity, absorption, and monetary approaches.
Relative price effects are introduced between a composite tradeable good (exports and imports are aggregated into a single
commodity, since their relative price is fixed for the small country) and a domestic nontradeable good. Excess demands for or
supplies of the tradeable good correspond to trade-balance deficits and surpluses. Absorption equals income less additions to cash
balances (money is the only asset held by individuals). In static
long-run stock equilibrium, there can be no increments to cash
balances – income equals absorption and the trade balance equals
zero. Dornbusch assumes that all prices and wages are flexible so
that full employment occurs at all times. He specifies that the
consumption of tradeable and nontradeable goods can be written
as functions of real expenditure and the relative price of the two
goods.

The first effect of devaluation is to raise the relative price of
tradeables in home currency by the amount of the devaluation.

---

26 Meade (1951, Chap. 12) uses an elasticities approach and handles the absorption problem by assuming that domestic policies vary to maintain internal balance as exchange
   rates change.

This shifts production from nontradeable to tradeable goods. Since real cash balances have decreased because of the increased price of tradeables, there is a reduction in absorption relative to income as domestic residents attempt to rebuild their cash balances. This reduction in absorption leads to a short-run increase in the trade balance. As the country rebuilds its real cash balances, however, absorption gradually increases relative to income until real cash balances achieve their original levels. A feature of the new equilibrium is that in the new stock equilibrium all real variables will be the same as in the original stock equilibrium before devaluation; real income, consumption of both goods, and real cash balances are unchanged. This results from the fact that the country's production-possibility curve for tradeables and nontradeables is unaltered by devaluation, and its community preference functions are also unaltered, so that there is a unique value of the relative price of tradeables to nontradeables that clears the two commodity markets. Since absorption equals income in the new stock equilibrium, we can have flow equilibrium only when the original relative price ratio is restored. Thus, in the process of adjustment after the devaluation, the price of non-tradeables also eventually rises by the percentage of the devaluation. This restores the original price ratio. For small countries and large countries alike (Dornbusch, 1971c), the only result of a change in exchange rates is a redistribution of the nominal world money supply toward the devaluing country. The devaluing country increases its holding of cash balances by the percentage increase in its prices.

The empirical implications of devaluation from the monetary approach are that, starting from stock equilibrium, there will be a short-run trade-balance improvement in order to replenish cash balances, but there can be no long-run change in trade flows after real balances have been restored. Starting from stock disequilibrium, on the other hand, exchange-rate changes can affect long-term flows in the sense that the initial nonzero trade balance differs from the ultimate long-term trade balance of zero. The motivation for devaluation in the stock-disequilibrium case is to restore stock equilibrium more rapidly than would have been possible through the market mechanism.[27]

Another empirical implication is that trade should be related

27 Dornbusch gives another case in which devaluation is useful. In a disequilibrium situation in which wages and prices of nontraded goods are rigid downward and are too high, causing unemployment, devaluation can lower the relative price of nontraded goods and restore both internal and external balance.

causally to expenditure rather than to income. This can be illustrated by an extreme case. If devaluation led a country to eliminate all expenditures in one period and use its entire income to accumulate cash through exports, imports would fall to zero. A model with imports related to expenditure would predict the drop in imports, while a model with imports related to income would not.

While the absorption and the monetary approaches to devaluation are not theoretically independent (in fact, their complete analytical interdependence has been demonstrated in the discussion here), the proponents of each approach emphasize different sides of the problem. Absorptionists are more concerned with the flow aspects of devaluation (the various means through which expenditure is cut below income), while monetarists dwell on stock aspects (portfolio balance and the long-run neutrality of the real economy to monetary and exchange-rate phenomena). Except for indirect evidence growing out of studies attempting to test the monetary approach to the balance of payments, I know of no empirical work that has attempted to apply this theory to exchange-rate changes.

Johnson (1967d) has written a good general paper on *monopolistic competition* theory and its application to international trade. Gray (1965) integrates explicitly the *rigid-price* phenomenon into the elasticities model of devaluation. Briefly stated, the empirical problem is that, when an exchange rate changes, product prices in one or both currencies may not change. Such rigidity could be attributable to a number of things: (a) trade by oligopolists, each of whom perceives a kinky demand curve for his product in foreign markets; (b) international price agreements or cartels; (c) long-run considerations of market entry, which dominate short-run price considerations and nonprice methods of market-share determination; (d) costs of price changes (such as accounting costs) and perceived loss of good will if prices are changed frequently; (e) expectations by exporters (whose currency has been devalued) that foreign countries will retaliate against their exports (increased tariffs, etc.) if their prices fall too rapidly in foreign currency; and (f) long-term contracts signed in terms of domestic currency for both exports and imports.

Consider the kinky-demand argument in an elasticities context. Assume that all pre- and post-devaluation marginal-cost curves intersect the marginal-revenue curve in the "vertical" segment. This has identical effects on a country's trade balance as when the supplies of its exports and imports are perfectly inelastic. Inserting values of 0 for s_x and s_m into equation (15) yields the following change in the trade balance in terms of the home currency:

$$dTB = kP_xX > 0 \ . \tag{19}$$

Thus the trade balance improves by the proportional devaluation times the initial value of exports. The observed price behavior would be an increase in the home price of exports by the percentage devaluation (no change in the foreign price) and no change in the home price of imports (the foreign price falls by the percentage devaluation). Thus, while the kinky-demand approach can explain stability of prices in one of the countries, it does not predict stability in both. Furthermore, the relative-price equation holds with kinky demand in the elasticities model just described.

However, we observe empirically that, in some imperfectly competitive situations, the relative-price equation does not always hold. In the most extreme case, devaluation of the dollar would lead to no change in the price of U.S. exports – either at home in terms of dollars or abroad in terms of foreign currency – and we would not observe any change in the quantity of trade (as in the case of the kinky-demand curve just investigated). There is some evidence from the 1971 changes in foreign-exchange rates that U.S. multinational corporations demonstrated such behavior. This pricing practice shifts entirely to the foreign subsidiary the profits obtained through the capital gain caused by the devaluation, and the improvement in the U.S. current account due to the devaluation appears in the repatriation of earnings on foreign investment rather than in the trade accounts.

The only empirical test of the validity of the critical relative-price equation (14) is provided by Dunn (1970). He tested the relative-price equation for trade between the United States and Canada during a period of flexibility in the Canadian exchange rate (1950–62). He chose six commodities that were traded by the United States and Canada throughout the entire period: copper, gasoline, crude oil, window glass, rolling-mill products, and coal. These were selected to test the imperfect-competition hypothesis that oligopolistic behavior (which applies to all the products except coal) may override the relative-price equation. The test regressed the percentage change in the relative prices of the commodity in the two markets on the Canadian–U.S. exchange rate. If the relative-price equation holds, the coefficient on the exchange-rate changes should be 1.0 and significant; the results indicated that this was not the case in any of the six markets. In only one case (copper) was there even near confirmation of the relative-price equation. Dunn concluded that the desire on the part of both buyers and sellers for stability in final prices led to the noncompetitive behavior he discovered. One problem with generalizing Dunn's results, however, is that they apply to a number of years in which there were relatively small variations in exchange rates. They also do not necessarily verify an imperfect-competition approach, since the relative-price equation can hold under imperfect competition, as we noted in the kinky-demand case. Finally, the reader should realize that there is no single coherent theory of devaluation under imperfect competition, but rather an amalgam of reasons why prices may not respond fully to exchange-rate changes.

We turn now to a comparison of the three devaluation models. One of the factors common to both the elasticity and the monetary approaches is the assumption that the relative-price equation holds. Dunn's (1970) agnostic empirical results on the validity of the relative-price equation in an imperfect-market situation throw some doubt on the validity of this assumption. If his results extend to cases of larger discrete foreign-exchange-rate changes, then future empirical work must develop separate explanations for the paths of adjustment in the competitive and noncompetitive components of total trade.[28] Failure of the relative-price equation to hold in the short-run may be one of several reasons why the currency realignment of 1971 had such a small impact on the U.S. trade balance in 1972. Other hypothesized explanations of this phenomenon include passthrough (Branson, 1972), the currency-contract problem (Magee, 1973b), long lags in the adjustment of trade to exchange-rate changes (Junz and Rhomberg 1973), dissynchronous cyclical behavior of U.S. and foreign incomes (Laffer, 1973a), and the general ineffectiveness of exchange-rate changes (Laffer, 1973b).

One shortcoming of the empirical work on devaluation is that, until Laffer's (1973b) paper, there had been no systematic examination of the effects of exchange-rate changes across countries in the postwar period. Laffer assembled 15 cases in which countries devalued. Of these, 12 involved small countries and 3

28 For a chronological taxonomy of the behavior of prices of internationally traded goods following a devaluation, see Magee (1973b). First comes a "currency contract" period in which capital gains or losses on outstanding contracts are observed; second, a "passthrough" period in which prices adjust to the new rates but quantitites of trade are not yet affected; and, third, a "quantity adjustment" period in which both quantities and prices move toward a new equilibrium. The trade balance can move in almost any direction in each of these three subperiods.

involved larger countries (France, twice, and the United Kingdom). The results seem to indicate that the devaluations had remarkably little effect on the trade balance. In 10 of the 15 cases, the countries had their largest trade-balance deficits in one of the three years *following* the year of the devaluation; 2 of the countries had their largest deficits in the year of the devaluation; only 3 had their largest deficits in one of the three years prior to the year of the devaluation. This study is important because of both its empirical revelations and its emphasis on the small-country cases, which would bias the results in favor of *improvement* following devaluation, both by the elasticities and the monetary approach. [Remember that, in equation (18), devaluations by small countries inevitably improve the trade balance. The prices of traded goods rise by the full amount of the devaluation in small countries, so the simplest monetary approach also implies that the post-devaluation trade balance will improve as domestic residents rebuild their cash balances.][29] Laffer's results, however, are subject to differences in interpretation. First, for 7 of the 8 episodes involving the largest devaluations, there was a noticeable improvement in the trade balance from the year before the devaluation to the year following the devaluation. (For the remaining cases, 4 showed virtually no change over the same time period, while 3 showed noticeable deterioration.) Second, in any uncontrolled, non–ceteris paribus experiment of this sort, it is hard to know if agnostic results are true or if the sample size is too small.

This concludes the discussion of the three competing theories of devaluation. While the theoretical issues are not resolved and the theories are not altogether independent, more research could throw light on the empirical importance of relative price changes, expenditure switching, expenditure reduction, and the real balance effects of exchange-rate changes. This new knowledge could, in turn, guide future theoretical work.

5. SUMMARY AND CONCLUSIONS

We return to the question raised in section 3 regarding the "Orcuttization" of empirical trade studies. *One of the reasons for the inadequate theoretical development of trade models has been the preoccupation with the mechanics of estimation and, specifically, with the*

---

29 In the simplest version of the monetary approach, capital flows and securities trading are omitted, so that an important element of portfolio adjustment is missing (see Branson, 1968b, for a general study of international capital flows and portfolio balance).

properties of the price coefficient. This concern with the price coefficient plus other factors has, for many years, held the standard empirical approach to international trade to an overly simple
variation of equation (2). The reasons for staying with this rather
limited approach for so long are intriguing.

First, the relatively simple specification of equation (2) made it
easy to estimate. It is easy to get highly significant and positive
income coefficients in most cases, and significantly negative price
elasticities of demand can be obtained about half the time.
Second, there is also a push from the theoretical literature on
devaluation toward the use of equation (2) and an "elasticities"
approach. For one thing, the Marshall-Lerner condition dictates
that the sum of the elasticities must exceed unity in absolute value
in order to achieve stability and for devaluations to yield the
expected effects on a country's trade balance. Since most international economists are free traders (which means they believe in
more or less free markets) and many are committed to flexible
exchange-rate systems, there is a subconscious desire for empirical justification of these normative judgments. Efforts to increase
the size and significance of the price coefficient help fulfill this
goal. But there is a second and more subtle cause for empiricists
in international trade to favor equation (2). The assumption of
the Marshall-Lerner condition in its simplest form (see Robinson,
1950) that the supplies of exports and imports are perfectly elastic
permits the reduction of a complicated criterion to the simple
summation of the price elasticities of demand for imports and
exports. This assumption appeals immediately to econometricians
because simultaneous-equation bias in estimating price elasticities
of demand disappears when supplies are perfectly elastic. Single-
equation systems are also popular because supply elasticities are
harder to estimate and identify than demand elasticities.

However, the theoretical and empirical convenience of assuming that the supply of exports and the supply of imports to a country are perfectly elastic is not matched by any a priori theoretical
justifications. For small countries, the standard assumption is that
the *demand* for exports and the *supply* of imports are perfectly
elastic, while the other two elasticities are less than infinite. For
large countries, all four elasticities are less than infinite in absolute
value. Thus we cannot justify the assumption of infinite supply
elasticities by any appeal to the large-country–small-country
distinction. The other assumptions used to justify highly elastic
supplies raise logical problems. On the other hand, the limited

empirical evidence on supply elasticities indicates they may be sufficiently high to minimize the importance of simultaneous-equation bias.

The preceding discussion should not be interpreted as a criticism of the use of price and activity variables per se as the empirical determinants of trade flows. Rather, it is an explanation of why these variables have been the nearly exclusive focus of empirical work and why they have been used in simplistic ways.

In summary, this paper has shown that the theoretical limitations of empirical trade studies can be classified in two ways. First, failure to integrate the pure theory into macroeconomic work has led to several problems – the assumption that the income elasticity of demand for imports must be positive; the failure to investigate the causes of income-coefficient instability in terms of reasonable pure-theory explanations (e.g., whether growth is anti-trade biased for portions of the period of estimation but not for others); the failure to test the extent to which the importance of trade in a national economy is influenced by distortions in product and factor markets; the failure to integrate empirical theories explaining the structure of trade with those explaining the levels of trade; and the failure to pursue adequately implications of the substitutability of factor flows for trade flows. The empirical evidence in these areas has shown almost no anti-trade-biased growth and only one solid case of negative income elasticities of demand for trade. On the other hand, rather considerable evidence has been presented of instability in both the income and price coefficients in trade models.

The second theoretical limitation involves specification errors of a more fundamental nature – the failure to capture the general-equilibrium interactions among trade, securities markets, and money markets. In few cases has the interaction of the goods and capital markets been successfully described using general-equilibrium approaches. This is a fruitful area for future research.

Orcutt's (1950) points regarding simultaneous-equation bias and aggregation problems, discussed in section 3, are still considerations of some importance; however, his discussions of observation errors and the timing and magnitude of price effects have been modified by subsequent literature or events. At the end of section 3, Orcutt's list was balanced by eight factors that can lead to an *overstatement* of the effects of prices on trade. Such biases include omission of nonprice rationing variables, upward disaggregation bias due to cross-price effects, upward bias due to the structure of trade, understatement of the length of price lags through the use of unit values, inversely correlated measurement errors in the prices and quantities of trade when demand is inelastic, use of aggregate prices in submarkets with inelastic demand, the tendency to drop positive price elasticities of components before aggregating, and overcompensation for Orcutt's points through data and specification mining in an effort to increase price coefficients. Empirical work on lags and the cyclical behavior of trade indicates that price effects can work for up to six years, while income effects are probably shorter. Studies have also shown that, because of price inflexibility, the quantity of both exports and imports responds nonlinearly to changes in the levels of economic activity, and these responses are in the expected directions. On the other hand, Mintz (1967) uncovered some paradoxical results in which the value of U.S. exports increased during upswings in the U.S. business cycle.

APPENDIX A

The Aggregation Problem

The aggregation problem in an elasticities context can be stated as follows: If we have an aggregate price elasticity that is a weighted average of several disaggregated price elasticities and we calculate an average price change from the disaggregated prices, the resulting aggregate quantity change may be greater than, equal to, or less than the product of the aggregate elasticity and the price change. Holding the component weights constant, the aggregate change depends on the correlation between the price changes and the elasticities at the disaggregated level. If high-elasticity components tend to have large price changes, the change at the aggregate level will be greater than if high-elasticity components tend to have relatively small price changes.

The following example will help to clarify this point. Suppose that we have two countries, 1 and 2, of equal importance in U.S. imports, so that the weights are $W_1 = W_2 = 0.5$ (column 1 in Table A1). Assume that the price elasticity of demand for U.S. imports from country 1 is -3 and from country 2 is -1. The weighted average price elasticity is -2. If there is a *uniform* price increase of 15 per cent, aggregate imports decline by 30 per cent ($-2 \times 15\%$). This is shown in Case A in Table A1. However, if the disaggregated price changes are not uniform, aggregate imports may change by more or less than 30 per cent.

Econometric models of trade and payments

Table A1   An Illustration of Aggregation Error

Component	Weight of Each Country (1)	Price Elasticity (2)	Three Price Changes		
			Case A (3)	Case B (4)	Case C (5)
Country 1	0.5	−3	15%	10%	20%
Country 2	0.5	−1	15%	20%	10%
Total or average	1.0	−2	15%	15%	15%
Change in aggregate quantity			−30%	−25%	−35%

In Case B, we assume that the component price changes are inversely related to the elasticities (in absolute values), while, in Case C, the converse is true. Since relatively small price changes occur in the relatively high-elasticity items in Case B, the aggregate effect is smaller than when the reverse is true in Case C. The important point is that an aggregate approach, in all three cases, gives a total predicted quantity change of −30 per cent. The aggregate approach gives correct results if (1) there is a uniform rate of price change at the disaggregated level, or (2) the disaggregated price changes are more or less uncorrelated with the product of the component elasticities and the component weights. Otherwise, the aggregate approach is subject to error.

Barker (1969) has discussed this problem with respect to U.K. imports; we can apply the same analysis, with some modification, to the United States. Consider the quantity of U.S. imports, m, which is a sum of several components, m_i:

$$m = \Sigma m_i . \tag{A1}$$

The aggregate demand for imports can be written

$$\log m = c + e_y \log y + e_p \log p , \tag{A2}$$

where y and p are U.S. income and import prices and e_y and e_p are the related elasticities. The component equations for each subcategory i can be written

$$\log m_i = c_i + e_{yi} \log y_i + e_{pi} \log p_i , \tag{A3}$$

where y_i and p_i are the relevant component income and import price series. From the aggregate equation, we know that the change in imports is

$$\frac{dm}{m} = e_y\,(dy/y) + e_p\,(dp/p), \tag{A4}$$

and, from the disaggregated equations, the change can be rewritten

$$\frac{dm}{m} = \Sigma\,\frac{dm_i}{m}$$

$$= \Sigma\,e_{yi}(dy_i/y_i)\,(m_i/m) + \Sigma\,e_{pi}(dp_i/p_i)\,(m_i/m). \tag{A5}$$

Sufficient conditions for the results in (A4) to be compatible with those in (A5) are that the first terms in both equations are equal and the second terms in both equations are equal. Thus

$$e_y\,(dy/y) = \Sigma\,e_{yi}\,(dy_i/y_i)\,(m_i/m), \tag{A6}$$

and

$$e_p\,\frac{dp}{p} = \Sigma\,e_{pi}\,(dp_i/p_i)\,(m_i/m). \tag{A7}$$

From these equations we can write total elasticities that will be consistent with the disaggregated data:

$$e_y = \Sigma\,e_{yi}\,(m_i/m)\,\frac{dy_i/y_i}{dy/y} \tag{A8}$$

$$e_p = \Sigma\,e_{pi}\,(m_i/m)\,\frac{dp_i/p_i}{dp/p} \tag{A9}$$

$$\text{(a)} \quad \text{(b)} \quad \text{(c)}$$

Thus the aggregate price elasticity, for example, is a function of three factors: the disaggregated (a) price elasticities, (b) shares of trade, and (c) variation of the component price i relative to the total price index. This last term is called the "distribution elasticity" and will be designated ed_{pi}. It can be estimated from the time series using the following equation:

$$\log p_i = c_i + ed_{pi} \log p. \tag{A10}$$

The aggregation problem can be illustrated with U.S. trade data. Consider, first, U.S. exports and imports in five commodity categories. The price and distribution elasticities are estimated from annual data, 1951–69, and the trade weights are for 1963. (These data are not shown here.) The results can be used to show two different aggregate price elasticities of demand for U.S. imports and exports. These elasticities are summarized in Table A2.

Method A (taking a weighted average of the components) has been commonly used in the past as a means of calculating aggregate elasticities, but it is improper because it fails to include the distribution elasticities. Method B is calculated from equation (A9) and is not subject to this defect. Notice how the pattern of elasticities changes from A to B. The larger distribution elasticities favor larger absolute values of the product of components (a) and (b) in equation (A9), and so the export elasticity rises slightly from A to B (-1.51 to -1.66). However, high elasticity-share items for U.S. imports are associated with smaller relative import price changes, as we might expect, so that the true aggregate import price elasticity associated with the period 1951–69 is not -2.23, but -1.15. An important point here is that simple weighted averages (Method A) show that imports are more responsive to price changes than exports, while in fact they are less responsive (Method B). Method A would give the appropriate historical price elasticity if the distribution elasticities had all equaled unity or had been uncorrelated with $e_{pi}(m_i/m)$, but this was not the case from 1951 to 1969.

Equation (A9) is related to Leontief's composite-good theorem: If relative prices between goods do not change, they can be treated as a single good. In equation (A9), if relative prices among the

TABLE A2   *Alternative Aggregations of Price Elasticities*

Method of Calculation	Aggregate Price Elasticities	
	U.S. Imports	U.S. Exports
A. Weighted average of the components $[\,\Sigma\, e_{pi}\,(m_i/m)\,]$	-2.23	-1.51
B. Weighted average including the distribution elasticities $[\,\Sigma\, e_{pi}\,(m_i/m)\,ed_{pi}\,]$	-1.15	-1.66

components do not change but all grow at the same rate, the distribution elasticities are all unity (since $dp_i/p_i = dp_j/p_j = dp/p$) and there is no aggregation problem. Remember, however, that the condition that the distribution elasticities equal unity is a *sufficient* but not a necessary condition for the absence of aggregation error; there will also be no error if the distribution elasticities and the product of the other two terms in (A9) happen to be uncorrelated.

APPENDIX B

An Expository Note on Constant-Market-Share Analysis

Economists unfamiliar with international competitive studies, or "shift and share" analysis, are initially puzzled when told that a country can experience large changes in its share of world trade even if it maintains its share of every product in every market. The purpose of this note is purely expository, namely, to derive a single equation that illustrates how a country's share of world trade depends on its product and market composition in addition to the trade performance of each of its products in each market. While the technique is old, the formula is new and provides some insight into constant-market-share analysis.

A body of empirical literature has developed, particularly in international trade, which uses this technique. Changes in a country's trade through time are decomposed into four components: changes due to (1) the growth of world trade, (2) differential product growth, (3) differential market growth, and (4) a residual or competitive effect.[30] If we are dealing with changes in market shares, only the last three are relevant because the growth of world trade is captured in the denominator of the share equations. It should be emphasized that this technique is sufficiently general to apply to multiproduct firms selling in many markets and to regional growth analysis as well as to international trade.

In this discussion, the following symbols will be used:
S the share of country k in world trade
X exports
g a growth rate expressed as proportion (e.g., 20 per cent growth implies $g = .20$)

---

30 See, for example, Balassa (1962), Baldwin (1958), Cooper (1962), Fleming and Tsiang (1956), and Stern (1965). Some problems with constant-market-share analysis have been raised by Richardson (1970, 1971a, 1971b, 1971c, 1972a, 1973).

R relative growth factor (e.g., for k's exports relative to world exports, $R = (1+g_k)/(1+g_w)$)

Superscripts:

i commodity number ($i = 1, \ldots, g$)

j market number ($j = 1, \ldots, m$)

Subscripts:

Time:

o base year

t terminal year

Exporter:

k the country under consideration

w the world

The absence of a superscript indicates that aggregation has been performed over that index. For example, if $X^{ij}{}_{ok}$ indicates exporter k's base-year exports of product i to market j, then $X^i{}_{ok}$ indicates exporter k's base-year exports of product i to all markets. The analysis below is general; it can be applied to current values or deflated values of trade, and the "world" category may include or exclude country k itself, depending on the user's needs. It can also be adjusted for non-base-year weighting schemes, although this problem is not considered here.

The relationship between country k's base-year share and its terminal-year share can be expressed

$$S_t = \frac{(1 + g_k)}{(1 + g_w)} S_o, \tag{B1}$$

where g_k and g_w are the proportional growth rates of exports of country k and the world, respectively. Whether the country experiences an increase, no change, or a decrease in its share between the base and terminal years depends on whether its relative growth factor, R, exceeds, equals, or is less than unity.

$$R = \frac{(1 + g_k)}{(1 + g_w)}. \tag{B2}$$

If a country's growth factor exceeds that of the world, its market share increases. The key to understanding how a country can experience radical changes in its share of world markets is found in decomposing the relative-growth factor.

First, to clarify the symbols used we can rewrite equation (B1) as

$$\frac{X_{tk}}{X_{tw}} = \frac{(1+g_k)}{(1+g_w)}\frac{X_{ok}}{X_{ow}} = R\,\frac{X_{ok}}{X_{ow}}. \tag{B3}$$

The term R can be written

$$R = \sum_i \frac{(1+g_k^i)}{(1+g_w)}\frac{X_{ok}^i}{X_{ok}}. \tag{B4}$$

Although the terms in the denominator contain no i superscripts, we have chosen to leave those terms to the right of the summation sign, for reasons which will become clear shortly. The numerator in equation (B4) can be expanded to read

$$\sum_i (1+g_k^i)\,X_{ok}^i = \sum_i \sum_j (1+g_k^{ij})\,X_{ok}^{ij}, \tag{B5}$$

so that equation (B4) can be rewritten

$$R = \sum_i \frac{1}{(1+g_w)\,X_{ok}} \sum_j (1+g_k^{ij})\,X_{ok}^{ij}. \tag{B6}$$

Multiplying the numerator and denominator of (B6) by $(1+g_w^i)\,X_{ok}^i$ yields

$$R = \sum_i \frac{(1+g_w^i)\,X_{ok}^i}{(1+g_w)\,X_{ok}} \sum_j \frac{(1+g_k^{ij})\,X_{ok}^{ij}}{(1+g_w^i)\,X_{ok}^i}. \tag{B7}$$

Multiplying the numerator and denominator of (B7) by $(1+g_w^{ij})$ yields

$$R = \sum_i \frac{(1+g_w^i)\,X_{ok}^i}{(1+g_w)\,X_{ok}} \sum_j \frac{(1+g_k^{ij})}{(1+g_w^{ij})}\frac{(1+g_w^{ij})\,X_{ok}^{ij}}{(1+g_w^i)\,X_{ok}^i}, \tag{B8}$$

which, when inserted in equation (B1) and (B3), yields

$$S_t = S_o \sum_i \left(\frac{1 + g_w^i}{1 + g_w}\right)\left(\frac{X_{ok}^i}{X_{ok}}\right)\sum_j \left(\frac{1 + g_k^{ij}}{1 + g_w^{ij}}\right)\left(\frac{1 + g_w^{ij}}{1 + g_w^i}\right)\left(\frac{X_{ok}^{ij}}{X_{ok}^i}\right). \qquad \text{(B9)}$$

$$\qquad\qquad\quad\;\; \text{(a)}\qquad\;\; \text{(b)}\qquad\qquad \text{(c)}\qquad\quad\; \text{(d)}\qquad\;\; \text{(e)}$$

The "order-sensitivity" problem discussed in the text hinges on the order in which the summations occur (here, it is "i" first and "j" second). The five terms in (B9) are lettered, for simplicity. Term (a) is the relative growth factor of product i in world trade: if (a) > 1, then product i grows faster than the average product and experiences an increase in its share of world trade. Term (b) is the share of product i in the base-year trade of exporter k. Term (c) is the growth factor of k relative to world trade for product i in market j, while (d) is the growth factor of market j relative to the world for product i. Term (e) is the share of market j in exporter k's base-year exports of product i.

Equation (B9) shows why a country may maintain its share of every product in every market and yet experience a change in its market share (i.e., $S_t = S_o$). If k maintains its share of every product in every market, then (c) $= 1$, and we can rewrite equation (B9) as follows:

$$S_t' = S_o R'$$

$$= S_o\left[\sum_i \left(\frac{1 + g_w^i}{1 + g_w}\right)\left(\frac{X_{ok}^i}{X_{ok}}\right)\sum_j \left(\frac{1 + g_w^{ij}}{1 + g_w^i}\right)\left(\frac{X_{ok}^{ij}}{X_{ok}^i}\right)\right] \qquad \text{(B10)}$$

$$\qquad\qquad\quad\;\; \text{(a)}\qquad\;\; \text{(b)}\qquad\qquad \text{(d)}\qquad\;\; \text{(e)}$$

Clearly, $S_t' = S_o$ if and only if $R' = 1$. There are two reasons why this may not occur, as the literature indicates. First, there may be a "product" effect, or positive (negative) correlation between products that grow rapidly (slowly) in world trade [i.e., term (a) > 1 (<1)] and the share of those products in base-year trade of country k, term (b). Second, there may be a "market" effect, or, for any given product i, positive (negative) correlation between markets that grow rapidly (slowly) in world trade [i.e., term (d) > 1 (< 1)] and the share of these markets in the base-year trade of country k, term (e). If a country's trade is weighted heavily toward fast-growing products and/or markets, it will experience market-share increases even if it is not aggressive in trying to increase individual product-market shares. A sufficient condition for $R' = 1$ is that all products and all markets grow at the same rate, so that (a) = (d) = 1. Of course, if we do not constrain the term (c) = 1 in equation (B9), a third effect, called a "residual" or "competitive" effect, indicates whether there is positive (negative) correlation between increases (decreases) in exporter k's share of product i in market j [i.e., term (c) > 1 (< 1)] and the share of product i in market j in k's base-year trade, term (e). Simply stated, the competitive effect is favorable if a country is able, on average, to increase its shares of individual product markets.

REFERENCES

Adams, F. G., *et al.*, *An Econometric Analysis of International Trade*, Paris, Organization for Economic Co-coperation and Development, 1969.
Adler, F. Michael, "The Relationship between the Income and Price Elasticities of Demand for United States Exports," *Review of Economics and Statistics*, 53 (August 1970), pp. 313–319.
Alexander, S. S., "Effects of a Devaluation on a Trade Balance," *IMF Staff Papers*, 2 (April 1952), pp. 263–278; reprinted in Caves and Johnson, eds. (1968, pp. 359–373).
"The Effects of Devaluation: A Simplified Synthesis of Elasticities and Absorption Approaches," *American Economic Review*, 49 (March 1959), pp. 222–242.
Armington, Paul S., "The Geographic Pattern of Trade and the Effects of Price Changes," *IMF Staff Papers*, 16 (July 1969a), pp. 179–201.
"A Theory of Demand for Products Distinguished by Place of Production," *IMF Staff Papers*, 16 (March 1969b), pp. 159–178.
"Adjustment of Trade Balances: Some Experiments with a Model of Trade Among Many Countries," *IMF Staff Papers*, 17 (November 1970), pp. 488–526.
Artus, Jacques R., "The Effect of Revaluation on the Foreign Travel Balance of Germany," *IMF Staff Papers*, 17 (November 1970), pp. 602–619.
"The Short-Run Effects of Domestic Demand Pressure on Export Delivery Delays for Machinery," *Journal of International Economics*, 3 (February 1973), pp. 21-36.

Balassa, Bela, "Recent Developments in the Competitiveness of American Industry and Prospects for the Future," in *Factors Affecting the United States Balance of Payments*, Subcommittee on International Exchange Payments, Joint Economic Committee, U.S. Congress, 1962, pp. 27–54.
Baldwin, Robert E., "The Commodity Composition of Trade: Selected Industrial Countries, 1900–1954," *Review of Economics and Statistics*, 40 (Supplement, February 1958), pp. 50–68.
"Implications of Structural Changes in Commodity Trade," in *Factors Affecting the United States Balance of Payments*, Subcommittee on Inter-

national Exchange Payments, Joint Economic Committee, U.S. Congress, 1962, pp. 55–72.

"International Trade in Inputs and Outputs," *American Economic Review,* 60 (May 1970), pp. 430–434.

Ball, R. J. ed., *The International Linkage of National Economic Models.* Amsterdam, North-Holland, 1973.

Ball, R. J., and Pamela S. Drake, "Export Growth and the Balance of Payments," *Manchester School,* 30 (May 1962), pp. 105–119.

Ball, R. J., and K. Marwah, "The U.S. Demand for Imports, 1948–1958," *Review of Economics and Statistics,* 44 (November 1962), pp. 395–401.

Barker, Terence S., "Devaluation and the Rise in U.K. Prices," *Bulletin of the Oxford University Institute of Economics and Statistics,* 30 (May 1968), pp. 129–141.

"Aggregation Error and Estimates of the U.K. Import Demand Function," in Kenneth Hilton and David E. Heathfield, eds., *The Econometric Study of the United Kingdom,* London, Macmillan, 1969, pp. 115–145.

Basevi, Giorgio, "Commodity Trade Equations in Project LINK," in Ball, ed (1973, Chap. 8, pp. 227–281).

Berry, R. Albert, and Stephen H. Hymer, "A Note on the Capacity to Transform and the Welfare Costs of Foreign Trade Fluctuations," *Economic Journal,* 79 (December 1969), pp. 833–846.

Bloomfield, Arthur I., "Recent Trends in International Economics," *Annals of the American Academy of Political and Social Science,* 386 (November 1969), pp. 148–167.

Branson, William H., "A Disaggregated Model of the U.S. Balance of Trade," *Staff Economic Studies,* No. 44, Board of Governors of the Federal Reserve System, February 29, 1968a.

Financial Capital Flows in the U.S. Balance of Payments. Amsterdam, North-Holland, 1968b.

"The Trade Effects of the 1971 Currency Realignments," *Brookings Papers on Economic Activity* (1, 1972), pp. 15–69.

Brems, Hans, "The Foreign Trade Accelerator and the International Transmission of Growth," *Econometrica,* 24 (July 1956), pp. 223–238.

Buckler, M., and Clopper Almon, "Imports and Exports in an Input-Output Model," Research Memorandum No. 38, Maryland Inter-Industry Forecasting Project, 1972.

Burns, Terence, "An Econometric Analysis of UK Imports 1958–68," Discussion Paper No. 16, London Graduate School of Business, Econometric Forecasting Unit, London, 1969.

Caves, Richard E., and Harry G. Johnson, eds., *Readings in International Economics,* Homewood, Ill., Irwin, 1968.

Cheng, Hang Sheng, "Statistical Estimates of Elasticities and Propensities in International Trade—A Survey of Published Studies," *IMF Staff Papers,* 7 (April 1959), pp. 107–158.

Cooper, Richard N. "American Competition in World Markets, 1953–1960," unpublished Ph.D. dissertation, Harvard University, 1962.

Currency Devaluation in Developing Countries, Essays in International Finance No. 86, Princeton, N.J., 1971.

Coppock, D. J., "The Alleged Case against Devaluation," *Manchester School of Economic and Social Studies,* 33 (September 1965), pp. 285–312.

Corden, W. M., *The Theory of Protection,* Oxford, Clarendon Press, 1971.

Courchene, Thomas J., "General Equilibrium Models and the World Payments System," *Southern Economic Journal*, 36 (January 1970), pp. 309–322.

Dornbusch, Rudiger, "Devaluation, Relative Prices and the Real Value of Money," Report No. 7130, Center for Mathematical Studies in Business and Economics, University of Chicago, 1971a.
"Notes on Growth and The Balance of Payments," *Canadian Journal of Economics*, 4 (August 1971b), pp. 289–395.
"Aspects of a Monetary Theory of Currency Depreciation," unpublished Ph.D. Dissertation, University of Chicago, 1971c.
"Taxes and the Robinson-Bikerdike-Metzler Condition," mimeographed, University of Chicago, 1972.
"Currency Depreciation, Hoarding and Relative Prices," *Journal of Political Economy*, 81 (July 1973a), pp. 893–915.
"Devaluation, Money, and Nontraded Goods," *American Economic Review*, 63 (December 1973b), pp. 871–880.
"A Note on Exchange Rates in a Popular Model of International Trade," mimeographed, University of Rochester, 1973c.
"Real and Monetary Aspects of the Effects of Exchange Rate Changes," in R. Z. Aliber, ed., *National Monetary Policies and the International Financial System* (Wingspread Conference, 1972), Chicago, University of Chicago Press, 1974, pp. 64–81.
Dunn, Robert M., "Flexible Exchange Rates and Oligopoly Pricing: A Study of Canadian Markets," *Journal of Political Economy*, 78 (January/February 1970), pp. 140–151.
Dutta, Manoranjan, "Import Structure of India," *Review of Economics and Statistics*, 47 (August 1965), pp. 295–300.

Edwards, John B., and Guy H. Orcutt, "Should Aggregation Prior to Estimation Be the Rule?" *Review of Economics and Statistics*, 51 (November 1969), pp. 409–420.
Ellis, H. S., and Lloyd A. Metzler, eds. *Readings in the Theory of International Trade*, Homewood, Ill., Irwin, 1950.
Emery, Robert F., "The Relation of Exports and Economic Growth," *Kyklos*, 20 (Fasc. 2, 1967), pp. 470–484.

Fleming, J. M., and S. C. Tsiang, "Changes in Competitive Strength and Export Shares of Major Industrial Countries," *IMF Staff Papers*, 5 (August 1956), pp. 218–248.
Frenkel, Jacob A., "A Theory of Money Trade and the Balance of Payments in a Model of Accumulation," *Journal of International Economics*, 1 (1971), pp. 159–188.

Gray, H. Peter, "Imperfect Markets and the Effectiveness of Devaluation," *Kyklos*, 18 (Fasc. 3, 1965), pp. 512–530.
Gregory, R. G., "United States Imports and Internal Pressure of Demand: 1948–68," *American Economic Review*, 41 (March 1971), pp. 28–47.
Griliches, Zvi, "Distributed Lags: A Survey," *Econometrica*, 35 (January 1967), pp. 16–49.
Grimm, Bruce T., "An Analysis of the Lagged Determinants of United States Import and Export Components," unpublished Ph.D. thesis, University of Pennsylvania, 1968.

246   **Econometric models of trade and payments**

Grunfeld, Yehuda, and Zvi Griliches, "Is Aggregation Necessarily Bad?" *Review of Economics and Statistics,* 42 (February 1960), pp. 1–13.

Harberger, Arnold C., "A Structural Approach to the Problem of Import Demand," *American Economic Review,* 43 (May 1953), pp. 148–159.
"Some Evidence on the International Price Mechanism," *Journal of Political Economy,* 65 (December 1957), pp. 506–521.
Harley, Charles K., "Empirical Literature on the U.S. Balance of Trade," *Staff Economic Studies,* Board of Governors of the Federal Reserve System, 1966.
Heien, Dale M., "Structural Stability and the Estimation of International Import Price Elasticities," *Kyklos,* 21 (Fasc. 4, 1968), pp. 695–712.
Helliwell, John F., *et al.,* "Econometric Analysis of Policy Choices for an Open Economy," *Review of Economics and Statistics,* 51 (November 1969), pp. 383–398.
Hemphill, W., "A Model of the External-Balance Constraint on Imports of Less-Developed Countries" mimeographed, IMF, 1973.
Hickman, Bert G., and Lawrence J. Lau, "Elasticities of Substitution and Export Demands in a World Trade Model," Research Memorandum No. 141, Stanford University, Research Center in Economic Growth, 1973 (forthcoming in the *European Economic Review*).
Hooper, Peter, "The Construction of a Trade Sector for the Michigan Quarterly Forecasting Model of the U.S. Economy, DHL-III," paper presented at the Winter Meetings of the Econometric Society, Toronto, Dec. 28–30, 1972 (unpublished paper, University of Michigan).
Horwell, D. J., "On Export Subsidies and Import Tariffs," *Economica,* 33 (November 1966), pp. 472–474.
Houthakker, Hendrik, "The Calculation of Bilateral Trade Patterns," a paper presented to the Workshop in International Economics, University of Chicago, Jan. 22, 1973.
Houthakker, H. S., and Stephen P. Magee, "Income and Price Elasticities in World Trade," *Review of Economics and Statistics,* 51 (May 1969), pp. 111–125.
Houthakker, H. S., and Lester D. Taylor, *Consumer Demand in the United States: Analyses and Projections,* Cambridge, Mass., Harvard University Press, 1970.
Hultman, Charles W., "Exports and Economic Growth: A Survey," *Land Economics,* 43 (May 1967), pp. 148–157.

Ikema, Makoto, "The Effect of Economic Growth on the Demand for Imports: A Simple Diagram," *Oxford Economic Papers,* 21 (March 1969), pp. 66–69.

Johnson, Harry G., *International Trade and Economic Growth,* Cambridge, Mass., Harvard University Press, 1967a.
Money Trade and Economic Growth, Cambridge, Mass., Harvard University Press, 1967b.
"International Trade Theory and Monopolistic Competition Theory," Chap. 9 in Robert E. Kuenne, ed., *Monopolistic Competition Theory: Studies in Impact,* New York, Wiley, 1967c, pp. 203–218.
Aspects of the Theory of Tariffs, Cambridge, Mass., Harvard University Press, 1972a.

Further Essays in Monetary Economics, London, Allen & Unwin, 1972b.

Johnston, J., and Margaret Henderson, "Assessing the Effects of the Import Surcharge," *Manchester School,* 35 (May 1967), pp. 89–110.

Junz, Helen B., and Rudolf R. Rhomberg, "Prices and Export Performance of Industrial Countries, 1953–63," *IMF Staff Papers,* 12 (July 1965), pp. 224–269.

"Price Competitiveness in Export Trade among Industrial Countries," Discussion Paper No. 22, Board of Governors of the Federal Reserve System, Division of International Finance, 1973.

Kafka, A., "The Elasticity of Export Supply," *Southern Economic Journal,* 32 (January 1966), p. 352.

Keesing, Donald B., "Labor Skills and Comparative Advantage," *American Economic Review,* 56 (May 1966), pp. 249–258.

Kemp, Murray C., "Errors of Measurement and Bias in Estimates of Import Demand Parameters," *Economic Record,* 38 (September 1962a), pp. 369–372.

The Demand for Canadian Imports: 1926–55, Toronto, University of Toronto Press, 1962b.

Kennedy, Charles, "Keynesian Theory in an Open Economy," *Social and Economic Studies,* 15 (March 1966), pp. 1–21.

Khan, Mohsin, "Import and Export Demand in Developing Countries, mimeographed, IMF, 1973.

Kindleberger, Charles P., *International Economics,* 5th ed., Homewood, Ill., Irwin, 1973.

Klein, L. R., "The Trade Effects of the 1971 Currency Realignments: Comment," *Brookings Papers on Economic Activity* (No. 1, 1972), pp. 59–65.

Komiya, Ryutaro, "Economic Growth and the Balance of Payments: A Monetary Approach," *Journal of Political Economy,* 77 (January/February 1969), pp. 35–48.

Kravis, Irving B., and Robert E. Lipsey, "International Price Comparisons by Regression Methods," *International Economic Review,* 10 (June 1969), pp. 233–246.

Price Competitiveness in World Trade, New York, Columbia University Press for National Bureau of Economic Research, 1971.

Kreinin, M. E., "Price Elasticities in International Trade, *Review of Economics and Statistics,* 44 (November 1967), pp. 510–516.

Krueger, Anne O., "Balance-of-Payments Theory," *Journal of Economic Literature,* 7 (March 1969), pp. 1–26.

Kwack, Sung Y., "The Determination of U.S. Imports and Exports: A Disaggregated Quarterly Model, 1960 III-1967 IV," *Southern Economic Journal,* 38 (January 1972), pp. 302–314.

Kwack, Sung Y., and George R. Schink, "A Disaggregated Quarterly Model of United States Trade and Capital Flows: Simulations and Tests of Policy Effectiveness," paper presented at the Brookings Conference on Econometric Model Building and Development, February 1972.

Laffer, Arthur B., "Do Devaluations Really Help Trade?" *Wall Street Journal,* Feb. 5, 1973a.

"Exchange Rates, the Terms of Trade and the Trade Balance," mimeographed, University of Chicago, 1973b.

Leamer, Edward E., and Robert M. Stern, *Quantitative International Economics*, Boston, Allyn and Bacon, 1970.

Linnemann, Hans, *An Econometric Study of International Trade Flows*, Amsterdam, North-Holland, 1966.

Lipsey, Robert E., and Merle Y. Weiss, "Analyzing Direct Investment and Trade at the Company Level," Proceedings of the American Statistical Association, reprinted from the 1972 Business and Economic Statistics Section, pp. 11–20.

MacDougall, G. D. A., "British and American Exports: A Study Suggested by the Theory of Comparative Costs, Part I," *Economic Journal*, 61 (December 1951), pp. 697–724.

"British and American Exports: A Study Suggested by the Theory of Comparative Costs, Part II," *Economic Journal*, 62 (September 1952), pp. 487–521.

Machlup, Fritz, "Elasticity Pessimism in International Trade," *Economia Internazionale*, 3 (February 1950), pp. 118–137.

Magee, Stephen P., "A Theoretical and Empirical Examination of Supply and Demand Relationships in U.S. International Trade," unpublshed study for the Council of Economic Advisers, 1970.

"U.S. Trade and the New Economic Policy," unpublished study for the Council of Economic Advisers, 1971a.

"U.S. Internal and External Balance in 1971," presented to the World Economy Study Group of the Adlai Stevenson Institute, December 6, 1971b.

"Tariffs and U.S. Trade," unpublished study for the Council of Economic Advisers, 1972a.

"The Welfare Effects of Restrictions on U.S. Trade," *Brookings Papers on Economic Activity* (No. 3, 1972b), pp. 645–701.

"Factor Market Distortions, Production, and Trade: A Survey," *Oxford Economic Papers*, 25 (March 1973a), pp. 1–43.

"Currency Contracts, Pass-through, and Devaluation," *Brookings Papers on Economic Activity* (No. 1, 1973b), pp. 303–323.

Marston, Richard, "Income Effects and Delivery Lags in British Import Demand: 1955–67," *Journal of International Economics*, 1 (November 1971), pp. 375–399.

Meade, J. E., *The Balance of Payments*, London, Oxford University Press, 1951.

Mintz, Ilse, *Cyclical Fluctuations in the Exports of the United States since 1879*, Studies in Business Cycles No. 15, New York, National Bureau of Economic Research, 1967.

Morgan, A. D., "Income and Price Elasticities in World Trade: A Comment," *Manchester School*, 1971, pp. 303–314.

Mundell, Robert A., *International Economics*, New York, Macmillan, 1968.

Monetary Theory, Pacific Palisades, Calif., Goodyear, 1971.

Narvekar, P. R., "The Role of Competitiveness in Japan's Export Performance, 1954–58," *IMF Staff Papers*, 8 (November 1960), pp. 85–100.

Negishi, Takashi, "Approaches to the Analysis of Devaluation," *International Economic Review*, 9 (June 1968), pp. 218–227.

Neisser, Hans P., "The United States Demand for Imports," *American Economic Review*, 43 (May 1953), pp. 134–147.

Neisser, H., and F. Modigliani, *National Incomes and International Trade*, Urbana, Ill, University of Illinois Press, 1953.

Niehans, Jurg, "Interest Rates and the Balance of Payments: An Analysis of the Swiss Experience," in R. E. Baldwin, *et al., Trade, Growth and the Balance of Payments*, Chicago, Rand McNally, 1965.

Officer, L. H., and J. R. Hurtubise, "Price Effects of the Kennedy Round on Canadian Trade," *Review of Economics and Statistics*, 51 (August 1969), pp. 320–333.

Ohlin, Bertil, "The Business Cost Account Approach to International Trade Theory," *Swedish Journal of Economics*, 72 (January 1970), pp. 12–20.

Olivera, J. H. G., "Is Free Trade a Perfect Substitute for Factor Mobility?" *Economic Journal*, 77 (March 1967), pp. 165–169.

Ooms, Van Doorn, "Models of Comparative Export Performance," *Yale Economic Essays*, 7 (Spring 1967), pp. 103–141.

Orcutt, Guy H., "Measurement of Price Elasticities in International Trade," *Review of Economics and Statistics*, 32 (May 1950), pp. 117–132; reprinted in Caves and Johnson, eds. (1968, pp. 528–552).

Patinkin, Don, *Money, Interest, and Prices*, 2d. ed., New York, Harper & Row, 1965.

Paul, Samuel, and Vasant L. Mote, "Competitiveness of Exports: A Micro-Level Approach," *Economic Journal*, 80 (December 1970), pp. 895–909.

Perkins, J. O. N., "Australia and the 1967 Devaluation of Sterling," *Economic Record*, 44 (March 1968), pp. 1–14.

Piekarz, Rolf, and Lois E. Stekler, "Induced Changes in Trade and Payments," *Review of Economics and Statistics*, 49 (November 1967), pp. 517–526.

Polak, J. J., *An International Economic System*, Chicago, University of Chicago Press, 1953.

"Monetary Analysis of Income Formulation and the Payments Problem," *IMF Papers*, 4 (November 1957), pp. 1–50.

Polak, J. J., and L. Boissonneault, "The Monetary Analysis of Income and Imports, and Its Statistical Application," *IMF Staff Papers*, 7 (April 1960), pp. 349–415.

Polak, J. J., and W. H. White, "The Effect of Income Expansion on the Quantity of Money," *IMF Staff Papers*, 4 (1954–55), pp. 398–433.

Poyhonen, Pentti, "Toward a General Theory of International Trade," *Ekonomiska Samfundets Tidskrift*, 17 (August 1963), pp. 69–77.

Prachowny, Martin F. J., *A Structural Model of the U.S. Balance of Payments*, Contributions to Economic Analysis Series No. 60, Amsterdam, North-Holland, 1969.

Prais, S. J., "Some Mathematical Notes on the Quantity Theory of Money in an Open Economy," *IMF Staff Papers*, 8 (May 1961), pp. 212–226.

"Econometric Research in International Trade: A Review," *Kyklos*, 15 (Fasc. 3, 1962), pp. 560–577.

Preeg, Ernest H., "Elasticity Optimism in International Trade," *Kyklos*, 20 (Fasc. 2, 1967), pp. 460–468.

Pulliainen, Kyosti, "A World Trade Study: An Econometric Model of the

Pattern of the Commodity Flows in International Trade in 1948–1960," *Ekonomiska Samfundets Tidskrift,* 17 (August 1963), pp. 78–91.

Review Committee for Balance of Payments Statistics, *The Balance of Payments Statistics of the United States: A Review and Appraisal,* Washington, Government Printing Office, 1965.

Rhomberg, Rudolf R., "Transmission of Business Fluctuations from Developed to Developing Countries," *IMF Staff Papers,* 15 (March 1968), pp. 1–29.

Rhomberg, Rudolf R., and Lorette Boissonneault, "Effects of Income and Price Changes on the U.S. Balance of Payments," *IMF Staff Papers,* 11 (March 1964), pp. 59–122.

"The Foreign Sector," in *The Brookings Quarterly Econometric Model of the United States,* Chicago, Rand McNally, 1965, pp. 375–406.

Richardson J. David, "Some Problems in the 'Constant-Market-Shares' Analysis of Export Growth," Seminar Discussion Paper No. 19, University of Michigan, Research Seminar in International Economics, 1970.

"Altering the World of Competitors in a 'Constant-Market-Shares' Analysis of Export Growth," Seminar Discussion Paper No. 36, University of Michigan, Research Seminar in International Economics, 1971a.

"Some Sensitivity Tests for a 'Constant-Market-Shares' Analysis of Export Growth," *Review of Economics and Statistics,* 53 (August 1971b), pp. 300–304.

"Constant-Market-Shares Analysis of Export Growth," *Journal of International Economics,* 1 (May 1971c), pp. 227–239.

"On Improving the Estimate of the Export Elasticity of Substitution," *Canadian Journal of Economics,* 5 (August 1972a), pp. 349–357.

"The Response of Imports and Domestic Demand to Price, Tariff, and Exchange Rate Changes: A Structural Estimation Study for Selected U.S. Manufactures," paper prepared for the Bureau of Economic Affairs, U.S. Dept. of State, 1972b.

"Beyond (But Back to?) the Elasticity of Substitution in International Trade," *European Economic Review* (No. 4, 1973).

Robinson, Joan, "The Foreign Exchanges," reprinted in Ellis and Metzler, eds. (1950, pp. 83–103).

Robinson, T. Russell, "Canada's Imports and Economic Stability," *Canadian Journal of Economics,* 1 (May 1968), pp. 401–428.

Romanis, Anne, "Relative Growth of Exports of Manufactures of United States and Other Industrial Countries," *IMF Staff Papers,* 8 (May 1961), pp. 241–273.

Rybczynski, T. M., "Factor Endowment and Relative Commodity Prices," *Economica,* 22 (November 1955), pp. 336–341; reprinted in Caves and Johnson, eds. (1968, pp. 72-77).

Savage, I. Richard, and Karl W. Deutsch, "A Statistical Model of the Gross Analysis of Transaction Flows," *Econometrica,* 28 (July 1960), pp. 551–572.

Schotta, Charles, Jr., "The Money Supply, Exports, and Income in an

Open Economy: Mexico, 1939–63," *Economic Development and Cultural Change*, 14 (July 1966), pp. 458–470.

Schotta, Charles, Jr., and Vittorio A. Bonomo, "A Cross-Spectral Analysis of the Real Balance Effect," *Western Economic Journal*, 5 (December 1966), pp. 77–78.

Sedjo, Roger A., "Price Trends, Economic Growth, and the Canadian Balance of Trade: A Three-Country Model," *Journal of Political Economy*, 79 (May/June 1971), pp. 596–613.

Severn, Alan K., "Exports and Economic Growth," *Kyklos*, 21 (1968 Fasc. 3), pp. 546–548.

Spiegelglas, Stephen, "World Exports of Manufactures, 1956 vs. 1937," *Manchester School*, 27 (May 1959), pp. 111–139.

Stern, Robert M., "Developments in the Commodity Composition, Market Distribution, and Competitiveness of Italy's Foreign Trade, 1955–1963," *Banca Nazionale del Lavoro Quarterly Review*, 72 (March 1965), pp. 58–76.

Steuer, M. D., R. J. Ball, and J. R. Eaton, "The Effect of Waiting Times on Foreign Orders for Machine Tools," *Economica*, 33 (November 1966), pp. 387–403.

Swan, T. W., "Longer-Run Problems of the Balance of Payments," in H. W. Arndt and M. W. Corden, eds., *The Australian Economy: A Volume of Readings*. Melbourne: Chesire Press, 1963, pp. 384–395; reprinted in Caves and Johnson, eds. (1968, pp. 455–464).

Taplin, Grant B., "Models of World Trade," *IMF Staff Papers*, 14 (November 1967), pp. 433–453.

"A Model of World Trade," in R. J. Ball, ed., *The International Linkage of National Economic Models*. Amsterdam, North-Holland, 1973, Chap. 7, pp. 177–223.

Tsiang, S. C., "The Role of Money in Trade-Balance Stability: Synthesis of the Elasticity and Absorption Approaches," *American Economic Review*, 51 (December 1961), pp. 912–936. reprinted in Caves and Johnson, eds. (1968, pp. 389–412).

Turnovsky, Stephen J., "International Trading Relationships for a Small Country: The Case of New Zealand," *Canadian Journal of Economics*, 1 (November 1968), pp. 772–790.

Tyszynski, H., "World Trade in Manufactured Commodities, 1899–1950," *Manchester School*, 19 (September 1951), pp. 272–304.

Vernon, Raymond, "International Investment and International Trade in the Product Cycle," *Quarterly Journal of Economics*, 80 (May 1966), pp. 190–207.

Waelbroeck, J., Y. Guillaume, and P. Kestens, "World Payments in Transition: An Evaluation of Orders of Magnitude," *Cahiers Economiques de Bruxelles*, No. 56 (4e trimestre, 1972), pp. 529–565.

White, William H., "Bias in Export Substitution Elasticities Derived through Use of Cross-Section (Sub-Market) Data," mimeographed, IMF, 1970.

Zellner, Arnold, "On the Aggregation Problem: A New Approach to a Troublesome Problem," in K. A. Fox *et al.*, eds., *Economic Models, Estimation and Risk Programming: Essays in Honor of Gerhard Tintner,* Springer-Verlag, 1969, pp. 365–374.

Zellner, Arnold, and Claude Montmarquette, "A Study of Some Aspects of Temporal Aggregation Problems in Econometric Analyses," *Review of Economics and Statistics,* 53 (November 1971), pp. 335–342.

THE MULTINATIONAL CORPORATION
AND DIRECT INVESTMENT*

G. C. Hufbauer

When a firm embarks on production in a foreign land, it faces new choices and opportunities. It must deal in a different currency, it must pay different factor costs, and it will be taxed under different laws. The corporate response to these fresh alternatives is an intriguing subject that has attracted much research.[1] But the problems of multinational production have assumed more than academic interest with the rapid expansion of U.S. direct investment abroad from $7 billion in 1935 to $86 billion in 1971. This expansion has aroused fears for the prosperity of home countries and for the sovereignty of host nations (Servan-Schreiber, 1968; Levitt, 1970).

Table 1 draws together figures for U.S. direct investment and for gross domestic product of host countries in a number of regions. On the whole, U.S. multinational corporate activity has ex-

* I am indebted to R. E. Lipsey, A. E. Scaperlanda, T. Horst, G. v. G. Stevens, and J. Bhagwati for valuable comments and suggestions. The paper was initiated while I was with the University of New Mexico. John Barnes, Mark Evans, and John Chilas helped gather sources and statistical data. A Fulbright-Hays award for research at King's College, Cambridge, enabled me to revise and extend the first draft. The views expressed here do not necessarily reflect the views of the Treasury Department.

1 Dunning (1958) and Wilkins (1970) trace the ancestry of multinational enterprise. The Harvard Business School (under Vernon), the University of Reading (under Dunning), New York University (under Hawkins), the United Nations Conference on Trade and Development (UNCTAD) (under Streeten, Lall, et al.), and the National Bureau of Economic Research (under Lipsey) have housed major research programs on the multinational corporation. Other agencies and institutes with active research programs are listed by Erb (1973). Bibliographies of the literature on multinational corporations have been prepared by Burtis, et al. (1971), Lea and Webley (1973), Aronson (1973), the UN Secretariat (1973), and, perhaps the most comprehensive, Lall (1973b). Among the leading essay collections, the works edited by Kindleberger (1970), Dunning (1970, 1971), Rolfe and Damm (1970), Machlup, Salant, and Tarshis (1972), and Brooke and Remmers (1972) and the studies compiled for the U.S. Senate Committee on Finance (1973a, 1973b) deserve mention. Brooke and Remmers (1970), Tugendhat (1971), Ragazzi (1973), Dunning (1973b), and Parry (1973b) offer good surveys. Corden (1974) has a useful analysis of the relationship between multinational corporations and orthodox trade theory, while Caves (1974b) has ably synthesized the relationships among international trade, investment, and imperfect markets. Leading books and papers have appeared over the names of Penrose (1956), Hymer (1960), W. C. Gordon (1962), Mikesell (1962, 1971), Dunning and Rowan (1965), Vernon (1966, 1971, 1972), Servan-Schreiber (1968), Stevens (1969b), Caves (1971), and Horst (1972a, 1972b). Topical reviews of multinational corporation issues have appeared in the *Wall Street Journal* (1973), *Newsweek* (1972), and *Fortune* (1973).

TABLE 1   *U.S. Direct Investment Compared with Host Region Gross Domestic Product* (billions of dollars and relative growth rates)

GROSS DOMESTIC PRODUCT

Year	United States	Canada	Western Europe Total	United Kingdom	Latin America	Australia, New Zealand, South Africa
1950	284	17	134	32	31	13
1955	396	24	211	47	33	18
1960	501	32	290	63	52	25
1962	557	41	385	68	61	29
1965	681	48	459	89	74	35
1970	970	70	681	103	102	53

U.S. DIRECT INVESTMENT

Year	Total	Canada	Western Europe Total	United Kingdom	Latin America	Other Countries and Unallocated Total	Australia, New Zealand, S. Africa
1950	11.8	3.6	1.7	0.8	4.4	2.1	0.4
1955	19.4	6.5	3.2	1.4	6.6	3.2	0.8
1960	32.0	11.2	6.7	3.2	8.4	5.7	1.2
1965	48.8	15.2	14.0	5.1	10.8	8.7	2.3
1970	78.1	22.8	24.5	8.0	14.7	16.1	4.3

RELATIVE GROWTH: U.S. DIRECT INVESTMENT
VS. GROSS DOMESTIC PRODUCT IN THE HOST REGION[a]

Period	Canada	Western Europe Total	United Kingdom	Latin America	Australia, New Zealand, South Africa
1950–55	2.0	1.5	1.6	8.3	2.2
1955–60	2.2	2.9	3.8	0.5	1.6
1960–65	0.7	1.9	1.4	0.7	2.1
1965–70	1.1	1.6	3.6	1.0	1.8

[a]The relative growth is the quinquennial percentage growth in direct investment divided by the quinquennial percentage growth in GDP. The relative growth (similarly calculated) for direct investment by all foreign countries in the United States was: 1950–55, 1.3; 1955–60, 1.3; 1960–65, 0.8; 1965–70, 1.2.

Sources: GDP figures were compiled from IMF (1972) and UN Statistical Office (1970, 1972). The figures are translated into U.S. dollars at prevailing exchange rates. U.S. direct-investment figures are from *Survey of Current Business* (various issues). These are book-value figures, compiled by adding annual direct-investment flows and retained earnings to benchmark census data on gross book values (before depreciation). Note that the figures pertain only to U.S. equity ownership of the foreign affiliate and debt of that affiliate to its parent; the ownership interest of foreign shareholders and banks is excluded. In making comparisons between gross domestic product in current prices and the book value of direct investment, I assume that the ratio between sales in current prices and the book value of the equity stake remained approximately constant between 1950 and 1970.

panded more rapidly than host-country gross product. During the years 1965–70, for example, U.S. direct investment in the United Kingdom grew 3.6 times as fast as U.K. gross product; in Western Europe as a whole it grew 1.6 times faster; and in Australia, New Zealand, and South Africa, 1.8 times faster. The principal exception to this pattern was Latin America, where, during the 1955–65 decade, U.S. direct investment grew more slowly than domestic gross product.

British direct investment overseas has also grown more rapidly than the domestic output of host countries, at least in the main industrial countries. The statistics appear in Table 2. Canada has been the principal area where U.K. investments have grown less rapidly than domestic product.

Direct investment by foreign countries in the United States and in the United Kingdom has likewise expanded more rapidly than gross product, a point brought out in the notes to Tables 1 and 2. Thus, faster relative growth is not restricted to the overseas operations of American or British multinational firms.

When multinational corporations grow at the same pace as their

TABLE 2   *U.K. Direct Investment Compared with Host Region Gross Domestic Product* (millions of pounds sterling and relative growth rates)

			U.K. DIRECT INVESTMENT				
						Other	Countries
							Australia,
		United		Western	Latin		New Zealand,
Year	Total	States	Canada	Europe	America	Total	South Africa
1962	3405	301	484	29	172	2419	919
1965	4210	387	531	42	213	3037	1242
1970	6415	762	716	91	264	4581	1901

RELATIVE GROWTH: U.K. DIRECT INVESTMENT
VS. GROSS DOMESTIC PRODUCT IN THE HOST REGION[a]

					Australia,
	United		Western	Latin	New Zealand,
Period	States	Canada	Europe	America	South Africa
1962–65	2.6	0.5	2.3	1.1	1.6
1965–70	2.3	0.8	2.4	0.6	1.0

[a] The relative growth is the period percentage growth in direct investment divided by the period percentage growth in GDP. The relative growth for direct investment by all foreign countries in the United Kingdom between 1962 and 1970 was 1.9.

Sources: Gross domestic product figures are from Table 1. U.K. direct investment figures are from U.K. Reference Division (1970) and U.K. Dept. of Trade and Industry (1973).

host economies, there is little to explain. When they grow more slowly, the question becomes: Why are they disadvantaged? The MNC story is not one of universal growth. Yet I shall concentrate on more rapid expansion, because growth has been the dominant theme for the last quarter-century.

A fundamental question that faces all explanations of MNC expansion is whether the postwar boom is a *stock-adjustment* phenomenon or a *continuous-flow* process (Branson, 1970). Will the expansion of MNCs relative to local firms stop in a few years, or will it continue for the rest of this century? The fact that American direct investment abroad grew more rapidly between 1945 and 1970 than between 1908 and 1940 suggests the durability of MNC expansion. Just as the nineteenth century witnessed the ascendancy of the national corporation, the twentieth century has given rise to the multinational firm (Kindleberger, 1967). Further evidence on the durability of MNC growth might be gained by examining both rates of corporate expansion as a function of length of time overseas and the recruitment of new firms to the MNC ranks (Richardson, 1971).

How should a multinational corporation be defined? There are degrees of multinational involvement, but most authors focus on a few firms with operations in several countries. Vernon (1971) used the following approach (which I shall also use): He examined U.S. manufacturing giants with establishments in six or more countries.[2] On this definition, there are some two hundred-odd U.S. multinational corporations (including nonmanufacturing concerns), and perhaps another hundred multinational giants based in Western Europe, Canada, and Japan.

Despite their multinational character, such firms are almost always controlled from a single country. Effective multinational ownership does occur, but rather infrequently. Western Europe has witnessed corporate marriages between national concerns: Royal Dutch/Shell, Unilever, Agfa-Gevaert, Dunlop-Pirelli. The ownership of Alcan is divided between Canada and the United States, while International Nickel is an American–British–Canadian venture. Joint ownership of a single affiliate by parent companies of diverse national origin occurs more frequently. This is particularly true of petroleum enterprises, for example in the Middle

---

2 In the terminology of U.S. official statistics, "affiliates" are establishments incorporated abroad that are controlled by American firms. Distinctions are further made between types of affiliates according to degree of parental control. "Branches" are unincorporated establishments operating abroad. Tax considerations largely determine whether an MNC opens branches or affiliates. I use the term "establishment" to encompass both types of operation.

East, and of banking ventures formed to enter the London capital market. Moreover, the multinational ownership of U.S. firms is growing, as foreign institutions acquire shares on the New York Stock Exchange (*Wall Street Journal*, June 22, 1973).

I shall attempt to divide the literature on multinational corporations into several channels, each corresponding to a basic theme.[3] In section 1, I review four major industry characteristics of multinational enterprise: access to cheap capital, portfolio diversification, technological rents, and industrial organization. In section 2, I examine the company choice between exports, foreign-affiliate production, and the licensing of independent foreign firms. Special attention is paid to the influence on this choice of tariffs and other government policy measures. In section 3, I review econometric forecasts of direct-investment flows and the balance-of-payments aspects of overseas investment. In section 4, I discuss welfare questions: the orthodox welfare analysis of capital flows and multinational enterprise, tax considerations and transfer pricing, the Marxist position, and the leading policy issues.

3   Data on multinational corporations have been collected by both public agencies and private scholars. I shall list the major sources by country. For official statistics, only the agency name is given; for privately collected data, a citation to the source listed in the bibliography is given. A statistical overview is provided by UN Department of Economic and Social Affairs (1973). Most of the available figures are restricted to book values of direct investment, some sales data, and a very limited body of data on trade flows between affiliates. More information should be published on the factor stocks and output levels of a given company's plants in different countries. Also, comparisons are needed between local and multinational firms operating in the same industry.

   United States. The U.S. Department of Commerce, Bureau of Economic Analysis (formerly Office of Business Economics), publishes data in the *Survey of Current Business* and also issues special reports. The U.S. Department of Commerce, Office of Foreign Direct Investment, issues special reports. *Fortune* magazine has an annual listing of the 500 largest U.S. manufacturing concerns and the 200 largest non-U.S. manufacturing concerns. Bruck and Lees (1968) have published a list of the foreign operations of the larger firms. The Harvard Multinational Enterprise Project has a bank of data, in addition to the published work by Vaupel and Curhan (1969).

   United Kingdom. The official statistics are regularly published in the U.K. Department of Trade and Industry's magazine, *Trade and Industry.* A compilation of data from 1962 to 1968 was issued by the U.K. Reference Division (1970). A wealth of unofficial data was published by Reddaway (1967, 1968). The University of Reading (under Dunning) has also gathered a bank of survey information. Dunning (1972) recently prepared an in-depth statistical study of U.S. industry operating in Britain. Forsyth (1972) has a survey of U.S. investment in Scotland. The Department of Trade and Industry sponsored a wide-ranging report by Steuer *et al.* (1973).

   Europe. Franko (1974) is working on a broad study of European-based multinational firms.

   Australia. The Commonwealth Treasury publishes an annual bulletin covering foreign investment in Australia. Brash (1966) put together the first unofficial survey.

   Canada. The Dominion Bureau of Statistics publishes surveys from time to time on U.S. companies that control manufacturing operations in Canada. Annual data are collected under the Corporations and Labor Unions Returns Act and published in the

1. INDUSTRY CHARACTERISTICS OF MULTINATIONAL ENTERPRISE

The familiar concept of comparative advantage furnishes a useful starting point. Certain industries in any given country enjoy an advantage over those same industries located abroad. The industries with a comparative advantage will exhibit a high ratio of foreign to domestic sales (including in foreign sales exports, sales from overseas affiliates, and some measure of the sales on which royalties are received).

The first question then is: Which industry characteristics enable companies in that field to enjoy a high ratio of foreign to domestic sales? The relevant industry characteristics are discussed under four headings: access to cheap capital, portfolio diversification, technological rents, and industrial organization. Some characteristics are invoked to explain only one type of foreign business, for

Annual Report of the Minister of Trade and Commerce. There are detailed official studies of the Royal Commission (1957), the Watkins Commission (1968), and the Gray Report (1972). Safarian (1966) has published his unofficial survey results. The Government of Canada Office of Economics (1971) has issued a bibliography on foreign investment in Canada.

France. Bertin (1972) of the University of Rennes has an ongoing program of research on multinational enterprise. The history of U.S. investment in France is traced by Kindleberger (1973a). *Revue Economique* (1972) published a special issue on multinational corporations.

Ireland. McAleese (1971/72) has assembled the available statistical material, and offers a good review of the fiscal incentives provided by the Irish Republic. P. J. Buckley of Reading University is writing a thesis based on a recent survey of multinational corporations operating in Ireland. Donaldson (1966) conducted one of the first surveys.

Japan. The basic statistics on Japanese direct foreign investment are collected by the Bank of Japan; they are summarized by Hamada (1972). Other nonofficial sources include Ozawa (1968), Kojima (1973), and Sherk (1973).

Netherlands. Stubenitzky (1970) has written about multinational firms operating in the Netherlands.

New Zealand. Official statistics are collected from time to time by the Department of Statistics and the Reserve Bank of New Zealand. The authoritative unofficial study, including extensive survey results, was written by Deane (1970).

Sweden. The Industrial Institute for Economic and Social Research in Stockholm is conducting studies both of Swedish overseas investment and of foreign investment in Sweden. Samuelsson (1973), Swedenborg (1973), and Thiel (1973) have written the first reports.

Other Countries. Ackerman (1971) lists some sources for Brazil. Hatti (1970) does the same for India, the principal source for that country being the Reserve Bank of India. May (1965) has data on Nigeria. UNCTAD commissioned a group at Oxford led by Streeten and Lall to gather data on selected foreign firms operating in Jamaica and Kenya (1970, 1972), India and Iran (1971, 1972), and Colombia and Malaysia (1973a). Drysdale (1972) had edited a volume on direct investment in Asia and the Pacific. Additional country studies are listed in the bibliographies by Burns *et al.* and Lall (1973b). The IMF's annual *Balance of Payments Yearbook* gives direct-investment flow figures by country.

example, sales by overseas affiliates; other characteristics are offered to explain two or more types of foreign involvement.

Cheap Capital

Early speculation on the nature of MNC comparative advantage centered on the idea that the MNC, based in a capital-rich country, would enjoy a cheaper supply of capital than the native firm. The MNC affiliate might work at a disadvantage in coordinating its activities with company headquarters, mastering local laws and customs, and developing a network of suppliers and distributors. But the MNC could overcome these disadvantages by its access to cheap funds from the mother country. This idea paralleled the Heckscher–Ohlin notion that capital-rich countries should export capital-intensive goods.

One way of looking at the cheap-capital thesis is to ask whether multinational corporations specialize in capital-intensive goods. The Tariff Commission (in U.S. Senate Committee on Finance, 1973b) posed this question and found a negative answer. Earlier, in a celebrated study, Leontief (1954) discovered that U.S. exports are not concentrated in capital-intensive goods.

More traditional applications of the cheap-capital argument as an explanation of overseas investment have compared foreign and domestic earnings. In some of the early studies, domestic returns were equated with the cost of capital, where "cost" was interpreted in an opportunity sense. Returns abroad were directly compared with returns at home, in the expectation that a positive differential would be associated with more rapid overseas expansion, while a negative differential would be associated with slower growth abroad. This formulation says nothing about the capital intensity of those industries dominated by multinational corporations. It is quite consistent with industry comparative advantage rooted in advanced technology, oligopolistic markets, or some other feature. The differential-returns formulation merely makes a general appeal to the importance of the mother country's capital abundance, as reflected in a lower domestic rate of return.

The differential-returns version of the cheap-capital thesis had considerable appeal in the late 1950s, when American manufacturing firms were rushing into Europe and the after-tax rate of return experienced by U.S. manufacturing subsidiaries consistently exceeded the return on U.S. domestic manufacturing by 3 to 4 percentage points (*Survey of Current Business*, September 1965). Second thoughts began to occur when U.S. firms again doubled their capital stake in European manufacturing between 1960 and 1965, although earnings there were no higher than at home. Faith in the differential-returns explanation was sorely tried when U.S. firms increased their holdings of European manufacturing assets by another 80 per cent between 1965 and 1970, even though higher rates of return could be obtained in domestic manufacturing during much of that period.

Indeed, the differential between U.S. and foreign returns has never correlated very well with the difference between the rates of home and foreign investment. Figure 1 provides a global comparison of these two differences. There is little apparent connec-

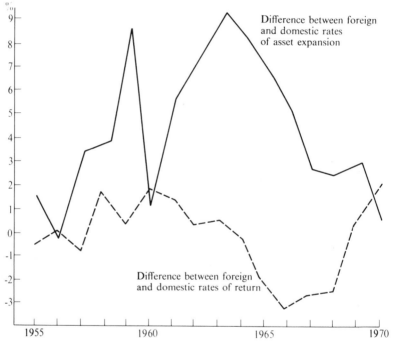

Figure 1. Comparison between foreign and domestic differential rates of asset expansion and differential rates of return.

Sources: Rates of return on domestic and foreign manufacturing investment are from *Survey of Current Business* (various issues). Foreign earnings are expressed on an after-local-tax basis; domestic earnings are expressed on an after-U.S.-tax basis. The rate of domestic-manufacturing asset expansion (book value of gross assets) is calculated from U.S. Department of Commerce (1971) and U.S. Department of Commerce Bureau of the Census (1972). The rate of manufacturing direct-investment expansion (book value of direct investment) is calculated from *Survey of Current Business* (various issues).

tion between the series. Weintraub (1967) likewise found no meaningful link between intercountry differences in rates of return and the flow of U.S. capital. Bandera and White (1968) could discern no effect of earnings on the year-end levels of direct-investment book value, while Bandera and Lucken (1972) could find no connection between relative earnings and the allocation of U.S. investment between the EFTA and the EEC.

Although the differential-returns hypothesis has not proven useful in explaining overall MNC growth, a variant of the hypothesis has appeared as a "straw man" explanation for the distribution of MNC investment among foreign countries. The variant notion is that MNCs should expand their activities most rapidly in countries providing the highest rates of return. That has not happened (Levitt, 1970, p. 171).

There are good reasons why observed differences in profit rates need not correspond with flows of foreign investment. First, the published earnings statistics tell us nothing about the subtleties of foreign tax rates, tax credits, and subsidies, let alone transfer prices. Reported profit rates for any one member of a multinational enterprise can be misleading, because tax and exchange-control regimes may make it worthwhile to shift profits between affiliates through artificial prices in interaffiliate transactions rather than through explicit capital movements. The fast growth of European petroleum facilities in the face of negative accounting earnings, for example, reflects both transfer pricing and tax arrangements.

Second, profit-rate differentials partly correspond to risk differentials. Exchange-rate variations, political instability, the threat of expropriation, and business fluctuations differ markedly from country to country. Considering these risks, observed differences in profit rates might reflect an equilibrium situation rather than a situation of stimulus for firms to expand in one area at the expense of another.

Third, in oligopolistic industries, earnings on new projects can differ substantially from returns on existing plants (Hymer, 1960; Vernon, 1971). And, in the available statistics, fluctuating returns on existing assets simply bury the effect of new investment on earnings. This is true both for investment abroad and investment within the United States. Thus, the available figures provide little help in analyzing expansion and retrenchment decisions at the margin.

These last two objections can be spelled out more formally if we assume that the MNC affiliate is characterized by a Cobb–Douglas production function:

$$X = \lambda L^{\beta} K^{\alpha} , \tag{1}$$

where X is output, L and K represent labor and capital, β and α are elasticities of output with respect to factor inputs ($\beta + \alpha = 1$), and λ is a neutral efficiency parameter. Note that λ is specified in a way that precludes factor bias in efficiency improvements.

Each affiliate will expand output to the point where the following relationships prevail between market wage, w, the cost of capital, c, and the price of output, p:

$$w = (\beta X/L) \left[X(dp/dx) + p \right]$$
$$c = (\alpha X/K) \left[X(dp/dx) + p \right] . \tag{2}$$

Suppose that the price of output is related to the volume of output through an elasticity parameter, η, which remains constant in the relevant range:

$$X = p^{-\eta} y^{\theta} , \tag{3}$$

where Y is national income and θ is the income elasticity of demand. The assumption of imperfectly elastic demand with respect to price sets a limit on the size of each firm. If demand were perfectly elastic, the size of each firm would be indeterminate, since production function (1) has no scarce factor.

The affiliate's rate of growth may be found by differentiating the logarithmic version of (1) with respect to time and by using equations (2) and (3) to substitute for the rates of growth in the firm's labor force and capital stock. The dot notation refers to the time rate of growth, for example, $\dot{X} = d \log X/dt$. Hence

$$\dot{X} = \eta (\dot{\lambda} - \beta \dot{w} - \alpha \dot{c}) + \theta \dot{Y} . \tag{4}$$

Equation (4) helps clarify why differential returns need not correspond to MNC rates of expansion in various parts of the world. The values of c assigned by the MNC to various countries may differ on account of risk, but in each area $\dot{c}$ could be zero. In these circumstances, output growth would be determined by differences in $\dot{\lambda}$, $\dot{w}$, and $\dot{Y}$ between areas, and have nothing to do with the differential in average returns.

The average rate of return in each area, r, would be given by the following equation:

$$r = (pX - wL)/K. \tag{5}$$

Using equation (2) to substitute for values of wL and K, and recalling that $(\alpha + \beta) = 1$, equation (5) may be written

$$r = c \left[1 + 1/(\alpha\eta - \alpha)\right]. \tag{6}$$

In other words, average returns will vary from place to place depending on the cost of capital, the elasticity of demand, and the value of α.

The difficulties with the cheap-capital thesis go beyond issues of measurement. The MNC phenomenon is probably *not* an outgrowth of capital abundance. MNCs do not necessarily specialize in capital-intensive sectors, just as American and British exports are not particularly concentrated in capital-intensive goods. Nor is there an observable connection between MNC expansion, cost of capital at home, and average earnings on investment abroad. The behavior of MNCs might have rather little to do with the classical theory of foreign investment.

Portfolio Diversification

According to the *Financial Times* (May 9, 1972, p. 10), there are "two major advantages to being multinational which outweigh all the disadvantages. First, there is the stability that comes from investments spread across many countries. . . ." Companies are not solely concerned with obtaining the highest mean return; they are equally anxious to produce stable earnings. The stock exchange welcomes growth, but it also welcomes a limited degree of fluctuation around the earnings trendline. A more sophisticated version of capital theory has thus been invoked to explain overseas investment. The new version incorporates risk as well as return.

At any given time, the firm can choose among different investments. Each investment is characterized both by an expected return and by an expected standard deviation attached to that return. Covariance may exist between the returns on the various investments. From its collection of investment alternatives, the firm can trace an optimal frontier, of the sort indicated by Figure 2. The frontier is formed by suitably combining various investments. Each point on the optimal frontier represents the highest possible return for a given standard deviation. The mathematics of deriving the frontier are spelled out by Mao (1969).

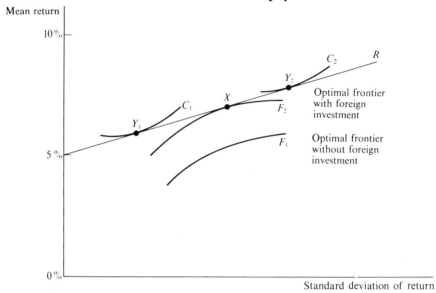

Figure 2. Risk-return alternatives facing the multinational corporation.

If the firm faces a single risk-free rate of return at which it can borrow or lend, more can be said. Suppose the risk-free rate is 5 per cent, as in Figure 2. The firm can then hold all or part of its net worth at the risk-free rate and invest the balance, or it can become a net borrower and invest more than 100 per cent of its own net, worth. Given these alternatives, it can choose any point along ray R in Figure 2. The point it chooses will represent a combination of the risk-free asset (or risk-free borrowing) and that portfolio mix with the return-variance characteristics of point X. Ray R is drawn tangent to the frontier at point X. Any other ray would involve either unattainable points (a ray originating at 5 per cent but steeper than R) or points that involve greater risk for a given return (a ray originating at 5 per cent but flatter than R).

The point the firm chooses along ray R will represent a combination of the risk-free asset (or risk-free borrowing) and that portfolio mix with the return-variance characteristics of point X. A conservative firm with indifference curve C_1 might choose the return-variance combination Y_1. Part of its investment would be committed to the risk-free asset and part to the portfolio mix of point X. A more adventurous company with indifference C_2 might choose the return-variance combination Y_2. It would borrow to invest more than 100 per cent of its own net worth in the portfolio mix of point X.

Whatever point the firm selects on ray R, its investment portfolio will reflect the composition of tangency point X (Tobin, 1958). If we know both the risk-free rate of return and the investment alternatives facing the firm, we can predict the firm's portfolio mix. The prediction requires no information on the firm's own indifference map. Such information would enable a forecast of the firm's "leverage" – its net borrowing or net holdings of the risk-free asset. But the location of the indifference map does not affect the firm's portfolio mix of "active" investments.[4]

How does this portfolio theory relate to overseas enterprise? The basic argument – which merits more empirical examination than it has so far received – is that foreign opportunities will shift the optimal frontier upward, from F_1 to F_2, as depicted in Figure 2. Foreign investments need not yield the highest possible return nor need they exhibit the lowest possible variance, but their combination of return and variance (and covariance with other investment projects) may entitle them to a place in the portfolio. In partial support of this argument, B. I. Cohen (1973c) found that an increase in the number of countries in which a firm operates significantly reduces its profit variance, while size and product variety have rather little effect.

A related portfolio argument, offered by Kenen (in a private communication), is that large firms with operations concentrated in a single industry will find greater appeal in locating abroad than conglomerate companies of the same size. Conglomerate companies can reduce their risk through involvement in a variety of domestic enterprises, but domestic expansion by an undiversified firm might attract the attention of the antitrust authorities. Horst (1972b) found no link between the number of 3-digit SIC products made by the firm and its multinational propensities. But a measure of the firm's concentration in a single industry – for example, its market share in principal product categories – might display a better connection with the decision to go abroad.

Another portfolio argument was advanced by Aliber (1970). He suggested that earnings are capitalized at a higher rate in the leading home countries than in host countries (he wrote before the New York and London stock markets began their protracted decline). An equally plausible version of the Aliber thesis is that

4 The portfolio mix of active investments can be affected by the position of the firm's return-variance indifference map when (as usually happens) the risk-free borrowing rate exceeds the risk-free rate of return available to the firm. Under such circumstances, a single ray R will not suffice to describe the firm's investment alternatives. Instead, there will be a discontinuity between the ray describing investment alternatives when the firm is a net holder of risk-free assets and the ray describing alternatives when it is a net borrower. If the firm's highest indifference curve touches the optimal frontier within the range of discontinuity, the precise point of tangency will determine the portfolio mix of active investments.

earnings are capitalized at a higher rate for big multinational firms than for small national companies. Earnings of the MNC might have lower variance because of geographic diversification; hence its shares may be bid up to a higher price/earnings ratio. The premium on earnings could enable an MNC to buy out small national firms or build new plants in a more aggressive fashion.

Turning to empirical work, Prachowny (1972) used the portfolio approach in an attempt to explain global levels of U.S. overseas investment during the period 1953–64. His dependent variable was the ratio of the book value of U.S. investment abroad to the *market* value of U.S. corporate stock. Nearly all the year-to-year variation in this ratio comes from the denominator, since the numerator is a smoothly rising variable. On the right-hand side, one of Prachowny's independent variables was the U.S. rate of return. To a large extent, therefore, his equation relates U.S. share prices and U.S. profit rates. A positive relationship would be expected, but this relationship has little to do with the riskiness of overseas investment.

The portfolio approach has been used with greater success to account for the geographic distribution of financial and direct investment. Grubel (1968), Levy and Sarnat (1970), and Agmon (1971) have calculated optimal frontiers for internationally diversified common-share portfolios. Levy and Sarnat, for example, found that if share holdings were spread across twenty-eight countries, a superior optimal frontier would emerge than if holdings were limited to eleven countries in Europe, North America, and Japan. Miller and Whitman (1970) showed that U.S. portfolio holdings of foreign securities were related to international bond yields and an assortment of proxy risk measures.

In the realm of direct investment, Stevens (1969a) used the portfolio approach to explain the proportion of American capital going to Latin America (A_i) and Canada (A_j), where r_i and r_j were five-year moving average rates of return, v_i and v_j were variances in the mean returns, and r^* was the risk-free return on U.S. Treasury bonds of five- to 10-year maturity. In logarithmic terms, the regression results were

$$\log (A_i/A_j) = -1.41 + 0.26 \log (r_i - r^*)$$
$$(4.5)$$

$$-0.46 \log (r_j - r^*) - 0.24 \log v_i + 0.00 \log v_j$$
$$(3.9) \qquad\qquad (2.1) \qquad\qquad (0.0)$$

$$R^2 = 0.94 . \qquad\qquad (7)$$

The numbers in parentheses under the coefficients are t-values. The coefficients are significant (with the exception of log v_j), but they are disquietingly smaller than unity, the value suggested by Tobin's (1958) theoretical equation. Moreover, on an individual-country basis, Stevens found that a simple neoclassical stock-adjustment model gave generally better results for Latin-American countries.

Paxson (1973) applied a stock-adjustment version of the port-folio model to explain the geographic distribution of assets. He first estimated the optimal geographical distribution of assets for American and British multinational firms. These estimates were based on historical earnings experience and the standard deviation and covariance of returns. He then calculated the difference between optimal and actual shares of the total portfolio held in various regions. These differences were compared with the percentage growth of assets in each geographical region between 1964 and 1970. As the stock-adjustment model would lead us to expect, the percentage growth of assets showed a positive rank correlation with the difference between optimal and actual port-folios.

Interestingly enough, the actual shares of assets held by American MNCs in the United States and British MNCs in the United Kingdom were far larger than the estimated optimal shares. This discrepancy could mean that the stock-adjustment process has just begun and that the foreign investment boom is far from over.

But a word of caution. When Paxson applied his analytic method to British–American Tobacco and the Unilever Group, he found that regional differences between optimal and actual portfolio shares were not at all correlated with investment behavior. Inappropriate data or the extensive use of artifical transfer prices (discussed later) could account for these findings. Nevertheless, care should be exercised in drawing macroeconomic conclusions from the portfolio approach when the microeconomic foundations remain to be established.

The portfolio approach has its critics (Leamer and Stern, 1970, p. 92). The argument that firms diversify as a way of reducing risk has been increasingly questioned by students of capital-asset pricing models. With a perfect capital market, the capital value of a given project will be determined solely by its own risk and return characteristics, not by the identity of the parent. Thus, in the absence of synergistic relationships, the market value of the multinational firm, like that of any other conglomerate, will equal the sum of its parts. A multinational enterprise does not become more valuable by combining safe and risky ventures. If investors want reduced risk, they can diversify their own portfolios; they have no need to turn to multinational corporations for financial inter-mediation. According to these critics, multinational enterprise must be explained by reference to the lumpiness of projects, mar-ket control, and technological leadership, not by application of portfolio-diversification models.

Even if we reject these criticisms, certain practical questions must be answered. Does serial correlation over time characterize the variance and covariance of returns for different classes of in-vestment? Unless the corporate manager can turn to past history for guidance on the extent and correlation of risks, he is not likely to employ the risk-return frontier as a tool in shaping investment strategy. And is it true that multinational corporations earn high-er returns, but with a larger variance, from their individual sub-sidiaries than national corporations earn from their regional divi-sions?

Perhaps the portfolio approach can offer useful insights into the geographical diversification of MNC assets. But beyond Ken-en's suggestion that large single-industry firms will find a stong appeal in overseas production, it has little to say about the kinds of industries that nurture exports or foreign investment. As far as portfolio analysis is concerned, tobacco and textile firms could be as internationally minded as chemical and computer companies. This is hardly so, however, and to understand the dif-ference we must turn to other explanations of industry compara-tive advantage.

Technological Rents

One promising hypothesis for understanding industry differences was mentioned by the *Financial Times* (9 May 1972, p. 10), "the economies of using knowledge over and over again." Various scholars have contended the peculiar MNC advantage reposes not in cheap capital but in knowledge (Vernon, 1966, 1971; Gruber *et al.*, 1967; Baranson, 1970; Horst, 1972b). The MNC can employ tangible factors with greater efficiency than local firms, so the ar-gument goes, and this advantage more than offsets any handicaps of doing business abroad. The growth of MNCs is thus attributed to the highly imperfect market for techniques of production and distribution. Sophisticated capital equipment, highly skilled engi-neers, and retail outlets can be bought and sold. But it takes some-thing more to make a successful enterprise. That "something more" is the firm's own proprietary knowledge – production secrets, organizational techniques, and marketing skills. This knowledge is not usually sold to outsiders.

Putting the matter more formally, equations (1), (2), and (3) may be combined to solve for each firm's equilibrium size of output:

$$X = \lambda \eta (1 - 1/\eta)^{\eta} (\beta/w)^{\beta/\eta} (\alpha/c)^{\alpha/\eta} Y^{\theta} \tag{8}$$

The technological parameter, λ, has now to be treated as including not only process techniques but also marketing skills and organizational talent. If the MNC enjoys a larger λ value, while other things are equal, its equilibrium size will be greater than that of the local firm. Many observers view the MNC boom as this kind of adjustment to technological possibilities. After World War II, American corporate giants emerged with a substantial technical edge over their European and Japanese competitors. The subsequent wave of international activity was designed to capture technological rents not by selling knowledge but by exporting research-intensive goods and producing abroad. More recently, European and Japanese giants have joined the game with their own accumulated expertise.

The important role played by technology and human skills in exports from the United States and Western Europe was stressed by Posner (1961), Keesing (1965), Vernon (1966), and Hufbauer (1966). Later, Gruber *et al.* (1967) discovered that U.S. manufactured exports and overseas manufacturing investment are both concentrated in research-intensive industries. Between 1958 and 1964, the four most research-intensive industries devoted a far larger percentage of their plant and equipment to overseas ventures than did the other fourteen industries. These same four industries (transportation, chemicals, electrical machinery, and nonelectrical machinery) exported a much larger fraction of their output than did the other industries. The Tariff Commission (U.S. Senate Committee on Finance, 1973b) likewise found a connection between research intensity, foreign investment, and exports.

Horst (1972a) carried the analysis further in a study of Canadian markets. When U.S. exports to Canada and foreign-affiliate production in Canada are taken *together,* the total for each industry shows a closer correlation to that industry's research intensity than either component taken by itself. Horst's findings were confirmed by Jud (1973). In another article, Horst (1972b) found additional evidence. He related coefficients indicating the industry's multinational propensities (these coefficients were estimated from an earlier set of regression equations) to industry research intensity (among other measures) and obtained significant results.

Technological leadership can also occur in industries that are not noted for their research and development outlays. Thus, the United States has spawned Hilton, Intercontinental, Sheraton, and other international hotel chains, while Danish firms, such as Ostermann-Petersen, have developed expertise in purveying wines, perfumes, and other luxury goods to the diplomatic corps of the world. The worldwide operations of Kellogg, Procter and Gamble, and Coca-Cola are based far more on marketing skills and brand names than on laboratory research and development (Horst, 1974).

Wilkins (1969, 1970), in her able history of American multinational enterprise prior to World War I, suggests that even in the early days fledgling multinational corporations were drawing on a superior storehouse of knowledge. Among the first important American direct-investment ventures were enterprises formed to promote rail and canal links between the Atlantic and Pacific Oceans across Nicaragua and New Granada (later Panama). In the 1840s and 1850s, there were clearly no local firms in Central or South America that could undertake such projects. After the Civil War, the sort of American company that established European footholds clearly had an image of superior know-how: American Radiator, Singer Manufacturing (Davies, 1969, has a delightful account of Singer's operations), the Standard Oil Companies, General Electric, National Cash Register, and International Harvester. The common basis for overseas activity was superior technology and marketing ability.

The preference of American multinational firms for entering large markets also provides an argument for the storehouse-of-knowledge thesis. As an explanation of U.S. manufacturing investment in the European Common Market, Bandera and White (1968) and Scaperlanda and Mauer (1969, 1971, 1972) both showed that market size was the most important variable. Perhaps markets must reach a threshold size before American technology can fruitfully come into play. The threshold could vary from industry to industry and even company to company, but, once it is reached, mass-production techniques learned in the American market can be profitably applied abroad.

In addition, plausible explanations can be offered for the more rapid improvement of techniques by large MNCs than by small local firms. Within the context of a large firm, research acquires the characteristics of a public good. Findings that are useless for one product line may be profitably applied in another. And a firm that is prepared to try a number of research ventures faces less risk of utter failure than a firm that can undertake only one or two trials (Brems, 1970). Big firms should thus experience a faster growth of research-induced productivity than small firms.

Recently, a literature has developed comparing the efficiency of American multinational firms with their local counterparts (Brash, 1966; Johns, 1967; Safarian, 1969, 1973; Rowan and Dunning, 1968; Dunning, 1970; Deane, 1969, 1970; Mason, 1970, 1973; B. I. Cohen, 1973b). But difficulties confront any attempt to assess the technological-rent thesis using standard efficiency ratios. From equations (2), the equilibrium relationships between value of output per unit of capital and per unit of labor are

$$pX/L = (w/\beta) \left[1/(1 - 1/\eta) \right]$$

$$pX/K = (c/\alpha) \left[1/(1 - 1/\eta) \right]. \qquad (9)$$

The value ratios are independent of λ, the efficiency level, provided there is no factor bias in efficiency gains.[5] Therefore, even if no differences are found between MNC affiliates and local firms in the standard value ratios, the technological-rent hypothesis could still hold. The MNC affiliate may be in equilibirum, facing the same income and price elasticities as its local competitor. The affiliate may be larger than its local competitor [equation (8)] and it may be growing faster [equation (4)], but it need not enjoy higher *average* profits [equation (6)], nor be more efficient measured in terms of value of output per unit of input [equations (9)].

There is another interpretation of the technological-rent thesis that admits the possibility of higher MNC profits in equilibrium and a larger value of output per unit of input. Adler (1970) and other exponents of the product-cycle hypothesis argue that the demand for new products is more income elastic and less price elastic than the demand for existing goods (but see the comments by Deppler, 1971). If the MNC affiliate specializes in newer products, with the result that it faces a lower price elasticity of demand than its local competitors, then, by equations (6) and (9), the MNC

5 However, the ratios of *physical* output per man and per unit of capital can depend on λ. Dividing equations (9) by p, it will be seen that X/L and X/K are functions of the price level. If the more efficient firm sells at a lower price, p will be inversely related to λ. Hence X/L and X/K will be larger for the more efficient companies. In practice, ratios of physical output are seldom available for manufacturing firms.

will exhibit a better average profit rate and higher ratios between value of output and quantity of inputs. Its growth rate need not be higher than the local firm's unless, in the context of equation (4), the higher income elasticity offsets the lower price elasticity.

Thus, a good deal of evidence can be interpreted in a way consistent with one version or another of the technological-rent thesis. Much work needs to be done before we can conclude that such interpretations are more than ad hoc exercises. Host-country statistical authorities should exert far greater efforts to publish and compare the size measures, growth rates, and key operating statistics of MNC affiliates and locally owned plants in the same business. With these statistics, it might be possible to decipher the role played in MNC expansion by alternative forms of technical superiority.

Industrial Organization

Another explanation of MNC growth is rooted in the theory of oligopolistic behavior. Technological-rent explanations are often intertwined with these industrial-organization explanations (Penrose, 1968; Kindleberger, 1969, Lectures 1 and 6; Caves, 1971, 1974a, 1974b; Vernon, 1971; Dunning, 1973b). The mixture is altogether natural, since the profitable exploitation of technology depends on some degree of monopoly. Unless secrets can be kept, knowledge will rapidly become a free good, and any gains from the superior technique will either be captured by tangible factors or distributed through lower product prices. Nevertheless, a distinction can be made between oligopolistic behavior that is based on sheer size and oligopolistic behavior that rests on superior technology.

Size, profitability, research and development, and advertising set the MNC apart from other firms (Vernon, 1971). The 187 U.S. multinational enterprises identified by Vernon had an average of $900 million sales in 1964, by comparison with $300 million sales for the remainder of Fortune's 500 largest American industrial firms. MNC after-tax earnings were 13.3 per cent of investment, as against 11.1 per cent for other firms on Fortune's list. Corporate-funded research and development was 2.5 per cent of 1964 sales for the MNCs, compared with 1.9 per cent of sales for the others. Horst (1972b, p. 261), however, has established that company size is the only important *company* determinant of multinational production by U.S. firms:

The conclusion I have come to, after an exhaustive examination of the data, is that once interindustry differences are washed out, the only influence of any separate significance is firm size. That is to say, once industry and size are taken into account, there are no consistent differences among the multi-national firms, the Canadian investors, and the total sample of 1191 manufacturing firms in the extent of vertical integration, labor or capital intensity, advertising or research effort, product diversity, or any other characteristic I could observe.

Comparable studies are not yet available on MNCs of European or Japanese parentage. Nor do we know how closely the *extent* of multinational production by American firms (in contrast to the status of *being* a multinational firm) is correlated with size. But suppose that the overall company ratio between foreign and domestic production (after allowing for industry characteristics) is principally determined by firm size. What would account for this phenomenon? Most explanations stem in one way or another from the causes and consequences of oligopoly (Hymer, 1960, 1970, 1972; Balassa, 1966; Caves, 1971, 1974a, 1974b; Vernon, 1971; Knickerbocker, 1973).

The oligopolistic organization of markets is often explained by reference to economies of scale. Exports and foreign production may require a threshold level of operation before reasonable profits can be earned. The threshold may preclude small companies. Thus Hirsch, in an unpublished piece of research, has found that small firms sell extensively to foreign nations within a regional trade grouping (such as the Common Market) but that large firms have a decided advantage when exports must cross the customary barriers obstructing international trade. Economies of scale in the organization of firms and the lumpiness of individual projects may prove even more decisive in limiting foreign production by small companies.

Turning to the consequences of oligopolistic organization, every firm would like to sell as a monopolist and buy as a monopsonist. The industrial-organization explanation of MNC expansion is the story of attempts by large firms to achieve this sort of antisocial market structure. But it is seldom attractive for large firms to expand more quickly than the overall growth of demand. Large firms, since they already hold a substantial share of the market, customarily face lower product-demand and factor-supply elasticities than do small firms. The sensible large firm will therefore enhance its monopolistic profits by expanding sales less rapidly than small competitors expand theirs. Thus, the story of international oligopoly is *not* a story of aggressive expansion by giant multinational companies in a predatory effort to crowd out small local firms. Quite the contrary. The dominant firms prefer a *status quo* strategy.

Kindleberger's (1971) oil-company example may be cited as an instance of less aggressive growth by established monopolists: "From a world of two major oil firms in the 1920s – Shell and Standard of New Jersey, with Socony Mobil a lesser factor – the world has moved to some twenty or thirty firms which have an impact on world oil." Tilton's (1971) study of the semiconductor industry likewise suggests that the established firms have not been the most aggressive proponents of new technology. Rowthorn's (1971) work on "Gibrat's law," or the "law of proportionate effect," also supports the notion of less aggressive growth by established firms. Gibrat's law on the size distribution of firms assumes that random market disturbances exert an impact proportional to initial firm size. But if large firms pursue a *status quo* strategy, they will in fact grow less rapidly than small firms when the random shocks are favorable movements in product and factor prices. Rowthorn (1971, p. 40) found that growth "was not an increasing function of size. Big firms did not grow faster than small firms. On the contrary, during 1962–7, firms which were small by international standards grew faster than the giants."

Because logic and facts argue against a general thrust by dominant firms to crowd out small competitors, the industrial-organization literature has focused on gamesmanship within the oligopoly. A principal theme is that MNC expansion can be interpreted in terms of counterthreat strategy. Large firms establish footholds in each other's markets as a means of preserving similar cost structures and favorable price levels. If each firm can discomfort its rivals in a variety of different ways, and if each firm has access to basic materials, labor, and capital at approximately the same cost, the *status quo* will be disturbed only after careful deliberation. This kind of deliberate care in an uncertain world serves as a principal buttress of monopolistic behavior in an oligopolistic industry. Thus the industrial-organization story is not so much concerned with exports (though they can be a useful weapon) as with the judicious worldwide placement of production facilities.

A fascinating work on gamesmanship is Knickerbocker's (1973) study of entry patterns. Using data gathered by the Harvard Multinational Enterprise Project, Knickerbocker calculated an entry concentration index (ECI) for each industry. The index shows the extent to which subsidiary start-up dates were bunched in time. The ECI was positively related to industry concentration, suggesting that oligopolies do react in a way that minimizes the possibility of one rival gaining a significant cost or marketing advantage over its competitors. The ECI was also positively related to the size of market, indicating that the reaction is all the more intense when a large market is at stake. The ECI was negatively related to the product diversity of MNCs and to the extent of MNC research and development efforts. These latter results suggest that oligopolistic reactions are dulled when a firm has diverse investment opportunities, or when its position rests on technological superiority.

Oligopolistic interdependence can spring, as Bhagwati (1972) has noted, from cooperation as well as competitive reaction. Joint ventures, licensing arrangements, and corporate marriages can provide the foundations for security. The Dunlop-Pirelli merger is cited as an example:

Long the friendliest of competitors, Dunlop and Pirelli neatly complement each other. Dunlop is primarily a manufacturer of conventional cross-ply tires, Pirelli concentrates on radials. In Europe, Dunlop has perhaps 18 per cent of the market, Pirelli 12 per cent, as against 12 per cent for Michelin, the next largest competitor. In Europe, Pirelli crosses Dunlop's path only in West Germany: Elsewhere, where Dunlop is active, Pirelli stays out; where Pirelli is active, Dunlop stays out. Outside of Europe, Pirelli is active mostly in Latin America, Dunlop in the Commonwealth and North America.

Another theme in the industrial-organization story holds that multinational corporations go abroad to secure their lines of supply. As a consequence of monopolistic pricing on intermediate inputs, the firm with an established marketing system can usually earn more from the development of foreign raw materials than an overseas firm with no marketing outlets in the advanced countries.[6] Vertical integration across national boundaries thus provides an attractive avenue of growth for firms in the raw-materials sector. Supporting this thesis, Horst (1972b) found a positive link between orientation toward natural resources and industrial production abroad.

2.   MODE OF FOREIGN INVOLVEMENT

The Product-Cycle Thesis

Suppose that a company is situated in an industry with the requisite characteristics for a high ratio between foreign and domestic sales – for example, a research-intensive oligopoly. What deter-

---

6 In this connection, it is significant that Arpan (1972) received no response from the oil companies in his study of intracorporate pricing.

mines the company's choice between exports, foreign-affiliate production, joint-venture arrangements, and licensing? Posner (1961), Vernon (1966), and Hufbauer (1966) were among the first to suggest a sequential choice between exports and foreign production. In the early phases, a new good would be exported from the innovating country. Later it would be manufactured abroad. Vernon (1966) cast the choice within the framework of company affairs. Early in the life cycle of a product, the company would choose to manufacture at home and export to foreign nations. Later, when foreign sales had grown to respectable volume, the company would establish manufacturing subsidiaries abroad. Still later, the firm might license production by other companies, or the technology might enter the realm of public knowledge. (Alternatively, licensing might be a totally different route, chosen by small companies that lack the resources to produce or market overseas.)

One reason given by Vernon for manufacturing at home first was to take advantage of receptive demand in a high-income country. Klein (1973, p. 183) has also stressed the empirical importance of learning conditions on the supply side: "Early in the production process, when learning is important, the U.S. has a comparative advantage in producing a new product. When learning becomes less important, it is then not surprising that comparative advantage should shift to a low wage country." Klein found just such a shift for the four pharmaceutical companies he studied. Learning can also explain implementation of new processes, involving *old* goods, in the home country first. Demand for the good could be well established abroad, but the firm may still prefer to try out new machinery and techniques at home.

The Role of Government Policy

The product-cycle concept offers a useful point of departure. Recent findings, however, have underlined the effect of policy measures on the choice between exports, foreign production, joint ventures, and licensing, both in the manufacture of new goods and in the implementation of new processes. Protection by a foreign country can accelerate the transition from exports to foreign-affiliate production. If the protection is severe enough, the export and foreign-affiliate phases may be bypassed altogether and the company may be forced to license its knowledge, or enter a joint-venture arrangement. Thus, the sequence envisaged in product-cycle models frequently yields to a sequence dictated by government policy.

The impact of policy measures can be better understood after a brief excursion into trade theory. Mundell (1957) developed the fundamental proposition (which can be traced to Pigou, 1906, and Ohlin, 1933) that trade and factor movements may act as substitutes for one another. Suppose there are two goods, two factors, and two countries, that competition prevails in product and factor markets, and that production functions are the same in both countries. Free trade, with factor immobility, will ensure that the same wage–profit ratio prevails in both countries. If Country A, which specializes in the labor-intensive good, restricts imports of the capital-intensive good, it will drive up the domestic rate of return. Now relax the factor-immobility assumption. Capital will flow to Country A until wage–profit ratios are once again equalized. The equalization of factor-price ratios implies the equalization of commodity-price ratios. Hence, if the tariff is now dropped, there will be no incentive for commodity trade. The export of capital from Country B has been substituted for the export of capital-intensive goods.

If a country wants to attract capital, it should thus protect its capital-intensive sectors. As we have seen, and as Borts (1974) has rightly emphasized, MNCs do not particularly specialize in capital-intensive goods. But if knowledge is viewed as a factor of production, and access to it rather than to capital is seen as the key ingredient of MNC comparative advantage, Mundell's analysis may be applied to the choice between exports and foreign production. When foreign countries protect their home markets, multinational corporations will respond by locating factories abroad sooner than they might otherwise have done. According to the product-cycle thesis, exports would eventually have been lost, but protection accelerates the natural sequence of events.

Protection comes in a variety of forms. Tariffs are an obvious example, but numerous nontariff barriers have also been devised. Quotas are set on imports; local standards are rigged to exclude foreign goods; sales and excise taxes are levied in a discriminatory manner; government bodies buy on a preferential basis from local producers; attractive production subsidies are offered to multinational firms. The quantification of nontariff barriers is a difficult task, and empirical study of the choice between exports and foreign production has necessarily focused on tariff barriers.

Horst (1972a) found that the ratio of U.S. exports to total U.S.

sales in Canada (exports plus foreign production) was negatively affected both by the height of the Canadian tariff and the size of the Canadian market. The size-of-market effect fits in naturally with the demand side of the product-cycle thesis, while the tariff effect shows the impact of policy measures. A given tariff should exert a greater impact on a larger market, but this implication was not tested by Horst. Horst did find that the ratios of U.S. exports to U.S. sales in the United Kingdom and the Common Market were negatively influenced by tariff levels. Horst's work on Canada was confirmed and extended by Jud (1973). Jud found that, in addition to Canadian tariffs and market size, a higher degree of industrial concentration stimulates the shift from exports to foreign production. This finding supports Knickerbocker (1973), who uncovered a pattern of reaction in oligopolistic industries. When one oligopolist goes abroad, others quickly follow suit. Thus a more concentrated industry will exhibit a lower ratio of exports to foreign production.

Horst and Jud used industry statistics to assess the influence of tariffs. Valuable work remains to be done at the company level. Interview studies do suggest that company choices are heavily influenced by the extent of domestic protection. Thus, Wells (1964), working on U.K. foreign investment, stressed the importance of protectionist measures; so did Polk *et al.* (1966) and Stobaugh *et al.* (1972), working on U.S. foreign investment; Brash (1966) and Parry (1973a) on foreign investment in Australia; Deane (1970) on foreign investment in New Zealand; Daniels (1971) on foreign investment in the United States; and McAleese (1971/72) on foreign investment in Ireland. Marshall *et al.* (1936) and Barber (1955) earlier used the same explanation to account for U.S. manufacturing investment in Canada.

Statistical attempts have been made to relate aggregate direct investment to tariff discrimination. Most of the analysis has concerned the European Common Market. Scaperlanda and Mauer (1969, 1971, 1972) found that their tariff proxy variable exerted no significant influence on U.S. direct investment in the Common Market. Their proxy variable was the ratio between U.S. exports to the EEC and internal EEC trade, a decrease in the ratio supposedly indicating greater effective tariff discrimination. The ratio has fallen since 1959, but the fall exerted no significant effect on the annual change in the book value of U.S. direct investment in the EEC. The only variable that exercised a significant impact was the size of the EEC market.

Leftwich (1973) undertook a similar analysis of direct investment by foreigners in the United States over the period 1952–71. As with Scaperlanda and Mauer, his dependent variable was the annual change in the book value of foreign investment. His tariff variable was the ratio of total U.S. tariff proceeds to the total value of dutiable imports. Presumably, the higher the ratio, the greater the incentive for foreign investment, but an insignificant negative relationship was found. (One can question the adequacy of the tariff variable.) The only significant relationship was between size of market, measured by U.S. GNP, and foreign investment. Ahlburg and Parry (1973) reached similar conclusions in a statistical study of U.S. investment in Australia. They used two trade-barrier variables, the level of imports and the percentage change in imports.

In an earlier study, Scaperlanda (1967) analyzed the EEC *share* of the overall book value of U.S. direct investment. His dependent variable was (K_{it}/K_t), where K_{it} is book value of total direct investment (as distinct from annual accretions to the total) in region i at the end of year t, and K_t is book value of direct investment in all regions at the end of year t. The EEC share rose steadily after 1951, and rose at a more rapid rate after the formation of the Common Market in 1959. However, Scaperlanda could detect no significant difference between the rate of increase in the EEC share and the rate of increase in the non-EEC European share over the entire period 1951–64.

D'Arge (1969) also investigated whether the formation of the EEC exerted an impact on U.S. direct investment. His dependent variable was the *change* in the EEC *share* of the overall book value of U.S. direct investment, or $(K_{it} - K_{it-1})/(K_t - K_{t-1})$. Among the independent variables was a term designed to capture any shift in the slope after 1959; d'Arge found a positive slope-shift coefficient, indicating an acceleration in the EEC share of U.S. direct investment between 1960 and 1965, but the coefficient was not statistically significant. A similar regression for the EFTA countries revealed a negative slope-shift coefficient. Schmitz (1970) argued that d'Arge's slope-shift coefficient findings support the tariff-discrimination hypothesis.

Wallis (1968) used Scaperlanda's (1967) equation and data but broke the time series into two periods, 1951–58 and 1959–64. The slope coefficient for the EEC share rose in the later period, while the slope coefficient for the non-EEC European share declined. Wallis interpreted these findings to favor the tariff-discrimination hypothesis (see the comment by Scaperlanda, 1968).

Schmitz and Bieri (1972) ran a new set of equations over the period 1952–66. The dependent variable was the share of book value of U.S. direct investment in region i (K_{it}/K_t), while the independent variables included a slope-shift term for 1959 and later years. The slope-shift coefficients were positive for U.S. direct investment in the EEC and EFTA but negative for U.S. direct investment in Canada (all coefficients were significant). Schmitz and Bieri find confirmation of the tariff-discrimination hypothesis in these results.

It appears that the supply of U.S. direct investment has been shifted toward the European Common Market and away from other areas since 1959. From the work of Franko (1974), it also appears that European MNCs have dispersed their production facilities across the Common Market in response to nontariff barriers. It might be useful to compare patterns of MNC location *within* the larger industrial countries with patterns *between* countries. The contrast between interregional and international response to market size would further illuminate the role played by trade barriers in stimulating the establishment of new plants.

Policy measures can affect not only the choice between exports and foreign production, but also the choice between production by wholly owned MNC subsidiaries, joint-venture arrangements, and the license of technology to local firms. Japan, for example, vigorously encouraged the import of technology and discouraged foreign investment during the postwar period (Ozawa, 1968; Sherk, 1973). Not until the 1970s did Japan tentatively relax its restrictions on multinational investment. So far, American and European corporations have established rather few wholly owned subsidiaries in Japan, but they have extensively licensed Japanese companies. And, of the 89 manufacturing subsidiaries established by American MNCs between 1960 and 1967, 79 were joint-venture arrangements (Stopford and Wells, 1972, p. 152). Spain, Ceylon, India, Mexico, and Pakistan have also encouraged licensing and joint-venture arrangements in preference to wholly owned subsidiaries. As another example, the Northrop Company licensed its F-5, a small fighter aircraft, for production in several countries, because, for military reasons, local governments did not want to rely on imports.

Government policy can also influence a new and potentially important mode of technology transfer – the takeover bid. The hallmark of companies acquired through international takeover bids has, in the past, been technical inefficiency. But takeover bids can also be aimed at firms that are rich in knowledge. Europeans sometimes accuse U.S. multinational firms of buying technology on the cheap through takeover deals. With devaluation of the dollar and lower price–earnings multiples on the New York Stock Exchange, the tide could turn. European and Japanese corporate giants might start purchasing technologically advanced American firms. De Gaulle demonstrated that takeover bids can be regulated by government policy. It remains to be seen whether the takeover of American firms will provoke a "Gaullist" reaction. The concern expressed in Washington about Japanese, German, and Arab acquisitions scarcely bodes well for the takeover challenge (*Wall Street Journal*, 22 Jan. 1974).

There is still another sphere in which government measures can influence business decisions. Foreign affiliates of the parent company sometimes sell their output in the home-country market. This is particularly true of raw materials, where capital movements and trade are more often complements than substitutes. Schmitz and Helmberger (1970), commenting on Mundell (1957), made an important distinction between primary and secondary industries. Secondary industries can be established in a wide variety of locations, but primary industries are tied to specific immobile factors. In primary industries, restrictions on trade will limit the flow of capital, while the freeing of trade will have an opposite effect. Accordingly, MNC investment in the primary industries can be much influenced by home-country trade policies. English overseas enterprise was originally inspired by the search for raw materials and this search enjoyed the warm support of the crown. Mikesell and his collaborators (1971) have likewise shown that U.S. investment in mining and petroleum enterprises is closely related to U.S. imports. Carrying the theme further, Kojima (1973) contends that Japanese direct investment is largely pro-trade oriented. Japanese multinational firms specialize in the exploitation of raw materials and the overseas manufacture of labor-intensive goods. Much of the output is then shipped back to Japan. By contrast, American multinational firms tend to manufacture their most sophisticated products abroad for locally protected markets.

If the relaxation of trade barriers continues, the definition of specific immobile factors might be extended to include cheap labor in less developed countries. Many manufactured goods, as well as natural-resource products, could then fall within the Schmitz–Helmberger category of primary industries.[7] Thus, a complementary relationship might emerge between direct investment and

7 The definition of primary industry could also be extended to encompass any situation in which decreasing returns to scale characterize the use of capital and labor. Berglas and Razin (1973) have begun to explore the role in trade theory of decreasing returns.

trade in manufactured goods, and the multinational corporation might become a major vehicle for the export of manufactures from less developed countries (B. I. Cohen, 1973a; Dunning, 1973a; Helleiner, 1973). Eventually, the pattern of multinational investment could come to resemble Kojima's portrait of Japan. But the outlook is far from clear. The nascent Border Industrial Program in Mexico (Fernandez, 1973) and "runaway" manufacturing plants in Singapore and Taiwan have already attracted hostile notice from American labor unions. Yet, in 1970, less than 8 per cent of the sales of majority-owned foreign manufacturing affiliates were imported by the United States (U.S. Dept. of Commerce, November 1972).

3. DIRECT INVESTMENT AND THE BALANCE OF PAYMENTS

Direct-Investment Forecasts

Forecasting equations have mainly been devised to explain year-to-year flows of either direct investment or foreign-affiliate plant and equipment expenditures. Because of data limitations, econometric work has focused on the investment activity of U.S. affiliates (Spitaller, 1971). Direct investment is usually defined as the change in the book value of equity in overseas affiliates and branches. Retained earnings of foreign affiliates are included in these changes, even though, from the standpoint of U.S. balance-of-payments accounting, such earnings are not included among direct-investment outflows.[8] As time passes, multinational corporations finance more and more of their expansion with both retained earnings and locally acquired funds. Thus, forecasts of direct investment are not the same as forecasts of plant and equipment expenditures; and neither forecast corresponds with actual financial outflows from the United States.

In short-run analysis, the national location of economic activity is taken as given, and direct-investment flows are explained on the basis of changes in overseas sales, corporate cash flows, the cost of capital, and government restraints. Short-run equations do not purport to say whether restrictions on direct investment are bypassed by other forms of private capital movement. After all, mul-

[8] In U.S. balance-of-payments accounting, branch earnings are treated as if they were repatriated but affiliate earnings are not, since the branch (unlike the incorporated affiliate) has no separate legal identity. This practice is inferior to U.K. accounting, which includes *all* retained earnings among "repatriated" earnings and direct-investment outflows.

tinational corporations are only one vehicle for the international integration of capital markets (Kindleberger, 1967). Thus, for a broad view of the interactions between economic activity and capital movements, we must turn not to the literature on direct-investment flows but to the work of authors such as Bloomfield (1968), Branson (1970), Bonomo (1971), Bryant and Hendershott (1972); to Borts and Kopecky (1972) for the growth approach to capital movements; or to Johnson (1972) for the monetary approach to the balance of payments.

Forecasting equations for direct investment bear a strong resemblance to investment functions estimated for the domestic economy. The short-run analysis of direct-investment flows has mainly been based on the standard neoclassical approach developed by Jorgenson (1963).[9] Assuming a goal of maximum profits, the basic equation for desired capital stock at time t, K_t^*, is

$$K_t^* = \alpha p_t Q_t / c_t , \tag{10}$$

where p_t is the product price, Q_t is output, α is the elasticity of output with respect to capital, and c_t is the rental price of capital. The rental price of capital is a function of the price of capital goods and its rate of change, the cost of money capital, the depreciation rate, and various tax rates. Starting from equation (10), investment is viewed as an adjustment of the actual capital stock to its desired level.

Using a modified form of the Jorgenson equation, Stevens (1969b) examined the investment behavior of seventy-one well-established foreign subsidiaries. He regressed plant and equipment expenditures, expressed as a proportion of the previous year's net fixed capital stock, against several variables. Subsidiary sales exerted the most significant impact. The previous year's profits and depreciation had a positive effect on direct investment, while dividends had a negative effect.

Lipsey (in a private communication) has argued that the proper variable to explain investment flows would be expected growth in sales. Past growth is a fair but imperfect proxy for expected

9 Aharoni (1966) suggests that corporations may have geographical "blind spots" in their pursuit of profit. However, Stevens (1974) points to a dearth of empirical work on theories that suppose some corporate goal other than profit maximization. The institutional argument that corporations place greatest stress on growth is, in many respects, complementary to the neoclassical profit-maximizing assumption. Growth requires profits and a profitable situation is conducive to further growth. Hence, the institutional and neoclassical approaches are not easily distinguished by empirical analysis.

growth. If the firm expects future growth to equal or exceed past growth, it will hold down dividends, while if it expects future expansion to be slower, it might declare higher dividends. Past sales growth and dividend payouts may thus be indicating the firm's predictions as to future sales. These predictions in turn provide the mainspring for investment flows.

The U.S. restraint program, voluntary in 1965 and mandatory in 1968 (Pizer, 1971), has prompted a good deal of econometric work at the aggregate level. Using the neoclassical model, Kwack (1972) obtained the following results:

$$I = \underset{(2.2)}{1.06} + \underset{(3.8)}{0.14\,C_{t-3}} + \underset{(2.6)}{0.023}\,\big[pQ/(r-p)\big]$$

$$\underset{(5.0)}{-0.094\,D_{t-1}} + \underset{(5.0)}{2.04DMY65} \qquad\qquad R^2 = 0.86\,, \qquad (11)$$

where I is direct investment, including retained earnings; C is the cashflow of U.S. nonfinancial corporations; pQ is a weighted average of the gross national products of Canada, Japan, the United Kingdom, and Germany, and the exports of developing countries; r is the long-term U.S. government bond yield; p is the rate of change in the U.S. GNP deflator; D is the direct-investment stock; and $DMY65$ is a dummy variable for the 1965 voluntary-restraint program. The subscripts refer to the lag period, expressed on a quarterly basis. The numbers in parentheses under the estimated coefficients are t values. Kwack's results agree with the micro work done by Stevens (1969b). Larger cash flows and an expansion of foreign sales cause the multinational corporation to expand its overseas investment, while a higher real cost of capital and a bigger existing stock of foreign assets exert the opposite effect. However, Stevens's equation was designed to explain plant and equipment expenditures, whereas Kwack's equation is addressed to direct-investment flows.

Herring and Willett (1972) devised equations of the following form to explain expenditure on overseas plant and equipment:

$$PE_f = \underset{(-3.5)}{-10110} + \underset{(11.6)}{138\,PE_{us}} + \underset{(3.0)}{152\,T} + \underset{(4.9)}{1038\,DMY\,57/58}$$

$$R^2 = 0.99\,, \quad (12)$$

where PE_f is plant and equipment expenditure of all overseas affiliates in millions of dollars; PE_{us} is plant and equipment outlays of U.S. business expressed in billions of dollars; T is a trend term; and DMY is a dummy variable to pick up the unusual 1957–58 events in the petroleum industry.

In addition to examining the effect of the restraint program on direct-investment flows, scholars have attempted to estimate these flows in relation to other variables. Scaperlanda and Mauer (1969, 1971, 1972) found that only the economic size of the EEC, measured by gross national products, exerted a significant impact on U.S. direct investment during the 1952–66 period. Building on this work, Scaperlanda and Mauer (1973) used various specifications of a dummy variable, together with EEC gross national product, to explain the impact of post-1965 controls on U.S. direct investment in the Common Market. The best results were obtained using a dummy variable that took the value zero through 1966:

$$I = -461 + 4.88Y - 512DMY \qquad R^2 = 0.90 . \qquad (13)$$
$$(11.1) \quad (4.4)$$

As before, I is direct investment, including retained earnings, in millions of dollars; Y is EEC gross national product; and DMY is the dummy variable. Equation (13) suggests that U.S. controls have reduced direct investment in the Common Market by some $500 million annually since 1967. Of this reduction, about $200 million is accounted for by lower investment in manufacturing and the balance by lower investment in other sectors, such as petroleum and retailing. In another piece of work, Scaperlanda (1972) found that GNP growth, the exchange rate, and the Canadian–U.S. automotive agreement all had an impact on direct investment in Canada, along with the customary neoclassical stock-adjustment variables.

The regression equations that succeed in explaining direct-investment flows, such as Kwack's and Scaperlanda's, are specified as if those flows reflect real investment decisions. As pointed out earlier, direct-investment flows are not the same as plant and equipment expenditures. Despite this misspecification, the neoclassical stock-adjustment model has few challengers in forecasting direct investment. The portfolio stock-adjustment model (discussed at an earlier juncture) has been used to explain the geographic distribution of MNC investment, but it is not the sort of model that can be used for short-term forecasting. In any event, the short-run analysis of direct investment would benefit from the same sort of hypothesis testing that Bischoff (1971) applied to alternative domestic-investment equations. Since, as Bischoff showed, it is fairly easy to obtain good retrospective fits, the decisive test should be the forecasting ability of alternative models.

Effects on the Balance of Payments

Johnson (1970) has rightly stressed that arguments for the control of balance-of-payments flows seldom have validity unless they represent an underlying combination of optimum-tariff, optimum-tax, and infant-industry arguments. If a country is unhappy with its balance of payments, appropriate remedies involve the broad sweep of fiscal and monetary measures and exchange-rate adjustments, rather than piecemeal policies of restraint. Even if, on some calculations, exports appear more helpful to the home country's balance of payments than direct investment abroad, licensing, or takeover bids, such calculations supply no independent argument for attempting to change the form of overseas business operations. The same dictum applies, with appropriate modification, to host countries.

Nevertheless the balance-of-payments effects of multinational enterprise have stimulated considerable comment, mainly with a view toward capital controls on direct investment [W. C. Gordon (1961, 1962); Bell (1962); Phillips (1964); Polk et al. (1966); Behrman (1966, 1968, 1969); Moffat, (1967); Reddaway (1967, 1968); Hufbauer and Adler (1968); Bruck and Lees (1968); Law and Contemporary Problems (1969); Dunning (1969a, 1969b); Adler and Hufbauer (1969a, 1969b); Lindert (1970); Fieleke (1971); Morley and Smith (1971); Lipsey and Weiss (1972a, 1972b); Hui and Hawkins (1972); Stobaugh et al. (1973); Wert (1973); UNCTAD (1970, 1971, 1972, 1973a, 1973b)].

W. C. Gordon (1961, 1962), an institutional economist, first challenged Cairnes's (1874) description of the foreign-investment process. According to Gordon, and contrary to Cairnes, countries investing abroad have had little need to run a merchandise surplus to accomplish the transfer of real resources. Within a short period, foreign enterprises have generated sufficient profits not only to accommodate future expansion but also to make remittances.

Bell (1962) looked at these questions quantitatively, taking into account initial exports of home-country capital equipment; subsequent exports of parts and components; dividend,[10] interest, and royalty remittances; and other transactions between the parent firm and its overseas affiliates. Bell's calculations made possible the estimation of balance-of-payments "recoupment periods" – the length of time before an initial investment would be matched by income flows from the foreign subsidiary. As Wert (1973) has pointed out, recoupment-period estimates may be placed in a product-cycle context. From the viewpoint of the home country, the early phases of a foreign investment project bring positive trade effects (more exports) and negative investment effects (capital outflows). The later phases bring negative trade effects (reduced exports and more imports) and positive investment effects (remittance of profits).

The estimation of recoupment periods critically depends on what would have happened in the absence of MNC activity – the "alternative position." Three possibilities were distinguished by Hufbauer and Adler (1968, p. 6). Under classical substitution assumptions, direct investment completely supplements host-country investment and completely replaces home investment. Under reverse classical assumptions, direct investment fully substitutes for foreign local investment and does not diminish home formation of capital. Under anticlassical assumptions, direct investment supplements host-country investment but does not diminish home investment. Under both classical and reverse classical assumptions, international capital flows do not affect the *total world volume* of investment. Anticlassical assumptions imply that international investment *increases* world capital formation.

Reverse classical assumptions reflect the tariff-discrimination hypothesis, known in this context as the defensive-investment argument. According to this argument, the choice between home and foreign production is mainly determined by tariff and tax considerations. Since host-country policies are often designed to promote self-sufficiency, the assumption is that export markets were doomed to disappear. The reverse classical framework principally applies to manufacturing investment. In the fields of agricultural and mineral exploitation, MNC activity has more frequently worked to promote international specialization. In these areas, the classical assumptions come nearer the mark.

The anticlassical framework, which implies an increase in world investment when firms go overseas, need not be altogether far-fetched. Multinational firms may carry out projects in the host

---

10 Since Bell wrote, Mauer and Scaperlanda (1972) and Kopits (1972) have explored the dividend behavior of multinational corporations.

countries that local firms were incapable of undertaking. A net addition could then be made to host-country investment. Meanwhile, two possible scenarios can be envisaged in the home country. The home country might lose exports, and for this reason home investment could decline in certain industries. However, the home government could offset this decline through expansionary policies, leaving total domestic investment unchanged. The other scenario (urged by Behrman, 1968) is that home-country exports will be unaffected, simply because the host country already pursued such highly protectionist policies that there were no exports of that particular kind to displace.[11] Accordingly, home investment would have no reason to decline.

Depending on which framework of assumptions is chosen, very different balance-of-payments recoupment periods emerge. The anticlassical scenario defended by Behrman (1968) leads to recoupment periods of two years or less. This is Gordon's thesis with a vengeance! On the other hand, the classical assumption can lead to recoupment periods of indefinite length.

Clearly, the estimation of recoupment periods is a speculative venture. More important, the recoupment period affords an incomplete guide to the welfare aspects of direct investment. Whether the recoupment period is long or short says little about the costs and benefits of multinational corporations to home and host countries. Nor does the recoupment period illuminate the basic institutional impact of the multinational corporation on the balance-of-payments adjustment process.

There are three major versions of the way in which policy measures work to restore balance-of-payments equilibria. The familiar elasticities approach (summarized by Kindleberger, 1973b) focuses on relative commodity prices at home and abroad and between traded and nontraded goods. To correct a deficit, the policy package must shift relative prices enough so that – given the elasticities of supply and demand – the payments gap is closed by an improvement in the trade balance. By contrast, the absorption approach stresses aggregate savings (Alexander, 1952). According to the Keynesian algebra of national accounts, a balance-of-trade deficit implies negative foreign investment and hence an unduly low level of domestic savings. Finally, the monetary ap-

---

11 The circumstances envisaged by Behrman (1968) imply that host-country real output grows more rapidly than it otherwise would, as a result of MNC investment. According to the monetary approach to balance-of-payments theory (Johnson, 1972), faster real growth of output must displace imports or enhance exports, assuming a constant supply of domestic money. Thus, while MNC production might not displace the same kind of import from the United States, it could displace some other type of import or accelerate exports.

proach (synthesized by Johnson, 1972) emphasizes the relationship between the demand for money, the stock of real assets, the flow of output, and the price level. Two kinds of money are available to the nation, domestic and foreign, and each kind can be converted into the other. To correct a deficit, the policy package must stimulate home demand for foreign money. By assumption, a single interest rate rules in the international capital market, and a single price rules in each international commodity market. Thus, according to the monetary school, devaluation creates a general rise in domestic prices. The rise in prices enlarges the demand for money; provided the domestic money supply is held constant, the larger demand will be satisfied by selling commodities and assets abroad.

The growing ascendancy of multinational enterprise compels, I think, greater emphasis on a monetary approach to the balance-of-payments adjustment process. The multinational firm unifies a wider range of capital and commodity markets (for both traded and nontraded goods), and restores a single price more quickly after some disturbance, than a collection of purely national firms might have done. The multinational enterprise is uniquely placed to know prices and costs in several nations at once and to use this knowledge in adjusting production and borrowing levels so that it pays the same marginal money cost and receives the same marginal money return for a given quantum of output everywhere in the world. To be sure, trade barriers and capital controls continue to separate national markets. But barriers and controls drive wedges of fixed magnitude between the prices ruling in different countries. Multinational firms can better ensure that price differentials in fact correspond to these fixed wedges than can national companies. Thus, a key assumption made by the monetary school – one market, one price – comes closer to realization under the new institutional framework.

Correspondingly, the elasticities approach begins to fade (though, in 1974, it still has lots of life). With one market, one price, fiscal, monetary, and even exchange-rate policies cannot so effectively create the price differentials either between home and foreign goods or between traded and nontraded products which prompt a shift of output toward export and import-competing markets. Moreover, the unification of capital markets means that adjustment problems cannot be analyzed solely in terms of the trade balance, a weakness shared by the elasticities and the absorption approaches. Instead, attention must also be given to the impact of policy measures on the capital account.

Misgivings are often voiced that the multinational corporation moves vast quantities of "hot money" around the globe, thereby worsening national balance-of-payments difficulties (U.S. Senate Committee on Finance, 1973b). But currency "speculation" can hardly be distinguished from the customary business practice of acquiring capital cheap and investing dear (Robbins and Stobaugh, 1973). No one worries about "hot money" moving in search of a higher return from one region to another within the United States, nor is anyone concerned when business tries to secure the cheapest available financing, but then we accept the unification of capital markets within a single country. At bottom, the objection to international "hot money" is an objection to the creation of an international capital market (Kindleberger, 1967).

4. WELFARE QUESTIONS

The Orthodox Statement

Classical welfare arguments start off with two assumptions: They assume competition and they assume that the MNC is engaged in shifting capital from one part of the world to another. Among MNCs, oligopoly is more prevalent than competition, and MNCs probably move more technology than capital around the globe. The classical analysis nevertheless serves as a useful beginning. The basic statement was laid down by MacDougall (1960).

Private capital movements were once seen as beneficial for both home and host countries. The analysis was based both on the differential-returns argument and on classical assumptions concerning the relocation of capital stock. Capital would supposedly flow from A to B until returns in the two countries were equated. (For the moment, I shall neglect the role of corporate taxes.) In Figure 3, home country A would experience a decline in domestically produced output of trapezoid *cdef,* but it would earn returns on foreign investment of rectangle *ghij.* The net gain to the home country is thus indicated by the shaded triangle lying above its marginal productivity of capital curve. In the host country, the addition to capital stock would increase output by trapezoid *gmij,* of which only rectangle *ghij* is paid to foreign capitalists. Thus, the triangle *hmi* remains as incremental income to the host country.

According to this analysis, the flow of capital simultaneously achieves three goals. World income is increased because capital is now equally productive in all countries. The home country is better off because it is earning a higher social return on its capital abroad than it would have earned had the capital remained at

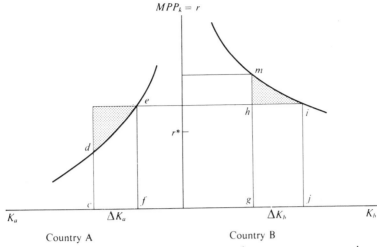

Figure 3. Gains from capital movement between two countries.

home. Finally, the host country is better off because higher returns to other factors absorb part of the gain in output resulting from a larger stock of capital.

The classical analysis implies that the return per unit of capital at home rises at the expense of other factors, while the reverse happens abroad. Thus, the flow of capital exerts a distributional effect. Relying implicitly on this analysis, the American labor movement has sought to halt "runaway plants" by altering U.S. tax laws and restricting trade (Cantor, 1972; Meany, 1972; Babson, 1973; Thurow, 1973).

One would also expect the MNC to depress returns to capital in the host country, as suggested by Figure 3. But Johnson (1970) has shown how the more efficient MNC can instead depress the price of labor in the host country. If the MNC improves the production isoquant for capital-intensive goods, the benefits may be distributed to the host community in two ways: either through a lower relative price for the capital-intensive good or through an altered factor-price ratio, with higher returns to capital and lower wages for labor. If the relative price of goods is fixed by international markets (as it may be for a small country with an open economy), the benefits will be passed on entirely in the form of an altered factor-price ratio. The MNC presence depresses the relative reward of labor, and it might even depress the absolute reward. Local labor suffers at the same time local capitalists are being displaced.

B. I. Cohen (1972) has amplified Johnson's basic case. Foreign ownership of capital might be so extensive that the higher profit rate could actually serve to decrease total income accruing to residents of the host country. The main difficulty with the Johnson–Cohen case is that MNCs do not particularly specialize in the production of capital-intensive goods. Even if they did, the foreign-owned capital stock is seldom large enough so that the introduction and diffusion of more efficient technology would actually diminish host-country income.

More important than its effect on overall returns to capital, the MNC may reap exceptional profits on the new technology it brings to the host country (Hogan, 1967; Dunning and Steuer, 1969; Mason, 1970; Streeten, 1972; Mansfield, 1974). If the MNC enjoys a monopoly in its branch of technology, the fruits of improved products and processes can for a long while leave the country. Only as competition prevails will technological gains be reflected in higher factor prices or lower commodity prices in the host nation. The important question is how long it takes before the fruits of technology are spread to the domestic economy. It would be well worth comparing the diffusion of "best practice" techniques in local industries that have multinational corporations and those that do not. [For an exposition of analytic methods, see Mansfield (1968, 1974) and Mansfield et al. (1971).]

The orthodox statement needs further qualification when there are infant entrepreneurs in the host country. It is often claimed that multinational corporations thwart local entrepreneurial effort (Levitt, 1970; Safarian, 1973). The argument can apply to the domestic formation of either capital or technology. If the infant-entrepreneur argument is valid, a first-best case may exist for restricting inward multinational investment and even, perhaps, for limiting the inward flow of technology. Clearly, we need studies on the development of a given industry in different countries to see if the extent of multinational presence makes any difference.

In addition, the orthodox statement needs qualification when there are domestic distortions. If domestic prices do not accurately reflect social costs, the MNC can impose a burden on the economy. The most important distortions are those created by tariff and nontariff barriers. Multinational corporations are attracted to protected markets like bears to honey. The result may be small and inefficient plants, as in the Australian chemical industry (Parry, 1973a). Or profits could be generously inflated, with multinational corporations sharing in the windfall earnings. For example, Vaitsos (1970) has shown that the combination of protection and domestic monopoly gave excessive profits to foreign investors in the Colombian pharmaceutical industry.

The prevalence of factor-market distortions in less developed countries raises the question of "inappropriate technologies." Do MNCs use techniques there that are too capital-intensive, given the abundance of labor? The techniques that MNCs use in less developed countries can be evaluated against two standards. They can be compared with the techniques adopted by local firms or with those that MNCs use in developed countries.

Mason (1973) examined 14 matched pairs of U.S.-owned and locally owned firms (9 matched pairs were located in the Philippines and 5 in Mexico), and concluded that American firms used more capital per employee. But B. I. Cohen (1973b) got mixed results when he compared the mechanization (measured by electricity consumption) of 4 U.S., 5 Japanese, and 10 matched Korean firms operating in Korea. Both the Mason and Cohen studies were conducted with great care, but the samples are small; more work is needed before a clear picture emerges. Turning to the second standard of comparison, Courtney and Leipziger (1973) estimated Cobb–Douglas production functions for some 1,484 U.S. affiliates operating in developed and less developed countries. In 9 of the 11 industries, the capital–labor ratios were lower in the less developed countries, indicating some degree of factor substitution. But Morley and Smith (1974) suggest that much of the observed "substitution" results from the correspondence between scale and capital intensity: larger plants enable the use of more automated production methods.

Other possible distortions qualifying the orthodox welfare statement deserve mention. Owing to an improper exchange rate, the MNC might purchase or sell foreign exchange at bargain prices; owing to the absence of environmental controls, it might degrade the environment. The national income of the host country can decline when an MNC introduces marginal-cost pricing to only one sector of the economy, while other sectors continue to use an average-cost approach in the employment of productive factors (B. I. Cohen, 1972). In the home country, the MNC might displace jobs rather than merely shift employment to alternative industries (Hawkins, 1972). At the international level, the multinatonal corporation might lead to the pervasive cartelization of world production and trade. Indeed, the question has been raised whether free competition in international markets can be reconciled with the free flow of capital and technology (Shaffer, 1972). Appropriate solutions to these various distortions are lower trade barriers, antitrust measures (on both the national and the international levels), correct exchange rates, and countervailing taxes and subsidies. Restriction of MNC activity is a possible second-best solution but not a very effective or enlightened one (Corden, 1967; Johnson, 1970).

Corporate Taxes and Transfer Prices

The taxation of corporate profits leads to a classic conflict between social rates of return (used by countries and economists to assess projects) and private after-tax rates of return (used by companies to guide investment). Furthermore, corporate taxation creates a difference between internationalist and nationalist criteria for appraising social rates of returns. Jasay (1960), MacDougall (1960), and Balogh and Streeten (1960) were among the first to raise the question of taxes in the context of direct investment. Perhaps, they argued, overseas investment was not so beneficial for the *home* country as the orthodox statement implies.

The major capital-exporting countries either allow a credit against their taxes to the extent of profit taxes paid abroad or they make no claim to tax foreign income. The complexities of tax credits and kindred arrangements are spelled out by Richman (1963), Krause and Dam (1964), Musgrave (1969), and N. N. Gordon (1971). Basically, these arrangements are designed to avoid "double taxation." If the corporate tax rates in the home and host countries are equal, the flow of capital will still serve to increase world income. Capital will be moving from a low-productivity country to a high-productivity country, and the result will be larger world income. But the home country may take a social loss from the outflow of capital. The relevant selfish comparison for the home country is between *before-tax* returns at home and *after-local-tax* returns abroad. Thus, if foreign investment is pushed by private companies to the point where after-tax returns are the same in both areas, the capital-exporting country is earning a lower social return on capital placed abroad than on capital employed at home. In terms of Figure 3, if host country B captures part of rectangle *ghij*, that amount is lost to the home country. If the MNC equalizes after-tax returns for both nations, say at point r^*, the domestic social earnings on foreign investment are much less than the before-tax contribution of capital to domestic output.

Grubel (1974) has applied these theoretical considerations to an analysis of private and social rates of return on U.S. manufacturing investments in Canada and Western Europe. In 1969, before-tax rates of return on equity averaged 24 per cent in the industrial host countries and 19 per cent in the United States. The effective rate of taxes collected by the host countries was about 46 per cent (taking into account dividend withholding tax), compared with a 40 per cent effective corporate tax rate in the United States. Thus, the private after-tax rate of return earned by U.S. manufacturing firms was about 12 per cent on equity in the United States and 13 per cent on equity in the industrial host countries. However, the social rate of return to the United States on domestic equity capital was 19 per cent (the before-tax return) compared with 13 per cent on equity capital located abroad (the after-local-tax return). The United States therefore lost about 6 per cent per year in social return on its manufacturing investments in Canada and Western Europe.

As these calculations suggest, the existence of corporate taxes leads to two quite different concepts of "tax neutrality." On the one hand, there is the international school, which says that capital should migrate to the location of highest (before-tax) return so as to increase world income. On the other hand, there is the national school, which asserts that a country should receive the same social return on its capital whether invested at home or abroad.

Under a tax-credit scheme, where the credit is limited to the amount of home tax otherwise payable, private capital movements will serve the international criterion for socially efficient allocation of capital (in the sense of leading to the worldwide equalization of before-tax returns), provided only that corporate tax rates are no lower in the capital-exporting country than in the capital-importing country.[12] But when the home nation asserts no claim to tax foreign income, the test is more demanding: private capital flows will serve the international criterion only if tax rates are the same in the capital-exporting and capital-importing jurisdictions. The United States and other capital-exporting nations have so far pursued the international criterion, mostly by using tax-credit schemes.

Private capital movements would serve the national criterion for efficient allocation of capital if the home jurisdiction taxed foreign income and allowed a deduction but no tax credit for corporate taxes paid to foreign countries. As Grubel (1974) has pointed

---

12 Note, however, that the deferral of corporate taxes until dividends are remitted from incorporated overseas affiliates is *not* an ingredient of the international approach. Deferral is even more inconsistent with the national approach. Corporate tax deferral, which has been standard U.S. practice for many years, amounts to an interest-free loan. It thus subsidizes the export of capital to jurisdictions that have lower tax rates than the United States.

out, whether tax arrangements based on the international criterion detract from the welfare of any particular country depends on that country's balance of direct investments. At the close of 1970, direct investments by U.S. firms abroad had a book value of $78 billion, while direct investments by foreign firms within the United States were $13 billion. The comparable U.K. figures were £6.4 billion and £3.4 billion. Thus, under present circumstances, these two countries might benefit from a national criterion of tax neutrality. The Burke–Hartke bill is intended to move U.S. tax practice part way toward the national criterion (see the essay by Senator Hartke in Kujawa, 1973). However, the static home-country gains from national tax neutrality might over time be offset by a lower rate of capital formation (Brownlee, 1974).

If the United States, the United Kingdom, and other MNC base countries shifted to a national criterion, the result might be a substantial diminution of MNC *ownership* of foreign affiliates. Yet the MNC form of business might well continue in the guise of managing agencies. The agencies could coordinate and control their overseas affiliates, exact a fee for this service and for the export of technology, but let local investors own the equity capital. Disputes might arise over transfer prices, dividend policy, and global strategy, but, as Gabriel (1967) points out, Hilton International has thrived for years on a management-contract basis.

Several interview studies have been designed to look at the impact of corporate tax practices and other fiscal measures (such as capital grants) on direct investment flows (Shulman, 1967; Duerr, 1972; Dunning and Yannopoulous, 1973). Dixon-Fyle (1967) concluded that tax concessions had not attracted much direct investment to Africa. Hughes and Seng (1969) found that tax concessions played little role in bringing foreign firms to Singapore. However, Schöllhammer (cited in Dunning and Yannopoulous, 1973) found that tax considerations ranked third in a list of nine locational determinants for the 140 MNCs he surveyed. Donaldson (1966) and McAleese (1971/72) found that fiscal incentives played an important role in bringing MNCs to Ireland and persuading them to locate away from the Dublin area. Forsyth (1972) suggests that British regional policy has attracted MNCs to Scotland. Dunning and Yannopoulous (1973) cite additional evidence on the effect of regional policy in Europe.

Mellors (1973) used the portfolio approach in an ingenious way to gauge the impact of corporate tax rates on the geographic location of British MNC investment. He asked whether the actual geographic distribution of company portfolios more closely resembled optimal portfolios predicted from the history of before-tax mean earnings and variance, or optimal portfolios predicted from the history of after-tax mean earnings and variance. The actual portfolios of sixteen manufacturing companies with operations in seven countries were in fact more similar to the after-tax optimal portfolios. The result suggests that tax rates do influence the geographic distribution of investment.

Not only do differing national tax arrangements influence the geographic distribution of MNC investment, but they also stimulate tax avoidance through the judicious use of transfer prices and misleading cost allocation in transactions between members of the corporate family. Arpan (1972) and Lall (1973a) have summarized the literature. There are two quite distinct management principles on which transfer pricing can be based. In the first approach, each affiliate is treated as a "profit center." The management of the affiliate is evaluated by its contribution to overall corporate profits. This approach requires that each affiliate be free to determine the price and quantity of intracorporate sales. Intracorporate pricing will then resemble an "arms-length" or "market price" standard.

In the second approach, the MNC seeks to maximize global profits. A profit-maximizing strategy requires marginal-cost pricing for sales *within* the corporate family. Otherwise, members of the family will buy unnecessarily from outside sources, thereby sacrificing global profits, and they will not expand sales to outsiders to the profit-maximizing point where corporate marginal cost equals marginal revenue.

The story becomes more complicated when affiliated firms operate in different countries. Corporate tax rates and customs duties differ between jurisdictions. A given before-tax income therefore has a different after-tax value depending on where it is realized. In addition, some jurisdictions may restrict capital flows. These considerations almost compel the MNC to adopt a global strategy rather than the profit-center philosophy.

Horst (1971) and Vaitsos (1972) have worked out the interactions between income taxes, tariff rates, and export duties when a global strategy is pursued. For example, in the Horst formulation, if τ is the tariff rate confronting imports by a firm from its foreign affiliate, and t_1 and t_2 are the effective profit-tax rates at home and abroad, the following conclusions may be drawn. When $\tau > (t_1 - t_2)/(1 - t_1)$, the firm will want to pay the lowest possible transfer price for the exports of its foreign affiliate. When the inequality runs in the other direction, the corporation will maximize global after-tax profits by paying the highest possible transfer price to its foreign affiliate.

Lall (1973a), however, points out that transfer pricing is often inspired not so much by the wish to minimize taxes as by restrictions on the movement of capital and profits, and by a corporate desire to conceal profits from the gaze of nationalists and trade unions. These latter considerations are particularly important in less developed countries.

Most industrial countries require (at least in principle) that transfer prices conform to an arm's-length standard. The arm's-length price is determined by reference either to market prices or, if those are not available, to some mark-up on prime costs or mark-down on final selling price. A totally different approach would require a formula for the allocation of profits among jurisdictions. Each company's global profits would be allocated among countries on the basis of some weighted function of capital, labor, and sales in each jurisdiction (Musgrave, 1972). However, the formula approach raises more problems than it solves (McLure, 1973). For example, all jurisdictions must agree on the formula. Otherwise, part of the tax base will be double-taxed and part not taxed at all.

Johnson (1970) has offered another suggestion, seconded by Vaitsos (1974) and Streeten (1972): MNCs ought to sell component products to their subsidiaries in the less developed countries at the marginal cost of production. No charge should be levied for research and overhead costs; supposedly, these costs have been fully met in the markets of the home country and other advanced nations. Horst (1973) rightly questions the wisdom of this supposition. If invoice prices were changed to the recommended marginal-cost basis, profit taxes and customs revenues would be relocated between taxing jurisdictions. The shifts might enlarge the *total* tax take of developed and less developed countries. But whether such changes would ultimately put more resources in the hands of LDC governments depends very much on the bargaining position of the countries and the companies.

Insofar as multinational firms can use transfer prices to shift profits from one country to another, their investment decisions need not correspond to the mean and variance of reported earnings in different nations. Perhaps this explains why Paxson (1973) discovered such a poor correspondence between optimal and actual portfolios of British–American Tobacco and the Unilever Group. If vertically integrated multinational companies were in fact forced to use arm's-length pricing for intracorporate sales, the portfolio approach might work better. Moreover, since there might be some increase in customs duties and corporate taxes, and some decrease in the freedom to shift capital around the globe, corporations might alter the geographical distribution of their investments. But it is debatable whether the geographic shift in production would benefit developing countries.

Optimal Taxes

Since the quantity of capital and technology flowing from one country to another affects their prices, there is always the unpleasant possibility that countries might go beyond the concept of national tax neutrality and impose optimal taxes on capital and technology flows, analogous to the optimal tariff on goods. The theory of optimal taxes was developed by Kemp (1962a, 1962b, 1969) and Jones (1967), and has been explored by Connolly and Ross (1970).

The optimal tax on capital could be exacted as a lump-sum levy when capital crosses the border, but the literature customarily speaks of an annual tax on earnings. A country's optimal capital tax will depend both on the nature of its commodity specialization and on its degree of trading power. A small country, completely specialized with little trading power, will not improve its welfare by taxing capital flows. A large, incompletely specialized country may benefit by applying a high capital tax, whether it imports or exports capital. Of course the benefits depend on an assumption of no retaliation, and this assumption becomes less plausible for larger countries.

Jones (1967) has analyzed cases in which the country is not free to vary tariffs because of international commitments (commercial policy is inactive) or is not free to tax the flow of capital (capital taxes are inactive). With one or the other of these restrictions, the country is not able to optimize its position. But provided one policy is active, a second-best optimum can be reached, since the imposition of tariffs will affect capital returns, while capital taxes will affect commodity prices.

Following the path laid down in Jones's analysis, an optimal technology tax could also be devised (Johnson, 1970). Second-best optimization might be applied to those technology flows which are inseparable from the sale of capital and skilled personnel services, although the analysis would be complex and tedious. But practical attempts to alter the selling price of technology are seldom cast in terms of optimal taxes. Instead, the focus is on the form of sale.

Technology may be sold through the export of goods, through the direct-investment process, or through the takeover of technology-rich firms. Governments often act on the belief that a given quantum of knowledge commands a different price depending on the form of sale. Official preferences also reflect a protectionist concern for the welfare of factors that complement technology. Thus, importing countries customarily favor licensing and joint-venture arrangements over wholly owned subsidiaries, and wholly owned subsidiaries over imports (Gabriel, 1967). Exporting countries prefer the reverse order, and they are least happy about takeover bids aimed at their technology-intensive firms. In different eras, Flanders, France, Britain, Germany, and the United States have attempted to keep vital production techniques within their national boundaries, preferring to export the finished product. In the long run, none of these attempts has worked. At the most, they temporarily slowed the diffusion of knowledge.

Government concern with the form in which technology is sold is partly dictated by the very real administrative difficulties of levying a tax on knowledge. Since knowledge is highly differentiated, since the costs of generating technology bear little relation to its value (at least in individual instances), since overt royalty payments often poorly reflect the value of transferred technology, and since technology sales are frequently commingled with the sale of capital and labor, the orthodox sort of tax, where a rate is applied to a base, can hardly be used to restrain the outflow or inflow of technology. Accordingly, governments have concentrated their efforts on modifying the form of technology sale.

To the extent that exporting countries attempt to modify the form of technology sale, their efforts could be misdirected. Sellers of knowledge are by definition quasi-monopolists. If the technology were widely available, no one would want to buy it; there would be no implicit payment for technology in the export of goods, direct-investment undertakings, or takeover bids. Thus, in order to justify national restraints on the sale of knowledge, there must be some evidence that owners of technology are not properly exploiting their monopolistic positions. After all, an optimal tax imposed by the government merely achieves the same goal for a competitive industry, in its dealings with foreigners, that a monopolist will gladly achieve for itself.

Countries that import technology have greater reason for official intervention, since they normally face monopolistic sellers. But intervention by buying countries can (and has) spurred countervailing intervention by selling nations. These measures could easily lead to a self-defeating spiral of retaliation. Moreover, the technology-importing country that insists on licensing and joint-venture arrangements may find itself acquiring risk as well as return.

As yet there is no evidence that the mode of technology sale significantly influences the ultimate diffusion of production techniques. Production techniques may leak out just as quickly when a good is exported as when an MNC establishes a foreign affiliate. Nor is there evidence of a systematic connection between mode of sale, average returns, and the variance of earnings on technology. The pronounced preference of MNCs for wholly owned subsidiaries, particularly when technology and marketing skills are key ingredients (Stopford and Wells, 1972), is suggestive but not conclusive.

Marxism and Imperialism

When I speak of a Marxist approach to economic imperialism, I am using labels loosely. Marx, himself, did not explicitly offer a theory of imperialism (Karsten, 1971, p. 35). Nevertheless, the critical literature linking imperialism to capitalism has been dominated by the Marxist school (Magdoff, 1969; Wolff, 1970). In the Marxist view, multinational corporations are agents of economic imperialism. B. J. Cohen (1973) has recently published an authoritative and highly readable account of imperialism, and I shall merely touch on the high points.

In the early socialist literature, which can be traced back to Sismondi (1819), economic imperialism was linked to underconsumption in the home country. According to this view, which was brought to popular notice by Hobson (1902), capital exports are necessary to take up the economic slack created by the pressures of the capitalist system. In modern parlance, the savings rate of the mother country was kept high, although the growth rate was low. Foreign investment was necessary to utilize capital and avoid home unemployment.

Abroad, the consequences of foreign investment were no better. Capitalism, together with wage slavery, would be exported to the host country. Not only is the capitalist system attacked as bad economics but it is also charged with unnecessary wars and the political subjugation of innocent people (Ackerman, 1971). As I do not have space to review the origins of war and subjugation, I shall instead concentrate on the economic aspects of imperialism.

The modern Marxist view concerning foreign investment

stresses the Baran and Sweezy "suction pump" thesis. Departing from Hobson's earlier theory, Baran and Sweezy (1966, pp. 107–108) argue that ". . . foreign investment far from being an outlet for domestic generated surplus, is a most efficient device for transferring surplus generated abroad to the investing country." Zweig (1973) has expressed the suction-pump thesis in the mathematical language of Domar (1950).

The suction-pump thesis pays no attention to the distinction between stocks of capital abroad and flows of current income (Nisbet, 1970, 1971; Du Boff, 1971). The role of reinvested earnings is neglected. Nor does the thesis consider the productivity of capital (part of which is captured by local income taxes) and the external effects of foreign enterprise. Thus, suction-pump statistics (remitted earnings vs. fresh capital outflows from the home country), such as those quoted by Levitt (1970, pp. 168–169), provide no reliable guide as to whether less developed countries gain or lose on balance from their total relationship with multinational corporations (Hunt, 1972).

Indeed, the suction-pump thesis is merely a Marxist attempt to draw policy guidance from balance-of-payments statistics. Interpreted sympathetically, the thesis seems to be addressed to this question: Regardless of total gains or losses over the corporate lifetime, at what point should the host country expropriate the foreign enterprise? When has the relationship "turned the corner" so that the host country loses from a continued MNC presence? This is essentially the golden-goose question raised by Bronfenbrenner (1955), debated by Garnick (1963), and explored in useful essays by Hirschman (1969), Kindleberger (1972), and Zink (1973). The golden-goose question raises complex analytic issues. Balance-of-payments statistics, as used by Marxist advocates, are quite inadequate to the problem. They take no account of the ability of the country to manage the enterprise, the impact of nationalization on capital and technology flows, or retaliation by the mother country. They furnish only the crudest indication as to when the corner has been turned. A much more comprehensive approach, which makes allowance for these objections, has been used in the studies commissioned by UNCTAD (1970, 1971, 1972, 1973a, 1973b), in which P. P. Streeten, S. Lall, and others at Oxford have examined foreign investment in Jamaica, India, Iran, Colombia, and Malaysia. The added realism of the UNCTAD studies makes their conclusions less clear-cut than the Marxist school might like.

Closely related to the golden-goose question is the concept of nationalism as a public good. This concept was introduced by Breton (1964), pursued by Johnson (1965), and emphasized in the multinational context by Kindleberger (1969). Foreign corporations encroach on national sovereignty in a fashion that antagonizes many people. France was greatly offended by the presence and manners of American multinational corporations in the early 1960s (Johnstone, 1965). Levitt (1970, p. 3) writes that American corporations "are manifestations of a new mercantilism of corporate empires which cut across boundaries of national economies and undermine the national sovereignty of the hinterland countries in which their subsidiaries and branch plants are located." Moreover, in the Marxist view, the state will be corrupted by foreign firms and become increasingly reluctant to take appropriate measures (Levitt, 1970, p. 17). The MNC, like any private or public bureaucracy, will of course attempt to persuade the government to pass favorable legislation and grant administrative favors. This is the stuff of political life. A celebrated example was the role played by the International Petroleum Company (a subsidiary of Standard Oil of New Jersey) in the politics of Peru for several decades prior to the 1968 expropriation (Pinelo, 1973). Another example was a Brazilian government instruction giving multinational corporations preferential access to foreign exchange (Ackerman, 1971). But despite the supposed MNC domination of economic events, the countries that have conspicuously nationalized MNCs during the twentieth century – Mexico, Cuba, and Chile – stand out for an abundance of foreign investment, not a lack of it (de Vries, 1969). Canadian and Australian hostility to the MNC likewise suggests that political antagonism increases with foreign presence.

Another element of economic imperialism is the displacement of local by foreign capitalists. Since capitalists are enemies of the people (in Marxist eyes), it might seem that nationality would make no difference. In fact, since foreign capitalists often invite more hostility than local capitalists, they could be viewed as better servants of the dialectic. But this is not the Marxist view. In Ackerman's (1971, p. 3) account, Baron Maua, a nineteenth-century Brazilian entrepreneur who suffered bankruptcy partly because of foreign machinations, comes across as a minor hero.

The orthodox reply to Marxist concerns is brief. The host government can redress any of the enumerated abuses that in fact exist. Through appropriate tax, trade, and antitrust policies, and with the help of honest public servants, the government can rectify the distribution of income, penalize parasitic firms, and end improper interference with public affairs. The government can even play to nationalistic sentiment, and favor domestic firms over MNCs. The Marxist retort is equally brief. Government policy is not independent of the underlying economic structure. As Levitt (1970, p. 17) puts it:

The economic power of producing organizations and the legislative power of government are believed [by orthodox economists] to be independent of each other: the former subordinate to the democracy of the market place, the latter to the democracy of the ballot box. In this cowboy and Indian world of nineteenth century make-believe, the will of the people can always be made to prevail by the appropriate stroke of the legislative pen.

According to Marxist litany, the make-believe never comes to pass, either because the host government is corrupted by overseas firms, or because the mother country employs its military, economic, and diplomatic strength to thwart local wishes (Levitt, 1970, p. 102). The only answer is revolution and expropriation.

Policy Agenda

Government dissatisfaction with the multinational corporation is rife, fueled as much by orthodox reservations as by Marxist complaints. In the United States, organized labor is vigorously promoting the Burke–Hartke bill (Meany, 1972). Senator Church has held hearings critical of the MNC. The Watkins Commission (1968) in Canada issued an unfavorable report. The twenty "eminent persons" chartered by the United Nations wrote a critical review of the impact of MNCs on less developed countries (UN Economic and Social Council, 1974). The MNC issue is making its way to the top of the UNCTAD agenda (Krause, 1972). And so on.

These rumblings point to a series of international conferences and perhaps ultimately to multilateral and bilateral agreements. Goldberg and Kindleberger (1970) and Bergsten (1974) have speculated on the scope of these negotiations. I shall briefly review some of the major themes.

The groundwork for negotiations has already been laid in various international agreements that regulate business practices (Smith, 1973). Mechanisms of consultation are provided in GATT procedures, OECD procedures, the EFTA agreement, and the Treaty of Rome. In addition, bilateral treaties of friendship, navigation, and commerce often provide for discussion of restrictive business practices by firms based in either country.

Home and host governments are unhappy with MNC practices

for different and often contradictory reasons. But just as countries sacrificed some of their own economic interests to negotiate the General Agreement on Tariffs and Trade, they might develop agreed rules for the conduct of multinational business operations. There are other morals in the GATT precedent. As Goldberg and Kindleberger (1970) point out, GATT was implemented only because it program for modest reform enlisted the support of the business community. Moreover, the agreement operates by mutual consent rather than legal sanction; there are numerous escape clauses for the dissatisfied member state. International agreements on the MNC will function in similar fashion.

The most important agenda item could be government forbearance on tax policy and investment controls as a device for inducing or thwarting the movement of capital and technology. The interaction between trade barriers and capital movements will also have to be considered, since many decisions on location of MNCs are taken in response to protection rather than taxes.

The sharing of potential tax revenues between member states is another agenda item. The problem is particularly acute between countries housing different layers of the same vertically integrated MNC family. Tariff revenues, income taxes, and – in the case of mineral resources – royalties are all involved. The bilateral-tax-treaty approach would set up government machinery to review transfer prices, in hopes of correctly attributing import values, export values, overhead costs, and ultimately profits to each affiliate. Another approach would allocate the global profits of each MNC to the member states by a formula that takes into account each country's share of capital assets, wage payments, sales, and other measures of economic activity.

Host countries may attempt to "untie the package" so that they can import technology alone or with little foreign investment (Gabriel, 1967; Hunt, 1972). But joint ventures and licensing arrangements are not panaceas; they involve a sharing of failure as well as success (Vernon, 1973). Meanwhile, home countries will want more equitable rules on compensation in the event of expropriation. As Vernon (1973) amply illustrates, corporate virtue provides no guarantee of corporate survival in the developing world.

The United States and other advanced nations may press for uniformity of wage and environmental standards, ostensibly as a means of protecting the host countries, but really as a device for slowing the migration of industry. There is little economic reason for harmonization, since countries differ greatly in their underlying conditions. Host countries would be well advised to resist the imposition of uniform standards.

Finally, there is the question of an effective international antitrust policy. Nations have long tolerated, and even encouraged, export and import cartels. OPEC is merely the latest chapter of a history that can be traced at least to the fourteenth century with Edward III's profitable control of the Staplers Company. But the cloak of respectability that has been laid on international price-fixing schemes must be replaced by an effective antitrust policy if we are to avoid the monopolistic use of multinational enterprise.

REFERENCES

Ackerman, Frank, "Industry and Imperialism in Brazil," *Review of Radical Political Economics,* 3 (Spring 1971), pp. 1–39.
Adler, F. M., "The Relationship between the Income and Price Elasticities of Demand for United States Exports," *Review of Economics and Statistics,* 52 (August 1970), pp. 313–319.
Adler, F. M., and G. C. Hufbauer, "Foreign Investment Controls – Objective Removal," *Columbia Journal of World Business,* 4 (May–June 1969a), pp. 29–39.
  "The Foreign Investment Controversy Continued," *Bankers' Magazine,* 208 (November 1969b), pp. 217–223.
Agmon, T. B., *Interrelations among Equity Markets – A Study of Share Price Movements in the United States, United Kingdom, Germany and Japan,* Ph.D. dissertation, University of Chicago, 1971.
Aharoni, Yair, *The Foreign Investment Decision Process,* Boston, Harvard Business School, 1966.
Ahlburg, D. A., and T. G. Parry, "Determinants of U.S. Direct Investment in Australian Manufacturing Industry," University of Reading Discussion Papers in International Investment and Business Studies No. 2, Reading, England, 1973.
Alexander, S. S., "Effects of a Devaluation on a Trade Balance," *IMF Staff Papers,* 2 (April 1952), pp. 263–278.
Aliber, R. Z., "A Theory of Direct Investment," in Kindleberger, ed. (1970).
Aronson, J. D., *The Multinational Corporation, the Nation-State, and the International System: A Bibliography,* Stanford University, Department of Political Science, June 1973.
Arpan, J. S., *International Intracorporate Pricing: Non-American Systems and Views,* New York, Praeger, 1972.

Babson, S., "The Multinational Corporation and Labor," *Review of Radical Political Economics,* 5 (Spring 1973), pp. 19–36.
Balassa, Bela, "American Direct Investments in the Common Market," *Banca Nazionale del Lavoro Quarterly Review,* 19 (June 1966), pp. 121–146.
Balogh, T., and P. P. Streeten, "Domestic vs. Foreign Investment," *Bulletin of Oxford University Institute of Statistics,* 22 (August 1960), pp. 213–224.
Bandera, V. N., and J. A. Lucken, "Has U.S. Capital Differentiated between EEC and EFTA?" *Kyklos,* 25 (1972), pp. 306–314.

Bandera, V. N., and J. T. White, "United States Direct Investments and Domestic Markets in Europe," *Economia Internationale,* 21 (February 1968), pp. 117–133.

Baran, P. A., and P. M. Sweezy, *Monopoly Capital: An Essay on the American Economic and Social Order,* New York, Modern Reader, 1966.

Baranson, Jack, "Technology Transfer through the International Firm," *American Economic Association Papers and Proceedings,* 60 (May 1970), pp. 435–441.

Barber, C. L., "Canadian Tariff Policy," *Canadian Journal of Economics,* 21 (November 1955), pp. 513–530.

Behrman, J. N., "Foreign Private Investment and the Government's Efforts to Reduce the Payments Deficit," *Journal of Finance,* 21 (May 1966), pp. 283–296.

Direct Manufacturing Investment, Exports and the Balance of Payments, New York, National Foreign Trade Council, 1968.

"Assessing the Foreign Investment Controls," *Law and Contemporary Problems,* 34 (Winter 1969), pp. 84–94.

Bell, Phillip, "Private Capital Movements and the United States Balance-of-Payments Position," in Joint Economic Committee, 87th Cong., 2d sess., *Factors Affecting the Balance of Payments,* Washington, 1962.

Berglas, E., and A. Razin, "Effective Protection and Decreasing Returns to Scale," *American Economic Review,* 63 (September 1973), pp. 733–737.

Bergsten, C. F. "Coming Investment Wars?" *Foreign Affairs,* 53 (October 1974), pp. 135–152.

Bertin, G. Y., *L'Expansion Internationale des Grandes Entreprises,* Paris, La Documentation Française, 1972.

Bhagwati, J., "Review of R. Vernon, *Sovereignty at Bay,*" *Journal of International Economics,* 2 (September 1972), pp. 455–459.

Bischoff, C., "Business Investment in the 1970's: A Comparison of Models," *Brookings Papers on Economic Activity,* 1 (1971), pp. 13–63.

Bloomfield, A. I., *Patterns of Fluctuation in International Investment before 1914,* Princeton Studies in International Finance No. 21, Princeton, N.J., 1968.

Bonomo, V., "International Capital Movements and Economic Activity: The United States Experience, 1870–1968," *Explorations in Economic History,* 8 (Spring 1971), pp. 321–341.

Borts, G. H., "The International Firm, the Tariff, and Long Run Capital Movements," in Dunning, ed. (1974).

Borts, G. H., and K. J. Kopecky, "Capital Movements and Economic Growth in Developed Countries," in Machlup *et al.,* eds. (1972).

Branson, W. H., "Monetary Policy and the New View of International Capital Movements," *Brookings Papers on Economic Activity,* 2 (1970), pp. 325–370.

Brash, D. T., *American Investment in Australian Industry,* Cambridge, Mass., Harvard University Press, 1966.

Brems, H., "The Profitability of Direct Investment, National and International," *Swedish Journal of Economics,* 72 (December 1970), pp. 278–300.

Breton, A., "The Economics of Nationalism," *Journal of Political Economy,* 72 (August 1964), pp. 376–386.

Bronfenbrenner, M., "The Appeal of Confiscation in Economic Development," *Economic Development and Cultural Change,* 3 (April 1955), pp. 201–218.

Brooke, M. Z., and H. L. Remmers, *The Strategy of Multinational Enterprise,* London, Longmans, 1970.

eds., *The Multinational Company in Europe,* London, Longmans, 1972.

Brownlee, O. H., "A Critique of Two Views," unpublished, University of Minnesota, Minneapolis, 1974.

Bruck, N., and F. Lees, *Foreign Investment, Capital Controls, and the Balance of Payments,* Institute of Finance Bulletin No. 48–49, New York, New York University, 1968.

Bryant, R. C., and P. H. Hendershott, "Empirical Analysis of Capital Flows," in Machlup *et al.,* eds. (1972).

Burtis, D., *et al., Multinational Corporation – Nation-State Interaction: An Annotated Bibliography,* Philadelphia, Foreign Policy Research Institute, 1971.

Cairnes, J. E., *Some Leading Principles of Political Economy,* London, Macmillan, 1874, pp. 424–437.

Cantor, A., "Tax Subsidies That Export Jobs," *AFL-CIO American Federationist* (November 1972).

Caves, R. E., "International Corporations: The Industrial Economics of Foreign Investment," *Economica,* 38 (February 1971), pp. 1–27.

"Multinational Enterprise and Industrial Organization," in Dunning, ed. (1974a).

International Trade, Investment, and Market Performance, Princeton Special Papers in International Economics No. 10, Princeton, N.J., 1974b.

Cohen, B. I., "An Alternative Theoretical Approach to the Impact of Foreign Investment on the Host Country," Yale Growth Center Discussion Paper No. 164, New Haven, 1972.

"The Role of the Multinational Firm in the Exports of Manufactures from Developing Countries," Yale Growth Center Discussion Paper No. 177, New Haven, 1973a.

"Comparative Behavior of Foreign and Domestic Export Firms in a Developing Economy," *Review of Economics and Statistics,* 55 (May 1973b), pp. 190–197.

"Foreign Investment by U.S. Corporations as a Way of Reducing Their Risk," Yale Growth Center Discussion Paper No. 151, New Haven, 1973c.

Cohen, B. J., *The Question of Imperialism: The Political Economy of Dominance and Dependence,* New York, Basic Books, 1973.

Connolly, M., and S. Ross, "A Fischerian Approach to Trade, Capital Movements and Tariffs," *American Economic Review,* 60 (June 1970), pp. 478–484.

Corden, W. M., "Protection and Foreign Investment," *Economic Record,* 43 (June 1967), pp. 209–233.

"The Multinational Corporation and International Trade Theory," University of Reading Discussion Papers in International Investment and Business Studies No. 10, Reading, England, 1974.

Courtney, W. H., and D. M. Leipziger, "Multinational Corporations in LDCs: The Choice of Technology," U.S. Dept. of State and Agency for International Development, Washington, 1973.

Daniels, John D., *Recent Foreign Direct Manufacturing Investment in the United States: An Interview Study of the Decision Process,* New York, Praeger, 1971.

d'Arge, R., "A Note on Customs Unions and Direct Foreign Investment," *Economic Journal,* 79 (June 1969), pp. 324–33.

Davies, R. B., "Peacefully Working to Conquer the World," *Business History Review,* 43 (Autumn 1969), pp. 299–325.

Deane, R. S., "Import Licensing: A Stimulus to Foreign Investment," *Economic*

Record, 45 (December 1969), pp. 1101–1107.

Foreign Investment in New Zealand Manufacturing, London, Sweet and Maxwell, 1970.

Deppler, M. C., "Elasticities of Demand for U.S. Exports: A Comment," *Review of Economics and Statistics,* 53 (May 1971), pp. 201–203.

de Vries, H., "Diplomatic Protection of Investments in Foreign Countries," *Columbia Journal of World Business,* 4 (September–October 1969), pp. 89–91.

Dixon-Fyle, S. R., "Economic Inducements to Private Foreign Investment in Africa," *Journal of Development Studies,* 4 (October 1967), pp. 109–137.

Domar, E. D., "The Effect of Foreign Investment on the Balance of Payments," *American Economic Review,* 40 (December 1950), pp. 805–826.

Donaldson, L., *Development Planning in Ireland,* New York, Praeger, 1966.

Drysdale, P., ed., *Direct Foreign Investment in Asia and the Pacific,* Canberra, Australian National University Press, 1972.

Du Boff, R. B., "Transferring Wealth from Underdeveloped Countries via Direct Foreign Investment: Comment," *Southern Economic Journal,* 38 (July 1971), pp. 118–121.

Duerr, M. G., *Tax Allocations and International Business,* New York, National Industrial Conference Board, 1972.

Dunning, J. H., *American Investment in British Manufacturing Industry,* London, Allen and Unwin, 1958.

"The Reddaway and Hufbauer/Adler Reports on the Foreign Investment Controversy," *Bankers' Magazine,* 207 (May–June 1969a), pp. 307–312, 354–360.

"The Reddaway and Hufbauer/Adler Reports on the Foreign Investment Controversy," *Bankers' Magazine,* 208 (July 1969b), pp. 21–25.

United States Industry in Britain, London, The Financial Times for the Economists Advisory Group, 1972.

"Multinational Enterprises and Trade Flows of Less Developed Countries," University of Reading Discussion Papers in International Investment and Business Studies No. 1, Reading, England, 1973a.

"The Determinants of International Production," University of Reading Discussion Papers in International Investment and Business Studies No. 4, Reading, England, 1973b.

Dunning, J. H., ed., *Studies in International Investment,* New York, Humanities Press, 1970.

The Multinational Enterprise, London, Allen and Unwin, 1971.

The Multinational Firm and Economic Analysis, Allen and Unwin, 1974.

Dunning, J. H., and D. C. Rowan, "British Direct Investment in Western Europe," *Banca Nazionale del Lavoro Quarterly Review,* 18 (June 1965), pp. 127–156.

Dunning, J. H., and Max Steuer, "The Effects of United States Direct Investment in Britain on British Technology," *Moorgate and Wallstreet* (Autumn 1969), pp. 5–33.

Dunning, J. H., and G. Yannopoulos, "The Fiscal Factor in the Location of Affiliates of Multinational Enterprises," in Centre de Recherches Interdisciplinaires Droit-Economie, *Vers une Politique Fiscale Européenne à l'égard des Entreprises Multinationales?* Brussels, Vander, 1973.

Erb, G. F., "Foreign Private Investment and Multinational Enterprises: Sources of Studies and Information," Washington, Overseas Development Council, 1973.

Fernandez, R. A., "The Border Industrial Program on the United States–Mexico Border," *Review of Radical Political Economics,* 5 (Spring 1973), pp. 37–52.

Fieleke, N. S., *The Welfare Effects of Controls over Capital Exports from the United States,* Essays in International Finance No. 82, Princeton, N.J., 1971.

Financial Times, "Unilever: Dr. Ernest Woodroofe on Unilever's Role as a Multi-National Business," 9 (May 1972), p. 10.

Forsyth, D. J. C., *U.S. Investment in Scotland,* New York, Praeger, 1972.

Fortune, 88 (August 1973), review of the multinational corporation; also annual listing of the largest firms.

Franko, L. G., "The Other Multinationals: The International Activity of Continental European Enterprise," Geneva, Centre d'Etudes Industrielles, 1974.

Gabriel, P. P., *The International Transfer of Corporate Skills: Management Contracts in Less Developed Countries,* Boston, Harvard Graduate School of Business Administration, 1967.

Garnick, D. H., "The Appeal of Confiscation Reconsidered," *Economic Development and Cultural Change,* 11 (July 1963), pp. 353–356.

Goldberg, M. A., and C. P. Kindleberger, "Toward a GATT for Investment: A Proposal for Supervision of the International Corporation," *Law and Policy in International Business,* 2 (Summer 1970), pp. 295–325.

Gordon, N. N., "Tax Aspects of U.S. Foreign Direct Investment," in U.S. Commission on International Trade and Investment Policy, *United States International Economic Policy in an Interdependent World,* Washington, 1971.

Gordon, W. C. "The Contribution of Foreign Investments: A Case Study of United States Foreign Investment History," *Inter-American Economic Affairs,* 14 (Spring 1961), pp. 35–56.

"Foreign Investments," *University of Houston Business Review,* 9 (Fall 1962), pp. 1–69.

Government of Canada, Office of Economics, Foreign Investment Division, *Foreign Direct Investment in Canada: Selected Bibliography to June 1971,* Ottawa, June 1971.

Gray Report, *Foreign Direct Investment in Canada,* Ottawa, Information Canada, 1972.

Grubel, H. G., "Internationally Diversified Portfolios," *American Economic Review,* 58 (December 1968), pp. 1299–1314.

"Taxation and the Rates of Return from Some U.S. Asset Holdings Abroad, 1960–1969," 82 (May/June 1974), pp. 469–487.

Gruber, W., D. Mehta, and R. Vernon, "The R & D Factor in International Trade and International Investment of U.S. Industries," *Journal of Political Economy,* 75 (January–February 1967), pp. 20–37.

Hamada, K., "Japanese Investment Abroad," in Drysdale, ed. (1972).

Hatti, N., "Growth of Private Foreign Investment in India, 1948–1960," *Economy and History,* 13 (1970), pp. 54–80.

Hawkins, R. G., "Job Displacement and the Multinational Firm: A Methodological Review," Center for Multinational Studies Occasional Paper 3, Washington, 1972.

Helleiner, G. K., "Manufactured Exports from Less-Developed Countries and Multinational Firms," *Economic Journal,* 83 (March 1973), pp. 21–47.

Herring, R., and T. D. Willett, "The Capital Control Program and United States Investment Activity Abroad," *Southern Economic Journal,* 39 (July 1972), pp. 58–71.

Hirschman, A. O., *How to Divest in Latin America, and Why,* Essays in International Finance No. 76, Princeton, N.J., 1969.

Hobson, J. A., *Imperialism: A Study,* New York, Pott and Company, 1902.

Hogan, W. P., "British Investment in Australian Manufacturing: The Technical Connection," *The Manchester School of Economic and Social Studies,* 35 (May 1967), pp. 133–166.

Horst, Thomas, "The Theory of the Multinational Firm: Optimal Behavior under Different Tariff and Tax Rates," *Journal of Political Economy,* 79 (September/October 1971), pp. 1059–1072.

"The Industrial Composition of United States Exports and Subsidiary Sales to the Canadian Market," *American Economic Review,* 62 (March 1972a), pp. 37–45.

"Firm and Industry Determinants of the Decision to Invest Abroad: An Empirical Study," *Review of Economics and Statistics,* 54 (August 1972b), pp. 258–266.

"The Simple Analysis of Multi-National Firm Behavior," in M. B. Connolly and A. K. Swoboda, eds., *International Trade and Money,* London, Allen and Unwin, 1973.

At Home Abroad: A Study of the Domestic and Foreign Operations of the American Food-Processing Industry, Cambridge, Mass., Ballinger, 1974.

Hufbauer, G. C., *Synthetic Materials and the Theory of International Trade,* Cambridge, Mass., Harvard University Press, 1966.

Hufbauer, G. C., and F. M. Adler, *Overseas Manufacturing Investment and the Balance of Payments,* Tax Policy Research Study No. 1, Washington, U.S. Treasury Department, 1968.

Hughes, H., and Y. P. Seng, eds., *Foreign Investment and Industrialization in Singapore,* Madison, University of Wisconsin Press, 1969.

Hui, C., and R. G. Hawkins, "Foreign Direct Investment and the United States Balance of Payments: A Cross Section Model," *American Statistical Association Proceedings of the Business and Economic Statistics Section,* 1972, pp. 21–28.

Hunt, S. J., "Evaluating Direct Foreign Investment in Latin America," Discussion Paper 23, Research Program in Economic Development, Woodrow Wilson School, Princeton, (July 1972).

Hymer, S., *The International Operation of National Firms: A Study in Direct Foreign Investment,* Ph.D. dissertation, M.I.T., 1960.

"The Efficiency (Contradictions) of Multinational Corporations," *American Economic Association Papers and Proceedings,* 60 (May 1970), pp. 441–448.

"The Internationalization of Capital," *Journal of Economic Issues,* 6 (March 1972), pp. 91–111.

IMF, *International Financial Statistics: 1972 Supplement,* Washington, 1972.

Jasay, A. E., "The Social Choice between Home and Overseas Investment," *Economic Journal,* 70 (March 1960), pp. 70–105.

Johns, B. L., "Private Overseas Investment in Australia: Profitability and Motivation," *Economic Record,* 43 (June 1967), pp. 233–261.

Johnson, H. G., "A Theoretical Model of Economic Nationalism in New and Developing States," *Political Science Quarterly,* 80 (June 1965), pp. 169–185.

"The Efficiency and Welfare Implications of the International Corporation," in Kindleberger, ed. (1970).

"The Monetary Approach to Balance-of-Payments Theory," *Intermountain Economic Review,* 3 (Fall 1972), pp. 1–13.

Johnstone, A. W., *United States Direct Investment in France,* Cambridge, Mass., M.I.T. Press, 1965.

Jones, R. E., "International Capital Movements and the Theory of Tariffs and Trade," *Quarterly Journal of Economics,* 81 (February 1967), pp. 1–38.

Jorgenson, D., "Capital Theory and Investment Behavior," *American Economic Association Papers and Proceedings,* 53 (May 1963), pp. 247–259.

Jud, C. D., "An Empirical Study of the Industrial Composition of U.S. Exports and Foreign Subsidiary Sales," paper read at meetings of the Southwestern Economic Association, March 1973.

Karsten, S. G., "Economic Imperialism: A Survey," *Intermountain Economic Review,* 2 (Spring 1971), pp. 30–44.

Keesing, D. B., "Labor Skills and International Trade: Evaluating Many Trade Flows with a Single Measuring Device," *Review of Economics and Statistics,* 47 (August 1965), pp. 287–294.

Kemp, M. C., "Foreign Investment and the National Advantage," *Economic Record,* 38 (March 1962a), pp. 56–62.

"The Benefits and Costs of Private Investment from Abroad: Comment," *Economic Record,* 38 (March 1962b), pp. 108–110.

The Pure Theory of International Trade and Investment, Englewood Cliffs, N.J., Prentice-Hall, 1969.

Kindleberger, C. P., "The International Firm and the International Capital Market," *Southern Economic Journal,* 34 (October 1967), pp. 223–230.

American Business Abroad: Six Lectures on Direct Investment, New Haven, Yale University Press, 1969.

"Magdoff on Imperialism: Two Views," *Public Policy,* 19 (Summer 1971), pp. 531–534.

"Direct Investment in Less-Developed Countries: Historical Wrongs and Present Values," in L. E. di Marco, ed., *International Economics and Development: Essays in Honor of Paul Prebisch,* New York, Academic Press, 1972.

"Origins of United States Direct Investment in France," MIT Department of Economics, Working Paper No. 105, 1973a.

International Economics, Homewood, Ill., Irwin, 1973b.

Kindleberger, C. P., ed., *The International Corporation,* Cambridge, Mass., M.I.T. Press, 1970.

Klein, R. W. "A Dynamic Theory of Comparative Advantage," *American Economic Review,* 68 (March 1973), pp. 173–184.

Knickerbocker, F. T., *Oligopolistic Reaction and Multinational Enterprise,* Boston, Harvard Business School, 1973.

Kojima, K., "A Macroeconomic Approach to Foreign Direct Investment," *Hitotsubashi Journal of Economics,* 14 (June 1973), pp. 1–21.

Kopits, G. F., "Dividend Remittance Behavior within the International Firm: A Cross-Country Analysis," *Review of Economics and Statistics,* 54 (August 1972), pp. 339–342.

Krause, L. B., and K. N. Dam, *Federal Tax Treatment of Foreign Income,* Washington, The Brookings Institution, 1964.

Krause, W., "UNCTAD III: Implications for Multinational Enterprise," paper read to the Association for Education in International Business, December 1972.

Kujawa, K., ed., *American Labor and Multinational Corporations,* New York, Praeger, 1973.

Kwack, S. Y., "A Model of U.S. Direct Investment Abroad: A Neoclassical Approach," *Western Economic Journal,* 10 (December 1972), pp. 376–383.

Lall, S. "Transfer-Pricing by Multinational Firms," *Oxford Bulletin of Economics and Statistics,* 35 (August 1973a), pp. 173–195.
  An Annotated Bibliography on Prviate Foreign Direct Investment, Oxford University, Institute of Economics and Statistics, 1973b.

Law and Contemporary Problems, 34 (Winter 1969), special issue on "Trans-Atlantic Investment and the Balance of Payments."

Lea, S., and S. Webley, *Multinational Corporations in Developed Countries: A Review of Recent Research and Policy Thinking,* Washington, British–North American Committee, 1973.

Leamer, E. E., and R. M. Stern, *Quantitative International Economics,* Boston, Allyn and Bacon, 1970.

Leftwich, R. B., "Foreign Direct Investments in the United States, 1962–71," *Survey of Current Business,* 53 (February 1973), pp. 29–40.

Leontief, W. W., "Domestic Production and Foreign Trade: The American Capital Position Re-examined," *Economia Internazionale,* 7 (February 1954), pp. 9–38.

Levitt, Kari, *Silent Surrender: The Multinational Corporation in Canada,* New York, St Martin's Press, 1970.

Levy, H., and M. Sarnat, "International Diversification of Investment Portfolios," *American Economic Review,* 60 (September 1970), pp. 668–675.

Lindert, P. H., "The Payments Impact of Foreign Investment Controls," *Journal of Finance,* 26 (December 1970), pp. 1083–1099.

Lipsey, R. E., and M. Y. Weiss, "Analyzing Direct Investment and Trade at the Company Level," *American Statistical Association Proceedings of the Business and Economic Statistics Association,* 1972a, pp. 11–20.
  "The Relation of United States Manufacturing Abroad to United States Exports," mimeographed, National Bureau of Economic Research, 1972b.

McAleese, D., "Capital Inflow and Direct Foreign Investment in Ireland, 1952 to 1970," *Journal of the Statistical and Social Inquiry Society of Ireland,* 22 (Part 4, 1971/72), pp. 63–99.

MacDougall, G. D. A., "The Benefits and Costs of Private Investment from Abroad: A Theoretical Approach," *Bulletin of the Oxford University Institute of Statistics,* 22 (August 1960), pp. 189–211.

Machlup, F., W. Salant, and L. Tarshis, eds., *International Mobility and Movement of Capital,* New York, Columbia University Press for the National Bureau of Economic Research, 1972.

McLure, C. E., "Taxation of Inter-State Corporations," Report Prepared for the UN Conference on Multinational Corporations, June 1973.

Magdoff, H., *The Age of Imperialism: The Economics of United States Foreign Policy,* New York, Monthly Review Press, 1969.

Mansfield, E. E., *Industrial Research and Technological Innovation,* New York, Norton for the Cowles Foundation, 1968.
  "The Multinational Firm and Technological Change," in Dunning, ed. (1974).

Mansfield, E. E., et al., *Research and Innovation in the Modern Corporation,* New York, Norton, 1971.

Mao, J. C. T., *Quantitative Analysis of Financial Decisions,* New York, Macmillan, 1969.

Marshall, H., *et al.*, *Canadian-American Industry: A Study in International Investment*, New Haven, Yale University Press, 1936.

Mason, R. H., "Some Aspects of Technology Transfer: A Case Study Comparing United States Subsidiaries and Local Counterparts in the Philippines," *Philippine Economic Journal*, 9 (First Semester, 1970), pp. 83–108.

"Some Observations on the Choice of Technology by Multinational Firms in Developing Countries," *Review of Economics and Statistics*, 55 (August 1973), pp. 349–355.

Mauer, L. J., and A. E. Scaperlanda, "Remittances from United States Direct Foreign Investment in the European Economic Community: An Exploratory Estimate of Their Determinants," *Economia Internazionale*, 25 (February 1972), pp. 3–13.

May, R. S., "Direct Investment in Nigeria – 1953–63," *Scottish Journal of Political Economy*, 12 (November 1965), pp. 243–266.

Meany, G., *A Modern Trade Policy for the Seventies*, Washington, American Federation of Labor and Congress of Industrial Organizations, 1972.

Mellors, J., "Corporate Taxation and the Location of Overseas Direct Investment: A Pilot Study," University of Reading Discussion Papers in International Investment and Business Studies No. 5, Reading, England, 1973.

Mikesell, R. F., *United States Private and Government Investment Abroad*, Eugene, University of Oregon Press, 1962.

et al., *Foreign Investment in the Petroleum and Mineral Industries: Case Studies of Investor–Host Country Relations*, Baltimore, Johns Hopkins Press for Resources for the Future, 1971.

Miller, N. C., and M. v. N. Whitman, "A Mean-Variance Analysis of United States Long-Term Portfolio Investment," *Quarterly Journal of Economics*, 84 (May 1970), pp. 175–196.

Moffat, G. G., "The Foreign Ownership and Balance of Payments Effects of Direct Investment from Abroad," *Australian Economic Papers*, 6 (June 1967), pp. 1–24.

Morley, S. A., and G. W. Smith, "Import Substitution and Foreign Investment in Brazil," *Oxford Economic Papers*, 23 (March 1971), pp. 120–135.

"Managerial Discretion and the Choice of Technology by Multinational Firms in Brazil," unpublished, Houston, Rice University, 1974.

Mundell, R. A., "International Trade and Factor Mobility," *American Economic Review*, 47 (June 1957), pp. 321–335.

Musgrave, P. B., *United States Taxation of Foreign Investment Income: Issues and Arguments*, Cambridge, Mass., Harvard Law School International Tax Program, 1969.

"International Tax Base Division and the Multinational Corporation," *Public Finance*, 27 (1972), pp. 394–413.

Newsweek, "Global Companies: Too Big to Handle?" (Nov. 20, 1972), pp. 96–104.

Nisbet, C. T., "Transferring Wealth from Underdeveloped to Developed Countries via Direct Foreign Investment: A Marxist Claim Reconsidered," *Southern Economic Journal*, 37 (July 1970), pp. 93–96; Comment by R. B. Du Boff, and reply by Nisbet, *Southern Economic Journal*, 38 (July 1971), pp. 118–124.

Ohlin, B., *Interregional and International Trade*, Cambridge, Mass., Harvard University Press, 1933.

Ozawa, T., "Imitation, Innovation, and Japanese Exports," in P. B. Kenen and

R. Lawrence, eds., *The Open Economy: Essays on International Trade and Finance*, Columbia University Press, New York, 1968.

Parry, T. G., "Plant Size, Capacity Utilisation and Economic Efficiency: Foreign Investment in the Australian Chemical Industry," University of Reading Discussion Paper in International Investment and Business Studies, No. 8, Reading, England, 1973a.

"The International Firm and National Economic Policy," *Economic Journal*, 83 (December 1973b), pp. 1201–1221.

Paxson, D. A., "The Territorial Diversification of Multinational Enterprises," University of Reading Discussion Papers in International Investment and Business Studies No. 6, Reading, England, 1973.

Penrose, Edith, "Foreign Investment and the Growth of the Firm," *Economic Journal*, 66 (June 1956), pp. 220–235.

The Large International Firm in Developing Countries: The International Petroleum Industry, London, Allen and Unwin, 1968.

Phillips, E., *The Long Run Implications of Direct Foreign Investment for the United States Balance of Payments*, Ann Arbor, University Microfilms, 1964.

Pigou, A. C., *Protective and Preferential Import Duties*, London, London School of Economics, 1935 (first published in 1906).

Pinelo, A. J., *The Multinational Corporation as a Force in Latin American Politics: A Case Study of the International Petroleum Company in Peru*, New York, Praeger, 1973.

Pizer, S., "Capital Restraint Programs," in United States Commission on International Trade and Investment Policy, *United States International Economic Policy in an Interdependent World*, Washington.

Polk, J., I. W. Meister, and L. A. Veit, *United States Production Abroad and the Balance of Payments: A Survey of Corporate Investment Experience*, New York, National Industrial Conference Board, 1966.

Posner, M. V., "International Trade and Technical Change," *Oxford Economic Papers*, 13 (October (1961), pp. 323–341.

Prachowny, Martin F. J., "Direct Investment and the Balance of Payments of the United States: A Portfolio Approach," in Machlup *et al.*, eds. (1972).

Ragazzi, G., "Theories of the Determinants of Direct Foreign Investment," *IMF Staff Papers*, 20 (July 1973), pp. 471–498.

Reddaway, W. B., *Effects of United Kingdom Direct Investment Overseas – Interim Report*, Cambridge, England, Cambridge University Press, 1967.

Effects of United Kingdom Direct Investment Overseas – Final Report, Cambridge, England, Cambridge University Press, 1968.

Revue Economique, 23 (July 1972), special issue on "L'Entreprise Multinationale."

Richardson, J. D., "On 'Going Abroad': The Firm's Initial Foreign Investment Decision," *Quarterly Review of Economics and Business*, 11 (Winter 1971), pp. 7–22.

Richman, P. B., *Taxation of Foreign Investment Income: An Economic Analysis*, Baltimore, The Johns Hopkins Press, 1963.

Robbins, S. M., and R. B. Stobaugh, *Money in the Multinational Enterprise*, New York, Basic Books, 1973.

Rolfe, S. E., and W. Damm, eds., *The Multinational Corporation in the World Economy*, New York, Praeger, 1970.

Rosenbluth, G., "The Relation between Foreign Control and Concentration in

Canadian Industry," *Canadian Journal of Economics,* 3 (February 1970), pp. 14–38.

Rowan, D. C., and J. H. Dunning, "Inter-Firm Efficiency Comparisons, United States and United Kingdom Manufacturing Enterprises in Britain," *Banca Nazionale del Lavoro Quarterly Review,* 85 (June 1968), pp. 132–182.

Rowthorn, R., in collaboration with S. Hymer, *International Big Business 1957–1967: A Study of Comparative Growth,* Cambridge, England, Cambridge University Press, 1971.

Royal Commission on Canada's Economic Prospects (Gordon Commission), *Final Report,* Ottawa, Queen's Printer, 1957.

Safarian, A. E., *Foreign Ownership of Canadian Industry,* Toronto, McGraw-Hill, 1966.

    The Performance of Foreign-Owned Firms in Canada, Canada, Canadian–American Committee, 1969.

    "Perspectives on Foreign Direct Investment from the Viewpoint of a Capital Receiving Country," *Journal of Finance,* 28 (May 1973), pp. 419–438.

Samuelsson, H. F., *Foreign Direct Investment in Sweden 1965–70,* Stockholm, Industriens Utredningsinstitut, 1973.

Scaperlanda, A. E., "The E.E.C. and U.S. Foreign Investment: Some Empirical Evidence," *Economic Journal,* 77 (March 1967), pp. 22–26.

    "The E.E.C. and U.S. Foreign Investment: Some Empirical Evidence – A Reply," *Economic Journal,* 78 (September 1968), pp. 720–723.

    "Trends, Composition and Determinants of United States Direct Investment in Canada," paper read at meetings of the American Economic Association, December 1972.

Scaperlanda, A. E., and L. J. Mauer, "The Determinants of United States Direct Investment in the E.E.C.," *American Economic Review,* 59 (September 1969), pp. 558–568.

    "Errata: The Determinants of U.S. Direct Investment in the E.E.C.," *American Economic Review,* 61 (June 1971), pp. 509–510.

    "The Determinants of United States Direct Investment in the E.E.C.: Reply to a Comment by M. A. Goldberg," *American Economic Review,* 62 (September 1972), pp. 700–705.

    "The Impact of Controls on United States Direct Foreign Investment in the European Economic Community," *Southern Economic Journal,* 39 (January 1973), pp. 419–423.

Schmitz, A., "The Impact of Trade Blocs on Foreign Direct Investment," *Economic Journal,* 80 (September 1970), pp. 724–731.

Schmitz, A., and J. Bieri, "E.E.C. Tariffs and United States Direct Investment," *European Economic Review,* 3 (October 1972), pp. 259–270.

Schmitz, A., and P. Helmberger, "Factor Mobility and International Trade. The Case of Complementarity," *American Economic Review,* 60 (September 1970), pp. 761–767.

Servan-Schreiber, J. J., *The American Challenge,* New York, Atheneum, 1968.

Shaffer, F. H., "International Trade, Capital Movements and Competitive Policy," paper read at meetings of the Western Economic Association, August 1972.

Sherk, D. R., *Foreign Investment in Asia: Cooperation and Conflict between the United States and Japan,* Federal Reserve Bank of San Francisco, 1973.

Shulman, J. S., "The Tax Environment of Multinational Firms," *The Tax Executive,* April 1967, pp. 173–187.

Sismondi, J. C. L. S. de, *New Principles of Political Economy,* translated and edited by P. C. Newman, A. D. Gayer, and M. H. Spencer, New York, Norton, 1954 (first published in 1819).

Smith, E. R., "Private Power and National Sovereignty," unpublished, Eugene, University of Oregon, 1973.

Spitaller, E., " Survey of Recent Quantitative Studies of Long-Term Capital Movements," *IMF Staff Papers,* 18 (March 1971), pp. 189–220.

Steuer, M. D., *et al., The Impact of Foreign Direct Investment on the United Kingdom,* London, Department of Trade and Industry, 1973.

Stevens, G. v. G., "United States Direct Investment in Latin America: Some Economic and Political Determinants," unpublished, The Brookings Institution, 1969a.

"Fixed Investment Expenditures of Foreign Manufacturing Affiliates of United States Firms: Theoretical Models and Empirical Evidence," *Yale Economic Essays,* 9 (Spring 1969b), pp. 137–206.

"The Multinational Firm and the Determinants of Investment," in Dunning, ed. (1974).

Stobaugh, R. B., *et al.,* "U.S. Multinational Enterprises and the U.S. Economy: A Research Study of the Major Industries That Account for 90 Per Cent of U.S. Foreign Direct Investment in Manufacturing," in U.S. Dept. of Commerce, *The Multinational Corporation: Studies on U.S. Foreign Investment,* Washington, Bureau of International Commerce, Vol. 1, 1972.

Stobaugh, R. B., P. Telesio, and J. de la Torre, *The Effect of U.S. Foreign Direct Investment in Manufacturing on the U. S. Balance of Payments, U.S. Employment and Changes in the Skill Composition of Employment,* Center for Multinational Studies Occasional Paper 4, Washington, 1973.

Stopford, J. M., and L. T. Wells, Jr., *Managing the Multinational Enterprise: Organization of the Firm and Ownership of the Subsidiaries,* New York, Basic Books, 1972.

Streeten, P. P., "Technology Gaps between Rich and Poor Countries," *Scottish Journal of Political Economy,* 19 (November 1972), pp. 213–230.

Stubenitsky, F. A., *American Direct Investment in the Netherlands Industry,* Rotterdam, Rotterdam University Press, 1970.

Swedenborg, B., *Den Svenska Industrins Investeringar i Utlandet 1965–1970,* Uppsala, Almqvist and Wiksell for Industriensinstitut, 1973.

Thiel, E., "The Profitability of Swedish Manufacturing Investment Abroad," *Columbia Journal of World Business,* 8 (Fall 1973), pp. 87–92.

Thurow, L. C., "Multi-National Companies and the American Distribution of Income," unpublished, Cambridge, Mass., Massachusetts Institute of Technology, 1973.

Tilton, J. E., *International Diffusion of Technology: The Case of Semi-conductors,* Washington, The Brookings Institution, 1971.

Tobin, J., "Liquidity Preference as Behavior towards Risk," *Review of Economic Studies,* 25 (February 1958), pp. 65–86.

Tugendhat, C., *The Multinationals,* London, Eyre and Spottiswoode, 1971.

U.K. Dept. of Trade and Industry, *Trade and Industry,* various issues.

U.K. Reference Division, *Britain's International Investment Position,* London, Central Office of Information, 1970.

UNCTAD, reports prepared by P. P. Streeten, S. Lall, *et al.,* mimeographed,

"Balance of-Payments Effects of Private Foreign Investment: Case Studies of Jamaica and Kenya," July 1970.

"Balance-of-Payments and Income Effects of Private Foreign Investment in Manufacturing: Case Studies of India and Iran," December 1971.

"Balance-of-Payments Effects of Private Foreign Investment in Developing Countries: Summary of Case Studies of India, Iran, Jamaica, and Kenya," April 1972.

"Some Reflections on Government Policies Concerning Private Foreign Investment," May 1973a.

"Methodology Used in Studies on Private Foreign Investment in Selected Developing Countries," May 1973b.

"Main Findings of a Study of Private Foreign Investment in Selected Developing Countries," May 1973c.

"Balance-of-Payments and Income Effects of Private Foreign Investment in Manufacturing: Case Studies of Colombia and Malaysia," June 1973d.

UN Department of Economic and Social Affairs, *Multinational Corporations in World Development*, New York, 1973.

UN Economic and Social Council, "The Impact of Multinational Corporations on the Development Process and on International Relations: Report of the Group of Eminent Persons to Study the Role of Multinational Corporations on Development and on International Relations," New York, Part I, May 1974; Part II, June 1974.

UN Secretariat, *Multinational Corporations: A Select Bibliography*, New York, 1973.

UN Statistical Office, *Yearbook of National Statistics*, New York, 1970, 1972.

U.S. Dept. of Commerce, *Fixed Nonresidential Business Capital in the United States, 1925–1970*, Springfield, Va., National Technical Information Service, 1971.

Special Survey of U.S. Multinational Companies, 1970, Springfield, Va., National Technical Information Service, 1972.

Bureau of the Census, *Statistical Abstract of the United States*, Washington, 1972.

Bureau of Economic Analysis, *U.S. Direct Investments Abroad – 1966: Part II*, Springfield, Va., National Technical Information Service, Vol. 1, 1971, Vol. 2, 1972, Vol. 3, 1972.

Bureau of International Commerce, *The Multinational Corporation: Studies on U.S. Foreign Investment*, Washington, Vol. 1, 1972, Vol. 2, 1973.

Office of Business Economics, *U.S. Direct Investments Abroad: Part I: Balance of Payments Data*, Washington, 1970.

Office of Foreign Direct Investments, *Foreign Affiliate Financial Survey: 1967–1968*, Washington, 1970.

Office of Foreign Direct Investments, *Foreign Affiliate Financial Survey: 1966–1969*, Washington, 1971.

Office of Foreign Direct Investments, *Foreign Direct Investment Program: Selected Statistics*, Washington, 1972.

U.S. Senate Committee on Finance, *A Compendium of Papers Submitted to the Subcommittee on International Trade*, 93rd Cong., 1st sess., Washington, 1973a.

Implications of Multinational Corporations for World Trade and Investment and for U.S. Trade and Labor, 93rd Cong., 1st sess., Washington, 1973b.

Vaitsos, C. V., "Transfer of Resources and Preservation of Monopoly Rents," mimeographed, Harvard Center for International Affairs Economic Development Report No. 168, 1970.

"Income Distribution, Welfare Considerations, and Transnational Enterprises," in Dunning, ed. (1974).

Vaupel, J. W., and J. P. Curhan, *The Making of Multinational Enterprise*, Boston, Harvard Business School, 1969.

Vernon, Raymond, "International Investment and International Trade in the Product Cycle," *Quarterly Journal of Economics*, 30 (May 1966), pp. 190–207.

Sovereignty at Bay: The Multinational Spread of United States Enterprises, New York, Basic Books, 1971.

The Economic and Political Consequences of Multinational Enterprise: An Anthology, Cambridge, Mass., Harvard Business School, 1972.

"Social Responsibility in Foreign Enterprises," unpublished, Cambridge, Mass., Harvard University, 1973.

Wall Street Journal, series on the multinational corporation (May 18, 19, 20, 23, 25, 1973); and other issues.

Wallis, K. F., "The E.E.C. and United States Foreign Investment," *Economic Journal*, 78 (September 1968), pp. 717–719.

Watkins Commission, *Foreign Ownership and the Structure of Canadian Industry*, Report of the Task Force on the Structure of Canadian Industry, Ottawa, Privy Council Office, 1968.

Weintraub, R., "Studio empirico sulle relazioni di lungo andare tra movimenti di capitali e rendimenti differenziali," *Revista Internazionale di Scienze Economica e Commerciali*, 14 (May 1967), pp. 401–415.

Wells, S. J., *British Export Performance: A Comparative Study*, Cambridge, England, Cambridge University Press, 1964.

Wert, F. S., "A Product Cycle Model of the Balance of Payments Impact of U.S. Based Multinationalism," *Journal of International Business Studies*, 4 (Fall 1973), pp. 51–64.

Wilkins, M., "An American Enterprise Abroad: American Radiator Company in Europe 1895–1914," *Business History Review*, 43 (Autumn 1969), pp. 326–346.

The Emergence of Multinational Enterprise: American Business Abroad from the Colonial Era to 1914, Cambridge, Mass., Harvard University Press, 1970.

Wolff, R. D., "Modern Imperialism: The View from the Metropolis," *American Economic Association Papers and Proceedings*, 60 (May 1970), pp. 225–236.

Zink, D. W., *The Political Risks for Multinational Enterprise in Developing Countries, With a Case Study of Peru*, New York, Praeger, 1973.

Zweig, M., "Foreign Investment and the Aggregate Balance of Payments," *Review of Radical Political Economics*, 5 (Spring 1973), pp. 13–18.

EMPIRICAL RESEARCH ON FINANCIAL CAPITAL FLOWS*

Ralph C. Bryant

This paper is concerned with the growing body of literature reporting on empirical research on international capital flows. The term "financial" capital flows (or, alternatively, "portfolio" capital flows) is used to connote capital flows other than direct investments. Readers interested primarily in research on direct investments and the multinational corporation should consult Hufbauer's paper and its references; it precedes mine in this volume.

The scope of this paper is restricted in another way as well. There have been a number of articles in recent years, primarily theoretical in nature, dealing with what might be termed macroeconomic models of international trade and capital flows. Some of this literature is discussed in Helliwell's paper in this volume. I have not attempted to cover this ground except insofar as it has a direct bearing on empirical research per se.

As a glance at the list of references at the end of the paper will show, most of the literature on financial capital flows is of recent vintage. Little of it pre-dates the 1960s; the major part was published within the last five or six years. This fact underlines the relatively underdeveloped state of econometric research on the capital account in the balance of payments. Econometric studies of the impacts of real activity and prices on the current account in the balance of payments have a much longer and more sophisticated history – not to mention the great volume of empirical research carried out on domestic financial markets, domestic expenditures on real goods and services, and the linkages between them.

I should caution the reader with one further introductory comment. This paper is not a *survey* as the word is often used; I have not tried to summarize comprehensively the literature bearing on empirical research on financial capital flows. The paper is most accurately described as a selective assessment of empirical knowledge and of the state of the art in research in this field.

Before plunging into a discussion of the strengths and weak-

* The analysis and conclusions of this paper represent the personal views of the author and should not be interpreted as reflecting the views of the Board of Governors of the Federal Reserve System or its staff.

nesses of the work done in this area, I think it is useful to provide a brief road map of the literature. That is the purpose of the following section.

1.   A BRIEF MAP OF THE LITERATURE

One method of mapping the literature is to classify it by the main country of interest and the extent of coverage of that country's capital account. The bulk of the research has been done on the United States and on Canada. Bilateral capital flows between the United States and Canada have received considerable attention. Recently, more intensive empirical work has begun on capital flows in the balance of payments of European countries and Japan. Empirical research on the Eurocurrency market, although showing promising signs of growth, is very much in its infancy.

The first systematic econometric work on the U.S. capital account was begun in the first part of the 1960s. The growth of interest in capital flows reflected in part a rising concern about weakness in the U.S. balance of payments and instability in the international monetary system. It also coincided with the development by academic economists of a literature on the so-called "assignment" problem; in much of this literature, it was suggested that monetary policy should be aimed at the balance of payments, while fiscal policy should be aimed at domestic policy objectives [see Mundell (1968, Chaps. 11 and 16–18) for several of the important early contributions, and Whitman (1970) for a survey]. Early publications by Bell (1962) and Kenen (1963), commissioned by the U.S. Government, drew attention to the area and stimulated further work [see, for example, Cohen (1963) and Kenen's (1973) subsequent research (carried out in 1964–67, but not made available for general circulation until 1973]. Stein's 1965 article in the *American Economic Review* had a similar effect in inducing critical comments (see Heckerman, 1967; Hendershott, 1967a; Laffer, 1967; Stein, 1967) and focused more attention on the exchange-market aspects.

By the end of the decade, a large volume of work had been done, employing increasingly sophisticated methodology and statistical techniques. Branson's important Ph.D. dissertation (published in 1968) was followed by further articles refining his work (Branson, 1970; Branson and Hill, 1971, pp. 11–26; Branson and Willett, 1972). The collaboration of Miller and Whitman resulted in three contributions (1970a, 1970b, 1972). Bryant and Hendershott (1970, 1972) focused on bilateral capital flows between the United States and Japan in order to illustrate the general problems confronting empirical research in this area.

Kwack (1971a; 1971b; Kwack and Schink, 1972) has estimated equations for the U.S. capital account as part of an ambitious effort to construct an econometric model for the U.S. balance of payments as a whole. Prachowny (1969) had a similar objective. Marston and Kwack (1973) have recently abridged Kwack's model as part of an effort to incorporate it into the Wharton School model of the U.S. economy. In a recent Princeton Ph.D. dissertation, Herring (1973) estimates an aggregate equation for net capital flows and compares the results with the disaggregated results of Branson and Hill (1971). The substantive contributions of these studies are discussed in subsequent sections.

Early contributions to the literature on the Canadian capital account included those of Rhomberg (1960, 1964) and Powrie (1964). Black (1968) studied bilateral U.S.–Canadian flows in the course of testing his extensions of Tsiang's (1959) model of exchange-market behavior. Arndt's (1968) study applied the partial-adjustment, distributed-lag model to U.S.–Canadian data, focusing on speculative behavior. Lee (1969) looked at U.S. residents' holdings of Canadian long-term securities; he was the first to apply explicitly the portfolio-adjustment theory (see below) to U.S.–Canadian flows. Still another paper employing bilateral U.S.–Canadian data was done by Hawkins (1968). Caves and Reuber (1971, 1972) have carried out extensive research on the Canadian capital account, with special emphasis on Canadian economic policy. Virtually all these studies are concerned in one way or another with exchange-market behavior; this preoccupation can be traced, no doubt, to the interest in and concern about this subject on the part of Canadian policymakers.

For full-scale econometric models of the Canadian balance of payments, one can turn to Officer (1968), the TRACE model constructed at the University of Toronto (Choudhry et al., 1972; Carr and Sawyer, 1973), and the impressive efforts sponsored by the Bank of Canada (see, for example, Helliwell *et al.*, 1971, and Stewart, 1972). Helliwell (1969, 1972) and Helliwell and Maxwell (1972, 1974) in particular have made original contributions to the capital-account part of this modeling effort (see section 2 below). The chapter by Helliwell *et al.* in the volume on Project LINK (Ball, 1973) is also relevant. Recent work on Canadian capital flows includes that of Charles Freedman; the empirical work itself has been published by the Bank of Canada (Freedman, 1974); see also Freedman (1973).

Econometric analysis of capital flows in the U.K. balance of payments is currently going forward at the London Business School as part of their project to model the U.K. economy (see, for example, Boatwright and Renton, 1972). Hodjera (1971), Branson and Hill (1971), and Herring (1973) have also reported equations for the United Kingdom.

The studies by Branson and Hill and Herring include research on the capital accounts of several other European countries. Additional work on German capital flows includes Willms (1971) and the interesting papers of Porter (1972), Kouri and Porter (1974), Argy and Kouri (1974), and Kouri (1973). These last papers are discussed in section 3. The University of Bonn model of the German economy incorporated in Project LINK now includes some equations for the German capital account (see Sandermann, 1972; Martiensen and Sandermann, 1973).

Kouri and Porter (1974) and Argy and Kouri (1974) report equations for the Netherlands and Italy. Empirical research on the capital account in the Italian balance of payments is being carried out by economists at the Banca d'Italia, and by Basevi and others at the Istituto de Scienze Economiche at the University of Bologna.

Australia is the fourth country studied by Kouri and Porter (1974) and also is the focus of Zecher's (1973) unpublished research done at the University of Chicago. The econometric model project of the Reserve Bank of Australia has also devoted attention to Australian capital flows.

Although I have worked on certain types of capital flow in the Japanese balance of payments (Bryant and Hendershott, 1970, 1972), I am not sure how extensive research has been on the Japanese capital account. To some degree, this area has been investigated as part of the econometric model projects at the Institute of Economic Research, Kyoto University, at the Economic Planning Agency in Tokyo, and at the Bank of Japan. Amano's forthcoming book (1973a) is one important source of information on this research.

In general, as a selective scanning of the volume on Project LINK (Ball, 1973) will show, most national econometric models have concentrated on the current account in the balance of payments. Given the relative underdevelopment of the monetary sectors of these models and the scarcity of reliable and accessible data for the capital account, the omission of equations for the capital account is not surprising. Several participants in Project LINK hope to see the financial and capital-flows aspects of LINK given greater attention in the future (see, for example, Basevi and Waelbroeck, 1973).

Theoretical modeling and empirical study of the Eurocurrency markets have only recently begun to grow rapidly. This lag can be attributed, at least in part, to the fact that appropriate and reliable data on the assets and liabilities of Eurobanks have been difficult to come by. Moreover, time series of sufficient length to allow medium-term econometric work became available only toward the end of the 1960s. Hendershott (1967b), Kwack (1971c), Argy and Hodjera (1973), Mills (1973b), and Herring (1973, Chap. 6) have all considered the determination of Eurodollar interest rates. Papers by Makin (1972) and Marston (1974) attempt to estimate equations explaining deposits in and borrowing from banks in the Eurodollar market. I, myself, have some uncompleted research (Bryant, 1971) on the demand by nonresidents of the United States for liquid dollar assets. Several recent papers by two economists at the IMF (Hewson and Sakakibara, 1973a, 1973b, 1974) are important contributions, for their more careful theoretical approach as well as for their empirical efforts.

Black (1971) studied the weekly behavior of the liabilities of U.S. banks to their foreign branches, a very important element of the behavior of the Eurodollar market during the period of his study; for two comments on Black's paper, see Valentini and Hunt (1972) and Massaro (1972). Mastrapasqua (1973) has also reported equations for the liabilities of U.S. banks to their foreign branches. Unpublished research bearing on this aspect of the Eurodollar market includes the University of Maryland Ph.D. dissertation of Bradshaw (1973) and a paper by Ciccolo and McKelvey (1971).

The distinction between "short-term" and "long-term" financial capital flows is in some respects not analytically interesting; as the discussion in section 2 makes clear, in principle they need to be considered together as part of an integrated theory. See also the discussion in section 3 of the appropriate degree and type of disaggregation. Moreover, existing statistical data distinguish between them (if they are separated at all) on quite arbitrary grounds – usually by asking whether the original maturity of the financial instrument is greater or less than one year. For these reasons, I have not emphasized this distinction here. Those especially interested in empirical research on portfolio capital flows of a longer-term nature should consult, inter alia, Spitaller's (1971) survey article, Miller and Whitman (1970a), Lee (1969), Boatwright and Renton (1972), and the relevant parts of Branson and Hill (1971), Kwack and Schink (1972), and Amano (1973a).

Another method of mapping this literature is to classify the contributions by the theoretical approach or specification employed by the researcher. A majority of the early contributions relied on what came to be called a "flow theory" (see section 2 for a discussion). This specification was used in part of Bell's work (1962; contrast the form of the equations in Appendices II and III) and is found, for example, in Kenen (1963), Rhomberg (1964), Powrie (1964), Stein (1965), Kenen (1973), Arndt (1968), Hawkins (1968), and Prachowny (1969).

More recently, the bulk of the research has been based on more or less sophisticated versions of a "stock adjustment" or portfolio-balance type of specification (again, see section 2). Branson (1968), Grubel (1968), and Hendershott (1967a) were among the first to criticize the theoretical shortcomings of the earlier research (discussed below). For a representative sampling of contributions based on the portfolio-adjustment approach, see Amano (1973), Branson and Hill (1971), Bryant and Hendershott (1970), Kwack (1971a), Lee (1969), and Miller and Whitman (1970a).

Most of the studies cited here, with the important exceptions of those dealing with the Canadian capital account, have not shown an especially strong interest in exchange rates and the foreign-exchange markets as such. Of the research focused on this area, Black (1968, 1973) and Helliwell *et al.* (see the various references cited above) stand out in importance. Additional studies that concentrate attention on exchange-market aspects of capital flows include Stoll (1968), Kesselman (1971), and Dooley (1974). See also Officer and Willett (1970) and Porter (1971) for related papers.

Hardly any empirical research motivated by a "monetary" approach to the balance of payments has yet been published. Theoretical papers such as Johnson's (1973), however, have prompted several researchers to try their hand. Examples are Zecher (1973) and Girton and Roper (1974). More work in this vein will probably be available in the near future. On the distinguishing characteristics of the monetary approach to the balance of payments, see Salop (1973).

Some recent empirical work coming out of the Research Department at the IMF (see, for example, Kouri and Porter, 1974) is difficult to characterize as either "monetary" or "portfolio balance" in its approach. In the minds of its authors, it constitutes a synthesis of both approaches.

Finally, to conclude this road map, I should alert the reader to a recent survey by Hodjera (1973), which in a different manner is also a map of the literature on international capital movements (although Hodjera restricts his survey to short-term capital flows).

In what follows I discuss selected aspects or results of a number of the studies mentioned above but do not try to summarize in any detail the theoretical specifications used or the empirical results reported. Instead, my limited objectives are to call attention to some important general issues that arise in connection with the theoretical specifications used in these studies, to point to some unresolved questions of strategy for future research, and to present my own assessment of how far the profession has progressed in our empirical work in this area. The following sections of the paper take up these topics in turn.

2. GENERAL ISSUES OF THEORETICAL SPECIFICATION

As already noted, the so-called "portfolio approach" to capital flows underlies the bulk of recent literature in this area. The basic ideas underlying this theoretical approach go back at least to the works of Markowitz (1959) and Tobin (1965).

At their lowest common denominator, all studies based on the portfolio approach imply an underlying specification of the following form:

$$F_1^* = f_1(S, R_1, \ldots, R_n, \sigma_1, \ldots, \sigma_n, X_1, X_2, \ldots)$$

$$F_2^* = f_2(S, R_1, \ldots, R_n, \sigma_1, \ldots, \sigma_n, X_1, X_2, \ldots)$$

$$\vdots$$

$$F_n^* = f_n(S, R_1, \ldots, R_n, \sigma_1, \ldots, \sigma_n, X_1, X_2, \ldots). \tag{1}$$

The variables $F_1^*, \ldots F_n^*$ (hereafter F_i^*) represent derived quantities of the financial instruments held in the decision-making unit's portfolio of assets and liabilities. These functional forms are, in the case of assets, *stock* demand functions; when F_i^* is a liability, the equation is a *stock* supply function. Ideally, the system of equations should refer either to an individual decision-making unit or to an aggregation of decision-making units that are reasonably homogeneous in character (see section 3 for a discussion of the appropriate degree and type of disaggregation in empirical applications).

The symbol S represents the "scale" variable indexing the size of the decision-making unit's portfolio. In the case of an individual household, for example, the scale variable would typically be taken as wealth (net worth). If the economic unit has no liabilities – that is, if expected returns from investing do not exceed expected costs of borrowing by enough to overcome the unit's risk aversion – total assets and net worth will be identical. In the more general case where expected asset yields exceed expected liability costs by an amount sufficient to make borrowing desirable, the portfolio will have a determinate scale if the unit has aversion to risk and its marginal utility of wealth is nonincreasing. (See Bryant and Hendershott, 1970, pp. 5–6, for a more detailed discussion.) In principle, with the entire portfolio correctly specified, a balance-sheet constraint will hold such that S will be equal to the sum of the F_i^* (where liabilities are treated as negative assets).

In a true general-equilibrium approach to the theory, the scale variable S would be determined endogenously and simultaneously with all the other components of the portfolio. In practice, both theory and empirical applications have assumed that the scale variable can be taken as exogenously determined. For households, this assumption is rationalized by arguing that income can be taken as predetermined (that is, based on past decisions) and that the saving-consumption decision can be analyzed independently of decisions about the composition of the balance sheet (see, for example, the discussion in Tobin, 1961). For firms, an analogous rationalization is that profits can be taken as predetermined and that the dividend-retained earnings decision can be studied independently of balance-sheet decisions.

The vector of returns in the set of equations, the R_i, and the vector of associated risks, the σ_i, are in principle the expected risks and returns associated with each of the assets in the portfolio. In the case of liabilities, these vectors are expected borrowing costs and the expected risks associated with these borrowing costs. Each composite return or borrowing cost may have several components: for example, the nominal interest rate, the expected capital gain or loss, and the expected changes in relevant exchange rates (when assets or liabilities denominated in several different currencies are part of the portfolio). In principle, each of the return and risk variables appears in the equation for every asset and liability in the portfolio.

The vector of variables X_1, X_2, etc., represents all those other variables that are relevant to demand or supply. An example would be the volume of transactions of the decision-making unit. If a variable X_j influences the demand or supply for one particular asset or liability, it must (because of the balance-sheet constraint) influence demand or supply for at least one other asset or liability.

Suppose that one or more of the F_i^* represent a claim on, or liability to, economic units outside the country in which the portfolio holder is resident. There is then the potential for international capital flows – changes in assets or liabilities involving transactions between residents of two different countries.

As an example, consider the simplified balance sheet in Table 1. The assets and liabilities of a Japanese city bank are broken down into twelve main categories plus net worth. Five of these categories – LAf, Lf, Df, Bus, and Be\$ – represent claims on or liabilities to nonresidents of Japan, three of which are denominated in foreign currency. Changes in any of these five components of the bank's balance sheet give rise to an international capital flow as recorded in Japan's balance of payments. An analysis of any one of these types of capital flow along the lines of the portfolio approach requires the specification of a consistent set of stock asset-

TABLE 1   *Hypothetical Balance Sheet of a Japanese City Bank* (June 30, 1973; billions of yen)

Assets		Liabilities and Net Worth	
Liquid assets denominated in yen	LAd	Deposit liabilities (in yen) to Japanese residents	Dj
Liquid assets held abroad denominated in \$ and other foreign currencies	LAf	Deposit liabilities (in yen) to foreign residents	Df
Loans and discounts (in yen) to domestic customers	Ld	Borrowing (in yen) from Bank of Japan and other Japanese commercial banks	Bj
Loans and discounts (in yen) to foreign residents	Lf	Borrowing denominated in \$ from U.S. banks	Bus
Security holdings (in yen)	Sd	Borrowing denominated in \$ from Eurodollar market	Be\$
Other assets (in yen)	OA	Other liabilities (in yen)	OL
		Capital accounts	NW

demand and liability-supply equations for each of the separately identified components (in this illustration, twelve) of the bank's portfolio.[1]

Typically, though not exclusively, it is assumed that the demand/supply functions for the decision-making unit are linear homogeneous in the scale variable:

$$F_1^* = g_1(R_1, \ldots, R_n, \sigma_1, \ldots, \sigma_n, X_1/S, X_2/S, \ldots) S$$

$$F_2^* = g_2(R_1, \ldots, R_n, \sigma_1, \ldots, \sigma_n, X_1/S, X_2/S, \ldots) S$$

.

.

.

$$F_n^* = g_n(R_1, \ldots, R_n, \sigma_1, \ldots, \sigma_n, X_1/S, X_2/S, \ldots) S. \qquad (2)$$

This assumption implies that an increase of z per cent in the scale variable S and in the nonreturn "distribution" variables X will, other things equal, raise the desired stock demand or supply F_i^* by z per cent. This particular specification of the equations has several practical advantages; among other things, it makes it easier for the researcher to enforce the balance-sheet constraint in empirical estimation. It also makes it easy to see that the impact on desired quantities of increments in the scale variable is dependent on the levels of the risk and return variables, and the impact of changes in the return and risk variables is dependent on the level of the scale variable. *Flow* demands or supplies – changes in *stock* asset demands or liability supplies – are the time rate of change, or first difference, of the above equations:

$$\Delta F_i^* = g_i(\ldots) \Delta S + S_{-1} \Delta g_i(\ldots)$$

$$i = 1, \ldots, n. \qquad (2a)$$

One can see from this last set of equations the now accepted

---

[1] The balance sheet illustrated here is similar to the consolidated balance sheet for all Japanese city banks studied by Bryant and Hendershott (1970, 1972). For another illustration, see the balance sheets specified in Black's (1973, pp. 5–14) "Two-country model."

conclusion that international capital flows, seen in a portfolio-balance perspective, have both "continuing flow" and "stock adjustment" components. Given a once-for-all change in returns or risks, the existing-stock effect produces capital flows that are also once-for-all in nature (a reallocation of existing portfolios), while the continuing-flow effect persists indefinitely as long as the change in the scale variable is not zero.

To digress for a moment, I should point out that much of the early empirical literature on international capital flows suffered from a lack of familiarity with contemporary trends in monetary theory, and hence prominently featured a confused debate on "stocks versus flows." For example, many studies regressed capital flows on levels of interest rates and other variables such as the level of trade flows. The specification of these equations took the basic form:

$$\Delta F_i = f(R_1, R_2, \ldots, X_1, \ldots), \tag{3}$$

where R_1, R_2, etc., were the levels of nominal interest rates and X might be the flow of imports or exports. This so-called "flow theory" had no theoretical justification when carefully examined. It implied that desired equilibrium stocks of assets or liabilities depend on the sum (integral) of the current and all past values of the relevant return variables, and thus that elasticities with respect to these returns are infinite.[2] Similar difficulties arose from the assumed dependence of capital flows (that is, changes in stocks) on the flow, rather than on changes in the flow, of imports or exports.

An alternative "stock theory" employed in the earlier literature did not suffer from the serious theoretical defects of equation (3), but was still incomplete. In this latter case, capital flows were regressed on changes in the levels of interest rates and, for example, changes in trade flows:

$$\Delta F_i = g(\Delta R_1, \Delta R_2, \ldots, \Delta X_1, \ldots). \tag{4}$$

This formulation can be interpreted as approximating the exist-

---

2 Examples of equations with this incorrect specification were reported by Kenen (1963; see also 1973), Powrie (1964), Rhomberg (1964), Stein (1967), Laffer (1967), Arndt (1968), Hawkins (1968), and Prachowny (1969). Bell (1962) was also unclear on this issue. A similar problem was prevalent in many of the theoretical contributions to the internal–external-imbalance literature, where capital flows were made a function of the level of interest rates. Comments on this stock-vs.-flows controversy include Hendershott (1967a), Willett and Forte (1969), and Branson (1970).

ing-stock responses, but it disregards the continuing-flow effects.[3] On theoretical grounds, therefore, the specification in the set of equations (2) above is clearly preferable to either (3) or (4).

One further important addition must be made to the preceding general description of the portfolio approach. Responses to changes in the variables determining desired demand/supply are typically not immediate. Therefore, a complete theoretical framework requires the specification of a relationship between short- and long-run desired holdings of the financial instruments, where demand/supply in the short run – F_i^s – is expressed as a function of current and lagged values of all the determinants of long-run desired holdings.[4]

Such, in the briefest of terms, are the theoretical underpinnings of the portfolio approach to capital flows.[5] How faithfully is this framework implemented in actual empirical research?

There are several important respects, I am afraid, in which all of us who have been working in this area tend to be cheating when we claim to be applying a Markowitz–Tobin type of theory to international capital flows. For one thing, many studies are embarrassingly sloppy in defining *which* decision-making units are actually being studied and what their aggregate balance sheets look like. In principle, studies dealing with the changes in assets and liabilities that constitute international capital flows are concentrating on a subset of the F_i^* for some particular aggregate of economic units.[6] In many cases, authors have not even thought their way through the problems at a conceptual level, so that readers of the literature on capital flows encounter difficulty in determining who the transactors are, let alone what other assets or liabilities they hold in their portfolios. There are egregious examples of this sloppiness in much of the early literature (written before the perspective of the portfolio approach became widespread). And even in the better recent studies – for example, Branson and Hill (1971) or Miller and Whitman (1972) – there is little or no empha-

---

3 Bell (1962) estimated equations of this so-called "stock" form. Branson's early work (1968) also employed specifications of this type.

4 Branson (1968) was among the first to incorporate an awareness of the importance of lagged responses into empirical research on capital flows. See also Hendershott (1967a).

5 For more detailed discussions of this theoretical framework and its applicability to empirical research, see, for example, Bryant and Hendershott (1970), Branson and Hill (1971), and Miller and Whitman (1970a).

6 To continue the example given in the hypothetical balance sheet in Table 1, Bryant and Hendershott (1970, 1972) were concentrating on changes in the variable Bus, aggregated over all Japanese banks.

sis on careful delineation of the decision-making units and their balance sheets.[7]

For another thing, many studies simply omit a large number of the variables that the theory argues should be relevant. These omissions sometimes occur for valid reasons. To illustrate, it is typically quite difficult to include all the return variables in any given empirical regression because of collinearity among them. If the collinearity is serious enough, the researcher may argue that he is justified in omitting some of the variables.[8] In other instances, however, the researcher may not even attempt to collect all the relevant return variables and may not even bother to argue for their exclusion on grounds such as multicollinearity. (Of course, if he makes no explicit attempt to specify the appropriate aggregate balance sheet, the researcher does not even know in theory which return variables are relevant.) Even when a careful researcher excludes certain variables because of practical considerations, we are bound to be uneasy. We know from studies such as that of Brainard and Tobin (1968) that a researcher can get into serious trouble in financial model building if he forgets about balance-sheet constraints and omitted variables.

In another respect, the literature pays little more than lip service to the theory. Risk variables may be mentioned in introductory paragraphs, or in a section describing the theoretical framework that supposedly underpins the empirical research.[9] The actual empirical work, however, seldom includes variables purporting to represent risks. The lip service varies from study to study, but the most that any has done is attempt on an ad hoc basis to create a few proxy variables to represent risk effects.

As an example of such an attempt, consider the Miller and Whitman (1970a, 1972) papers. They argue that the riskiness of domestic assets in the United States is inversely correlated with the fluctuations of aggregate economic activity about its long-term trend (1970a, pp. 182–183). They further posit a relationship be-

---

7 See also section 3, where there is a discussion of the decision a prospective researcher must make about the appropriate degree and type of disaggregation of aggregative data.

8 Interest rates in Canada and the United States, for example, tend to be strongly correlated, and this difficulty plagues all the research on Canadian–U.S. capital flows. Eurodollar and U.S. interest rates move closely together. The problem of collinearity is still more severe among interest rates within a particular country; as is clear from equation (1), many of these play an important, separate role in the portfolio decisions of transactors resident within the country.

9 See Grubel (1968) for one of the earlier discussions of risk aversion as an explanation for the international diversification of portfolios.

tween the capital-control programs of the U.S. government and the riskiness to U.S. asset holders of foreign lending. Finally, they argue that:

. . . . since risk is a manifestation of imperfect information, the risk-estimate associated with an asset should diminish as information concerning the probable return on the asset increases. For this reason, we hypothesize that there has been a secular downward trend in σ_K (the risk of investing abroad), stemming from the increase in knowledge and communications, which symbolizes the gradual movement toward integration of international short-term capital markets since World War II (1972, p. 264).

In actual practice, what are Miller and Whitman's empirical proxies? They are deviations of U.S. GNP (not seasonally adjusted) from its trend regression line over the estimation period; a dummy variable equal to zero until the first quarter of 1965 and unity thereafter; and a simple time trend. The reader can judge for himself whether these variables seem convincing proxies for the risks discussed in portfolio theory.[10]

The portfolio-choice theory worked out by Markowitz and Tobin also argues that covariances among returns are important. The existing empirical literature on capital flows does not even bother to pay lip service to these covariances. They are typically not mentioned at all in the paragraphs of a study describing its theoretical framework.[11] (The same criticism also applies to the exposition above.)

I noted earlier that the returns and risks which are relevant in the theoretical specifications are *expected effective* returns and risks. Most of the existing empirical research sidesteps altogether the question of expectations and the formation of expectations. It simply uses observed values of the variables, making no effort to collect data on expectations or to formulate proxy variables thought to be correlated with the theoretically appropriate expected values. An outstanding exception is Black's (1973, pp. 22–27, 39–52) application of the rational-expectations hypothesis to exchange markets.

How important are such divergences between the theory believed to be relevant and the equations that are actually estimated? If we answer this question honestly, we have to admit that we do not know.

In all empirical work, it is true, there are serious problems in

---

10 Miller and Whitman pay more attention to this problem than most researchers, and therefore deserve *less* criticism than the average study.

11 Miller and Whitman show the covariance terms in their theoretical discussion but do not try to incorporate them in the empirical analysis.

obtaining empirical approximations for the theoretical constructs that the theory says are relevant. These problems in obtaining suitable empirical approximations may not be any more difficult in the area of international capital flows than in other areas of empirical research. Moreover, we often hear the argument – intended to be comforting – that the empirical equations actually estimated would not fit very well if the omitted considerations were really important. In other words, it is argued, we need not worry about the divergences between theory and empirical practice so long as our estimated equations fit the data reasonably well.

This line of reasoning, while it has some validity, does not comfort me very much. It reminds me of the story of a woman approaching a street corner who finds a man standing there snapping his fingers and looking all around. The woman asks the man: "Why are you standing on this street corner snapping your fingers?" The man replies, "I'm snapping my fingers to keep the tigers away." The woman, with a puzzled look on her face, asks the man: "You don't expect me to believe that story, do you?" And the man, continuing to snap his fingers while he looks over his shoulder, says: "You don't see any tigers hereabouts, do you?"

The argument that our estimated equations would not fit very well if we had failed to include all the explanatory variables that are quantitatively important is somewhat analogous to the man's contention that the tigers are staying away because he keeps snapping his fingers. For a high value of the coefficient of determination in a reported regression is not sufficient evidence that the regression actually represents a good approximation to economic behavior. Few researchers are rigorous in specifying a hypothesis and then testing that hypothesis alone. It is tempting to rerun equations to see what would happen if this variable were included or that variable omitted. By the end of such a process – which can easily, often inadvertently, turn into a fishing expedition – we ought to have greatly reduced confidence in the final results. Strictly speaking, the traditional tests of statistical significance are not valid. Certainly, it cannot be convincingly claimed that any considerations which are theoretically relevant but not embodied in the empirical estimates really are unimportant (for a similar view, see Rhomberg, 1972, pp. 314–318).

For purposes of comparison, Bryant and Hendershott (1972, pp. 227–236) reported a number of deliberately misspecified equations for the same set of data. Several of the misspecified equations had standard errors of estimate that compared favorably with those from more correctly specified equations. Yet the misspecified equations implied implausible or even ludicrous economic behavior. These results demonstrate all too clearly that a researcher may frequently be unable to discriminate, in purely statistical terms, between alternative imperfect specifications, and that fishing expeditions are virtually bound to be "successful" if one is satisfied with merely finding some specification that will give a good statistical fit for the sample period.

Another illustration of the gap between theory and empirical practice is furnished by the set of problems arising in connection with the scale variable. There are, of course, enormous headaches involved in obtaining adequate data either for the international capital flows themselves or for an appropriate scale variable. Lack of adequate data forces rather drastic compromises. One possible compromise is to omit the scale variable altogether from the estimated equations. This, for example, is the route chosen by Branson and Hill (1971, pp. 27ff.) in their study of capital movements among OECD countries. Whatever the empirical consequences of this assumption, omission of the scale variable clearly guts the theory. Another compromise is to make some rather strong arbitrary assumptions about the scale variable. An example here would be the studies by Miller and Whitman (1970b, 1972) of short-term capital flows in the U.S. balance of payments. Their theory calls not only for a scale variable representing the net worth of economic units resident in the United States, but also for a scale variable representing the aggregate net worth of foreigners. Data for the latter scale variable are of course impossible to obtain in practice. It is difficult even to construct a weighted average of foreign GNPs to serve as a proxy. Miller and Whitman therefore resort to an arbitrary assumption that the ratio of the foreign scale variable to the domestic scale variable is constant over the period of their study. It is impossible to justify this assumption on the basis of theory, and it even stretches the imagination a bit to believe the ratio was approximately constant in practice.

Even if data are available for the scale variable, the assumption of linear homogeneity – see equation (2) above – cannot be justified on the basis of the portfolio-balance theory per se.[12] Tests of this homogeneity assumption, moreover, are seldom attempted. Branson and Hill (1971) did make an effort to allow for the possibility of nonhomogeneity in their empirical specification for certain capital flows in the U.S. balance of payments. I suspect, however, that, in the few equations in their study where there is an

---

12 For a more extended discussion of this point, see Bryant and Hendershott (1970, p. 7). See also Norman Miller's discussion of this point in his comments in this volume.

apparently significant departure from homogeneity (see, for example, the equation on p. 18 for U.S. short-term liabilities to foreigners), other factors are at work in the equations and the empirical estimates do not represent a good test of the homogeneity assumption. Bryant and Hendershott (1972, pp. 224–225) made an explicit attempt to test this assumption within the context of a nonlinear regression program. In effect, they estimated an equation of the following form:

$$F_i^s = g_i(\dots) S^\phi. \tag{5}$$

Instead of assuming that the parameter ϕ was equal to unity, they allowed the parameter to take on any positive value. In fact, the estimate of ϕ was close to unity, lending some apparent support to the use of the homogeneity assumption. But this isolated test is hardly conclusive evidence about the general applicability of the assumption.

Another deficiency of the specifications used in the empirical literature is their failure adequately to incorporate the effects of exchange-rate changes. Here, again, most studies pay lip service to the importance of exchange rates, while doing little, if anything, to take these effects into account. The most careful and interesting work of which I am aware has been done by Black (1973) and by Helliwell and his colleagues (Helliwell, *et al.*, 1971; Helliwell and Maxwell, 1972, 1974).[13] A distinguishing feature of these studies is the endogenous determination of spot and forward exchange rates within a model that specifies all the demands and supplies for foreign exchange. This is a big improvement over specifications that either ignore exchange rates altogether or include them simply as an exogenous element in the return variables entered on the right-hand side of the equation.

In view of the international monetary upheavals of the 1971–73 period, which produced dramatic alterations in exchange regimes, an explicit consideration of exchange rates in research on international capital flows has become even more important. Indeed, now that a majority of major exchange rates are floating subject to management via official intervention, researchers studying capital flows have no reasonable alternative: they must, by a quantum jump, increase the sophistication with which they handle this set of problems.

---

13 For earlier studies that recognized the importance of the problem, see Stein (1965) and Black (1968). Readers especially interested in the relationships between capital flows and exchange rates should also consult Stoll (1968) and Kesselman (1971). Dooley (1974) has recently completed a paper that I have not yet had time to study carefully.

To make matters still more difficult, basic questions of research strategy are involved for those who in their empirical work try to tackle the capital account in the balance of payments as a whole. The traditional approach (see, for example, Kwack, 1971a, 1971b, or Branson and Hill, 1971) has been to estimate separate equations for each component of the capital account other than the change in official reserves, with the exchange rate assumed to be determined exogenously. The change in reserves (the official settlements balance) is then derived from the balance-of-payments identity. Even with an exchange regime of the Bretton Woods type, this approach had unsatisfactory features.[14] With widespread floating of exchange rates, the rationale for this traditional approach has been seriously undermined.

The line of attack followed in the papers of Helliwell and his various collaborators may turn out to be more promising. This alternative approach involves direct specification of one or more equations describing the intervention behavior of monetary authorities in the exchange market. (Looked at from another perspective, these equations can be construed as modeling the official demand for reserves.) Such equations, taken together with current-account and certain capital-account net demands for foreign exchange, simultaneously determine the exchange rate and the change in official reserves. The residual item derived from the balance-of-payments identity is then that part of net capital flows not already explicitly accounted for by behavioral equations. The strength of this approach lies in its possibilities for the modeling of many alternative exchange regimes (including, of course, managed floating) and for the specification of official exchange-market intervention as an important *endogenous* component of the model.

Note, however, that even this latter approach runs into great difficulty in circumstances of widespread floating. The Canadian models of Helliwell and his colleagues could reasonably use the Canadian dollar/U.S. dollar cross rate as "the exchange rate" so long as any change in the Canadian dollar vis-à-vis the United

14 Within the Bretton Woods exchange margins, spot exchange rates were endogenous variables; forward exchange rates were not even constrained by margins. Moreover, movements of both spot and forward rates had important effects on exchange-rate expectations (see, for example, White, 1963), which in turn were influential determinants of capital flows (especially at times when the ability or willingness of governments to maintain the spot margins were suspect). To complete the circle, capital flows often triggered changes in the spot margins. Hence, especially over some longer time period, there were many elements of artificiality in treating exchange rates as exogenously determined outside one's model of the capital account.

States also involved a similar change against third currencies. With widespread floating, no single cross rate – even for a country such as Canada – can serve as an adequate proxy for "the exchange rate." One has no choice but to resort to concepts such as the "effective exchange rate" and attempt to approximate them empirically with various weighted averages. Yet this path runs right through the middle of the familiar swamp of index-number problems. Difficulties of this sort are particularly severe when specifying the exchange regime for a model of the U.S. balance of payments.

My main purpose here has been to point out some respects in which the empirical literature relies on specifications that tend to be theoretically invalid or inappropriate. Still another important illustration is the failure of the literature to incorporate the effects of governmental restrictions on international capital flows. None of the studies with which I am familiar, with the exception of Bryant and Hendershott (1970, 1972), has even tried to cope with this problem when setting out the theoretical framework. Instead, researchers have done something ad hoc when it comes time actually to run a regression. Typically, simple off-on dummy variables are inserted ad hoc into the empirical regressions, with no attempt to blend the underlying theory of the capital flows with the governmental restrictions that prevent private individuals from carrying out their portfolio decisions.[15] Needless to say, the form of such dummy variables, which is usually highly arbitrary, forces a particular (arbitrary) interpretation of the effectiveness of the capital controls.

As an example, consider the equation reported in Branson and Hill (1971, pp. 13–15) for changes in short-term claims of U.S. residents on foreigners:

$$\Delta C_t^s = f \text{ (U.S. wealth variable, U.S. interest rate, U.K. interest}$$
$$\text{rate, U.S. merchandise exports) + seasonal dummies}$$
$$- 392\,IET1 - 607\,DF1 - 213\,DF2.$$

In this equation, $IET1$, $DF1$, and $DF2$ are all dummy variables. Branson and Hill explain:

Since the target of the [U.S. capital control] programs is the *stock* of outstanding claims, we would expect the annual tightening of the programs to be associated with continuing inflows, or reduced outflows, of capital. Thus we have added two dummy variables to the analysis to reflect the programs. The first, $DF1$, is set

15 For a useful summary of the limited work that has been done in this area, see Cheng (1973). See also Kwack (1973), Cooper (1965), Herring and Willett (1972), Lindert (1971).

to unity in 1965I–1965III and zero elsewhere, reflecting the fact that the largest change in the program occurred with its initial imposition. A second dummy, *DF2*, is set to zero through 1965III, and unity from 1965IV on to reflect the continued tightening of the programs. These variables may be crude, but exact quantification of increases in pressure through "moral suasion" and a change from voluntary to mandatory is impossible.

The *IET* dummy is 1.0 in 1963III. This dummy was added because of a large unexplained (the *IET* applied only to long-term capital) residual in that quarter, and effectively drops that observation from the regression data.

As Branson and Hill acknowledge, the Interest Equalization Tax did not even apply to the capital flows explained by their equation, so that their IET dummy variable serves only to throw out an awkward observation; it certainly does not indicate that the Interest Equalization Tax reduced U.S. short-term claims on foreigners by $392 million in the third quarter of 1963. The other two dummy variables, if taken at face value, suggest that the U.S. Voluntary Foreign Credit Restraint (VFCR) program reduced the flow of U.S. short-term lending to foreigners by $607 million (compared with what it otherwise would have been) in each of the first three quarters of 1965, and in each quarter thereafter reduced the flow by $213 million.

The arbitrary specification of the impacts of the VFCR program by Branson and Hill may be contrasted with an equally arbitrary – and incompatible – specification in the Miller and Whitman studies of the same capital flow. As noted above, Miller and Whitman employ a dummy variable equal to zero through the first quarter of 1965 and equal to unity in each quarter thereafter. They also employ a "partial adjustment" specification in an effort to capture lagged responses, which, inter alia, imposes upon their VFCR dummy variable the same geometrically decaying lag pattern forced on all other explanatory variables in their equation. Since Miller and Whitman estimate a low (0.25) "speed of adjustment" coefficient in their preferred equation (1972, pp. 272–278), their results taken at face value suggest that the restraining effects of the VFCR program on U.S. short-term lending to foreigners were still gradually building up by the first quarter of 1966 and were still having only two-thirds of their eventual impact.

To put the point mildly, neither the estimates – more precisely, the assumptions – of Branson and Hill nor those of Miller and Whitman inspire confidence as reliable indications of the impacts of the VFCR program.[16]

If government controls affect rates of return or other variables

---

16 Yet the dummy variables in *both* the Branson–Hill and Miller–Whitman studies are highly significant by the customary statistical tests!

in a way that can be specified more or less exactly, it is preferable to attempt to adjust the rate of return directly to take these effects into account. For example, in studying purchases of foreign securities by U.S. residents or long-term lending by U.S. banks to foreigners in the 1963–73 period, one can add the rate of the Interest Equalization Tax directly to the appropriate rates of return used in the regression. Similar quantitative adjustments can be made if negative interest charges or reserve requirements are imposed on bank liabilities.

But usually the problem is more complicated. It is worst of all when the governmental restraint or stimulus is carried out purely by administrative guidance (commonly known by such euphemisms as jaw-boning, ear-stroking, threatening to use the big club in the closet, etc.). One suggestion made by Bryant and Hendershott (1970) is that, except in cases where controls are known to be strictly binding on all economic units, the researcher can assume that the tightening or relaxation of controls will reduce or increase, but not suppress altogether, the response of desired quantities to changes in their economic determinants. For a particular capital flow, this view can be represented formally in the following way:

$$F_i = \alpha F_i^s \tag{6}$$

$$\alpha = h(C_1, C_2, C_3, \dots), \tag{7}$$

where F_i is the observed quantity of asset demand or liability supply, and, as before, F_i^s is short-run desired demand. In this formulation, alpha would equal unity when the controls are absent or not binding at all, and would be less than unity when the controls keep the observed quantity below the desired quantity. In the case of controls that governments use to stimulate capital flows, alpha could take on values greater than unity. This treatment of the effects of capital controls requires the researcher to construct variables – C_1, C_2, etc. – that reflect changes in the intensity of the different controls.[17] This is, of course, an extremely difficult task. But it has the merit of forcing the researcher to try to specify explicitly how the controls have their impacts and how the intensity of the controls varies over the period of the study – something that

---

17 For example, Bryant and Hendershott (1970, pp. 60–62) attempted to construct a variable to measure the effects of the U.S. VFCR program. See Bryant and Hendershott (1972, pp. 228–230) for comparisons of alternative specifications (including the use of an off-on dummy variable).

should be attempted in any case.[18] This type of specification also tends to force the researcher to use nonlinear estimation techniques. These techniques involve added expense and inconvenience, but the costs may not be too high if the alternative is the use of ad hoc dummy variables that do nothing more than alter the constant term in regression equations.

The use of capital controls has been much more the rule than the exception throughout the postwar period. For a survey of countries' practices, see, for example, Mills (1968, 1972, 1973a) or the annual reports of the IMF on exchange restrictions; see also Johnson (1973). Moreover, governments have been increasingly prone to utilize these controls in recent years. Thus, despite the practice in the literature so far, it is simply not possible to downplay the importance of these controls and still do valid empirical research on the capital accounts of most countries' balances of payments.

I have said little up to this point about estimation problems per se, and for a good reason: no estimation technique, however powerful or sophisticated, can produce satisfactory empirical results if the theoretical specification itself is inappropriate. Moreover, inadequate theory or faulty empirical approximations of theoretical constructs are the most frequent causes of estimation difficulties (e.g., serial correlation of the residuals).

Nonetheless, it is probably useful here to remind the reader that the simultaneous-equations problem – already referred to implicitly in the discussion of exchange rates – is an important complication in empirical research on capital flows. Turn back for a moment to the set of equations (1), in which the various F_i depend on the vector of rates of return, the R_i. In principle, this causation is not just one-way; the return R_j on some financial instrument j will be determined by all the demands and supplies for j, including the particular demand or supply F_j of the transactor whose portfolio is specified in (1). The more important the particular economic unit being studied in relation to the market for j – and, a fortiori, if one is studying a large aggregation of units – the less valid will it be to estimate the influence of R_j on F_j while ignoring the simultaneous influence of F_j on R_j.

For many purposes, therefore, and especially in macroeconomic studies, it may be necessary to specify a theoretical model in which *both* F_j and R_j appear as endogenous variables. To be useful in quantitative research, of course, such a model must be well

18 Perhaps this point should be put even more strongly: A researcher has no business applying econometric techniques to the data *until* such an attempt has been made!

enough articulated to yield explicit equation specifications that can be empirically tested.

Stein (1965) was one of the first to stress the need for a simultaneous-equations approach in the context of international capital flows. For additional references, see Black (1968), Miller and Whitman (1970b), Bryant and Hendershott (1970, Appendix A), Kouri and Porter (1974), Herring (1973), and Norman Miller's comments in this volume. For two examples of papers that derive reduced-form equations from a more complete model, thus solving out an endogenous variable and removing one source of simultaneous-equations bias, see Kouri and Porter (1974) and Black (1973).

3. SOME UNRESOLVED QUESTIONS OF STRATEGY FOR FUTURE RESEARCH

As the preceding discussion indicates, there is no shortage of inadequacies in the existing literature to which current and future researchers, aspiring to remedy deficiencies in the work of their predecessors, can address themselves. Quite the contrary: there is a surfeit of opportunities, and only a shaky foundation of existing knowledge on which to build.

To make matters still more difficult for the prospective researcher, he must grapple at the outset with several major questions of research strategy. At present, we simply do not know enough even to give sound advice on the most appropriate resolution of these questions of strategy. No wonder, then, that the choice of research topics and methods of attack cannot yet be narrowed down to a small range of possibilities which can confidently be declared to have the highest payoff for future research.

One of the most important strategic questions facing the prospective researcher is the degree to which he should pursue a "structural," as contrasted with a "reduced form," approach. The ramifications of this initial choice may be particularly important if he aspires to carry out research relevant to government policy decisions.

To see why this may be so, the reader should ask himself how far existing empirical research in this area carries us toward the objective of improving the formulation of economic policy. In an open economy, the effects of monetary policy on capital flows may be so important that they alone determine whether or not monetary policy can be successful in facilitating the attainment of desired levels of real activity, employment, and prices. Yet the bulk of the empirical research surveyed in this paper does not allow us to trace the impacts of a change in a policy instrument (e.g., an open-market sale of securities by the central bank) all the way through the financial and real sectors of the economy to the ultimate effects on the balance of payments, domestic activity, and the price level. Typically, the estimated equations for capital flows contain explanatory variables – for example, interest rates or activity variables – that are rather far removed in the chain of causation from the policy instruments themselves. Before we can predict the impact of changes in policy instruments on capital flows, therefore, we must predict their impact on the explanatory variables in the estimated equations. Since this prediction is very difficult (the relevant empirical research being either nonexistent or at a relatively primitive stage), the estimated equations for capital flows by themselves are of limited help to policymakers.

Appreciation of this dilemma has led some researchers to attempt to estimate "reduced form" equations, with policy instruments appearing explicitly in the estimated equations as regressors. If successful, such an approach would obviate the need for an elaborate system of structural equations or the full-scale econometric models that would otherwise be required.

Interesting work along these lines has been done recently at the IMF by Pentti Kouri, Michael Porter, and Victor Argy (see Kouri and Porter, 1972, 1974; Porter, 1972; Argy and Kouri, 1972; and Kouri, 1973). They begin with a simplified portfolio-adjustment model focused on aggregative economic behavior in a small open economy. By solving out the domestic interest rate, they are left with an estimating equation that relates capital flows to various monetary-policy variables, the current account in the country's balance of payments, the change in domestic income, and the change in a foreign interest rate. Foreign variables, in particular foreign interest rates, are assumed to be exogenous; that is, the country is assumed to be small enough in relation to the rest of the world so that foreign monetary conditions and real activity can be taken as independent of monetary conditions and activity in the country being studied. As noted above, this research at the IMF has produced some interesting empirical regressions for capital flows in the balances of payments of Germany, Italy, the Netherlands, and Australia.

From the point of view of policy, however, it can be argued that equations of the type estimated by Kouri and Porter – even if they turn out to be reliable relationships – may not get us much further than the traditional equations in the literature that purport to be closer to "structural" relationships. In order to use the empirical results of Branson and Hill, Kwack, or Miller and Whitman to forecast the impacts of monetary policy on capital-flow aggregates, separate predictions of domestic activity and domestic interest rates are required, as well as predictions of foreign explanatory variables. The equations of Kouri and Porter require separate predictions of foreign variables, domestic activity, and the current account in the balance of payments. The practical difference between the two approaches in their present incarnations depends, then, on whether one is in a better position to predict the current account in the balance of payments or domestic rates of return. The record of explaining and forecasting changes in the current-account balance is not especially good, as we know from the research surveyed elsewhere in this volume by Magee, Stern, and Klein. Another drawback of the Kouri–Porter approach that limits its usefulness in many circumstances is its heavy reliance on the small-country assumption. Without an explicit relaxation of this assumption, for example, the approach could not be applied to the United States.

Further work needs to be done along the lines pursued by Kouri and Porter before we can confidently judge the relative merits of this approach and its usefulness to policymakers. But this work, as well as recent empirical studies that take the "monetary" approach to the balance of payments as their starting point (see section 1), does serve to emphasize the need for prospective researchers to be more self-conscious about their research objectives. In particular, they should carefully consider the balance they want to strike between analyzing behavioral, structural relationships and finding a reduced-form shortcut to predicting the effects of policy instruments on ultimate target variables.

The choice of emphasis between structural and reduced-form approaches would pose no problem, of course, if one could be confident of the success and reliability of a reduced-form approach. With such a happy state of affairs, those primarily interested in the structural relationships underlying economic behavior would focus their efforts on those relationships, while everyone else would clearly choose the shortcut of going directly to the reduced forms. But, in practice, there is substantial uncertainty as to whether reliable shortcuts actually exist. Unfortunately, in other words, it is still essentially a matter of personal hunch and judgment – not of verifiable fact – whether reliable predictions of the effects of policy instruments on target variables can be made without first spelling out the underlying structural models.

My own personal bias is to doubt the existence of both free lunches and reliable shortcuts. Yet I feel sure that a full-blown "structuralist" approach to the empirical study of international capital flows will take years, if not decades, to come to real fruition. Important policy decisions will continue to be made in the meantime – for the most part, in a glass darkly. Under the circumstances, it seems fully justifiable – at least for a further exploratory period lasting several years – to have available resources dispersed all along the spectrum from the structural microeconomic extreme to the other extreme of highly aggregative reduced-form equations.

Regardless of the balance he strikes between a structural and a reduced-form approach, but especially if he is inclined to emphasize structural relationships, a researcher in this area must resolve another major question of strategy at the outset of his work: What is the appropriate degree and type of disaggregation?[19] As in the preceding case, the researcher's answer will partly depend on the specific objectives of his research; if he is interested in the behavior of capital flows generated by commercial banks, for example, he must obviously disaggregate the capital-flow data sufficiently to eliminate changes in the assets and liabilities of nonbanks. But suppose his primary objective is to obtain, for a given country, predictions of the capital account as a whole. At what point do the additional costs associated with further disaggregation come to outweigh the incremental benefits (if such benefits actually materialize) of more precise and reliable predictions?[20]

The question of the appropriate *degree* of disaggregation turns out, in practice, to be inseparable from decisions about the appropriate *type* of disaggregation. There are three main conceptual possibilities: disaggregation by transactor (type of decision-making unit), by geographical region (origin or destination of the capital flows), or by instrument (characteristics of the assets or liabilities being exchanged).

A moment's recollection will make it evident that the theoretical framework spelled out at the beginning of section 2 presupposes *all three* types of disaggregation, since it assumes the existence of detailed data on the balance sheets and income accounts of in-

---

19 Leamer and Stern (1972) discuss this question in their survey of the problems in the theory and empirical estimation of international capital movements. See also Leamer and Stern (1970).

20 Contrast, for example, the approaches of Kwack (1971a, 1971b), Kwack and Schink (1972), and Herring (1973), who wish to produce estimates for the U.S. capital account as a whole. Herring employs a single equation for the entire capital account (including U.S. government capital and direct investment). Kwack's model is the most disaggregated of any that deal with the entire capital account.

dividual economic units. In practice, researchers in this area seldom can acquire such data for individual economic units. And, to repeat, even if these data were available, the researcher's objective will often be to analyze or predict capital flows at a more aggregative level. To make his research germane to policy decisions, his conclusions must certainly have a bearing on aggregative data. Hence the familiar problem of all empirical research: the microtheory of individual behavior has to be supplemented with numerous additional assumptions and questionable approximations before it is possible to carry out any empirical testing at all.

When data are aggregated over a set of relatively homogeneous economic units, one can hope that resort to an aggregate function taking the same general form as the individual functions will not introduce an unacceptably high degree of aggregation bias. The more heterogeneous the individual economic units and the more heterogeneous the economic environments in which they operate, however, the less confidently one can hold to such a hope.

There is a strong rationale for some significant disaggregation of aggregative data by type of decision-making unit. Commercial banks, nonbank financial institutions, nonfinancial corporations, government agencies, and households, for example, all face different constraints and regulatory environments. Differences in their asset preferences or in other aspects of their economic behavior may be quite important. Moreover, some disaggregation by type of transactor may be essential if one is to match data for capital flows with appropriate data for the relevant economic determinants (e.g., the scale variable S).

Some of the greatest disparities among economic units and economic environments are those created by or embodied in national political boundaries. Certainly, the nature and timing of national economic policies – to take the most pertinent example, policies intended directly to influence international capital flows – differ markedly across countries. Even in instances where it is less difficult to swallow one's doubts about the heterogeneity of environments across countries, there are no easy, clearly appropriate ways to consolidate economic conditions across a group of countries into a few summary variables.[21] These considerations argue strongly for some significant degree of disaggregation by geographical region.

21 For example, in the study of any given capital flow, what weights should be used to construct weighted-average variables for GNP, or monetary aggregates, or short-term interest rates in the countries of the European Economic Community? We are back again in the swamp of index-number problems as soon as we ask such questions.

Some data on international capital flows are collected by type of financial instrument, with little or no cross-classification by type of transactor or geographical region. Moreover, *published* data for most countries tend to be in this format. Thus the data may well satisfy a researcher's need, based on his theoretical framework, for some disaggregation along this third line.

Even if adequate data were available to allow a significant degree of disaggregation along all three lines simultaneously (typically they are not), researchers in this area would still be faced with an enormously difficult judgment. To put the matter bluntly, the requirements of theory and the dictates of practicality conflict violently. And I know of no easy generalizations with which to help or comfort those who must make the awkward compromises.[22]

The problem of the availability and reliability of data deserves a comment in its own right. Here, too, prospective researchers must resolve for themselves a strategic question – how much effort to devote to data collection per se. There is, of course, the inevitable difficulty that "whatever we measure is never quite the thing that represents, or closely corresponds to, the theoretical concept of our theories" (Machlup's "Introduction," in Machlup, *et al.*, eds., 1972). Nonetheless, many researchers may lean too heavily on this fact of life as a rationalization for avoiding the effort to acquire institutional knowledge and for devoting as little time as possible to the tedious job of examining carefully all potential sources of data. Yet innovative, diligent searching can often turn up information that will either greatly improve a data set or, alternatively, prevent an investigator from drawing unwarranted inferences from statistics that purport to measure one thing and actually measure something else.[23]

Careful scrutiny and compilation of the data are especially important in the field of international capital flows because far too few data are available, and much of what is available is of poor quality. Any researcher who has used balance-of-payments data for the United States in an empirical study but has not read the report of the Bernstein Committee (Review Committee, 1965)

---

22 As suggested earlier, it is the "structural" purist who most agonizes over these inevitable compromises. The pure monetarist who aspires to explain the entire balance of payments with a single reduced-form equation may feel he has hurdled the dilemma entirely. Everyone else must suffer to a greater or lesser degree.
23 Compare Machlup's "grumble" (1972, p. 4): "Too often researchers do not question the meanings of the terms with which they work; they are diving into piles of third-rate statistical data which they believe, or assume, to be suitable proxies for the vague or ambiguous concepts with which their supposedly first-rate models are furnished."

should be put in a straitjacket until he has done so – perhaps twice.[24] For a study that discusses data problems in some detail and attempts to construct an integrated matrix of capital flows across individual countries for the 1950–54 period, see Michael (1971). Smith's (1967) paper also highlights problems with the consistency and reliability of the data. For examples of serious data problems in the context of an empirical study, see the discussion in Bryant and Hendershott (1970, Appendices B and C).

There is more than a little doubt in my mind whether empirical research on international capital flows *can* make great progress in the future in the absence of substantial improvement in the availability and quality of the basic data. In fact, it would be surprising if this were not so. No one has yet discovered a way to squeeze blood out of a turnip.

4.   CONCLUDING COMMENT: HOW FAR DOES EXISTING
EMPIRICAL KNOWLEDGE TAKE US?

One way to assess the empirical research in the area surveyed by this paper is to ask: How much do we know now that we did not know fifteen years ago? My summary answer to this question is that we do have some useful knowledge we did not have then, but we still know much less than we need or would like to know.

One thing about which we have definitely learned something is the responsiveness of international capital flows to changes in monetary conditions. There is ample evidence from a number of recent studies that capital flows are quite interest elastic. Representative results may be found in Branson and Hill (1971), Kwack's research (see Kwack and Schink, 1972), the studies of Miller and Whitman (1970b, 1972), those by Bryant and Hendershott (1972), Helliwell's work on Canadian capital flows (see Helliwell and Maxwell, 1972), Black's (1973) recent work, and Herring's (1973) Ph.D. dissertation.

The evidence from these recent studies contrasts sharply with the conclusions drawn from some of the earliest research in this area. Neither Bell (1962) nor Kenen (1963), for example, thought that changes in interest rates would produce sizable impacts on the capital account (see also Cohen, 1963). Today, as Kenen notes in the introduction to his 1973 monograph, there tends to be little

---

24 Another useful document, which contains some of the details (including reporting forms) of how U.S. data on international capital flows are collected and processed, is the guide to international financial statistics compiled by the Federal Reserve Bank of Atlanta (1972).

dispute: "Scholars and practitioners alike are thoroughly persuaded that monetary policy has an immediate, pervasive effect on private capital movements" (1973, p. 3).

Branson and Hill, and Kwack, have carried their work far enough to be able to put forward estimates of the total net effect on the overall U.S. balance of payments of a change in relative monetary conditions in the United States and abroad.[25] Herring (1973), following the lead of Branson and Hill, has attempted the ambitious objective of estimating equations for both interest rates and the net capital account for six major industrial countries. In his concluding chapter, Herring has pulled these estimates together so as to describe, albeit very roughly, the linkages that (partially) integrate national financial markets into the beginnings of a world market for money and capital.[26] Although all these estimates are subject to the problems noted in section 2, and hence probably have very large margins of error, they nonetheless represent the best quantitative evidence we have so far on the interrelationships between international capital flows and national monetary conditions.

The evidence is also fairly strong that many individual capital flows are associated with trade flows of one sort or another. Lending by banks or intercompany credits often have an important element of trade financing. For examples, note the relationship between Japanese imports and borrowing by Japanese banks from the United States studied by Bryant and Hendershott (1970,

25 For an overview of Kwack's quantitative results, see Kwack and Schink (1972, especially pp. 18–27). For an overview of the quantitative results for the United States in Branson and Hill (1971), see the table of stock-shift multipliers on page 25 and the associated discussion in the text. The following quotation indicates the order of magnitude of the Branson-Hill estimated effects on the net financial private capital account (KA) as a whole: "For example, a one-point increase in the U.S. short-term rate, by itself, will temporarily reduce the KA deficit (or increase the surplus) by a one-time stock-shift effect of $2.6 billion over three quarters. With assets growing at about 7 percent per year, this would give a continuing improvement in the KA balance equal initially to $180 million at an annual rate. But if the Eurodollar rate adjusts point-for-point to movements in the U.S. rate, the total coefficient of a one-point change in the U.S. rate on KA is $1.5 (= 2.6−1.1) billion, while the effect of a one-point change in the Eurodollar rate relative to the U.S. rate is $1.1 billion. Thus in this case the one-point increase in the U.S. bill rate would give a $1.5 billion net stock-shift effect over three quarters, with an initial continuing-flow effect of about $77 million at an annual rate. If the U.S. bill rate increase was accompanied by an increase in velocity of about 0.1, not unreasonable in U.S. experience, another $602 million would be added to the stock-shift effect, and $42 million to the initial level of the continuing-flow." For a discussion of how such results might be used for projections of the capital account, see Branson (1970, pp. 253–257); note, however, that the empirical results used in this 1970 article were superseded by the later estimates in Branson and Hill (1971).

26 Herring estimated a single, aggregative equation for the capital account as a whole (for the United States as well as for each other country). An overview of his results can be found in Chap. 7, pp. 287–315; see especially Tables 7.4 and 7.5.

1972), or the dependence of several components of the U.S. capital account on trade flows or the trade balance in Kwack's model (Kwack and Schink, 1972). On the subject of the relationship between capital movements and trade flows, see also Hansen (1961).

We know rather less about the relationships between capital flows and fluctuations in growth and business activity. It is true that variables representing the level of, or fluctuations in, business activity appear in many of the empirical equations that have been estimated. But the interpretation of these results is often strained. For example, as noted above, Miller and Whitman regard deviations from trend in business activity as a proxy for risk. Others interpret real activity variables as saying something about the demand for money (Kouri and Porter, 1974). In my view, it may be some time before we know how to interpret the correlations that have been observed in the empirical work already done.

I have already stressed in section 2 the failure of equation specifications adequately to incorporate the effects of exchange-rate changes. It is hardly surprising, therefore, that we have a very imperfect understanding of the relationships between capital flows, spot and forward exchange rates, and exchange-rate expectations. What knowledge we do have is mostly qualitative and tends to come, not from empirical research, but from the exploration of theoretical models. The main exceptions to this generalization, as already noted, are Black (1973) and Helliwell and his collaborators (Helliwell, *et al.*, 1971; Helliwell and Maxwell, 1972).[27]

I am even less confident that we have useful knowledge about the time patterns of the various responses of capital flows to their economic determinants. The estimation of lagged responses is still very difficult and problematical in all empirical research. But it is a fair judgment on the vast majority of work done so far on international capital flows to call it unsophisticated relative to advanced empirical work in other areas. The existing studies often resort to crude techniques, such as the inclusion of the lagged dependent variable in the equation.[28] The potential pitfalls associated with this formulation are notorious.[29] Quite apart from problems of statistical bias, inclusion of the lagged dependent variable can generate superficially plausible results even though the basic economic relationship is seriously misspecified. (In an extreme case, lagged values of a dependent variable – if it is a rather smooth

27 Black's analysis of and inferences about private speculative behavior (1973, pp. 39–52) are especially interesting. He concludes that "the flexible exchange markets of 1936 to 1938 were not destabilizing. In most cases, they facilitated the response of participants in the markets to the destabilizing political events of the period" (p. 53).

28 See, for example, Arndt, 1968, and the Miller and Whitman studies.

29 For a discussion of the state of the art as of 1966, see Griliches's useful survey (1967).

economic time series – can alone "explain" the dependent variable quite well, suggesting a "significant" and slow speed of adjustment even when the equation contains no theoretically appropriate variable to which the dependent variable is allegedly adjusting.)[30] In other cases, researchers have made use of polynomial interpolation techniques, but again in ways that are rather ad hoc and that do not inspire much confidence in the results.[31]

We are in the poorest position of all to appraise the effects of governmental restrictions on capital flows, for two reasons. First, as discussed in section 2, the techniques used to study capital flows directly subject to governmental restraints are inadequate. We therefore know little about the quantitative impacts of the restraints, even on those specific capital flows at which the restraints are aimed. Second, and especially important when we are interested in the *net* effects of restrictions on a country's capital account or balance of payments as a whole, we know virtually nothing about the quantitative impacts of the controls on capital flows *other than those at which the controls are aimed.* Substitutions or "leakages" of funds through noncontrolled channels are typically an important phenomenon – too important to be safely ignored. Yet, by and large, they have been ignored in the empirical literature so far.[32]

These gaps in what we know about the effects of capital controls would not be troublesome if the use of controls were more the exception than the rule, or even if the controls were seldom varied in intensity. As noted earlier, however, this is not the case, and the deficiencies in our knowledge are serious.

---

30 Bryant and Hendershott (1972) give some illustrations of the consequences of misspecification of equations that include a lagged dependent variable.

31 Branson's early work (1968), for example, made extensive use of the polynomial interpolation technique developed by Shirley Almon.

32 Consider the following examples pertaining to the effects of capital restrictions imposed by the U.S. government. Because of the Interest Equalization Tax (IET), foreigners purchased foreign securities issued outside the United States that otherwise would have been issued in New York and bought by U.S. residents. Similarly, because of the program administered for direct investors by the Commerce Department Office of Foreign Direct Investments (OFDI), foreigners purchased a greatly increased volume of securities issued outside the United States by U.S. direct investors; absent the OFDI program, direct investors would probably have borrowed more from U.S. residents. But to what extent did foreign investors therefore buy fewer U.S. securities than they otherwise would have purchased? (There were, of course, no controls requiring foreigners not to reduce the rate at which they otherwise would have accumulated such securities.) Branson and Hill (1971, pp. 19–20) do not even bother to test for this possibility in their equation for U.S. long-term liabilities to foreigners. Analogous problems arise in connection with the Voluntary Foreign Credit Restraint (VFCR) Program restraining U.S. banks. Branson and Hill, and Kwack, both include a dummy variable in their equations explaining U.S. bank loans to foreign residents but do not discuss the possibility that foreigners reduced their deposits in U.S. banks (compared with what they otherwise would have been) as an indirect result of the VFCR program.

Although the empirical research in this area has produced limited but useful additions to our knowledge, it has not carried us very far toward the objective of improving the formulation of economic policy, and monetary policy in particular.[33] It is all very well, for example, to note that capital flows are sensitive to changes in interest rates, so that monetary policy can have a powerful influence on private capital movements. But can this influence and the other ways in which economic policies help to determine capital flows be described in a fashion that is helpful to policymakers? By and large, they cannot; there is a huge discrepancy between what economists know and what policymakers need to know in order to formulate policy intelligently.

To be sure, the existing empirical evidence puts a modest amount of flesh on the bones of the so-called "portfolio adjustment" view of capital movements. This view, it will be remembered,[34] argues that, in response to a change in monetary conditions or some other determinant of a given capital flow, there is a stock-shift effect which, though it may be spaced out over several quarters, represents a once-for-all adjustment in portfolios – and therefore gives rise to a once-for-all capital flow. (Under a regime of flexible exchange rates, the stock-shift effect gives rise to a once-for-all change in the level of the exchange rate.) Simultaneously, the change in monetary conditions induces a continuing-flow adjustment (an altered pattern of investing increments to wealth) that persists more or less indefinitely. Recently, the better studies in the field have all been based on formulations that allow both types of effects, and the resulting empirical estimates support the view that the size of the stock-shift effect is a good deal larger (while it is taking place) than the continuing-flow effect.[35]

This latter point, taken together with evidence that capital flows are highly interest elastic, has important implications for the use of monetary policy to influence the capital account in the balance of payments. It suggests that monetary policy can have sizable, but *mainly transitory*, impacts on the capital account and/or the exchange rate. Thus, with exchange rates pegged at a certain level, monetary policy – if used for external objectives – should be thought of mainly as an instrument for bringing about a one-time

---

33 On this point, see also the discussion at the beginning of section 3 on the relative merits of the structural and reduced-form approaches.

34 See the discussion of the portfolio approach in section 2.

35 Strictly speaking, the existing empirical estimates do not constitute a test of the portfolio-adjustment view of capital movements; the specifications employed force this theory on the data.

change in reserves (compared with what they otherwise would have been). It can be much less effective in bringing about an *enduring* change in the capital account. The counterpart of this argument for the case when exchange rates are floating is that monetary policy should be regarded primarily as an instrument for inducing a once-for-all shift in the level of the exchange rate (compared with what it otherwise would have been).

Although important, these conclusions about the impacts of monetary policy on capital flows and exchange rates tell policymakers very little of what they need to know. Consider the following representative illustration of the choices and uncertainties that confront policymakers in the United States. Suppose the Federal Reserve is contemplating the possibility of tightening monetary policy via open-market sales of Treasury bills. Suppose further that a proposal is being considered to lower the Regulation M and D reserve requirements on Eurodollar borrowings by U.S. banks. The Federal Reserve must project not only the effects of these proposed actions on real activity, employment, prices, and financial conditions, but also their *net* effects on the balance of payments and the value of the dollar in exchange markets.[36]

What analytical steps are required? In principle, one must project the effects of the proposed actions on the portfolio behavior of all categories of economic units and thus on the whole structure of interest rates and credit availabilities in U.S. financial markets. These changes in financial conditions will have an influence on domestic activity and prices, which in turn will feed back and induce further changes in financial conditions. With the United States such an important part of the world economy, activity, prices, and financial conditions in the United States will have significant impacts on activity levels, prices, and interest rates in other countries. If exchange rates are being held relatively fixed by official intervention, these impacts will be transmitted in part

[36] For the purpose of the discussion in the test, the motives underlying these contemplated actions are not relevant, since – whatever the motives – judgments have to be made about the effects of the actions on all important macroeconomic variables. Situations that might conceivably give rise to such actions include the following: (a) Prices have been rising too rapidly, domestic demand is thought to be expanding at too high a rate, while the balance of payments has been weak (or the dollar has been depreciating on exchange markets). (b) Domestic demand is judged not to have been growing at an excessive rate, but the balance of payments or exchange value of the dollar has been very weak. (c) Domestic demand has been expanding excessively, but the balance of payments or the exchange value of the dollar has not been weak; in this case, the Regulation M and D actions might be under consideration primarily for regulatory reasons (e.g., to alter competitive inequities between U.S. banks and foreign banks), and there might be concern that taking both actions would strengthen the external position excessively.

through changes in reserves. In the absence of significant official intervention in exchange markets, exchange rates will change and help to transmit the impacts. In any case, it is clear that large numbers of international channels of causation and feedback loops need to be taken into account. For example, the proposed change in reserve requirements on Eurodollar borrowings might have particularly important impacts on the international assets and liabilities of U.S. banks, and hence on the Eurocurrency markets, and hence on conditions in financial centers in other major countries. The analysis has to be able to cope, on the one hand, with the many influences of economic activity and financial conditions – both in the United States and abroad – on capital and trade flows and, on the other hand, with the many feedback influences of capital and trade flows on economic activity and financial conditions.

Seen against this background of complex, interdependent transactions, how artificial an intellectual experiment it is for the Federal Reserve to ask how much the capital account of the U.S. balance of payments would improve as a result of an increase of, say, 100 basis points in U.S. interest rates, *with interest rates and other financial conditions in the rest of the world remaining unchanged.* For any large, open economy – but a fortiori for the United States – it cannot be plausibly assumed that the rest of the world will stand still. But in what manner, and by how much, will the rest of the world move? Economists' lack of quantitative knowledge of the determinants of international capital flows is even exceeded by our quantitative ignorance about the manner in which capital flows link national financial markets together.[37]

Just to complete the picture, there is the small matter of having a less than perfect understanding of the linkages and inter-

---

37 Herring's Ph.D. dissertation (1973), which I have already mentioned, is a commendable first effort to tackle this area of ignorance. On the same subject, see also Argy and Hodjera (1973). In an important recent paper, Girton and Henderson (1973) investigate these problems in terms of a two-country theoretical model.

If Herring's empirical results are taken at face value, they suggest that a tightening of monetary policy in the United States so as to bring about a 100-basis-point increase in U.S. interest rates would exert so much upward pressure on other national interest rates that a weighted-average interest differential between the United States and the rest of the world would be increased by only 36 basis points (Chap. 7, Table 7.6). Herring's aggregative capital-flow equations yield the result that a 100-basis-point increase in U.S. interest rates, in the absence of any adjustment in foreign interest rates, would produce a $3½ billion capital inflow into the United States; the resulting inflow to the United States would be only $1¼ billion when it is assumed that foreign interest rates adjust to their new equilibrium levels (as calculated in Herring's interest-rate equations). I have considerable misgivings, as has Herring himself, about his specific estimates. But they do constitute a step forward on a path, as yet unmarked and uncleared, along which many more researchers will have to tread.

dependence between financial conditions, real activity, and the price level – for the United States or for any other economy. The unfortunate truth, therefore, is that the economics profession does not have sufficient knowledge about any of the requisite analytical steps to enable the Federal Reserve or any other monetary authority to make reasonably accurate projections of the first-round and ultimate effects of any of their proposed actions.

I would not want the preceding remarks to be misinterpreted. Even the meager theoretical and empirical knowledge we do have is often sufficient to prevent policymakers from falling into gross errors – such as, for example, ignoring the key interrelationships between domestic monetary conditions and monetary conditions abroad, or expecting an alteration in the relative levels of domestic and foreign interest rates to have as large an enduring impact on capital flows or changes in exchange rates as the initial, stock-adjustment impact. And I certainly do not share the views of those who are so agnostic as to doubt the value of a major additional expenditure of research resources in this area.

My argument, however, does amount to an overall critical judgment of the empirical literature on international capital flows. Fifteen years from now, we will almost surely look back and see that by 1973 this area of research, if not in its infancy, was at best beginning to struggle with adolescence. I leave it to the reader to judge, since that depends on one's own perspective and rate of time preference, whether this is basically an optimistic or a pessimistic assessment.

REFERENCES

Amano, Akihiro, "International Capital Movements: Theory and Estimation," in Ball, ed. (1973).
  "An Econometric Model of the Japanese Balance of Payments," mimeographed, 1973a. (Forthcoming in Contributions to Economic Analysis series, Amsterdam, North-Holland.)
Argy, Victor, and Z. Hodjera, "Financial Integration and Interest Rate Linkages in the Industrial Countries, 1958–1971," *IMF Staff Papers*, 20 (March 1973).
Argy, V., and Kouri, P. J. K., "Sterilization Policies and the Volatility in International Reserves," in R. Z. Aliber, ed., *National Monetary Policies and the International Financial System* (Wingspread Conference, 1972), Chicago, University of Chicago Press, 1974.
Argy, Victor, and Michael G. Porter, "The Forward Exchange Market and the Effects of Domestic and External Disturbances under Alternative Exchange Rate Systems," *IMF Staff Papers*, 19 (November 1972).
Arndt, Sven W., "International Short-Term Capital Movements: A Distributed

Lag Model of Speculation in Foreign Exchange," *Econometrica*, 36 (January 1968), pp. 59–70

Ball, R. J., ed., *International Linkage of National Economic Models*, Amsterdam, North-Holland, 1973.

Basevi, G., and J. Waelbroeck, "World Financial Constraints in Project Link," unpublished paper presented at 1973 annual meetings of LINK.

Bell, P. W., "Private Capital Movements and the U.S. Balance of Payments," *Factors Affecting the United States Balance of Payments*, Joint Economic Committee, 87th Cong. 2nd Sess. 1962.

Black, Stanley W., *Theory and Policy Analysis of Short-term Movements in the Balance of Payments*, unpublished Ph.D. dissertation Yale University, 1965, abridged version published in *Yale Economic Essays*, 8 (Spring 1968).

"An Econometric Study of Euro-dollar Borrowing by New York Banks and the Rate of Interest on Euro-dollars," *Journal of Finance*, 26 (March 1971).

International Money Markets and Flexible Exchange Rates, Princeton Studies in International Finance No. 32, Princeton, N.J., 1973.

Boatwright, B. D., and G. A. Renton, "A Preliminary Analysis of U.K. International Transactions in Private Long-term Capital," Discussion Paper No. 3, Econometric Forecasting Unit, London Graduate School of Business Studies, 1972.

Bradshaw, Robert C., *A Theoretical and Empirical Analysis of U.S. Bank Euro-dollar Borrowing, 1966–71*, Ph.D. dissertation, College Park, University of Maryland, 1973.

Brainard, William C., and James Tobin, "Pitfalls in Financial Model-Building," *Papers and Proceedings of the American Economic Association*, 58 (May 1968).

Branson, William H., *Financial Capital Flows in the U.S. Balance of Payments*, Amsterdam, North-Holland, 1968.

"Monetary Policy and the New View of International Capital Movements," *Brookings Papers on Economic Activity*, No. 2, Washington, D.C., 1970.

Branson, W. H., and R. D. Hill, "Capital Movements in the OECD Area: An Econometric Analysis," *OECD Economic Outlook*, Occasional Studies, 1971.

Branson, W. H., and T. D. Willett, "Policy toward Short-term Capital Movements: Some Implications of the Portfolio Approach," in F. Machlup *et al.*, eds. (1972).

Bryant, Ralph C., "The International Demand for Liquid Dollar Assets," unpublished manuscript, 1971.

Bryant, Ralph C., and Patric H. Hendershott, *Financial Capital Flows in the Balance of Payments of the United States: An Exploratory Empirical Study*, Princeton Studies in International Finance No. 25, Princeton, N.J., 1970.

"Empirical Analysis of Capital Flows: Some Consequences of Alternative Specifications," in F. Machlup *et al.*, eds. (1972).

Carr, J. L., and J. A. Sawyer, "The Balance of International Payments and the Foreign Exchange Rate in TRACE Mark IIIR," unpublished manuscript, Institute for the Quantitative Analysis of Social and Economic Policy, University of Toronto, 1973.

Caves, Richard E., and Grant L. Reuber, "International Capital Markets and Canadian Economy Policy under Flexible and Fixed Exchange Rates, 1951–1970," in *Canadian-United States Financial Relationships*, Proceedings of a conference held in September 1971, Federal Reserve Bank of Boston, 1972, pp. 9–40.

Caves, Richard E., Grant L. Reuber, and others, *Capital Transfers and Economic Policy: Canada, 1951–1962*, Cambridge, Mass., Harvard University Press, 1971.

Cheng, Hang-Sheng, "The Balance-of-Payments Impact of the U.S. Capital-Control Programs: Evidence from Recent Econometric Studies," mimeographed, 1973.

Choudhry, N., Y. Kotowitz, J. A. Sawyer, J. W. L. Winder, *The TRACE Econometric Model of the Canadian Economy*, Toronto, University of Toronto Press, 1972.

Ciccolo, John H., Jr., and Edward F. McKelvey, "Large Bank Liability Creation in the 1960's," mimeographed, 1971.

Cohen, Benjamin J., "A Survey of Capital Movements and Findings Regarding Their Interest Sensitivity," included in *The United States Balance of Payments*, Hearings before the Joint Economic Committee, 88th Cong., 1st Sess., 1963.

Cooper, Richard N., "The Interest Equalization Tax: An Experiment in the Separation of Capital Markets," *Finanz Archiv*, 24 (December 1965), pp. 447–471.

Dooley, Michael P., "A Model of Arbitrage and Short-term Capital Flows," International Finance Discussion Paper No. 40, Washington, D. C., Federal Reserve Board, 1974.

Federal Reserve Bank of Atlanta, Research Department, *Guide to International Financial Statistics Collected and Processed by the Federal Reserve Bank of Atlanta*, 1972.

Freedman, Charles, "International Capital Flows, Interest Rates, and the Money Supply," Discussion Paper No. 73–32 of the Center for Economic Research, Minneapolis, University of Minnesota, Department of Economics, 1973.

The Foreign Currency Business of the Canadian Banks: An Econometric Study, Staff Research Studies No. 10, Bank of Canada, 1974.

Girton, Lance, and Dale Henderson, "Two-Country Model of Financial Capital Movements as Stock Adjustments with Emphasis on the Effects of Central Bank Policy," International Finance Discussion Paper No. 24, Washington, D.C., Division of International Finance, Federal Reserve Board, 1973.

Girton, Lance, and Don E. Roper, "A Monetarist Model of Fixed and Floating Exchange Rates Applied to the Canadian Experience," unpublished draft, 1974.

Griliches, Zvi, "Distributed Lags: A Survey" *Econometrica*, 35 (January 1967), pp. 16–49.

Grubel, H. G., "Internationally Diversified Portfolios: Welfare Gains and Capital Flows," *American Economic Review*, 58 (December 1968), pp. 1299–1314.

Hansen, Bent, *Foreign Trade Credits and Exchange Reserves: A Contribution to the Theory of Capital Movements*, Amsterdam, North-Holland, 1961.

Hawkins, Robert G., "The Stability of Flexible Exchange Rates: The Canadian Experience," *Bulletin*, New York University Institute of Finance, Part II of No. 50–51 (July 1968).

Heckerman, Donald, "International Short-Term Capital Movements: Comment II," *American Economic Review*, Vol. 57 (June 1967).

Helliwell, John F., "A Structural Model of the Foreign Exchange Market," *Canadian Journal of Economics*, 2 (February 1969).

"The Effects of Revaluation on Trade and Capital Flows between Canada and the United States," in *Canadian-United States Financial Relationships*, Proceedings of a conference held in September 1971, Federal Reserve Bank of Boston, 1972, pp. 83–97.

Helliwell, John F., and Tom Maxwell, "Short-Term Capital Flows and the Foreign Exchange Market," *Canadian Journal of Economics*, 5 (May 1972), pp. 199–214.

"Monetary Interdependence of Canada and the United States under Alternative Exchange Rate Systems," in Aliber, ed., *National Monetary Policies and the International Financial System* (Wingspread Conference, 1972), Chicago, University of Chicago Press, 1974.

Helliwell, John F., H. T. Shapiro, G. R. Sparks, I. A. Stewart, F. W. Gorbet and D. R. Stephenson, *The Structure of RDX2*, Parts 1 and 2, Bank of Canada Staff Research Studies, No. 7, 1971.

Hendershott, Patric H., "Comment IV," *American Economic Review*, 57 (June 1967a).

"The Structure of International Interest Rates: The U.S. Treasury Bill Rate and the Eurodollar Deposit Rate," *Journal of Finance*, Vol. 22 (September, 1967b).

Herring, Richard J., "International Financial Integration: Capital Flows and Interest Rate Relationships among Six Industrial Nations" Ph.D. dissertation, Princeton, N.J., Princeton University, 1973.

Herring, Richard, and T. D. Willett, "The Capital Control Program and U.S. Investment Activity Abroad," *Southern Economic Journal*, 39 (July 1972).

Hewson, John, and Eisuke Sakakibara, "A General Equilibrium Approach to the Euro-dollar Market," unpublished draft, 1973a.

"The Effects of U.S. Controls on U.S. Commercial Bank Borrowing in the Euro-dollar Market and the Euro-dollar Interest Rate," unpublished IMF Department Memorandum, December, 1973b.

"The Euro-dollar Deposit Multiplier—a Portfolio Approach," *IMF Staff Papers*, 21 (July 1974).

Hodjera, Zoran, "Short-Term Capital Movements of the United Kingdom, 1963–1967", *Journal of Political Economy*, 79 (July-August 1971).

"International Short-Term Capital Movements: A Survey of Theory and Empirical Analysis," *IMF Staff Papers*, 20 (November 1973).

Johnson, Harry G., "The Monetary Approach to Balance-of-Payments Theory," in M. B. Connolly and A. K. Swoboda, eds., *International Trade and Money*, Toronto, University of Toronto Press, 1973.

"International Capital Movement Controls" (Report on a conference held in Geneva in June 1973 under the sponsorship of the International Center for Monetary and Banking Studies), *Euromoney* (August 1973).

Kenen, Peter B., "Short-Term Capital Movements and the U.S. Balance of Payments," included in *United States Balance of Payments*, Hearings before the Joint Economic Committee, 88th Cong., 1st Sess., 1963.

"Portfolio Capital and Monetary Policy" (3 vols.), mimeographed, Working Papers in International Economics, Princeton, N.J., Princeton University, Department of Economics, International Finance Section, 1973.

Kesselman, J., "The Role of Speculation in Forward-Rate Determination: The Canadian Flexible Dollar 1953–60," *Canadian Journal of Economics*, 4 (August 1971), pp. 279–298.

Kouri, Pentti J. K., "The Hypothesis of Offsetting Capital Flows: A Case Study of Germany," paper presented at the 4th Konstantz Seminar on Monetary Theory and Monetary Policy, June 1973.

Kouri, Pentti J. K., and M. G. Porter, "Interest Rates, Capital Flows and Exchange Rate Expectations," IMF Staff Memorandum DM/72/84, 1972.

"International Capital Flows and Portfolio Equilibrium," *Journal of Political Economy*, 82 (May/June 1974).

Kwack, Sung Y., "A Disaggregated Model of Financial Flows between the United States and Foreign Regions," mimeographed, 1971a.

"A Disaggregated Model of Capital Flows between U.S. Banks and Foreign Regions," mimeographed, 1971b.

"The Structure of International Interest Rates: An Extension of Hendershott's Tests," *Journal of Finance*, Vol. 26 (September 1971c).

"A Note on the Balance of Payments Effects of the U.S. Capital Controls Programs: Simulation Estimates," mimeographed (forthcoming in *Journal of Finance*).

Kwack, Sung Y., and George R. Schink, "A Disaggregated Quarterly Model of the United States Trade and Capital Flows: Simulations and Tests and Policy Effectiveness," paper presented at Brookings Conference on Econometric Model Building and Development, February 1972.

Laffer, Arthur B., "Comment III," *American Economic Review*, 57 (June 1967).

Leamer, E. E., and R. M. Stern, *Quantitative International Economics*, Boston, Allyn and Bacon, 1970.

"Problems in the Theory and Empirical Estimation of International Capital Movements," in Machlup *et al.*, eds. (1972).

Lee, C. H., "A Stock-Adjustment Analysis of Capital Movements: The United States-Canadian Case," *Journal of Political Economy*, 77 (July/August 1969).

Lindert, P. H., "The Payments Impact of Foreign Investment Controls," *Journal of Finance*, Vol. 26 (December 1971).

Machlup, Fritz, *et al.*, eds., *International Mobility and Movement of Capital*, New York, Columbia University Press for National Bureau of Economic Research, 1972.

Makin, J. H., "Demand and Supply Functions for Stocks of Eurodollar Deposits: An Empirical Study," *Review of Economics and Statistics*, 54 (November 1972).

Markowitz, Harry M., *Portfolio Selection*, New York, Wiley, 1959.

Marston, Richard C., *American Monetary Policy and the Structure of the Eurodollar Market*, Princeton Studies in International Finance No. 34, Princeton, N.J., 1974.

Marston, Richard C., and Sung Y. Kwack, "A U.S. Capital Account Sector for the Wharton Model: Some Preliminary Results," unpublished manuscript, 1973.

Martiensen, Joern, and Guenter Sandermann, "A Quarterly Model of the Monetary and Balance of Payments Sectors of the West German Economy," Discussion Paper No. 47, Institut fur Gesellschafts-und Wirtschaftswissenschaften, University of Bonn, 1973.

Massaro, Vincent, "An Econometric Study of Euro-dollar Borrowing by New York Banks and the Rate of Interest on Euro-dollars: Comment," *Journal of Finance*, 27 (September 1972).

Mastrapasqua, Frank, "U.S. Bank Expansion via Foreign Branching: Monetary

Policy Implications," *The Bulletin,* New York University Graduate School of Business Administration, Institute of Finance (January 1973).

Michael, Walther P., *Measuring International Capital Movements,* Occasional Paper No. 114, New York, Columbia University Press for National Bureau of Economic Research, 1971.

Miller, Norman C., and Marina von N. Whitman, "A Mean-Variance Analysis of United States Long-Term Portfolio Foreign Investment," *Quarterly Journal of Economics,* 84 (May 1970a).

"Alternative Theories and Tests of U.S. Short-Term Investment," unpublished manuscript, 1970b.

"The Outflow of Short-Term Funds from the United States: Adjustment of Stocks and Flows," in Machlup *et al.,* eds. (1972).

Mills, Rodney H., Jr., "The Regulation of Short-Term Capital Movements: Western European Techniques in the 1960's," Federal Reserve Board Staff Economic Study No. 46, 1968.

"The Regulation of Short-Term Capital Movements in Major Industrial Countries," Federal Reserve Board Staff Economic Study No. 74 (October, 1972).

"An Evaluation of Measures to Influence Volatile Capital Flows," University of Geneva, Graduate Institute of International Studies, Conference on Capital Movements and Their Control, June 14–15, 1973a.

"Structural Change in the Euro-dollar Market: Evidence from a Two-Equation Model," International Finance Discussion Paper No. 33, Federal Reserve Board, Division of International Finance, 1973b.

Mundell, Robert A., *International Economics,* New York, Macmillan, 1968.

Officer, Lawrence H., *An Econometric Model of Canada under the Fluctuating Exchange Rate,* Cambridge, Mass., Harvard University Press, 1968.

Officer, L. H., and T. D. Willett, "The Interest Arbitrage Schedule: A Critical Survey of Recent Developments," *Journal of Money, Credit and Banking,* 2 (May 1970).

Porter, Michael G., "A Theoretical and Empirical Framework for Analyzing the Term Structure of Exchange Rate Expectations," *IMF Staff Papers,* 18 (November 1971).

"Capital Flows as an Offset to Monetary Policy: The German Case," *IMF Staff Papers,* 19 (July 1972).

Powrie, T. L., "Short-Term Capital Movements and the Flexible Canadian Exchange Rate, 1953–61," *Canadian Journal of Economics and Political Science,* 30 (February 1964), pp. 76–94.

Prachowny, Martin F. J., *A Structural Model of the U.S. Balance of Payments,* Amsterdam, North-Holland, 1969.

Review Committee for Balance of Payments Statistics ("Bernstein Committee"), *The Balance of Payments Statistics of the United States, A Review and Appraisal,* Washington, Government Printing Office, 1965.

Rhomberg, R. R., "Canada's Foreign Exchange Market: A Quarterly Model," *IMF Staff Papers,* 7 (April 1960), pp. 439–456.

"A Model of the Canadian Economy under Fixed and Fluctuating Exchange Rates," *Journal of Political Economy,* 77 (February 1964).

"Comment," in Machlup *et al.,* eds. (1972).

Salop, Joanne, "A Note on the Monetary Approach to the Balance of Payments," International Finance Discussion Paper No. 36, Federal Reserve Board, Division of International Finance, 1973.

Sandermann, Gunter, "A Balance of Payments Model for West Germany," mimeographed, University of Bonn, Institut fur Gesellschafts-und Wirtschaftswissenschaften, 1972.

Smith, John S., "Asymmetries and Errors in Reported Balance-of-Payments Statistics," *IMF Staff Papers*, 14 (July 1967).

Spitaller, Erich, "A Survey of Recent Quantitative Studies of Long-term Capital Movements," *IMF Staff Papers*, 18 (March 1971).

Stein, Jerome L., "International Short-Term Capital Movements," *American Economic Review*, 55 (March 1965).

"Short-Term Capital Movements: Reply," *American Economic Review*, 57 (June 1967).

Stewart, Ian A., "RDX2 Research Department 'Xperimental' Model Version 2," *Bank of Canada Review* (April 1972), pp. 3–28.

Stoll, H. R., "An Empirical Study of the Forward Exchange Market under Fixed and Flexible Exchange Rate Systems," *Canadian Journal of Economics*, 1 (February 1968).

Tobin, James, "Money, Capital, and Other Stores of Value," *Papers and Proceedings of the American Economic Association*, 51 (May 1961).

"The Theory of Portfolio Selection," in F. Hahn and F. P. R. Brechling, eds., *The Theory of Interest Rates*, New York, Macmillan, 1965.

Tsiang, S. C., "The Theory of Forward Exchange and Effects of Government Intervention on the Forward Exchange Market," *IMF Staff Papers*, 7 (April 1959).

Valentini, John J., and Lacy H. Hunt II, "Euro-dollar Borrowing by New York Banks and the Rate of Interest on Euro-dollars: Comment," *Journal of Finance*, 27 (March 1972).

White, W. H., "Interest Rate Differences, The Forward Exchanges, and the Scope for Short-Term Capital Movements," *IMF Staff Papers*, 10 (November 1963).

Whitman, Marina von N., *Policies for Internal and External Balance*, Special Papers in International Economics No. 9, Princeton, N.J., 1970.

Willett, Thomas D., and F. Forte, "Interest Rate Policy and External Balance," *Quarterly Journal of Economics*, 83 (May 1969), pp. 242–262.

Willms, M., "Controlling Money in an Open Economy: The German Case," *Federal Reserve Bank of St. Louis Review*, 53 (April 1971).

Zecher, Richard, "Monetary Equilibrium and International Reserve Flows in Australia," mimeographed, 1973.

DISCUSSION

PRICES, INCOMES, AND FOREIGN TRADE: A COMMENT*

Grant B. Taplin

My comments will focus on Magee's paper and, in particular, on areas that Magee points out explicitly or in passing as needing further research. In general, his suggestions can be summarized as a need for more complete models. I agree with him. However, I should like to elaborate on a few of his points as well as raise some others, all within the context of world trade modeling. In addition to their usefulness in forecasting, we are interested in world trade models in order to investigate questions such as the effect on trade balances – and some day, on the balance of payments – of domestic and international price changes, income developments, and exchange-rate adjustments.

One area that could profit from further theoretical and empirical research is the import behavior of less developed countries, mentioned by Magee in footnote 1. In world trade models, these countries are often treated as one or a small number of groups, frequently by continent. In some empirical work, foreign-exchange availability is used as a proxy for economic activity for imports by less developed countries.[1] In other instances, foreign-exchange availability has a different meaning. Rhomberg-Boissonneault (1964) treated all less developed countries as one group (that group also included Canada, Japan, Australia, New Zealand, and South Africa) and set the value of their imports as equal to current foreign-exchange earnings, specifically exports plus net capital inflows less changes in reserves. This identity is an example of the most simple import-exchange equation and is based on the notion that less developed countries spend all their current receipts on imports in the current period. This approach has been applied by others in studies dealing with effects on the balance of payments of reductions in U.S. economic and military assistance. In a second type of import-exchange equation for less developed countries, the level of international reserves is included in a stan-

---

* The views expressed represent the opinions of the author of this note and should not be interpreted as official Fund views.
1 Polak (1954) employed exports as a proxy for economic activity.

dard type of import function [see, for example, equation (2) of Magee's paper] as a proxy for the tightness of restrictions. However, other variables may include economic activity and prices. The mixing of real and balance-of-payments variables often encounters the problem of double counting and simultaneous-equations bias. A third form of equation has imports as a function of balance-of-payments phenomena alone (see, e.g., Rhomberg, 1968). A behavioral relationship is specified, in contrast to the identity discussed above, but the two sets of determinants of imports are not mixed, as in the second set. Hemphill (1973a, 1973b) has provided a theoretical justification for an import-exchange equation in terms of balance-of-payments adjustment, showing that this type of function holds even when restrictions are not used. He has shown, moreover, that for the less developed countries imports and reserve changes should be considered as jointly determined according to balance-of-payments adjustment needs.

Turning to a second consideration, Magee notes that in simple single-equation demand equations for imports, the supply elasticities with respect to price are implicitly infinite. He points out later that some of his work and that of Hooper and of Richardson have been directed toward estimating export-supply and import-demand equations by simultaneous-equation techniques. the export-supply equation suggested, equation (4), is simple but nonetheless represents an important step toward reality. [He failed to note that similar equations were used by Rhomberg and Boissonneault (1964, in particular, pp. 89–92), although they estimated by ordinary least squares.] This does point out one important area of future work – estimating the supply side of international trade. It is not sufficient in the framework of policy to know that the Marshall–Lerner conditions hold; it is of utmost importance to know the magnitudes of responses to price changes. We have very little information indeed on the supply side, and our knowledge of the magnitude of responses is accordingly very small.

Magee emphasizes the need to build feedback mechanisms into our models of world trade. With this I agree wholeheartedly. We need to know how trade and other components of the balance of payments influence domestic income, employment, production, and prices; most of the existing empirical literature deals with how trade is influenced by those forces. This is especially true for countries with a large foreign sector. Feedback is a broad term, however. It can apply to the joint determination of trade and GNP, and to foreign and domestic prices. Substantial steps forward in the treatment of both types of feedback have been taken in Project Link, which is discussed more fully in the paper by Klein in this volume. There are other important examples, including work on EEC countries by Waelbroeck *et al.* (1972), on Canada by Helliwell *et al.* (1973), and on Japan by Moriguchi and Tatemoto (1973). In these models, income and prices in other countries are used as explanatory variables in the home-country equations, and in some instances these variables are jointly determined along with the home-country variable.

As Magee notes, we have had some success at the Fund with building in a feedback mechanism (see Taplin, 1973). We have a model which in its present form divides the world into 27 countries and regions (25 individual developed countries and 2 regions, the centrally planned economies and the rest of the world). There is an import and export equation for each country or region. The activity variable in the import equation is typically the sum of investment, government expenditure, and exports of goods and services. In simulation, the model solution of merchandise exports is used to determine a country's imports, and the model is iterated until a joint solution of each country's or region's imports, exports, and, in addition, activity variable is obtained. The next step in refining the model will be endogenizing prices.

Another area deserving further study is the way in which import demand is distributed among supplying countries. Bilateral import equations, whether for total imports or on a commodity-by-commodity basis, are cumbersome. There are too many prices if the equations are specified correctly, and it is not worth doing otherwise. This means that one could make full use of Armington's (1969) two-step separation procedure: first, determine imports from all sources by reference to income, prices, and other relevant variables; second, determine the market shares of supplying countries in that import market.

The export-share matrix for distributing import demand across supply countries is common to the Project Link system and some of the trade-modeling work at IMF. Market shares are implicitly used in most trade models, other than those that look explicitly at exports market by market. In the simplest cases, a country's exports are considered to be a constant share of world exports; in more complicated formulations, economic activity, prices, and other variables in the principal markets are brought together by using shares to form a few composite variables. A share matrix can be used to cover the entire world in more detail than is implicit in the use of, say, total world trade, and, furthermore, the world-trade constraint of exports equaling imports (after adjustment for freight and insurance) is satisfied. The basic problems are how to account for the changes of shares through time, and how to relate these changes to relative price movements, shifts in preferences, and other relevant variables. A theoretical derivation of shares as a function of relative prices can be found in Armington's (1969) work. Some important steps forward in estimating share functions have been taken, particularly by Hickman, by Moriguchi and Johnson, and by Klein (see Klein's paper in this volume for fuller references to these works). Thus, in the Project Link system, foreign trade prices, along with domestic prices, are endogenous. Nevertheless, many problems remain.

Another important element needing further work, as Magee notes, is the question of time lags on imports and exports, and the reconciliation of the two. The work to date shows short responses on the import side and long responses on the export side. Until we are quite confident of our results, measures taken to correct, say, balance-of-payments deficits may be too large and too frequent. For example, was the lack of substantial improvement in the U.S. balance of payments during 1972 due to an insufficient change in the exchange rate or to the long lags required for adjustment?

Looking at the import side first, the usual form of import equation is given by Magee in equation (2). When using annual observations, there is not enough information to estimate polynomial lags, and there is too much multicollinearity to introduce each lagged variable individually into the equations. We would expect to obtain a better view of the lag structure by using quarterly data, but that has not been the case. Of the statistical results summarized in Magee's Table 2, only the equations of Houthakker and Magee have lags, and they are of the Koyck variety, which, as Magee points out, means that price and income effects follow the same geometrically declining lag pattern. Furthermore, the bulk of the effects are worked out within a year. In a more recent use of quarterly data, Kwack (1972) has no lag term at all; in his model, imports on a quarterly basis adjust without lags to concurrent changes in activity and prices.

On the export side, as Magee points out, the evidence looks very different. Junz and Rhomberg (1973), in particular, looked at the changes of export shares of each of the industrial countries in fourteen industrial markets, and how these changes related to changes in the exporting country's prices relative to a weighted average of all exporting countries' prices, market by market. Using pooled cross-section and time-series data, Junz and Rhomberg obtained the following sequences of elasticities of changes in market shares to changes in relative prices, from year t to year t-5, respectively: -0.52, -0.29, -0.58, -0.98, -0.24, -0.27. The coefficients for the first, third, and fourth years have t-statistics greater than 2. Three points are particularly worthy of mention: first, the peak of the lag occurs three years after a price change; second, the response during both the fourth and fifth years is as great as the response during the first year following a price change; and third, very little of the variation in shares is explained by price variation, indicating that we are a long way from understanding fully all the factors influencing shares.

As Magee notes, there has been some interesting work on nonprice rationing variables and trade, but much remains to be done here as well. Observed price series do not fully capture implicit price movements such as discounts and credit terms. Furthermore, certain elements such as waiting time and delivery lags are nonprice rationing mechanisms. These nonprice variables could be combined with price variables to construct hypothetical price series that could be used in the trade models. Alternatively, observed price and the nonprice variables could be used in the same import or export equation. In the OECD model, for example, variables such as excess inventory stock and the ratio of excess unfilled orders to deliveries are used in the same equation as relative prices (see Adams *et al.*, 1968). There are other examples, but the work of incorporating nonprice rationing and implicit price variables needs to be extended. Adjustments to excess demand and excess supply are not exclusively via prices. Rather, adjustment to excess or deficient demand is via trade, prices, and inventory changes. What is needed, therefore, is more elaborate modeling dealing with all the above factors simultaneously. Only in this way will we have a full understanding of how the economy reacts to developments at home and abroad.

In summary, Magee and I would agree on the need for more elaborate, more complete trade models. We have made substantial progress in the past decade, but much more remains to be done. The 1970s will be an opportune time for fruitful work because of recent events in the international system. For example, price changes have been sharper and more frequent. Our model building will be challenged to trace and explain these events.

REFERENCES

Adams, F. G., et al., An Econometric Analysis of International Trade, Paris, OECD, 1969.

Armington, Paul S., "A Theory of Demand for Products Distinguished by Place of Production," IMF Staff Papers, 16 (March 1969), pp. 159–178.

Helliwell, J. F., et al., "Comprehensive Linkage of Large Models: Canada and the U.S.A.," in Ball, ed. (1973).

Hemphill, W., "A Model of the External-balance Constraint on Imports of Less-developed Countries," mimeographed, 1973a.

  "The Effect of Foreign Exchange Receipts on Imports of Less Developed Countries," mimeographed, 1973b.

Junz, Helen B., and Rudolf R. Rhomberg, "Price Competitiveness in Export Trade among Industrial Countries," Division of International Finance Discussion Paper No. 22, Washington, Board of Governors of the Federal Reserve System, 1973.

Kwack, Sung Y., "The Determination of U.S. Imports and Exports: A Disaggregated Quarterly Model, 1960 III-1967 IV," Southern Economic Journal, 38 (January 1972), pp. 302–314.

Moriguchi, C., and M. Tatemoto, "An Econometric Analysis of a Bilateral Model of International Economic Activity in Japan and U.S.A.," in Ball, ed. (1973).

Polak, J. J., An International Economic System, London, Allen & Unwin, 1954.

Rhomberg, R. R., "Transmission of Business Fluctuations from Developed to Developing Countries," IMF Staff Papers, 15 (March 1968), pp. 1–29.

Rhomberg, R. R., and Lorette Boissonneault, "Effects of Income and Price Changes on the U.S. Balance of Payments," IMF Staff Papers, 11 (March 1964), pp. 59–122.

Taplin, G. B., "A Model of World Trade," in Ball, ed. (1973).

Waelbroeck, J., et al., "World Payments in Transition: An Evaluation of Orders of Magnitude," Cahiers Economiques de Bruxelles, 56 (4th Quarter, 1972), pp. 59–65.

THE MULTINATIONAL CORPORATION AND DIRECT INVESTMENT: A COMMENT

Thomas Horst

According to the product-cycle hypothesis, new and old products differ from one another in the stability and diversity of their technologies. With newer products, everything is in a state of flux. Capital–labor ratios are shifting, the product is continually redesigned, new markets are explored, new distribution channels are established, etc. Competing producers are often pursuing radically different strategies, each of which seems to offer opportunities for profitability and growth. As the product matures, however, these different strategies tend to stabilize around a common norm. Producers who started out in what later proved to be the wrong direction correct their course if they can. If not, they either enter some new line of business or exit from the industry altogether.

Gary Hufbauer has the unenviable task of reviewing the development of a comparatively new industry. The length of his survey reflects not only his patience and perseverance in covering current research, but also the diversity and, alas, confusion of our current methods. Although the multinational firms themselves have been around for some time, only lately have international economists worried about integrating their behavior into the general theory of international trade and investment. This is no easy task, for the typical multinational firm bears little resemblance to the atomistic seller of goods or services envisaged by conventional, general-equilibrium theory. The tendency has been to turn increasingly to industrial-organization analysis, which assumes *imperfect* competition. Since foreign *direct* investment assumes both ownership and control, and since control matters only where markets are imperfect, the appeal of industrial-organization analysis is apparent.

The problem with industrial-organization analysis, or with virtually any other approach except general-equilibrium analysis, is its incompleteness. The emphasis on the long-run, structural characteristics of industries becomes a disadvantage in evaluating short-run phenomena, such as balance-of-payments adjustment. Likewise, this approach tends to emphasize positive issues and say little about normative and distributive issues. In short, any review of the broad range of economic issues raised by the behavior of multinational firms is bound to be either eclectic or incomplete. While one might wish that more order could be made of this seeming chaos, I share Hufbauer's opinion, implicit in the length and diversity of his survey, that further simplification is not possible. Not yet, anyway.

EMPIRICAL RESEARCH ON
FINANCIAL CAPITAL FLOWS: A COMMENT

Norman C. Miller

It is difficult to say anything critical about the excellent paper that Ralph Bryant has written. It is up to date, thorough, and clearly written. I find no points of disagreement with either the details of his exposition of past work or his assessment of what still remains to be done. Therefore, my comments will merely augment or expand some of the many topics that he has covered. These comments concern four topics: direct foreign investment and portfolio capital flows, the scale variable, exchange-rate variations and capital flows, and the simultaneous-equation approach to capital flows.

Direct Foreign Investment and Portfolio Capital Flows

The many papers on portfolio capital flows and on direct foreign investment ignore the fact that the direct foreign investment figures contain both short-term and long-term portfolio types of assets. U.S. direct investment abroad is defined by the U.S. Department of Commerce to include *any* increase in U.S. claims on foreign enterprises (which include foreign branches and subsidiaries as well as other foreign businesses) if either (1) one American person or firm has more than 10 per cent control of that foreign enterprise or (2) all americans combined have more than 50 per cent control of that foreign enterprise. Thus, if you buy a share of common stock in a foreign corporation, this transaction appears either as long-term portfolio foreign investment or direct foreign investment in the balance-of-payments accounts, depending on whether or not the foreign corporation is controlled by Americans. Also, changes in short-term or long-term portfolio claims between a U.S. parent and its foreign subsidiary or branch always appear in the direct foreign investment account.

With a few exceptions, most of the studies dealing with direct foreign investment tend to reject the Tobin–Markowitz model on the grounds that real capital goods cannot be bought and sold without high transactions costs, and thus firms do not adjust their portfolios of real assets in the manner required by the Tobin–Markowitz portfolio-adjustment theory. This is true, but multinational firms can constantly change the location of their net worth without buying and selling factories. This can be done simply by changing the location of their short-term or long-term portfolio claims or liabilities. What we need are microdata on multinational firms so as to be able to apply the Tobin–Markowitz model to direct foreign investment.

The Scale Variable

In the typical mean-variance model we have an equation such as $F = \phi S$, where F is claims on foreigners, S is the scale variable that represents the size of the investor's portfolio, and ϕ is the portfolio ratio. The researcher must be careful to change the manner in which he defines and measures S as he changes the definition of F. For example, if F is all foreign assets held by the investor, S should be the value of all assets in the investor's portfolio. S is not the investor's net worth. On the other hand, S should be the investor's net worth if F is defined as the investor's net holdings of foreign assets (i.e., assets minus liabilities).

The researcher is not free to make assumptions about the homogeneity of the scale variable, that is, about whether or not F changes by the same percentage as S, independently of other assumptions in the model. The Tobin–Markowitz model as extended by Sharpe places constraints on this homogeneity, depending on the definitions of F and S and the type of utility function used. If F includes only *risky* foreign assets, and it is usually assumed that *all* foreign assets are risky in the sense that there is a nonzero variance in their expected rate of return, then Tobin's separation theorem can be used to show that F is homogeneous of degree 1 in S. This theorem holds provided that S is defined as all *risky* assets held by the investor. In other words, the ratio of one class of risky assets, F, to the total portfolio of risky assets, S, will be independent of the size of the portfolio. On the other hand, if S is defined as all assets (both risky and riskless) held by the investor, F will be homogeneous of degree less than 1 in S if the typical quadratic utility function is used. This occurs because a quadratic utility function shows increasing risk aversion. The larger the size of the portfolio, the smaller the proportion of it that will be held in the form of risky assets.

Exchange-Rate Variations and Capital Flows

It is common knowledge that a permanent change in the level of the exchange rate will not affect the optimum portfolio ratios for assets whose annual payout is fixed in nominal terms. Thus, there are no permanent capital flows associated with the exchange-rate variation. We get only a temporary flow of capital toward the strong-currency country in anticipation of the exchange-rate change, and then a return flow later to reap profits. Presumably, all the capital returns home if there is no expectation of further exchange-rate adjustments. For example, a doubling of the dollar price of marks will double the dollar price of all German assets, but it will also double the nominal dollar value of the earnings that are fixed in terms of marks. Consequently, the rate of return on German assets is unchanged, optimum portfolio ratios are unaffected, and there is no net flow of capital after speculation has been completed.

The conventional wisdom has it that an exchange-rate change may cause a permanent capital flow if the exchange-rate adjustment significantly alters the relative profitability of export and import-competing industries between countries. That is, if the variation in the exchange rate alters the relative rates of return on investment in different countries, permanent capital flows will occur. It does not appear to be commonly known that an exchange variation can cause permanent capital flows even if the rate of return and, hence, optimum portfolio ratios are unchanged. This will take place if, for example, U.S. investors have old foreign assets that are denominated in marks. The U.S. investors are likely to calculate portfolio ratios in terms of dollar values. A doubling of the dollar price of marks may not change the *optimum* portfolio ratios, but it will change *actual* or existing ratios. The proportion of mark-denominated assets in U.S. portfolios will double in this example. If optimum ratios are unchanged, U.S. investors will sell some of their mark-denominated assets and the U.S. will experience a capital inflow.

Another neglected aspect of the relationship between exchange-rate changes and capital flows is the possible effect of exchange adjustments on expected inflation rates, and the impact of the latter on output, prices, and capital flows. Milton Friedman's so-called "natural rate" hypothesis says that the government cannot permanently alter the level of unemployment via monetary or fiscal policy on either side of the natural rate of unemployment. Any temporary expansion in output will cause more inflation, which will raise workers' expectations about future inflation. This will lead to higher nominal wage demands and a leftward shift in the aggregate supply-of-output curve; that is, any given output now requires a higher selling price. In other words, the expectation of higher inflation will shift the Phillips curve upward and to the right, so that we get a higher unemployment rate for any given inflation rate. In sum, in the short run the expectation of a higher inflation rate leads to lower output, higher prices, and increased unemployment.

Now suppose that we accept Friedman's hypothesis and also assume that a devaluation of the home currency (with the possibility that future devaluations may also take place) leads to expectations of a higher inflation rate. According to Friedman, this will cause home output to fall and prices to rise faster. These movements in prices and output are consistent with the findings of Richard

Cooper in his well-known study of devaluations. Moreover, a number of papers on portfolio capital flows have found an inverse relationship between capital outflows and the business cycle; capital flows out faster in a recession. Thus, if a devaluation stimulates output and income, as the textbooks have it, then it may lead to a capital inflow. If, however, a devaluation raises the expected rate of inflation and if Friedman's hypothesis operates in the short run, a devaluation may lead to a recession and a capital outflow.

The Simultaneous-Equation Approach to Capital Flows

Current and future research on portfolio capital movements is likely to center on the simultaneous-equation approach, which is in sharp contrast to the single-equation models employed in earlier works. Researchers must distinguish between two basically different types of "reduced form" capital-flow equations. One approach builds a partial-equilibrium type of demand and supply for foreign (or domestic) capital model. In such a model, the capital flow or the level of claims on, or liabilities to, foreigners is endogenous and one or more interest rates are endogenous. To my knowledge no one has yet (1) produced such a model; (2) solved the demand and supply functions for the reduced-form interest rate and capital-flow equations as *functions of the same set of exogenous variables;* (3) estimated the two reduced-form functions with existing data; and (4) gone back and calculated the values of the parameters in the structural equations. Until now, the so-called simultaneous-equation models have fallen short on one or more of these four steps.

A second simultaneous-equation approach that is now becoming popular is to build a general-equilibrium type of macro model with bond-market and money-market equations The macro model can then be solved for a reduced-form capital-flow equation. Such models are appealing because they give total capital movements as functions of exogenous variables that can include any desired set of policy instruments. This allows for the direct estimation of the effect of, say, monetary and/or fiscal policy on aggregate capital flows. Moreover, the overall effect of controls on capital flows can be estimated in this type of model. In doing so, we avoid the danger of attributing too much influence to a control on a particular type of capital movement. The control may appear to limit effectively the desired component of capital flows, but it may simply channel funds into uncontrolled areas and have no effect on total capital movements.

In sum, I believe that future work on portfolio capital flows will (1) try to uncover and explain the portfolio capital flows that are hidden in the direct foreign investment data; (2) pay close attention to the definition, measurement, and theoretical use of the scale variable in Tobin–Markowitz models; (3) investigate carefully the relationship between exchange-rate variations and portfolio capital flows; and (4) work with reduced-form partial-equilibrium models and with general-equilibrium macro models of capital flows.

ECONOMETRIC MODELS OF TRADE AND PAYMENTS:
A COMMENT

Lawrence B. Krause

Part II covers subject matter directly relating to changes over time, as distinct from Part I, which looked at structural factors. The great advantage of structural analysis in econometric work is that it often permits the use of cross-section data alone or in combination with time series. In my view, changes over time raise much more interesting questions, but I have the distinct feeling that we have made much less progress on them – as can be seen in the contrast between the Magee and Stern papers.

At a recent hearing of the Joint Economic Committee, the whole profession was accused by Senator Proxmire of failing to inform, and indeed of misleading, the Congress and the public as to the outlook for the U.S. trade balance following the Smithsonian devaluation of the dollar, and he had justification.

Too frequently, we keep the degree of our uncertainty to ourselves and make public statements as if we had confidence in our predictions. In usual econometric work on foreign trade, it is not very easy to find a standard error of estimate of the trade balance – obviously of some interest in evaluating predictions. Furthermore, when observed values fall outside the expected range, we are much more likely to reestimate the model with a slightly different specification to capture the experience than to face our misuse of the laws of probability (for instance, by overestimating the real degrees of freedom in our work). We use scientific method, but are most of us really scientific in the sense of building upon previous work and trying to add to the accumulation of usable knowledge? Too often, our resources are spent on differentiating our product rather than on integrating incremental bits of knowledge.

Many of the points that I consider important are raised in the useful paper by Stephen Magee. Magee gives us a comprehensive review of where we stand and describes areas of needed improvement in our work. I would like to emphasize a particular shortcoming of existing research which encompasses a number of his points. We are not attempting to build macro models from a believable micro base. Our models do not seem to rest on the theory of the firm and the theory of household behavior and usually do not include the government as a separate actor, even though governmental policies are incorporated. I am encouraged by the work of Paul Armington and some others, but much more needs to be done. Until we have solid building blocks, the structure is likely to be unstable. Of course, there are aggregation problems – Magee points out that theory suggests their existence – but we do not make progress by assuming them away. Rather, efforts should be made to find what can be aggregated properly without suppressing important behavior relations in the system. Then we could develop an incremental-scientific approach to our research. We could try to see what is involved in the development of multinational firms in international commerce; or learn how to incorporate savings behavior and asset management, as well as consumption flows, in our models; or capture the elements in the growth process that affect trade so importantly in Japan.

Of course, we would not have finished our work just by specifying the micro–macro relations; we would still need to link countries together to get the full dimensions of the international system. But my impression is that we have made more progress on the linking process – as described in Klein's paper – than we have in producing the national models that are to be linked together.

Section 2 of Magee's paper deals with developments in theory, and this is the least satisfying part. I wish more space had been devoted to covering the interesting attempts that are being made to include money and bond markets with trade flows. Monetary approaches to balance-of-payments analysis should be brought into perspective to make the necessary distinction between saying "money matters" and "only money matters." As I understand it, this work is mainly oriented toward long-run equilibrium; in order to explain the apparent perpetuation of disequilibria, it would have to include endogenous reaction functions of the monetary authorities. Thus the proper response to the question raised at the beginning of proposition 26, "If the long-run effects of devaluation are neutral, why do countries change exchange rates?" is that devaluations (revaluations) are undertaken in response to a disequilibrium situation in order to speed the adjustment of real flows back to their equilibrium values. These values would be achieved anyway in the long run, but the devaluation (revaluation) helps reach them more easily and quickly.

Magee's review of empirical studies utilizing the single-equations approach makes me wonder if such studies have not reached the end of their usefulness. One is forced to ask for what purpose they might be utilized. As a description of the past, they still have some interest, but, for purposes of forecasting even a few quarters into the future, serious questions arise as to the stability of parameters. Furthermore, more advanced econometric techniques are available for short-term forecasting than are usually used in single equations of exports or imports. These techniques make use of the knowledge of observed errors at the end of the sample period. For longer-run predictions or for policy making, the instability of measured parameters is even more fatal. Some interesting work might be done by using the measured income and price parameters for various countries as dependent variables and trying to explain their differences, but this work also could not easily be accomplished by simple methods.

The more sophisticated models are more promising, and it is encouraging to see work going on in this direction. Large models are inherently more difficult to understand, but unfortunately the real world is complicated.

It is well that Magee reminds us of what still needs to be done, lest anyone be under the impression that all the good problems have already been solved.

PART III

PAYMENTS ADJUSTMENT
AND THE MONETARY SYSTEM

ADJUSTMENT UNDER FIXED AND FLEXIBLE EXCHANGE RATES

John Helliwell

The topic of international adjustment under alternative exchange-rate systems can be defined broadly enough to cover almost all of international economics. In my efforts to narrow the topic to manageable proportions, I shall intentionally run the risk of ignoring important issues in order to make more specific comments about existing empirical work and some potential lines for future research.

I shall interpret "adjustment" broadly to refer to the whole range of changes in expenditures, employment, prices, savings, interest rates, exchange rates, and so on, that follow any exogenous change in the balance of payments. The simple fact underlying our interest in the subject is that national policy makers are always looking for easier ways to meet domestic employment and output goals, subject to some constraints, including that of a viable balance of payments. From their point of view, the purpose of learning more about the empirical facts of alternative exchange-rate systems is to choose the one that makes their job easier. From a broader point of view, we must assess the congruence of the balance-of-payments targets chosen by national policy makers and consider the processes that come into play when the goals do not mesh. In this paper, I start somewhat farther back and concentrate on the empirical evidence describing various adjustment processes under fixed and flexible exchange rates. No policy conclusions of importance are reached, for the question of how to identify a better adjustment process when you see one is raised only at the end of the paper and is not answered.

Section 1 lists some of the specific problems whose solutions depend on information about international adjustment processes. A summary of theoretical requirements is made in passing. Section 2 presents a theoretical skeleton with which to relate the main alternative quantitative approaches. Section 3 surveys empirical attempts to compare the relative ability of alternative exchange systems to handle adjustment problems, based on the Canadian experience. Section 4 makes some suggestions for future research in the areas of trade equations, long-term capital flows, foreign-exchange markets and short-term capital flows, and overall model structure. Some concluding comments are supplied in section 5.

1. SOME ADJUSTMENT PROBLEMS IN WHICH
THE EXCHANGE-RATE SYSTEM MATTERS

The Transfer Problem

In contemporary dress, the problem is how best to accommodate large capital transfers. If the exchange rate is flexible, how far will it have to move to effect the transfer? If the exchange rate is fixed, what are the processes whereby trade flows or other capital flows are altered? Alternatively, what are the consequences of accommodating the capital transfer by altering the foreign-exchange reserves of either the source or the recipient nation?

The transfer problem is usually one of digesting shocks that disturb an initial balance-of-payments equilibrium. As in the case of most digestive problems, the choice of a remedy will depend upon the frequency and size of the disturbances, as well as on the timing and side effects of the cure.

Persistent Imbalance of Trade and Long-Term Capital Flows

Some identify a "balance-of-payments problem" with any continuing excess of merchandise imports over exports. Broader and more symmetric definitions are available. In the absence of growth, a problem is posed by any continuing imbalance of total trade in goods and services. If there are net savings and investment, however, there is scope for long-term capital flows. Under these circumstances, a balance-of-payments problem requiring adjustment exists if the "basic" balance (of trade and long-term flows) is substantially positive or negative on a continuing basis. The use of exchange-rate changes to restore balance is intrinsic to flexible exchange systems and is a possible feature of all systems in which par values are adjustable under certain circumstances. The effects of using changes in par values to remove persistent flow imbalances depend on the conditions under which the par values are permitted to shift, and on the relation between par values and market values. The nature of exchange speculation has obvious importance for the choice of methods to adjust par values and for comparisons of adjustable systems with flexible exchange rates. If the comparison is between flexible and truly fixed exchange rates, however, the emphasis switches to the processes by which money-wage and price adjustments can restore external balance when exchange rates are fixed. From the many theoretical studies considering whether depreciation will serve to remove a flow disequilibrium, the consensus seems to be (e.g. Tsiang, 1961; Johnson

1961) that full account must be taken of domestic income-expenditure balance in money terms [the "absorption approach," named by Alexander (1952)], jointly with the relative price changes immediately due to the depreciation [the "elasticities approach" emphasized by Robinson (1937), Machlup (1955), and others].

More recently, emphasis has been placed on "the monetary approach to the balance of payments," a version of the absorption approach that focuses on the international substitutability of national currencies under fixed exchange rates (e.g., Johnson, 1973), and on the real balance effects of exchange-rate changes (e.g., Dornbusch, 1974). In terms of empirical work, the requirement is therefore for full macroeconomic models that show not just the standard multiplier effects of trade changes but the whole process whereby monetary equilibrium is restored under the new exchange rate.

Growing Imbalances of Trade

The chief causes of growing imbalances of trade are internationally differing rates of inflation. Unlike the persistent nongrowing imbalances discussed above, growing imbalances cannot be dealt with by once-and-for-all changes in exchange rates or prices. Two main classes of solution are possible. If the international differences in rates of inflation are considered necessary or desirable, then the system must accommodate repeated or continuous exchange-rate changes, preferably by some method that avoids periodic speculative surges. Otherwise, international coordination of monetary and fiscal policies, or some other form of gold-standard discipline, is required. Recent developments in the monetary approach to balance-of-payments theory, as outlined by Mundell (1971) and by Johnson (1973), have helped to emphasize the necessary features of models designed to deal with international differences in rates of inflation. If transition is contemplated from one inflation rate to another, then models must distinguish real and nominal rates of interest both at home and abroad, and take some care to specify the price and exchange-rate expectations governing trade- and capital-allocation decisions.[1]

1 There is a complex linkage between the correct specification of rates of return and expected exchange rates. International differences in nominal rates of interest are relevant when exchange rates are expected to be constant, or when loans are covered in the foreign-exchange market. By contrast, uncovered movements of capital ought to be governed by differential real rates of return if investors believe that exchange rates will exactly offset differential rates of inflation over the investment horizon. Since actual data do not relate to either of these polar states of equilibrium, realistic models must be more complex.

Insulation of the Domestic Economy from External Shocks

In order to avoid some or all domestic consequences of foreign shocks to trade and payments, more freedom must be gained to concentrate policies on domestic problems. Under fixed exchange rates, one solution is to let foreign-exchange reserves absorb the shocks. Nice calculations are required to compare the opportunity costs of holding higher average reserves with the costs of a devaluation forced by a series of autocorrelated shocks. The stakes are high, as speculation is a game any number can play, and the international system can be driven to crisis when fixed rates come unstuck too often. If successful, this strategy avoids exchange-rate movements, but the full aggregate-demand effects of trade shocks are felt on the domestic economy. If the shocks arise in the capital account rather than the trade account, the fixed exchange rate plus sterilization of monetary effects provide complete insulation. In effect, the investment in question is financed from official reserves if it is an outflow or added to reserves if it is an inflow.

Under flexible exchange rates, the tables are turned. The exchange rate is allowed to move as far as necessary to restore balance. If only trade flows are affected by the exchange rate (a crucially unrealistic assumption), then trade shocks do not affect the net trade balance in nominal terms. Given that the terms of trade and the relative prices of traded and nontraded goods are changing, insulation is far from complete. However, aggregate activity is less affected than under the fixed-exchange-rate strategy outlined above. If the shocks arise in the capital account, the parallel with the transfer problem is most complete. The flexible rate permits some degree of transfer and, to that extent, does not insulate aggregate activity. Quantification of these comparisons between exchange-rate systems requires specification of all monetary and expenditure linkages between the foreign and domestic sectors, with special attention to timing.

Effectiveness of Domestic Monetary and Fiscal Policies

A large body of literature has grown up dealing with the assignment of monetary and fiscal policies to domestic and external policy objectives. In this paper, we are interested in these questions only to the extent that the answers depend on the degree to which exchange rates are flexible.

One strand of research has been concerned with the comparative advantages of monetary and fiscal policies in achieving internal and external balance. Following Meade (1951) and Mundell (1961, 1962, 1963), most of the models employ comparative-static methods and assume that trade surpluses offset by capital-account deficits, or vice versa, suffice to define external balance. These simple two-target, two-instrument linear models pose no great conflicts to the policy makers under any exchange system, so that they furnish no strong grounds for choosing between fixed and flexible exchange-rate systems. Some comparisons of the "effectiveness" of particular policies under alternative exchange-rate systems have been surveyed by Helliwell (1969), Whitman (1970), and Kenen (1972). Such comparisons are important in the choice of an exchange system only if there are costs attached to bigger shifts of the policy levers. In most of the models I surveyed, monetary policy retains its comparative advantage in dealing with external balance, whether focused on the change in reserves or the level of the exchange rate. This is of interest only if there is an "assignment problem" requiring that each policy instrument have a specific assigned target.

Qualitative models with matching targets and instruments have been improved upon in several ways. Even within the same basic model structure, recognition of uncertainty (Brainard, 1967) breaks down any comfortable pairing of instruments with targets. Under uncertainty, the usual portfolio-diversification principles come into play, counseling a judicious mixture of all available policies. Similar conclusions follow if one recognizes diminishing returns or higher costs from larger doses of an instrument. Under these circumstances, a gain is possible from dropping a target, since the available instruments can then be focused more precisely on the remaining targets. This suggests a possible advantage for flexible exchange rates, but only if the exchange rate does not itself become a target.

The whole range of comparative-static flow-equilibrium models fails to distinguish portfolio-realignment effects from changes in the allocation of new savings and, further, fails to link the latter flows to growth in the domestic and foreign economies. Simple no-growth models of international portfolio allocation can be used to show (Willett and Forte, 1969) that attempts to use higher interest rates to shore up the balance of payments lead eventually to a net weakening; eventually, there are no further capital inflows to offset the higher current-account payments for debt service. If portfolio growth and realignment are both to be taken into account, as they should be, there seems to be no alternative to quantitative models.

The monetarist approach summarized by Johnson (1973) contrasts in several respects with the models discussed above. There is full employment, one world interest rate, and one world price level. Under these conditions, which are presumably relevant only with rigidly fixed exchange rates, there are no income and employment targets to worry about. Monetary policy influences the balance of payments because faster domestic credit expansion implies a loss of reserves, given that income, prices, and interest rates are fixed and that domestic and foreign currencies are perfect substitutes. A simple extension of this model to flexible exchange rates presumably allows nations' rates of monetary growth and prices to differ. Abstracting from uncertainty about rates of monetary growth, each country has its own rates of growth of money and prices, and nominal interest rates differ by the expected rate of exchange depreciation, which is also equal to the international difference in rates of inflation. This type of theoretical model can be made more realistic in many ways: by the separation of traded and nontraded goods (Parkin, 1974), the recognition of heterogeneous markets for goods and capital, and the treatment of adjustment costs and lags. As with the Keynesian-type models discussed previously, the addition of accessory features reduces the clarity of the conclusions, brings back the need for policy instruments, and soon requires empirical work to support any conclusions.

A final improvement of the earlier analysis of monetary and fiscal policies in open economies has been the increasing attention to international interdependence. The generalized foreign-trade multipliers of Metzler (1950) have been estimated by Beckerman (1956) and Morishima and Murata (1972). In the context of Project LINK (see Ball, ed., 1973, and Lawrence Klein's paper in the present volume), the multinational foreign-trade model is being generalized by the endogenous determination of foreign-trade prices and export shares, as well as of imports and the components of final demand. Theoretical two-country models of policy making with trade and capital flows have been presented by Mundell (1968, pp. 262–271), Cooper (1969), and others. A multinational model must recognize that there are likely to be inconsistencies among national targets for the balance of payments and exchange rates. The development of dynamic binational and multinational models with endogenous policy responses is just beginning; interesting suggestions for a game-theoretic approach have been made by Hamada (1974).

Enough taxonomy. The catalog of problems must not be

allowed to dominate this paper, whose main purpose is to assess present or potential empirical results bearing on the relative ability of fixed and flexible exchange systems to handle adjustment problems.

2. THEORETICAL SKELETON

The brief discussion here of alternative ways of modeling the balance of payments and the foreign-exchange market under alternative exchange-rate systems is intended to provide a basis for the empirical comparisons in the next section. Consider a simplified balance-of-payments identity:

$$X\$ - M\$ + FIL + FIS = B ,$$

where all flows are measured in current dollars, and

$X\$$ = exports of goods and services
$M\$$ = imports of goods and services
FIL = net capital inflows in long-term forms
FIS = net capital inflows in short-term forms
B = balance of payments, the domestic-currency equivalent of
        the change in foreign-exchange reserves.

The standard theoretical models of policy making under fixed and flexible exchange rates (e.g., Mundell, 1968, pp. 250–271) assume that net exports depend negatively on domestic activity and prices, and positively on foreign activity and prices. The price of foreign exchange (*PFX*), measured as the number of units of domestic currency required to purchase one unit of foreign currency, is assumed to have a positive effect on the trade balance. Exchange-rate expectations are ignored, short-term capital flows are assumed away, and net long-term capital inflows depend positively on the difference between domestic and foreign interest rates. In the fixed-exchange-rate version, the change in reserves is simply the sum of the balances on capital and current accounts. In the flexible-exchange-rate version, *B* is assumed to be zero, and the exchange rate moves until the balances on trade and long-term capital accounts are exactly offsetting.

One fairly straightforward result of these flexible-rate assumptions is worth explaining, because it is overturned by empirical results reported in the next section. In a bilateral situation, if the home country expands its domestic money supply, capital flows out in response to any drop in domestic interest rates. The resulting increase in the price of foreign exchange has the usual expansionary effects at home and depressive effects abroad. The amount by which the price of foreign exchange has to rise in order to call forth the necessary home-country exports depends upon the interaction of all the usual elasticity and absorption parameters, but the direction of the change in foreign income and in the exchange rate is definite. The depressive effect on foreign income requires that capital flows be responsive only to interest differentials but does not require Mundell's (1968, p. 263) assumption of perfect capital mobility (see, e.g., Krueger, 1965, p. 206). To see how this result can be reversed, we need first to consider more realistic ways of dealing with short-term capital flows and the foreign-exchange market.

I find it enlightening to focus attention on the foreign-exchange market, and to assume that, at least in the absence of exchange controls, the market clears on a continual basis. The net official demand (FXO) for foreign exchange, expressed in units of foreign currency, is equal to B/PFX. The net private demand (FXP) for foreign exchange is equal to the negative of the official demand. If particular components of the private demand can be isolated, they can be separately treated. A parallel structure can be used for forward exchange of every maturity. Explicit official-demand equations for spot or forward exchange can be estimated if official behavior is sufficiently stable and there is enough variance in the resulting time series.[2] The corresponding net private-demand equations also depend on there being sufficient variance in the time series for FXO.

The rigidly fixed and freely flexible exchange systems are special cases. With the rigidly fixed rate, the official "behavior rule" is to deal freely at the posted price; thus $FXO = -FXP$. Since there is usually lots of variance to the FXP series in these circumstances, the private-demand equation can be directly estimated, as a func-

---

2 Basevi (1972) has recently argued that there is no neat correspondence between any country's balance of payments and transactions in its currency. He draws the inference that it may therefore be a mistake to model the foreign-exchange market using national balance-of-payments data. I would prefer the matter to be stated slightly differently: For any country, especially one linked closely to international short-term capital markets, the demand for foreign exchange is determined not just by interest rates, the net short-term liability position, and the history of net balances on trade and long-term capital accounts, but also by the panoply of regulations and preferences influencing all the participants in short-term capital markets. Basevi emphasizes the importance of Eurobanks shifting their net currency balances, but the basic point was relevant even before the growth of Euromarkets. For example, the U.S. dollar business of Canadian banks has long been substantial enough to make separate modeling possible for bank and nonbank short-term capital flows. None of the basic theory is altered by such a split, but emphasis can be more clearly placed on institutional factors not directly related to Canada's balance of payments.

tion of trade and long-term capital flows, as well as other factors (such as interest rates, expected future exchange rates, and the forward-exchange differential) influencing "leads and lags" and other elements of short-term capital flows. With B determined simply as $(PFX)(FXO)$, net short-term capital inflows are determined by the balance-of-payments identity.

In the flexible exchange-rate system with no intervention, FXO and FXP are both zero – FXO because the authorities are not in the market, and FXP because the exchange rate moves far enough for the various private demands to sum to zero among themselves. The same situation exists for any forward-exchange market in which there is no official intervention. As will be seen in the next section, the usual modeling strategy in these circumstances is to renormalize the private-demand equation so that the exchange rate is the dependent variable. Similar treatment is given to the markets for forward exchange. Once again, the balance-of-payments identity is used, with $B=0$, to solve for net short-term capital inflows. Note that, in this scheme of things, there is no requirement, even under fully flexible exchange rates, that an increase in long-term capital outflows should be immediately offset by an increase in net exports induced by a change in the exchange rates . The rate could remain immobile in the case of strongly held inelastic expectations leading to short-term capital inflows. Alternatively, expectations could be so extrapolative that an increase in long-term capital outflows would be accompanied by an increase in short-term capital outflows.

Thus we have found sufficient theoretical reason to overthrow the earlier assumption that an easier monetary policy under flexible exchange rates would lead to higher activity at home and lower activity abroad. Sufficiently inelastic exchange-rate expectations could assure that induced capital inflows would be positive for the country initiating a faster rate of monetary growth.

The theoretical framework illustrated above for the special cases of rigidly fixed and freely flexible exchange rates can also be used for exchange-market and balance-of-payments modeling under more general circumstances. As illustrated elsewhere (Helliwell and Maxwell, 1972 and 1974), countries operating under systems of limited exchange-rate flexibility are suitable candidates for the "full treatment" – estimation of separate equations for private and official demands for foreign exchange. These two equations can then be solved, making use of the market-clearing condition that $FXO = -FXP$, to determine simultaneously the exchange rate and the change in reserves.

3. ADJUSTMENT UNDER ALTERNATIVE EXCHANGE SYSTEMS:
      SOME CANADIAN COMPARISONS

Quantitative attempts to compare fixed and flexible rates on a macroeconomic basis have been made by Rhomberg (1964), Caves, Reuber, *et al.* (1971), Choudhry *et al.* (1972), and Helliwell and Maxwell (1974). All the studies except that of Caves and Reuber are based on macroeconometric models.

The Rhomberg Model

Rhomberg's (1964) pioneering assessment of the Canadian experience has stood the test of time remarkably well. The seventeen stochastic equations and two identities are rudimentary. The equations are fitted using quarterly data from 1952 to 1959, all safely within the flexible-rate period that ran from October 1950 to May 1962 The balance-of-payments structure is similar to that outlined in the last section; there are equations for imports of goods and services, exports of goods and services, two categories of net long-term capital inflows, and the spot foreign-exchange rate. The balance-of-payments identity is therefore used to determine net short-term capital inflows.

Rhomberg measures the exchange rate as $1/PFX$, the number of U.S. dollars required to purchase one Canadian dollar. Thus care must be taken when making comparisons with more recent Canadian models using PFX, the number of Canadian dollars required to purchase one U.S. dollar. Rhomberg's capital-flow equations are of the "flow equilibrium" type, in which continuing flows result from an altered differential between domestic and foreign interest rates. It is therefore not possible to distinguish portfolio reallocation from the allocation of new savings, and there are not mechanisms showing how, in the absence of new net savings, portfolios would adjust so as to eventually choke off net capital flows. The model's results should thus be interpreted in a short-term context, assuming average rates of portfolio growth.

Rhomberg has two fixed-exchange-rate versions of the model, both obtained by interpreting the exchange-rate equation as a short-term capital-flow equation, and using the balance-of-payments identity to solve for the change in reserves. This renormalization is slightly different from that suggested in the last section but is natural in the context of Rhomberg's model, in which the functional form of the flexible-exchange-rate equation is derived by a renormalization of a short-term capital-flow equation. The two fixed-exchange-rate versions differ from one another in their assumptions about domestic credit creation. The "endogenous money" version may be regarded as an application of gold-standard rules, or of one aspect of the monetarist model outlined in section 1. In this version, any increase in foreign-exchange reserves implies an equal increase in the stock of money in circulation in Canada. In the monetarist model, this result would be obtained by treating foreign-exchange reserves as part of the money stock. In the Rhomberg version, the monetary authorities can expand the domestic money stock, and it will stay larger until the cumulated reserve losses are sufficient to bring the money supply back to its original level. Because of Rhomberg's "pure flow" equations for capital movements, this result is inevitable. In the monetarist version, these induced reserve losses are assumed to take place immediately, so that interest rates, at least in real terms, remain the same at home and abroad.

The second fixed-exchange-rate version of Rhomberg's model involves an exogenous money supply, implying that induced changes in reserves lead to offsetting changes in interest-bearing government debt rather than in the money supply. This sterilization is possible in the context of Rhomberg's model because the increasing stock of government debt has no impact on any behavior equation.

Rhomberg linearizes his model and computes dynamic response paths (separately for the flexible-rate and the two fixed-rate versions) for a continuing increase in bond-financed government expenditure and for a once-and-for-all increase in the money supply. There are also impact and equilibrium multipliers listed for changes in other exogenous variables.

A feature of Rhomberg's results is that monetary expansion in Canada leads to increases in income and to deficits in the balance-of-payments under fixed exchange rates, although both results are transitory in the case where reserve losses come out of the money supply. Under flexible exchange rates, Canadian monetary expansion leads to depreciation of the Canadian dollar (an increase in *PFX*). After eight quarters, the domestic-income effects of monetary expansion under flexible exchange rates are about twice as great as they are under fixed exchanges with exogenous money, and more than four times as great as in the fixed-exchange system based on gold-standard rules. The effect of higher income on imports is dominated by the exchange-rate effects, so that domestic monetary expansion leads to higher real net exports, and hence to a reduction in aggregate demand in other countries. As indicated in the last section, this result is not implied by the theory of the model but is an empirical conclusion dependent on a number of the estimated parameters. If the model's stabilizing exchange-rate expectations were more inelastic, or if the interest elasticity of capital flows and the exchange-rate elasticity of trade flows were smaller in relation to the income elasticity of net imports, things might have been different. Then the model could have produced the fixed-exchange-rate result of higher real domestic net imports and hence higher aggregate demand abroad in response to Canadian monetary expansion. In any case, Rhomberg's results for Canadian monetary expansion are broadly consistent with those described below based on linked simulations of larger econometric models of Canada [*RDX2*, described in Helliwell *et al.* (1971)] and the United States [*MPS*, detailed in Ando and Rasche (1971)].

Rhomberg's model does not permit firm conclusion about the effects on Canada of foreign monetary policies, because foreign interest rates and income are not linked by an analytical framework. There is not much point in performing the calculations in detail using output from *MPS* or some other model, because the Rhomberg model does not contain the portfolio-balance constraints and the distinctions between real and nominal rates of return that are crucial to longer-term monetary simulations.

With respect to fiscal policy (increased government expenditure in nominal terms), the Rhomberg model shows the greatest effects under fixed exchange rates with endogenous money, slightly smaller effects under sterilization, and the smallest effects under flexible rates. The differences are not extreme, however, as the peak income effects under flexible rates are about 60 per cent as large as under fixed exchanges with endogenous money, and occur two or three quarters sooner. The predominance of the effects of monetary tightness on capital inflows shows up again. The higher income in Canada creates enough extra demand for money to induce capital inflows larger than the induced decline in net exports; hence, an expansionary fiscal policy with an unchanged money supply leads to an appreciation of the Canadian dollar.

Caves and Reuber

The original Caves, Reuber, *et al.* (1971) book was chiefly concerned with the effects of capital movements on Canadian income and employment between 1951 and 1962. Perhaps their most important finding, for our present concerns, was that portfolio and short-term capital flows alike responded in a stabilizing way to changes in the foreign exchange rate during the flexible-rate period (Table 2.2, p. 90). Their more general conclusions about the role of the flexible exchange rate in the transfer process are somewhat ambiguous and difficult to interpret. The main problem is that they use evidence from a variety of sources and do not use internal consistency constraints.

The more recent Caves and Reuber (1972) paper is of considerable relevance to the comparision of fixed and flexible exchange rates, because it contains the results of searches for structural shifts between flexible and fixed exchange eras. Equations for several components of the capital account of the Canadian balance of payments are estimated for part (1Q52 to 4Q61) of the flexible-rate period, for part (1Q63 – 4Q69) of the subsequent experience with pegged exchange rates, and for the two data samples considered together. Caves and Reuber find significant shifts between the two periods and report an apparent decline in the interest sensitivity of capital flows in the fixed-exchange-rate period. In explaining this result, Caves and Reuber (1972, p. 33) emphasize the difference between occasional speculative flurries and a variety of regulations and guidelines introduced to control capital flows.

TRACE

A recent book by Choudhry, Kotowitz, Sawyer, and Winder (1972) presents the TRACE model of the Canadian economy with annual data from periods of fixed and flexible exchange rates. Policy simulations starting in 1957 and 1964 are compared to expose some of the differences between flexible- and fixed-exchange systems. For the flexible-rate period, the exchange market is modeled by an equation for the spot exchange rate, with short-term capital flows determined by the balance-of-payments identity. The exchange-rate equation is similar in structure to that of Rhomberg, although the expected signs are different because TRACE uses the price of foreign exchange *(PFX)*, rather than the price of Canadian dollars, to define the exchange rate. The coefficients in the TRACE equation show the exchange rate to be several times as responsive to trade pressures, and twice as responsive to interest-rate differentials, as the Rhomberg equation. The coefficient on the lagged exchange rate is about 0.5 in both equations, implying the same ratio of impact to equilibrium effects, but the equation based on quarterly data implies faster adjustment. Looking at all the coefficients as a group, the Rhomberg equation suggests smaller exchange-rate variations and hence a more active stabilizing role for short-term capital flows. In neither model is there any mechanism forcing the exchange rate to move far enough eventually to restore the basic balance of trade and long-term capital flows.[3]

One result emphasized by the authors of TRACE is that fiscal policy is much more inflationary under flexible than under fixed exchange rates, but only slightly less effective in altering real GNP. The fixed-exchange-rate simulation involves a constant money supply and is thus comparable to Rhomberg's "exogenous money" case; capital flows are implicitly sterilized by compensating open-market operations. In the Rhomberg model, the split of fiscal-policy effects between price increases and real-income increases is about the same in fixed- and flexible-exchange systems, using the "exogenous money" case for fixed exchange rates (Rhomberg, 1964, pp. 14, 18). Both effects under flexible rates are about 75 per cent as large as under fixed rates. Only a series of detailed calculations or simulations could pinpoint the exact causes of this difference between the TRACE and Rhomberg models. The proximate reason, as explained under "The Rhomberg Model" in this section, is that in the Rhomberg model the higher interest rates induced by higher income pull in so much foreign capital that the price of foreign exchange, and hence of imports, goes down. In TRACE, by contrast, the price of foreign exchange rises, capital inflows being too small to offset the demand for foreign exchange to pay for the induced imports.

For a given change in interest rates, the capital-flow consequences under flexible rates are fairly similar for the TRACE and Rhomberg models, as are the total effects on real expenditure. The price effects of monetary expansion in TRACE are about five times greater under flexible than under fixed exchange rates. This result is due primarily to the rise of import prices caused by

3 The most recent version (no.III) of TRACE alters this situation by ceasing to define short-term capital flows as a residual item. There are explicit equations for short- and long-term capital flows, as well as for trade flows, and the exchange rate is determined so that the balance of payments, $B = (FXO)(PFX)$, is zero. The equation for short-term capital flows under flexible exchange rates is driven primarily by interest-rate differentials and provides no role for exchange-rate expectations. Thus the exchange rate must move far enough within each year to achieve basic balance of trade and long-term capital flows, augmented by interest-induced short-term capital flows. Adjustment to balance-of-payments disturbances therefore involves greater exchange-rate movement in TRACE III than in TRACE I because short-term capital flows are not allowed to play their usual part in stabilizing exchange-rate fluctuations.

the higher price of foreign exchange, and not to supply constraints in the domestic economy, because the inflationary effects are almost as great for simulations in the slack year 1960. In TRACE, import prices enter final demand prices and affect the price of domestic output. Choudhry *et al.* (1972, p. 39) think that the estimated elasticity of 0.4 for the response of the latter price to import prices is too high; I agree. Using this 0.4 figure, along with the direct impact of import prices, the price of equipment investment has an estimated elasticity of over 0.8 with respect to the import price.

TRACE shares the Rhomberg model's property that monetary expansion raises income at home and lowers it abroad. This was to be expected, given that the two models show similar domestic-expenditure effects for monetary policy, and given also the smaller stabilizing role played in TRACE by short-term capital flows. For a specified increase in real domestic income obtained by monetary policy, TRACE has a larger induced trade surplus than the Rhomberg model[4] and therefore gives a lower ratio of domestic gains to foreign costs. As suggested earlier, the main reason for this difference between the models is the greater sensitivity of TRACE's exchange-rate equation to a balance-of-payments surplus or deficit; hence the rate moves more quickly and further to reinforce the effects of domestic monetary policy under flexible exchange rates.

Linked Simulations with Quarterly Models

The *RDX2* quarterly model of Canada (Helliwell *et al.*, 1971) was designed with open-economy policy assessments and linked simulations in mind. Thus considerable attention was paid to explaining international movements of goods, services, capital, and people in ways that reflect the appropriate consequences of changes in exchange rates, inflation rates, portfolio growth rates, and a variety of monetary and fiscal policies. This required a good deal

---

4 For a 12-basis-point (0.12 per cent) first-year drop in the short-term interest rate in TRACE, the exchange rate shifts by three-fourths of 1 per cent, the constant-dollar annual export surplus increases by about 35 million 1957 dollars, while the current-dollar export surplus is virtually unchanged. Long-term capital flows from the United States are reduced, by over 50 million per year, accommodated by offsetting increases in short-term capital inflows. By comparison, if the short-term interest rate is reduced by 12 basis points in the Rhomberg model, the exchange rate shifts 0.14 of 1 percent, the export surplus increases by the equivalent of 18 million 1957 dollars on an annual basis, and total long-term capital inflows are reduced by 25 million on an annual basis. These are impact results for both models, but the Rhomberg model's lags in terms of quarters are not unlike many of TRACE's lags in terms of years.

of asset accounting and endogenous valuation adjustments for private, government, and business sectors. Financial tightness and the associated switches in borrowing and spending patterns are influenced by cash-flow constraints and measures of portfolio disequilibrium, as well as by various market rates of return in real and nominal terms. Because the resulting combinations of price and nonprice adjustments are rather complicated, it is difficult and often not revealing to quantify the partial effects by reference to single equations. The dynamics of the model's adjustment mechanisms are also more extended and complex than those of TRACE and the Rhomberg model, so that comparison of impact or equilibrium multipliers is not revealing.

One or two general comparisons may be helpful. The balance-of-payments structure of *RDX2* differs from that of the Rhomberg and TRACE models and from that of its predecessor, *RDX1*, by introducing endogenous portfolio-balance constraints into the determination of short- and long-term capital flows. Thus the private demand for foreign exchange in the various pegged exchange-rate systems depends on the net stock of private short-term liabilities as well as the balance-of-payments flows. The flexible-exchange-rate equation, which is a renormalization of the private demand for foreign exchange, thus also contains the stock of short-term liabilities; it therefore forestalls the possibility of a perennial imbalance of the combined trade and long-term capital-flow accounts. Similar mechanisms exist in the equations for private long-term capital flows, most of which are tied to growth in specific foreign or domestic portfolios. In the absence of portfolio growth, capital flows in response to rate-of-return differentials approach zero as portfolio realignment is completed. International payments and receipts of interest and dividends are also tied to the rates of return and to the stocks of assets and liabilities, thus exposing the longer-term consequences of using capital flows to offset a current trade imbalance. Most of this background is available elsewhere (Stewart, 1972; Helliwell *et al.,* 1971).

RDX2 has been simulated between 1964 and 1968 under four alternative exchange-rate systems – the rigidly fixed and freely flexible systems studied by Rhomberg and the TRACE group, as well as two systems with limited exchange-rate flexibility. These are the Bretton Woods system adhered to by Canada between 1962 and 1970, and a moving-peg system in which limited changes in the par value are triggered by movements of the market rate within the band. Market rates in both systems are determined by the intersection of private and official excess-demand functions. The simulations for all four exchange systems are reported elsewhere; they examine the effects of Canadian and U.S. monetary policies (Helliwell and Maxwell, 1974) and fiscal policies (Helliwell, 1972b). Here I shall describe only the polar cases of rigidly fixed and flexible exchange rates, noting in passing that the Bretton Woods results differ sufficiently to suggest that it is misleading to treat rates with 2 or 4 per cent band widths as though they were fixed. That is, exchange-rate movements within the 2 per cent band were large enough, in the Canadian context, to alter reserve changes substantially from what they would have been under rigidly fixed exchange rates.

All the simulations were performed with *RDX2* linked to the *MPS* quarterly model (Ando and Rasche, 1971) of the United States. The effects of Canadian policies on the United States are not large relative to the size of the U.S. economy; hence there are relatively few repercussions reflected on Canada, especially as we have not yet attempted to model U.S. policy responses to imbalance of payments.

Restrictive Canadian monetary policy decreases income at home and increases it abroad under flexible exchange rates, a result parallel to that described above for TRACE and the Rhomberg model. Under fixed rates, the domestic real-income and employment effects are less than half as large as under flexible rates, and the price effects represent a decreasing fraction as the simulation extends across several years (Helliwell and Maxwell, 1974).

Canadian fiscal policy (defined as a debt-financed change in government expenditures) has effects in Canada that are slightly larger under flexible than under fixed exchange rates. This result is different from that reported for the TRACE and Rhomberg models and is due in part to the presence of an endogenous monetary policy in *RDX2*. If a deflationary fiscal policy is instituted, the monetary authorities facilitate it, in part, by cutting the money supply, while also letting nominal interest rates decline somewhat. Because nominal interest rates do not fall as far as would be implied by a fixed monetary base, the induced capital outflows are not as large and the price of foreign exchange falls more, thus increasing the deflationary effects relative to the "exogenous money" cases studied for TRACE and the Rhomberg model.

The most important results from the linked simulations are those showing how Canada is affected by U.S. monetary policy under flexible exchange rates. The domestic-expenditure effects of U.S. monetary restriction are so large, as modeled in *MPS*, that the decline in Canadian net exports due to lower U.S. activity and prices is large enough to offset the expansionary effect of interest-induced southbound capital flows (which raise the Canadian price of foreign exchange). The theoretical discussion in section 2 paved the way for this result by showing how it could occur in any system in which exchange-rate movements are stabilized, whether by official support or private speculation. Without such stabilization, U.S. monetary policy under flexible exchange rates has opposite expenditure effects at home and abroad. The process is as follows: If capital flows are influenced only by interest rates and not by exchange-rate expectations, U.S. monetary restriction draws in Canadian capital and drives up the Canadian price of U.S. dollars, thereby expanding Canadian exports and aggregate demand. But if the exchange rate is sufficiently stabilized by private expectations or official capital flows, U.S. monetary restriction can cut aggregate money demand in Canada, just as it does in Colorado. In order for this result to come about, however, it is necessary for the domestic expenditure effects of monetary policy to be very substantial. None of the three Canadian models produced this result with respect to the international transmission of the effects of Canadian monetary policy. Gordon (1974) has suggested that this may be because *RDX2* and, presumably, the other models do not contain the necessary links between money and spending. However, *RDX2* has more channels for price and non-price credit effects than has the *MPS* model, so the explanation must lie deeper. Only detailed experiments with fully compatible models will show whether the modeled differences in the north- and southbound transmission effects are due to genuine differences in the economies or to unjustified differences between the models. We suspect that the double counting of nonwage income, problems in dealing with capital gains in the *MPS* consumption equation, and an overestimate of the elasticity of share prices with respect to interest rates may lead to an overstatement of the size and speed of the interest-induced wealth effect in the *MPS* model.[5]

Assessment

It is clear from the variety of results reported above that there is much to be done before past Canadian experience with flexible

---

5 The *MPS* model was revised in 1973 in two respects that influence our linked simulations. The dividend/price-ratio equation now exhibits a lower elasticity of share prices with respect to inflation rates, and share prices now enter the consumption equation with a longer lag. The revised model alters the results reported in Helliwell and Maxwell (1974) by dampening somewhat the MPS responses to monetary policy.

exchange rates is efficiently utilized. The range of experiments performed has not begun to distinguish and address appropriately the variety of questions posed in section 1. Good dynamic models must be used, and attention must be devoted to designing criteria by which to prefer one set of adjustment processes to another.

4. SUGGESTIONS FOR FURTHER RESEARCH

Trade Equations

As indicated in section 1, each theoretical approach to balance-of-payments adjustment has given rise to a related body of empirical work. Before and since the important study by Orcutt (1950), the "elasticities approach" has focused attention on estimating the effects of relative prices on a single country's imports and exports. Much of this work has been surveyed by Leamer and Stern (1970, Chap. 2). From the point of view of the present paper, a key problem with existing studies is the scant attention paid to the way that f.o.b. product prices, exchange rates, freight costs, and import tariffs are combined in trade prices. Part of the difficulty lies in the data used to construct the official statistics (see, e.g., Kravis and Lipsey, 1971), which often do not represent what purchasers actually pay. More subtle problems arise in the *ex ante* context, where the product, exchange-rate, and tariff components of the landed import price may each be connected with a different expectation process. Both types of problem are crucial in assessing the effects of different types of exchange-rate changes. For example, the following questions must be answered before we can confidently assess the effects of exchange-rate changes: To what extent are administered prices used (as suggested by Dunn, 1970) to absorb exchange-rate changes? Do the measured trade prices reflect such cushioning? What foreign-exchange rates are used as a basis for trade decisions – current spot rates, forward rates applicable to the date of payment (as argued by Sohmen, 1969), expected spot rates, central or parity rates, or some notional average? Is exchange-rate variation ignored unless large changes (such as major parity changes) are expected? In cases where decisions commit trade flows over an extended period, how are expected exchange rates and expected national price levels entwined in the determination of the relative prices governing trade decisions? What is the role of third- and fourth-country prices in bilateral trade decisions? And so on. This sample of questions reveals how far we are from bringing econometric evidence fully to bear on the effect of exchange-rate variations on the level and variance of trade flows.

The "absorption approach" has given rise to national multinational applications of multiplier analysis, as mentioned in section 1. The approach becomes relevant to the analysis of exchange systems only when it is extended to include the effects of relative prices. A more important by-product of the multinational linkage of national-income-determination models has been the attention focused on the obvious fact that one country's imports are another's exports. Some puzzles arise from aggregate import and export equations that are fitted independently. For example, it is fairly common to estimate larger price elasticities for exports than for imports, and to have the degree of domestic-capacity utilization contribute importantly to the explanatory power of equations for imports but not for exports. Little theoretical work has been done to explore the differences in aggregation between imports and exports that would rationalize these results. As flows are progressively disaggregated by commodity and country, the characteristics of import and export equations must begin to converge.

If the focus of attention is on bilateral trade flows, as with the *RDX2* equations for trade flows between Canada and the United States, then symmetry of specification is quite naturally imposed. As might be expected, the two countries measure differently the volume and prices of the bilateral trade flows, even within the unifying framework of the SITC. Research to reconcile such differences on a consistent time-series basis must be given priority. If attention is concentrated on multilateral trade flows, as with project LINK, then data limitations and sheer complexity forbid separate explanations of all pair-wise trade flows. The alternative methods used in project LINK are explained by Lawrence Klein in his paper in this volume; their common feature is the inclusion of commodity-specific import equations and export price equations in each country model and some variant of a trade-shares matrix to allocate total imports of each commodity class among the potential exporting countries. The problems involved in finding consistent explanatory roles for output prices, shipping costs, exchange rates, tariffs, and quotas in such a framework are formidable.

Most of the theory and estimation of trade equations has dealt with flows of goods measured in real terms. Elasticities of trade volume with respect to price (including exchange-rate) variation are estimated and combined with estimated prices to yield value flows. By contrast, equations for service payments (see the chapter by Sawyer in Ball, 1973) are estimated at current prices, usually without taking adequate account of the effect of changes in exchange rates. The difficulties are greatest with respect to interest and dividends, and freight and shipping. International lending takes place in a variety of currencies, so that detailed knowledge of the currency composition of liabilities is required to indicate the appropriate impact of exchange-rate changes. In the absence of accurate vintage accounting of liabilities (usually impossible because of trade in outstanding securities), some guesswork is required to link interest payments accurately to liabilities, coupon rates, and exchange rates (see pp. 86–91 of Part 1 of Helliwell *et al.*, 1971, for further discussion). Dividend payments are relatively simple, as the dividends are usually declared and paid in the currency of the host country. Income flows related to direct investment, especially by large multinational firms, expose many possibilities for exchange-rate effects, because of the non–arm's-length nature of the transaction. Freight and shipping are complicated because long-term charters and other contracts may often be expressed in a variety of currencies, not that of the purchasing country. Thus it is difficult to calculate the short-run effects of currency realignments.

Long-Term Capital Flows

The crucial distinctions in the consideration of long-term capital flows are between direct and portfolio investment, between bonds and shares, and between borrowers and lenders. The first distinction is usually considered necessary to get behaviorally apt equations. The second distinction is needed partly to distinguish categories responding to different impulses, and partly to permit interest and dividend flows to be separately explained. The third is essential if portfolio-balance constraints are to be considered in explaining capital flows. For example, it is necessary to distinguish sales of Canadian securities by U.S. residents from purchases of U.S. securities by Canadian residents.

All three of these distinctions are used in the *RDX2* equations for long-term capital flows between Canada and the United States. Two more distinctions are also important in *RDX2*, although unlikely to be so important for other countries less closely related to one big neighbor. New issues of Canadian bonds in the United States are explained separately for businesses and for provinces and municipalities, and depend primarily on requirements for funds and domestic borrowing conditions, with some account taken of U.S. portfolio proportions. Trade between the

United States and Canada in outstanding Canadian bonds, by contrast, is explained entirely by relative rates of interest and U.S. portfolio-balance considerations. This distinction between "borrower" and "lender" behavior is natural in the case described and introduces the often-neglected features of the borrower's liability structure. No systematic study has been undertaken, in *RDX2* or elsewhere, of the effect of exchange-rate variability on the degree of diversification across currencies desired by either borrowers or lenders.

Quantitatively, two chief influences of exchange rates on capital flows have been identified. During Canada's flexible-exchange-rate period, portfolio capital flows responded to dampen exchange-rate variations, high values of *PFX* leading to net inflows to Canada, and vice versa. The second influence is less direct but has a similar equilibrating effect. Direct-investment inflows are very sensitive to the net investment expenditures of domestic firms. An increase in the price of foreign exchange (i.e., a devaluation of the domestic currency) increases net exports. This increase in aggregate demand operates through some variant of an accelerator mechanism to expand domestic investment expenditure and hence direct-investment inflows. There is a reverse line of causation, running from direct investment to capital expenditure and thence to imports. This reverse pattern, whose first component is difficult to distinguish from the simultaneous use of direct investment to finance capital expenditures, is emphasized by Caves, Reuber, *et al.* (1971, Chap. 4). Where both lines of causation are modeled, subsequent simulations must be set up with some care. If one wishes to assess the effects of an interest-induced change in the proportion of capital expenditure financed by direct investment, one would not want the induced direct investment to lead directly to new capital expenditures by the route hypothesized by Caves and Reuber. On the other hand, if one wishes to assess the impact on the balance of payments and the domestic economy of a new direct-investment project involving extra domestic investment expenditure, then the channel emphasized by Caves and Reuber is of chief importance. Ideally, the direct-investment and capital-expenditure equations should be specified precisely enough for each influence to come into play in the appropriate circumstances. The matter is of more than passing importance, as experiments with *RDX2* suggest (Helliwell, 1972a) that almost half of the balance-of-payments effects of a revaluation of a pegged Canadian dollar might be due to induced declines in direct-investment inflows to Canada.

A number of recent papers by IMF staff members (Porter, 1973; Kouri, 1974; Kouri and Porter, 1974) have argued, in a manner consistent with the monetarist models described in section 1, that capital flows are so responsive to interest differentials, and interest rates are so responsive to capital flows, that the estimation of capital-flow equations with interest rates as independent variables gives rise to results which understate international capital mobility. As an alternative, they suggest explaining capital flows by changes in the domestic and foreign monetary bases. For countries on fixed exchange rates, however, this alternative faces a similar source of bias. To the extent that capital inflows arise from causes other than credit restraint, they lead to reserve accumulation. If the authorities attempt to insulate the total money supply from the effects of the capital inflow, there will be an increase in the foreign component and a matching decrease in the domestic component of the monetary base. Whether a reduced-form monetarist approach is more appropriate than the usual alternatives thus depends on the mix of reasons for capital movements, the degree and speed of interest-induced capital flows, and whether the monetary authorities attempt to offset the monetary effects of capital flows. Simultaneous-equation estimation methods may help to resolve the issue by avoiding the biases that might otherwise result from using endogenous interest rates or monetary stocks as independent variables in equations explaining capital movements. Some efforts in this direction are reported by Argy and Kouri (1974).

Foreign-Exchange Markets and Short-Term Capital Flows

This part of the topic had substantial exposure in sections 2 and 3. It is obvious that the specification of exchange-market equations is central to the comparison of adjustment processes under alternative exchange-rate systems. Of key importance are assumptions concerning official exchange-market behavior and the nature of private expectations about future exchange rates.

Official behavior in the spot exchange market is trivially easy to specify when exchange rates are immutably fixed. The difficulty comes when exchange rates are supported only within a band, and the par or central value is itself subject to shifting under pressure. Because exchange rates are neither regarded as the highest-priority targets nor ever ignored entirely, the choice in practice is never between rigidly fixed and freely floating exchange rates. Thus our data samples are made up of "fixed" rates that wobble before jumping and "flexible" rates that are subject to being talked down like aircraft in a fog, influenced by direct official operations in the spot or forward-exchange markets or used as intermediate targets for domestic policy decisions. Thus realistic models of "fixed" exchange-rate systems ought to indicate how and when official resolve breaks down, and how and when private speculative activity becomes intense. The problem facing empirical work is the small number of instances; it is not hard to find a theory to fit them all, especially if realistic allowance is made for changes in preferences. For "flexible" rate systems, it may be possible to treat official purchases as exogenous and find expectations processes that hold good for several years, at least until moral suasion comes heavily into play.

In both fixed and flexible exchange-rate regimes, expectations are crucial. As noted in sections 1 and 2, theoretical models have not explored the possibilities thoroughly, perhaps because almost anything is possible. One way of making expectations explicit is to introduce forward-exchange markets. For example, Argy and Porter (1972) supplement a simple theoretical model of income and payments flows with a forward exchange rate determined by expectations of the future spot exchange rate. Capital flows are then made a function of the interest-rate differential plus the forward-exchange premium. If capital flows are very responsive to this differential, and if exchange-rate expectations are very inelastic, this model operates with virtually fixed exchange rates, easily available private arbitrage funds providing the counterpart of official exchange reserves. None of this is surprising in the light of the theoretical skeleton of section 2; indeed, the explicit treatment of one or more markets for forward exchange adds nothing essential to a theoretical model in which exchange-rate expectations are already explicit. From the viewpoint of empirical work, the value of forward-exchange data lies in what they can reveal about exchange-rate expectations. For example, Kesselman (1971) has recently used data on Canadian forward exchange rates to test expectations processes enriched by the addition of variables providing current information about potential future exchange-rate changes.

For the exchange market, the research requirements are extensive and the available data are scanty. Brief bits of Canadian history, U.S. data for the late 1930s (Black, 1973), some of the story of the French franc in the 1920s (Aliber, 1970), and several episodes in the last century (see the paper by Yeager in Mundell and Swoboda, eds., 1969) do not provide a powerful testing ground for general theories of expectations under flexible exchange rates, so that our ambitions must be modest. Much more can be done with experience drawn from exchange markets with pegged exchange rates, preferably using models that can be altered to represent alternative exchange-rate systems.

Overall Model Structure

The preceding paragraphs have dealt with the balance of payments and exchange markets. Comprehensive assessment of adjustment under alternative exchange systems requires much more. How and when are domestic prices, wages, interest rates, money supplies, expenditures, and asset preferences altered in response to disturbances in the balance of payments? Which are the important nonclearing markets, and what are their disequilibrium dynamics? What are the political, social, and economic costs of slow or erratic adjustment in various activity levels or prices? What are the expected frequencies of the various types of problem listed in section 1? What are the costs and consequences of international cooperation as opposed to independent or competitive policies? If these questions are valid, they require a solid base of quantitative dynamic models, supplemented by brave attempts to categorize better and worse exchange-rate systems according to their ability to cope with hypothetical history. As ever, many issues will be left to be settled as matters of taste.

5. CONCLUDING COMMENTS

What have we learned from existing studies, and what ought to be the next empirical and theoretical steps? What have empirical studies of the Canadian experience taught us about the operation of fixed and flexible exchange systems?

1. We have learned that, subject to short-run shocks, flexible exchange-rate systems may in practice operate much like fixed exchange-rate systems, in the sense that short-term private capital flows may for a while play a role analogous to that played by changes in foreign-exchange reserves. This result follows from the exchange-market structure implicit in the various estimated equations for the Canadian price of U.S. dollars. It is also the conclusion of a number of studies of Canadian private short-term capital flows under flexible exchange rates.[6]

6 These include Hawkins (1968), Arndt (1968), Powrie (1964), Rhomberg (1960), and Eastman (1958).

2. This result provides for the possible overthrow of a theoretical assumption established with Keynesian-type models that monetary expansion in a flexible exchange-rate system would in the short run raise income at home and depress it abroad. The overthrow occurs only where the domestic expenditure effects of monetary policy lead to activity-induced increases in net imports that exceed exchange-rate-induced decreases in net imports. What is *not* at stake here is the direction of the exchange-rate change: An expansionary monetary policy leads to depreciation of the home currency, come what may.

The above points illustrate that empirical results sometimes force us to rethink and amend our theoretical assumptions about the differences between fixed and flexible exchange rates. The following points are of less general applicability, being based on the Canadian experience, which includes an amalgam of pegged, flexible, and semiflexible exchange rates.

3. There is some evidence that long-term portfolio capital flows have also responded to exchange-rate changes in such a way as to reveal inelastic exchange-rate expectations and hence to play a stabilizing role.

4. There is no conclusive evidence about the comparative interest elasticity of capital movements under flexible and pegged exchange rates. As Caves and Reuber suggest, their evidence of lower interest elasticity under pegged exchange rates may reflect the various crises and guidelines controlling the 1962–70 Canadian peg period. On semiflexible exchange systems, the evidence is even more scanty.

5. Simulations of Canadian and U.S. macro-models linked by full trade and capital accounts indicate that a crawling peg whose movements are triggered by movements in exchange rates or reserves would require substantial official support, in the short term, unless monetary and fiscal policies were designed to avoid such support. Without persistent gains or losses in reserves, however, the rate would bobble about from upper to lower support points and not provide much aid in righting a basic imbalance.

6. The evidence on the Canadian pegged exchange-rate system, however, suggests that even a 2 per cent band of variation around par value can substantially lessen reserve fluctuations. This result ceases to hold when it is widely expected that the par value will be shifted by a substantial amount.

7. In capsule, my reading of the evidence from the Canadian experience is that, in the short run, exchange systems of limited and full flexibility operate in very similar ways. The differences

become crucial on those occasions when an officially or unofficially supported rate is considered unrealistic by wealthy pixies, gnomes, and reasonable men. These occasions just do not arise under a moderately clean float. Empirical work on the trigger mechanism is next to impossible. Crises are still small in number (their monthly frequency in early 1973 must be regarded as exceptional, if not a debasement of the term "crisis"). The costs of crises must be measured in terms of the stop–go policies used to stave them off or to guarantee the "success" of the resulting exchange-rate shift. On this matter, which I suspect to be of vital importance, our quantitative work to date has little to contribute. So let us turn to consider what other questions remain for us to answer.

What do we need to know, especially now that everyone has had at least some recent experience of unpegged exchange rates?

1. Better data about the currencies, exchange rates, and prices involved in trade transactions are crucial even to measure the results of exchange-rate changes. Perhaps more data-gathering agencies will ascertain and report the currencies in which international interest payments and other service payments are contracted.

2. More flexible specification and more survey information are required to assess the relations between measured trade prices, exchange rates (whether spot or forward), and the expectations so crucial to trade and capital-flow decisions. These expectations are vital to many transactions, such as long-term debt issues, that cannot be laid off in the forward-exchange market.

3. Such information about the Canadian experience may help to reveal how easy it will be to generalize from the Canadian experience to the prospects for other countries.

4. Models of the Canadian foreign-exchange market typically assume that foreign exchange (of any particular maturity) is a unique commodity whose price is represented by the price of the U.S. dollar in terms of the Canadian dollar. The price of third-country currencies in terms of U.S. dollars is therefore considered exogenous to the Canadian foreign-exchange market. Given that the measured series are built by this method of indirect quotations for Canadian dollar prices of third-country currencies, and given the relatively small size of Canada, this procedure was appropriate when Canada was floating more or less alone. But under more generally flexible exchange rates some need arises to consider jointly the determination of at least $n - 1$ exchange rates linking n currency blocs. If triangular arbitrage does not serve to keep the

remaining $(n - 1)^2$ bilateral exchange rates consistent with any arbitrary set of $n - 1$ rates linking n currencies, then the modeling problem will achieve awesome scope. I suspect that for the spot market, and possibly, in time, for a ninety-day forward market, triangular arbitrage would permit $n - 1$ reduced-form exchange-rate equations to do the job. Some data reduction would be required to permit estimation, especially if n is large. If a symmetric system evolves in which national currencies are linked to a redefined SDR or some other pivot defined in terms of a fixed-weight bundle of currencies, the obvious data reduction would be to explain each country's exchange rate in terms of the new pivot, by methods similar to those now used for the Canadian foreign-exchange market. If quoted cross rates do not reflect adequate arbitrage, then it will be necessary to investigate whether the extra search costs and wider buy-sell margins reflect a resource cost intrinsic to flexible exchange rates[7] or slow adaptation by exchange traders.

Harking back to the types of problem listed at the beginning of the paper, let me note how far we are, even in the fairly well-plumbed Canadian case, from having comprehensive answers. The issues require first measuring and then evaluating adjustment processes and the transactions costs coming into play under fixed and flexible exchange rates. Whether a country is better off as part of a multinational currency bloc, floating alone, or even having flexible regional currencies within the nation, must depend on the nature of the disturbances to be digested, the mobility of goods and factors, the degree of community of macroeconomic preferences and structure, and the extent to which the efficiency of a monetary system depends upon the size and number of currency areas.[8] The empirical work surveyed in this paper deals only with the first two or three of these matters, for only one or two countries, and not in a manner that will permit all the pros and cons to be quantified on a comparable basis. I doubt any claim that this situation is likely to change materially in the future. We will continue to learn more, in quantitative terms, about how flexible exchange systems work in practice, but never in a form that

---

7 An alternative attempt has been made by Aliber (1972) to use interest-rate data to evaluate the greater exchange-market costs due to exchange-rate uncertainty.

8 That much, if little more, has been shown in the literature concerned with the size of optimum currency areas. See the paper by Kenen and comments thereon, especially those by Johnson (pp. 395–396), in Mundell and Swoboda, eds. (1969). See also the subsequent conference volume edited by Johnson and Swoboda (1973), especially the attempts by Laffer and by Mundell to make explicit some of the risk-pooling benefits provided by exchange rates fixed rigidly enough to constitute a common currency area.

will justify the choice of an exchange system, or the size of a currency area, on the basis only of comparably measured costs and benefits.

Until we have acquired and assessed contemporary experience of several countries operating under flexible exchange rates, doubts will remain about conclusions derived solely from Canadian evidence. It may dumbfound Canadians more than Europeans that the Canadian dollar marched down lockstep with the U.S. dollar, when the driving force was supposed to be Watergate. When currency dealers and traders act as if Canada and the United States were parts of the same currency area, and the Canadian monetary authorities ratify their actions, it is difficult to use equations based on Canadian experience to make general conclusions about the stability of flexible exchanges.

REFERENCES

Alexander, S. S., "Effects of a Devaluation on a Trade Balance," *IMF Staff Papers*, 2 (April 1952), pp. 263–78.
Aliber, Robert Z., "Speculation in the Flexible Exchange Revisited," *Kyklos*, 23 (Fasc. 2, 1970), pp. 303–312.
   "Uncertainty, Currency Areas, and the Exchange Rate System," *Economica* 39 (November 1972), pp. 432–441.
Aliber, Robert Z., ed., *National Monetary Policies and the International Financial System* (Wingspread Conference, 1972), Chicago, University of Chicago Press, 1974.
Ando, Albert, and Robert Rasche, "Equations in the MIT-Penn SSRC Econometric Model of the United States," mimeographed, Philadelphia, 1971.
Argy, Victor, and Pentti J. K. Kouri, "Sterilization Policies and the Volatility in International Reserves," in Aliber, ed. (1974).
Argy, Victor, and Michael G. Porter, "The Forward Exchange Market and the Effects of Domestic and External Disturbances under Alternative Exchange Rate Systems," *IMF Staff Papers*, 22 (November 1972), pp. 503–528.
Arndt, Sven W., "International Short Term Capital Movements: A Distributed Lag Model of Speculation in Foreign Exchange," *Econometrica*, 36 (January 1968), pp. 59–70.

Ball, R. J., ed., *International Linkage of National Economic Models*, Amsterdam, North-Holland, 1973.
Basevi, Giorgio, "Balances of Payments and Exchange Markets," Discussion Paper 7209, University of Bologna, Institute of Economic Science, November 1972.
Beckerman, W., "The World Trade Multiplier and the Stability of World Trade, 1938–1953," *Econometrica*, 24 (July 1956), pp. 239–252.
Black, Stanley W., *International Money Markets and Flexible Exchange Rates*, Princeton Studies in International Finance No. 32, Princeton, N.J., 1973.
Brainard, William C., "Uncertainty and the Effectiveness of Policy," *American Economic Review*, 57 (May 1967), pp. 411–425.

Caves, Richard E., and Grant L. Reuber, "International Capital Markets and Canadian Economy Policy under Flexible and Fixed Exchange Rates, 1951–1970," in *Canadian–United States Financial Relationships*, Proceedings of a conference held in September 1971, Federal Reserve Bank of Boston, 1972, pp. 9–40.

Caves, Richard E., Grant L. Reuber, *et al.*, *Capital Transfers and Economic Policy: Canada, 1951–1962*, Cambridge, Harvard University Press, 1971.

Choudhry, N., Y. Kotowitz, J. A. Sawyer, and J. W. L. Winder, *The TRACE Econometric Model of the Canadian Economy*, Toronto, University of Toronto Press, 1972.

Cooper, R. N., "Macroeconomic Policy Adjustment in Interdependent Economies," *Quarterly Journal of Economics*, 83 (February 1969), pp. 1–24.

Dornbusch, Rudiger, "Real and Monetary Aspects of the Effects of Exchange Rate Changes," in Aliber, ed. (1974).

Dunn, Robert M., Jr, "Flexible Exchange Rates and Oligopoly Pricing: A Study of Canadian Markets," *Journal of Political Economy*, 78 (January/February 1970), pp. 140–151.

Eastman, Harry C., "Aspects of Speculation in the Canadian Market for Foreign Exchange," *Canadian Journal of Economics and Political Science*, 24 (August 1958), pp. 355–372.

Gordon, Robert J., "Models of Monetary Interdependence," in Aliber, ed. (1974).

Hamada, Koichi, "International Financial Systems and the Interdependence of Monetary Policies," in Aliber, ed. (1974).

Hawkins, Robert G., "Stabilizing Forces and Canadian Exchange-Rate Fluctuations," *Bulletin of the New York University Institute of Finance*, No. 51 (July 1968), pp. 28–79.

Helliwell, John F., "Monetary and Fiscal Policies for an Open Economy," *Oxford Economic Papers*, 21 (March 1969), pp. 35–55.

"The Effects of Revaluation on Trade and Capital Flows between Canada and the United States," in *Canadian–United States Financial Relationships*, Proceedings of a conference held in September 1971, Federal Reserve Bank of Boston, 1972a, pp. 83–97.

"North American Interdependence under Alternative Foreign Exchange Systems," paper prepared for the European Meetings of the Econometric Society, Budapest, 1972b.

Helliwell, John F., and Tom Maxwell, "Short-Term Capital Flows and the Foreign Exchange Market," *Canadian Journal of Economics*, 5 (May 1972), pp. 199–214.

"Monetary Interdependence of Canada and the United States under Alternative Exchange Rate Systems," in Aliber, ed. (1974).

Helliwell, John F., H. T. Shapiro, G. R. Sparks, I. A. Stewart, F. W. Gorbet, and D. R. Stephenson, *The Structure of RDX2*, Parts 1 and 2, Bank of Canada Staff Research Studies No. 7, Ottawa, 1971.

Johnson, Harry G., "Towards a General Theory of the Balance of Payments," in *International Trade and Economic Growth: Studies in Pure Theory*, Cambridge, Mass., Harvard University Press, 1961, pp. 153–168.

"The Monetary Approach to Balance-of-Payments Theory," in M. B. Connolly and A. K. Swoboda, eds., *International Trade and Money*, Toronto, University of Toronto Press, 1973.

Johnson, Harry G., and Alexander K. Swoboda, ed., *The Economics of Common Currencies*, London, Allen & Unwin, 1973.

Kenen, Peter B., *The Analytics of External Balance: An Extended Taxonomy*, Working Papers in International Economics, International Finance Section, Princeton, N.J., 1972.

Kesselman, Jonathan, "The Role of Speculation in Forward-Rate Determination: The Canadian Flexible Dollar 1953–1960," *Canadian Journal of Economics*, 4 (August 1971), pp. 279–298.

Kouri, Pentti J. K., "The Hypothesis of Offsetting Capital Flows: A Case Study of Germany," paper presented at the 4th Konstantz Seminar on Monetary Theory and Monetary Policy, June 1973.

Kouri, Pentti J. K., and Michael G. Porter, "International Capital Flows and Portfolio Equilibrium," *Journal of Political Economy*, 82 (May/June 1974), pp. 443–467.

Kravis, Irving B., and Robert E. Lipsey, *Price Competitiveness in World Trade*, New York, Columbia University Press for National Bureau of Economic Research, 1971.

Kreuger, Anne O., "The Impact of Alternative Government Policies under Varying Exchange Systems," *Quarterly Journal of Economics*, 79 (May 1965), pp. 195–208.

Leamer, Edward E., and Robert M. Stern, *Quantitative International Economics*, Boston, Allyn and Bacon, 1970.

Machlup, F., "Relative Prices and Aggregate Spending in the Analysis of Devaluation," *American Economic Review*, 45 (June 1955), pp. 255–278.

Meade, J. E., *The Balance of Payments, Mathematical Supplement*, London, Oxford University Press, 1951.

Metzler, L. A., "A Multiple Region Theory of Income and Trade," *Econometrica*, 18 (October 1950), pp. 329–354.

Morishima, M., and Y. Murata, "An Estimation of the International Trade Multiplier, 1954–1965," in M. Morishima, ed., *Essays on the Working of Macroeconometric Models*, London, Cambridge University Press, 1972.

Mundell, Robert A., "Flexible Exchange Rates and Employment Policy," *Canadian Journal of Economics and Political Science*, 27 (November 1961), pp. 509–517.

"The Appropriate Use of Monetary and Fiscal Policy for Internal and External Stability," *IMF Staff Papers*, 9 (March 1962), pp. 70–77.

"Capital Mobility and Stabilization Policy under Fixed and Flexible Exchange Rates," *Canadian Journal of Economics and Political Science*, 29 (November 1963), pp. 475–485.

International Economics, New York, Macmillan, 1968.

Monetary Theory, California, Goodyear, 1971.

Mundell, Robert A., and Alexander K. Swoboda, eds., *Monetary Problems of the International Economy*, Chicago, University of Chicago Press, 1969.

Orcutt, G. H., "Measurement of Price Elasticities in International Trade," *Review of Economics and Statistics*, 32 (May 1950), pp. 117–132.

Parkin, Michael, "Inflation, the Balance of Payments and Domestic Credit Expansion in a Fixed Exchange Rate Open Economy," in Aliber, ed. (1974).

Porter, Michael G., "Capital Flows as an Offset to Monetary Policy: The German Experience," *IMF Staff Papers,* 19 (July 1973).

Powrie, T. L., "Short-Term Capital Movements and the Flexible Canadian Exchange Rate, 1953–1961," *Canadian Journal of Economics and Political Science,* 30 (February 1964), pp. 76–94.

Rhomberg, Rudolf R., "Canada's Foreign Exchange Market: A Quarterly Model," *IMF Staff Papers,* 7 (April 1960), pp. 439–456.

"A Model of the Canadian Economy under Fixed and Fluctuating Exchange Rates," *Journal of Political Economy,* 72 (February 1964), pp. 1–31.

Robinson, J., "The Foreign Exchanges," *Essays in the Theory of Employment,* New York, Macmillan, 1937.

Sohmen, Egon, *Flexible Exchange Rates,* rev. ed., Chicago, University of Chicago Press, 1969.

Stewart, Ian A., "RDX2 Research Department 'Xperimental' Model Version 2," *Bank of Canada Review* (April 1972), pp. 3–28.

Tsiang, S. C., "The Role of Money in Trade-Balance Stability: Synthesis of the Elasticity and Absorption Approaches," *American Economic Review,* 51 (December 1961), pp. 912–936.

Whitman, Marina vN., *Policies for Internal and External Balance,* Special Papers in International Economics No. 9, Princeton N.J., 1970.

Willett, T. D., and F. Forte, "Interest Rate Policy and External Balance," *Quarterly Journal of Economics,* 83 (May 1969), pp. 242–262.

INTERNATIONAL RESERVES AND LIQUIDITY

Benjamin J. Cohen

Analytical discussions of the international monetary system are conventionally divided into the three separate problems of adjustment, liquidity, and confidence. This trichotomy goes back to the deliberations of Fritz Machlup's celebrated international study group of thirty two economists in 1964 (Machlup and Malkiel, eds., 1964). The adjustment problem is understood to relate to the capacity of countries to maintain or restore equilibrium in their international payments. As this is the subject of the preceding paper in this volume, it will not be addressed directly here. Instead, the present paper will concentrate on the remaing two problems of the monetary system, which together comprise the general subject of international reserves and liquidity. A major theme of this paper, however, will be the need for more explicit recognition of the relationship between this subject and the problem of payments adjustment than has been customary in the literature in the past.

The liquidity problem is generally understood to relate to the issue of the *quantity* of international monetary reserves. The confidence problem is generally understood to relate to the issue of the *composition* of reserves – specifically, to the issue stemming from the coexistence of several different kinds of reserve assets, and therefore the possibility of disturbing shifts among them. It is also understood that lurking in the background of both these problems is a third fundamental issue relating to the *distribution* of international reserves. These three issues define the scope of the present paper.

The literature on international reserves and liquidity largely grew out of normative concerns about these three issues. What is the appropriate quantity of reserves, and at what rate should reserve supply be increased? What is the appropriate composition of reserves, and in what form(s) should new reserves be created? What is the appropriate distribution of reserves, and to whom should the benefits of new reserve creation be distributed? Many writers have addressed themselves to these issues explicitly from the point of view of normative policy judgment (prescription). Many others have been concerned as much or more with positive economic analysis (description) of the determinants and effects of the quantity, composition, or distribution of reserves. This paper will review each of these three issues in turn. In each case, recent research and new developments will be surveyed from both the positive and the normative points of view. The purpose of the paper will be to help point the direction for future research in this important area of international policy.

Before beginning, a word or two about definitions would be appropriate. Virtually all writers agree on the meaning of the term "international reserves." "A country's reserves may be broadly defined as all those assets of its monetary authorities that can be used, directly or through assured convertibility into other assets, to support its rate of exchange when its external payments are in deficit" (Group of Ten, 1965, p. 21). Thus, reserves are generally defined gross (rather than net), to include total central-bank holdings of gold, convertible foreign exchange, Special Drawing Rights, and reserve positions in the IMF. On the other hand, over the years there has been rather less agreement on the meaning of the term "international liquidity." In the earliest postwar years, a few economists insisted on using the term as a qualitatively descriptive adjective applicable to any *given* reserve asset: international liquidity, by analogy with conventional domestic monetary usage, described the adequacy or usefulness of specific reserve assets in meeting foreign payments contingencies (Arndt, 1947; Goodman, 1956). Later, others insisted on using the term as a qualitatively descriptive adjective applicable to *all* of a country's, or the world's, reserve assets: international liquidity described the adequacy or usefulness of total national or global reserve supplies – adjusting gross reserves for such factors as the availability of external credit or borrowing facilities, the outstanding level of privately owned foreign-exchange assets or liabilities, domestic money-supply reserve requirements, and so on (Brown, 1955; Gemmill, 1960; Clement, 1963; Williamson, 1963; Cohen, 1964; Kane, 1965). In effect, international liquidity described a country's ability to finance a payments deficit without resorting to "undesirable" (Williamson, 1963) adjustment measures. In the words of one writer, "a nation's international liquidity is best regarded as a probabilistically weighted sum of its various foreign assets, liabilities, commitments, and lines of credit" (Kane, 1965, p. 29). However, today neither of these meanings is favored in the literature. Since the deliberations of Machlup's international study group, international liquidity has been defined simply as "the sum of owned reserves and unconditional drawing rights"

(Machlup and Malkiel, eds., 1964, p. 31) – in other words, simply as a synonym for international reserves, a *quantitatively* descriptive expression. This will be the meaning of the term in the present paper.

1. THE QUANTITY OF RESERVES

What is the appropriate quantity of reserves, and at what rate should reserve supply be increased? Of the three issues to be surveyed in this paper, this is the one that has traditionally received by far the most attention in the formal literature. As long ago as the Genoa Conference of 1922, academic economists and public officials alike were expressing grave concern over the problem of reserve adequacy and reserve growth. At the time, they called it a "gold shortage"; later, it became part of what was known as a "dollar shortage"; more recently yet, it has gone under the name of a possible "liquidity shortage." However, whatever the label, the problem itself has remained very much the same: to determine the optimal rate at which reserves should grow through time. When Triffin wrote his landmark *Gold and the Dollar Crisis* (1960), he was reviving an old debate, not initiating a new one.

Triffin himself, of course, was persuaded that a world liquidity shortage was imminent. He was particularly critical of a major IMF study (IMF, 1958) for its much more sanguine appraisal of prospective reserve adequacy. His own conclusion was that comprehensive new measures would be needed to provide for global reserve growth in the future. In this conclusion, at least, if not in the details of his personal proposals for reform, Triffin was joined by most of the academic community. Official opinion, however, remained publicly unconvinced even as late as 1965 (Group of Ten, 1965). It was only in 1966 that the tide began to shift (Group of Ten, 1966), and then it moved swiftly. By 1968 the agreement on Special Drawing Rights was formally signed. By 1970 the facility was already in operation. In its first three years of activation (1970–72), a total of almost 9.5 billion of SDRs was created and added to global reserves.

The SDR has put a new twist on the old debate about the quantity of reserves. In practical terms, the policy question has now become: At what rate should *Special Drawing Rights* grow through time? The answer to this question depends on two vital pieces of information that can be obtained only through positive economic analysis – first, an estimate of total world demand for reserves and, second, an estimate of how much of this demand is likely to be satisfied through growth of reserve assets still not under conscious international control. Given these two desiderata, an appropriate rate of SDR creation can then be directly calculated as a residual. This may be considered an adequate rate of growth. On the other hand, it need not be considered an optimal rate of growth; under some circumstances, it may be desirable to adjust the calculated rate of SDR creation, thereby forcing a modification of national reserve behavior, in order to approximate more closely a global supply optimum. That is a matter for normative policy judgment.

The remainder of section 1 will consider what contribution empirical research can make toward solution of these problems of positive and normative analysis.

The Demand for Reserves

What factors determine or influence the demand for international monetary reserves? This is a matter for positive economic analysis. Fundamentally, the demand for reserves derives from the commitment of national governments to some kind of limitation on exchange-rate flexibility. If the rate of exchange between home and foreign currencies were not constrained in any way, there would be no need at all for official monetary reserves. That need arises only because the national authorities have been traditionally reluctant to leave determination of the foreign-currency price of home currency solely in the hands of the private market.

Other things being equal, individual governments would always prefer more reserves to less. In this respect, their psychology is not different from that of any economically rational individual in the marketplace. A given level of reserves yields more utility than any lower level of reserves because it gives the authorities more elbow room in the management of the domestic economy. The higher the level of reserves, the greater the ability to finance external deficits without resorting to adjustment measures such as a reduction of domestic expenditure, devaluation, or controls. All such measures may be difficult to impose and inconvenient, because they can result in unemployment, distortions of resource allocation, and a reduced rate of real economic growth. These represent the (potential) cost of not holding reserves. (With opposite sign, they represent the utility of holding reserves.)

But there is also an opportunity cost of acquiring and holding reserves. Reserves represent a claim on real resources that might otherwise be employed to expand output, improve the allocation of resources, and stimulate the pace of real economic growth. The hoarding of reserves in excess of a country's needs represents a real sacrifice in terms of consumption or investment foregone. It is in this regard that Machlup (1966) was right to instruct us on the differences among the notions of "demand," "desire," and "need." Governments may be assumed to have a virtually unlimited *desire* for reserves (just as any economically rational individual is assumed, other things being equal, to have a virtually unlimited desire for things of utility in the marketplace). They may also be assumed to have a very considerable *need* for reserves, in the sense that certain possibly undesirable consequences are apt to arise if the needed reserves are unavailable. But these are both very different from the notion of a national demand for reserves, which implies a willingness to offer something of value in exchange for the reserves being demanded. Demand involves a balancing of the marginal costs of holding and not holding reserves. (This may also be viewed as a balancing of the marginal cost and marginal utility of alternative levels of reserves.) The higher the net cost of holding reserves, the lower the effective demand for reserves will be.

Numerous attempts have been made to construct empirical indicators of the demand or need for reserves. Much of this literature has already been surveyed on at least four other occasions – by Clower and Lipsey (1968), by Niehans (in IMF, 1970), by Grubel (1971), and by Williamson (1973). The present survey will try to concentrate less on what has already been accomplished by various writers and more on what useful work still remains to be done on the subject.

By necessity, all empirical studies are based on the assumption that actual reserve holdings can tell us something meaningful about the effective *demand* for reserves. However, it does not follow that observed reserve behavior is all that is necessary to tell us something meaningful about the individual *need* for reserves. To talk about a single country's need for reserves, its individual reserve adequacy, is really to shift the focus of analysis to the normative point of view. The outcome depends on one's value judgment concerning the consequences that are apt to arise for that country if its stock of reserves is at one level rather than another. That is a quite different thing from the positive analytical question of what are the actual determinants of a country's demand for reserves. Many writers fail to make clear precisely which of those notions they are talking about – the demand for reserves or the need. They seem to feel that the two notions can be freely substituted for one another without serious loss of logical consistency. In fact, the risks of inconsistency are considerable. In particular, as we shall see below, the distinction has a great bearing on the issue of whether a global supply of reserves that is defined as "adequate" may therefore also be regarded as "optimal."

The earliest attempts to use positive economic analysis to estimate the demand for reserves of individual countries were based mainly on ratio comparisons. Typically, reserves were compared with the level of imports, on the assumption that the demand for reserves could somehow be expected to grow in line with the overall volume of foreign trade (Harrod, 1953; IMF, 1953, 1958; Triffin, 1960). These measures have been strongly criticized by Machlup and others (Machlup, 1966; Heller, 1968) on the grounds that the demand for reserves is properly related to the variability of trade and payments rather than to their overall volume. There is much justice to these criticisms. Obviously, monetary reserves are not held for transactions purposes, to pay for all of a country's imports of foreign production and assets. They are held rather for precautionary purposes, to finance all *discrepancies* between foreign payments and receipts. Nonetheless, such criticisms may be overdone.

In the first place, we must distinguish between the short run and the long run. The ratio of reserves to imports may perhaps provide a fairly accurate description of the *long-run* demand function for reserves, if not of the *short-run* function relating to the transitional disturbances against which reserves are presumably held (Niehans in IMF, 1970). In the second place, some form of the reserves/imports ratio may perhaps provide a fairly accurate description of the reserve demand function even in the short run. This would be the case if it happens that imports are a faithful proxy for the relevant payments disturbances – in other words, if there exists some direct relationship between the volume of trade (and payments) and the variability of trade (and payments). In the domestic economy, it has long been assumed that for individual economic units such a relationship does in fact exist. The relationship is described by the so-called "square-root law," which states that the transactions demand for cash balances tends to increase with the square root of the overall volume of transactions. Why should not some similar relationship be assumed to hold at the international level?

Theoretical reasons for expecting at the international level a relationship like the square-root law have been suggested by Olivera (1969). Unfortunately, few writers have sought to follow up this lead with empirical research – and those who have tried to do so have come up with contradictory results. Rhomberg (1966, p. 391), for example, concluded that "the statistical results do not . . . contradict the hypothesis that . . . payments imbalances tend to increase in proportion to gross transactions." And Flanders (1971, p. 47) found parallel evidence suggesting that there is a virtually one-for-one relationship between the reserve holdings of individual countries and the overall volume of their imports. These results would appear to imply that there are no scale economies at all in the demand function for reserves. However, there are also indications to the contrary. An IMF study (1969, p. 26), for instance, concluded that "as a whole, it would appear that imbalances have risen more slowly than trade." And Frenkel (1974; in Aliber, 1974) found evidence that the import elasticity of demand for reserves may actually be significantly lower than unity. These results imply that something like the square-root law could indeed hold after all. In view of these mixed results, one observer has aptly suggested that "It may not be possible for a long time to settle in a conclusive way whether any such relationship exists" (Polak in IMF, 1970, p. 512). Clearly, there is room here for additional statistical work.

Grubel (1971, p. 1152) has objected to the use of any kind of reserves/imports (or reserves/payments) measure on different grounds: "This analogy between the demand for cash and reserves is imperfect because cash holders initiate transactions on their own while reserve holders tend to react passively to the consequences of private transactions." Again, though there is much justice to this criticism, it too seems overdrawn. After all, even if reserve holders do not initiate international transactions, they certainly do not lack for policy instruments to encourage or discourage them. Governments are hardly passive when it comes to the balance of payments. Taking the entire range of national macro- and microeconomic policy tools into account, it does not seem to do too much violence to reality to treat individual countries in the international economy as if they were analogous to individual economic units in the domestic economy.

As an alternative to the reserves/imports ratio, Brown (1964) attempted to compare reserves directly with the variability, rather than with the volume, of trade and payments, as indicated by annual data on various countries' "net overall external balance." This represented something of an advance over earlier studies. However, because he continued to use the older ratio approach, his procedure generated some truly strange statistical results, particularly in years when a country's net external balance happened to be small or positive. Even more important, his procedure ignored the simultaneity problem inherent in the use of *ex post* rather than *ex ante* measures of the magnitude of payments imbalance. Realized movements in the balance of payments tend to reflect policy measures previously adopted. But since policy measures actually adopted tend to be influenced, directly or indirectly, by the level of reserves outstanding, actual variability in the balance of payments and actual holdings of monetary reserves tend in large part to be determined simultaneously. A procedure that relies, therefore, on observed or realized outcomes rather than on anticipated or potential outcomes cannot tell us very much about the determinants of the demand for reserves.

The simultaneity problem has been characteristic of much subsequent work as well. For example, Thorn (1967), in commenting on an earlier study by Kenen and Yudin (1965), tried to estimate the demand for reserves in terms of imports and a target ratio of reserves to imports, using regression techniques. However, as Kenen and Yudin (1967) pointed out in a rejoinder, Thorn's procedure contained a serious tautological element because of his reliance on realized or observed levels of reserves. As an alternative procedure, Kenen and Yudin (1965, 1967) developed a stochastic approach to the subject, stressing the probability distribution of potential reserve outcomes. (Specifically, they postulated that each country's reserve changes could be described by a simple Markov process.) Although Kenen and Yudin themselves also relied on realized levels of reserves to measure payments variability, their use of a stochastic approach to the problem of estimation represented a significant improvement over earlier demand studies.

Most demand studies since the middle 1960s have, like those of Kenen and Yudin and of Thorn, employed regression techniques in preference to the older ratio approach. For obvious reasons, this too represented a significant improvement over earlier studies, in particular because the procedure allowed for the inclusion of more independent variables in the analysis and for more sophisticated specification of relationships with the dependent variable. A variety of independent variables have been employed by different writers.

The most obvious variable to employ, as Brown (1964) understood, is some measure (or combination of measures) of payments variability. The approach has been used by Kenen and Yudin (1965), by Courchene and Youssef (1967), by Clark (1970a), by

Kelly (1970), by Archibald and Richmond (1971), by Flanders (1971), by Hipple (1974a), and by Frenkel (1974; in Aliber, 1974). The empirical results have been promising. Only Flanders, using several measures of export instability in a sample of less developed countries, found that "the results were a dismal failure" (1971, p. 43). Most of the other writers, by contrast, found some highly significant relationships between reserve holdings and various measures of payments variability. More work could surely be done along these particular lines. The main technique used so far has been to estimate instability indices for individual countries from time series, and then to employ these indices in demand-function estimates based on cross-sections of countries. It is apparent that improvements of methodology would be possible. For example, further effort could be devoted to adding theoretical and statistical refinement to the measures of payments variability that have been developed. (In particular, more should be done to eliminate the simultaneity problem.) More attention might also be paid to increasing sample size in the studies, perhaps by following the lead of Kelly (1970) and Frenkel (1974; in Aliber, 1974) in pooling cross-sections of countries with time-series data.

A second variable sometimes employed in these studies is the domestic money supply (or related domestic monetary variables). The theoretical justification for this "monetarist" approach, which has been most elegantly stated by Johnson (1973, Chap. 9), originates in the proposition that any balance-of-payments disequilibrium is fundamentally a monetary phenomenon. A deficit reflects an excess of aggregate expenditures over aggregate receipts, and since any deficit must therefore have its counterpart in a reduction of cash balances, the conclusion follows that the demand for international reserves will be determined essentially by what is happening to the domestic money supply. Governments will seek to hold enough reserves to withstand potential exposure to the withdrawal of cash balances either into foreign currency or into increased aggregate demand for goods and services. Like the reserves/imports approach, the monetarist approach probably has considerable merit in helping to explain reserve behavior in the long run, even if not in the short run. (In the short run, the causal relationship may perhaps run more the other way, the money supply being determined essentially by what is happening to reserves.) However, despite the qualified endorsement that the monetarist approach has received from writers such as Niehans (in IMF, 1970, pp. 60–62), it has not been tested much empirically except by Machlup (1966), using ratios, and by Courchene and

Youssef (1967), using regression techniques. Machlup concluded that current domestic liabilities may indeed be a determinant of official demand for reserves (to the extent that officials do have an identifiable demand for reserves, which Machlup questions). Courchene and Youssef found an even stronger relationship of reserve demand to domestic money supply. These results suggest that more tests of the monetarist approach might be worthwhile.

A third variable employed in some recent studies is aggregate national wealth. Heller (1970) suggested that as a country acquires greater total wealth, its demand for all types of assets, including international monetary reserves, should be expected to increase. Tests by Heller (1970) and Hipple (1974a), employing current output measures as proxies for national wealth, have turned out to be statistically significant, suggesting that, at least in part, official reserve holdings may indeed reflect rational management of an economy's total portfolio of assets. This approach, too, probably has considerably more merit in explaining reserve behavior in the long run than in the short run. Further tests of this approach also might be worthwhile.

A final variable employed in these studies is the opportunity cost of holding reserves. Several proxies for this variable, including the long-term rate of interest, domestic per capita income and growth rate, and the balance of international indebtedness, have been variously tested by Kenen and Yudin (1965), by Heller (1966), by Courchene and Youssef (1967), by Kelly (1970), by Clark (1970a), by Flanders (1971), and by Hipple (1974a). Unfortunately, except in the case of Courchene and Youssef, who in some instances found a strong relationship between reserve demand and the domestic long-term interest rate, the results of these tests have by and large been meager. However, this should not be taken as evidence that the opportunity cost of holding reserves is therefore unimportant. Quite the contrary, it indicates rather that there is a vital need to improve the technical specification of this particular variable. There can be no doubt in logic that opportunity cost to the nation must play a role in determining the demand for reserves of individual countries. To believe otherwise is to deny that central bankers have any trace at all of economic rationality. However appealing such a thought may be to some members of the economics profession, it can hardly provide a firm foundation for much useful empirical research.

The key advantage of including the opportunity-cost variable is that it enables the researcher to construct a complete model of the short-run demand function for reserves consistent with what theory (as well as common sense) tells us is relevant. The government can be treated as no different from any other economic unit attempting to maximize its own economic welfare under conditions of risk and uncertainty. Like all other units, the government can be assumed to have a (social) utility function and to make decisions rationally by weighing the marginal benefits and marginal costs to the nation of alternative options for behavior. The national demand for reserves can then be estimated directly in terms of an explicit optimizing procedure. Early starts in this direction were made by Kane (1965) and by Heller (1966). Heller correctly summarized the principal factors relevant to such an optimizing procedure as the probability of reserve depletion, the cost of the alternative policy measures that would be required if reserves were depleted, and the opportunity cost of holding reserves. The approach was subsequently refined and elaborated in papers by Clark (1970a, 1970b), by Kelly (1970), by Agarwal (1971), by Britto and Heller (1973), and by Hipple (1974a). However, none of these writers can be said by any means to have provided the last word on the subject. Much more could certainly be done to improve on their pioneering efforts.

Indeed, insofar as the positive analysis of reserve demand is concerned, here is where I think most research resources should be allocated in the future – at the level of theory as much as at the level of empirical testing and application. At the level of theory, much further elaboration of existing models is called for. Clark (1970b) and Hipple (1974a) have stressed the need to introduce the element of time and the speed of adjustment explicitly into the analysis. Even more important is the need to account explicitly for the differing costs of alternative sources and types of external disturbances, as well as for the differing costs of the whole range of alternative policy measures that may be available to the authorities if reserves are depleted. Earlier models (Heller, 1966; Clark, 1970a, 1970b; Kelly, 1970; Agarwal, 1971) did not distinguish among alternative sources and types of disturbances, and they tended to assume that just a single policy measure – domestic expenditure reduction – was available to the authorities in the event of disequilibrium. The implication, therefore, was that adjustment and financing were perfect substitutes for one another – in other words, that there was a straight trade-off between the costs of holding and not holding reserves (the marginal utility of holding reserves always declining, the marginal cost of holding reserves always rising). This was hardly a realistic assumption. Instances do arise, as Kenen (in Fellner *et al.*, 1966, p. 152) has reminded us, when "financing and adjustment should be considered as complements rather than rivals." The marginal utility of a high level of reserves, for example, may be considerably greater than that of a low level of reserves if it induces governments to put into effect slower, more efficient methods of adjustment. The marginal utility of any given level of reserves may vary substantially depending on the nature of anticipated balance-of-payments disturbances. More recent models of reserve demand have been expanded to allow for some specific instances such as these (Britto and Heller, 1973; Hipple, 1974a).

At the level of empirical testing and application, what is mainly called for is further technical refinement of the three central arguments of the government's utility function. I have already commented on the need for improved specification of the measures of payments variability (proxy for the probability of reserve depletion) and of the opportunity cost of holding reserves. However, it is undoubtedly the third variable – the cost of the alternative policy measures that would be required if reserves were depleted – that requires the most fresh effort. This relates back directly to the point made in the previous paragraph. The standard assumption of earlier models, that the only alternative policy measure available was domestic expenditure reduction to cut imports, was obviously a caricature of reality. The authorities are not confined to a simple choice of either using owned reserves or deflating the domestic economy. There is a whole range of other possible options. If governments prefer not to use owned reserves (unconditional liquidity) to finance a deficit, they may be able to use borrowed reserves (conditional liquidity) or they may be able to use interest-rate changes (financial correctives) to attract private short-term capital inflows. If they prefer not to use expenditure-reducing techniques to adjust a deficit, they may be able to use one or another expenditure-switching technique, such as devaluation or selective restrictions. Any of these policy measures may be used in some given circumstances; they may be used singly, or, if instruments are subject to diminishing returns (increasing marginal cost) or their impacts are uncertain, they may be used in combination. All ought to be investigated for their potential influence on the demand for reserves (to hold). Unfortunately, to date only two empirical studies (Flanders, 1971; Hipple, 1974a) have even tried to examine the influence on reserve-holding behavior of such variables as the availability of external credit or the willingness to devalue, and these were not very successful. An alternative method of incorporating the availability of external credit into existing models was suggested by Salant (in IMF, 1970, p. 280), but has never been tested.

The main reason why the standard assumption of earlier models was so unsatisfactory is that it undoubtedly exaggerated the true cost of adjustment. If the only alternative to using owned reserves is domestic expenditure reduction to cut imports, the cost of adjustment to external disturbances will be determined directly by the size of the foreign-trade multiplier. Optimal reserves will vary negatively with the marginal propensity to import. If, on the other hand, account is taken of the whole range of other policy options available to the authorities, the estimate of cost is likely to be considerably reduced. Although the theory of adjustment costs is still in its infancy (Cohen, 1966), in recent years a number of efforts have been made to quantify the real costs associated with alternative policy measures (Cohen, 1971a, Chap. 7; Heller and Kreinin in Sellekaerts, ed., 1973; Sellekaerts and Sellekaerts, 1973; Hipple, 1974b). One thing we now know is that, in all but the most open economies, switching techniques of adjustment generally tends to be far less costly in terms of national income foregone than domestic expenditure reduction. In the case of the United Kingdom, for instance, Cohen (1971a, Chap. 7) estimated that the cost of restricting either trade or capital movements was far less than that of deflating the domestic economy. Sellekaerts and Sellekaerts (1973) found that in many circumstances financial correctives tend to be even less costly. Governmental decisions on reserve holding are undoubtedly influenced by such considerations.

These considerations are important because they have a direct and crucial bearing on the issue of the appropriate rate of interest to pay on SDRs. Currently, the interest rate on SDRs created by the Fund is set in the vicinity of 5 per cent per annum. However, a number of writers (Mundell, 1971, Chap. 17; Clark, 1972; Johnson, 1973, Chap. 10; Grubel, 1973) have urged an increase in that rate to more commercially competitive levels; the issue has become one of the most hotly debated of all aspects of world monetary reform. The principal argument in favor of a higher interest rate on SDRs is that it will "lead to higher average reserve holdings, lower speed of adjustment, and increased overall efficiency of the international payments mechanism" (Grubel, 1971, p. 1164). But is this argument necessarily correct? Must higher average reserve holdings and a lower speed of adjustment necessarily mean an increase in the overall efficiency of the international payments mechanism? The argument is necessarily correct only if the real cost of adjustment is in fact very high – in other words, if the standard assumption of earlier demand models is in fact accurate. On the other hand, if it happens that the standard assumption of earlier models tends to exaggerate the real cost of adjustment, then a relatively high rate of interest on SDRs could actually decrease the overall efficiency of the international payments mechanism by encouraging governments to hold onto their SDRs when instead they ought to be using them. The speed of adjustment could actually be reduced to below its international optimum.

The standard assumption of earlier models has also been criticized by Hipple (1974a) and by Frenkel (1974; in Aliber, 1974). Both authors proposed considering the opposite assumption – namely that the alternative to using owned reserves be expenditure switching via a change in the terms of trade instead of domestic expenditure reduction. The theoretical implication of this assumption appears to be that in most circumstances optimal reserves will then vary *positively* with the *average* propensity to import, rather than (as conventionally thought) *negatively* with the *marginal* propensity to import. This implication was confirmed both by Frenkel and by Hipple in empirical tests. Unfortunately, no comparable tests of the relationship of reserve holdings to the marginal propensity to import have yet been made. All existing studies are critically flawed, first, by the procedure (owing to data limitations) of using the average propensity to import as a proxy for the marginal propensity to import (Heller, 1966; Clark, 1970a; Kelly, 1970), and, second, by the failure to distinguish adequately between alternative sources and types of external disturbances. A negative correlation between the marginal propensity to import and optimal reserves in fact would be expected to hold only in the case of disturbances originating abroad. In the case of disturbances originating at home, a high marginal propensity to import would mean a substantial spillover into the balance of payments and thus imply a positive, rather than a negative, correlation between the two variables.

The fundamental point being made here is that there is a need for much greater sophistication in the handling of the relationship between the demand for reserves and the process of adjustment than has generally been true in the past. As Clower and Lipsey (1968, p. 592) have stressed, "the calculation of optimal reserves is extremely sensitive to the set of policy alternatives considered." Because of this, several authors have expressed grave doubt whether meaningful empirical indicators of reserve demand may even be possible (Yeager, 1959; Clower and Lipsey,

1968; Sohmen in IMF, 1970; Niehans in IMF, 1970). In the words of one skeptic: "The circumstances . . . are such as to defy any attempt at quantitative evaluation" (Sohmen in IMF, 1970, p. 29). In the words of another:

> Since the demand for reserves depends on their utility and cost which, in turn . . . depend on many highly variable aspects of the macroeconomic system, we cannot expect any relatively simple demand function to be valid for many countries over considerable periods of time. . . . In view of these circumstances, it would not be surprising if the demand for reserves of a single country turned out to be a rather elusive concept which might be difficult to quantify" (Niehans in IMF, 1970, p. 57).

One can only agree with the sentiment that quantification may be difficult in practice. But that does not therefore mean that quantification is necessarily impossible in principle. It all depends on the ingenuity as well as the perseverance of researchers. That is always the challenge of trying to make the transition from theory to application. In this case, the transition would be particularly eased by better theory about the costs of adjustment and about the trade-offs between adjustment and financing.

The Supply of Reserves

Unlike studies of the demand for reserves, in which the focus of attention is necessarily on individual countries, positive economic analysis of the supply of reserves must concentrate on the world as a whole. The question is: What determines or influences the global supply of international monetary reserves? Global reserve supply (international liquidity) in the monetary system today, as noted above, has four components: gold, convertible foreign exchange, SDRs, and reserve positions in the IMF. Two of these, gold and foreign exchange, are still not under formal international control. The prospective growth of their supply, therefore, must be estimated in advance before decisions can be taken on an appropriate rate of creation of SDRs.

Prior to 1968, analysis of the determinants of the supply of monetary gold was of considerable topical interest. (Monetary gold is defined to include IMF holdings as well as the holdings of central banks.) The estimation problem was twofold: first, to identify the trend of physical production in the (non-Communist) world, and, second, to calculate how much of this new output was likely to be absorbed by the arts and industry and by private demand for hoarding. Only the residual, adjusted for any sales by the Soviet Union, represented net additions to monetary gold stocks. An authoritative early study by Altman (1958) predicted that annual increases of gold reserves would average at least $700 million over the next decade. However, by the middle of the 1960s it was already clear that the pace of new output could hardly keep up with the rising level of private demand at the then prevailing price of $35 an ounce. When Soviet sales fell off after 1966, official gold holdings actually began to decline until governmental support of the price in the private market (through the Gold Pool) was withdrawn in March 1968. The United States and other major financial powers agreed to refrain completely from either buying or selling gold in the private market. Following establishment of the two-tier gold-price system, changes in the supply of monetary gold were minimal, apart from changes in the valuation of existing physical stocks necessitated by the two U.S. formal devaluations of December 1971 and February 1973.

Are significant changes in the supply of monetary gold likely to occur in the future? Most observers have expected to see gold gradually phased out of the international monetary system. Yet gold may still have an important practical role to play as an international reserve asset. In November 1973 the self-denying ordinance of March 1968 was terminated, governments restoring to themselves the privilege of either buying or selling gold in the private market. Whether this will in fact lead to substantial changes in monetary gold holdings will depend on what happens to the private price for gold, and this in turn will depend on what happens, on the one hand, to physical production and, on the other hand, to the private demand for gold (adjusted for net hoarding or dishoarding). With respect to both sides of the equation, our present knowledge is extremely limited. There have been few satisfactory studies recently of prospects for gold production in the years ahead (but see Hirsch, 1968). There have been even fewer systematic studies of the prospects for private demand, though there have been some educated guesses (Machlup, 1969; Davies, 1969). Unfurrowed fields lie here to be tilled.

The other important issue to be considered in this connection is what determines the size of the foreign-exchange component of reserves. This will continue to be an important issue in supply analysis at least until such time as the monetary system is reformed to remove all dollars and other national currencies (mainly the Deutsche mark, pound sterling, and French franc) from international reserves. Whether or not reform along such lines would be a desirable objective is a normative question best considered under the heading of the composition of reserves. For positive supply analysis, the existence and growth of foreign-exchange reserves must simply be taken for granted.

The main source of growth of foreign-exchange reserves has of course been the deficit in the U.S. balance of payments. (Official holdings of secondary reserve currencies, other than of the Deutsche mark, have not increased significantly in the postwar period.) The question is: What determines the supply of official dollar liabilities? Over the years, two contrasting types of answer were developed in the literature. One type, distinctly a minority view, argued that the deficit in U.S. payments was merely a reflection of the liquidity objectives of the rest of the world (Kindleberger, 1965; Despres *et al.*, 1966; McKinnon, 1969). Other countries set their targets for reserve accumulation; the United States suffered the consequences in the form of a deficit in its balance of payments. The supply of dollar reserve liabilities therefore was essentially "demand-determined." There was no fundamental disequilibrium in the international system. In the opinion of Kindleberger (1969, p. 5), "this is not a deficit in any meaningful sense but international financial intermediation, a useful economic function which supplies liquidity to the world when and as needed."

The alternative type of explanation, by contrast, argued that there *was* a deficit in a meaningful sense: there *was* a fundamental disequilibrium in the international system (even prior to the massive deterioration of the U.S. balance of payments in 1970–71). The supply of official dollar liabilities did not bear any systematic relationship to the reserve-accumulation objectives of other countries. Instead, it reflected considerably more basic economic and policy phenomena – variously said to be excessive monetary and demand inflation in the United States, excessive devaluations of European and Japanese currencies earlier in the postwar period, inappropriate interest-rate differentials, excessive U.S. remittances and capital exports, excessive protectionism in Europe and Japan, structural changes in tastes and technology, or whatever. This was a "supply-determined" explanation of the U.S. deficit – the United States supplying dollars in excess of the rest of the world's overall demand for liquidity. It has been the prevailing view on the subject ever since the initial statement by Triffin (1960).

Which of these two explanations really tells the tale? The question is important. For example, if the minority view happens to be even partially right over the long term, then the prevailing view that the U.S. deficit must be totally eliminated is not only misguided but actively pernicious. Any corrective measures by the United

States (unless compensated by an appropriate change in the rate of creation of SDRs) will sooner or later generate matching efforts by other countries to maintain their targeted rate of reserve accumulation. As a result, unless foreign demand for reserves declines, the end-product could turn out to be a reduced rate of worldwide economic growth or a heightened level of international trade and capital restrictions. According to Kindleberger (1965, p. 25), "Objective circumstances of strength can be turned into chaos by subjective judgments."

On the other hand, if the prevailing view is *not* misguided, and the U.S. deficit is in fact supply-determined over the long term rather than demand-determined, current efforts to bring the global stock of reserves under conscious international control may be doomed to failure by unilateral American policies. Even before the convertibility of the dollar was formally suspended in August 1971, Johnson (in IMF, 1970, p. 149) warned that if the United States were not constrained by the same need to maintain an adequate level of reserves as other countries – other countries instead being obliged to accept dollars in whatever amounts the United States happened to create them – then effective control of the growth of international liquidity would rest with the American government and not with the collective decision-making machinery in the IMF for creation of SDRs. The dollar's present inconvertibility has of course had precisely that effect. For this reason, many observers now argue that in the future the United States must be required to finance its deficits exclusively through variations on the assets side of its reserve portfolio, rather than as at present through variations on the liabilities side; this has become another of the more hotly debated aspects of monetary reform. As Williamson (1973) has duly noted, the real issue underlying the convertibility controversy is precisely this question of who will determine the global quantity of reserves.

Unfortunately, remarkably few attempts have yet been made to test empirically whether there has ever been any validity at all to the minority view of the U.S. deficit. Indeed, apart from some rather cursory inspections of the statistics (Triffin, 1966; Aliber, 1969; Lamfalussy in Kindleberger and Shonfield, eds., 1971), only one study relating to the question has so far appeared in the literature embodying formal econometrics (Laffer in Machlup *et al.*, 1972b), and this offered at best only minimal confirmation of the minority view. The jury is still out on this crucial issue. There is a rather obvious need for more sophisticated statistical investigation.

Adequacy and Optimality

This brings us back to our initial question: What is the appropriate quantity of reserves, and at what rate should reserve supply be increased? A number of writers have denied even the possibility of identifying a precise "adequacy" in global reserves. Some, already mentioned above, are skeptics because of the extreme sensitivity of empirical demand estimates to the set of policy alternatives considered. Others are skeptics because they doubt that governments do in fact tend to set any specific targets for reserve accumulation. Reserves, they suggest, instead constitute only a *constraint* on policy, in the sense that if reserves (or reserve growth) fall below some minimum level (or rate), certain actions will be forthcoming; but so long as reserves (or reserve growth) remain above such a critical minimum, governments will be more or less indifferent to what is actually happening in this respect. Machlup (1966, p. 207), for example, has insisted that "There is no 'need' for any particular sum of monetary reserves in the world. There is no sense, therefore, in which it can be said that the world total of monetary reserves is inadequate." However, this is a rather extreme position. Cooper (in IMF, 1970), for instance, even while admitting that over certain ranges countries may be indifferent to changes of reserve level (or growth rate), nevertheless concluded that it is a safe generalization to speak of reserves as an explicit objective of policy. In any event, the various studies described above have already produced considerable evidence of well-defined national demand functions for reserves. Reserve holdings do not appear to be random.

Another skeptic is Flanders, who in 1969 (p. 528) argued that because the only alternative to financing is adjustment, and adjustment necessarily involves a real-resource cost to the community, "It follows from this that no amount of international reserves, short of infinity, can ever be enough. . . . [T]here is likely always to be a 'shortage' of reserves, whatever the actual level of reserves may be." (This position was only slightly modified in her 1971 study (p. 43), which meanwhile tended to confirm her skepticism on empirical grounds.) This argument rests on a total denial of central-bank rationality. In effect, it confuses the desire for reserves, which admittedly is virtually unlimited, with the demand for reserves, which is undoubtedly limited by the opportunity cost of holding reserves. If it can be assumed that central bankers are economically rational (and to assume otherwise, as I have already suggested, can hardly provide a firm foundation for much useful empirical research), it follows that their demand for reserves will fall far short of infinity.

Most students of international liquidity today seem prepared to concede that central bankers do act rationally. Most also are prepared to assume that countries do set approximate reserve targets, and that the quantification of national demands for reserves is not impossible in principle. This was apparently the majority view, for instance, at the special conference convened by the IMF in 1970 to explore various aspects of the liquidity issue (IMF, 1970). On this basis, adequacy in global reserves can be identified directly by summing the demands for reserves of all individual countries (ignoring any possible sources of interdependence among national demands). Furthermore, an approximate rate of SDR creation can be calculated directly by deducting from the sum of country demands any prospective increases in the total of official dollar liabilities (assuming that the United States is somehow constrained like all other countries to maintain an adequate level of its own reserves). The residual represents adequacy in the growth of global reserves. "Adequacy" here means the quantity and rate of increase of reserves that are sufficient to enable all countries together to reconcile their separate payments objectives.

However, *adequacy* in this sense, as Grubel (1971, p. 1162) has correctly warned us, is not necessarily the same thing as *optimality:*

If one uses demand equations . . ., one can calculate what reserves would be demanded by the world at the future date and at assumed levels of determinants. The supply of such reserve quantities is defined to be "adequate" in permitting the world economy to operate with the same level of restrictions on trade and capital flows and adjustment policies as were used during the period from which the data for the demand equation estimate were taken. This level of restrictions and adjustment policies, and therefore the projected "adequate" level of reserves, may or may not be "optimal." For the supply of reserves to be "optimal" certain other criteria have to be met. . . .

What are these other criteria? Here we are obliged to return, once more, to the relationship between the demand for reserves and the process of payments adjustment. We have seen that the estimated demand of each individual country, its own optimizing procedure, depends heavily on the range of alternative policy options considered. In the same way, the estimated demand for the world as a whole, the global reserve optimum, must also be conceived as depending heavily on the range of alternative policies considered. Specifically, it depends on the range of alternative adjustment *systems* considered. The discussion is raised to a *systemic* level. The criteria required are those for choosing between alternative adjustment systems.

Empirical demand studies, since they are based on past behavior, naturally take the existing adjustment system for granted. Under these conditions, a supply of reserves equal to estimated aggregate demand could be defined as adequate (in the sense of enabling all countries to reconcile their separate payments objectives). But it would not be an optimal supply if some alternative adjustment system could be conceived permitting reconciliation of payments objectives at a lower level of trade and capital restrictions or via the use of more efficient adjustment techniques. Such a system might involve, for example, wider margins of flexibility around parity and quicker adjustment of par values, or even some managed version of floating exchange rates; alternatively, it might involve more international supervision of national policies within the traditional Bretton Woods pegged-rate framework. Whatever its characteristics, if the level of world welfare associated with it is greater than that associated with the existing adjustment system, then a reserve supply which is adequate under given conditions does not represent a global optimum for all conditions. There is only a single global optimum in this sense. It is the supply of reserves which is adequate (in the sense described) for the adjustment system associated with the highest possible level of world welfare.

This explicitly welfare-oriented interpretation of the problem of estimating an appropriate reserve quantity and growth rate was pioneered early by Fleming (1961, 1967) and was later formalized by Johnson (1973, Chap. 10), extending parallel discussions concerning the optimum quantity of money for the domestic economy (Friedman, 1969). Implicitly, it formed the basis for most of the contributions to the IMF conference in 1970 (IMF, 1970). Although a number of the participants seemed uncertain as to whether one could actually speak of such a thing as an optimal *supply* of reserves, little doubt was expressed that it was possible at least to speak of an optimal *rate of growth* of reserves. The general consensus was that reserve creation through SDRs should be viewed as a deliberate policy instrument capable of influencing and modifying national reserve behavior in desirable directions – specifically, toward choosing the lowest possible level of restrictions and the most efficient possible techniques of adjustment. This viewpoint, that there is such a thing as an optimal rate of growth of SDRs, has dominated official and academic discussions ever since.

Ideally, what the viewpoint calls for is specification of an aggregate welfare function for the world. Alternative models of the adjustment system *qua* system could then be compared directly for their ability to maximize this world function, subject to the usual behavioral and institutional constraints. The optimal supply of reserves would be identified as that quantity which is adequate (again, in the sense described) for the best of these alternative systems. SDRs would be created at a rate designed to approximate this global optimum. Needless to say, this direct route of investigation has never yet been tried in empirical research: our understanding of the marginal costs and benefits of alternative adjustment systems is still much too rudimentary to allow it. This puts emphasis once again on the need for better theory about the costs of adjustment and about the trade-offs between adjustment and financing. Indeed, if one is looking for new problems for study at the level of pure theory, here might be a useful place to begin.

In the meantime, in place of the ideal one must settle for the practical. Fleming (1967, pp. 15–18) noted that insofar as empirical application of the welfare-oriented interpretation is concerned, either of two indirect approaches might be substituted for the more direct (but presently impracticable) route of investigation. One is an individual-country approach, the other a global approach. Both involve the use of positive economic analysis. Both are promising areas for research in the future.

The individual-country approach looks directly at how different countries react to changes of reserve supply. As Fleming (1967, pp. 17–18) described it,

[The approach] begins by asking *for each country* the following question: Given the actual level of reserves, what rate of reserve growth would produce the "best" effects on policy as to the goals of full employment, price stability, and liberalization of international transactions, etc.? . . . After these figures are estimated for each country, they can be aggregated . . . to provide an estimate of the global optimal rate of reserve growth.

Actually, there are two questions here: First, is it possible to predict the effects of reserve changes on national policies? And, second, is it possible to know what the "best" policies are? The second is obviously a question for normative evaluation. It calls for value judgments concerning the consequences that are apt to arise if reserves are at one level rather than another. This emphasizes again the imperative to keep clear the distinction between reserve demand and reserve need. It is assumed that countries develop a demand for a quantity of reserves that they can consider adequate or optimal for their own purposes. They demand what they "need" to avoid certain consequences. But some of these consequences might actually be desirable from the point of view of maximizing world welfare. For example, more vigorous use of expenditure policy or exchange-rate change might be what the *sys-tem* says a country "needs," even if it does necessitate greater pain of dislocation and resource reallocation locally. The cosmopolitan interest dictates that the international distribution of adjustment costs must be taken into account. The interest of each country is to minimize its own share of the total burden of adjustment. The "best" policies, therefore, may be those which redistribute part of that burden. As Fleming (1967, p. 17) stressed, "This 'best' is judged more from an international than a national standpoint."

The first question, by contrast, is a subject for positive economic analysis. It is, in fact, what the study of individual-country reserve demand is presumably all about. Some writers doubt the relevance of demand studies in this connection (Grubel, 1971). But so long as it can be assumed that countries do have well-defined demand functions for reserves, these can provide much of the necessary input for predicting the effects of reserve changes on national policies. Indeed, the only way of improving on these studies would be to build a comprehensive macroeconomic model of the world in which the use of adjustment policies and the state of the balance of payments in individual countries would be determined simultaneously with other principal economic objectives. In time, this may be accomplished through the efforts of "Project LINK"; some of the conceptual and data problems that must be confronted in attempting to design such a model have been outlined by Rhomberg (1970). Until then, however, it would not be a waste of intellectual resources to continue seeking improvements in the positive analysis of reserve demand.

What of the alternative global approach? This approach shifts the focus of investigation to the state of the international economy as a whole. Instead of attempting to predict the effects of reserve changes on individual-country behavior, it concentrates rather on the effects of such changes on the behavior of the world economy overall. The principle is to measure directly the most relevant common targets of policy, such as employment, output, prices, and growth. The procedure then is to ask what rate of reserve growth (given the actual level of reserves) would produce the "best" global performance of these several macroeconomic variables. (Again, this implies that there is a normative issue here of what is "best," as well as a question for positive economic analysis.)

One variant of the global approach would focus on the changing level of national trade and capital restrictions as the best indicator of stringency or excess in the rate of growth of reserves. An alternative variant would focus on the monetarist theory of the balance of payments, which, as indicated earlier, assumes that payments disequilibrium is fundamentally a monetary phenomenon. Since monetarist theory also assumes that changes of the money supply primarily affect prices rather than real macroeconomic variables such as output or employment (except in the very short run), the conclusion follows that it is impossible to control the real level of reserves internationally through manipulation of the nominal level of reserves (just as it is impossible, presumably, to control the real money supply domestically through manipulation of the nominal money supply). The best the authorities can hope to do is increase the overall supply of reserves at a rate conducive to world price stability. According to the monetarist variant of the global approach, therefore, there is really only one valid indicator of best global performance and optimal reserve growth – the index of international prices (Mundell, 1971, Chap. 17; Johnson, 1973, Chap. 10).

To date, there have been no systematic empirical studies formally embodying any variant of the global approach, though a number of possible research methods have been evaluated by Rhomberg (in IMF, 1970). The approach has received the enthusiastic endorsement of a number of writers (Niehans in IMF, 1970, pp. 83–84):

[An] assessment of national reserve needs may be quite unnecessary. The creation of reserves by an international institution is in many respects analogous to the creation of commercial bank reserves by a central bank. But domestic monetary policy never starts out from an evaluation of cash requirements of individual banks, firms, and households, and this was never regarded as a handicap or deficiency. In fact, economists have hardly ever bothered about the adequacy of cash balances of individual agents at a given moment of time. All discussions of monetary theory and policy have really been about aggregates and "representative" individuals. An analysis of individual cash balances has always appeared as both impossible and unnecessary.

The same is likely to be true for international reserves. International monetary authorities should be able to formulate workable guidelines for the aggregate supply of, say, special drawing rights, without considering the reserve needs of individual countries. These guidelines would probably be based on certain broad facts about the development of the world economy in much the same way that domestic monetary policies are based on broad facts about the national economy.

There can be no doubt that the global approach has considerable merit and deserves far more attention in formal empirical research than it has received until now. However, it is neither likely nor desirable that the approach would ever supplant completely the individual-country approach. Niehans's analogy is imperfect. It is true that the domestic monetary authorities mainly concern themselves with aggregates rather than with individuals – but at a cost. The cost is the failure to take into account (except, possibly, indirectly) any sectoral or regional imbalances that may be concealed within these broader aggregates. There is little enough excuse for this failure at the domestic level. There can be none at all at the global level, where considerations of national sovereignty and (as we shall see below) world wealth distribution obviously oblige the international authorities to keep the reserve (and other) needs of individual countries very much in mind. The global approach and the individual-country approach must be treated as complementary rather than as substitutes. Both can be useful in determining the optimal rate of growth of SDRs through time.

2. THE COMPOSITION OF RESERVES

What is the appropriate composition of reserves, and in what form(s) should new reserves be created? This issue has traditionally received rather less attention in the formal literature than the issue of the quantity of reserves – in large part because, until Triffin (1960), few observers fully recognized the inherent instability of a gold-exchange standard. During the interwar period, of course, there was much concern with "hot money" flows, and with the problem of divided responsibility among the principal reserve centers. But the conventional wisdom of the time – embodied in the Tripartite Agreement of 1936 as well as in the IMF Charter negotiated at Bretton Woods – was that the system itself could surely be stable if only it was managed properly. The great contribution of *Gold and the Dollar Crisis* lay in its demonstration that the question was really one of fundamental structure, not merely of superficial management. As long as the international monetary system continued to rely mainly on cumulative deficits in the U.S. balance of payments to avert a liquidity shortage, the progressive deterioration in the American reserve position would almost certainly in time undermine global confidence in the dollar. Indeed, eventually, in Triffin's opinion at least, the growing relative scarcity of monetary gold might possibly become so serious that a massive "run on the bank" could develop, causing the system to collapse altogether (as in 1931).

Essentially, the instability inherent in a gold-exchange standard is the same as that described by the old formula of Gresham's Law. The instability stems directly from the coexistence of several different kinds of reserve assets (gold, dollars, sterling, etc.) in what is supposed to be a fixed-price relationship to one another.

The problem is how optimally to cope with international shifts of confidence or attempts to alter the composition of reserve holdings that threaten to upset this fixed-price relationship.

In principle, there are three alternative ways to cope with a Gresham's Law problem. One is to adjust the relative supplies of the several assets to correspond to the asset preferences of holders. The second is to adjust the asset preferences of holders by altering various of the attributes of the several assets (the most important of these attributes being interest income, convertibility risk, and exchange risk). The third is to reduce the total number of assets to a single-money system. During the 1960s a variety of reforms were proposed by academic experts and others embodying one or another of these three approaches to solution of the international confidence problem. Some reforms would have adjusted for the growing relative scarcity of monetary gold via a uniform revaluation of the official price of gold in terms of all national currencies (Harrod, 1965). Others would have adjusted for the convertibility risk and exchange risk of foreign-exchange reserve balances via the provision of exchange guarantees (Kenen, 1963a). And still others would have created a single-money system based variously on gold (Rueff in Cassell, ed., 1965), on the dollar (Despres in Joint Economic Committee, 1966), on some internationally created fiduciary reserve asset (Triffin, 1960), on a composite reserve unit (CRU) representing a pool of all existing monetary assets (Bernstein in Joint Economic Committee, 1968), or on an international stockpile of storable basic commodities (Hart *et al.* in United Nations, 1965).

In practice, however, remarkably little was actually done along any of these three lines. At the intergovernmental level, efforts were concentrated largely on the development of a variety of credit and borrowing facilities – reciprocal currency (swap) arrangements, the General Arrangements to Borrow, the Gold Pool, etc. – to provide an elastic supply of liquidity to governments in the event of short-term speculative crisis. (This was "crisis" liquidity, as contrasted with the provision of "trend" liquidity through the creation of SDRs.) These efforts could be interpreted as a marginal tinkering with the attributes of foreign-exchange reserve balances to reduce somewhat their convertibility risk and exchange risk. But they could hardly be described as constituting a fundamental solution of the international confidence problem. In fact, no really meaningful action was ever taken during the period after 1960 to moderate substantially the instability inherent in the system, either by adjusting significantly for the growing relative scarcity of monetary gold or by reducing the number of reserve assets. Establishment of the two-tier gold-price system in 1968, for instance, though it did succeed in halting the drain of monetary gold into private hoards, was essentially a compromise as far as the future reserve role of gold was concerned. The SDR agreement of 1968 actually resulted in an increase in the number of reserve assets in the system. And the suspension of the dollar's convertibility in 1971 only suppressed the Gresham's Law problem, it did not eliminate it.

Today, the prevailing view seems to be that the Gresham's Law problem would be best solved by immediately reducing the number of reserve assets, preferably by means of some sort of consolidation or funding of all dollar and other foreign-exchange reserve balances. (This also implies a return to dollar convertibility in the sense discussed above of asset financing of all future U.S. deficits.) A longer-term objective, as indicated earlier, would be eventually to phase out the monetary role of gold as well. Thus, ultimately, SDRs (together with reserve positions in the IMF) would constitute the sole medium of international reserves. There would no longer be any confidence problem at all at the intergovernmental level. New reserves would be created exclusively in the form of SDRs.

This approach has intuitive appeal, particularly because it would bring the entire supply of international liquidity under formal international control for the first time in history. But would it necessarily be the *optimal* approach to solution of the confidence problem? That is *not* so intuitively obvious. There are still many experts who are prepared to argue for the merits of alternative solutions based either on gold (Gilbert, 1968; Oppenheimer, 1969; Humphrey in Bergsten and Tyler, eds., 1973) or the dollar (McKinnon, 1969; Mundell in Acheson *et al.*, eds., 1972; Johnson, 1972). Once again, this is a question for normative policy judgment. And, once again, the answer calls for a contribution from positive economic analysis. To make the normative policy choice, we should be able to predict what the practical economic consequences would be of each of these alternative lines of reform. In particular, we should be able to predict what the impact of each would be on the adequacy of world reserves. What would the effect of each be on the global demand for reserves? What would the effect of each be on the global supply?

Curiously, the empirical literature is largely silent on these crucial matters. As a result, virtually all aspects of the normative policy choice remain shrouded in uncertainty. For example:

a. *The price of gold.* Advocates of a solution based on gold assume that a uniform revaluation of the official gold price would have a positive impact on global reserve supply, not only by upvaluing existing gold stocks but also by favorably influencing new inflows of gold into the world monetary system. But what, exactly, is the price elasticity of the supply of monetary gold? Just how big would a gold revaluation have to be to get the "right" result (if there is any such thing as a single "right" result)? I have already mentioned our limited knowledge of the determinants of the supply of monetary gold. There have been no systematic studies at all of the price elasticity of that supply. Gold-standard loyalists have preferred enunciation to demonstration.

b. *The Eurodollar market.* Advocates of a solution based on the dollar generally recognize that their approach is complicated somewhat by the existence of the Eurodollar market. It is known, for instance, that the market can substantially influence the recorded level of official dollar reserves through a process of currency "pyramiding" involving central banks: dollars received by central banks and then deposited in the market (either directly or through the Bank for International Settlements) and subsequently re-lent to private borrowers may eventually end up being sold back again to the official authorities. It is also known that, because of the closer integration of financial markets fostered by the Eurodollar market and the increased opportunities for currency speculation that the market provides, there may be a substantial influence on the level of reserve demand as well. However, as yet there have been no satisfactory studies of the impact of the market on either the demand or the supply side of the equation. We have hardly any idea at all what the quantitative relationship of the market is to the adequacy of world reserves. We are not even sure what the quantitative relationships are within the market itself – what the size is of the Eurodollar deposit multiplier, for instance, or even if there is one (Machlup in Machlup *et al.*, 1972a).

c. *The relationship between composition and demand.* All advocates of single-money systems – whether based on the SDR, gold, or the dollar – seem to assume that the coexistence of several different kinds of reserve assets tends to inflate the demand for reserves above what it would otherwise be, because of the structural instability inherent in a Gresham's Law situation. The *quantity* of reserves presumably must be greater to compensate for the diminished *quality* of certain of the assets in the system. However, just what the connection is between the quantity and "quality" of reserves has never been subjected satisfactorily to empirical investigation. It may be that total demand for reserves is not all that much affected by variations in the composition of reserve supply. It may even be that the coexistence of several different kinds of reserve assets tends to *reduce* the demand for owned reserves below what it would otherwise be, because of the greater variety of credit and borrowing facilities (the greater elasticity of supply of "crisis" liquidity) that a mixed system makes available. This question is perhaps the most important of all of those bearing on the composition issue. It is one that could use a good deal more work, at the level of pure theory as well as at the level of testing and application. Research might begin by extending the probabilistic notion of liquidity first proposed by Kane (1965). Various other possible methods have been outlined by Salant (in IMF, 1970, pp. 277–280).

Clearly, on all these matters there is a real need for more rigorous statistical investigation. Reduced uncertainty would permit greater rationality in the normative choice among proposed alternative solutions of the confidence problem.

Until now, virtually all the empirical literature concerned with the confidence problem has focused on the determinants of the reserve-asset preferences of central banks within the framework of the traditional gold-exchange standard. An elementary portfolio approach to reserve-asset composition, emphasizing the variables of risk and yield, was first proposed by Kenen (1960), in effect formalizing the verbal argument outlined by Triffin in *Gold and the Dollar Crisis.* Subsequent studies incorporating this approach (Kenen, 1963b; Greene in Kenen and Lawrence, eds., 1968; Hagemann, 1969; Stekler and Piekarz, 1970; Makin, 1971b) all found evidence that rational portfolio-management considerations do play a role in determining the composition of reserves as between gold and dollars. Key to the portfolio approach is the assumption that asset preferences are determined independently and that, in attempting to maximize their own utility, central banks do not recognize their mutual interdependence. Officer and Willett (1969), however, argued that in fact central banks (at least the major central banks) do recognize their mutual interdependence, and that as a result reserve-composition policies (specifically, conversions of dollars into gold) are apt to be significantly modified for the sake of avoiding a collapse of the system. Several studies (Kenen, 1963b; Høst-Madsen, 1964;

Greene in Kenen and Lawrence, eds., 1968; Makin, 1971a) also found evidence of such cooperative restraint in official gold purchases prior to 1971.

It must be emphasized that all these studies concentrated exclusively on the portfolio choice between gold and dollars. No systematic research has yet appeared extending the analysis to consider the effect on reserve-asset preferences of the introduction of SDRs as a third element in the choice. Would SDRs be treated as a kind of "outside money," like gold, or would they be treated as "inside money," like the dollar? At the theoretical level, the question was first addressed by Aliber (1967), who concluded that an internationally created fiduciary asset would more probably be treated as an inside money – that is, as a substitute for the dollar rather than for gold. In effect, therefore, introduction of what he called the "new reserve unit" (NRU) would exaggerate the relative attractiveness of the outside money, gold, in central-bank portfolios. However, Goldstein (1969), in a comment on Aliber's argument, and Hirsch (1971) both concluded just the opposite – that the gold-value guarantee attached to SDRs would make them a closer substitute for gold than for the dollar, and so would instead enhance the relative attractiveness of the inside money, the dollar, as a constituent of reserves. Unfortunately, the time period from the first allocation of SDRs at the start of 1970 until the formal suspension of dollar convertibility in mid-1971 was too short to permit accumulation of sufficient data to settle the question conclusively. In any event, designation rules controlling the use of SDRs have prevented significant shifts between the SDR and other reserve media.

Today, the empirical literature on reserve-asset preferences is of rather less topical interest than it was before the dollar became inconvertible. Its main relevance at present is in connection with the question of how payments imbalances between countries with different reserve-asset preferences may influence the total recorded supply of international liquidity. However, since in the future the composition of reserve holdings is most likely to be determined by mutual agreement, rather than by independent portfolio-management considerations, the really relevant questions from now on will be those on which the literature has so far been largely silent – in particular, the question of the relationship between the quantity and quality of reserves (i.e., the effect of reserve composition on demand). Here is where most research resources should be allocated in the future insofar as the positive analysis of reserve composition is concerned.

3. THE DISTRIBUTION OF RESERVES

What is the appropriate distribution of reserves, and to whom should the benefits of new reserve creation be distributed? Like the composition issue, the issue of the distribution of reserves has traditionally received rather less attention in the formal literature than the issue of the quantity of reserves. In fact, it was only during the negotiations leading up to the SDR agreement of 1968 that for the first time the distribution issue began to be discussed at all systematically (Group of Ten, 1965, 1966). The seminal contribution in this regard was made by Machlup (1965), who pointed out that the distribution issue simply *had* to be faced: there was no way to avoid it. The substitution of any type of a fiduciary reserve asset for a commodity money like gold involves a saving of real resources – the cost of producing and administering a fiat money is clearly less than the cost of mining and storing gold – and this "social saving" must be distributed to someone in some way. Distribution is the name of the game:

> The discovery that international money can be produced with cheap ink and paper, and need not be produced with hard work applied to metal dug out of the ground, affords a large saving. . . . The saving in the production of the low-cost substitute must be distributed somehow. . . . the saving will benefit someone and its distribution must needs be arbitrary (Machlup, 1965, pp. 353–355).

In principle, there are two ways in which the social saving may be distributed. If the fiat money is produced under conditions of total monopoly, the saving will accrue entirely to the issuer of the asset himself in the form of "seigniorage." (Originally, "seigniorage" referred to the difference between the circulating value of a coin and the cost of bullion and minting. Later the term was extended to describe the gain of real resources, over and above costs of production and administration, to the issuer of any kind of money – including also international money.) If, on the other hand, the issuer is confronted by competition from other sources of money, then his (net) seigniorage gain will be correspondingly reduced, since he will be obliged to pay a rate of interest on his liabilities in order to induce foreign depositors to retain their holdings; part of the social saving will accrue instead to the holders of the asset in the form of these interest payments. Indeed, the greater the competition from other sources, the higher the rate of interest will have to be. At the extreme, where the fiat money is produced under conditions approximating perfect competition and free entry, no significant seigniorage at all may be expected to accrue, on a net basis, to the issuer; asset holders, rather than the issuer, will receive the full benefit of the social saving.

In the past, the only issuers of international fiat money have been national governments – reserve-currency centers such as the United States and the United Kingom. The advantage of including convertible foreign exchange such as the dollar or sterling in monetary reserves has always been the flexibility provided to the system to economize on the inherited commodity base of gold. One of the disadvantages has always been the rather uncertain distribution of the social saving that was produced. A number of writers have attempted to quantify the relative distribution of the social saving as between holders (collectively) and issuers, usually as part of a broader survey of the costs and benefits of being a reserve center (Aliber, 1964; Grubel, 1964; Kirman and Schmidt, 1965; Karlik in Kenen and Lawrence, eds., 1968; Cohen, 1971a, 1971b). In general, the conclusion that can be drawn from these investigations seems to be that even in the case of the United States, some part of the (net) seigniorage gain has been effectively bid away by holders in the form of higher interest payments. In the case of the United Kingdom, it appears that virtually all the gain, on a net basis, may have been redistributed to overseas sterling holders (Cohen, 1971b).

One advantage of SDRs, in contrast to national currencies, in reserves is that they permit a reduction in the uncertainty surrounding the distribution of the social saving The benefits of new reserve creation can be distributed consciously in accordance with any preconceived set of political or economic criteria. As before, that distribution can be accomplished in two ways – either by way of the interest yield paid to SDR holders, or, alternatively, in the absence of a significant rate of interest on SDRs, by way of the initial allocation of the newly created reserves (which, as they are first spent, produce an effect equivalent to a reserve center's seigniorage). Currently, of course, with the interest rate on SDRs as low as it is, the latter dimension of new reserve creation is decisive in this respect.

Under the agreement of 1968, new SDRs are supposed to be (and until now have been) allocated initially simply in proportion to each country's quota in the IMF. The rationale for this method is that it is distributionally neutral, in the technical sense that it conforms strictly to the demand for reserves to hold, rather than to the demand for reserves to spend. The key assumption of the method is that Fund quotas do, in fact, reflect each country's average long-term demand for reserves, so that on average and over the long term cumulative allocations of SDRs will be held rather than used to acquire or lend real resources through the monetary system. There will be no permanent unrequited redistribution of wealth internationally.

What would be the effect of raising the interest rate on SDRs to more commercially competitive levels, as some writers, mentioned above in section 1, have urged? Quite probably, there would be an impact on the overall demand for reserves, as I suggested earlier. Furthermore, as long as national currencies and gold continue to be included in international reserves, there might be some impact on reserve composition as well, to the extent that variations in the interest rate on SDRs tend to influence the reserve-asset preferences of central banks. But there would need be no impact at all on the distribution issue, since – insofar as the social saving is concerned – the interest-rate approach is in principle no less neutral than allocation on the basis of IMF quotas is supposed to be. Again, there would be no permanent unrequited redistribution of wealth.

However, it must be emphasized that distributional neutrality is only *one* possible criterion for distributing the benefits of new reserve creation. There are others. In particular, there is the alternative possibility that the social saving might be redirected to the poorer nations of the world, as many writers, following the early lead of Stamp (1958), have advocated (Cohen, 1966; Karlik, 1969; Scitovsky in Joint Economic Committee, 1969; Triffin, 1971; Park, 1973). This is the so-called "link" proposal – the argument, based mainly on equity considerations or on grounds of convenience (but see Cohen, 1966), for a link between the creation of monetary reserves for the system and the provision of international aid for less developed countries. An equally impressive list of experts have argued against a link of any sort (Johnson in Joint Economic Committee, 1969; Haberler, 1971; Roosa in Council on Foreign Relations, 1972). In fact, by now the link proposal has become one of the most prominently discussed questions in the entire literature.

Obviously, what is involved here is yet another question for normative policy evaluation: What is the *optimal* way to distribute the social saving from new reserve creation? This plainly calls for explicit value judgments. It also calls for two pieces of objective information that can be provided only through positive economic analysis – first, an estimate of the total magnitude of the potential social saving and, second, an estimate of what the real-resource effects would be of alternative patterns of distribution.

With regard to the magnitude of the potential social saving, the estimation problem is twofold – first, to estimate the resource cost of producing and storing commodity money, and, second, to compare this with the cost of creating and administering a fiduciary-reserve substitute. The latter, of course, is apt to be negligible, though undoubtedly nonzero. Grubel (1973) suggested something on the order of $35 million as the expense in 1970 of producing and servicing the then existing stock of internationally created reserve assets (SDRs and reserve positions in the Fund); in fact, the figure is reputed to be probably even smaller than that. Cost-benefit studies of reserve-currency centers have implied roughly comparable dimensions to the expense of producing and servicing the foreign-exchange component of international reserves. By contrast, the resource cost of producing and storing commodity money is apt to be nonnegligible, though precisely how great it may be in real-resource terms is not at all clear from the literature. The cost of using gold for monetary purposes, for instance, was estimated by Oppenheimer (1969) and by Laidler (1969), with sharply differing results. And even sharper differences resulted from attempts to quantify the potential cost of using an alternative for gold in the form of a so-called "commodity-reserve currency" – that is, a reserve asset based on an international stockpile of storable basic commodities (Harmon, 1959; Hart *et al.* in United Nations, 1965; Grubel, 1965; Hart, 1966). The only firm conclusion that can be drawn from this literature is that use of a commodity-reserve currency would in all likelihood be considerably more expensive than continued use of the traditional commodity money, gold, mainly because of the greater costs of storage and depreciation involved. But just what the magnitude of the potential saving would be of withdrawing all commodity moneys from international circulation still remains to be determined. Here again is an area where more useful work could surely be done.

With regard to the real-resource effects of alternative patterns of distribution, the estimation problem focuses specifically on the demand for reserves to hold. It does not matter what type of fiduciary reserve asset we are talking about – whether about national currencies or about CRU or about SDRs. All imply an initial pattern of distribution of the social saving. Whether that pattern will be neutral in wealth terms, or whether it will lead to a permanent unrequited redistribution of wealth among nations, depends entirely on how the initial pattern compares with the pattern of national demands for reserves. For example, under the 1968 agreement, current initial allocations of SDRs may actually tend to shift world resources internationally, specifically to the rich, if it is true (as some suspect) that IMF quotas in fact underestimate the average long-term demand for reserves of LDCs. This was the conclusion of at least one recent empirical study (Hawkins and Rangarajan, 1970). Continued use of national currencies in international reserves, on the other hand, may well act to shift world resources away from (two of) the rich, if the interest rate paid on the existing stock of dollar or sterling balances exceeds the desired growth rate of reserves among the poor. The point is: We need to know the reserve demand function of every country in the system before we can provide a practical answer to the normative question of how "best" to distribute the social saving. This of course brings us full circle, back to where the survey began. It especially emphasizes again the importance of the individual-country approach, as a complement to the global approach, in analyzing optimality in international liquidity.

4. CONCLUSIONS

The conclusions of this paper may be summarized briefly.

On the issue of the *quantity* of reserves, the principal question is: What is the optimal growth rate of SDRs? As a first approximation, this calls for a comparison of total world demand for reserves with the prospective growth rate of reserve assets still not under conscious international control. Much more research will be needed in the future to make that comparision feasible. First of all, more work will be needed to improve existing empirical indicators of the demand for reserves. The main effort should be to construct a complete model of the national short-run demand function for reserves in terms of an explicit optimizing procedure. The principal factors relevant to such an optimizing model are the probability of reserve depletion, the cost of the alternative policy measures that would be required if reserves are depleted, and the opportunity cost of holding reserves. All three determinants need to be refined and tested for their influence on the demand for reserves of individual countries. It would also be useful to test for the influence of possible longer-run determinants of the demand function for reserves, such as the level of imports, the domestic money supply (or related domestic monetary variables), or aggregate national wealth.

Similarly, more work will be needed to improve understanding of the growth rate of reserve assets still not under conscious international control The main effort here should be to test for the validity, if any, of the "minority" (demand-determined) view of the U.S. payments deficit. It might also be worthwhile to investigate prospects for the price of gold in the private market, focusing on trends in physical production and in demand for nonmonetary uses.

As indicated, the comparison of total world demand for reserves with the prospective growth rate of reserve assets still not under conscious international control gives us only a first approximation of the optimal growth rate of SDRs. The reason is that the procedure takes the existing international adjustment system for granted. The residual represents "adequacy" in the growth of global reserves for the given adjustment system; to determine what would represent "optimality" in the growth of global reserves, the calculation must be adjusted for the best (in welfare terms) of all possible alternative adjustment systems. Here, again, much more research will be needed in the future. In the absence of sufficient theory to permit specification directly of an aggregate world welfare function, two indirect approaches to the problem are conceivable – the individual-country approach, which would concentrate on the effects of reserve changes on the economic policies of each nation separately, and the global approach, which would concentrate on the effects of such changes on the world economy overall. More work is needed to develop the methodology of both these analytical approaches.

On the issue of the *composition* of reserves, the principal question is: What is the optimal approach to solution of the confidence problem? This calls for predicting the impact of alternative lines of reform on the adequacy of world reserves. Further research will be needed to investigate a variety of crucial aspects of this question. Perhaps the most important of these concerns the relationship between the quantity and "quality" of reserves: What is the effect of the composition of reserves on the demand for reserves? More work could also usefully be done on the quantitative relationship of the Eurodollar market to global reserve adequacy. Gold-standard loyalists are obliged to seek more precise specification of the price elasticity of the supply of monetary gold.

On the issue of the *distribution* of reserves, the principal question is: What is the optimal way to distribute the social saving from new reserve creation? Further research will be needed here also, first to estimate the total magnitude of the potential social saving, and second to calculate the real-resource effects of alternative patterns of distribution. This latter emphasizes again the imperative to improve existing empirical indicators of the demand for reserves.

REFERENCES

Acheson, A. L. K., J. F. Chant, and M. F. J. Prachowny, eds., *Bretton Woods Revisited,* Toronto, University of Toronto Press, 1972.

Agarwal, J. P., "Optimal Monetary Reserves for Developing Countries," *Weltwirtschaftliches Archiv,* 107 (March 1971), pp. 76–91.

Aliber, Robert Z., "The Costs and Benefits of the U.S. Role as a Reserve Currency Country," *Quarterly Journal of Economics,* 78 (August 1964), pp. 442–456.

"Gresham's Law, Asset Preferences, and the Demand for International Reserves," *Quarterly Journal of Economics,* 81 (November 1967), pp. 628–638.

Choices for the Dollar, Washington, National Planning Association, 1969.

Aliber, Robert Z., ed., *National Monetary Policies and the International Financial System,* (Wingspread Conference, 1972), Chicago, University of Chicago Press, 1974.

Altman, Oscar L., "A Note of Gold Production and Additions to International Gold Reserves," *IMF Staff Papers,* 6 (April 1958), pp. 258–288.

Archibald, G. C., and J. Richmond, "On the Theory of Foreign Exchange Requirements," *Review of Economic Studies,* 38 (April 1971), pp. 245–263.

Arndt, H. W., "The Concept of Liquidity in International Monetary Theory," *Review of Economic Studies,* 15 (October 1947), pp. 20–26.

Bergsten, C. Fred, and William G. Tyler, eds., *Leading Issues in International Economic Policy: Essays in Honor of George N. Halm,* Lexington, Mass., Heath, 1973.

Britto, Ronald, and H. Robert Heller, "International Adjustment and Optimal Reserves," *International Economic Review,* 14 (February 1973), pp. 182–195.

Brown, Weir M., "The Concept and Measurement of Foreign Exchange Reserves," *Economic Journal,* 65 (September 1955), pp. 436–440.

The External Liquidity of an Advanced Country, Studies in International Finance No. 14, Princeton, N.J., 1964.

Cassell, Francis, ed., *International Monetary Problems,* London, Federal Trust for Education and Research, 1965.

Clark, Peter B., "The Demand for International Reserves: A Cross Country Analysis," *Canadian Journal of Economics,* 3 (February 1970a), pp. 577–594.

"Optimum International Reserves and the Speed of Adjustment," *Journal of Political Economy,* 78 (March/April 1970b), pp. 356–376.

"Interest Payments and the Rate of Return on International Fiat Currency," *Weltwirtschaftliches Archiv,* 108 (December 1972), pp. 537–564.

Clement, M. O., "A Functional Approach to the Concept of International Reserves," *Kyklos,* 16 (1963), pp. 415–435.

Clower, Robert, and Richard Lipsey, "The Present State of International Liquidity Theory," *American Economic Review,* 58 (May 1968), pp. 586–595.

Cohen, Benjamin J., "A Note on the Definition of International Liquidity," *Economia Internazionale,* 17 (August 1964), pp. 491–501.

Adjustment Costs and the Distribution of New Reserves, Studies in International Finance No. 18, Princeton, N.J., 1966.

The Future of Sterling as an International Currency, London, Macmillan, 1971a.

"The Seigniorage Gain of an International Currency: An Empirical Test," *Quarterly Journal of Economics*, 85 (August 1971b), pp. 494–507.

Council on Foreign Relations, *The Smithsonian Agreement and Its Aftermath: Several Views*, New York, 1972.

Courchene, T. J., and G. M. Youssef, "The Demand for International Reserves," *Journal of Political Economy*, 75 (August 1967), pp. 404–413.

Davies, Jack L., *Gold: A Forward Strategy*, Essays in International Finance No. 75, Princeton, N.J., 1969.

Despres, Emile, Charles P. Kindleberger, and Walter S. Salant, "The Dollar and World Liquidity: A Minority View," *The Economist*, Feb. 5, 1966, pp. 526–529.

Fellner, William, Fritz Machlup, Robert Triffin, and eleven others, *Maintaining and Restoring Balance in International Payments*, Princeton, N.J., Princeton University Press, 1966.

Flanders, M. June, "International Liquidity is Always Inadequate," *Kyklos*, 22 (1969), pp. 519–529.

The Demand for International Reserves, Studies in International Finance No. 27, Princeton, N.J., 1971.

Fleming, J. Marcus, "International Liquidity: Ends and Means," *IMF Staff Papers*, 8 (December 1961), pp. 439–463, reprinted in Fleming (1971).

Toward Assessing the Need for International Reserves, Essays in International Finance No. 58, Princeton, N.J., 1967, reprinted in Fleming (1971).

Essays in International Economics, London, Allen and Unwin, 1971.

Frenkel, Jacob A., "The Demand for International Reserves by Developed and Less-Developed Countries,"*Economica*, 41 (February 1974), pp. 14–24.

Friedman, Milton, *The Optimum Quantity of Money*, Chicago, Aldine, 1969.

Gemmill, R. F., "Notes on the Measurement of International Liquidity," *Journal of Finance*, 15 (March 1960), pp. 56–59.

Gilbert, Milton, *The Gold-Dollar System: Conditions of Equilibrium and the Price of Gold*, Essays in International Finance No. 70, Princeton, N.J., 1968.

Goldstein, Henry N., "Gresham's Law and the Demand for NRU's and SDR's," *Quarterly Journal of Economics*, 83 (February 1969), pp. 163–166.

Goodman, Bernard, "The Price of Gold and International Liquidity," *Journal of Finance*, 11 (March 1956), pp. 21–28.

Group of Ten, *Report of the Study Group on the Creation of Reserve Assets*, 1965.

Communiqué of Ministers and Governors and Report of Deputies, 1966.

Grubel, Herbert G., "The Benefits and Costs of Being the World Banker," *National Banking Review*, 2 (December 1964), pp. 189–212.

"The Case against an International Commodity Reserve Currency," *Oxford Economic Papers*, 17 (March 1965), pp. 130–135.

"The Demand for International Reserves: A Critical Review of the Literature," *Journal of Economic Literature*, 9 (December 1971), pp. 1148–1166.

"The Case for Optimum Exchange Rate Stability," *Weltwirtschaftliches Archiv*, 109 (September 1973), pp. 351–381.

Haberler, Gottfried, "The Case against the Link," *Banca Nazionale del Lavoro Quarterly Review*, 24 (March 1971), pp. 13–22.

Hagemann, H. A. "Reserve Policies of Central Banks and Their Implications for U.S. Balance of Payments Policy," *American Economic Review,* 59 (March 1969), pp. 62–77.

Harmon, E. M., *Commodity Reserve Currency,* New York, Columbia University Press, 1959.

Harrod, Roy F., "Imbalance of International Payments," *IMF Staff Papers,* 3 (April 1953), pp. 1–46.

Reforming the World's Money, New York, St. Martin's, 1965.

Hart, Albert G., "The Case for and against an International Commodity Reserve Currency," *Oxford Economic Papers,* 18 (July 1966), pp. 237–241.

Hawkins, Robert G., and C. Rangarajan, "On the Distribution of New International Reserves," *Journal of Finance,* 25 (September 1970), pp. 881–891.

Heller, H. Robert, "Optimal International Reserves," *Economic Journal,* 76 (June 1966), pp. 296–311.

"The Transactions Demand for International Means of Payment," *Journal of Political Economy,* 76 (January/February 1968), pp. 141–145.

"Wealth and International Reserves," *Review of Economics and Statistics,* 52 (May 1970), pp. 212–214.

Hipple, F. Steb, *The Disturbance Approach to the Demand for International Reserves,* Studies in International Finance No. 35, Princeton, N.J., 1974a.

"The Estimation of the Cost of Adjustment to External Disequilibria," *Review of Economics and Statistics,* 56 (November 1974b), pp. 450–455.

Hirsch, Fred, "Influences on Gold Production," *IMF Staff Papers,* 15 (November 1968), pp. 405–490.

"SDRs and the Working of the Gold Exchange Standard," *IMF Staff Papers,* 18 (July 1971), pp. 221–253.

Høst-Madsen, Poul, "Gold Outflows from the United States, 1958–63," *IMF Staff Papers,* 11 (July 1964), pp. 248–261.

International Monetary Fund, "The Adequacy of Monetary Reserves," *IMF Staff Papers,* 3 (October 1953), pp. 181–227.

International Reserves and Liquidity, Washington, 1958.

Annual Report 1969, Washington, 1969.

International Reserves: Needs and Availability, Washington, 1970.

Johnson, Harry G., "Political Economy Aspects of International Monetary Reform," *Journal of International Economics,* 2 (September 1972), pp. 401–423.

Further Essays in Monetary Economics, Cambridge, Mass., Harvard University Press, 1973.

Joint Economic Committee, *New Approach to United States International Economic Policy,* Hearings, Washington, 1966.

Next Steps in International Monetary Reform, Hearings, Washington, 1968.

Linking Reserve Creation and Development Assistance, Hearings, Washington, 1969.

Kane, Edward J., "International Liquidity: A Probabilistic Approach," *Kyklos,* 18 (1965), pp. 27–48.

Karlik, John R., *On Linking Reserve Creation and Development Assistance,* Washington, Joint Economic Committee, 1969.

Kelly, M. G., "The Demand for International Reserves," *American Economic Review,* 60 (September 1970), pp. 655–667.

Kenen, Peter B., "International Liquidity and the Balance of Payments of a Reserve-Currency Country," *Quarterly Journal of Economics,* 74 (November 1960), pp. 572–586.

"International Liquidity: The Next Steps," *American Economic Review,* 53 (May 1963a), pp. 130–138.

Reserve Asset Preferences of Central Banks and Stability of the Gold-Exchange Standard, Studies in International Finance No. 10, Princeton, N.J., 1963b.

Kenen, Peter B., and Roger Lawrence, eds., *The Open Economy,* New York, Columbia University Press, 1968.

Kenen, Peter B., and Elinor B. Yudin, "The Demand for International Reserves," *Review of Economics and Statistics,* 47 (August 1965), pp. 242–250, reprinted in Kenen and Lawrence (1968).

"The Demand for International Reserves: A Reply," *Review of Economics and Statistics,* 49 (November 1967), pp. 626–627.

Kindleberger, Charles P., *Balance-of-Payments Deficits and the International Market for Liquidity,* Essays in International Finance No. 46, Princeton, N.J., 1965.

"The Euro-Dollar and the Internationalization of United States Monetary Policy," *Banca Nazionale del Lavoro Quarterly Review,* 22 (March 1969), pp. 3–15.

Kindleberger, Charles P., and Andrew Shonfield, eds., *North American and Western European Economic Policies,* London, Macmillan, 1971.

Kirman, Alan P., and Wilson E. Schmidt, "Key Currency Burdens: The U.K. Case," *National Banking Review,* 3 (September 1965), pp. 101–102.

Laidler, D., "The Case for Raising the Price of Gold: A Comment," *Journal of Money, Credit and Banking,* 1 (August 1969), pp. 675–678.

Machlup, Fritz, "The Cloakroom Rule of International Reserves," *Quarterly Journal of Economics,* 79 (August 1965), pp. 337–355.

"The Need for Monetary Reserves," *Banca Nazionale del Lavoro Quarterly Review,* 19 (September 1966), pp. 175–222.

"Speculations on Gold Speculation," *American Economic Review,* 59 (May 1969), pp. 332–343.

Machlup, Fritz, and Burton G. Malkiel, eds., *International Monetary Arrangements: The Problem of Choice,* Princeton, International Finance Section, 1964.

Machlup, Fritz, Armin Gutowski, and Friedrich A. Lutz, *International Monetary Problems,* Washington, American Enterprise Institute, 1972a.

Machlup, Fritz, Walter S. Salant, and Lorie Tarshis, eds., *International Mobility and Movement of Capital,* Columbia University Press for National Bureau of Economic Research, New York, 1972b.

McKinnon, Ronald I., *Private and Official International Money: The Case for the Dollar,* Essays in International Finance No. 74, Princeton, N.J., 1969.

Makin, John H., "Swaps and Roosa Bonds as an Index of the Cost of Cooperation in the 'Crisis Zone'," *Quarterly Journal of Economics,* 85 (May 1971a), pp. 349–356.

"The Composition of International Reserve Holdings: A Problem of Choice Involving Risk," *American Economic Review,* 61 (December 1971b), pp. 818–832.

Mundell, Robert A., *Monetary Theory,* Pacific Palisades, Calif., Goodyear, 1971.

Officer, Lawrence H., and Thomas D. Willett, "Reserve-Asset Preferences and the Confidence Problem in the Crisis Zone," *Quarterly Journal of Economics,* 83 (November 1969), pp. 688–695.

Olivera, Julio H., "A Note on the Optimal Rate of Growth of International Reserves," *Journal of Political Economy,* 77 (March/April 1969), pp. 245–248.

Oppenheimer, Peter M., "The Case for Raising the Price of Gold," *Journal of Money, Credit and Banking,* 1 (August 1969), pp. 649–665.

Park, Y. S., *The Link between Special Drawing Rights and Development Finance,* Essays in International Finance No. 100, Princeton, N.J., 1973.

Rhomberg, Rudolf R., "Trends in Payments Imbalances, 1952–64," *IMF Staff Papers,* 13 (November 1966), pp. 371–397.
"Possible Approaches to a Model of World Trade and Payments," *IMF Staff Papers,* 17 (March 1970), pp. 1–28.

Sellekaerts, Willy, ed., *International Trade and Finance: Essays in Honour of Jan Tinbergen,* London, Macmillan, 1973.

Sellekaerts, Willy, and Brigitte Sellekaerts, "Balance of Payments Deficits, the Adjustment Cost, and the Optimum Level of International Reserves," *Weltwirtschaftliches Archiv,* 109 (March 1973), pp. 1–18.

Stamp, Maxwell, "The Fund and the Future," *Lloyds Bank Review* (October 1958), pp. 1–20.

Stekler, L., and R. Piekarz, "Reserve Asset Compositions for Major Central Banks," *Oxford Economic Papers,* 22 (July 1970), pp. 260–274.

Thorn, Richard S., "The Demand for International Reserves: A Note on Behalf of the Rejected Hypothesis," *Review of Economics and Statistics,* 49 (November 1967), pp. 623–627.

Triffin, Robert, *Gold and the Dollar Crisis,* New Haven, Yale University Press, 1960.
The Balance of Payments and the Foreign Investment Position of the United States, Essays in International Finance No. 55, Princeton, N.J., 1966.
"The Use of SDR Finance for Collectively Agreed Purposes," *Banca Nazionale del Lavoro Quarterly Review,* 24 (March 1971), pp. 3–12.

United Nations, *Proceedings of the U.N. Conference on Trade and Development,* Vol. 3, New York, 1965.

Williamson, John, "Liquidity and the Multiple Key-Currency Proposal," *American Economic Review,* 53 (June 1963), pp. 427–433.
"International Liquidity: A Survey," *Economic Journal,* 83 (September 1973), pp. 685–746.

Yeager, Leland B., "The Misconceived Problem of International Liquidity," *Journal of Finance,* 24 (September 1959), pp. 347–360.

THE LINK MODEL OF WORLD TRADE,
WITH APPLICATIONS TO 1972–73

L. R. Klein, C. Moriguchi, and A. Van Peeterssen

1. MOTIVATIONS AND PARTICIPATION

Given that there are large, on-going econometric-model studies in many of the main industrial countries, how can these be linked together in a consistent way to analyze world trade flows and, more generally, the international transmission mechanism?

By and large, each national model is customarily simulated by itself or, at best, in a two-country model with a superficial treatment accorded to "the rest of the world." It is possible to construct theoretical models with full cross-country interrelatedness, but the empirical implementation of such a system must necessarily give fairly sweeping and uniform treatment to each national component. The LINK approach is quite different. We try to use the full detail and intimate knowledge that each national model builder has imparted to his own system by taking what is already available and concentrating efforts on building the linkages among all the parts.

Some basic decisions were taken when the LINK project was begun in 1968:

a. Each national model will provide estimates of import equations, with exports being determined from international-share relationships. Short of building a complete set of bilateral relationships, we had to decide whether to work primarily on the side of imports or exports in national models. We chose the former.

b. Imports of goods are to be valued f.o.b. and split into a fixed number of categories for each country:

SITC 0, 1 food, beverage, and tobacco
  2, 4 basic materials
  3 mineral fuels (mainly oil)
  5–9 manufactures.

Services are treated in a separate category.

Many countries find it important to disaggregate their imports in more detail. That is all right, provided the end results can always be aggregated into the above groupings for goods and services.

National models in LINK can be quarterly or annual. There is, in principle, no size restriction, but it would be difficult to accommodate some of the larger models now being produced (500 to 1,000 or more equations). We have mainly stayed with systems containing no more than approximately one hundred equations.

The main industrial countries are explicitly included in the system. Some smaller countries are grouped together in a residual block. The special treatment given the developing countries and the socialist countries will be detailed below.

The system has evolved; models have changed (and are still changing); new features are regularly being incorporated. As it existed during November 1972, the system consisted of the following components:

Austria:	Annual model of the Institute for Advanced Studies.
Belgium:	Quarterly model of the Free University of Brussels.
Canada:	Annual (Trace) model of the University of Toronto.
France:	Small interim model built at the University of Pennsylvania.
Germany:[1]	Annual model of Bonn University.
Italy:	Small interim model built at the University of Pennsylvania.
Japan:	Quarterly model of the Kyoto University Institute of Economic Research and the Central Electricity Board Research Center.
Netherlands:	Annual model of the Central Planning Bureau.
Sweden:	Annual model of the Institute of Economic Research.
United Kingdom:	Quarterly model of the London Business School.
United States:	Quarterly Wharton model, Mark III.
LDC:	Annual regional models of developing countries by UNCTAD (Latin America, Africa, Middle East, South/East Asia).
CMEA:	Annual trade models by UNCTAD (Bulgaria, Czechoslovakia, East Germany, Hungary, Poland, Rumania, and U.S.S.R.).

This list is undergoing change. A model built by a research team from the University of Bologna has just been inserted into

---

[1] The separate model and trade calculations for Germany refer to West Germany throughout this paper. East Germany is included in the CMEA model.

the system in place of the interim Italian model. The Reserve Bank of Australia model is being made ready for inclusion, as is the Bank of Finland model. All these are quarterly systems. Individual small models like those cited above for France and Italy are now available for other developed countries and are being programmed for inclusion in the system. The interim French model will, in the near future, be replaced by a newly constructed French model under the supervision of Y. Guillaume of Brussels. The developing countries' models are being changed. Some large developing countries will eventually be represented by their own model. More structural detail is being provided for the socialist-country (CMEA) models by UNCTAD.

These are the main changes under way as far as enlargement or improvement of the system is concerned. Each individual country model is continuously being improved. LINK is also asking each model proprietor to introduce export-price equations for the four separate SITC categories, to include a monetary sector, and to include a balance-of-payments sector.

2. SPECIFICATION OF THE LINK SYSTEM

A central feature of the LINK system is the use of the world-trade matrix. This is used by SITC grouping but, for expository purposes, only one of the matrix relationships will be analyzed. Let us define

X_{ij} =   flow of goods from country (region) i to country (region) j, measured in numeraire units (U.S. dollars)

$\sum_i X_{ij} = X_{.j}$ = imports of j

$\sum_j X_{ij} = X_{i.}$ = exports of i

$a_{ij} = X_{ij}/X_{.j}$ = share coefficients.

We use the matrix relationships

$$X = AM \qquad (1)$$

to compute the export vector X from the import vector M given the trade matrix A. By construction, equation (1) must hold exactly if X, A, M all refer to the same accounting period. The issue, particularly in forecasting trade flows, is to use a base-period matrix and projected imports and exports. We then have

$$X_t = A_0 M_t + R_t \tag{2}$$

where R_t is a vector of residuals (discrepancies). These arise because of shifts in A over time, and much of our analysis deals with techniques for projecting A.

Since the columns of A sum to unity, by construction, it follows that world exports computed from (1) are equal to world imports.

$$X_1 = a_{11} M_1 + a_{12} M_2 + \ldots + a_{1n} M_n$$

$$X_2 = a_{21} M_1 + a_{22} M_2 + \ldots + a_{2n} M_n$$

.

.

.

$$\frac{X_n = a_{n1} M_1 \quad + \quad a_{n2} M_2 \quad + \ldots + \quad a_{nn} M_n}{\Sigma X_i = M_1 \, \Sigma a_{i1} + M_2 \, \Sigma a_{i2} + \ldots + M_n \, \Sigma a_{in}}$$

$$= \Sigma M_i$$

If we were to ignore R_t in (2) as being negligible, the computed value of exports, $A_0 M_t$, would sum to the total of imports, and the basic world-trade accounting identity would hold. We would gain consistency by assuming that the world-trade matrix is fixed, but we would lose accuracy by the amount R_t. If we try to project R_t, we run the risk of losing the accounting balance $\Sigma X_i = \Sigma M_i$. Later we shall discuss methods of projecting A or estimating R_t that give either exact or approximate accounting balance.

First, let us neglect R_t, estimate X_t from $A_0 M_t$, and describe the fundamental LINK algorithm for obtaining a consistent estimate of world trade. In each country or regional model, there will be a solution for endogenous variables given initial values for lags and exogenous inputs for the solution period. Symbolically, the *reduced-form* equations for the jth country model will be of the form

$$y_{it}^j = f^j(y_{1, t-1}^j, \ldots, y_{n, t-p}^j, z_{1t}^j, \ldots, z_{mt}^j). \tag{3}$$

The jth country's fiscal, monetary, and other policies will be described by the z_{Kt}^j variables. Among these will also be exports from j, or world trade, which will, in turn, determine exports.

Given an initial assumption about the jth country's exports, $(z_{et}^j)^0$, and all the other lagged or exogenous inputs, there will be a solution for its imports, $(y_{mt}^j)^0$. These will be in own-currency units and can be converted at stated exchange rates into a numeraire quantity. If this is done for all countries, we obtain a vector $(M\$)_{1t}^{(0)}, \ldots, (M\$)_{nt}^{(0)}$. From the trade matrix, we compute

$$(X\$)_t^{(1)} = A_0 (M\$)_t^{(0)} \tag{4}$$

The trade matrix A_0 is defined in terms of current-dollar flows, although the exercise could also be worked out in constant-dollar flows. The export vector computed from (4) can be revalued in terms of own-currency units and re-inserted as $(z_{et}^j)^{(1)}$ in each country's model for computing a new solution (1). This iterative process continues until the total real volume of world trade measured as ΣM_{it}, in constant dollars, does not change from iteration to iteration.

There is yet another way in which the trade matrix is used in the iteration process. In equation (4), we are using *rows* of A_0 to transform import values into export values. In a *dual* procedure we use *columns* of A_0 to transform export prices into import prices. Conventionally, single-country national models are constructed with import prices exogenous and export prices endogenous. The latter depend on domestic costs, inflation rates, and possibly also on import prices. The LINK system therefore complements individual national models by generating, on a world basis, some external variables that are conventionally exogenous:

	National Models	LINK System
Import volume	endogenous	endogenous
Import prices	exogenous	endogenous
Export volume or world trade	exogenous	endogenous
Export prices	endogenous	endogenous

The price transformation equations are

$$\Delta(PM\$) = A_0' \, \Delta(PX\$). \tag{5}$$

Each element of the vectors $\Delta(PM\$)$ and $\Delta(PX\$)$ is understood to be a percentage change of an import or export price, reckoned in dollars.

The iteration of national-model solutions seeks an adjustment through changing trade flows (measured as weighted averages of imports) and changing price levels (measured as weighted averages of export prices). We have already indicated that imports are endogenously computed from reduced-form equations (3) from a whole system; similarly, export prices are computed from other reduced-form equations in each country's system. Imports and export prices are then passed through the trade matrices A_0 and A_0' as in (4) and (5). After dollar import prices are derived from (5) in each iteration, they are converted into indexes of import prices in own-currency units at prevailing exchange rates, but care must be taken to distinguish between current exchange rates and base-period exchange rates when converting price indexes on a fixed base.

There are three exceptions to this general specification and solution algorithm for LINK. They are (a) developing countries (LDC), (b) socialist countries (CMEA), and (c) other nonsocialist developed countries (ROW). These three groupings of countries are represented in the world-trade matrix by single rows and columns for each. It need not be done this way, but this is the approach we followed. For individual countries in the A matrix, the diagonal entries, a_{ii}, are zero by definition. For groups of countries, the diagonal entries represent intratrade and are substantially different from zero.

The four regional models built for groupings of developing countries by UNCTAD generate imports and export prices as endogenous variables for each region. The four import values obtained from the models (all in U.S. dollars) are summed to give the LDC import total. This total is then entered as a single element in the vector $(M\$)$. Correspondingly, an element of $(X\$)$ gives an export total for the developing countries as a whole. This total export value is split into four components for use in the separate regional models by using the proportions obtained from the export equations from each model.

$$\frac{(X\$)^{(r)}_{(i)}}{\sum\limits_{i=1}^{4} (X\$)^{(r)}_{i}} = \pi^{(r)}_{i}$$

gives the proportion of (X$) associated with each LDC group on the rth iteration. This proportion is multiplied into the LDC export total computed from the trade matrix in (4) on the $(r + 1)$th iteration. The resulting figures are input values for the LDC regional model on the $(r + 1)$th iteration of their solution. While conventional export equations are overridden by trade-matrix calculations for individual industrial countries, they are not suppressed in the LDC models.

Individual aggregative models have been built by UNCTAD for each LDC region. The approach for dealing with socialist countries is quite different. UNCTAD economists have estimated reduced-form export and import equations for each CMEA member and combined them with an intra-trade matrix in the following equation system:

$$X_i^{ns} = b_{0i} + b_{1i} (TW)^{ns} \qquad (6.1)$$

$$X_i^s = X_i^T - X_i^{ns} \qquad (6.2)$$

$$X_i^s = \sum_{j=1}^{7} X_{ij}^s \qquad (6.3)$$

$$M_j^s = \sum_{i=1}^{7} X_{ij}^s \qquad (6.4)$$

$$M_i^T = c_{0i} + c_{1i} Y_i + c_{2i} X_i^T \qquad (6.5)$$

$$M_i^{ns} = M_i^T - M_i^s \qquad (6.6)$$

$$X_{ij}^s = d_{ij} X_j^T . \qquad (6.7)$$

In this notation, X stands for exports; M stands for imports; a superscript s denotes socialist; a superscript ns denotes nonsocialist; a superscript T denotes total; TW stands for world trade; and Y stands for net material product of the socialist countries. All variables are measured in constant U.S. dollars.

The first six equations hold for each CMEA country. There are thus seven equations implied for each country in (6.1) to (6.6). The set in (6.7) defines elements in the trade matrix, with the understanding that diagonal entries are zero.

Equation (6.1) states that exports from socialist to nonsocialist countries depend linearly on total trade of the nonsocialist countries. This is currently being modified to take into account supply conditions within socialist countries. These are stochastic equations and have been estimated from available time-series data.

In contrast, equations (6.2) to (6.4) and also (6.6) are definitional equations. Equation (6.2) notes that total exports are the sum of exports to socialist and to nonsocialist countries. Equation (6.3) states that the ith socialist country's exports to other socialist countries can be obtained from the sum of all bilateral flows from it within the CMEA group. Similarly, (6.4) defines the jth socialist country's imports from other CMEA countries as the sum of all bilateral flows coming in. Equation (6.6) is the import-side counterpart of (6.2).

Equation (6.5) is a stochastic import equation. The ith socialist country's total imports depend on its aggregate production and on its total exports. The latter variable is an indicator of the availability of foreign exchange that must be used to purchase goods from abroad.

A key group of equations is contained in (6.7), defining the trade-share coefficients as the ratio of the flow from country i to country j to j's total exports. This again, as in (6.5), emphasizes the foreign-exchange limitation on a socialist country's ability to import. Trade coefficients based on the definition in (6.7) were worked out by Beckerman (1956) in a paper written in quite another context some years ago, but they seem to be unusually applicable to the case of CMEA trade flows. The matrix concept coming out of (6.7) has not been unchallenged. It departs significantly from the treatment used for the trade matrix of the rest of the LINK system because it focuses on an export vector rather than an import vector for projecting trade performance for individual countries. A reasonable way to study the issue would be to conduct time-stability tests for different definitions of the trade-shares matrix, D, but these have not yet been carried out. We do not assume (d_{ij}) to be constant and, in fact, let individual elements follow simple trends, much as in the case of A for the market economies.

To solve equations (6.1) to (6.7), we go through the following steps in the extended LINK algorithm:

1. Reduce (6.2), (6.3), and (6.7) by substitution to

$$X_i^T - X_i^{ns} = \sum_{j=1}^{7} d_{ij} X_j^T$$

or

$$X^T = (I - D)^{-1} X^{ns}$$

2. Compute X^{ns} from LINK estimates of TW^{ns}, substitute in step (1) above, and solve for X^T.
3. With external estimates of Y (from the Economic Commission for Europe, for example) and the values just obtained for X^T, evaluate M^T from (6.5).
4. M^s can be evaluated directly from (6.4), where the right-hand-side variables come from the trade-matrix elements computed after step 1 using (6.7).
5. M^{ns} can be obtained directly from (6.6).

These steps provide estimates of CMEA trade, given $(TW)^{ns}$. The latter variable comes from an iteration of the LINK system. On subsequent iterations, the CMEA component of $(M\$)_{t}^{(r)}$ will come from the CMEA model and influence the whole LINK solution. When the iterations stop at equilibrium, there will be a last-round input of (TW) into the CMEA model and a final CMEA projection of total trade flows for each country, including bilateral CMEA flows.

The CMEA countries account for an aggregate row and column in the LINK trade matrix, generating values for their total exports. If these do not agree with the values produced from (6.1), we use the latter to form proportions of the total for allocation among individual CMEA countries. Thus, we distribute total LINK exports for CMEA countries to individual socialist countries in the same manner as for the LDC group. In a sense, in the LINK conception, the CMEA model forms a satellite to the world economy as a whole. We also have to scale the total of CMEA imports from each of the nonsocialist countries so that the socialist column of the LINK trade matrix agrees with the total import values in the CMEA model.

Temporarily, the ROW countries are given very superficial treatment in LINK. Calculations of their imports are based on the simple rule that they form a constant fraction of the world total

(*TW*). Their total exports are then estimated from (4). The unsatisfactory nature of this superficial treatment is shown by the big gap in their export/import position in the estimated-trade tables. Small models for each of the countries in ROW have been estimated for LINK at Stanford University. These countries are Australia (now a separate LINK model), Denmark, Finland (now a separate LINK model), Greece, Iceland, Ireland, New Zealand, Norway, Portugal, South Africa, Spain, Switzerland, Turkey, and Yugoslavia. The models will be introduced in much the same way as in the LDC models, and this should significantly improve estimates for ROW trade.

3. METHODS OF PROJECTING THE TRADE MATRIX

Clearly, the trade matrix plays a critical role in the specification of the LINK system. For expository purposes, a constant trade matrix was used to show complete system properties and the design of the basic algorithm. Equation (4), as it stands, would give poor results in applied work; it is essential to use the formulation in (2), but then we have to account for the discrepancies in R_t.

An obvious approach is to model R_t in terms of trends, autoregressive errors, and similar mechanical time-series methods of correction. Dominant trends like growth in the Japanese share of world trade or the corresponding U.K. decline would be accounted for in this way, at least as historical correlations. It is more fundamental, however, to model R_t as functions of price movements.

In the first LINK-system calculations, we used the mechanically fitted formulas

$$X_{it} = a_i + b_i \left(A_{i0} M_t \right) + c_i t$$

$$A_{i0} = \text{ith row of the 1969 trade-share matrix.} \qquad (7)$$

The second term on the right-hand side gives computed exports, determined from an application of (4). The coefficient b_i varies above and below unity, according to whether the country's share is growing or falling.

A difficulty in the use of equation (7) is that it produces trade estimates that fail to satisfy the basic accounting identity that equates world exports and world imports. Equation (7) may be formulated in either current or constant prices, but either way it does not satisfy the identity. Another defect of (7) is that it does not attach explicit coefficients to price movements in determining exports. This is an especially important defect in a period when large relative-price changes are being induced by exchange re-alignments. Relative prices, through exchange revaluation, have some effect in the use of (7) with the LINK algorithm, because M_t must be transformed from own-currency units for use in each country model. But this seems to be an inadequate treatment of price in trade relationships.

We have accordingly developed two alternative methods for projecting the trade matrix so as to account explicitly for the role of price. One method attempts to model the elements of the A matrix directly and project them individually through time. The other method examines the discrepancy between X_{it} and $A_{i0}M_t$ and explains that as a function of relative price. In some respects, the second approach may be more robust, but it gives less infor-mation about the effects on bilateral trade flows.

The first method, developed for LINK by Moriguchi and John-son (1972) has some analogies with the RAS method of adjusting input-output matrices through time. Their formula is

$$\log a_{ijt} = \alpha_i + \beta_i \log \frac{(PX)_{it}}{(PMC)_{ijt}} + \gamma_i \log \frac{(X)_{it}}{(M)_{jt}}$$

$$+ \sum_{j=1}^{n} \delta_{ij} D_j$$

a_{ijt} = element of trade-share matrix from current-price data

$(PX)_{it}$ = export price of country i

$(PMC)_{ijt}$ = $\sum_{k \neq i} w_{kj} (PX)_{kt}$; $\sum_{k \neq i} w_{kj} = 1$

= price of goods competitive with i in jth market

$(X)_{it}$ = total exports of i in constant dollars

$(M)_{jt}$ = total imports of j in constant dollars

D_j = dummy variable (0 or 1) for the jth country.　(8)

Since (8) is estimated for each row in A_t, the calculations of the coefficient values are done from pooled data across time periods and countries. The coefficients, except for the country dummy variables, depend only on i and not on j. In the RAS method, the elements of an input-output table are revised from base-year values according as the joint product of row and column totals vary. In this case, the current-value coefficients vary according as some generalization of the product of current-dollar row and column totals vary. If β_i and γ_i were equal, we would have a_{ijt} directly depend on $(PX)_{it}.X_{it} / [(PMC)_{ijt}.M_{jt}]$. Equation (8) is more general, since it attributes separate effects to price and to quantity changes. The estimates of β_i and γ_i from a pooled sample are given for SITC 5–9 in Table 1.

TABLE 1   *Estimates of Export Coefficients for SITC 5–9*
(*t*-ratios in parentheses)

| | Estimates of Export Coefficients | | |
	β	γ	R^2
Austria	−0.304	0.681	0.958
	(1.41)	(5.58)	
Belgium	2.761	−0.049	0.956
	(3.89)	(0.42)	
Canada	−1.127	−0.204	0.893
	(1.20)	(1.10)	
France	−1.622	0.048	0.963
	(2.62)	(0.46)	
Germany	0.028	0.138	0.982
	(0.07)	(2.18)	
Italy	−1.676	0.281	0.969
	(5.18)	(3.48)	
Japan	−2.539	0.636	0.875
	(2.94)	(4.03)	
Netherlands	−0.385	0.180	0.956
	(0.98)	(1.77)	
Sweden	−1.424	0.106	0.967
	(3.10)	(1.00)	
United Kingdom	−0.422	0.424	0.970
	(1.40)	(8.14)	
United States	−1.209	0.218	0.964
	(3.00)	(1.74)	
LDC	−1.342	0.748	0.894
	(0.62)	(4.74)	

   The alternative approach is modeled after a variant of the linear expenditure system (LES).

$$(X\$)_{it} = \alpha_i (PX)_{it} + \beta_i [A_{i0} (M\$)_t] + \gamma_i (PMC)_{it} + \delta_i^t. \qquad (9)$$

If

$$\beta_i = 1, \quad \sum_{i=1}^{n} \gamma_i \, (PMC)_{it} = -\sum_{i=1}^{n} \alpha_i \, (PX)_{it},$$

then we have the LES model. Actually, if β_i fluctuates about 1.0 from country to country, and if $\gamma_i = -\alpha_i$ for the definition

$$(PMC)_{it} = \sum_{j=1}^{n} \lambda_{ij0} \left[\sum_{k \ne j} \alpha_{kj0} \, (PX)_{kt} \right]$$

$$\lambda_{ij0} = \frac{X_{ij0}}{\sum_j X_{ij0}},$$

it turns out that, in a practical sense, the basic accounting identity comes close to holding. The definition of competing prices $(PMC)_{it}$ is taken from Hickman (1972).

Equation (9) states that exports depend on the computed value from a base-period trade matrix and on the comparison between competing prices in other markets and own price. If both sides of (9) are divided by $(PX)_{it}$, we see that real exports depend on the real value of computed exports and on the price ratio between $(PMC)_{it}$ and $(PX)_{it}$.

In many respects, (9) is like the ordinary total export function that appears in most country models. Instead of using the standard specification that real exports depend on the real volume of world trade and on relative prices – own price in comparison with competing prices – we use (9) with world trade being replaced by the expression $A_{i0}(M\$)_t$. This is a weighted sum of other countries' imports. It is simply a different weighting scheme for measuring world trade. It is therefore evident that (9) comes close to matching the usual export equation, although some specific properties of the trade matrix are used in getting

$$\sum_{j=1}^{n} a_{ij0} \, (M\$)_{jt} .$$

Estimates of the LES-model parameters are given in Table 2.

TABLE 2   *Parameter Estimates of Export Equations, SITC 5–9, 1960–69* (t-ratios in parenthesis)

	α	β	γ	δ	Residual Variance	Own-Price Elasticity (1963 Value)
Austria	0.119	0.912			0.001	−0.92
	(6.930)	(29.515)				
Belgium	0.306	0.955			0.008	−0.92
	(6.764)	(47.210)				
Canada	−0.476	1.046			0.052	−1.17
	(−4.504)	(21.709)				
France	−5.369	1.0	5.742		0.012	−1.91
	(−5.542)	–	(1.941)			
Germany	−11.441	0.958	12.022		0.070	−1.87
	(−2.790)	(28.958)	(0.958)			
Italy	−7.932	1.0	7.219		0.038	−3.03
	(−13.615)	–	(4.362)			
Japan	−4.427	1.288			0.038	−1.90
	(−43.183)	(52.586)				
Netherlands	−0.169	1.008			0.003	−1.06
	(−0.573)	(56.113)				
Sweden	0.027	0.996			0.001	−0.99
	(1.214)	(48.503)				
United Kingdom	3.778	0.628	1.234		0.067	−0.61
	(3.097)	(16.680)	(0.338)			
United States	−15.583	1.0	16.718		0.097	−2.03
	(9.383)	–	(3.301)			
LDC	−3.424	1.0	2.615	0.075	0.008	−1.69
	(−1.053)	–	(0.270)	(5.596)		
ROW	−7.439	0.772	7.289	0.348	0.016	−2.28
	(−2.886)	(3.052)	(0.842)	(1.352)		
CMEA	0.0	1.0	0.0	(No endogenous export price)		

4.   APPLICATIONS TO THE TRANSMISSION MECHANISM, 1971–73

The LINK system had been used for the estimation of world trade in 1970 and 1971. By and large, the first simple applications were perceptive in picking out the major shifts in total volume of world trade in this period. Progressively, the system became more detailed and complicated. New country models were added; better models were constructed for the developing countries; more price effects were introduced in import equations; and better techniques were developed for projecting the trade matrix. A unique opportunity presented itself when we were faced with the U.S. policy changes of August 1971, known as the New Economic

Policy, and the subsequent realigning of exchange rates according to the Smithsonian Agreement. The most important single feature of the evolving system that needed attention for NEP/Smithsonian simulations was more adequate treatment of prices in import and export relationships, for the new alignments are essentially relative price changes.

Various simulations have been made to study these policy changes. First, let us consider forecast implementations of the Smithsonian Agreement by introducing, for 1972 and 1973, the vector of exchange rates agreed upon in December 1971, with allowance for midyear 1972 adjustment by the United Kingdom (see Table 3). In these calculations, policy inputs for domestic monetary, fiscal, and trade variables (or parameters) were assumed to be those known to model proprietors in each country as of spring and summer 1972. The LES version of LINK exports was used.[2] Exchange rates and exogenous inputs changed for 1973 after these calculations were made; therefore, they are not suitable as forecasts for 1973, but they are directly relevant, retrospectively, to 1972. They indicate, as estimates, what would have happened in 1973 if the Smithsonian rate structure had been preserved.

From the many magnitudes of interest produced by the separate national models, regional models, and trade matrices, we

TABLE 3   *Exchange Rates for Simulation Calculations:*
U.S.$/Domestic Currency

	1971	1972	1973
Austria	0.03866	0.04001	0.04323
Belgium	0.02060	0.02251	0.02251
Canada	0.99021	0.99411	1.00000
France	0.18148	0.19329	0.19329
Germany	0.28768	0.30956	0.30956
Italy	0.00162	0.00169	0.00169
Japan	0.00288	0.00320	0.00320
Netherlands	0.28650	0.31072	0.31072
Sweden	0.19592	0.20731	0.20731
United Kingdom	2.44420	2.45000	2.50000
United States	1.00000	1.00000	1.00000
LDC	1.00000	1.02500	1.02500
ROW	1.00000	1.00000	1.00000

2 The RAS-type model is simulated for 1972 and 1973 by Moriguchi (1973).

select for discussion the estimates of world trade, real national production, and bilateral trade flows for 1971–73.[3]

Most national model builders and economic forecasters concentrate attention on GNP (GDP) as a central variable for macroeconomic analysis. Models are often built for the purpose of projecting GNP (GDP) and are validated by comparing such projections with actual data. In project LINK, we first concentrated attention on projections of total world trade, as the most important aggregative variable of the international system. The LINK estimates of world trade for 1971 and 1972 in Table 4 are both too low; they are a good deal closer in terms of estimated change. This is especially true of real trade, since the amount of price inflation was underestimated in 1972. As early as 1970, LINK forecasts of world trade were on the side of moderation, following a period of rapid expansion, but in 1972 it was apparent from simulation calculations that growth in world trade would accelerate. It is projected at a rate of 10.4 per cent for 1973, whereas the model estimates show an increase of only 7.9 per cent from 1971 to 1972. The actual growth was approximately 8.3 per cent. The revised estimates for 1973 presented below raise the figures for 1973 to 11.8 per cent. Table 5 shows LINK estimates of real GNP (GDP) for each of the countries or areas for 1972 and 1973.

To give an impression of the degree to which the LINK system has interpreted the business-cycle situation in advance, we present in Table 6 estimates of real growth rates projected for individual countries for 1971–72, just after the introduction of the Smith-

TABLE 4   *World Trade, Estimates (E) and Observations (O)* (in billions of U.S. dollars)

	1971		1972		1973
	(E)	*(O)*	*(E)*	*(O)*	*(E)*
Nonsocialist world trade at 1963 prices	257.5	264.2	277.9	286.2	306.7
Nonsocialist world trade at current prices	305.7	311.7	344.1	366.3	386.9
Total world trade at current prices (exc. Mainland China, N. Vietnam, N. Korea, Albania)	342.5	345.4	386.4	403.8	433.5
Nonsocialist world-trade price index (1963 = 100)	118.7	118.0	123.8	128.0	126.1

3 The 1971 estimates from the LINK model (Klein, Moriguchi, and Van Peeterssen, 1972b) are presented here for comparison purposes only.

TABLE 5   *Real GNP (GDP) Estimates after Linkage, 1972–73*

	Units[a]	1972	1973
Austria	1964 S	332.7	355.4
Belgium	1961 FR (Belgian)	1,010.9	1,058.9
Canada	1961 $ (Canadian)	71.9	74.8
France	1963 FR (French)	651.1	688.1
Germany[b]	1954 DM	396.0	439.2
Italy	1963 L	46.6	49.1
Japan	1965 ¥	66.6	75.8
Netherlands	1963 f	87.9	92.7
Sweden	1959 KR (Swedish)	107.4	115.1
United Kingdom	1963 £	33.9	35.4
United States	1958 $ (U.S.)	788.1	838.8
Africa	1960 $ (U.S.)	42.3	44.6
Latin America	1960 $ (U.S.)	138.9	147.1
Middle East (incl. Libya)	1960 $ (U.S.)	42.2	45.1
South and East Asia	1960 $ (U.S.)	132.2	139.9

[a]All units in billions except Italian lira and Japanese yen, which are in trillions.

[b]*Private* GDP.

sonian exchange rates. The most serious error was in the overestimate of West German growth. The estimate for the Netherlands was equally poor, but not as serious for world trade.

For 1972, the LINK projections for activity levels in the various constituent economies were correctly in line with the basic notion that Western Europe and the United Kingdom would grow moderately, that Japan would recover nicely, but not excessively, from the preceding year of growth recession, and that North America would respond well to domestic stimuli. As we reported earlier in

TABLE 6   *Real Growth Rates, Estimates and Observations, 1971–72* (in per cent)

	LINK Estimates	Observations
Belgium	3.0	4.9
Canada	6.1	5.8
France	4.2	5.5
Germany	5.6	2.9
Italy	3.0	3.4
Japan	8.2	9.2
Netherlands	1.9	4.5
Sweden	2.4	2.2
United Kingdom	2.5	3.4
United States	5.7	6.1

1972 to the second UNCTAD in Santiago, the developing countries would not be restrained in the near term by the new world
currency alignments (Klein, Moriguchi, and Van Peeterssen,
1972a). The pattern projected was not uniform, however, and
stronger growth was foreseen for the Middle East than for other
LDC areas, as indicated in Table 5.

The principal reason for the moderate LINK projections of
world trade in 1970–71 and 1971–72 was the restraining "feedback" effect on the world economy of moderate real growth in the
main trading countries – the worldwide recession, if you like –
first in North America and then in Western Europe, the United
Kingdom, and Japan, as revealed in solutions of internationally
linked models. By the same token, renewed growth in world trade
is associated with increased real growth in 1973 for many key
countries. The effect of the linkage technique on the various
country solutions has not been large in most individual cases, but
the degree of shift in own-country projections compared with
LINK projections depends heavily on individual assumptions
about own-country export prospects. In the case of the United
Kingdom, the solutions after linkage for 1972 were significantly
divergent from pre-linked estimates. The former were more
bearish on real growth and more inflationary, as turned out to be
the case for that year.

The third LINK tabulation of interest from this exercise is the
estimated matrix of bilateral trade flows presented in Tables 7
and 8.[4] The figures in the lower right-hand corner of these matrices are the total-world-trade estimates given in Table 4. The
five row entries for each country or area represent the four standard LINK commodity classifications (SITC 0,1; 2,4; 3; 5–9) and
the total value of commodity trade, all valued in billions of U.S.
dollars at current prices f.o.b. These detailed bilateral flows are
mainly indicative of what we hope to get from the LINK system
when it is perfected.

For 1972 we overestimated the West German surplus, although
it was in fact substantial. We also underestimated Japan's surplus.
The main consequence of this discrepancy was an underestimation of the U.S.–Japanese bilateral balance, which is closer to
−$4.0 billion for the United States than to the −$2.4 billion estimated. The total U.S. deficit is correspondingly underestimated.
The 1973 estimates show a continuing U.S. deficit, though smal-

---

4 Since exports are adjusted by equation (9), the row entries do not necessarily sum to the
right-hand column totals. More recently, we have introduced a final RAS correction to
balance the whole table.

ler. This was a realistic picture of the cumulative lagged effect of the Smithsonian realignment that was taking place, all too slowly, at the time of the February 1973 currency crisis. (The 1973 estimates are hypothetical, since they are based largely on Smithsonian rates.)

The socialist countries' trade is shown in the aggregate by row (exports) and column (imports) of Tables 7 and 8 for 1972 and 1973. The trade results of going through the model outlined in equations (6.1) to (6.7) are shown in Tables 9 and 10. The aggregate socialist-country entries in Tables 7 and 8 show a near balance between exports and imports in 1972 and a small surplus in 1973. Two points must be kept in mind in evaluating these estimates, however. First, it should be noted that Tables 7 and 8 are in current U.S. dollars, while Tables 9 and 10 are in 1963 U.S. dollars. Second, the large grain purchases from the West in 1972–73 are not exogenously added to imports, and revaluation of the ruble (with respect to the dollar) in 1973 is not taken into account. These calculations are mainly indicative of what might be achieved in future applications of the linkage process. A particular bilateral flow that is worthy of citation in this connection is the export-import balance of trade between socialist and developing countries. For 1972, there is a projected socialist-country surplus (4.61 − 2.56 = 2.05), which is calculated to grow in 1973 (5.11 − 2.64 = 2.47). Apart from revaluation effects (which may, in fact, increase this kind of trade balance), socialist-country economists have questioned whether such a trade gain is plausible.

The projection of the entire matrix of bilateral trade flows is a formidable undertaking. A projection intermediate between aggregate world trade and the trade matrix is the vector of total imports and total exports by country or area. This more limited projection is actually better suited to the LINK methodology than is the complete bilateral projection. The marginal totals (row and column) of the trade matrices for 1971 and 1972 are given in Tables 11 and 12, with comparison against actual data in order that the accuracy of this calculation can be judged. The 1971 estimates are those associated with the estimates of total world trade in Table 4. The 1972 estimates come directly from Table 7.

The CMEA figures used in Tables 11 and 12 are taken from observations adjusted for the purpose of obtaining a complete world-trade matrix and balance, while those implied in Table 4 are taken directly from *International Financial Statistics;* therefore, the figures are not comparable in all respects. Actually, the observed data for LDC, ROW, and CMEA countries are subject to

TABLE 7 *Trade Matrices for 1972 (in billions of current U.S. dollars)*

	Belgium	Canada	France	Germany	Italy	Japan	Neth.	Sweden	U.K.	U.S.	Austria	LDC	ROW	CMEA	All
Exports															
Belgium and Luxembourg:															
0,1	...	0.00	0.26	0.12	0.03	0.01	0.11	0.01	0.02	0.01	0.00	0.03	0.02	0.00	0.63
2,4	...	0.00	0.14	0.21	0.05	0.01	0.16	0.01	0.09	0.02	0.01	0.03	0.03	0.03	0.77
3	...	0.00	0.03	0.16	0.01	0.00	0.08	0.02	0.09	0.01	0.00	0.01	0.07	0.00	0.47
5-9	...	0.08	2.74	3.50	0.54	0.10	2.77	0.19	0.36	1.06	0.07	0.69	1.36	0.26	13.40
0-9	...	0.08	3.17	3.99	0.62	0.12	3.12	0.22	0.55	1.11	0.08	0.75	1.48	0.29	15.28
Canada:															
0,1	0.01	...	0.01	0.01	0.02	0.24	0.02	0.01	0.20	0.78	0.00	0.11	0.03	0.06	1.51
2,4	0.03	...	0.08	0.25	0.08	0.26	0.14	0.03	0.64	1.86	0.01	0.17	0.18	0.02	3.74
3	0.00	...	0.00	0.00	0.00	0.04	0.00	0.00	0.00	1.09	0.00	0.00	0.00	0.00	1.13
5-9	0.05	...	0.09	0.15	0.04	0.18	0.11	0.02	0.58	11.18	0.00	0.57	0.58	0.00	13.54
0-9	0.10	...	0.18	0.42	0.15	0.72	0.27	0.06	1.41	14.90	0.01	0.85	0.79	0.08	19.92
France:															
0,1	0.17	0.02	...	0.47	0.34	0.07	0.15	0.03	0.13	0.13	0.01	0.23	0.23	0.02	1.99
2,4	0.11	0.00	...	0.30	0.29	0.00	0.07	0.02	0.09	0.02	0.01	0.11	0.08	0.02	1.13
3	0.02	0.00	...	0.15	0.02	0.00	0.04	0.00	0.08	0.01	0.00	0.02	0.10	0.00	0.46
5-9	2.13	0.17	...	3.82	1.41	0.13	0.96	0.22	0.43	1.13	0.14	2.75	3.12	1.04	18.06
0-9	2.43	0.19	...	4.75	2.06	0.20	1.23	0.27	0.73	1.29	0.15	3.11	3.53	1.07	21.64
Germany:															
0,1	0.03	0.00	0.11	...	0.20	0.02	0.07	0.03	0.02	0.05	0.05	0.05	0.09	0.01	0.75
2,4	0.05	0.00	0.13	...	0.23	0.00	0.21	0.05	0.05	0.03	0.08	0.11	0.12	0.02	1.08
3	0.12	0.00	0.21	...	0.08	0.00	0.16	0.01	0.03	0.00	0.11	0.01	0.13	0.00	0.88
5-9	4.08	0.46	5.54	...	2.87	0.58	4.46	1.20	1.31	4.34	1.74	3.44	10.32	2.33	42.54
0-9	4.28	0.46	5.99	...	3.37	0.61	4.88	1.29	1.41	4.43	1.99	3.61	10.67	2.37	45.26
Italy:															
0,1	0.02	0.01	0.13	0.23	...	0.00	0.02	0.04	0.06	0.08	0.05	0.04	0.16	0.02	0.86
2,4	0.01	0.00	0.05	0.12	...	0.00	0.02	0.01	0.03	0.03	0.02	0.04	0.05	0.03	0.41
3	0.04	0.00	0.04	0.13	...	0.00	0.08	0.02	0.07	0.11	0.03	0.06	0.13	0.00	0.71
5-9	0.71	0.15	2.38	3.35	...	0.12	0.74	0.15	0.37	1.84	0.21	1.64	3.07	1.22	14.72
0-9	0.77	0.17	2.60	3.83	...	0.13	0.86	0.22	0.52	2.05	0.30	1.78	3.41	1.27	16.70
Japan:[a]															
0,1	0.00	0.01	0.01	0.02	0.01	...	0.00	0.00	0.04	0.17	0.00	0.18	0.04	0.00	0.48
2,4	0.00	0.00	0.00	0.02	0.01	...	0.02	0.01	0.01	0.04	0.00	0.29	0.03	0.03	0.46
3	0.00	0.00	0.00	0.00	0.00	...	0.00	0.00	0.00	0.01	0.00	0.08	0.00	0.00	0.04
5-9	0.22	0.69	0.17	0.65	0.18	...	0.30	0.09	0.36	7.90	0.02	6.38	2.87	1.37	25.07
0-9	0.22	0.70	0.18	0.69	0.20	...	0.32	0.10	0.41	8.12	0.02	6.87	2.94	1.40	26.05
Neth.:															
0,1	0.14	0.01	0.28	0.57	0.14	0.05	...	0.06	0.15	0.16	0.01	0.15	0.13	0.01	1.86
2,4	0.06	0.00	0.12	0.48	0.06	0.01	...	0.08	0.12	0.03	0.02	0.06	0.07	0.03	1.14
3	0.09	0.00	0.06	0.56	0.01	0.00	...	0.02	0.20	0.04	0.01	0.03	0.07	0.00	1.10
5-9	1.79	0.08	1.13	2.84	0.43	0.06	...	0.17	0.50	0.47	0.11	0.65	1.36	0.37	11.94
0-9	2.08	0.09	1.60	4.45	0.64	0.11	...	0.34	0.97	0.70	0.15	0.88	1.64	0.41	16.04

Origin	SITC	1	2	3	4	5	6	7	8	9	10	11	12	13	14	15
Sweden:	0, 1	0.13	0.00	0.05	0.00	0.00	0.01	0.02	⋮	0.00	0.00	0.02	0.01	0.01	0.00	0.00
	2, 4	1.73	0.06	0.20	0.07	0.01	0.02	0.52	⋮	0.16	0.00	0.09	0.42	0.14	0.00	0.05
	3	0.07	0.00	0.06	0.00	0.00	0.00	0.01	⋮	0.00	0.00	0.00	0.00	0.00	0.00	0.00
	5-9	7.13	0.44	3.21	0.53	0.10	0.55	0.53	⋮	0.28	0.07	0.13	0.73	0.31	0.11	0.19
	0-9	9.06	0.50	3.52	0.61	0.11	0.57	1.10	⋮	0.43	0.08	0.24	1.16	0.46	0.11	0.24
U.K.:	0, 1	1.00	0.00	0.21	0.17	0.01	0.34	⋮	0.05	0.02	0.06	0.02	0.03	0.05	0.03	0.02
	2, 4	0.60	0.05	0.12	0.10	0.01	0.04	⋮	0.04	0.04	0.01	0.05	0.07	0.04	0.02	0.01
	3	0.46	0.00	0.21	0.03	0.00	0.03	⋮	0.05	0.07	0.00	0.01	0.06	0.01	0.00	0.01
	5-9	20.74	1.18	8.47	3.70	0.25	2.93	⋮	0.66	0.98	0.40	0.59	1.38	0.99	0.96	1.22
	0-9	22.79	1.23	9.01	3.99	0.26	3.34	⋮	0.81	1.10	0.46	0.66	1.54	1.09	1.01	1.26
U.S.:	0, 1	4.39	0.02	0.41	0.95	0.01	⋮	0.26	0.10	0.17	1.58	0.13	0.19	0.12	0.39	0.05
	2, 4	4.93	0.07	0.31	1.47	0.01	⋮	0.36	0.10	0.49	0.71	0.31	0.49	0.10	0.45	0.07
	3	1.71	0.00	0.09	0.14	0.00	⋮	0.04	0.01	0.06	0.93	0.08	0.09	0.03	0.20	0.01
	5-9	38.97	0.26	5.84	8.44	0.06	⋮	1.83	0.43	1.49	2.49	1.21	2.54	1.59	11.91	1.45
	0-9	49.99	0.35	6.65	11.00	0.08	⋮	2.50	0.65	2.22	5.70	1.74	3.32	1.85	12.96	1.58
Austria:	0, 1	0.10	0.00	0.00	0.00	⋮	0.01	0.01	0.01	0.00	0.00	0.05	0.00	0.00	0.00	0.00
	2, 4	0.36	0.01	0.03	0.03	⋮	0.00	0.01	0.00	0.01	0.00	0.15	0.11	0.00	0.00	0.00
	3	0.09	0.00	0.00	0.00	⋮	0.00	0.00	0.00	0.00	0.00	0.00	0.08	0.00	0.00	0.00
	5-9	2.83	0.55	0.93	0.15	⋮	0.16	0.15	0.11	0.12	0.02	0.11	0.83	0.09	0.05	0.05
	0-9	3.38	0.58	0.97	0.18	⋮	0.17	0.16	0.12	0.13	0.02	0.31	1.03	0.09	0.05	0.06
LDC:	0, 1	11.77	0.52	1.04	1.38	0.07	3.82	0.82	0.25	0.26	1.65	0.44	0.59	0.71	0.11	0.11
	2, 4	12.73	1.25	0.63	2.82	0.07	1.49	1.58	0.11	0.41	1.20	0.65	1.32	0.92	0.16	0.12
	3	22.29	0.01	1.63	2.31	0.01	2.95	2.58	0.12	1.12	5.74	1.69	2.24	1.19	0.43	0.26
	5-9	17.41	0.78	1.31	3.21	0.03	5.12	1.29	0.20	0.26	1.29	0.49	1.64	0.72	0.23	0.99
	0-9	64.20	2.56	4.62	9.71	0.18	13.38	6.28	0.68	2.05	9.88	3.28	5.79	3.55	0.93	1.48
ROW:	0, 1	6.10	0.16	0.41	0.46	0.06	1.24	1.48	0.38	0.07	0.77	0.37	0.35	0.19	0.11	0.05
	2, 4	5.88	0.31	0.33	0.47	0.05	0.32	1.47	0.15	0.27	0.60	0.52	0.82	0.46	0.03	0.08
	3	0.89	0.00	0.06	0.08	0.02	0.02	0.06	0.06	0.03	0.48	0.01	0.04	0.02	0.00	0.00
	5-9	20.87	1.96	4.04	2.71	0.49	2.23	2.21	1.16	0.58	0.51	0.73	2.84	1.08	0.24	0.52
	0-9	33.73	2.44	4.84	3.72	0.62	3.80	5.22	1.76	0.95	2.35	1.63	4.05	1.75	0.39	0.64
CMEA	0, 1	2.61	0.80	0.19	0.55	0.07	0.08	0.14	0.07	0.04	0.18	0.24	0.15	0.09	0.00	0.02
	2, 4	4.35	1.72	0.17	0.60	0.09	0.03	0.45	0.09	0.09	0.25	0.23	0.43	0.16	0.01	0.02
	3	2.09	0.48	0.41	0.14	0.22	0.00	0.00	0.06	0.01	0.25	0.22	0.19	0.10	0.00	0.01
	5-9	33.31	24.73	2.09	3.32	0.14	0.20	0.58	0.17	0.18	0.29	0.19	0.88	0.31	0.11	0.14
	0-9	42.36	27.73	2.87	4.61	0.52	0.30	1.18	0.39	0.32	0.96	0.87	1.65	0.66	0.12	0.18
Total world trade:	0, 1	34.17	1.65	3.02	4.29	0.33	6.87	3.34	1.04	0.95	4.62	2.02	2.75	1.95	0.69	0.61
	2, 4	39.30	3.63	2.34	6.36	0.38	3.92	5.41	0.72	2.08	3.05	2.71	5.04	2.35	0.69	0.61
	3	32.39	0.51	2.96	2.84	0.41	4.26	3.17	0.39	1.66	7.44	2.11	3.70	1.70	0.64	0.57
	5-9	280.53	36.47	48.66	38.20	3.36	39.09	10.47	4.77	13.19	6.24	8.91	25.13	17.13	15.24	13.55
	0-9	386.39	42.26	56.98	51.69	4.48	54.13	22.40	6.92	17.88	21.34	15.75	36.62	23.14	17.26	15.35

^{a} Custom clearance basis.

TABLE 8   *Trade Matrices for 1973 (in billions of current U.S. dollars)*

							Imports (f.o.b.)								
Exports	Belgium	Canada	France	Germany	Italy	Japan	Neth.	Sweden	U.K.	U.S.	Austria	LDC	ROW	CMEA	All
Belgium and Luxembourg:															
0, 1	...	0.00	0.29	0.14	0.04	0.02	0.13	0.01	0.02	0.01	0.00	0.03	0.03	0.00	0.71
2, 4	...	0.00	0.16	0.24	0.05	0.01	0.18	0.01	0.09	0.02	0.01	0.03	0.03	0.03	0.87
3	...	0.00	0.03	0.18	0.01	0.00	0.09	0.02	0.10	0.01	0.00	0.01	0.07	0.00	0.53
5-9	...	0.08	3.12	4.46	0.62	0.12	3.15	0.20	0.40	1.15	0.10	0.76	1.50	0.26	15.65
0-9	...	0.08	3.61	5.02	0.72	0.14	3.55	0.24	0.62	1.20	0.11	0.83	1.63	0.29	17.76
Canada:															
0, 1	0.01	...	0.02	0.02	0.03	0.28	0.02	0.01	0.23	0.78	0.00	0.12	0.03	0.06	1.62
2, 4	0.04	...	0.09	0.29	0.10	0.30	0.16	0.03	0.67	1.95	0.01	0.18	0.20	0.02	4.02
3	0.00	...	0.00	0.00	0.00	0.04	0.00	0.00	0.00	1.20	0.00	0.00	0.00	0.00	1.25
5-9	0.06	...	0.10	0.19	0.05	0.22	0.12	0.03	0.65	12.16	0.00	0.63	0.64	0.00	15.00
0-9	0.11	...	0.20	0.50	0.18	0.84	0.30	0.07	1.55	16.09	0.01	0.94	0.87	0.08	21.88
France															
0, 1	0.19	0.02	...	0.53	0.39	0.08	0.18	0.03	0.15	0.13	0.01	0.26	0.25	0.02	2.23
2, 4	0.12	0.00	...	0.35	0.34	0.00	0.08	0.02	0.10	0.02	0.01	0.12	0.09	0.02	1.26
3	0.03	0.00	...	0.17	0.02	0.00	0.05	0.00	0.09	0.01	0.00	0.03	0.11	0.00	0.51
5-9	2.34	0.18	...	4.88	1.62	0.16	1.10	0.24	0.49	1.23	0.19	3.05	3.44	1.03	20.70
0-9	2.67	0.20	...	5.93	2.37	0.24	1.40	0.29	0.82	1.40	0.20	3.45	3.89	1.07	24.70
Germany:															
0, 1	0.03	0.00	0.12	...	0.23	0.03	0.08	0.03	0.02	0.06	0.05	0.06	0.10	0.02	0.84
2, 4	0.05	0.00	0.14	...	0.26	0.00	0.23	0.05	0.05	0.03	0.07	0.13	0.13	0.02	1.18
3	0.13	0.00	0.24	...	0.09	0.00	0.19	0.01	0.04	0.00	0.12	0.01	0.15	0.00	0.98
5-9	4.48	0.49	6.30	...	3.29	0.71	5.06	1.32	1.48	4.72	2.40	3.81	11.38	2.31	47.10
0-9	4.70	0.50	6.81	...	3.88	0.74	5.56	1.41	1.60	4.81	2.64	4.00	11.76	2.35	50.10
Italy:															
0, 1	0.02	0.01	0.14	0.26	...	0.01	0.02	0.04	0.07	0.08	0.05	0.04	0.17	0.02	0.95
2, 4	0.01	0.00	0.06	0.14	...	0.00	0.02	0.01	0.03	0.03	0.01	0.05	0.06	0.03	0.45
3	0.04	0.00	0.05	0.14	...	0.00	0.10	0.02	0.08	0.12	0.03	0.06	0.14	0.00	0.79
5-9	0.77	0.16	2.71	4.27	...	0.14	0.84	0.16	0.42	2.00	0.29	1.82	3.38	1.21	16.96
0-9	0.85	0.18	2.96	4.82	...	0.15	0.98	0.24	0.59	2.23	0.38	1.97	3.75	1.26	19.15
Japan:[a]															
0, 1	0.00	0.01	0.01	0.02	0.01	...	0.01	0.00	0.05	0.17	0.00	0.19	0.04	0.00	0.52
2, 4	0.00	0.00	0.01	0.02	0.01	...	0.02	0.01	0.01	0.04	0.00	0.32	0.03	0.03	0.51
3	0.00	0.00	0.00	0.00	0.00	...	0.00	0.00	0.00	0.01	0.00	0.03	0.00	0.00	0.04
5-9	0.24	0.74	0.20	0.83	0.21	...	0.35	0.09	0.40	8.59	0.03	7.07	3.17	1.36	27.91
0-9	0.25	0.75	0.21	0.88	0.23	...	0.37	0.11	0.46	8.81	0.03	7.61	3.24	1.39	28.98
Neth.															
0, 1	0.15	0.01	0.32	0.64	0.17	0.05	...	0.07	0.17	0.16	0.01	0.16	0.15	0.01	2.07
2, 4	0.07	0.00	0.14	0.55	0.07	0.01	...	0.08	0.13	0.03	0.02	0.06	0.07	0.03	1.26
3	0.10	0.00	0.07	0.63	0.01	0.00	...	0.02	0.22	0.04	0.01	0.03	0.08	0.00	1.22
5-9	1.97	0.08	1.29	3.63	0.49	0.08	...	0.19	0.57	0.51	0.15	0.72	1.50	0.37	13.61
0-9	2.99	0.09	1.82	5.45	0.73	0.14	...	0.36	1.08	0.75	0.18	0.98	1.80	0.41	18.17

Exporter / SITC														
Sweden														
0, 1	0.00	0.00	0.01	0.01	0.02	0.00	…	0.03	0.01	0.00	0.00	0.05	0.01	0.14
2, 4	0.05	0.00	0.16	0.48	0.10	0.18	…	0.55	0.02	0.00	0.08	0.22	0.06	1.91
3	0.00	0.00	0.00	0.00	0.00	0.00	…	0.01	0.00	0.00	0.00	0.06	0.00	0.08
5-9	0.21	0.12	0.35	0.93	0.15	0.30	…	0.60	0.60	0.13	0.59	3.54	0.44	8.07
0-9	0.26	0.12	0.52	1.42	0.27	0.49	…	1.20	0.62	0.14	0.67	3.88	0.50	10.20
U.K.														
0, 1	0.02	0.03	0.05	0.03	0.02	0.02	0.05	…	0.35	0.01	0.19	0.23	0.00	1.07
2, 4	0.02	0.02	0.05	0.08	0.06	0.05	0.05	…	0.04	0.01	0.11	0.13	0.05	0.66
3	0.01	0.00	0.01	0.06	0.01	0.08	0.06	…	0.03	0.00	0.03	0.23	0.00	0.50
5-9	1.34	1.04	1.13	1.76	0.68	1.11	0.72	…	3.19	0.34	4.10	9.34	1.17	22.84
0-9	1.38	1.09	1.24	1.94	0.76	1.25	0.88	…	3.60	0.36	4.42	9.93	1.23	25.07
U.S.														
0, 1	0.06	0.42	0.13	0.21	0.15	0.19	0.11	0.30	…	0.01	1.05	0.45	0.03	4.98
2, 4	0.07	0.49	0.12	0.57	0.36	0.56	0.11	0.38	…	0.01	1.63	0.34	0.07	5.48
3	0.01	0.22	0.04	0.10	0.09	0.07	0.01	0.05	…	0.00	0.16	0.10	0.00	1.92
5-9	1.59	12.85	1.81	3.24	1.40	1.70	0.47	2.08	…	0.08	9.35	6.44	0.26	44.07
0-9	1.74	13.98	2.10	4.13	1.99	2.52	0.70	2.80	…	0.10	12.19	7.33	0.35	56.45
Austria:														
0, 1	0.00	0.00	0.00	0.01	0.06	0.00	0.01	0.01	0.01	…	0.00	0.01	0.00	0.11
2, 4	0.00	0.00	0.01	0.12	0.17	0.01	0.00	0.01	0.00	…	0.03	0.04	0.02	0.41
3	0.00	0.00	0.00	0.09	0.00	0.00	0.00	0.00	0.00	…	0.00	0.00	0.00	0.10
5-9	0.06	0.05	0.10	1.06	0.12	0.14	0.12	0.17	0.17	…	0.17	1.02	0.55	2.54
0-9	0.06	0.05	0.11	1.28	0.36	0.15	0.13	0.18	0.18	…	0.20	1.07	0.57	3.15
LDC:														
0, 1	0.12	0.12	0.81	0.67	0.51	0.80	0.26	0.94	3.87	0.07	1.53	1.14	0.55	12.81
2, 4	0.13	0.17	1.05	1.52	0.75	0.46	0.11	1.66	1.56	0.06	3.13	0.70	1.32	13.96
3	0.29	0.46	1.36	2.50	1.94	1.28	0.12	2.85	3.25	0.01	2.55	1.80	0.00	24.98
5-9	1.09	0.25	0.82	2.09	0.56	0.30	0.22	1.46	5.57	0.05	3.55	1.45	0.77	19.81
0-9	1.62	1.00	4.08	6.77	3.77	2.34	0.72	6.92	14.25	0.18	10.76	5.09	2.64	71.57
ROW:														
0, 1	0.05	0.12	0.22	0.39	0.43	0.08	0.40	1.69	1.25	0.06	0.51	0.45	0.17	6.73
2, 4	0.09	0.04	0.52	0.95	0.59	0.31	0.16	1.55	0.34	0.04	0.52	0.36	0.33	6.46
3	0.00	0.00	0.03	0.04	0.01	0.03	0.06	0.06	0.02	0.03	0.09	0.07	0.00	0.99
5-9	0.57	0.26	1.23	3.63	0.84	0.66	1.28	2.50	2.42	0.68	3.00	4.45	1.94	23.71
0-9	0.71	0.42	1.99	5.01	1.88	1.09	1.90	5.81	4.03	0.81	4.12	5.34	2.44	37.89
CMEA:														
0, 1	0.02	0.01	0.10	0.16	0.27	0.05	0.07	0.17	0.08	0.07	0.61	0.21	0.92	2.94
2, 4	0.03	0.01	0.18	0.49	0.26	0.10	0.09	0.48	0.03	0.07	0.66	0.19	1.99	4.87
3	0.01	0.00	0.12	0.21	0.25	0.01	0.07	0.00	0.00	0.24	0.15	0.45	0.55	2.35
5-9	0.15	0.12	0.35	1.12	0.22	0.21	0.19	0.65	0.21	0.19	3.68	2.81	28.49	38.23
0-9	0.20	0.13	0.75	2.00	1.00	0.37	0.42	1.30	0.32	0.58	5.11	3.16	31.94	48.39
Total world trade:														
0, 1	0.69	0.74	2.18	3.09	2.32	1.06	1.09	3.83	6.95	0.35	4.76	3.33	1.81	37.73
2, 4	0.68	0.74	2.62	5.74	3.11	2.31	0.75	5.70	4.09	0.31	7.05	2.58	3.99	43.30
3	0.63	0.69	1.90	4.11	2.43	1.84	0.39	3.49	4.71	0.44	3.15	3.27	0.56	36.23
5-9	15.10	16.35	19.11	31.72	10.23	14.64	5.23	11.84	42.43	4.64	42.38	53.71	40.08	316.20
0-9	17.11	18.52	25.81	44.66	18.08	19.85	7.47	24.85	58.18	5.73	57.35	62.89	46.44	433.46

[a] Custom clearance basis.

TABLE 9 *Results of UNCTAD Model for the Socialist Countries, 1972* (in millions of 1963 U.S. dollars)

Exports:			East					Imports			
	Bulgaria	Czech.	Germany	Hungary	Poland	Romania	U.S.S.R.	Intra	Extra	Total
Bulgaria		126	215	47	86	33	1,406	1,913	632	2,545
Czechoslovakia	102		482	218	368	141	1,652	2,962	1,485	4,447
East Germany	234	566		272	404	144	2,310	3,929	1,005	4,934
Hungary	33	261	242		202	67	1,168	1,973	836	2,805
Poland	95	374	185	195		85	1,514	2,447	1,518	3,965
Romania	29	185	129	70	73		725	1,211	1,007	2,218
U.S.S.R.	1,407	1,504	2,391	998	1,213	430		7,945	6,581	14,525
Intra	1,900	3,014	3,644	1,801	2,346	901	8,773	22,379	13,063	35,442
Extra	650	1,449	1,332	862	1,619	1,499	4,334	11,746		
Total	2,550	4,463	4,976	2,664	3,965	2,400	13,108	34,125		

TABLE 10 *Results of UNCTAD Model for the Socialist Countries, 1973* (in millions of 1963 U.S. dollars)

Exports:			East					Imports			
	Bulgaria	Czech.	Germany	Hungary	Poland	Romania	U.S.S.R.	Intra	Extra	Total
Bulgaria		140	248	53	99	38	1,633	2,211	729	2,940
Czechoslovakia	118		540	239	416	154	1,849	3,316	1,645	4,961
East Germany	270	643		310	443	164	2,586	4,416	1,117	5,533
Hungary	35	291	272		234	76	1,353	2,261	935	3,196
Poland	110	427	192	226		97	1,734	2,785	1,695	4,480
Romania	34	213	144	80	83		812	1,366	1,155	2,521
U.S.S.R.	1,626	1,678	2,682	1,135	1,342	431		8,894	7,369	16,263
Intra	2,192	3,392	4,078	2,044	2,617	960	9,966	25,250	14,644	39,894
Extra	427	1,561	1,489	814	1,243	1,768	4,245	11,546		
Total	2,619	4,953	5,567	2,858	3,860	2,728	14,211	36,796		

TABLE 11   *Exports and Imports, Estimates and Observations, 1971* (in billions of current U.S. dollars f.o.b.)

	Exports		Imports	
	LINK Estimates	Observations	LINK Estimates	Observations
Belgium and Luxembourg	13.3	12.4	13.7	12.9
Canada	17.6	17.7	16.0	14.7
France	19.8	20.3	18.7	20.0
Germany	38.4	39.0	30.5	31.7
Italy	14.4	15.1	14.0	15.3
Japan	21.5	24.0	19.3	15.8
Netherlands	12.4	14.0	15.7	15.6
Sweden	8.0	7.4	6.6	6.6
United Kingdom	23.2	22.3	18.2	21.4
United States	44.9	43.5	44.4	45.1
LDC	58.6	59.7	52.3	66.3
ROW	33.6	34.7	58.1	47.2
CMEA	36.8	36.4	34.9	34.1

TABLE 12   *Exports and Imports, Estimates and Observations, 1972* (in billions of current U.S. dollars f.o.b.)

	Exports		Imports	
	LINK Estimates	Observations	LINK Estimates	Observations
Austria	3.4	3.9	4.5	5.3
Belgium and Luxembourg	15.3	16.2	15.4	15.6
Canada	19.9	20.9	17.3	18.3
France	21.6	26.4	23.1	25.8
Germany	45.3	46.7	36.6	37.9
Italy	16.7	18.5	15.8	18.9
Japan	26.1	28.7	21.3	19.2
Netherlands	16.0	16.8	17.9	18.1
Sweden	9.1	8.8	6.9	7.7
United Kingdom	22.8	24.3	22.4	25.5
United States	50.0	49.7	54.1	56.1
LDC	64.2	70.2	51.7	74.1
ROW	33.7	39.3	57.0	48.8
CMEA	42.4	36.9	42.3	36.1

alternative interpretations and comparatively large measurement error. The correspondence is not always good for these groupings, but the observed data for the developed market economies are more reliable.

In 1971, the principal error was in the underestimation of the Japanese trade balance; LINK estimates were too low for exports and too high for imports. Furthermore, U.K. import demand was underestimated. In 1972, we again underestimated U.K. imports and were off the mark for France and Italy. It is expected that Italian estimates for 1973 and subsequent years will be better with the introduction of the new Bologna model into the system. When the new POMPOM model for France is introduced, the French trade estimates should improve.

In spite of the deficiencies in the 1972 projection, it is apparent that the system identified the main imbalances with which the Smithsonian rates were unable to cope, namely, the large U.S. deficit and correspondingly large surpluses for Germany and Japan. The year 1972 was extremely difficult to project because of the major changes introduced, but the LINK system did provide some insight into the workings of the disequilibrium process.

Exchange rates changed again in February and March 1973. We accordingly recalculated the simulations for 1973, with the new rates averaged over the weeks in which they were actually or assumed to be in effect. After the March changes, when world currency markets reopened, we assumed that rates would not change again during the year. Also, the rates assumed in Table 3 underestimate changes for the LDC and ROW countries. The calculations and comments are left in original Conference form (with some post-Conference revision) as an *ex ante* forecast for 1973. As these pages have been edited, proofread, set in type, and proofread again, events of the year 1973 have become retrospective. The oil crisis, high oil prices, further exchange-rate changes, and other international events had a large bearing on the actual outcome, which naturally differs in important respects from this forecast scenario.

For comparison, two cases are presented in Table 13: (a) a baseline calculation that assumes no change in exchange rates from year-end 1972 (basically, Smithsonian rates) and (b) a calculation with the rate changes of February and March prorated over the year, assuming that two-thirds of the changes are "passed through" in export prices. Inputs of exogenous and lagged variables for all the country models were brought up to date for early 1973, and the new Italian model (Bologna) was introduced into the system. Agricultural deliveries from the United States to CMEA countries were raised to a level of $1.0 billion for 1973.

The LINK system projects better balance in world patterns as a result of the second wave of revaluations. The U.S. deficit is ex-

TABLE 13   *Revised Trade Simulations for 1973*
(in billions of U.S. dollars f.o.b.)

	Base-Line Case		2/3 Passthrough	
	Exports	Imports	Exports	Imports
Austria	4.3	5.8	4.4	6.1
Belgium and Luxembourg	18.3	16.7	19.0	17.0
Canada	24.0	19.3	24.6	19.8
France	26.2	27.5	27.2	28.7
Germany	52.7	42.8	54.0	44.9
Italy	20.3	21.7	21.4	22.3
Japan	32.5	25.0	33.2	26.1
Netherlands	18.0	19.8	18.7	20.6
Sweden	10.0	7.3	10.3	7.7
United Kingdom	26.3	27.9	27.3	29.2
United States	57.9	64.5	61.2	65.9
LDC	74.9	76.4	78.0	80.4
ROW	42.7	54.9	44.4	56.9
CMEA	48.5	47.1	50.4	48.8

pected to be reduced by about $2.0 billion, with help from both Japan and Germany as their surpluses are each reduced by about $0.5 billion or more. In contrast with the Smithsonian round, we now expect that the developing countries will experience some deterioration in their aggregate balance. Of course, the oil-exporting nations will increase their net export position; this shows up clearly in the full set of calculations, where the Middle East region records a large surplus of more than $10 billion. If basic commodity prices in lines other than petroleum continue to rise throughout 1973, the expected adjustment for developing countries could prove to be incorrect. There are some signs that the CMEA countries are moving into a reduced surplus position.

The estimated volume of world trade (nonsocialist countries) is $310.8 billion in 1963 prices. This figure decreases by approximately $1.0 billion (1963 prices) for each one-third of passthrough.

The major point of disequilibrium in the world trade pattern, causing the exchange crisis of 1971 and giving rise to the Smithsonian Agreement, was the large U.S. deficit. LINK calculations bearing on the size of that deficit were on the pessimistic side for the following reasons: (a) The state of world Konjunktur was unfavorable. There was growth recession throughout Western Europe and Japan. Furthermore, the strong recovery phase in

North America stimulated imports. It is a feature of the LINK system that economic prospects for individual countries figure importantly in the trade calculations. (b) The relevant price elasticities in the LINK models are not large, especially in the short run. They are much smaller than the elasticities used in many official calculations. (c) The amount of passthrough was expected to be small.

The LINK estimate of the U.S. merchandise deficit for 1972 was $4.0 billion. While this was smaller than the actual deficit, it was substantially larger than the 1971 deficit ($1.6 billion). The estimate for 1973 is quite different. The system predicts reduction in the deficit because (a) the lag effects of the Smithsonian Agreement are building up (this is consistent with LINK import equations); (b) the state of world Konjunktur is now favorable, with recovery and strong growth in Western Europe and Japan; (c) agricultural shipments to CMEA countries are large in 1973; (d) the degree of passthrough should be larger. Our simulations give very different outcomes for the system in two realistic situations.

5. SOME LINK PROSPECTS

The LINK model is a living system, in the process of development. The research project has proceeded since 1968 by adding pieces each year and by steadily increasing the degree of sophistication. In this section, we shall try to outline the principal lines of development that are being followed or contemplated at this time.

A system like this is never finished. It can always be extended and improved. Certainly, an obvious development is to include more countries in explicit models. As there is a limit to our ability to function effectively as a group research team, we shall not add more large-country models simply because they become available, but we do expect to have a working French model in the system during 1974. Among countries not now explicitly represented, Switzerland appears to be a likely candidate for inclusion in the near future. There is much to be desired in better treatment and prediction for "other nonsocialist developed countries" (ROW), and we shall try to include small usable models for GNP determination, together with trade flows, for each of the ROW countries. This, too, may be accomplished in 1974.

The CMEA countries are being worked on by UNCTAD economists, and a system that is better than the present one may become available in 1974. The same is true of the LDC regional models.

Africa, in particular, needs much more research – from data preparation to equation estimation and system simulation.

This work is now in progress at UNCTAD. At the same time, research is going on aimed at the separate inclusion of important individual developing countries such as India, Brazil, Argentina, and Mexico.

As we have inserted new and better models into the system, improvement has been clearly discernible both for the specific country or region and for the world economy as a whole. During the past year, the inclusion of a new Italian model distinctly improved the Italian trade projections. We therefore look for gradual improvement in the whole system as models are included for new countries or as individual country models are significantly improved. This line of research knows no end.

Apart from the individual constituent models, the most important analytical piece in the LINK system is the world-trade matrix for computing exports. The linkage process would be much more straightforward if the elements of this matrix, expressed in ratio form, were to remain constant through time. This is clearly not a reasonable assumption and research must continue on methods of projecting the trade matrix through time. Two methods described in section 3 are now in experimental use. Other methods proposed by Grant Taplin and jointly by Hickman and Lau are candidates for further research in the context of complete system solutions. The Hickman and Lau (1973) technique is a linear approximation to complete projections of all bilateral-flow coefficients in the matrix that would follow from Armington's (1969) CES formulation of trade relationships.

The simulations of the LINK system presented in the previous section were for isolated years. There were successive simulations for 1972 and 1973. A year earlier, the corresponding simulations were for 1971 and 1972. The system is so large, and the programming difficulties sufficiently cumbersome, that provision in the coding and programming has not yet been made for indefinite successive solution in time.[5] This deficiency is now being remedied, and medium-term simulations of five years or possibly a decade will be undertaken. Programming is not the sole bottleneck, however; that obstacle is readily being overcome. A deeper issue is the development of lengthy input records for the individual models and the working out of meaningful longer-range simulations from short-term business-cycle types of models. Enough of the individual systems have, however, been simulated over quinquennia

5 The complexity of program structure is outlined in Klein and Van Peeterssen (1973).

and decades with reasonable results that it appears possible to develop multi-year LINK simulations. Since the lags in adjustment to changes in the world trade and payments system are presumed to be fairly long, it is important to make these longer-range simulation studies.

Of great importance for the trade performance of the developing countries are economic activities in basic commodity markets. Many developing countries are major exporters to the whole world in a few narrow commodity lines (minerals, fibers, foods, oils, and other commodities). In some cases, commodity imports are also strategic for them. We should be able to make better trade projections for developing countries if we can combine commodity and country models in one fully linked system. In a number of cases, basic commodities are also strategic for the industrial market and socialist economies. The whole system should benefit from this expanded dual treatment of world commodity and country models. An experimental case of a world copper model within the LINK system is presently being researched.

Both longer-run analyses and the introduction of basic-commodity models are attractive for socialist-country participants in LINK, but the greatest improvement for this analysis will surely come through the introduction of full system models for the internal-external workings of individual socialist countries. An inventory of interesting models is being accumulated for individual CMEA countries (especially Hungary, Poland, and Czechoslovakia). The time is not distant when the CMEA countries will be separately represented in the LINK system, as are individual European countries. And, as China trade grows, steps will have to be taken to include the rest of the socialist world in the system.

The original design of the LINK system centered around a trade-flow model. Even if this model is developed along the lines indicated in this concluding section, large questions will remain unanswered, especially those having to do with exchange-rate determination. We must try to supplement linked trade models with linked payments models. Many of the individual country models have jointly expanded their monetary sectors and their international capital-flows sectors. Balance-of-payments models are now available or are being prepared for Japan, Canada, the United States, the United Kingdom, Germany, and Australia. Others will be following soon. Some bilateral linking studies, through balance-of-payments models, are being made already. Simulations of balance-of-payments models together with domestic real-sector and monetary-sector models have been made. When a complete collection of balance-of-payments models becomes available, we shall undertake another major project development in trying to link international capital flows.

REFERENCES

Armington, Paul, "A Theory of Demand for Products Distinguished by Place of Production," *IMF Staff Papers,* 16 (March 1969), pp. 159–178.

Beckerman, W., "The World Trade Multiplier and the Stability of World Trade, 1938 to 1953," *Econometrica,* 24 (July 1956), pp. 239–252.

Hickman, Bert G., "Prices and Quantities in a World Trade System," Project LINK, Working Paper No. 1, 1972.

Hickman, Bert G., and Lawrence Lau, "Elasticities of Substitution and Export Demands in a World Trade Model," *European Economic Review,* 4 (1973), pp. 347–380.

Klein, L.R., C. Moriguchi, and A. Van Peeterssen, "Impact of the Present International Monetary Situation on World Trade and Development, Especially in the Developing Countries," TD/140/Supp. 4, Santiago, Chile, Apr. 18, 1972a.

"NEP in the World Economy: Simulations of the International Transmission Mechanism," Project LINK, Working Paper No. 2, 1972b.

Klein, L. R., and A. Van Peeterssen, "Forecasting World Trade within Project LINK," in R. J. Ball, ed., *The International Linkage of National Econometric Models,* Amsterdam, North-Holland, 1973.

Moriguchi, C., "Forecasting and Simulation Analysis of the World Economy," *American Economic Review, Papers and Proceedings,* 63 (May 1973), pp. 402–409.

Moriguchi, C., and K. Johnson, "A New Approach to Estimating Export Price Elasticities and Simulation Analysis of the International Currency Realignment: An Interim Report," Kyoto Institute of Economic Research, Discussion Paper No. 058, Kyoto University, Japan, 1972.

DISCUSSION

ADJUSTMENT UNDER FIXED AND FLEXIBLE
EXCHANGE RATES: A COMMENT

Richard E. Caves

The copious theoretical research on macroeconomic policy in the open economy has finally begun to induce some empirical work. One line of research, represented by Michaely (1971), explores the way in which governments actually manipulate their policy instruments in response to the signals of external and internal balance. Another undertakes to compute the effects a government can expect when it pulls on a policy lever. Helliwell summarizes the extant research on Canada of the latter type, leaping from a selective summary of the underlying policy theory to parametric revelations about our Northern Neighbor. Following the spirit of his paper, I shall comment on several aspects of the interplay of theory and empirical research in this obviously important area.

The underlying policy theory is in comparative-static form, whereas empirical estimates of policy leverages can hardly ignore the explicit time path of adjustment. The conventional methods of handling large-scale models yield estimates of ultimate effects, of course. But, aside from verifying the stability of the system, these hardly hold much interest for policy makers, who want to know the effect their handiwork will have by the next election. The results summarized by Helliwell derive from time-explicit simulations, as they should. But many model builders seem disinclined to devote great efforts to assuring that the short-run dynamics of the key relations have been captured as accurately as possible. The trouble is that almost any of the popular lag-structure formulations tend to fit the data reasonably well, and to discriminate among them is a dirty job without much theoretical interest. Yet the empirical significance of a good vs. bad approximation is surely great. I wonder, in particular, if we have given enough attention to the differences in lag structures between the real and monetary sectors: economists regularly counsel governments to expect several years' wait for the effect of devaluation on the trade balance, while the minimum time needed to gain or lose a billion dollars of reserves is asymptotically approaching zero!

Empirical estimation of these policy responses has already

proved suggestive for further development of theory, and one can hope for more interchange. An example, at least insofar as it originated with Caves and Reuber (1971), is the influence of private exchange-rate expectations on the policy system under any exchange rate that is less than fully pegged. We found this influence, rightly stressed by Helliwell, impressive both in its implications for the theory of economic policy and in the size and apparent pervasiveness of expectations effects in practice. To the extent that the public speculates on the expectation that future values of a flexible exchange rate will be those of the past, they are simply doing the job that an exchange-stabilization authority would do under fixed rates. Yet we may be in danger of losing perspective on this expectations effect. Just as capital flows are regularly dissected into their stock-adjustment and flow aspects, we should notice that the magnitude of speculative responses can hardly be independent of the recent history of disturbances and *ex post* movements of the exchange rate. We need to make at least as sharp a distinction between short and long run in the empirical analysis of expectations as in the analysis of interest-sensitive capital flows. The same proposition, incidentally, may well hold for certain influences on trade. Oligopolistic exporters undoubtedly delay the adjustment of the foreign prices of their goods when an exchange-rate disturbance is expected to be temporary, and lag the adjustment when the disturbance proves cumulative. Thus one would expect the cushioning effect of their behavior also to be transitory rather than permanent. These problems reassert the importance of getting the dynamics right in our empirical estimates.

I shall not comment on Helliwell's summary of the evidence from various econometric models of Canada, if only because the models themselves are not officially on the table for inspection. One curious result, however, demands attention. When Canada eases its monetary policy, while maintaining a flexible exchange rate, we expect a rise in output and employment at home and a reduction abroad (e.g., in the United States). The reduction abroad is due to the effect of the monetary change on the exchange rate, depressing the price of the Canadian dollar and switching expenditure toward Canadian and away from foreign goods and services. This adversary relationship could be avoided only if capital flows are not very interest-elastic or speculation stabilizes the external value of the Canadian dollar. Then the direct positive effect of monetary expansion on Canadian income and imports could raise income abroad through the conventional foreign-trade multiplier. Helliwell reports that the econometric models of Canada all give the conventional result: monetary policy with a flexible rate raises Canadian and lowers foreign income. The MPS model of the United States, however, delivers the opposite verdict on the effect of U.S. monetary expansion: its direct effect on expenditure in the United States is strong enough to make the income-induced increase in demand for Canadian exports dominate (and thus raise) Canadian income.

This result is worth noting for its theoretical interest – the literature on policy assignment having been largely restricted to consequences for a single national economy. I wonder, though, whether the difference in the sizes of the two economies has been pondered as an explanation. Baguley (in Caves and Reuber, 1971) found that the response of Canadian interest rates to changes in corresponding U.S. rates was much greater than could be explained by the associated displacement of capital flows. In other words, Canadians expect Canadian interest rates (securities prices) to follow those in the United States. This fact tends to produce the reported asymmetrical result: U.S. monetary expansion reduces North American interest rates and causes interest-sensitive expenditures to increase in Canada, but the Canada-to-U.S. relationship contains no detectable counterpart.

Helliwell's agenda for future research is fine as far as it goes. Many of the lacks he notes demand not only improved specification of large-scale econometric models but, prior to that, research bearing directly on the underlying microeconomic structure. The pricing behavior of exporters of manufactures is a case in point. Theoretical models happily develop the implications of "traded goods" whose prices are everywhere the same, yet we know next to nothing empirically about the tightness of international price adjustments. This is an instance of the extraordinary backwardness of applied behavioral research in international economics – a backwardness resulting not from a lack of sophistication in the investigations we do undertake but in the spotty and arbitrary selection of the topics that draw our research efforts.

REFERENCES

Caves, R. E., G. L. Reuber, *et al.*, *Capital Transfers and Economic Policy: Canada, 1951–1962*, Cambridge, Mass., Harvard University Press, 1971.
Michaely, M., *The Responsiveness of Demand Policies to Balance of Payments: Postwar Patterns*, New York, Columbia University Press for National Bureau of Economic Research, 1971.

INTERNATIONAL RESERVES AND LIQUIDITY: A COMMENT

Ronald I. McKinnon

Cohen's comprehensive survey of conceptual and econometric issues bearing on the international reserve problem identifies many gaps in what we need to know before supply and demand relationships can be quantified. On the demand side, Cohen posits the level of foreign trade, its variability, GNP, domestic money supplies, interest rates, domestic costs of macroeconomic adjustment, the degree of exchange-rate flexibility, and so on as possible explanatory variables for each individual country. On the supply side, he mentions the uncontrolled growth of gold and official foreign-exchange holdings (some in Eurocurrencies) that must somehow be compensated by an appropriate issue of Special Drawing Rights if the optimum global quantity of reserves is to be obtained. He then examines the pros and cons of greater or lesser reserve creation by the International Monetary Fund, as if the Fund could operate directly on the quantity of real reserves in the system.

The issues are indeed complicated, as indicated by Cohen's elaborate taxonomy, and they lead him to call for more broadly based research on a variety of issues rather than for a narrower focus on the subject. But the very diffuseness of the subject seems to be the greatest barrier to meaningful research. A sharper focus can be obtained, I believe, by treating the problem of international reserve creation more purely as a monetary one, and then applying to the analysis all the normal ground rules of monetary theory.

Consider for a moment a single closed national economy. Monetary theorists have long recognized that a central bank cannot operate directly to change the real stock of domestic money (i.e., cash balances divided by some comprehensive commodity price index). While the authority can operate directly on the stock of nominal money, no simple one-to-one correspondence exists between nominal and real money, because the price level and real output may both vary over suitably defined time horizons. In contrast, most of the literature on international finance implicitly assumes that an increase in nominal reserves – whatever its sources – is quantitatively equivalent to an increase in real reserves. Cohen follows this intellectual tradition by discussing the pros and cons of different reserve levels in real terms. Possible price-level effects are noted only briefly.

There are good historical reasons why the literature on international reserve creation has developed without making the real-nominal distinction. Immediately after World War II, severe portfolio imbalance existed in the sense that the reserves of European countries and Japan were much too low relative to their flows of international trade or GNP, at price levels that were more or less pegged in dollar terms by the dominant position of the United States in the world economy. Since currency depreciation and severe price inflation within Europe and Japan were not desirable, it was essentially correct at that time to treat the shortage of reserves (portfolio imbalance) as a "real" problem that severely impeded the clearing of payments deficits or surpluses across countries. Hence, the return to convertibility and the removal of trade restrictions were associated with the buildup of nominal reserves (or lines of credit from the IMF) that was indeed equivalent to an increase in real reserves (denominated in dollars) under the relatively fixed exchange rates of the old Bretton Woods system. The emphasis was always on a "shortage" of international liquidity rather than a surplus, and new reserve creation was associated (correctly, I believe) with trade liberalization – an improvement in the clearing mechanism.

Needless to say, economic conditions have changed. Major trading countries have had many years to select their official reserve portfolios, and the severe "accidental" shortfalls of the immediate postwar period have been eliminated. If anything, overinvestment in officially held reserves may have taken place. Correspondingly, international capital markets, as manifested in Eurocurrencies and lines of credit between central banks, have revived completely, so that credit-worthy borrowers – private or public – have no trouble obtaining loans at market rates of interest. This access to credit and buildup in reserves have both been important in liberalizing foreign trade and achieving greater balance in trading relationships and per capita incomes among industrial countries. Concomitantly, it is now more difficult economically, and less desirable politically, for any one nation or state to provide an international numeraire and assume responsibility for pegging the world price level of tradeable goods in its own currency.

These great institutional changes suggest that the IMF (and related institutions) should begin to behave more purely as an international central bank whose principal role is to provide a stable international numeraire and medium of exchange that is widely used. Success is critically dependent on maintaining the value of the medium of exchange in terms of some comprehensive price index of internationally traded commodities. Hence, the rate of international price inflation, and the influence of nominal reserve creation on that rate, should become the focus of IMF policy. Correspondingly, the IMF need be less immediately concerned with "structural" imbalance as manifested in reserve deficiencies on the part of individual countries. or with measuring the macroeconomic costs of adjustment to the payments imbalances of individual countries. By analogy, when a national central bank uses domestic open-market operations or rediscounting to create high-powered base money, it concerns itself with prices and the aggregate level of activity in the economy as a whole. Regional payments imbalances are left to be accommodated by the domestic capital market. This last point is important in the current international milieu, because one need not worry about imbalances at the individual-country level if credit-worthy nations can borrow freely at a rate of interest that approximates the opportunity cost of capital.

Besides focusing international monetary policy on the price level as the key target variable, this altered conceptual viewpoint can also simplify future quantitative research. It emphasizes a few key *global* determinants of the demand for reserves, such as the aggregate flow of international trade, the sum of national money supplies (including offshore currencies), world GNP, the degree of exchange-rate flexibility, and so on. One would not have to analyze in detail structural imbalance in particular countries and worry about directing more reserves toward country A as opposed to country B. Cohen certainly recognizes the important simplifications inherent in a global approach, although most of his analysis is in the older tradition where no distinction is made between real and nominal reserve creation. He suggests that the structural and global approaches are complementary and that research on both should be carried forward together. Unfortunately, adherence to the structural approach loses the conceptual simplicity necessary for underpinning tractable econometric estimation procedures in future research efforts.

While generally very sympathetic to most of the points Cohen makes, I think the absence of a well-defined monetary model shows up most clearly in his discussion of the proposal for a "link" between new reserve creation and aid for developing countries. He assumes that the distribution of newly created reserves (SDRs) is mainly a normative problem in allocating seigniorage between rich and poor countries, divorced from the efficiency with which international reserves might be used and the way in which the

IMF's role as a central bank might evolve. Essentially, he envisages a two-stage decision procedure for issuing SDRs, where first the optimal increment in global reserves is estimated, and then possible distribution procedures are considered according to their welfare or equity implications.

The literature on the optimum quantity of money suggests, however, that if money is to be used efficiently its holders must see a return or deposit rate of interest that is close to the average returns to be earned on bonds or physical capital. Otherwise, individuals (countries in the international case) will unduly economize on their holdings of money (reserves) in favor of other interest-bearing assets. Indeed, on a growth path satisfying the golden rule of accumulation of physical capital and balanced inflation, all newly created nominal money would be paid out to depositors. The real rate of growth and the deposit rate of interest would be the same.

In the international context, the only practical way the IMF can convince potential individual holders of SDRs to hold large stocks voluntarily (apart from those imposed by collective agreement) is to pay out the new increments of SDRs to existing holders at a pace that is more or less consistent with the stability of world prices in terms of SDRs. An attractive rate of return on SDRs is particularly important if the SDR facility is to be broadened and voluntarized, perhaps eventually to be used by commercial banks and other private individuals and corporations. Hence there is direct conflict between equity and efficiency. If the interest rate on using SDRs is kept low enough that their allocation involves a significant income transfer to less developed countries, as under the link proposal, potential holders (who see the same low rate of return) will demand an amount of SDRs below that which is efficient in a global monetary sense. The evolution of the IMF into an effective world central bank will be substantially hampered if the holders of its liabilities are taxed, however worthy the recipients of the tax proceeds.

INTERNATIONAL RESERVES AND LIQUIDITY: A COMMENT*

Rudolf R. Rhomberg

Although my main assignment is to discuss Cohen's paper, I would like to comment briefly on Helliwell's topic. Fluctuating ex-

* The views expressed are those of the author and not necessarily those of the International Monetary Fund.

change rates were once of interest chiefly to academic economists and to Canadians, but they have now attracted worldwide concern. Moreover, I expect that this topic will be important for some time to come and that it therefore merits serious renewed study. Not only are major currencies floating today, but recent international negotiations refer explicitly to the usefulness of floating exchange rates in certain circumstances. How long the international monetary system will operate under the interim regime of generally floating rates may be influenced by how well or badly this interim system works. The present regime of floating can, at any rate, serve to buy time for thoughtful and thorough reconstruction of the international monetary system. In fact, some experience with floating rates may well be necessary for the proper specification of certain aspects of the reformed system.

There are here two principal questions: First, how clean or dirty will the float be? If monetary authorities pursue mutually inconsistent exchange-rate aims, their efforts at market intervention will be frustrated and, moreover, get the system out of gear. As Kindleberger foresaw correctly many years ago, floating currencies are not likely, in practice, to float freely. Second, are speculative short-term capital movements going to fulfill their necessary stabilizing function? In the very short run, when demand elasticities are close to zero, the exchange market resulting from trade flows alone must be unstable and can be stabilized only by official intervention or speculative private capital flows motivated by stabilizing expectations. It remains to be seen whether stabilizing expectations can establish themselves quickly and firmly enough to impart a reasonable degree of stability to the present system of floating rates.

I now come to my main task of commenting on Cohen's paper. One of the discussants in an earlier session remarked that survey papers are difficult to write. They are also difficult to discuss, particularly when they are as comprehensive, well-organized, and full of insights as this one. In making an effort to fulfill his function as critic, the discussant is tempted to blame the surveyor for the shortcomings of the area surveyed. At the risk of falling into this trap, I must confess to a certain disappointment that even so penetrating an analyst as Cohen can give us in many cases only the most general guidance on the research tasks that lie before us in the area of international reserves and liquidity.

In Cohen's discussion of the quantity of reserves, which occupies about half the paper, the operational problem is to determine the optimal rate of creation of SDRs. Under the assumption – of which I am somewhat doubtful – that the composition of reserves does not influence the optimal global quantity, the problem can be posed as one of subtracting the volume of non-SDR reserves likely to be supplied during a period from the optimal volume of total reserves. The global optimal volume is likely to be somehow related to the demand for reserves by individual countries, and this leads to the positive analysis of the determinants of the demand for reserves. The theoretical formulation is not difficult when we envisage – and why not? – optimizing monetary authorities that equate marginal cost and marginal utility of reserve holdings. The utility of reserves lies in not having to adjust external expenditures in the face of changes in external receipts, and the opportunity cost lies in the yield of alternative investments less the interest on the reserve asset. But empirical testing and prediction are very difficult. One of the crucial concepts is the variability of certain aggregates, such as exports or current receipts; this concept must be defined over a substantial time period to make any sense at all, so that in practice only one observation per country is available.

The problem of predicting the reserve holdings of an individual country is akin to that of predicting the cash balances of an individual company or household. Since there is no good way to do it, we may have to deal with the representative, or typical, company or household; this is not very helpful when size and importance of units vary as much as they do among countries. Unlike Cohen, I am therefore on the side of the skeptics who are not confident that more theoretical and empirical research will substantially extend our knowledge about the reserve behavior of individual countries. It might have been useful under this heading to ask whether the analysis of the demand for reserves is best couched in nominal or real terms and, if the latter, what deflator should be used.

Knowledge of the demand functions for reserves of all countries would not enable the IMF to determine optimal SDR creation any more than knowledge of the demand functions for money of households and companies would enable a central bank to decide upon the quantity of money it should put in circulation. The demand for money will always be satisfied, regardless of the volume supplied, but the attending circumstances as to interest rates, employment, price levels, etc., will vary with the amount supplied. Similarly, different volumes of reserves, though always satisfying the demand, will do so at different rates of change of the world price level, different interest levels in the major coun-

tries, different tendencies with regard to trade and payments restrictions in the world economy, etc. Most of these effects take
place through the influence on domestic and external policies of
the degree of reserve stringency felt by the monetary authorities.
We cannot, therefore, avoid consideration of the effect of variation in the supply of reserves on the policies of countries and,
through them, on world welfare. I must disagree with Cohen
when he implies that this is precisely the information we can get
from countries' demand functions for reserves. Countries can
react to a shortfall or excess of reserves, relative to the desired level, with a number of policy responses. We do not know which ones
they will choose, and there may be only limited scope for inferring
the most likely choice from the postulate of optimizing behavior.
Ideally, countries would adhere to an internationally desirable sequence of policies. For instance, when reserves expand, they
might first liberalize trade and payments until no restrictions remain, expand demand until full employment is reached, then appreciate the exchange rate, and never inflate. In the opposite case,
when the degree of reserve ease diminishes, they might first stop
inflation, then devalue, then – but only rarely – allow a temporary
shortfall of aggregate demand from its full-employment level,
and never introduce or increase trade restrictions. Unfortunately,
adherence to such a desirable sequence of policy actions cannot be
assumed, and this makes determination of the optimum rate of
increase in global reserves much more difficult than it would otherwise be.

The IMF has used two approaches to the assessment of the
appropriate amount of global reserves. The first consists of extrapolating certain relations, such as the ratio of reserves to imports or to money, from a base period during which the degree of
reserve ease is judged to have been about right. The second relies
on inferences about the existing degree of reserve ease or stringency from its manifestations in the conduct of countries' policies.
Under this approach, which Cohen does not discuss, an increase
in reserve ease could be inferred from tendencies in the world
economy toward (1) reduced reliance on restrictions on outpay-
ments (or increased reliance on restrictions on capital inflows), (2)
an increase in the volume of foreign aid or a reduction in the degree of tying, (3) a predominance of revaluations over devaluations, (4) reduced reliance on balance-of-payments credits, and (5)
pursuit of more expansionary demand policies than would be appropriate from the point of view of internal balance alone.

These manifestations must be evaluated in the light of the interest yield on reserve assets. If the yield of reserve assets were artificially kept below the yield on alternative investments, a volume of reserves that would be judged suboptimal from the international viewpoint could coexist with a predominance of balance-of-payments policies designed to reduce, rather than increase, reserve holdings. The relation between nominal interest rates on reserve assets, their valuation in terms of currencies, their implied real yield, and the pattern of their use is a topic which until recently was quite neglected and which deserves further study.

In the sections dealing with the composition and distribution of reserves, I was sorry to note the uncritical acceptance of the bogus classification of "reserves to hold" and "reserves to spend." One need only make the mental experiment of transferring this distinction to domestic monetary analysis – "money to hold" versus "money to spend" – to convince oneself that it will yield no great analytical insights. The direct social cost of an international monetary standard, to which Cohen pays some attention, is an easily overrated issue. In comparison with amounts of trade, reserves, and related aggregates measured in billions or hundreds of billions, annual material or administration costs are counted in millions. What could weigh much more heavily is the loss of world welfare from choosing the cheapest international standard, if it should turn out to be an inefficient one.

May I be permitted, in conclusion, to present my own short list of favorite future research tasks? I believe a twofold gain is possible from further development of normative models of reserve behavior by individual countries: It may help monetary authorities to make decisions on balance-of-payments and reserve policy, and it may also improve our ability to assess the optimal global supply of reserves under various circumstances. A second area for research concerns the typical policy responses of monetary authorities to externally induced changes in their reserves. Both these subjects need to be studied under alternative exchange regimes, excluding of course the limiting case of freely fluctuating rates without intervention, under which these questions would not arise. From findings in these two areas, indicators might be developed for optimal changes in the supply of global reserves. The last research task, already mentioned, would be the investigation of the relation between the demand for reserve assets and their yield, that is to say, the international liquidity-preference function.

PAYMENTS ADJUSTMENT AND
THE MONETARY SYSTEM: A COMMENT*

Thomas D. Willett

I have been asked to take primary responsibility for commenting on the paper by Klein *et al*. This is a pleasure, as I found it to be a useful description of a project whose purpose I strongly applaud. I think the LINK effort to model the interactions between domestic activity and international trade and financial flows is a major contribution to economic research and policy analysis.

The results reported in Klein's paper indicate that, while the forecasting ability of the project is still well below what one hopes is its long-run potential, significant progress has been achieved. Klein and his colleagues appear to be well aware of the major directions in which further work is crucial – for example, with respect to the problems associated with the use of the fixed-trade-share matrix and the need to include much more on the monetary and financial sides of the model. I have no question that systematic national-economy models, linked by fully developed balance-of-payments models, such as the one developed at the U.S. Treasury by Sung Kwack, are essential for good analysis and prediction of international monetary developments.

I do feel, however, that the more aggregate econometric study of international payments adjustment, as represented by Klein's and Helliwell's papers at this session, should be supplemented by a good deal more work at the microeconomic level, on the industrial-organization aspects of international payments adjustment. In the remainder of this paper, I shall sketch out some possible lines of research in this area and then turn to the policy implications of findings that the adjustment process is more sluggish than we had perhaps thought.

Two of the most important questions highlighted by recent international monetary developments are the length of the lags in the process of adjustment to exchange-rate changes and the so-called "passthrough" question, the extent to which relative prices change in response to exchange-rate adjustments.[1] The second question is important both because of its relation to the questions

---

* The following discussion does not necessarily reflect the views of the U.S. Treasury.
1 For a good recent discussion of these questions, see William H. Branson, "The Trade Effects of the 1971 Currency Realignments" and the following discussion in *Brookings Papers on Economic Activity* (No. 1, 1972), pp. 15–70.

of the terms-of-trade and inflationary impacts of exchange-rate adjustments and because of the information it gives on the distribution of adjustment between consumer and producer initiatives. This distribution, in turn, may influence both the speed of adjustment and its total magnitude.

The most noticeable effect of the degree of passthrough is probably on the timing of adjustment (see, for instance, the discussion by Branson, pp. 22–23). Where the effects of realignments are not passed through to consumers, the effects on suppliers' profits would, over the long run, induce entry and exit and hence eventually bring about supply adjustments. There is no necessary reason, however, why such supply responses would, over the long run, be of the same magnitude as demand responses. Conceptually, it would seem that they could be either larger or smaller. In imperfect market situations, however, the amount of entry or exit generated by changes in profitability will generally be less that in competitive situations. Hence, market structure may have an important influence on the total amount of adjustment as well as on its timing.

A number of interesting studies could be undertaken on industry responses to exchange-rate realignments. Such work would be an extremely valuable complement to the more aggregate econometric studies of the adjustment process. One might also find that some of the "non–profit maximizing" theories of the firm that have been developed in recent years have particular applicability in the international area, for instance, with respect to the behavior of Japanese trading firms. Recent interest in the multinational corporation has stimulated work combining aspects of industrial organization and international economics. The adjustment process is another area in which this kind of work would be worthwhile.

Another microeconomic area ripe for research is the impact of exchange-rate adjustments on relative prices. Careful examination of recent experience might give useful insight into the size of the tradeable-goods sectors for a number of countries. Too often we use figures on the value of goods actually traded as a proxy for the whole tradeable-goods sector, without knowing how good a proxy it is. We should also be able to secure valuable information on the empirical relevance of the monetarist view of Mundell, Laffer, and others that there is little if any exchange-rate illusion left in the international monetary system.

The list of topics for future research could be expanded considerably, but I think these suggestions should be sufficient to indi-

cate the opportunity for useful microeconomic studies of responses to the recent exchange-rate adjustments. The discrete
changes in the dollar parity and the simultaneous floating of a
number of major currencies have provided economic researchers
a wealth of interesting experience for analysis.

Let me turn briefly to a discussion of possible policy implications of findings about the speed and strength of the adjustment
process in response to exchange-rate changes. While it seems that
elasticity optimists probably still outnumber elasticity pessimists
within our profession, both casual observation and recent econometric work suggest that adjustments to large, discrete exchange-rate adjustments may be neither as rapid nor as large as
many of us had previously believed.

I am somewhat concerned that such findings may be interpreted as arguments against the movement toward greater exchange-
rate flexibility in the international monetary system. I would
arrive at just the opposite conclusion – that evidence that the
process of adjustment to the recent exchange-rate changes is relatively more difficlult than had been anticipated should increase
the case for greater exchange-rate flexibility.

The low or slow effectiveness of large, discrete exchange-rate
adjustments is probably indicative of the difficulty of inducing relatively large shifts in the structure of an economy in a relatively
short period of time. Under the adjustable peg, disequilibrium
has frequently tended to mount over a period of years. With an
overvalued exchange rate, resources would slowly shift out of export industries. After eventual devaluation it would take considerable time for them to be drawn back again. Conversely, in surplus
countries such as Germany and Japan, industrial capacity in the
export sector was gradually built up over time, and substantial resource adjustments are necessary for balance to be restored. Until
those resource adjustments are made, the effects of the exchange-
rate adjustments on the trade balance will be relatively small.

The implication I would draw from this is that it may be even
more important than we had thought that exchange rates not be
allowed to get very far out of line in the first place. Exchange-rate
adjustments to *maintain equilibrium* in the face of differential
macroeconomic trends could be quite effective even where effective short-run elasticities were so low that exchange-rate adjustments to *remove large disequilibrium* were not very effective.[2]

---

2 There is, of course, no way to eliminate the need for resource adjustments in response
  to real microeconomic factors, but greater exchange-rate flexibility could substantially
  reduce the magnitude of resource adjustments that have occurred under the adjustable
  peg because of continual payments disequilibrium.

The more difficult is resource adjustment, the more important it is to stay close to equilibrium in the first place. Hence I believe there is need for considerably greater exchange-rate flexibility than we had under the adjustable peg. I suspect that it would require a considerable amount of instability within a system of flexible exchange rates to match the extent of resource misallocation and adjustment costs that have occurred under the operation of the adjustable-peg system.

PART IV

AN OVERVIEW AND AGENDA

WHAT WE NEED TO KNOW: PANEL DISCUSSION

Charles P. Kindleberger

I have been asked to open this panel discussion, which is designed to explore the directions in which future research in international economics should go. I shall do so by trying to provoke the distinguished panelists with a few questions not covered by the discussions at earlier sessions, questions which seem to me worth investigation. In particular:

1. How general is the Canadian case under which capital continues to flow after the adoption of a floating exchange rate?

2. With a floating pound sterling, will capital continue to move, as with the Canadian dollar, or dry up under the pressure of increased exchange risks?

3. How realistic is it to attempt to devise a system that is in all respects symmetrical, or is asymmetry inherent in the relations between trading and financial centers?

4. Is there room in international economic research for economic history, as opposed to econometrics, to examine more deeply how the prewar gold standard functioned with very little liquidity by modern standards, how the Franco-Prussian indemnity was transferred, how the Baring crash was surmounted, how the Latin Monetary Union functioned, and so on?

5. To move to current matters, in the determination of foreign-exchange and balance-of-payments policy, are econometrics and rigorous mathematical analysis adequate substitutes for experience with, and a feeling for, markets? I have the impression that the passive attitude toward the devaluation of February 1973 was determined in Washington, without much input from the market experts in New York. It is evident that we need a feel for markets as well as econometric studies when the Treasury sets government bond rates. I should have expected the same expertise to inform policy in the foreign-exchange field, but I do not know that it does.

Hollis B. Chenery

I would like to concentrate on one of the several topics raised by Carlos Diaz-Alejandro, namely, the relationship between trade policy and development policy in developing countries. Despite efforts over the past decade or more to integrate trade and development theory, the two are still largely separate in both their underlying assumptions and their policy conclusions. In particular, trade policy is often judged in terms only of short-run balance-of-payments objectives rather than of its total effects on development over a longer period of time.

The most useful framework for this discussion is Tinbergen's formulation of the relationships between economic objectives and policy instruments. In an overall analysis of economic policy, the balance of payments appears as a constraint on the performance of the system rather than as an objective in itself. In the short run, it is necessary to balance the demand for imports against the supply of foreign exchange from exports and external capital. In the longer run, trade policy also has to take account of the exhaustion of natural resources, changes in world markets, and other structural changes that are necessary to permit sustained growth. The need to satisfy these longer-term constraints may lead us to different judgments about the effectiveness of instruments such as tariffs and quotas than those we reach by examining only their efficiency in achieving a balance of trade in the short run.

In discussing this problem, we need to make a basic distinction between the trade problems of developing countries and those of the countries which have already industrialized and whose trade is largely in manufactures. To continue to expand with given trading opportunities, the developing countries must "restructure" their economies first by shifting from primary production to manufacturing and subsequently by shifting from primary to industrial exports. The effectiveness of this process can be determined only over a period of twenty years or more.

The instruments of trade policy – tariffs, quotas, export incentives, etc. – have been relied on heavily by developing countries to bring about the necessary adaptation of their productive structures. The price mechanism alone is less effective for this purpose than for short-term adjustment because future changes in the availability of foreign exchange – and especially in primary exports – are not reflected in the existing exchange rates or relative prices. For example, in an optimal long-term plan for allocating resources, it may be desirable to plan to produce steel five or ten years from now. There may be nothing in the price system of today to indicate the future desirability of this investment or to stimulate producers to make the necessary investments in such related fields as transportation and mining. To get an idea of the optimal patterns of structural change, we need to include production lags, learning curves, and other limits on the system and to project programs of investment and trade that are consistent with them. Solutions to such programming models (of which Bruno's 1970 analysis of the Israeli economy is a good example) give us some idea of comparative advantage in the long-run sense.

In any attempt to derive lessons for trade policy from the experience of developing countries over the past twenty years, the test should be primarily the contribution made to overall development and only secondarily the cost per unit of foreign exchange earned or saved. In an optimal plan, the least-cost method of earning or saving foreign exchange is of course to be preferred to more expensive methods. However, when we are comparing several second-best alternatives, this test may be less important than other effects on growth.

In this respect, it seems to me that the comparisons of Little, Scitovsky, and Scott (1970) may be quite misleading because they use a static measure of efficiency and do not consider the extent to which trade bottlenecks or learning phenomena may have affected growth. In several of the worst cases cited by them (Argentina and Brazil), excessive protection amounted to a subsidy to the manufacturing sector on the order of 4 or 5 per cent of GNP. By implication, the capital–output ratio in the protected sectors may be some 25 to 30 per cent higher than it might have been with optimal policies. If this were the only effect of resource misallocation, however, even in these extreme cases, it would reduce the growth rate by less than 1 per cent. In most countries, this type of static inefficiency is much less important than the ability to secure important imports for investment and the maintenance of existing productive capacity so that the economy can continue to grow. In other words, the dynamic effects that are not measured in looking at levels of protecion are likely to be more important than the type of inefficiency that is measured.

I have argued elsewhere (Chenery and Carter, 1973) that this latter type of dynamic inefficiency has affected a large number of countries and is one of the main sources of variation in development performance over the past twenty years. It would follow that we should be more concerned with avoiding bottlenecks and devising a broader range of instruments for the reallocation of resources and less worried about the excessive use of resources that may occur during certain phases in this process. For example, when seen in a fifteen-year perspective, Brazil's high protection in the early 1960s may in fact have contributed to the development of an industrial base that supported its exports in the 1970s. Although Brazil is now on its way to becoming an efficient exporter of automobiles and machinery, a period of apparently inefficient import substitution may well have been necessary to structural change in both production and exports.

My research agenda follows this diagnosis of where our theory of policy is lacking. First, we need a long-term trade theory that includes frictions, economies of scale, learning phenomena, etc. Once we specify a model of that sort empirically, however, we will not be able to get simple rules for policy out of it. We will have to simulate realistic alternative policies and compare them, rather than rely on oversimplified neoclassical assumptions.

Second, we need empirical research that enables us to analyze the effects of specific instruments, as Cooper has started doing in his very useful comparison of devaluations, or as Bhagwati and Krueger (1973) are doing in studying actual policy changes that enable us to see the full interaction of policies.

Finally, we should think of trade policy as one element in an overall development strategy and judge it against alternative means of accomplishing the structural changes required by long-term growth. The developing countries that have had the greatest success in achieving growth objectives during the past ten or fifteen years – Taiwan, Korea, Turkey, Yugoslavia, Brazil, Mexico, Thailand – are distinguished more by having devised a set of policies sufficient to bring about the structural changes needed for rapid growth than by the efficiency of their trade policies or any other single policy element.

REFERENCES

Bhagwati, J. N., and A. O. Krueger, "Exchange Control, Liberalization, and Economic Development," *American Economic Review,* 63 (May 1973), pp. 419–427.

Bruno, Michael, "Development Policy and Dynamic Comparative Advantage," in R. Vernon, ed., *The Technology Factor in International Trade,* New York, Columbia University Press for National Bureau of Economic Research, 1970.

Chenery, H. B., and N. G. Carter, "Foreign Assistance and Development Performance, 1960–1970," *American Economic Review,* 63 (May 1973), pp. 459–468.

Little, I., T. Scitovsky, and M. Scott, *Industry and Trade in Some Developing Countries,* London, Oxford University Press, 1970.

Jagdish Bhagwati

I shall be brief, not merely because I have a stern Chairman who insists on the ten-minute ration for the panelists, but because to be asked to tell this distinguished audience what we should all be doing in the coming years is to be asked to cast pearls before prima donnas.

I would like to address myself principally to the issues raised in the first session [Part I], on trade policy and development in particular. That is the area where I have comparative advantage when I put on my empirical hat. Also, at MIT where I now teach, one learns that Paul Samuelson has absolute advantage in everything, so that everyone has to teach according to comparative advantage (and Paul does not have to teach at all).

The interaction of trade policy (in its widest sense, including exchange-rate policy) with economic variables such as income, growth rates, income distribution, and employment is an intricate problem. It is by no means settled, in my view, and is still open to much more research – despite the excellence of the Little–Scitovsky–Scott (LSS) analysis and contrary to the main burden of the intervention at the earlier session by some of the participants commenting on Diaz-Alejandro's paper.

The current state of research in this area was indeed well surveyed by Diaz-Alejandro, who captured very well the "temperament," as he calls it, that I would like to see more people bring to this field. Commenting on the role of economic history and of economic theory in comprehending reality, a wit has observed that one says precisely nothing and the other says nothing precisely. Diaz-Alejandro takes correctly the more prosaic and realistic view that both disciplines offer useful insights *but that* our missionary spirit to change things over to "free trade" or "export promotion" or the like needs to be moderated by a healthy skepticism and desire for yet more research.

I applaud this position, and not merely because, like the Hindu in E. M. Forster's *A Passage to India,* I have an infuriatingly eclectic approach to the important things of life such as Economics, an approach that corresponds to Diaz-Alejandro's equally noncommittal and skeptical Hispanic stance. It is also because my occasional involvement in empirical research in this field has made me somewhat skeptical of the *unqualified* claims concerning the cost of protection, the misallocation of resources, the wastefulness of import substitution, etc., which some believe to be established by economic *science* as exemplified by the theoretical *and* empirical research to which I have myself contributed. As I elaborate on the somewhat dubious nature of these claims, let me also speculate why they flourish in our profession.

1. Partly, I think that the reaction against the LDC import-substitution strategies of the 1950s and 1960s has been the result of

the swing of the pendulum that so often occurs in the philosophy of economic policy (as on fixed versus flexible rates).

2. Partly, it is also a result of the fact that the LDCs have pursued their import-substitution policies at a time when world trade has grown rapidly – a growth that has been significantly affected by Japan's phenomenal expansion, which is not sufficiently allowed for in reaching judgments on this issue. (Even if Japan were not accumulating surpluses, a balanced-trade growth by Japan at its remarkable postwar rate, combined with Japan's high propensity to import and consequent need to export, would imply, for a faster-growing world economy, continuing shock waves requiring continuous adjustments. Part of the U.S. problem in recent years has been that Japan's rapid export expansion has affected the United States more drastically than Japan's import intake.)

At the same time, some LDCs have clearly managed remarkably better export performance than others, leading to the view that exports could be increased by *all* LDCs – although (a) some LDCs have prospered at the expense of other LDCs (e.g. Pakistan and India on jute exports), (b) the ability to exploit some markets has depended on political and cultural ties (e.g., the Korean access to the U.S. market?), (c) it is not conceivable that all LDCs could have expanded exports at high rates without running into DC protectionism, and (d) higher rates of export expansion could not be high enough in some cases to alter significantly the import-substitution strategy [e.g., even significantly accelerated exports did not seem to make for a dramatic shift in the industrialization level or income expansion when Srinivasan and I used the Eckaus–Parikh multisectoral programming model to examine this issue for India in the National Bureau of Economic Research (NBER) Bhagwati–Krueger project].

3. I think that, among the important psychological reasons for the disillusionment of many economists with the import-substitution strategy has been the shock of finding that LDC governments (as much as DC governments in other areas of economic policy) have import-substituted in an economically chaotic way! In our theory classes, we spend a lot of time discussing why the Invisible Hand may not work or, as Joan Robinson once put it graphically, why it may work by strangulation. When, however, we go and see the actual nature of the intervention, and the maze of controls, quantitative restrictions, and automatic protection in many LDCs, we find the intervention chaotic and comprehensive. As a friend of mine in Ghana lamented, "The Invisible Hand is nowhere to be

seen!" It is easy then to lose one's balance and reach an extreme conclusion like the one quoted earlier by Hufbauer from Johnson in respect of multinational corporations:

It is evident that with sufficient analysis one can construct cases in which there is a second-best argument for restriction of inward foreign direct investment. The fundamental problem is that, as with all second-best arguments, determination of the conditions under which a second-best policy actually leads to an improvement of social welfare requires detailed theoretical and empirical investigation by a first-best economist. *Unfortunately, policy is generally formulated by fourth-best economists and administered by third-best economists;* it is therefore very unlikely that a second-best welfare optimum will result from policies based on second-best arguments. [Italics inserted.]

Needless to say, such prescriptions ignore the evidence of useful interventions in a number of areas of policy as well as the evident failures of the market system when left completely to itself. But such prescriptions and attitudes do tend to be the result of exposure to the reality of LDC policy.

4. And, finally, once one is so shocked, it is easy to fall into the two major pitfalls of economic research and inference: (a) the production of simple regressions, with the right R^2's, which support these views; and (b) the calculation of dubious numbers based on dubious concepts, accepted by us with relative ease because they seem to validate the disillusionment with what has been observed to be a chaotic policy.

The distinction between Economics and Econometrics may cynically be said to be that Economics is based on casual empiricism and Econometrics on selective empiricism. It is not uncommon for the best of us to regress (implicitly or explicitly) growth of income on protection levels or to argue that labor productivity has grown less in countries with reliance on import substitution. We then convince most people that this proves import substitution to be bad even when we know that labor productivity is *not* a proper index or that, if this hypothesis is indeed to be tested, it may be more useful to take a cross-section among industries in the same country and see if the export-oriented industries do better on technical change than import-substituting industries (something which Srinivasan and I have tried to do, with no clear results, in our study of India for the Bhagwati–Krueger India project). And we have all succumbed in varying degrees to the fallacy of *post hoc ergo propter hoc,* as Diaz-Alejandro reminded us in an earlier session in the context of arguments attributing more rapid growth rates to preceding liberalizations – an example which is matched in my country by the reverse assertion that the difficulties in India's economy after the liberalization attempt of 1966 were "obviously" the result of the liberalization.

In the area of trade policy and development, where the phenomena involved are fairly complex, it is relatively easy to be seduced subconsciously into accepting as confirmation of one's ideas the limited aspect of reality that is consistent with one's thesis, and even into thinking that this reality is somewhat more consistent with one's notions than it really might be. A good example is provided by the contrast between Taiwan and India in the OECD series of country studies. In their excellent overall volume, LSS are fairly cautious and guarded in many of their sound recommendations, and they are always scholarly. But I cannot help detecting, as in their argument that Taiwan (which performed very well) "give[s] an impression of more moderate [protection] rates than in other countries, except Mexico (another fine performer)" (p. 185), a tendency, as in the work of nearly all of us, to underplay the limitations of such "impressions." One should really highlight much more the tenuous character of all these estimates of protection, the noncomparability of these estimates across countries owing to differences in data quality, the nature of protection (e.g., quantitative restrictions versus ad valorem tariffs versus specific tariffs), and the sensitivity of these estimates to the classifications used and the aggregation implied. I cannot help feeling that we are all tempted to conclude that Taiwan must be following more closely the prescriptions of LSS (who, I am often chided, relied heavily on Bhagwati–Ramaswami for their theory and Bhagwati–Desai for their policy lessons) because Taiwan has done better economically! In fact, the secret of Taiwan's success may lie elsewhere. Indeed, looking at the chaotic nature of Taiwan's governmental intervention in investment allocation, which the OECD study of Taiwan itself suggests very strongly, I would be inclined to consider other factors myself, much as I have a vested interest in showing that the Bhagwati–Ramaswami–Johnson prescriptions on how to run trade policy are very important in practice! I cannot help mentioning Mexico also in this context. Was Mexico's relative success the result of her better trade policy? The interventions were again rather extensive, and by no means suited to our prescriptions in any manifest fashion. But, arriving at an explanation that would suit the strategy which we would consider (with them) eminently sensible, LSS found that internal competition and "smuggling" from the United States must have helped to reduce the protection to which Mexico otherwise would have been condemned! In short, Mexico's policies were not too good, but her proximity to the United States saved her for the LSS strategy and for economic prosperity. My good friends, Little, Scitovsky, and Scott, will forgive me, I hope, if I say with levity and obvious exaggeration that they are almost turning on its head the famous remark of Porfirio Diaz: "Poor Mexico! How far from God and how near to the United States!"

I must confess also that I am not much impressed by the statistical description of tariff structure, whether nominal or effective, which Corden cited in his review as having illuminated much of what is to be known from an economic viewpoint about the trade policy of LDCs. These tariff numbers have little meaning outside the policy and economic context, which also must be assessed. A 400 per cent tariff, calculated implicitly from a high import premium, may be the result of restrictive industrial licensing and not merely an import quota: it does *not* then signify a successful and massive pull of resources. A system of automatic protection may signify a different qualitative insight into the process of industrialization than the resulting tariff structure calculated at any one point in time; it would imply a tariff structure *adjusting* to changing competitiveness and therefore have allocational effects quite different from those of an unchanging tariff structure. One must go way beyond these simpleminded descriptions toward understanding *functionally* the economic system of the LDC in question (as the NBER project explicitly tries to do). The trouble is that this does hamper cross-section regression analysis and it also calls for more intensive analytical "country studies." Fortunately, this is no longer difficult. Fraser, the great evolutionary anthropologist, in the pre-Malinowski–Radcliffe–Brown era, was asked if he had ever visited the exotic areas he wrote about. He is reported to have said: "I only write about savages, I don't mix with them." Thanks to the Foundations, AID, the Bank, and the eager jetsetting propensity of the modern economist, we need no longer fear that our search for knowledge, if not pleasure, will be handicapped by Fraserian attitudes.

As for the use of analytically dubious concepts and the conclusions based thereon to take (wittingly or unwittingly) to task the import-substitution strategy, I could draw on a large sample indeed. But one example should suffice. It has become fashionable to say that LDC growth rates would look even less attractive if one evaluated them at international prices; indeed, as in other areas where numbers seem to emerge with rapidity even before the concept is shown to make sense, we are already told that protected economies like Argentina and Pakistan show reduced "real" rates of growth on that basis (and God knows how many more empirical theses on this subject are underway). Two years ago, Bent Hansen and I showed (in a paper now published in the Rosenstein–Rodan *Festschrift*) that growth rates measured at domestic prices in fact made excellent sense from a welfare viewpoint and that growth rates measured at international prices could yield misleading results on both conceptual and measurement grounds. Lo and behold, LSS, who are widely credited with having suggested that growth rates be reevaluated at international prices, have informed us after protracted correspondence that they too wanted to evaluate growth rates at *domestic* prices — a conclusion conveyed to us by Scott.

In this context, I would also like to enter a strong caveat against the practice of using simple exercises to reach quantitative conclusions on empirical issues and preaching them as if they were scientifically watertight. Take, for example, the cost-of-protection estimates which are thrown at us with even the first decimal place calculated. Not merely are these based on estimates of protection which are far less than accurate, they have necessarily to use estimates of general-equilibrium supply and demand elasticities (and the latter, in principle, ought to be based on a well-behaved lump-sum-transfer-generated social-utility function unless cardinality is explicitly assumed and *its* implications carefully worked out) which are critically dependent on the number and size of price changes carried out in the system – things no one really knows! Why not say therefore that the estimates are no more than "illustrative," instead of saying: "So and so has shown that the cost of protection for Argentina is 10.63 per cent of GNP"? It is not surprising that we tend to be dismissed as charlatans whenever we confront anyone who really *knows* what is going on.

In conclusion, while there are many serious questions about the trade policies of LDCs in the last two decades, and indeed the excellent analytical work of the OECD authors and the detailed statistical descriptions of tariffs turned up by the IBRD projects under the able guidance of Bela Balassa have helped to raise them, we are *not* very close to saying: "Definitive knowledge gained, let us now turn to other things." This conclusion also bears on the issue that came up in an earlier session: Corden and Johnson, among others, asked for work on why politicians refuse to accept our wisdom (and related work on what political forces constrain them to act as they do). Are we to disregard the fact that this wisdom of ours changes and is fickle on both a cross-section among economists and a time series for any given economist? It would be very entertaining, if not instructive, to study the policy advice of economists on this panel (including myself) over the last ten years: You would probably find that the conviction with which any one of us considers governments to be senselessly recalcitrant in taking economic advice varies positively with the number of times one has changed one's mind on important policy issues! But let us suppress such self-destructive thoughts. We are *still* left with two alternative explanations:

One, produced by Johnson with eloquence in an earlier session, is that politicians *use* economists to justify selectively what they wish to do anyway: Economics becomes the handmaiden of political perfidy. This is an egocentric, econocentric view. My experience does not really coincide with it. Political leaders have rarely sought to justify industrialization in a strictly economic sense; images of modernization, reaching technological maturity, national military power, etc., have.played a much more important role in the ideology of industrialization and import substitution. Few politicians have bothered to convince our profession that they were right.

The alternative explanation, to which I am partly inclined, is that policymakers have *something* on their side. Recall that deficit spending as an instrument to create aggregate employment preceded the *General Theory*. Economists should be a little more cautious in assuming that policy wisdom is necessarily on *their* side. And in the area of trade and development policy, I have given enough reasons to doubt that we are immensely smarter than the policymakers.

So we need to know more, to do more research. Let me throw out a few things that worry me, as the results of the NBER Bhagwati–Krueger project come in, where more research seems to me to be needed.

1. Instead of the chaotic selectivity of the incentive policies for "import substitution," which seems to be the main focus of our trade-theoretic analysis, a more *important* inhibition on growth may in practice be the speed with which "import substituting" industrialization is geared toward "export promotion." Here, again, as the Korean study in the Bhagwati–Krueger project seems to underline, the key to success is not the absence of detailed, selective, and target-oriented export promotion; Korea shows as much variation in domestic resource costs as you could now expect to find among the import-substituting industries in "inward-looking" countries. And, as Bent Hansen's study of Egypt for the same

project also shows, you can have low variance among domestic resource costs even when trade and other incentive policies seem to be chaotically set!

The distinguishing feature of superior economic performance seems to be the pursuit of "indiscriminate" and "chaotic" but *energetic* policies to promote exports from industries which have been nurtured under protection in the first place.

If this is true, however, we will not find in our standard Bhagwati–Ramaswami–Johnson models the sources of superior performance. We have to look elsewhere. (This seems to have been the case with Japan since 1898 as well – as suggested by a detailed, original study, by Ippei Yamazawa, of Japan's extensive resort to protection during this period, sponsored under the Bhagwati–Krueger project.) Krueger and I expect to develop this theme at greater length in the overall volumes which will cap the NBER country studies, much as the LSS volume grew out of the OECD country studies, but some preliminary thoughts on this issue were spelled out in our paper at the AEA meetings in Toronto in December 1972. This is clearly an area that needs to be explored much more intensively than we will – with both theoretical and empirical work of the highest quality.

2. Among the issues related to the possible advantage of rapid export promotion is the question of the impact of import-substituting LDC strategies on technical change and X-efficiency. I must admit to thinking, as did most economists who pondered these issues in the last decade, that sheltered markets generated by quantitative restrictions destroyed incentives for research and development. We should have known better. There is evidence of growing R & D in India, little evidence that it is stronger in export-oriented firms, much evidence that it springs out of the desire generated by the trade regime to promote the use of locally available materials – a variant of the Kennedy-type thesis on technical change – and ample evidence that large firms matter in this game. Is such R & D desirable? What does it do to growth and hence to our overall evaluation of the import-substituting growth strategy from which it springs? There is clearly need for more research here. One has only to recall Japan's transition from shoddy manufacture under bad imitation to decent manufacture under good imitation to excellent manufacture under outstanding imitation to innovative manufacture, and the growing evidence that India is beginning to transit to decent manufacture, to at least pause and ask if there is much more to our choice of strategies than meets our trade-theoretic and cost-benefit-analysis-oriented eye.

Historical, current-LDC-oriented *and* theoretical research in this difficult area is urgent.

3. Let me next join with Johnson in suggesting that we re-introduce political and sociological factors into our analysis of trade policy and development. This is necessary if we are really going to understand complex phenomena such as the impact of policies on growth. As we all know by now, first-best policies applied in second-best contexts can be counterproductive. The Bhagwati–Krueger project again helps to illustrate this very nicely. Unlike the OECD project, ours extends the analysis to specific attempts at liberalizing trade regimes, putting this analysis into its specific political context. Thus, the Israeli and Indian liberalization attempts of the 1960s demonstrate clearly that import liberalization is unsuccessful when it results in greater domestic competition but is eminently successful when it involves only greater access to non-competitive imports: the influence of pressure groups created by the earlier "automatic protection" type of strategy is evident. Similarly, the analysis of the 1966 Indian devaluation brings out the specific interaction between the success and repeatability of a liberalization package and the political framework (especially the pressure from the Aid Consortium) within which the package was implemented. I am convinced that a full analysis of the feasibility and success of liberalization would have to take into account these and similar political factors, and that a "scientific" economic analysis cannot ignore them altogether; the distinction sometimes drawn between "political economy" and "scientific economics" is really a false one.

I am sure that we should now also be addressing ourselves to much more developed-country research of a similar type. The original Marshall–Taussig concern with the criteria by which tariff protection was actually granted (at the LDC level, one such detailed analysis is Padma Desai's volume on the Indian Tariff Commission) needs to be revived and supplemented by examination of such questions as the characteristics of the industries which managed to get exemptions in the Kennedy Round (a task in which John Cheh at MIT is now engaged). If we knew more about why tariff exemptions are granted, we could construct interesting and relevant theories of tariff retaliation which would add to the otherwise esoteric literature to which theorists such as Johnson and Gorman have contributed in the past.

4. Finally, let me emphasize the need for more research on the impact of multinational corporations on LDCs. In this area, we have had diverse theories: (a) the "dualism" notions of the Dutch

sociological school, leading to the *enclave* models and approach, where the MNCs bypassed the hinterland, having no effect, either malign or benign; (b) the *benign neglect* model, which has emphasized the beneficial side-effects of MNCs in the guise of diffused technology, increased competitiveness for domestic entrepreneurs, and the like; (c) the *malign intent* model, which finds its validation in the experience of the Union Minière du Haut Katanga, the United Fruit Company, and the ITT of recent vintage; and (d) the *malign neglect* model, which focuses on how the presence of MNCs exercises adverse influence on LDCs via a Hirschman-type inhibition of domestic entrepreneurship or a Sunkel-type accentuation of taste formation, which distorts the pattern of development away from a preferable, more equitable mold or affects the income distribution (as when the granting of salaries comparable to the MNC salary levels to local nationals creates an upward pull on the salary levels of the elite groups in the host LDCs, at the expense of egalitarian ideas). We know far too little about these issues at an empirical level, even about the relatively more tractable issues such as the diffusion of technology; our theories are correspondingly inadequate to the important task of relating the MNCs to the past and future performance of the LDCs.

Richard N. Cooper

There are many subjects intrinsically more interesting than economics but relatively few that are as useful. I view the discipline of economics as instrumental in improving the human condition rather than as an intellectual end in itself. This "practical" perspective does not imply, however, that the most important research is empirical or is aimed at immediate and pressing problems. Two of the three areas of research in international economics that I believe deserve top priority are, on the contrary, highly theoretical and abstract.

The first is really a branch of monetary theory, for it concerns the marketplace for monies. A monetary economy is obviously superior to a barter economy. We teach that in introductory economics and we all know it to be true. But, paradoxically, money plays no integral role in our theory of consumption, except as a component of wealth; in our theory of the firm; or in long-run general-equilibrium theory. Implicitly, money is apparently like a catalyst in a chemical reaction: it facilitates the reaction without actually participating in it. We have not specified the exact catalytic functions of money in a monetary economy. Indeed, we are behind the chemists in discovering just how catalysts do perform their empirically important function.

Our capacity to experiment with economic systems is limited. It is therefore necessary to understand the nature of the catalytic role of money before we can assess properly alternative monetary regimes. Is it really true, as is frequently alleged, for example, that a regime of anticipated inflation has no economic costs, provided that interest can be paid on cash balances? Or, to take an issue closer to the subject matter of this conference, is it really true, as is frequently alleged, that a regime of freely floating exchange rates is the least-cost balance-of-payments adjustment mechanism? Under what conditions does free floating begin to interfere with the moneyness of money? How much oil can one put on a catalyst before it ceases to perform its catalytic function and real efficiency losses are incurred?

The homogeneity postulate that we use in microeconomic theory and its macroeconomic analogue, the separation theorem, are both long-run relationships. Most economists have abandoned the separation theorem in short-run macroeconomic theory – stabilization theory. We recognize there that money matters to the real economy.

We simply do not know at what point interfering with the moneyness of money begins to impinge seriously on the efficiency of a monetary economy. Some work has been done on the importance of money in bridging discrepancies in timing between receipts and payments. Some work has also been done on the importance of money in lowering transactions costs. I suspect that the essence of money goes beyond these factors and involves the transmission of information in a world in which, contrary to our usual theoretical assumptions, it is costly to surmount ignorance. Surely the great advantage of a money economy over barter is that the former economizes greatly on search costs. A monetary regime with a stable price level greatly reduces the "search costs" of distinguishing relative from absolute price changes and thus also reduces the costs of erroneously interpreting the latter as the former and acting on that misconception.

To the extent that search costs are potentially important, the role of money is not completely separable from what is occurring on the real side, and it does therefore affect the efficiency of the economy. In any case, we cannot resolve the debate on flexibility versus fixity in exchange rates, or ascertain the proper degree of flexibility and the optimum size of currency areas, until this fundamental area of theory is developed. It is an essential part of any cost–benefit analysis of an exchange-rate regime and is highly pertinent to the issues on which international economists are frequently questioned these days.

A second area that requires fundamental research concerns the advantages and disadvantages of alternative time paths in returning to equilibrium from an initial disequilibrium. Caves, in his remarks at an earlier session, emphasized the importance for empirical work of looking at alternative time paths, and he expressed some skepticism about the mathematically simple lagged responses that are usually used, on the ground that they have no basis in theory. I agree fully with those remarks and suggest that there is much room for theoretical development to find not only time paths based plausibly on behavioral theory but also socially optimal time paths.

This issue comes up in many guises, not all of them international. It arises in moving a domestic economy from a condition of unemployment to one of full employment, or in trying to restore monetary stability to an economy that has gone into an inflationary spiral – a problem that is no longer peculiar to less developed countries.

On the international side, we have the problem of correcting a balance-of-payments disequilibrium that has been allowed to develop. Should adjustment measures be abrupt, or should they be smoothed over a period of time? The same question arises for the removal of tariffs. Should smoothing accompany the removal or not?

The question should have arisen with respect to international capital movements. At least in retrospect, it now seems clear that by 1959 there was a major disequilibrium in the allocation of the world's capital stock. That is true whether one takes a risk and rate-of-return view or a market-structure view of what motivates capital movements. During the 1950s international capital movements were relatively modest. They underwent a big surge in the 1960s, presumably because European currencies became convertible and because the barriers of geographical insecurity were swept away as a result of strategic military developments. We therefore faced the need for a large stock adjustment in the world's allocation of capital. How fast should the adjustment have taken place? Should the United States have maintained tighter controls than it did on the outflow of capital – not for balance-of-payments reasons, for there are better measures to deal with the balance of payments, but to assure an optimal path of reallocation? Or should it have devalued the dollar at once to facilitate more rapidly the necessary real transfers?

McKinnon mentioned a related problem of the same genre. Immediately after World War II there was a widely recognized maldistribution of international reserves, and to rebuild their reserves the European countries maintained tight controls over trade, which were gradually relaxed during the 1950s. Was that the right way to do it? Instead of trade controls, should the United States have made large loans, on the lines of the Anglo-American Loan only bigger, followed by an exchange-rate adjustment sufficient to amortize the loans over some specified period of time?

The same problem is raised by the diffusion of new knowledge that has been proven by application in one country. We normally assume that diffusion of new knowledge should take place as rapidly as possible. But if investment in plant and labor skills has taken place, that investment might be wasted if diffusion is too rapid. This issue is now of lively concern to American labor and influences its perceptions of multinational corporations. Moreover, one also must assess the extent to which very rapid diffusion will blunt the incentive to innovate. The patent is only one device, demonstrably suboptimal, to permit some control on diffusion. One weakness of the patent is that not all the costs of adjustment to diffusion are internal to the patent-owning firm. So, once again, we need a better theoretical framework for considering optimal paths of adjustment to equilibrium. This class of questions has not been adequately addressed.

The general point is that there are costs to reallocation, there are real costs to structural unemployment, there are psychic costs to declines in real income, and the magnitude of these costs is related to the speed of adjustment, since there is a natural turnover to all factors of production such that with sufficient time no unemployment need result. We require greater application of optimal-control theory to economic problems. Unfortunately, this area of theory is complicated by the fact that optimal adjustment paths will often depend on the "initial conditions," that is, the precise nature of the initial disequilibrium, and the logical possibilities are therefore legion.

The third area requiring more research is very empirical. It concerns the realism of the assumptions underlying the case for liberal trade – or, to put the same point the other way around, the factual validity of the many claims that are increasingly made for restrictions on trade. Liberal trade policy is at present under attack from many directions, attacks that have been given intellectual respectability by the "theory of second-best." But second-best theory does *not* urge that we eschew liberal trade; it just urges that we be cautious in applying to a complex reality normative principles derived under "ideal" assumptions. It is totally agnostic as to the direction of its findings, and indeed may frequently turn up instances (like the case of domestic monopoly) which may reinforce rather than weaken the traditional arguments for liberal trade. While we have been taught to be more cautious about normative generalizations, we may have become too willing to accept all the old and new arguments for protection against imports. Since various considerations point in opposite directions for tariff policy, what we need now is careful empirical work on the quantitative importance of the factors in whose name protectionist arguments are invoked: economies of scale external to the firm, learning curves, factor-market distortions, terms-of-trade effects, and the like. For example, have relative costs fallen over the years in the great and growing manufacturing centers of the developing world – New Delhi, São Paulo, Karachi, etc. – as the claims for economies of agglomeration would predict? How many countries have enough market power to influence their terms of trade by a consequential amount? To what extent do wages in developing countries really differ from labor's marginal product? How important are restrictive import policies in protecting local monopolies? Answers to questions such as these will be necessary to advance beyond the sterile claims and counterclaims regarding the merits of liberal or restrictive trade policy.

Wilson Schmidt

I was hit awfully hard by problems with the data in some work I did during my two years at the Treasury as Deputy Assistant Secretary for Research. My first experience was the Thursday that the staff came in with an extraordinary increment in the size of the U.S. balance-of-payments deficit. It was so large that none of us could believe it. So we sent some of the people back to work to find out why. It turned out that it was a reporting error by one bank attributable to one individual with, I assume, a green eyeshade and a pencil that had gotten awfully dull and who had no eraser. Ever since that first exposure to the problems of reporting, I shook every Thursday or Friday when those numbers came in and I asked myself what we had missed this time.

Still another example of problems with data is the extraordinary disparity between the U.S. and the Canadian trade figures.

When we realize that policy debates between the Canadians and ourselves were raised to shouting matches largely over what data were correct, we see how important the data can become not just to econometricians but to real people!

If we look at the transportation accounts, we realize that some information is reported by foreign governments in a way that cannot be checked at all by anyone on this side of the ocean. The way in which the interest payments are estimated should frighten us. The coverage of nonbank reporters in the Treasury system is extraordinarily poor.

In additon to problems with the data, problems stem from the dynamics of the data base. The things that ought to be reported are constantly changing. One example is the decision a number of central banks made to buy agency bonds. Our statistical reporting did not pick up these purchases until we changed the system, with some effort and a considerable lag. The development of leasing as a new form of international transaction on a wide scale is another example.

Of course, problems with the data come as no surprise to this group. So far as I can count, with possibly one exception, everybody has mentioned at least one problem with the numbers. The unit-price indices seem to be the leading candidate, but we have also had mention of problems with reconciling data in the United States and other places. So I need not waste my words here on problems in the data.

But the graduate students I have talked to in the recruiting process do not show the healthy disrespect for the data which many people around this table already have, and I worry about this. It seems that econometricians do more poorly than ordinary people who have an awareness of the marketplace and the institutions, the facts of life in the forecasting process. The problem here is that we are no longer manufacturing in the graduate schools the kind of person who can do this work. We may have a structural decline in the quality of our forecasting in the years ahead, because very few people we turn out are willing to get into the nitty and gritty of the data as a lot of people in the U.S. government still are. At the very least, we should be turning out people with a healthy disrespect for the numbers.

I am also surprised by the infrequency of requests by academics to government agencies (the one I was involved with in particular) for special runs of data. In the future, many more around this table should ask for information and special runs than have so far been willing to do so.

What bothers me most of all is how difficult it is to get budgetary support for improvements in the quality of the data with which all of us deal. That was the toughest fight that I had in the work we did. The effort to improve the unit-value indices is floundering because of inadequate budget support and is now increasingly delayed. I know about the inadequacies of the series for which I was responsible and how hard it is to get additional people to work on them. What are the problems here? One is that the people at the highest level who have to make decisions on policy and budgetary resource allocations simply do not have the time. But, more important, they probably do not even have the interest, because the gestation period for the improvement of numbers is so long that most of those who must make the decsions will be out of office by the time the high-quality numbers arrive. The people who do really care about the numbers are the civil servants down the line, but they are too far down the line to have the impact necessary to get quantum jumps in quality. Most important, there is also disrespect at the higher levels for those civil servants because they seem to be perfectionists. This again stems from the fact that the high policymaker does not really have time and will be out of business before the numbers can be improved.

My strongest suggestion is, first, that when you testify next and Senator Proxmire screams that you have misled his Committee, tell the Senator that it is because the numbers are bad. Persuade those who hold the pursestrings to furnish budgetary support for improving the quality of numbers. Second, in the revision of your papers, put far more emphasis on the deficiencies of the data. All of us are reluctant to tell the truth about our numbers, because if we use them to prove something and then disparage them, our case falls to the ground. So let us be a little more humble. Let us complain about the numbers not because the civil servants do not know that they are deficient but because we have to start educating a great many more people about their quality. The general outlook for the econometricians around this table is not particularly good, because the data are not improving nearly as fast as the techniques.

Milton Gilbert

The question before us, namely, what we need to know now, could be answered in various ways. I would be inclined to say that we need to know mostly how to stop high personalities from making so many statements. The official world has lost credibility with the market to such an extent that almost any statement has an adverse effect. For example, the market price of gold took a large jump recently and then was beginning to settle down. The idea appeared in the newspapers that perhaps it would be a good thing for central banks to sell some gold so as to bring down the price. When an American official was asked whether the United States would be willing to sell gold for this purpose, he said that it might be willing; in the face of this threat, the market price went up immediately by $1.80.

But to answer the question more seriously, I would like to make two points about the kind of econometric studies we have been discussing. First, Schmidt said that we ought to have a healthy disrespect for the numbers. I think that we ought also to have a certain disrespect for the models. Dressing things up in a model is not a substitute for good judgment. I have this skepticism because it seems to be so easy to work out a model that supports the conventional wisdom. For example, in the calculated models that lay behind the Smithsonian realignment, it just happened that the figure for the change required in the U.S. current-account balance agreed with the view held by the Europeans and Japanese rather than with the change which the United States believed essential. On top of this, the changes in exchange rates which were supposed to bring about the calculated swing in the U.S. current account were obviously too small. It was as if the Smithsonian exchange-rate changes had been determined not by calculation from a model but by a vote. And maybe in the end they were.

The second point I want to make is that we need more discrimination in what we are trying to measure. Cohen said we need more sophistication in measuring this and that, but my point is that we need more sophistication in what we measure altogether. There is need for deeper understanding of the process of official decision-making, of the impact of political considerations on economic policy decisions, and generally about the complexity of government objectives.

May I call your attention to all the discussions we heard, and all the work that has been done, about measuring the demand for reserves by central banks. I find this all off the mark because I do not believe that central banks have a demand for reserves. The accumulation of reserves has always been the residual result of the package of policy decisions about other matters more important to the government concerned than the size of the increase in reserves. Of course, the authorities try to act as promptly as they can to avoid losing reserves, but that is quite another thing from acting to gain reserves. As usual, one must judge official policy not by what it claims to be but by what is actually done. For example, all during the 1950s the authorities in London were saying that an increase in reserves was needed to support sterling as a reserve currency. However, it is not easy to find a time when they did anything about it. It was certainly an objective that had a very low priority and hardly one that could be considered a demand for reserves.

The only central bank which tried to express explicitly a demand for reserves was the Nederlandsche Bank. It had worked out a formula to show how much Dutch reserves should increase, and this was printed in its Report for several years. To show that this formula could not serve as a guide for the international monetary system as a whole, I calculated its implications if it were applied to all countries. The result was that an aggregate increase in reserves of $8 billion per year would be required. The formula was then dropped from the Annual Report.

Cohen also spoke of dividing the problems of reserves into those of quantity, composition, and distribution, saying that the most important question was quantity. I find it very difficult to believe that the quantity of reserves has ever been a problem, because all that countries need do about quantity is to have a meeting and agree on an increase. Indeed, it is amazing to see what amount of reserves can be created on a Sunday afternoon. No, the really important problem about reserves has been their composition; the system broke down over the problem of composition, not the problem of quantity.

Harry G. Johnson

The title of this panel discussion is "What We Need to Know," and instead of presenting a world view of trade theory and trade research, I would like to concentrate on a few things that have come out of the discussion. The first, growing mainly out of the first session [Part I], concerns in a broad sense what Kindleberger said about the need for some understanding of history. We have had enough of a historical run in the postwar period to begin to think historically again. In particular, one thing that has emerged is that our concept of the political debate seems to be pretty naïve. That does not seem to trouble Chenery, who likes to divide the world into structuralists and neoclassicists – and we all know who he means! I feel that this is a nonsense way to proceed. What is the point of acquiring a great deal of analytical technique, including

elaborate general-equilibrium systems, if we reduce our understanding of politics and debate to a contrast between two extremely simple myths about the world, of which our own must be
correct and the other person's must, by definition, be wrong?

Among the specific issues that emerge is, first of all, the attempt
to extend economic analysis to provide an understanding of why
governments do what they do. Here quite a case might be made
for looking at the economic forces that play on government. For
example, various developments are influencing the rapid conver-
sion of the United States into an increasingly protectionist country, one which is making exactly the same kinds of noises and the
same faces the Europeans used to make in the immediate postwar
period, when they were laughed out of court for their naïvete and
lack of economic understanding.

The second issue, which comes out of Diaz-Alejandro's paper,
is in what sense, if any, we can say that countries have become
more protectionist or less protectionist. Diaz-Alejandro made the
point that the success stories have really been a matter of retaining
most of the existing protection but not extending it. Some kind of
establishment of standards for that and for evaluation of the evidence would be useful. A possible hypothesis is that economic
growth would go on in spite of man, providing man does not tin-
ker too much with the machinery. Dennison's work on economic
growth, for example, shows that no matter what happens you get
a .75 per cent productivity increase per annum; it has taken a mir-
acle of mismanagement in Britain to prevent even that increase! It
may well be that it does not matter very much what policy you
choose so long as you do not keep changing it.

Turning to another major issue concerning the monetary field,
there has been a certain tendency to assume that recent developments mean we are moving toward a permanent regime of floating exchange rates, and that this is going to change everything. I
do not believe it will, since it is fairly clear that the U.S. administration still has in mind for the long run a regime of fixed rates,
and this is probably true of the Europeans as well, making the
present period transitional. So research on the impact of devaluation seems still to be worth doing. I do not think the time has yet
come to extend ourselves into the range talked about earlier –
namely, trying to develop models which contain $n-1$ exchange
rates moving simultaneously, as compared with the standard
practice of assuming that one exchange rate moves and analyzing
the devaluation by that country.

Various issues have come out of the discussion. One which has been mentioned extensively is the whole question of how prices change in response to devaluation. Schmidt's appeal for more and better numbers is essentially an appeal for building ourselves a second line of defense against our own errors by blaming the statisticians in government and developing sociological theories of why they are so bad. It does not really answer the question. We do need to look into the question of prices and how they respond to devaluation. We should do that with some sophistication, understanding that devaluations may come as a great surprise but that any rational businessman will have them in mind and will design the structure of contracts, etc., to try to minimize the cost of possible changes. I had an experience with this a few years ago. Most Malayan rubber was being sold under long-term contracts for dollars, so that changes in the exchange rate of the pound against the dollar did not really make that much difference. One could not analyze the situation as if prices were changed by the devaluation.

That brings us to another question which has been lurking under the surface of the conference – namely, the influence of oligopoly pricing. This needs investigation, partly because, without serious investigation, anybody's word goes. If something does not work, we can just say that it is because, contrary to the beliefs of the neoclassicists but according to what we structuralists would have said had we thought about it, markets are not competitive. We need to work out what the implications of oligopoly are.

Another point which has emerged is that, if devaluations work with a very long lag, other things happen in the meantime. Hence, rather than go in for very elaborate econometric exercises and cross-section analyses, it might be useful to make detailed case studies which attempt to allow for the other policy changes that are introduced around or following devaluations and the impact of changes in other countries' policies. It is not all that obvious that even very sophisticated models based on a static general-equilibrium analysis are going to tell us much if the time span of the operation is long enough. If it takes a long time for a devaluation to work, devaluation models constructed on theoretical grounds may miss most of the important changes that occur.

Finally, this suggests that more needs to be done on the monetary side of the picture. There is a whole area here which needs investigation, contingent on my presumption that there will not be a rapid and important change toward an enduring regime of generally fluctuating exchange rates, that the old structure will reemerge as the basis of the system. We need to look at such issues as international reserves, SDRs, and devaluations, attempts to stop inflation by price ceilings, and many other phenomena, in the context of a world system in which inflation is a monetary phenomenon. For that purpose, we need a lot of new statistics. Mundell has made this point before: if we really believe in a world system, we have to treat system phenomena accordingly, and this means we have to look at devaluations and inflation in terms of world money supply, world production, and things of that kind. It may be more fruitful to think of individual countries as operating within a world context and against world trends than to treat them, as we often do, as independent and in control of their own destinies. The world context does emerge in the material that has been surveyed on policy mixes, fixed versus floating rates, etc. But even those surveys presume, theoretically at least, that the world system outside is a stable-price, full-employment world, when really we are dealing with changes against the trend, a trend that is determined by the outcome of many decisions in many countries.

My agenda for research is contained in these remarks.

Charles P. Kindleberger

It is hard to see that this concluding panel discussion has given us a completely new agenda for research in international economics. For the most part, our discussants have dealt with familiar topics. Schmidt's plea for more and better statistics comes from a man who has suffered while trying to make government policy recommendations on the basis of inadequate data. But our other practical economist in the developed-country field, Gilbert, rather negated the import of Schmidt's message by suggesting that there were enough numbers and models, and that what is needed is more insight into the political process. I suspect that, with time, the technical economist is going to have to dilute his rigor with a deeper understanding of the political processes of decision-making. Political scientists are beginning to realize that international economic relations, and such matters as devaluations and how much international liquidity to create in the form of SDRs, are highly political and deserve analysis along with territorial claims.

If the pleas of Cooper for research on money and optimal time paths from disequilibrium to equilibrium, of Bhagwati and Chenery for sorting out of the issues of export-led growth versus import substitution, and of Johnson for further work on devaluation and macroeconomic policies in an interdependent world are not startling in their originality, we can be grateful, I think, that we did not hear much in this discussion about optimal growth paths or effective rates of protection. I choose to think that the failure to dwell here on the multinational corporation was an oversight, while the omission of effective tariff rates was deliberate, but this may be wish fancy.

If I may exercise the privilege of chairman and senior citizen at this conference, perhaps I may be allowed to say that I find the most important areas for research in the issues framed by Cooper and Johnson dealing with how interrelated the economies of the world will be. One can interpret the loosening of exchange-rate relations of the last two years as a pause for regrouping in the march to a world money, which, as Cooper puts it, will reduce transactions costs between nations in the same way that domestic money is regarded as superior to barter within national economies. The United States has been wearied by interdependence with the economies of the world and has been seeking autonomy. In my judgment, it is nowhere to be found in an interdependent world.

GLOSSARY OF FREQUENTLY USED ACRONYMS

CES	constant elasticity of substitution
CMEA	Council for Mutual Economic Assistance
EEC	European Economic Community
EFTA	European Free Trade Association
GATT	General Agreement on Tariffs and Trade
GDP	gross domestic product
GNP	gross national product
IMF	International Monetary Fund
IBRD	International Bank for Reconstruction and Development
LDC	less developed country
MNC	multinational corporation
OECD	Organization for Economic Cooperation and Development
R & D	research and development
SIC	standard industrial classification
SITC	standard international classification
UNCTAD	United Nations Conference on Trade and Development
VES	variable elasticities of substitution

AUTHOR INDEX

Page numbers refer to authors cited in the body of the text. No listings are given for References at the end of each paper.

531

INTERNATIONAL TRADE AND FINANCE
Essays in Honour of Jan Tinbergen

Edited by Willy Sellekaerts

One of three volumes conceived as a
substantive tribute to the Nobel Laureate.
The companion volumes are *Economic
Development and Planning* and
Econometrics and Economic Theory.

This volume consists of original articles
in the field of international trade and
finance, one of the areas in which
Tinbergen did important work. The
contributors include some of the world's
leading economists, and their essays deal
with a broad range of significant
problems.

The introductory essay appraises
Tinbergen's contributions to economics.
A selected bibliography of his work is
appended.

Willy Sellekaerts is a Visiting Professor at
Temple University, Philadelphia, and
Professor of Economics at the University
of Ottawa. Educated at the Free
University of Brussels, the University of
Michigan and Michigan State University,
he has also taught at all three universities
and has done research in international
finance at Princeton.

Professor Sellekaerts has published
articles in English, French and German
on such topics as international trade and
finance, micro and macro aspects of
inflation, and comparative economic
systems.